# CorelDRAW™ 8

**Inventive Techniques &
Outrageous Effects**

**Shane Hunt**

**CorelDRAW 8 f/x**
Copyright © 1998 by Shane Hunt

**Library of Congress Cataloging-in-Publication Data**
Hunt, Shane.
CorelDRAW 8 f/x / Shane Hunt. —1st ed.
p.    cm.
Includes index.
ISBN 1-56604-803-6
1. Computer graphics.  2. CorelDRAW!.  I. Title.
T385.H85  1997
006.6'869—dc21     97-40466
  CIP

First Edition 9 8 7 6 5 4 3 2

Printed in the United States of America

Ventana Communications Group
P.O. Box 13964
Research Triangle Park, NC 27709-3964
919.544.9404
FAX 919.544.9472
http://www.vmedia.com

Ventana Communications Group is a division of International Thomson Publishing.

**President**
Michael E. Moran

**Associate Publisher**
Robert Kern

**Editorial Operations Manager**
Kerry L. B. Foster

**Production Manager**
Jaimie Livingston

**Brand Manager**
Jamie Jaeger Fiocco

**Art Director**
Marcia Webb

**Creative Services Manager**
Diane Lennox

**Acquisitions Editor**
Christopher D. Grams

**Project Editor**
Amy Hayworth

**Development Editor**
Paul Cory

**Copy Editor**
Judy Flynn

**CD-ROM Specialist**
Shadrack Frazier

**Technical Reviewer**
Brian Little

**Desktop Publisher**
Patrick Berry

**Proofreader**
Jessica Ryan

**Indexer**
Ann Norcross

**Interior Designer**
Patrick Berry

**Cover Illustrator**
Lisa Gill

## About the Author(s)

Shane Hunt is a graphic artist and freelance writer and coauthor of *The CorelDRAW WOW! Book*. He has been using CorelDRAW since its initial release in 1989, and has worked directly with Corel corporation as a tester and consultant in an effort to continually improve the product. His column on computer design theory and technique appears monthly in *Corel Magazine*, and he is responsible for the CorelDRAW question and answer FAQ on the *Corel Magazine* Web site.

# Acknowledgments

I would like to thank my friends and family for their support, even when at times they have no idea what I am doing! It takes supportive and loving people to put up with my stream-of-consciousness dialog and ever-wandering mind, not to mention help remind me about the real world, and drag me into it now and again! I have to thank my great aunts Lisa and Margot, and my grandparents Rupert and Anni. Their long distance support is not without appreciation—Vielen Dank!

I would like to thank the brilliant staff at Ventana, who somehow balanced letting my creativity go wild with keeping within the boundaries of sensible publishing. The man most responsible for this is Paul Cory, who had the thankless task of editing my raw material and whipping me into shape. Thanks Paul for your great work! Also, of course, Amy Hayworth, who was chief whip-cracker and quality-controller in charge of the monumental task of controlling the project on a daily basis. Go Amy! Also Shadrack Frazier for his work on the CD-ROM, especially for his patience. I kept changing things right up until the last minute, making his life miserable. And thanks to all of the talented people working to put this book together. You can not believe how many people work on a project like this, and each one a prodigy in their own right. Thank you all!

And I must thank Chris Grams, who was determined to make this project unlike any other book available, and hunted me down to ensure just that. In a wishy-washy world, it's nice to see some visionaries willing to try something different (and to entrust a lunatic like myself with his reputation). He's the one who made this book happen, and he is the driving force behind many exciting new titles entering the market. Good luck on those other titles Chris, but I know this one is killer!

# Dedication

I would like to dedicate this book to my parents, Annemarie and Arnie. They have always been loving and supporting, even when they didn't always agree with the directions I was taking in my life.

# Contents

# Foreword

With computer technology advancing so quickly, the demand for exceptional computer graphics is growing, and the imaging power once reserved for an elite few is now in the hands of millions.

CorelDRAW™, winner of more than 270 international first-place awards, offers the precision and ease of use today's artists need. Dominating the PC illustration arena with over 85% market share*, CorelDRAW is a revolutionary leader in the graphic design industry.

The first book of its kind, CorelDRAW 8 f/x will help you discover the full potential of this world-class graphics suite. Hundreds of pages filled with useful techniques, time saving tips, and original artwork let you create professional graphics more efficiently than ever before. Learn effectively with hands-on training using the Companion CD-ROM, an invaluable learning aid and art resource. Whether you're a novice or a seasoned professional, this material will allow you to design graphics that will make others sit up and take notice.

With so many powerful, easy-to-use tools and features, CorelDRAW 8 lets you unleash your creativity. Join Shane Hunt and explore the possibilities as you advance through the pages of CorelDRAW 8 f/x.

Corel Corporation

---

*Market Share—Drawing & Painting Software. PC Data, 1996 Unit Sales. Percentage representation based on unit sales of top 4 competitors in the vector illustration and image editing software category only.

# Introduction

Humans are by nature predators, aggressive creatures responding instinctively to a constant bombardment of visual stimuli. Although the majority of us no longer need to hunt and kill to survive (at least not in a literal sense), millions of years of evolution can't be undone. We are visual beings that rely almost entirely on our sense of sight to survive and succeed in the modern world. For this reason we find ourselves in a society that relies heavily on visual imagery for communication. Everything from the mundane to the sublime is represented graphically to enhance interest and comprehension.

I have always been excited by visual imagery. I would devise ingenious schemes in grade school to finish all of my work early, so me and my buddy could focus our efforts on what was really important: art! We would draw these giant, elaborate scenes on big rolls of butcher paper, while our peers still toiled over the day's lesson plan. Big, scaly monsters attacking cities, armies attacking the monsters, jets, tanks, machines, fire, destruction, and in general, chaos. Moms and teachers were not very excited about our scenes of mass destruction, but every one of my classmates loved them. What made the murals interesting was the meticulous level of detail, from the rivets on the tank skin to blue-print like diagrams describing such features as the dual-furnace flame reservoirs in the dragon's torso.

Today computer graphics continue to indefinitely broaden the visual horizon. The potential has become virtually limited only by your imagination (which in my case is pretty twisted). Now even time and raw talent can be minimal, with the aid of computers, clip art, and wizards to help anyone create pretty pictures. Computer hardware is continuing to get better and cheaper, and software more and more powerful. Is this a great time to be a designer, or what?!

CorelDRAW™ is without question the most popular (and I argue the most powerful) object-oriented illustration package on the planet. What started out as an outcast application in the Apple Mac dominated graphics community has grown to be the premier suite on any operating system (CorelDRAW is available on the Mac, OS/2, Unix, Windows 2, 3.1, 95 and even NT). And although the journey at times has been troubled, in the end CorelDRAW has emerged a champion.

Which brings us to now, CorelDRAW 8, the result of almost a decade of evolution. There has never been a better program! More speed, more tools, more effects, more potential than ever. And in this world of change, where one minute you are designing a print-ad graphic and the next minute asked to make it dance in a Web page, this kind of power and flexibility isn't just a bonus, it's necessary for survival. To be really successful in today's highly competitive market, you need creativity and tenacity that you can't find in a box. You need to go beyond what everyone else is doing in order to stand out from the crowd. The fact that you purchased this book already makes you one step ahead, with a desire to learn and get more out of what is already the premier design package available on the market today. With that kind of passion for design, powerful hardware and unlimited software, the world is your oyster.

# chapter 1

# Overview of CorelDRAW 8

CorelDRAW is the world's most popular design package. It also has the largest percentage of users who have little or no formal art background. CorelDRAW artists are computer professionals working in a variety of applications for which they need some kind of computer-generated graphics. They also need speed and flexibility. So for simple business graphics, high-end advertising, and everything in between, CorelDRAW has become an integral part of their workday.

CorelDRAW's speed and flexibility, not to mention its use by professional artists, make it stand out from the other computer art programs on the market. We are not here just to make pretty pictures, but to put those images to work for us. You may have some art background or experience using traditional design tools, or no experience at all. I am assuming you are like me; that you want to get as much accomplished as you can with the smallest amount of effort and in the shortest amount of time. I have been working as a designer for over eight years and as a computer professional over half my life. I love art, I love pretty pictures, I love computers, and I even love my job. But, I am guessing, like me, you would prefer to finish your work as quickly as possible and get the heck out of the office!

## Getting to Know CorelDRAW 8

This book is about working smart. I have tried to use real-world examples and ideas you can use in your everyday work environment. My tips are from years of real-world experiences dealing with CorelDRAW on a daily basis and crunching out artwork for a living. Even if you are not a commercial artist and creating art is not the focus of your job (and that is many of you), I think you will appreciate the nature of this book. I have tried to make this a CorelDRAW book by and for Corel artisans!

In my experience, the CorelDRAW community, despite its size, has been a very close and friendly one. I hope to continue this tradition and will endeavor to make myself available for any questions or comments that may arise along the way. Hey, this is all a big adventure for me too!

## Object-Oriented Package

CorelDRAW is an object-oriented illustration package. This means everything breaks down into individual shapes that have their own outline and fill attributes, which the computer sees as a set of mathematical coordinates and settings. A CorelDRAW image file is essentially a set of computer instructions that the program uses to build your objects and in turn create your design. Object-oriented illustration with CorelDRAW objects is very efficient.

The object-oriented nature of CorelDRAW brings with it a level of flexibility unique to the medium. You can select an object and change it any time within the life cycle of your design, something you can't do when you are working with a bitmap program or traditional paint brush or pen and ink. What this means is that when a client says, "I love it, except instead of a fire theme, let's try ice...," you don't have to start over; you only have to change the attributes of the objects already in place. Or, before the client even asks, you can save multiple copies of the same artwork, recolor each uniquely, and present them with a variety of options. CorelDRAW artwork is flexible, and flexibility is synonymous with *power*.

In today's competitive design climate, the advantages of working with an object-oriented, vector-based application are many. Throughout this book you will see many effects and examples used for a specific application, but the nature of the program is such that you can use the artwork in almost any imaginable way. Artwork designed for the Web can become, with virtually no additional effort, high-end color printed material, oversized banners, coffee mugs, almost anything you can imagine. CorelDRAW images are ready to be ported to printing presses, onscreen applications, slides for presentations, even other design programs. It is a flexibility unrivaled by any other application. There is no hidden cost, file sizes are not huge or unmanageable, and output is not difficult. CorelDRAW is a commercial artist's best friend—and closest ally.

What this also means is that you never have to be satisfied with a design. You can go back and fine-tune an image and tweak a design until it is exactly what you want. Or you can take an image and refine it for another application. You can customize an ad campaign to hit multiple demographics smack between the eyes. Whatever your needs, the power is yours, limited only by your imagination and your energy.

## Vector Art vs. Bitmaps

CorelDRAW objects are *vector* artwork. They are a series of mathematical coordinates connected with a line, like an electronic dot to dot. This keeps the objects infinitely scaleable and also relatively small in size. A bitmap, on the other hand, is made up of a collection of colored pixels, the size and density of which determine the physical size and resolution of the image. A bitmap may have too much or too little image information depending upon its size and the needs of the current project. You can always generate a bitmap from vector artwork, but the reverse is not always true. That's why CorelDRAW is a superior starting point even for projects that will eventually become bitmaps.

Vector artwork is much more flexible than bitmaps because it is, like I said, basically a collection of coordinates. You can enlarge or reduce a CorelDRAW image without degrading the resolution or changing the file size because the computer basically needs only to reset a scale attribute for the new size. A bitmap, which is a fixed-resolution entity, does not have this flexibility.

On the left side of Figure 1-1, an Apache helicopter vector image off of the CorelDRAW clip-art CD (\clipart\aircraft\helicopt) is duplicated and enlarged to create a second one in the foreground. If you try and do the same with a bitmap (on the right side of Figure 1-1), the resolution is fixed and becomes pixelated upon enlargement. On the other end of the spectrum, if you have a large bitmap and then duplicate it and reduce it, your image will look fine but your file size will be large. Even though you made the bitmap smaller on the screen, it still contains all of the image information of the original, and therefore you end up working with redundant information that just increases your file size.

*Figure 1-1: Unlike a bitmap (on right), CorelDRAW vector artwork (left) can be enlarged or reduced without affecting file size or resolution.*

Although the focus of CorelDRAW has been creating and manipulating vector objects, you could also perform limited actions on imported bitmaps within all versions of the program. Corel has always bundled PHOTO-PAINT™, their powerful bitmap manipulation package, along with CorelDRAW for advanced bitmap massaging. Introduced in version 7 and getting better in version 8, you can create and modify bitmaps within the CorelDRAW environment itself.

Now, after I just explained why bitmaps are a pain, why would you then want to convert your nice vector artwork into such a beast? Well, there are times you just can't get the look you are after if your artwork is a crisp CorelDRAW object. Because of the hard-edged nature of object-oriented vector artwork, there are times you will want to convert to a bitmap to create a soft, anti-aliased edge or to use a filter or built-in bitmap effect that simply will not work on vector artwork at all.

For example, our hero Albert Einstein (\clipart\carictre\historic) in Figure 1-2 (on left) is in the CorelDRAW native vector format. On the right, a shape placed in front of this artwork is given a Fish Eye lens from the Lens roll-up (Alt+F3). Notice how only the vector artwork in the face is distorted and not the checkerboard pattern (this checkerboard is a two-color pattern fill set from the Pattern Fill dialog, accessed from the Fill flyout). Despite being native CorelDRAW entities, pattern fills and texture fills are not vector information; they are bitmaps. The Fish Eye lens effect will not distort the bitmap information in CorelDRAW fills.

*Figure 1-2: The Fish Eye lens will not distort some bitmap information, such as bitmap pattern fills or texture fills.*

Now we could redraw the checkers as individual vector box objects and then the Fish Eye lens would work. However, the easier solution is to use the Convert to Bitmap feature from the Bitmap menu (Figure 1-3). Notice that this image was converted to 24-bit color and not grayscale. Why? Well, it turns out that the KPT filter doesn't work on grayscale files. (There, now you just learned something that I spent 20 minutes going crazy trying to figure out!) With the image as a bitmap, it can now be easily manipulated with any of the effects listed under the Bitmap menu. You can also install any Photoshop-compatible aftermarket plug-in. The figure on the left was created using the KPT 3.0 Spheroid Designer, and the figure on the right was created with the 3D Rotate option from the 3D Effects flyout.

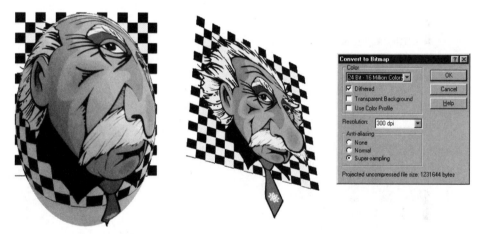

*Figure 1-3: You can use the Convert to Bitmap dialog to change vector art to a pixel-based image within the CorelDRAW work space. This allows for even more image manipulation within the program than ever before.*

The bottom line is getting the results you want, regardless of whether the image is vector or bitmap. (I preach the philosophy of *ruthless creativity*, which is getting what you want no matter what it takes or how potentially unconventional the means.) CorelDRAW has always provided a great way to generate bitmaps, only now you can do it easier and directly within the program. This new functionality blurs the line a bit between CorelDRAW and bitmap manipulation programs such as PHOTO-PAINT, but as you will see, the focus of each program is still pretty clear. As this is a CorelDRAW book and not a PHOTO-PAINT book, the discussion will focus on DRAW's bitmap features.

However, as PHOTO-PAINT is bundled with CorelDRAW, and PHOTO-PAINT runs circles around DRAW when it comes to bitmaps, I will not hesitate to turn to that program for help (as in Chapters 22 and 29, when PHOTO-PAINT power is critical to the techniques).

This is a book about working smart, so there is no need to be masochistic and force ourselves to work entirely in CorelDRAW when PHOTO-PAINT may be the better solution! Along those same lines, the final chapter looks at working with CorelDREAM 3D, the 3D modeling application. All images created with CorelDREAM 3D are bitmaps, so obviously they are a perfectly viable entity for commercial publishing projects. The main thing to remember with bitmaps is to create images at a high enough resolution and appropriate color depth for their intended purpose.

▼ **Rendering Images**

Although CorelDRAW is a vector-based art application, there are many applications that need bitmaps. You don't see many people using the Corel Presentation Exchange Filter (CMX) filter on Web pages to make the native vector format Internet friendly, for example (even though the technology exists). The much more practical and useful solution is to render the CorelDRAW images as 72-dpi bitmaps at 16 million colors (RGB) for all to see! You can take any CorelDRAW image and make it a bitmap using the Export (Ctrl+H) dialog. Here you can pick a resolution and color model appropriate for your project, be it four-color printing (CMYK at 300 dpi) or onscreen applications. You can also render a CorelDRAW file as a bitmap and then manipulate it further in PHOTO-PAINT. There are many applications when a bitmap is necessary (as we will see throughout this book), and CorelDRAW is ready to foot the bill!

## How to Use This Book

This book was written so that you can either read it straight through or just flip to a section that interests you. Some of the later chapters, however, do assume that you have learned techniques from previous chapters. Where this is the case, you will find a chapter reference so you can just jump back and review the material as needed.

## The Book

As I wrote this book, I tried to keep in mind how I would use it. I buy a techniques book like this one because there is something of specific interest in the color section that makes me think, "Cool. I want to do that!" I take the book home, flip to that section, and work through the tutorial. Yippee! Instant gratification!

Then I flip through the book some more, looking at the pictures and the step-by-step instructions until curiosity gets the better of me and I find myself checking out another chapter. I then peruse the CD-ROM and check out all of the goodies on it. Hey, I know the drill!

So I have tried to tailor this book to both the "jumpers" and the truly dedicated, who will plow through all of the material sequentially, unable to sleep until they have milked the pages dry of every secret and tip. It's up to you how you use this book. It's all here, and there is no expiration date! Use and enjoy at your own pace.

To entice you to read through the whole book and work through the tutorials, I was able to sneak in little funny stories and silly life experiences here and there. Hey, I know how dull computer books can be to read (trust me, I've written enough to feel your pain!). I couldn't stand to write another boring technical manual. I hope you will find this book both entertaining and educational.

## The Companion CD-ROM

One thing that has always bothered me about computer books is that the artwork in print is not always available digitally. I hate that. Sometimes, no matter how good a set of instructions are, nothing beats loading the file and digging around in it first-hand. With an object-oriented program like CorelDRAW, this is especially true.

The reason most books don't include all of the artwork on the CD-ROM is simple. Most books use a collection of artwork from other artists who, although excited to have their images in print, are not at all excited about letting people dig through their precious art files, learn all of their secrets, and steal the images for their own use. This is perfectly understandable.

However, I tossed sanity and convention to the wind and have used only my own original artwork in this book. I have drawn from almost a decade of material to mix and match images to provide a variety of artwork; I've also provided each and every example on the Companion CD-ROM. The files are there primarily so you can fully understand the techniques we are discussing, but feel free to pilfer the images and use them as you like! Consider it the "Crazy Uncle Shane" clip-art collection, a double bonus for buying this book!

Each chapter in the book has a matching directory on the Companion CD-ROM that contains the finished art and sometimes other support pieces (scans of illustrations, stock photography, etc.). I will point out in the text the name and location of the files in question so you can load them and see what is going on. For the most part, each file coincides with a page in the color section as well, so you can flip there and see what we are going to work on before you load the file or read the chapter. For chapters dealing with animation or onscreen artwork (Web pages, multimedia applications, etc.), I have also included the HTML code to view with your Web browser and self-running movies or animations to demonstrate a technique. There are a few extra files with art I thought fit a chapter or technique, and I will point them out to you as we go along.

Also on the Companion CD-ROM are the bonus fonts, utilities, and images that all computer books have these days. I tried to make it a CD that I would want if I were buying a computer book, so I think you will be really happy with what you find there! In my opinion, the CD-ROM alone is worth the price of this book! So don't miss out. Load it up—I guarantee there is something on there that will bring a smile to your face or add something useful to your design day.

## Newbie to Necromancer

CorelDRAW has evolved over the years from an entry-level package to a full-scale professional design suite. Along the way, with the never-ending addition of tools and functions, it has become a bit more intimidating to new users. With so much potential, the perceived learning curve seems pretty steep.

Fear not all, CorelDRAW 8 is as accessible to the seasoned pro as it is to the new kid on the block. The tutorial is great, the Template Wizard's awesome, and the documentation very complete. It should take no time at all to get up to speed and feel comfortable working in the program.

If you are new to the program, I suggest that you go through the tutorial and work through a few projects to get used to everything before you try the examples outlined in this book. Everyone has to crawl a bit before they can walk.

Users of all levels should be able to follow along in the tutorials. I have used keyboard shortcuts throughout to make it easy to just punch up the desired roll-up or dialog box. You can, of course, orient yourself with the pull-down menus and use their commands instead of the shortcuts. (I actually almost never use keyboard shortcuts. I am definitely a mouser by nature!) In CorelDRAW, you can customize your work space and modify your work habits to suit your exact needs, and I encourage you to do so. I know I have my own quirky work habits that will haunt me until I go to my grave (I *refuse* to use anything but the traditional zoom flyout, for example). If you think the way I create something can be achieved in some other and perhaps easier way, try it. CorelDRAW is a universe full of wonder and magic, and even I have yet to uncover it all. With yearly upgrades and constantly added features, I don't think I will ever end this journey of discovery! So let's get to it.

## Moving On

Okay, enough of the basic introduction, bring on the f/x! In the next chapter, we literally start with a bang as we explore fire and explosions. Like a match to gasoline, the first tutorial ignites instantly to create hot and fiery effects. So get out your protective gear, as things are going to get hot and furious right off of the bat. I'm sure that you can handle it, but maybe you should have a fire extinguisher nearby....

# chapter 2

# Fire, Explosions & Pinwheels

Somehow, I'm still fascinated with scenes of chaos like those I drew as a kid! The scribbles of yesterday become the inspiration for design elements today as fire, flames, and explosions still seem to creep into the mix. This is no surprise, as fire is such an interesting design element. It's bright and dynamic and has exciting visual and social connotations. Fire comes in many varieties, and like every project, the way this element takes shape is dictated entirely by the needs at hand. This chapter covers a handful of flaming-hot examples for a variety of applications, all completely inappropriate for "nonsmokers."

In this chapter we will explore several techniques to render fire and explosions. Making elaborate flame shapes is much easier with a few duplication/flipping tricks, and the key to looking good is the coloring. We will also look at using the Interactive Transparency tool to give smoke a wispy feel and finally end things with a "bang" using the Blend function to create dynamic explosions and fireworks.

This introductory chapter is sizzling with my philosophy of ruthless creativity. Basically, it's just a no-holds-barred approach to design, where you use your available resources to the fullest and don't hesitate to experiment or try new ways to use old tools. Just do whatever it takes to get what you want, even if it seems unconventional or even strange. Also embodied in this philosophy is approachable coolness. I have tried to keep everything in this book within a reasonable amount of effort. Personally, I hate spending too much time on one particular design, preferring shortcuts and tricks that still have a high visual payoff. Take what I give you and run from there, massaging and tweaking the techniques and examples in your own twisted little ways!

## Hot! Hot!

*Figure 2-1: CorelDRAW objects allow for greater design flexibility than a scanned photo would allow. You can stack objects front to back, duplicate, stretch, flip, and rotate to create a customized art piece, which can be output at any size without loss of any resolution.*

As irony would have it, I spent the day watching a raging brush fire on a hillside not far from my home here in southern California. What struck me was not how interesting the flames looked, but rather what a huge smoky mess it all was! This was a refreshing reminder of why graphic artwork created with CorelDRAW is so powerful, and that's the concept of *idealized reality*. The real world tends to be inherently inflexible, sticky, and messy, and photographs of real flames simply do not afford the kind of design opportunities and resolution flexibility that a collection of vector art does. In Figure 2-1 (and also in the color section), we see how with CorelDRAW objects we can manipulate our flames and smoke as we please, positioning objects in front of and behind our ad copy. This first example is a perfect place to start, as it looks cool, is not that difficult, and is great example of working smarter, not harder!

The premise behind this piece is the classic hot theme. I cannot tell you how many times I have set the word *hot* on fire for one reason or another! To start this project, I turned to the CorelDRAW clip-art book for ideas. Clip art?! *Heck yes!* Why reinvent the wheel when more than likely there is something useful at hand? The power of CorelDRAW includes the peripheral support material, including the rich font and clip-art libraries. Here is how to ignite the clip art into something much hotter:

1. With CorelDRAW running, start a new graphic (Ctrl+N).

2. Open the Import dialog (Ctrl+I), and with the CorelDRAW clip-art CD in your system, click on the CD icon. Now navigate down to the \clipart\fire subdirectory and click on the file called Fire3.cdr. Click on Import to bring in this file (see Figure 2-2).

*Figure 2-2: To save time and effort, use the Corel clip-art libraries for both inspiration and images. This image is from the \clipart\fire subdirectory.*

3. Ungroup (Ctrl+U) these objects so that you can manipulate them individually. Now deselect the group (Esc), select the tree objects, and delete them (Delete key). Also delete the front-left fire object until you have only the flame and smoke pieces as seen in Figure 2-3.

*Figure 2-3: Delete unnecessary objects from the original clip-art image to get just the flame and smoke parts.*

4. Drag-select all of these objects, and then click on the selection to reveal the rotation arrows. Now drag a corner arrow around until the flames are in a horizontal orientation.

5. Click and hold the Shape tool icon on the Toolbox to open the flyout, and then select the Knife tool (see Figure 2-4).

*Figure 2-4: The Knife tool is located on the Shape tool flyout.*

6. Switch to Wireframe under the View menu. This makes it easier to see the boundaries of objects. With the Knife tool, click on the bottom right where the flame just ends on the wireframe. Then move to the opposite side and click again to make the cut. The Knife tool cuts across the object and separates the pieces into two objects as seen in Figure 2-5.

7. Now toggle back to the Pick tool (tap the spacebar), select the bottom piece, and delete it. Back in the Normal view (see Figure 2-6), we should have a nice flame image, which will serve as a base for our design.

Figure 2-5: The Knife tool cuts objects into smaller pieces.

Figure 2-6: The clip art is reduced down to just the desired shapes.

8. The first thing I did was recolor the flames. Select the flame-top group and give it a solid red fill by left-clicking the red onscreen color well. Then select the bottom flame group and open the Fountain Fill dialog (F11), which is shown in Figure 2-7. From here, set the Type option to Radial, offset the center –43%, and change the Color Blend option to Custom. Now make the starting color orange (click on the swatch just above the color ramp on the left side and then click on the orange color well) and the final color white (the right swatch on top of the color ramp).

Then by double-clicking on the top of the color ramp, create a new color point. Make this color point yellow. A custom fountain fill gives you a broader color range than the default Two Color option (see Figure 2-7). This fill gives a "white-hot" center, cooling out to yellow and orange tones on the tips. Move the yellow point on the color ramp to the left or the right for more or less white in your blend.

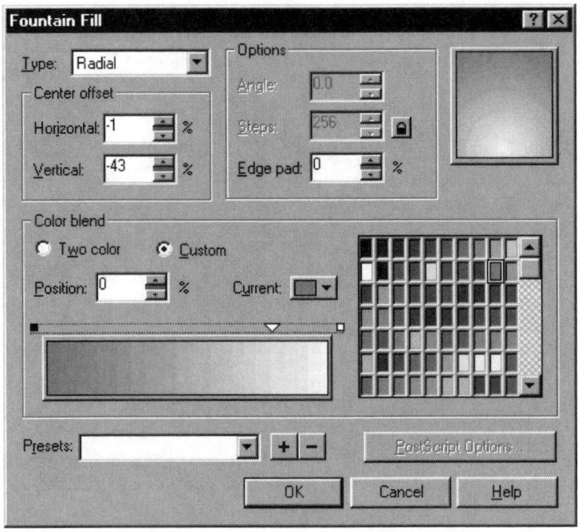

*Figure 2-7: The Fountain Fill dialog with a three-color custom color blend. The horizontal box in the center is the color ramp. Double-click above it to assign a color point. Select the starting or ending color points to change those colors.*

9. To add contrast to the flames and make them stand out, draw a box with the Rectangle tool, fill it with black, and then send it to the back (Shift+PgDn).

10. To make the smoke less harsh, I decided to make it semi-opaque. Shift-select all of the smoke objects and then click on the Interactive Transparency tool. Now click-drag from the center of the flames upward almost to the top of the highest object and release. What this does is make the smoke pieces solid at the starting point and fade out completely by the time they reach the ending point (see Figures 2-8 and 2-9).

*Figure 2-8: Dragging across your objects with the Interactive Transparency tool establishes a start point of 100% opacity, which fades out to an end point of 100% transparency.*

*Figure 2-9: You use the Property Bar for the Interactive Transparency tool to change its parameters. The default settings of Fountain transparency from 0–100% are shown.*

11. Drag-select all of the flame and smoke objects and open the Scale & Mirror roll-up (Alt+F9). Now click the Horizontal Mirror button, and Apply to Duplicate. This will create a flip-flopped duplicate of the smoke and flame on top of our original. Grab the top-center sizing handle and squash this duplicate down. Now grab the right-center sizing handle and

drag outward while holding down the Shift key to widen the selected objects. By flipping and resizing the duplicate, we disguise the clone to so that it looks unique, and at the same time, we make our fire hotter (see Figure 2-10)!

*Figure 2-10: Duplicating, flipping, and resizing the original results in a design that looks more complex without looking repetitive.*

12. Next, click on the screen with the Text tool and type **HOT**. Switch to the Pick tool and select the text object.

**TIP** *There is no shortcut back to the Pick tool from the Text tool. Esc does not deselect and the spacebar only adds spaces to your text! Move the cursor to the Pick tool and click.*

13. With your text selected, open the Format Text dialog (Ctrl+T) and from the Font tab, pick a typeface that suits your taste. I used SerpentineDBol at 36 points. Click OK to change the face.

14. Position the word *HOT* below our flame object and color it red. Now duplicate it and position the duplicate to the top and right of the original (drag or use the arrow keys to nudge). From the Arrange menu, choose Weld to open the Weld roll-up. Now click the Weld To button and then click on the front fire object (see Figure 2-11). This will merge the two objects into one. Because you welded the word to the flame object, which was behind the text, the red copy of *HOT* is now on top. Select it, and from the Arrange | Order submenu, choose Behind. Then click on the flame object. Voila!

*Figure 2-11: The Weld function merges two objects into one.*

**TIP** *Change the Nudge value in the Options dialog (Ctrl+J) to a much smaller increment, such as .005 or even .003 inches. This makes it easier to move your object in precise, tiny steps. To regain the functionality of a big nudge, simply up the Super Nudge multiplier value to something like 50. Now when you hold the Control key and nudge with the arrow keys, you "super-nudge" greater distances. In this way, you get micro-adjustments with the Nudge arrows and big moves with Super Nudge.*

15. The final step was to throw on some ad copy, which I set in the Faktos font in solid white. The type is set behind some of the smoke objects and in front of others. Use commands in the Arrange | Order submenu to move the text forward or backward until you are satisfied.

This is just one quick-and-dirty way to get the flaming look. This file is called Hot.cdr and is in the \Chapt2\ subdirectory on this book's Companion CD-ROM and is also in the color section. Open it up and experiment with the different settings, especially the Interactive Transparency tool to arrive at different variants. The "smoke" objects, for example, can make the text obscure and far away or pop out up close, depending on how subtle you make the transparency (see Chapter 9 for more on atmospheric perspective). Also, I gave these flames a stark, almost cartoony coloring scheme. You could recolor them to look more real, or you could color them in icy blues for a frozen flame paradox! Go crazy—I won't tell anyone!

## Goddess of Fire

*Figure 2-12: Using a bitmap for reference, flame shapes are hand-drawn and laid on top of each other. The Contour tool was used to give the flames the crisp, double-outline look. Then they are grouped as one, duplicated, and flipped horizontally on top of the original to add more flames without much effort.*

In my entryway I have a series of portraits in black ink that greet visitors to my studio. I wanted to take the faces and somehow incorporate them into an animation sequence, which eventually will replace the static images with a row of computer monitors, perpetually displaying the movies. The project will eventually have many animations representing elements or seasons (I can't decide!) but will certainly include this Goddess of Fire piece. This project is a good example of what I call hot rod flames; fire that has crisp, sweeping curves and multiple sets of outlines.

To start this project, I took photos of two pieces of artwork I had lying around. One was the pen-and-ink portrait and another a pastel flame-ball thing I had created for a racing helmet design. My studio is a bit chaotic, with many projects scattered around, but from this study in entropy I derive plenty of inspiration! Never hesitate to turn to unusual sources for ideas and imagery.

I scanned the photos using a flat-bed scanner, but you could use the tracing technique with any bitmap or illustration available. As with all the examples in this book, I don't expect you to repeat the process verbatim but instead tailor it to your own needs. Here is how to create the cartoony flames you see in Figure 2-12:

1. Import (Ctrl+I) the flame image onto a new CorelDRAW page. To prevent accidental moving of the bitmap, place it on its own layer and lock it. Open the Layers roll-up (Ctrl+F3) and from the submenu choose New. Now you have a new Layer 2 on top of Layer 1, which contains the bitmap. Click on the Pencil icon next to Layer 1 to disable editing on that layer. Now the bitmap is locked in place (see Figure 2-13).

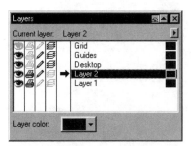

*Figure 2-13: The Layers roll-up (also called the Layer Manager) lets you manage your artwork by placing different objects on their own physical layer. Deselecting the Pencil icon disables editing on that layer, ensuring that the reference bitmap is not accidentally moved during the manual tracing process.*

2. Using the Bezier tool, click around to follow the contour of a section of flame.

**TIP** *The Bezier tool is good for quickly creating objects. If you click from point to point, you create straight lines, but you can also drag while you create to make a curve.*

*Don't worry about perfection, as it is easier to edit a line later with the Shape tool than it is to try and get it right the first time with the Bezier tool. When drawing on top of a bitmap, set the default outline color to something bright like white or yellow so that it stands out (see Figure 2-14).*

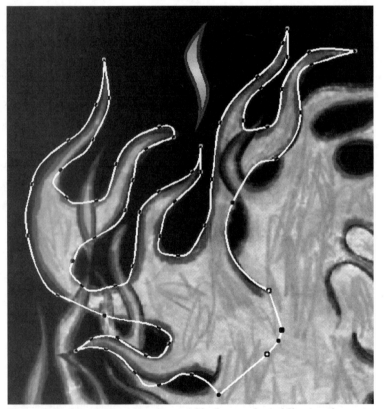

*Figure 2-14: Use the Bezier tool to quickly draw a shape following the contours of the flames. Perfection is not necessary, as it is easier to edit a curve later than it is to try and get it perfect the first time.*

**TIP**
*To set the default color, select nothing (click on an empty space or press the Esc key) and then right-click on an onscreen color well. CorelDRAW will prompt you that you are about to change the default, as nothing is selected. Make sure the Graphic box is checked and click OK.*

3. With the Shape tool, smooth out the curves and fine-tune the flames by dragging and manipulating the nodes. Double-click on a node to open the Node Edit roll-up. Then use the Make Node Smooth button to get a nice sweeping curve for the body of the flames. On the tips, use the Cusp button to make a sharp point (see Figure 2-15).

*Figure 2-15: Use the Shape tool to node-edit your shape to smooth out the curves. Use the Make Node Smooth button on nodes to get smoother transitions, and use the Make Node a Cusp button for the sharp pointy ends.*

I repeated this process for the entire flame until I had re-created it entirely with CorelDRAW objects. I drew many separate pieces in later steps to facilitate the illusion of the flames interweaving (see Figure 2-16).

*Figure 2-16: Drawing a shape with the Bezier tool and then fine-tuning it with the Shape tool results in smooth shapes for the entire flame ball.*

**TIP** *In a circular application such as this, to save time you could just create one quarter-section and then duplicate and rotate around three more times to finish off the circle. I liked my original design, so I just decided to go the long route and re-create the whole thing.*

When you are finished using the reference bitmap, click on the pencil on the bitmap layer and then select and delete the bitmap.

4. To create the illusion that the flames are weaving in and out of each other, I created many smaller individual shapes. These shapes would need to align perfectly on top of each other for the illusion to work. To get the edges to match, you could manually node-edit the pieces, but that sucks! Instead, use this Intersection/Trim trick. Select the overlapping object and open the Intersection roll-up from the Arrange menu. Now

click the Intersect With button, and then click on the curve you want to butt up against. Because the objects cross in three areas, the result is three new shapes (see Figure 2-17).

*Figure 2-17: The Intersection function results in shapes wherever objects overlap. All but the rightmost object will be deleted, which will trim away the key overlap area, resulting in the objects touching perfectly flush to one another.*

5. Break apart (Ctrl+K) this curve and delete all but the rightmost shape. Now select the remaining shape and change the Intersect roll-up to the Trim roll-up by clicking on Trim in the top window of the roll-up (see Figure 2-17). CorelDRAW groups related functions like these into one roll-up to speed things along. Now click the Trim button and then click on the original small flame object. This will trim away the key area where the flames overlapped, resulting in a perfect fit (see Figure 2-18).

Repeat this process wherever flame pieces need to appear to be overlapping. This process is necessary because you cannot bend a CorelDRAW object. An object can not be in front of another on the left and then behind it on the right. It must be either in front of or behind the entire object, so the smaller pieces are necessary to fool the eye into thinking the flames bend around each other (see Figure 2-19).

Figure 2-18: *Using the piece from the Intersection step, the Trim function then cuts away the area of overlap, resulting in a perfect fit.*

Figure 2-19: *The flames are broken into smaller objects to give the illusion that they bend and twist around each other. They have all been assigned the same radial fill in this image so you can see how some sections remain large while others are broken into smaller pieces.*

6. In order to outline the yellow flames in both red and blue, make two smaller copies of each flame curve using the Contour roll-up (Ctrl+F9). Select a curve and open the roll-up. Then set the parameters to Inside, Offset .006, and Steps 2. If you click the color-wheel tab and change the fill value to yellow, you will also save yourself a coloring step later. Click Apply to generate the new shapes (see Figure 2-20).

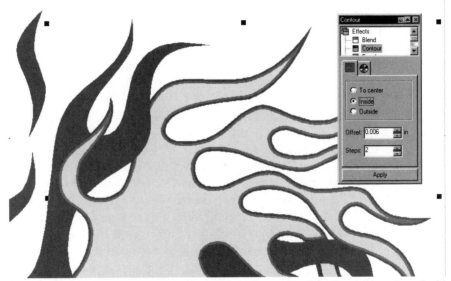

*Figure 2-20: The Contour roll-up creates two smaller copies of the flame objects for a double-outline effect.*

7. Arrange | Separate the Contour group and then ungroup (Ctrl+G) once more. Now select the green-colored interim shape and color it red by left-clicking an onscreen color well. This process was repeated on all of the flame objects to create a uniform look. The Contour roll-up will retain the settings from the previous use, so you only need to click on a new flame shape and then click the Apply button to generate uniform contour shapes for all of the flame objects.

**TIP**

*The problem with contouring the flame shapes is that it also creates contours in the shapes that were butted up against each other to suggest the weaving effect, which detracts from the look a bit. You could just leave things as they are, but I chose to use the Shape tool to drag the nodes of the contour shapes back into an overlapping configuration (see Figure 2-21). As they say, the devil is in the details!*

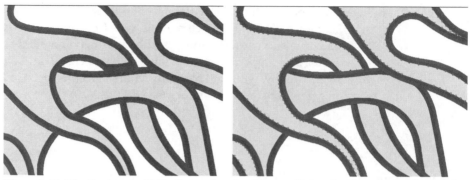

*Figure 2-21: The Contour tool kills the overlapping illusion. Using the Shape tool to drag nodes modifies the shapes so they look correct again.*

8. To make the flames look solid, an object was drawn over the open space in the center with the Bezier tool and given a solid yellow fill with no outline. This finished the flame ball, but somehow it looked very square to me. Drag-select all of the flame pieces and group them (Ctrl+G). Then from the Envelope roll-up (Ctrl+F7), depress the Single Arc button and then the Add New button. Drag the center right control node outward while holding down the Shift and Control keys to create a round envelope shape. Now click the Apply button on the Envelope roll-up to distort the artwork into the rounded envelope (see Figure 2-22).

9. As in the previous flame example, a duplicate of this flame shape will make the image look more interesting without much effort. Select the flame group and open the Scale & Mirror roll-up (Alt+F9). Enable the Vertical Mirror button and then click Apply to Duplicate to finish up the flame shape. For a bit of a glow effect, draw a circle over the flames and give it a black to white radial fountain fill. Hold down the Ctrl key while dragging the Ellipse tool to draw a perfect circle. Send this circle to the back (Shift+PgDn); then draw a black box around everything and send it to back (Shift+PgDn) to add even more contrast.

10. The Corel OCR-Trace utility is the best way to convert bitmaps into a usable CorelDRAW format (and how I turned my ink illustration into objects I could manipulate). See Chapter 18 for more on this conversion process. Start the application and open the bitmap you wish to convert (you can use the face.tif file in the \Chapt2\ subdirectory on the Companion CD-ROM if you want to practice this technique). Your scan should be as crisp as possible from a black-and-white source for the best trace results. You can convert anything into CorelDRAW objects with

**CD-ROM**

OCR-Trace, but color bitmaps just result in chaos. Trust me; I tried to save time by tracing the original pastel flames as well only to get a huge unusable file as a result! With your black-and-white image loaded, choose Trace Settings from the OCR-Trace menu and change from the default settings to Accurate. Now from the Image menu, choose Convert To and Black and White. This will give you the results closest to your original ink drawing. Now click on the Outline Trace button to perform the translation and then choose File | Save | Vector to save the converted data. OCR-Trace saves files in the Corel Presentation Exchange (CMX) format, which is supported by all Corel products. Exit without saving the changes to the bitmap file.

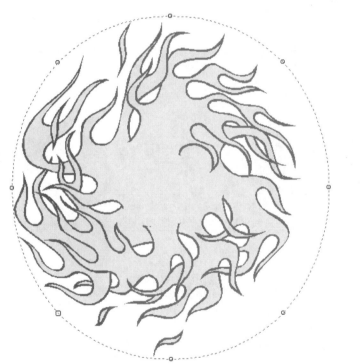

*Figure 2-22: An envelope distorts the flame objects into a rounder shape.*

11. Back in CorelDRAW, import (Ctrl+I) the CMX file into your workspace and ungroup (Ctrl+U) the objects. Delete the background box and give the face shape the same yellow fill as the flames. To get color in the lips, draw a shape behind the curves and assign it a red fill. Be aware that when you imported the CMX file, CorelDRAW created a new layer to

hold this data. This is very irritating! To get everything back on one layer, choose Select All from the Edit menu; then from the Layers roll-up (Ctrl+F3) flyout, click Move To and then click on your main layer (usually Layer 1). I almost never use layers because they make things so darn confusing—you can edit objects across multiple layers, but if you create something, it ends upon the selected layer. To add color to the eyes, select the white shapes in the dark areas and color them blue. Shift-select the finished pieces and group them (Ctrl+G). The face is now ready to be placed inside the flames to finish things off (see Figure 2-23).

*Figure 2-23: The Corel OCR-Trace utility converts bitmaps (left) into CorelDRAW objects (center). They can then be manipulated like any other CorelDRAW object. You can add fill and outline attributes (right), for example.*

The face was the final touch that brought this image to life (see color section for the final results). This file is called Goddess.cdr and is in the \Chapt2\ subdirectory on the Companion CD-ROM. Open it up and see how everything fits together. Also, I used this file to create the animation to use eventually in my greeting kiosk and for my Web site. The animation file, Goddess.avi, is also in the \Chapt2\ subdirectory. (Chapter 30 thoroughly describes the process for turning a collection of CorelDRAW images into an animation using Corel PhotoPaint.) To get motion in the Goddess.avi file, I simply selected and rotated the inner and outer flame objects in opposite directions in 15-degree increments (if you hold down Ctrl when you drag a rotation handle, it constrains to the default of 15 degrees) before exporting each frame of the animation as a bitmap using the CorelDRAW Export (Ctrl+H) feature. I find this animation quite mesmerizing, but then, it could just be the magic in those bewitching eyes.

## Explosions

COLOR
STUDIO

*Figure 2-24: Blending multiple sets of circles using the Acceleration feature results in a nice explosion! The nervous jet is straight out of the \clipart\aircraft\jets collection; the motion blur was made with the Interactive Transparency tool.*

What's fun about CorelDRAW is exploring the unknown. From solving a specific design problem to just open-ended experimentation, CorelDRAW gives you a powerful universe to explore. I was trying to get an explosion effect without investing too much effort when I discovered this technique. What thrills me is being able to get big payoffs with little creative effort! Here is how to blow things up:

1. Use the Ellipse tool to draw a circle. Duplicate this circle (use the + key on the numeric keypad) and then move the duplicate over and down slightly. Now drag-select both circles and repeat the duplication process until you have a blob of some 60 or so circles. Group them (Ctrl+G) and then fill them solid yellow by left-clicking the yellow swatch (to the right of the screen). Remove any outline by right-clicking the "no fill" color well (it looks like an *x*). Figure 2-25 shows what you will end up with.

*Figure 2-25: Start with a single circle and duplicate with the + key on the numeric keypad. Keep duplicating and moving until you have a blob of circles. This is the core of the explosion effect.*

2. Duplicate this group and color the duplicate magenta. Now ungroup the circle objects (Ctrl+U) and deselect them (click on nothing to deselect or press the Esc key). One by one, select and drag each of the magenta circles away from the center to form a scattered circle around the yellow cluster. When you are finished scattering, drag-select all of the pieces (or choose Select All from the Edit menu); during this process, you will also select the original yellow cluster. Hold down the Shift key and click on the yellow cluster to deselect it, leaving only the desired outside circles. Now, group these objects (Ctrl+G). See Figure 2-26 for the result.

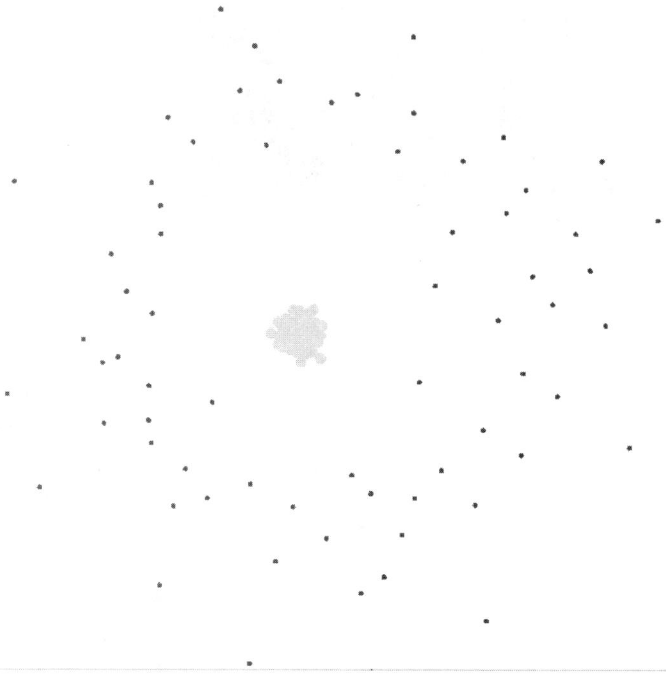

*Figure 2-26: The original set of circles is duplicated, and the duplicates scattered around one by one. This is the extent of the manual labor necessary for this effect! The Blend function will do the rest.*

3. Now shift-select both object groups and open the Blend roll-up (Ctrl+B). Change the number of steps from 20 to 50 and click Apply (see Figure 2-27). Pow! That was easy!

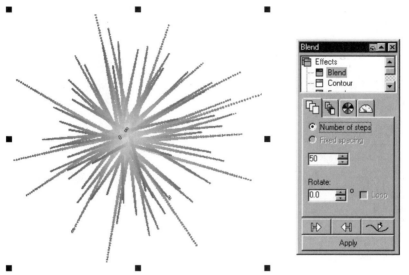

*Figure 2-27: Blending the scattered objects to the inner cluster results in a convincing explosion.*

4. Click on the second tab on the Blend roll-up to reveal the acceleration settings. Now drag the top Accelerate Objects slider almost all the way to the left and the Accelerate Fills/Outlines slider just a tad to the left. The Accelerate Objects setting will cluster the blend closer to the center, while the Fills/Outlines setting will result in the blend objects staying yellow longer. Click Apply to see the new blend. After applying the acceleration settings, it looks more like fragments are being thrown violently away from the hot center (see Figure 2-28).

5. I duplicated the explosion blend group to create vapor trails. Change the fill color of the outer control group objects to 40% black and the inner control group to white. When working with complex blends, it is a good idea to switch to Simple Wireframe from the View menu. In this mode, only the control objects in a blend are shown, hiding the dizzying array of in-between objects! Now switch back to Normal view, click on the blend group, and open the Blend roll-up once more. This time, slide the Accelerate sliders to the right and then click Apply (see Figure 2-29).

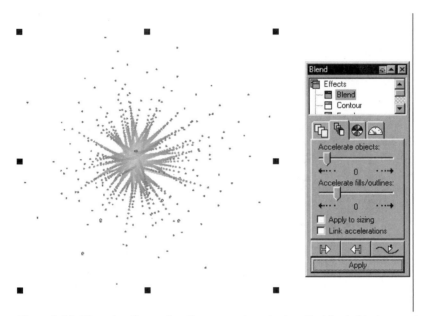

*Figure 2-28: Changing the acceleration parameters clusters the blend objects more in the center while delaying the blend from the inner to the outer color.*

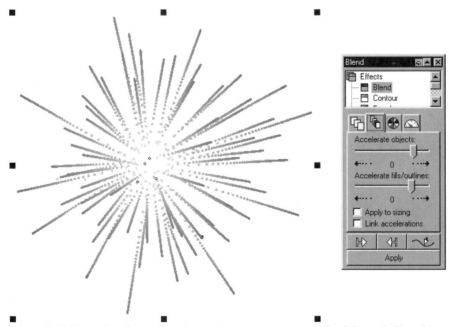

*Figure 2-29: Reversing the acceleration settings creates vapor trails of the exploding objects.*

6. Arrange the second vapor trails blend behind (Shift+PgDn) the first. Now your exploded pieces seem to leave a trail of smoke as they blast through the cosmos! Look at Figure 2-30 to see the effect.

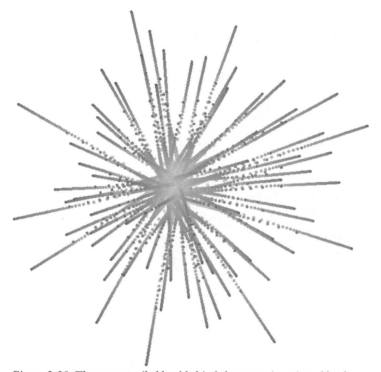

*Figure 2-30: The vapor trails blend behind the scattering pieces blend creates the explosion. Bang!*

For a glowing center, I placed my explosion on top of a perfect circle with a white to dark radial fountain fill. It is easy to duplicate the explosion; simply select the control groups and recolor them for a sky full of unique bursts. The great thing about this effect is that an explosion group will reblend itself at any size, so like a real explosion, it is small and compact and expands as you enlarge it. See the Explode.avi file in the \Chapt2\ subdirectory on the Companion CD-ROM for an example of how you can animate this technique. I threw on the jet I had from another project to create a battle scene. To manipulate the explosions for yourself, open the explode.cdr file from the \Chapt2\ subdirectory and you will appreciate the "live" nature of a blend. Enlarge or reduce the whole blend group or just the control groups to see how CorelDRAW recalculates your blend each time.

## Volcano

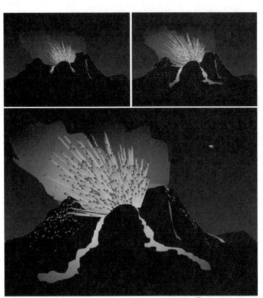

*Figure 2-31: Using the same blend technique we used with the explosion, you can create the hot magma of an erupting volcano. You can animate the eruption by simply enlarging the bend group, which recalculates to the new size and creates the explosion effect.*

As one thing leads to another, a news report of volcanic activity in Mexico led me to try and modify the explosion effect to simulate hot magma. It is essentially the same process, only the outside bits are not scattered in a big circle as with the explosion but rather in a 90-degree arc. Again, it's pretty easy, and I think the results are very cool! I actually made these images in reverse, starting with the full explosion with the lava drips and spatters (nothing more than radial-fountain-filled freehand shapes). Reducing the explosion blend, covering up the flowing lava shapes with black shapes, and deleting pieces reduced the explosion in several steps. You can choose any stage of explosion for your image, increasing or decreasing the chaos! Here is how to make a volcano erupt.

1. With the Freehand tool, I quickly drew out some mountain shapes in black. I started with a piece in the back and then drew some in front. The front pieces were to obscure the origin of the explosion blend later on. If you start and finish a curve at the same point, it becomes a solid object. If you are close, but the curve does not form a solid, click the Auto Close button on the Property Bar. Use the Freehand tool to quickly draw the

mountain shapes as well as some smoke objects. Working in Wireframe mode, it is easy to map out your objects first and then assign, color, and arrange them later. This way you don't flip-flop between tools or views, which for me is faster, but everyone has their own way of working. You can also use both views simultaneously (see tip below and Figure 2-32).

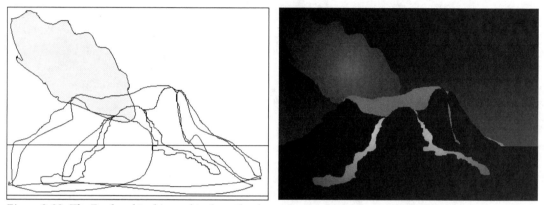

*Figure 2-32: The Freehand tool is used to draw the shapes for the mountain, smoke, and flowing lava.*

**TIP**  *To work in both the Wireframe and Normal viewing mode simultaneously, choose New Window from the Window menu. Then choose Window | Tile Horizontally (or Vertically, your choice) to view both windows at the same time. Now select one of the views and choose Wireframe or Normal from the View menu. Now you can see your object in both views simultaneously. If you have multiple files open when you do this, all of them will scatter across the screen when you choose one of the Tile options, so you may want to close all but the file you are working on at the moment to maximize viewing area.*

2. The Rectangle tool creates a boundary box; when the boundary box is given a black, to blue, to pink custom fountain fill at –90 degrees from the Fountain Fill dialog (F11), it becomes a colorful evening sky. Set the From color to black, and the To color to magenta and click to enable the Custom option. Then by double-clicking on the top of the preview ribbon, you create a new color point. Make this point blue by clicking on the blue color chip in the color selection area. In the Fountain Fill dialog, as in any dialog where you can assign fill values, if you want a color not available as a color chip, click on the Others button to open a color picker dialog, which works just like the Uniform Fill dialog (Shift+F11) to choose colors (see Figure 2-33).

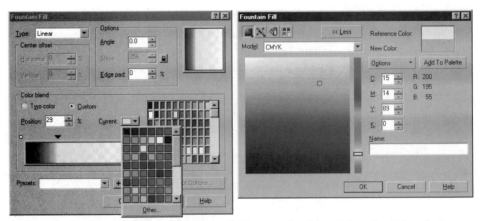

*Figure 2-33: To choose a custom color not available as a color chip, click on the Others button. This will open a dialog that is similar to the Uniform Fill dialog and works exactly the same way to mix and choose a specific color.*

3. The smoke objects were given a 40% black fill and then made semi-opaque with the Interactive Transparency tool. Creating a radial fountain transparency is a bit tricky, as it seems to be the reverse logic of a linear fountain transparency. With your object selected, click on the Interactive Transparency tool, which should make the settings for the tool appear in the Property Bar as None. Change the setting from None to Fountain (click on None and then on Fountain when it appears). Click on the second option button to toggle to Radial Fountain. Now the shape has a transparent center to a solid perimeter, which is exactly opposite from what we want (see the image on the left in Figure 2-34). To correct this, you need to reverse the black and white colors on the Interactive Transparency fill control points. These points just control how the transparency works and not the actual color of the object. Drag from the white onscreen color well and release over the black Interactive Transparency tool control point. Now drag from the black onscreen color well and release over the white Interactive Transparency tool control point to "fix" this fill and let the smoke fade away into nothing (see the image on the right in Figure 2-34).

4. The hot lava eruption is created in the same way as the explosions. Create a bunch of circle objects, group (Ctrl+G) them, and color them yellow. Duplicate this group (+) and color the duplicates red. Now ungroup the red circles (Ctrl+U) and one by one, drag each one out in a fan shape to become the extreme edge of the exploding magma. Shift-select all of the red circles again and group them (Ctrl+G). Now shift-select the original group of yellow circles and open the Blend roll-up

(Ctrl+B). Change the number of steps to 50, and from the Acceleration tab, move the Fills/Outlines slider way to the left. This will keep the blend yellow longer, leaving the red dots as obvious entities at the end of the explosion. I didn't change the Accelerate Objects slider this time, as I liked the way the standard blend scattered the objects more uniformly. Fiddle with these settings as you wish to change the way the eruption looks! You can see the results I got in Figure 2-35.

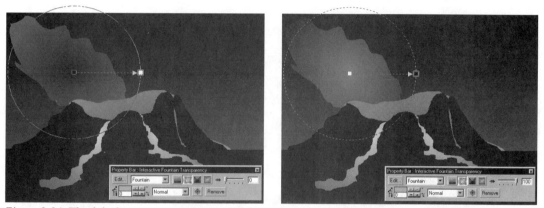

*Figure 2-34: The default arrangement for a radial fountain transparency is clear to opaque, the opposite of what we want in this example. Drag colors from the onscreen color wells onto the Interactive Transparency tool control points to change this.*

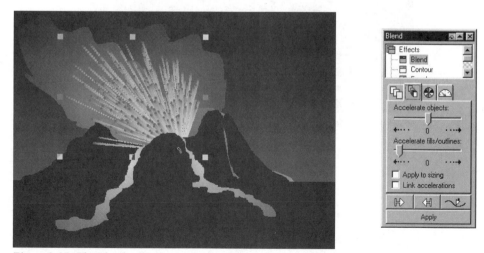

*Figure 2-35: The Blend roll-up once again results in a neat explosion effect. Only the Accelerate Fills/Outlines slider was moved this time, to keep the lava bits yellow/orange all the way to the end of the blend.*

This is one of those techniques that you can just play with indefinitely to get many crazy results (and boy have I!). Open the Volcano.cdr file in the \Chapt2\ subdirectory on the Companion CD-ROM to take apart and examine this file. The volcano looks as if it's erupting as the file builds onscreen!

## Pinwheels

*Figure 2-36. Modifying the parameters of the explosion from the Blend roll-up instantly transforms bursts into spinning, flaming pinwheels. Check out this image in the color section along with another color page describing the effects of the Rainbow function on these pinwheels.*

While experimenting with explosions, I stumbled upon this spinning pin-wheel variant; the veritable definition of serendipity—just another random, delightful discovery! You need to follow steps one through three of the "Explosion" section of this chapter to create the blend control objects that you need for this pinwheel derivative. Here is how to spin the wheel.

1. Start with the explosion blend group. Color the inner control objects yellow and the outer ones red. Select the blend and open the Blend roll-up (Ctrl+B). Now increase the number of steps to 100 and change the rotation value to 180. This puts the spin on the pinwheel. Click on the Acceleration tab and move the sliders to zero, or adjust the object acceleration to taste. Finally, click on the Colors tab and click on the Clockwise Rainbow selection. This will advance the pinwheel blend objects through the rainbow as the blend is calculated (see the color section for more on the Rainbow feature and Figure 2-37 for a look at the roll-ups used in this step).

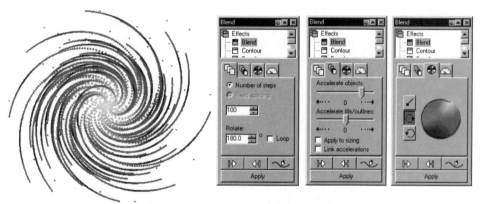

*Figure 2-37: Use the Rotate and Rainbow functions to create a pinwheel effect from the explosion blend control groups.*

2. Duplicate the pinwheel blend group (+) and play with the settings to get all kinds of different pinwheel looks! Figure 2-38 shows one of the effects I came up with.

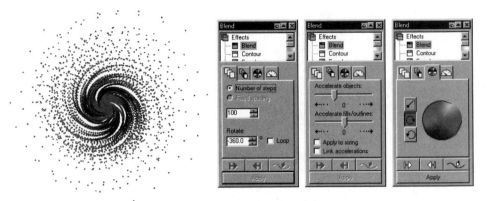

*Figure 2-38: Change the number of steps, the Rotate value, and Rainbow functions to create all kinds of different pinwheel effects.*

**CD-ROM**

To finish off the Fourth of July image, I imported and recolored a flag from the \clipart\flags\flying directory. Open the July4th.cdr file in the \Chapt2\ subdirectory of the Companion CD-ROM to spin the pinwheels firsthand! I feel so patriotic that I think I'll drive my Jeep down to the local American Legion Hall and drink some domestic beers with the Shriners! I'll do anything to wear a Fez!

## Moving On

This chapter mercilessly tossed you right out of the frying pan into the fire (excuse the pun). Along the way, we hit on many cool tools and functions (Blend, Interactive Transparency, Weld, Trim, Intersection, Contour, fountain fills, and so on), and my philosophy of ruthless creativity. We shall maintain this frantic pace to squeeze the most out of your design day, this book, and CorelDRAW itself!

In the next chapter, we switch from fire to water, just to cool off a bit! The water effects don't use the Blend roll-up, so you and your computer can take a breather from stepping for a spell. However, don't think your CPU won't be smokin' while it is working out the hard-core lens effects used in the next chapter! This book isn't for wimps or wimpy PCs, so keep your hands and feet inside the car at all times, and make sure the safety bar is down and locked. Off we go!

# chapter 3

# Pools of
# Mysterious Fluid

Along with the other natural forces, water and liquids are popular design
themes. When trying to replicate fluids, the challenge lies in making something look transparent, yet reflective. Using a few tricks, we can bring even
this enigmatic substance to life in CorelDRAW.

To create the illusion of liquid, we will need to create shadow and highlight
effects. The great thing about CorelDRAW objects is that you can also use
them to modify other CorelDRAW objects (like a cookie cutter on dough). We
will use duplicates of the main object shape, for example, to create the highlight and shadow shapes. Then we'll uniquely color each element to create the
illusion of depth and reflected light. It is a relatively simple process that instantly adds depth and personality to your design. Just add water and stir!

This chapter will cover some of the cool effects you can achieve with liquid.
We'll start with creating drops and puddles and move on to converting type
into liquid. Then we'll create the illusion of a liquid-filled impression and finally
add a spray of realistic drops of water to an illustration. So, ready to get wet?

## Drops of Liquid

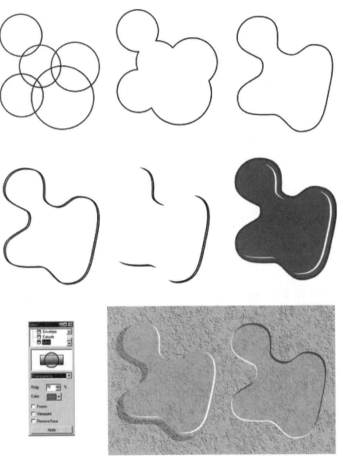

**COLOR STUDIO**

*Figure 3-1: Here a few circle objects are welded together to form a larger droplet. Use the Trim function to make duplicates of the original shape become the shadow and gleam elements. Finally, the order of assembly and the colorizing process creates water either on the surface or recessed in a puddle.*

There are always times when a few drops of liquid add flavor to your design. It could be clear water droplets on a photo, thick blood trails on the floor, or an acid-etched puddle. The potential is unlimited, but the process is pretty simple. The key is the creation of highlight and shadow shapes, which give the illusion of depth and a slippery surface. This technique is simple and has many applications (see Chapters 4 and 7 for more examples). Here we transform a group of circles into a shiny puddle.

1. With the Ellipse tool, draw a collection of perfect circles. Holding down the Ctrl key as you drag will keep the circles perfect. Drag-select the circles and from the Arrange menu, choose Weld to open the Weld roll-up. Now click the Weld To button and then click again on one of the circles. All of the objects should merge into one (see Figure 3-2).

*Figure 3-2: Use the Weld command from the Arrange menu to merge several objects into one.*

**TIP**  *If you don't know which button is which, use the right-mouse button in CorelDRAW. Move the pointer over the button in question, and click on the right-mouse button to reveal the "What's This?" menu. Click on "What's This?" and CorelDRAW will pop open a window explaining the function and the name of the tool/button/dialog in question.*

2. Use the Shape tool to soften the edges of the droplet by smoothing the nodes. Drag-select the nodes of the object and then open the Node Edit roll-up (Ctrl+F10). First, click on the Auto-Reduce button and then click on the Symmetrical button to really smooth out the curves (see Figure 3-3). These two steps are usually enough, but you may have to go back and fix/delete any odd-looking control nodes.

3. Duplicate the droplet shape (by using the + key on the numeric keypad) and offset it from the original to the right and down, say .05 inches. From the Arrange menu, choose the Trim command to open the Trim roll-up. Under Leave Original, select the Other Objects option. Now select the left object, click on the Trim button, and then click on the right object. The result should be a new set of gleam objects (see Figure 3-4).

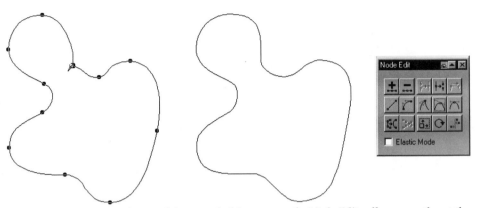

*Figure 3-3: The Auto-Reduce and Symmetrical buttons on the Node Edit roll-up smooth out the curves of the droplet.*

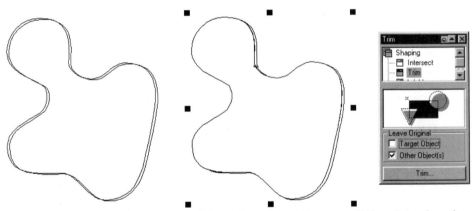

*Figure 3-4: The Trim tool creates a set of gleam shapes by cutting away all the points where the two objects overlap.*

4. Position the gleam objects over and on the right side of your drop shape. You may want to downsize the objects by dragging the center sizing handles inward. The more toward the center the gleam shapes are, the taller the liquid will look (see Figure 3-5).

**TIP**   *For gleam shapes deep in your object, use the Contour roll-up to first create a smaller copy on the inside of the original. Then duplicate this smaller contour, and then perform the trimming process to create a smaller set of gleam shapes. Keep in mind that you must always ungroup a contour shape, (even if it is only one object) before a function like Trim will work on it.*

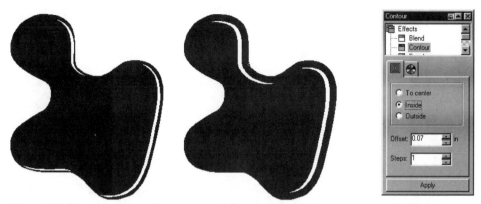

*Figure 3-5: Move the gleam shapes on top of the original and color to suggest a highlight. For an even deeper gleam, use the Contour roll-up to create a smaller copy inside of the original to serve as a parent shape for the gleaming process.*

5. Duplicate the original again (+); only this time, move the duplicate down and to the left to create shadow shapes. Select the original, and from the Arrange menu, open the Trim roll-up. Now click the Trim button and then click on the duplicate to create the shadow objects (see Figure 3-6).

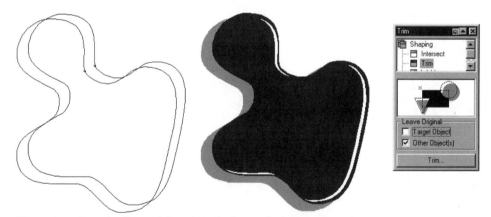

*Figure 3-6: Use a duplicate of the original offset to the left and down for a shadow shape. The Trim function once again cuts away the overlap, leaving just the shadow shape.*

6. In order for the illusion of transparency to work, the objects really need to be on top of something. Draw a rectangle and then from the Fill tool flyout, open the Texture Fill dialog. From there, change the Texture Library to Samples 7 and select Concrete from the Texture List.

Click OK and then click OK again to fill the object with the texture. Then send it to back (Shift+PgDn). Figure 3-7 shows the dialogs used in this step.

### When Math Meets Art

Texture fills are bitmaps rendered by CorelDRAW using special algorithms, but the default resolution is usually too low. To up the resolution, click on the Options button and then change the values in the Texture Options dialog. Increasing these numbers generates more image information when the program renders the texture; however, it also increases the file size and memory requirements of your image. I set the Bitmap Resolution to 300 (all bitmaps in this book are output at 300 dpi), and upped the Maximum Tile Width to the maximum setting of 2049 pixels. This makes for a big image, but one that is more appropriate for publishing.

Although increasing the resolution and size limit values on a texture fill will increase file complexity, there is a way to limit its increase in actual file size. Introduced in CorelDRAW 7, there is a way to compress certain CorelDRAW objects when you save the file to disk. In the Save Drawing dialog, click on the Advanced button. From the dialog that appears, you can enable several very efficient file-squishing strategies, including the Rebuild Textures When Opening the File option. It takes a little longer to save and retrieve, but these options dramatically reduce the amount of disk space needed to save your files.

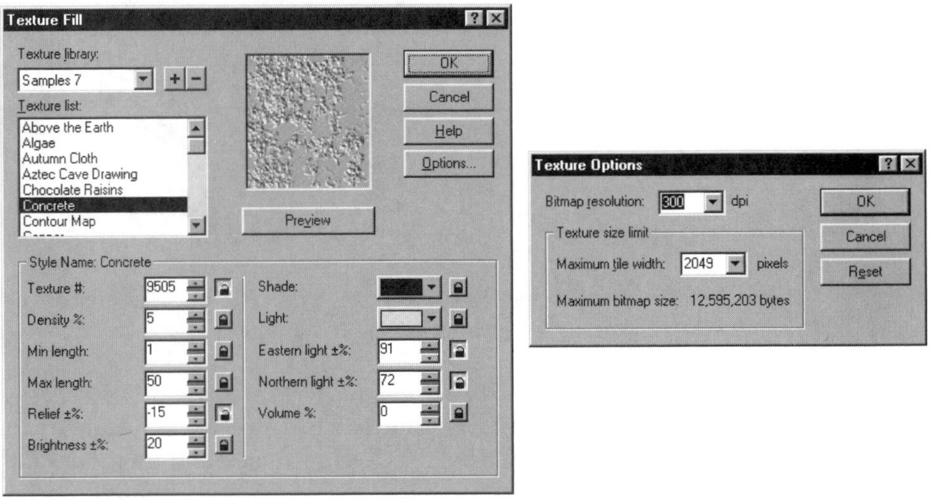

*Figure 3-7: For an interesting background behind the liquid, use a texture fill. Using the Texture Options dialog, you can alter the default values depending on the intended use of the illustration: down for use on the Internet, up for use in traditional publishing.*

7. Now select the shadow shape and give it a solid black fill. Open the Lens roll-up (Alt+F3), choose the Transparency option, change the Rate value to something like 80%, and then click Apply. In general, the more transparent your liquid is, the softer the shadow will be. Select the liquid shape and fill it with 100% cyan. In the Lens roll-up, change the Rate value to 50% and click Apply. This should let the texture below shine through but still look bluish. You can also soften the highlight shapes with a Transparency lens, although I chose the solid white. To create liquid beneath the surface, you go through the same process, only the gleam and shadow shapes are about the same size, not offset from the original, and colored with the shadow shapes on the top (see "Impress" later in this chapter). Figure 3-8 shows the result of using the Transparency lens.

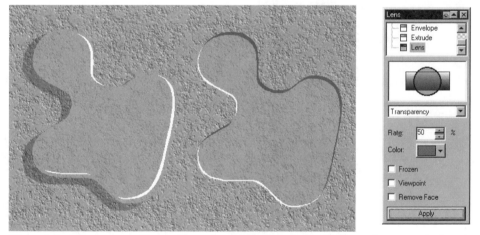

*Figure 3-8: A Transparency lens with a rate of 50% gives the liquid the semi-opaque coloring. A lens is also used on the shadow shape so that the texture of the object below shows through. The same process with slight modification and a reversed color scheme becomes an inset puddle.*

That's it! It really isn't difficult to give any object a shadow or highlight and instantly add the illusion of depth. Check out the final image in the color section. You will see that I use this shadow/highlight technique a lot—one, because I like the way it looks, and two, because I'm lazy!

For a firsthand look at this artwork, load the file liquid.cdr from the \Chapt3\ subdirectory of the Companion CD-ROM and see how things come together. To appreciate the flexibility of this process, select the background and change the texture fill from Concrete to anything else. Flexible artwork that's easy to change is great for creating, for example, a corporate ID. This is important when your client says, "Hmmm, I like the concrete, but can I see it on chocolate raisins?"

## Mysterious

*Figure 3-9: The gleam and shadow objects created with copies of the original using the Trim roll-up can transform any object, including text, into wet-looking droplets. Some fluids are more opaque than others (blood versus water, for example), but by changing the transparency of the fill and the contrast of the shadow elements and by varying the background texture, you can create a convincing look for each. To suggest that the liquid is magnifying the image below, use a Magnify lens instead of a Transparency lens; the Magnify lens will work on a texture fill (or a bitmap) and beneath it.*

Using the liquefying effect on type makes for an interesting diversion from plain text. Many, if not all, design projects involve type, and converting it into an interesting visual element makes for a more successful publication. You can really change the mood or tone of a design by incorporating headline text into the graphic. Just tell me that any word written in blood isn't more chilling than the same thing written in Helvetica Bold?! The process of converting type is exactly the same as converting any other shape into a liquid (as described in "Drops of Liquid" earlier in this chapter). To save time, however, you should pick a font that is more suitable to this technique rather than try to round out square text. I used the Croissant font for this image. You can perform the Trim functions directly on the text, but the resulting objects will obviously be curves.

## Bloody Mysterious

Here is how to give your text the look of an opaque liquid like blood:

1. I am assuming you already have the parent shape, the shadow, and the highlight objects as outlined in the previous section. Select the parent shape and give it a thick black outline (3.5 points) and black fill.

2. Duplicate the parent shape (using the + key) and give the duplicate a red hairline outline and red fill. Now select these two objects and blend them together using the default 20 steps. This will give your liquid a rounded edge, but it only works for nontransparent liquid (see Figure 3-10).

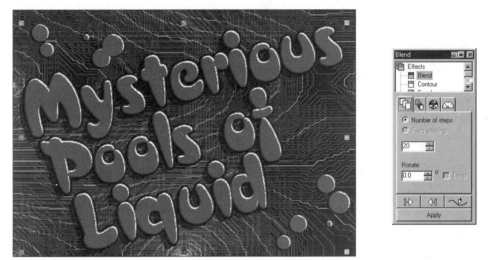

*Figure 3-10: Blending a thick-outlined copy of the text to a thin duplicate directly on top of it creates a rounded edge.*

**TIP** *Selecting objects stacked directly on top of one another can be difficult. You could select the top object and super nudge it to the side to reveal the bottom object, but this disturbs the placement of the objects. It is easier to use the Tab key to change the current selection. So to blend two stacked objects, select the top one and then press the Tab key to toggle the selection to the object beneath it. Now shift-select the top object again and perform the blend. Simple!*

## Transparent Mystery

Instead of using a Transparency lens on the main text element, try using the Magnify lens instead. The Magnify lens will give the subtle illusion of water refracting light, by distorting the image below the lens object. The distortion alone (without darkening or lightening the artwork below) makes for a more subtle graphic, but that can also be more convincing! Here is how to add light refraction to your liquid:

1. Start again with your basic parent, shadow, and highlight shapes. To make the refraction obvious, place a pattern behind the lens object that has linear elements the eye can follow (such as wood grain). This way, you see the grain distort in the text. I used a full-color bitmap pattern loaded from the \tiles\ subdirectory on the CorelDRAW clip-art CD for the wood look.

2. Now select the parent object and open the Lens roll-up (Alt+F3). Change to the Magnify lens and set the Amount value to 1.5 times. The Magnify lens does not change the colors; it just enlarges the image below at the factor set in the Amount box. Click Apply to see what I mean! Figure 3-11 shows how the wood grain is enlarged behind the lens object, creating the refraction illusion.

## Semitransparent

To change both the magnification and the coloring of your text, try stacking lens objects. To make your liquid refracted and colored, try this:

1. Select the Magnify lens and duplicate it (using the + key). (You may want to work in Wireframe mode while you build this so you won't have to wait for recalculation.)

2. Now from the Lens roll-up, switch from Magnify to Transparency. Change the Rate value to 50% (or more for less color), change to the desired color, and click Apply. There you go! (This example is on the Companion CD-ROM, but not in print.) Figure 3-12 shows the results of stacking the two lens objects.

*Figure 3-11: The Magnify lens creates an illusion of refraction by enlarging the image slightly inside the text.*

*Figure 3-12: Placing another lens object with a 50% Transparency rate on top of the Magnify object changes the color of the text element while retaining the enlarged background image.*

Check out the file on the Companion CD-ROM called mystery2.cdr in the \Chapt3\ subdirectory. It's pretty big and complex. You may wish to load it and delete all but the section you want to explore (choose Select All from the Edit menu, shift-drag around the selection you want to keep to deselect, then press the Delete key). Experiment with the Magnify lens feature and see how changing the value makes for subtle or dramatic image shifts. Also, try different background fills and watch the lenses recalculate the new images. The results of my experiments can be seen in the color section.

## Impress

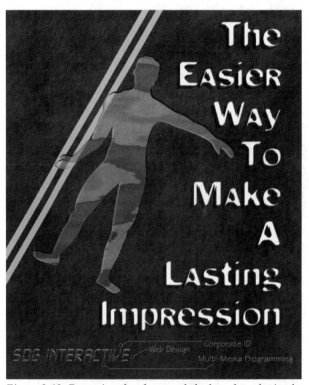

*Figure 3-13: Reversing the gleam and shadow shape logic of water on the surface creates liquid in a recessed puddle. A texture fill can also be given transparent qualities, to suggest clear water and also reflect clouds from above, with the Interactive Transparency tool.*

Admittedly, my brain isn't wired right, as the result of my free association with the word *impression* suggests! My first thought was the impression of a body in the ground, as if someone had fallen into the street and made a body-shaped dent. Using a technique similar to the one used to add gleams and highlights to suggest liquid on the surface, you can also create the illusion of water in a puddle. If this body-outline example isn't useful to you, use the same process on a different shape—say, dinosaur footprints (also found in the Tracks library in the Symbols roll-up) or even text again. Here is how to make a indented shape and fill it with water:

**TIP** *If you do not have the Symbols libraries installed on your system, you can copy them off of the CorelDRAW CD-ROM. From the \fonts\symbols\ttf\ directory on the CD-ROM, copy the desired symbol libraries to the \corel\draw(70 or 80)\symbols directory on your hard disk.*

1. The body outline is from the Symbols roll-up, Animals 1 font. Open the roll-up (Ctrl+F11), change to the desired library name, and then scroll through the images until you find the one you like. To get it on to your design, simply drag it off the roll-up and onto your page. (There is another body outline in the Tracks symbol font, suggesting perhaps that someone shares my twisted sense of humor!) To move the arm from the side so that it points out straight, use the Shape tool to rotate the nodes. With the Shape tool, select all of the nodes in the right arm (hold down the shift key to select multiple nodes). When you have all the nodes selected, click on the Rotate and Skew button on the Node Edit menu, which will make a set of rotation arrows and rotation axis appear around the nodes. Drag the axis of rotation (the little dot within a circle) to the shoulder area and then drag the bottom right arrow around to move the arm out. Repeat this process on the left leg. Additional little node tweaks will fine-tune the body outline shape (see Figure 3-14).

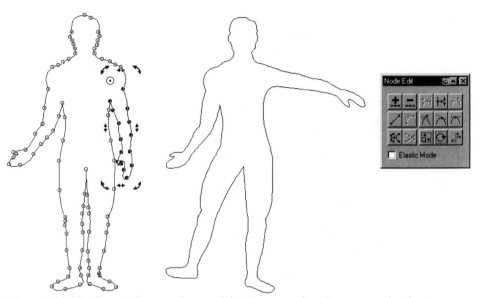

*Figure 3-14: The Shape tool can perform modifications on each node or group of nodes in an object. Here the Rotate and Skew button results in rotation arrows around the selected nodes, allowing you to spin them along the axis of rotation, which appears as a circle-dot that you can move to any desired position.*

2. With the body shape adjusted, map out the major elements in a boundary box to get an idea of how things will fit. To get the double-yellow lines to fit within the confines of the box, use the Intersection roll-up. With the line shape selected, open the Intersection roll-up from the Arrange menu, then click the Intersect button, and finally, click on the boundary box. Depending on which Leave Original options you have enabled, you may have to delete any redundant shapes when performing Intersection functions. (I find it is easier to deal with redundant shapes than try and remember each time which is the "target" and which is the "other" original. I am too impatient!) The font in the original comp is Kabel, while the final is MonkeyCaughtStealing from Garage Fonts (see Figure 3-15).

3. Duplicate the body shape (using the + key) and offset the duplicate to the right and up a tad. Select the left shape and open the Trim roll-up from the Arrange menu. Click the Trim button and then click on the right body shape, which should result in the shadow shapes. Super-nudge these shapes to the side for a moment by holding down the Ctrl key while tapping an arrow key. Now select the right body shape, deselect the Target Object Leave Original option, click the Trim button, and click

the left body shape to generate the highlight shapes. Now select the shadow shapes and super nudge them back into place. This should leave you with the shadow, highlight, and main body shapes (see Figure 3-16).

*Figure 3-15: To get a feel for the way the elements would come together, lay out the pieces first in Wireframe mode and then color them later. Use the Intersect roll-up to trim down objects to fit inside of a boundary box.*

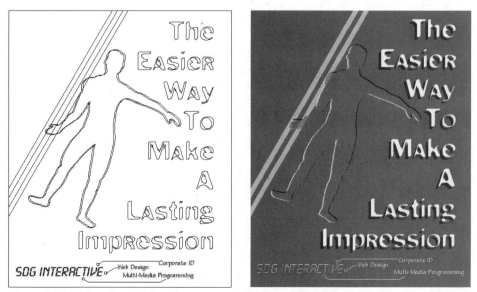

*Figure 3-16: Using the Trim function on a set of duplicate body shapes results in objects for the shadow and gleam of the "impressed" body.*

**TIP**

*Sometimes you need to move an object out of the way temporarily to work with objects below it. This is true when creating shadow and gleam shapes, which because they share the same contour of the parent, can make selection difficult.*

*The easiest way to move something aside with a guarantee that you can move it back exactly where it was is with the super nudge function. Hold down the Ctrl key and tap an arrow key to nudge your object off to the side. When you need it back, simply super nudge it back into place by tapping the opposite arrow key the same number of times. Another trick is to cut the object to the clipboard (Ctrl+X) and out of the way and then paste it back into place later (Ctrl+V). The cut/paste trick is easier, but if you forget about your copy on the clipboard and copy something else, you will lose it forever!*

4. Give the boundary box a texture fill to simulate asphalt. With the object selected, open the Texture Fill dialog from the Fill tool flyout. Set the Texture Library to Samples 7 and select Moss from the Texture List. This texture is correct, but the coloring is obviously wrong! Click on the color chip for First Mineral and change it to black, set the Second Mineral color chip to a dark gray, and finally, set the Light value to a light gray. Bump the values in the Texture Options dialog to increase the image information in the Texture fill.

**TIP**

*Texture fills only calculate in the RGB color model, even if you change the color model to CMYK. This is because there are fewer variables in RGB than any other color scheme, and therefore the RGB color model is easier to use when generating the textures. This makes choosing and controlling colors very difficult. For a better onscreen representation for process-color printing, make sure you have the Color Correction option set to Accurate from the View menu in CorelDRAW 7 (choose View | Color Correction | Accurate). Color correction enabled is the default in CorelDRAW 8.*

5. A texture fill gives the illusion of clouds reflected in the water of the body shape. From the Texture Fill dialog, change the Texture Library to Styles and pick the Water 3 Colors texture. I didn't like the way the default setting for this texture rendered, so I let the computer randomly generate another. When you click the Preview button in the Texture Fill dialog without making any other changes, CorelDRAW creates a random variant of the current texture. Keep clicking until you find a variant you like, and then click OK to fill your object.

6. To give the water a translucent look, select it and click on the Interactive Transparency tool (a lens will not work on all objects). On the Property Bar, change the type from None to Uniform, and move the slider to change the opacity to your taste (I left it at the default 50). Figure 3-17 shows the translucent water.

*Figure 3-17: To add an interesting effect, use the Interactive Transparency Tool to give a texture-filled object a uniform transparency. Not only can you see through the fill to the texture below, but you can also see a reflected set of images, such as clouds, above.*

So the result of my word association for the day is a body indentation in the street (see the color section). I'm sure my mother would not approve! This file is called impress.cdr and is in the \Chapt3\ subdirectory on the Companion CD-ROM if you want to examine it (or the crime scene) more closely. Select the top object with the texture fill and uniform transparency. Change the texture fill or dabble with the Interactive Transparency tool to see how it works. Instead of a uniform fill, drag the tool across the shape to make a fountain-filled transparency.

## Air Ski

*Figure 3-18: CorelDRAW lets you combine hand-drawn images with native objects. Here an ink illustration is scanned and saved as a black-and-white (1-bit) bitmap. When it is imported into CorelDRAW, you can change the white fill to transparent and then add CorelDRAW shapes underneath to colorize the image. Many fountain-filled circle shapes make up the water spray, and the colorful water and sky objects are filled with Custom Linear fountain fills.*

My graphics career started with a T-shirt shop that a buddy and I opened while I was in college; we called it Slimy Dog Grafix (which explains why you will see this name and logo now and again). Our early designs relied heavily on ink illustrations, which we manipulated electronically in CorelDRAW after scanning them into the computer. Although at first the program was used more as a type-setting tool, we eventually used CorelDRAW to finish the designs. The jet ski ink illustration that was scanned for this image had dithered shaded areas, which is fine for T-shirt art, but looks a bit grainy in print!

Water themes often branch out to include water sports or other related events. You can use the techniques for replicating liquid on any headline text to enhance the "wet" feel. The technique of creating the water spray is simple, but useful. Here is how to work with a black-and-white bitmap, render the wet water spray, and solve several color blend problems:

1. Import (Ctrl+I) the black-and-white scan into a new CorelDRAW file. The default fill is white and the outline black. If you assign no-fill, by left-clicking on the no-fill onscreen color well, the image becomes black ink on a clear sheet. You can also change the black area of the bitmap to any other color by changing the outline value (see Chapter 12 for more on this technique). In this example, we want the black image on a no-fill box (see Figure 3-19).

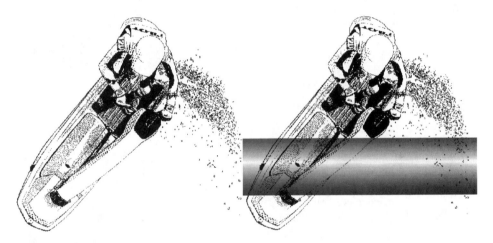

*Figure 3-19: A black-and-white (1-bit) bitmap imports with a solid white fill and black image. You can change the fill value to any other color, or none at all, for many different possibilities.*

2. Because the image is clear, you must create solid objects wherever you wish color to appear, including white. Working in Wireframe view, I used the Bezier tool and the Freehand tool to create solid shapes to place under the bitmap, giving the illusion of a solid, colorized object (see Figure 3-20).

**TRAP**  *If you have the bitmap selected when you click on either the Bezier or Freehand tool, you will activate the Tracing mode (see the tip on this page), so be sure to deselect the bitmap (Esc) before you use these tools.*

*Figure 3-20: Drawing solid objects behind the illustration will create the illusion that the bitmap object is colorized.*

**TIP**  *CorelDRAW has some limited automation to aid in creating shapes to colorize a black-and-white bitmap. With the bitmap selected, grab the Freehand tool, which will now be in the Tracing mode (crosshairs with a little dotted line to the right). Now when you click, CorelDRAW will try to scan to the right and around to create a shape. This tool works poorly, however; and you can draw more accurate shapes more quickly by hand. To make the tracing more or less accurate, right-click on the Freehand tool and then choose Properties from the flyout. You can then change the Autotrace tracking value for varied results.*

4. Use a custom fountain fill to transform the rectangle behind the skier into a colorful desert sky. Draw the rectangle and open the Fountain Fill dialog (F11). Change to a custom color blend and make the starting color dark blue and the ending color yellow. Now double-click on a point above the color blend preview ribbon about 1/4 of the length of the ribbon to the left of the yellow end point. Color this spot magenta, create another color point 1/4 of the way from the other end, and make it cyan. Change the angle to –90 and click OK to color the sky. Easy!

5. The progressively darkening lake water is also a custom fountain fill. To get a nice fade from blue to black, there is one coloring trick to note. Open the Fountain Fill dialog (F11). The starting color is black, and the ending color is cyan, with one more dark blue color point in between. The black needs to be altered to include the blue or the fill turns to gray before it goes black and does not look as good.

**TIP** *You will notice this a lot in CorelDRAW art—fountain fills seem to have washed-out interim steps. It is not the program that is at fault, just the artist who used a bad color combination for the program to calculate. Here is how you fix it. Select the black starting point, click on the Current button to open more coloring options, and then click on the Others button. Now a dialog exactly the same as the Uniform Fill dialog appears. Instead of assigning only black ink, add 100% cyan and 100% magenta to the mix. Adding the colors into your black that are found in the next "fade-to" color will allow CorelDRAW to calculate your fountain fill much more smoothly. Click OK, and then click OK again to assign the fill to your lake object.*

6. The spray of water droplets are just many little hand-drawn shapes filled with a cyan-to-white radial fountain fill. Tiny circle shapes would also do the trick. Open the Fountain Fill dialog (F11) and change the Type value to Radial. Now change the From color to cyan and the To color to white. Click OK to create a water drop. At the tiny size and in great numbers, the fountain-filled circles look like watery spray. The fountain fill just adds enough variation to make each object unique (see Figure 3-21).

▼ **Overprinting**

Depending on the process, it is a good idea to *overprint* the bitmap. What this does is print the black on top of whatever color is beneath rather than knock a hole in the underlying color. Overprinting helps compensate for registration problems during the printing process. In the jet-ski water illustration, if overprinting is not enabled, and if the black moves slightly, every tiny dot in the dithered shading areas would print as white holes knocked out of the color below. This would really accentuate even a small registration problem. To eliminate this problem, select the bitmap and right-click to open a dialog box. Now click on Overprint Outline for this object. I also trapped the outlines on the arrow shapes and the white text object. Enabling the Overprint Fill option ensures that there are no accidental white areas around the black text in the water should there be a registration problem.

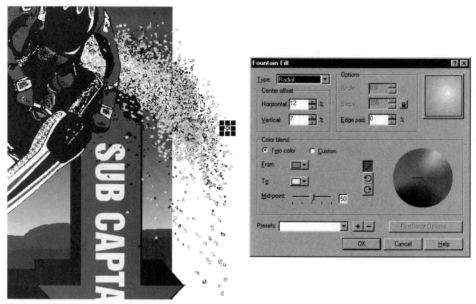

*Figure 3-21: Tiny circle shapes each filled with a radial fountain fill stack up to create the illusion of water spray. Some of the lines in the water were in the scanned illustration, so placing droplets on top or behind can soften the harsh black lines.*

This file is called airski.cdr and is in the \Chapt3\ subdirectory on the Companion CD-ROM, with the final image also in full glory in the color section. You can see how chunky the bitmap halftones are and how overprinting helps eliminate trapping problems. Open it and experiment with the bitmap object, changing the outline and fill colors, and also use the No Color option for each. Also examine the custom color blend fountain fills to see how the colors are mixed to include neighboring colors for smoother blends.

## Moving On

In this chapter we looked at creating effects that simulate liquids, flat or foamy. The basic trick is to suggest translucency, either literally with a Transparent lens or by coloring with fountain fills. Liquids are shiny and reflect the light sources around them, but they also affect the way images behind them appear.

The techniques for generating the highlight and shadow objects on the liquid elements are essential to other techniques, as we will see in the next chapter where we use them to add depth to solid materials. CorelDRAW images are all liquid in the sense that you can constantly change the way the design looks by altering the coloring scheme. You can turn stone into water, or fire into ice, as we will see next!

### Beyond f/x

Creating translucent images is a technique that you will find yourself using more than you think. The old saying "if you want to get someone's attention, whisper" also works well in design in some cases. This kind of image that is there, but not obtrusive, can be seen almost constantly on television these days. Networks subtly stick their logo, altered to look translucent, in the bottom corner of the screen as a subtle reminder of what station you are watching. You can make use of the same technique on your Web page graphics, to add a control panel that allows the main graphics to show through, while still providing a hint of buttons in "glass". Of course reflective water effects work right into specialized advertising, for such products as, well, water for example! The highlight and shadow tricks can add depth and substance to almost anything you can think of, as we will see in the examples coming up.

# chapter 4

# Ice, Stone & Other Building Materials

Although CorelDRAW is known for its crisp, vector-like imagery, you can also texturize objects to give them the look of almost any material. Texture fills and full color bitmap patterns can give your objects a very realistic appearance by making use of pixellated technologies while still retaining the power and flexibility of CorelDRAW vector objects. Adding shadow and highlights gives the objects even more depth, for more convincing objects.

In this chapter we will use the CorelDRAW bitmap pattern fills and texture fills to create objects that look like ice and stone. Also, we will create the look of depth and dimension using the highlight and shadow tricks covered in the previous chapter, and I'll introduce the concept of automatic depth and shading using the many features of the Extrude roll-up. Finally, we will use the Blend function to scatter snowflakes in an icy blizzard.

## Hearts

*Figure 4-1: Texture fills and full color bitmap fills make for an almost unlimited number of coloring options for your CorelDRAW objects. You can easily change the mood and tone of your design by simply choosing a different fill type.*

The great thing about CorelDRAW objects is that they remain infinitely flexible. You can change the outline or fill attributes at any time, making the pieces modifiable throughout the life of a project. Even if a design attempt is not exactly what you want, you can use all or just a few of the pieces in your next session, saving you time and energy. Forget the planet—recycle to save your sanity! These hearts all share basic shapes, but with just a few changes, each has a completely different mood. Once you create the main shapes, it is easy to recolor them for a handy assortment of love or hate notes. Here is how to create a heart of "stone":

1. With the Ellipse tool, draw a perfect circle. Hold down the Ctrl key as you drag to keep the circle perfect. Duplicate and enlarge the circle by dragging a corner control handle outward while holding the Shift key. Open the Symbols docker (was a roll-up in V. 7) (Ctrl+F11). In the Zapf

Dingbats font there are several nice heart shapes. Drag one onto your document. Make the heart taller by dragging the top center control handle upward. Now shift-select the inner circle and open the Align and Distribute dialog (Ctrl+A). Select both Center options and then click OK. Now combine (Ctrl+L) the two shapes and give the new curve a black fill. When you combine a smaller object inside of a bigger one, it knocks a hole (or *counter*) in it. Anything behind the object will show through the hole (see Figure 4-2).

*Figure 4-2: The symbol fonts are a great source for shapes, such as this heart. Combining two objects together cuts a hole in the shape of a heart in the center of a circle.*

2. With the Rectangle tool, draw a brick shape. Then from the Fill tool flyout, open the Texture Fill dialog. Now from the Styles Texture Library, pick the Surfaces texture. I changed the light color to a dark honey and the shade to a dark brown to make the texture look more like an old stone. Click OK. Duplicate the brick shape (using the + key) and move the brick over and flush to the right. Continue until you have five bricks across and then create a second row of bricks. For the half-bricks on the ends, simply reduce a rectangle by dragging a center sizing handle inward. Now select both rows, duplicate (+), move down, and continue this process until you create an entire wall. Drag-select all of the bricks and group them (Ctrl+G). Now open the Envelope roll-up (Ctrl+F7) and click the Add Preset button. From the flyout, select the perfect circle shape and click Apply. This will make the wall of bricks look rounded. To enhance the round look, use the Freehand tool to draw in highlight shapes and fill them with pure white (see Figure 4-3).

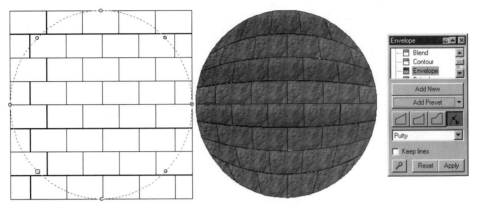

*Figure 4-3: An envelope distorts the brick wall into a round-looking shape. Although textures technically do not distort, because each shape is distorted, every texture renders differently enough to look right. The Wireframe view on the left shows the added envelope shape before it's applied.*

3. The brick ball is centered behind the heart-shaped cutout. Then another circle is drawn to serve as a guide to fix some text to. Use the Text tool to lay out some text elements in the desired font and size (I used a font called CommercialScript). Then shift-select the guide circle. From the Text menu, select Fit Text to Path. This will wrap the text along the top of the circle. Set your second piece of type and shift-select the guide circle again. Now in the Property Bar, change the vertical placement (second window from left) to the icon of text butting up against the top of the line. Then change the Text Placement to on the bottom of the circle, and finally, enable the Place on the Other Side option. This will place your text above and below the heart object. Positioning the text is the final step (see Figure 4-4).

**TIP** *If you drag the Artistic Text tool over a path, the cursor will change from crosshairs to the "Text on Path" cursor. You can then click and your text will wrap to the path below it. This shortcut is nice, but it will always place text at the top and outside of a circle. For the other options, you will need to use the Fit Text to Path Property Bar.*

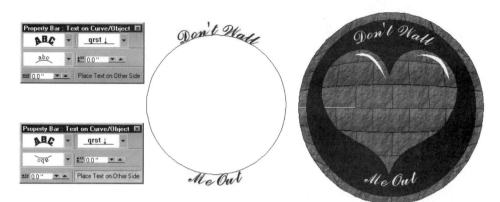

Figure 4-4: *Use the Fit Text to Path function to wrap text along a curve. Change the settings to place the text along the top or along the bottom of a curve.*

I found a nice use for my stone heart, but I wanted a more 3D-looking image and at the same time needed more flexibility for my alternative Valentines. I used the pieces from this first heart to create a template that would easily accept any fill type from ice to wood and that also had highlight and shadow elements that added much more depth. Here is how to set up the template shapes for a three-dimensional, textured object:

1. Select and delete brick shapes from the previous example. Draw another perfect circle around the heart/circle object and align them (Ctrl+A) Center-Center. Now combine them (Ctrl+L) to create a shape with a solid heart and outline but with an open area in between (see Figure 4-5).

Figure 4-5: *When you combine three objects, you get a cutout surrounded by two solid areas.*

**TIP** *CorelDRAW 8 now lets you use single-key shortcuts without opening the Align and Distribute Dialog at all. The same single key shortcuts that work within the dialog (Top, Center, Bottom, Left, Center, Right) now work any time directly from the keyboard. You still can open the Align and Distribute Dialog (Ctrl+A) as before for more options.*

2. The solid shape will serve as the parent to create highlight and shadow shapes as we did in Chapter 3. Duplicate the original (+ key), and offset it to the top and right. Using the Trim function from the Arrange menu, generate the necessary shapes. Give the shadow shapes a solid black fill and the highlights solid white. Draw an additional circle behind the heart shapes so that the cutout area can also be given a fill attribute (see Figure 4-6).

*Figure 4-6: Using the Trim function from the Arrange menu, use a duplicate of the shape to create highlight and shadow shapes. A circle behind everything allows for a fill attribute in the cutout area.*

3. An additional copy is used to create a deep shadow shape. As only the pieces inside the medallion are needed, the shapes are broken apart (Ctrl+K), the shape outside deleted, and then the pieces combined (Ctrl+L) again. These shapes are given a solid black fill, and then from the Lens roll-up (Alt+F3), a 50% Transparency rate. All the shadow and highlight shapes are given a 50% Transparency lens (see Figure 4-7).

This completes the medallion parents. With lens effects in place, you can shift-select the main heart shape and the background fill circle and experiment with different fill options. This is the great thing about the dynamic nature of lens effects and CorelDRAW in general. You can easily change the look of the medallion by choosing one of the literally hundreds of fill options. Let's start with a full color bitmap pattern for another spiteful stone heart, which at this point, only takes a paragraph to create!

*Figure 4-7: One more deep-shadow shape is created with the Trim roll-up. All of the highlight and shadow shapes are given a 50% Transparency lens from the Lens roll-up.*

Shift-select both the main heart shape and the background fill circle. Now from the Fill tool flyout, open the Pattern Fill dialog. Change to the Bitmap option and then tag the Load button. Now locate the CorelDRAW clip-art CD that contains the \Tiles\ subdirectory and find the \Tiles\Marble\Medium folder. From here pick your favorite and click Open. Now change the Tile option to Large if necessary and click on OK. That's it! Your lenses should do their magic and create a nifty 3D-looking medallion. You can experiment with different tile sizes and images until you find something that you like (see Figure 4-8).

*Figure 4-8: The Bitmap pattern fill option lets you fill an object with a variety of different images supplied with CorelDRAW; you can even make your own. Creating your own bitmap patterns is a bit tricky, especially hiding the repeat. See Chapter 28 for more on tiling.*

In addition to choosing from the bitmap pattern fills, you can also choose from the almost endless varieties of texture fills. This file is called hearts.cdr and is in the \Chapt4\ subdirectory on the Companion CD-ROM, and of course, it is also in the color section. The fire and ice examples are both texture fills from the Texture Fill dialog, accessed via the Fill tool flyout. Open the file, delete all but the fire medallion, and experiment with different texture fills and bitmap patterns. I really like the way the image looks using a wood bitmap pattern, for example.

## Ice Queen

*Figure 4-9: Using essentially the same explosion technique we used in Chapter 2, snowflake shapes are scattered into a randomized pattern using the Blend roll-up.*

As often as I find myself aimlessly experimenting, I also find myself trying to capture a specific image. I see images in my mind that I sometimes sketch out, but lately I just try to realize them directly in CorelDRAW. At this point, I might as well sketch in CorelDRAW, as then at least my efforts can literally work their way into a final composition. This was the case with the Ice Queen, another one of the eventual guardians to my studio. Here is how to create the icy portrait with the dancing snowflakes (which, like all this book's examples, appears in the color section).

1. I had a pose in mind for this image, but I had no illustrations of my own that fit the bill. Turning once again to the CorelDRAW clip-art book, I found exactly the source material I needed. An image from the \clipart\portrait\entertai\ subdirectory on the CorelDRAW clip-art CD-ROM, schiffe1,-was exactly what I needed. The snowflake shape is from the Symbols docker (Ctrl+F11), located in the Stars1 library. Drag it onto your document for manipulation later (see Figure 4-10).

*Figure 4-10: A portrait from the \clipart\portrait\entertai\ clip-art CD-ROM and a snowflake shape from the Stars1 symbol library serve as the starting point for the Ice Queen.*

2. Draw a boundary box with the rectangle tool around the portrait, but zoom in more around her face. Now select and ungroup (Ctrl+U) the portrait objects, and delete the pieces that make up the hair details while leaving the overall hair object intact. The hair details are not necessary for the image I had in mind. Select the boundary box, and from the Arrange menu, open the Intersection roll-up. Disable the Leave Original Target Object option, and click on shapes that extend beyond the boundary box. This will trim down the pieces to fit within the box, such as her hair, shoulders, and so forth. Only objects that are to be in the final image are trimmed down with the Intersection process. Everything else, including the large black pad underneath everything , should be deleted (see Figure 4-11).

*Figure 4-11: The Intersect roll-up cuts objects down to within the boundary box. Unnecessary objects are simply deleted.*

3. To eliminate the holes in the body where the halter top straps were, draw objects over the areas with the Freehand tool, then, from the Arrange menu, choose Weld to merge them to the other shoulder pieces. To suggest an icy tone, I changed all of the skin tones to white and the lip and cheek blends to blues. I also changed the eyes to turquoise and the eyeliner color to a plum and made the hair a baby blue color. Finally, the snowflake was given a white-to-cyan radial fountain fill and no outline and was reduced and moved to the top of the forehead.

4. A nice feature in CorelDRAW is that you can assign a blend to follow along a curve or object. I wanted the snowflakes to blend around the contour of the face. Select the face object and duplicate (+ key). The face shape also contains cutouts for the eyes, nose, and eyebrows, which need to be eliminated. With the Shape tool, select and delete the nodes that make up the nose, eye, and eyebrow and delete them. You will get wacky curves left over, which you should just select and then click on the Convert to Line button in the Node Edit roll-up (Ctrl+F10). This should create a new shape for our first snowflake blend (see Figure 4-12).

*Figure 4-12: Use the Shape tool and the Node Edit roll-up to prepare a duplicate of the face object for the snowflake blend.*

**TIP**

*There are a few new shortcuts in CorelDRAW 8 for the Shape tool that might throw you off. Double-clicking on a node no longer opens the Node Edit roll-up, rather it deletes the selected node. Double-clicking on a line also won't open the roll-up, but now adds a node. The Node Edit roll-up can be opened with Ctrl+F10, but as all of the functions are available on the Property Bar as soon as you select the Shape tool, you may not even bother!*

5. Duplicate the snowflake object and shift-select both. Open the Blend roll-up, change the number of steps to 65, and click Apply. Yippee, nothing happened! Before you can assign a path to a blend, it must first actually be a blend, so you have to go through this anticlimactic step to get things started. Now click on the Path button and New Path from the flyout. Click on the simplified face object that we created in step 4, and then enable the Blend Along Full Path and the Rotate All Objects options before clicking Apply. There, now something really did happen (see Figure 4-13).

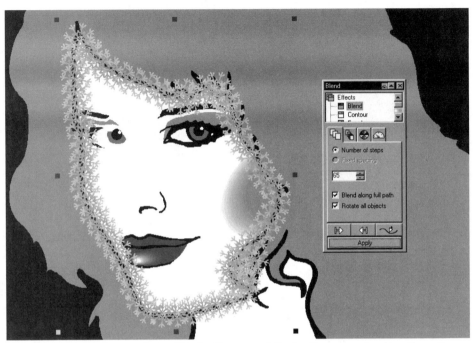

*Figure 4-13: Assigning a path to a blend will space out the duplicates evenly along the entire path and rotate the objects if you select those options in the Blend roll-up.*

6. With the blend still selected, choose Separate from the Arrange menu. Then hold the Shift key and click on the control curve shape to deselect it, and with the other three objects left, choose Ungroup All from the Arrange menu. This will separate all the blend pieces into individual objects again. With all 67 objects still selected, group them (Ctrl+G) again. Whew! It's a lot of little steps, but you can not blend a live blend, so you must first freeze a blend into its individual units. You can then blend a group of objects in the next step.

7. Duplicate (+) and enlarge the group by dragging a corner sizing handle outward. Now ungroup (Ctrl+U) all of these slightly larger snowflakes, and just like we did in the explosion technique, scatter them randomly around. When finished, shift-select all of the larger, scattered snowflakes again and group them (Ctrl+G) once more. Finally, select both the scattered group and the group around the face contour and open the Blend roll-up once more (Ctrl+B). Change the number of steps to 10, and add a rotation value of the maximum 360 degrees. Click Apply to watch the

snowstorm! Click the Acceleration tab, move the Accelerate objects slider to the right slightly, and click Apply once more until you are happy with the scatter pattern of the snowflakes (see Figure 4-14).

*Figure 4-14: With rotation enabled, the snowflakes twist and scatter as one group blends into the other.*

8. With the snowflake blend group selected, choose Behind from the Arrange | Order submenu. Click on the face object and the snowflakes will now build behind it. The final step is to select the hair object and instead of a solid blue, use a custom linear fountain fill at 90 degrees. Open the Fountain Fill dialog (F11), choose Custom, create a white, blue, white, blue, white, blue color scheme along the preview ribbon, and click OK. If you prefer, you can create the blend using the Interactive Fountain Fill tool. Select the tool and drag from top to bottom to create a blend. Now you can simply drag colors from the onscreen color wells to their spot on the blend (see the Ice Queen in the color section for more on the drag-and-drop technique).

This file is called queen.cdr in the \Chapt4\ subdirectory on the Companion CD-ROM. You can select the outer snowflake control group and spin it to watch the snowflakes rescatter. Scattering and exporting the image one frame at a time, which I of course did, could result in another animation idea. This animation is on the Companion CD, called queen.avi in the \Chapt4\ subdirectory as well.

## Cold Beer & Hot Rocks

*Figure 4-15: The Extrude roll-up will not only add depth and shading to your objects, it will also allow you to use the Bevel function to create a chiseled look. This feature adds a great deal of depth and interest to an otherwise flat object and will automatically recalculate if you change the fill value of the parent shape.*

Have you ever wanted to create those cool 3D-logos but didn't want to learn CorelDream? Well fear not, my friend! CorelDRAW has an awesome function known as Extrude. This feature can create the illusion of depth by building shaded 3D elements behind and on top of your two-dimensional shape. This tool got even more power with the addition of the Beveling option, which will add a chiseled look on top of your object. The really cool thing about the Extrude function is that it works on almost all types of CorelDRAW fills, such as textures and even full color pattern fills, and the program will automatically re-create the shapes should you pick a new fill pattern. The downside to all this automation is speed, with even the zippiest of computers plodding along at a snail's pace to render these images! Much like the heart medallions at the beginning of this chapter, you can create a parent object that will regenerate itself every time you change the fill attribute. To speed things along, you should make your objects as simple as possible by reducing the number of nodes. Here is how to reduce the nodes in your objects:

1. Set your type using the Artistic Text tool. I used a font called Boink, which has a simple, almost comic-book feel to it. Convert the text to curves (Ctrl+Q), and then with the Shape tool, drag-select all of the nodes and open the Node Edit roll-up (Ctrl+F10) or use the Property Bar.

2. Now click on the Auto-Reduce button to simplify the shape and reduce the nodes. The result will look essentially the same but have fewer nodes (136 reduced to 94; see Figure 4-16). The Extrude function uses the nodes as reference points, and the more there are, the more complex the extrusion will be. In the font Boink, the change wasn't dramatic, but some fonts have many control points along the curves, making for overly complex extrude calculations. It takes just a few steps to reduce the nodes and speed things up later.

*Figure 4-16: Before performing an extrude, convert your text to curves and then reduce the number of nodes using the Auto-Reduce function on the Node Edit roll-up or Property Bar.*

**TIP** *Node count varies from font to font, but it is a good idea to reduce the number of nodes when you can. Each node is a tiny chunk of memory and also a potential output snag. Where this step becomes absolutely essential is with CorelTrace objects, which are just infested with redundant nodes. Be sure to use the Auto-Reduce function to trim down these potentially problematic objects.*

Almost any fill will work and look convincing with the Extrude function. Things only go goofy when you spin some types of pattern fills (see "Dinosaur Land" in Chapter 5). In the beer examples, I first used a simple cyan-to-white radial fountain fill, which renders much, much faster than extrudes using bitmap patterns or texture fills. I like to work out the extrude parameters using a simple fill first to save time. You can also use a bitmap pattern fill, as I did in the top right example in Figure 4-15. For the bitmap pattern, I used a water pattern from the \Tiles\Nature\medium\ directory on the CorelDRAW clip-art CD-ROM. The last beer example uses a texture fill from the Samples 7 Texture library called Polar Surface (see Chapter 3 for more on how to use bitmap pattern fills and texture fills). The Extrude function will work on all of the fill options, but because most CorelDRAW patterns do not twist or tilt, some fills do not result in convincing extruded shapes. Anything other than solid or fountain fills will result in really complex and slow computations, so be prepared to wait! Here is how to reproduce the lava look:

1. Use the texture fill called Aerial Clouds from the Samples Texture library; change the default colors to yellow and red.

2. Select your text and open the Extrude roll-up (Ctrl+E). Set the options on the Vanishing Point page to Small Back and VP Locked to Object.

3. Click the Edit button to reveal the vanishing point, and a dotted-line box around your object will show how the extrude will build. Drag the vanishing point around into an orientation that you want (see Figure 4-17).

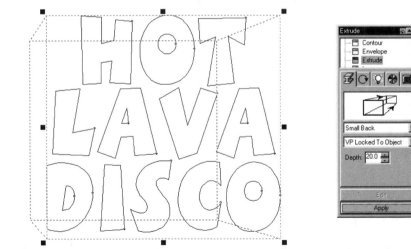

*Figure 4-17: The dotted lines serve as a preview for the Extrude settings. Drag the vanishing point around to change the orientation of the extrude shapes.*

**TIP**  *CorelDRAW 8 has an Interactive Extrude tool. From the Interactive Blend flyout, choose the Extrude option and drag from the center of your object outward to create the extrusion. From the Property Bar, you can then control the Extrude parameters. The Extrude roll-up has more options (such as the Corel logo 3D spin interface), which offer more control, but it is not as fast or convenient as the Interactive tool for simpler extrusions. Personal preference and the project parameters will dictate which method works best for you (see Figure 4-18).*

*Figure 4-18: The Interactive Extrude tool is faster but not as powerful as the Extrude roll-up. Like many of CorelDRAW's functions, there are several ways to do the same thing. Each Corel artisan uses their own pattern of keyboard/mouse shortcuts, menu options, roll-ups, and interactive tools to their own preference.*

4. Switch to the Lighting tab and click on the first lightbulb button to enable shading based on the active light source. Click on Apply to see the simpler extrude take shape (see Figure 4-19).

*Figure 4-19: With a single light source and a depth of 20, already the extrude is starting to come together.*

5. Click the Bevel tab and enable the Use Bevel function. The default settings are almost never usable, so change the Bevel Depth value immediately to .02 inch and then click Apply. If you accidentally click Apply with the default settings, don't fret, but your shapes will mutate into a spider-web glob of unusable mayhem! This final step adds a set of shapes to chisel the front of your extruded objects (see Figure 4-20).

*Figure 4-20: By simply enabling the Bevel function and reducing the Bevel Depth value to something reasonable, your objects take on a deep, carved look.*

**TIP**
*For most applications, the default bevel depth is way too big, resulting in total mayhem on the screen. It sometimes seems that even if you change this value initially, it will switch back to the default when you click Apply. To make sure your values sink in, key in the new Bevel Depth value and then click the mouse on the Bevel Angle box. This should ensure that the new Depth value is registered. You can then click the Apply button.*

**CD-ROM**
To see the different versions in a better light, check out the finished image in the color section. This file is called lava.cdr in the \Chapt4\ subdirectory on the Companion CD-ROM. The beer images can be found in the same directory, in a file called, yep, you guessed it, beer.cdr. The lava example is converted to curves, but the beer images are still text, saved with the TrueDoc option enabled so that even if you do not have the Boink font installed on your system, you will still be able to open and view the file correctly. I warn you that the extrudes take forever to render! Switch the view immediately to Wireframe and delete all but one of the examples for examination.

**TIP**
*Introduced in CorelDRAW version 7, TrueDoc technology is a great feature to aid in no-font-hassles file transfer. From the Save Drawing dialog, simply enable the Embed Fonts Using TrueDoc option to embed the font information into your file. With this option enabled, if you open your file on a system that does not have the fonts installed, CorelDRAW will extract them from within the file information itself. It will not automatically install the font on your system, however; it will only allow the font to work for the file that has the information associated with it.*

## Moving On

This chapter introduced the idea of template shapes, which you can use to generate a myriad of different looks by simply changing the fill attribute. This is very handy, especially for presenting a handful of design ideas to a client. You can simply duplicate the original and change the fill, and the whole image will look totally different and unique. Your client will think you slaved over the different logos, but you and I know it was CorelDRAW voodoo magic!

In the next chapter, we will look at some of the limitations of using the CorelDRAW pattern fills and how to circumvent them. Also, in the next section, we introduce the lens freeze function and how to use it to shave steps off of the design process. Until now we have been using the Blend function to create many scattered objects, as in the explosions from Chapter 2 or the snow-flakes in this chapter. In the next chapter, we will explore the Blend function and how to use multistep compound blends to create shiny, round-looking objects. Put on your rubber gloves—things are going to get scaly and slimy!

### Beyond f/x

Transforming an object from something flat and boring into a dimensional entity made from a recognizable material is a popular way to enhance artwork. A flat company logo comes to life when chiseled out of rock or marble and made to look solid and shiny. The choice of material brings new connotations to the artwork, and new themes you can play off of in advertising. Your client's start-up company suddenly seems reliable when their logo is given the stone treatment for a "like a rock" campaign. Or run with themes like "melting high prices" or "freezing interest rates" using the ice textures. Wood or brick can suggest crafts-manship, or the lack thereof (as in the three little pigs story). Recoloring artwork also changes the mood, as we saw when we made our model into an ice queen. You can make people hot or cold, soft or stony, and change the entire meaning of your artwork with a single click. Not a bad trick. And you thought only Mother Nature had such powers!

# chapter 5

# Scales & Slippery Textures

For every task, be it building a house or creating a computer illustration, there is the right tool for the right job. Because CorelDRAW is an object-oriented illustration package, there is a lot of built-in flexibility. This lets you change the look of your objects almost indefinitely until you get a look that you like, making CorelDRAW the tool of choice for computer illustration.

However, there are some limits to what the program can do, especially when it comes to manipulating patterns or texture fills. For every limitation, though, there is a creative solution, as the examples in this chapter of making flat objects scaly and slippery will show. We will look at different ways to create *scaly* objects (flat, distorted, and placed in perspective), how to recolor objects using the Color Styles feature, and also how multipart blends can be used to create shiny, slippery objects.

## Dinosaur Land

*Figure 5-1: Although textures and pattern fills look great and add a lot of coloring depth to your CorelDRAW objects with little effort, they are not especially flexible. If you attempt to rotate or, in this case, use the Perspective tool on an object, you will find that the fill does not reflect the change. This limitation can be circumvented using CorelDRAW native objects and a little creativity.*

When I first started dabbling with a scaly image, my first intentions were to generate an interesting but flat logo using the CorelDRAW patterning feature for a "Jurassic Park" sort of design (see Figure 5-1). I was happy with the results, but things went sour when I went to place the logo in a 3D orientation. When I tried to add perspective to the image, the pattern did not redraw correctly. In order to make this look work, I had to come up with a way to convert the pattern into something that would distort. Chapter 28 discusses making and manipulating your own bitmap pattern files, so here we will look at a manual patterning technique to circumvent any limitations that CorelDRAW pattern fills have. Here is how to manually make scales that you can then manipulate with the Perspective tool:

1. Set your text with the Artistic Text tool. I used a font called UGANDA (which is essentially the "Jurassic Park" font with extra pieces). To re-move the inside pieces, break apart (Ctrl+K) the text, and delete the inside parts. Drag-select the *R* pieces and rotate them so that they are slightly out of sync with the others. Now shift-select the letters of each word and combine (Ctrl+L) them into two separate shapes. This way you can enlarge *land* to fit better under *dinosaur*. When all of the pieces fit to your taste, shift-select both objects and combine (Ctrl+L) them. Now open the Contour roll-up (Ctrl+F9) to generate a slightly larger shape outside of our text. Set the Offset value to .1 and the Steps value to 1, select Outside, and then click Apply to generate the shapes. Choose Arrange | Separate, and with only the new contour shape selected, ungroup (Ctrl+U) it. You need to go through the ungroup process be-cause many effects (such as extrusion) will not work on a group of ob-jects (see Figure 5-2).

*Figure 5-2: Ordinary text is converted into a unique logo by resizing, repositioning, and using the Contour roll-up.*

2. Duplicate the contour shape and set it aside. Now shift-select both the original text and the contour element, and combine (Ctrl+L) them. This will result in two unique shapes, one large solid outline and one cut-out outline shape. We need both of these shapes to perform two different extrusions later (see Figure 5-3).

*Figure 5-3: Combining the original and the contour shape results in a cut-out outline shape. A duplicate of the contour is needed for the extrusion to come.*

3. Select the large solid outline contour shape and give it a green color by left-clicking the onscreen color well. Now open the Extrude roll-up (Ctrl-E). On the Vanishing Point property page, change the Depth value to 15 and then toggle to the second Vanishing Point options property page (click on the little page button). Key in 0 for the Horizontal and Vertical Vanishing Point values after selecting the Object Center option. This will make it easier to match up these extrude shapes later. Now tab to the 3D Rotation property page, grab the left cube of the Corel symbol, and drag left. This will spin the text in space. The dotted outline box around your object will give you an idea of the orientation of your extrusion. Now tab to the Lighting property page, and click on the button with the "1" light bulb to enable a light source in the upper right-hand corner. Tab to the Fill Color property page, enable the Use Object Fill option, and click Apply to create the extrusion (see Figure 5-4).

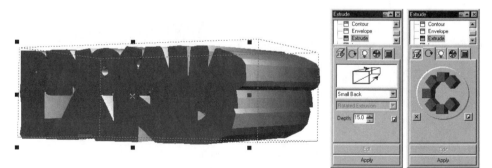

*Figure 5-4: The Extrude roll-up will create objects to simulate a third dimension. Use the 3D Rotation tool (in the form of the Corel logo) to twist your object in 3D space.*

4. Now select the other outline shape, and from the Effects | Copy submenu, choose Extrude From and then click on the first extrude shape. This will make all of the settings identical to the first. Notice, however, that it does not look correct. The vanishing point goes perquacky for some reason! So tab to the Vanishing Point property page, key in zeros for the Horizontal and Vertical values, and click Apply to correct this (see Figure 5-5).

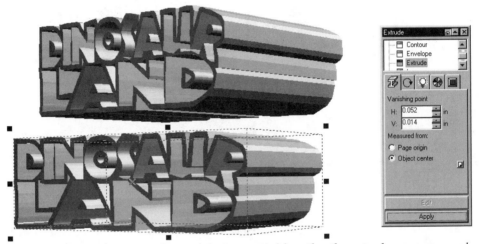

*Figure 5-5: Although the extrude properties were copied from the other extrude group, you need to manually adjust the Vanishing Point settings to ensure both objects are in the identical orientation.*

5. Tab to the Bevel property page on the Extrude roll-up. Select Use Bevel and Show Bevel Only. This will eliminate the redundant extrusion shapes and create only a beveled front. Change the Bevel Depth value to .017 in and the Bevel Angle value to 45 degrees. When you click Apply, the front face will now have a beveled highlight and shadow (see Figure 5-6).

*Figure 5-6: The Bevel feature will cut and chisel the face of your object to create interesting shadow and highlight shapes. If you enable the Show Bevel Only option, the rest of the extrusion will be eliminated from the final rendering.*

6. The beveled text will eventually be placed on top of the extruded back to create a final fat and chiseled look. Now the task is to create scales in the same orientation. First draw a perfect circle with the Ellipse tool. Hold down the Ctrl key to make a perfect circle. Next, open the Fountain Fill dialog (F11) to create a custom radial color blend. Create a blend that is black, to green, to lime, to green, and back to black. Then offset the center vertically around 48 percent by dragging the center upward in the preview window. Click OK to finish. Drag this circle to the right and tap the right mouse button as you release. This will duplicate and move in one step. Because it is one step, you can repeat it (Ctrl+R) to create a row of scales quickly. Duplicate this row, and move below and offset the original. While it is still selected, send the duplicate row to the back (Shift+PgDn). Continue the duplicate, move, send to back process until you have a wall of scales (see Figure 5-7).

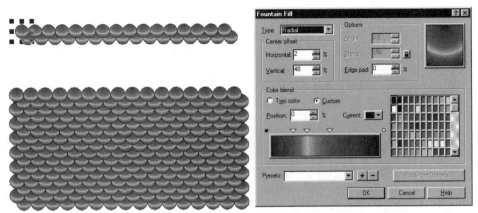

*Figure 5-7: Use the Fountain Fill dialog to give a circle a scaly coloring scheme. Then duplicate and arrange the circles into a wall of slippery scales.*

7. Now drag-select a section of the scales and group (Ctrl+G) them. Select the fat background extrude group, and from the Arrange menu, choose Separate. Now you should be able to select the front object only and bring it to the front (Shift+PgUp). Position your scale group so that it is centered to the front object, and then from the Effects menu, choose Add Perspective. Now a grid will appear around your scale group, and the Shape tool will be selected. Grab the top-left node and drag down while depressing both the Shift and Ctrl keys. This will bring the bottom-left node up simultaneously. Stop when the scales are in the same orientation as the extrude group (see Figure 5-8).

*Figure 5-8: Use the Add Perspective function to place the scale shapes in the same general orientation as the extrude group.*

8. With the scale group still selected, choose Place Inside Container from the Effects | PowerClip flyout. Now click on the front extrude object, and kapow! The scales are in the correct orientation and also inside the dinoland shape (see Figure 5-9). The PowerClip command is discussed at greater length in Chapter 8.

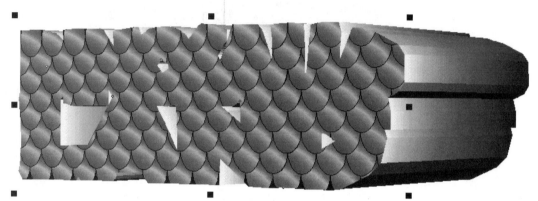

*Figure 5-9: The PowerClip function places the distorted scales inside the extrude shape.*

The only thing left to do is position the beveled front on top of this scale group. You could create another, lighter scale group and use the PowerClip function to squeeze them inside the smaller bevel group shape for a more scaly bevel. In fact, I went back and did just that! To see what I did, load the file (called dinoland.cdr and located in the \Chapt5\ subdirectory on the Companion CD-ROM) and look at the PowerClipped objects. The file also contains an earlier version of the logo that I abandoned. Live and learn!

**CD-ROM**

**TIP**  *To manipulate pieces within a PowerClip curve, choose Edit Contents from the Effects | PowerClip submenu. The screen will block out all but the contents of the PowerClip, which you can then edit like any other CorelDRAW objects. This makes it easy to work with objects already PowerClipped inside a curve. When finished, again from the Effects | PowerClip submenu, choose Finish Editing This Level. You can also yank all of the pieces out of a PowerClip curve with the Effects | PowerClip | Extract Contents command.*

## Goldfish

*Figure 5-10: The Lens function can be used not only to distort objects, but with the Frozen option enabled, it can also trim them to fit within a shape (rather than constrain them within a shape via a PowerClip). The Color Styles feature allows you to substitute colors in a selection easily, which makes recoloring clip art, for example, an easy task.*

To create a fish-food logo, I wanted each letter to look like a fat, happy fish (see Figure 5-10). I could squeeze the scales into each letter using the PowerClip function, but that would not generate the "bulging" look I was after. The PowerClip function is great to constrain images within other objects, but there are other ways to get similar results, sometimes quicker and easier. In this example, the Frozen option on the Fish Eye Lens roll-up lets you distort and constrain in a single step (fewer steps = less time = less work = happiness). Also introduced here is the Color Styles feature, which makes color substitution very quick and easy. The art is kind of goofy, but the time-saving tricks are worth a look-see! Here is how to use the frozen Fish Eye lens feature and also recolor with Color Styles:

1. I started by copying the scales from the dinosaur land example to save time. With all of the scales selected, open the Fountain Fill dialog (F11) and change the color values to be more appropriate for goldfish. The custom color blend was from cyan, to yellow, to white, to yellow, to orange. The white acts as a highlight on a shiny surface. With the Artistic Text tool, I set my type in a font called Stubby and positioned the text over the scale objects (see Figure 5-11).

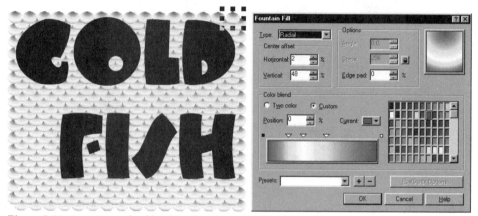

*Figure 5-11: A custom color blend in the Fountain Fill dialog changes reptilian scales into fishy ones.*

2. To make each letter look round, the Fish Eye lens is perfect (this is getting so *fishy*). For the most dramatic effect, each letter should be manipulated individually, so first select the text and convert to curves (Ctrl+Q). Duplicate (+) this object so you have a whole copy later on for the highlight and shadow steps. Now break apart the letters, shift-select the letter pieces (the inside and outside of the *o* for example), and combine (Ctlr+L) them back into their correct forms again. Shift-select all letters, open the Lens roll-up (Alt+F3), and select the Fish Eye option. Change the Rate value to 150 percent, and enable the Frozen option. Lenses don't normally change your design, just how they appear through the lens, which CorelDRAW recalculates each time you preview or output the design. When you "freeze" an image with the Frozen option, CorelDRAW actually creates a group of objects based on the current lens setting. This eliminates the lens and replaces it with objects that simulate

the lens effect. The advantage is that you eliminate all the lens recalculation, you can manipulate the resulting objects, and as in this case, the pieces are in a desired shape. With the frozen duplicates in place inside the letters, you can now delete the original scale objects (see Figure 5-12).

*Figure 5-12: The Frozen option on the Lens roll-up creates a new group of objects rather than just changing the look of the design during preview or output with a lens.*

3. Use the copy of the text curve to create a gleam shape with the Trim command as outlined in Chapter 3. You may also wish to place the copy with a thick black outline behind the scaly copies for more contrast. A box filled with the Water 5 Colors texture fill in the Styles Library gives the liquid background look. A goldfish was imported from the \clipart\fish\ subdirectory and placed behind the text. To add depth, I wanted the fish to cast a shadow. The quickest way to generate the shadow shapes is to duplicate the fish group, ungroup it (Ctrl+U), and then choose Weld from the Arrange menu. Now click the Weld To button, and click on one of the objects in this group. This should result in a solid shape, which you should then give a 50 percent black Transparency lens and no outline to create a shadow (see Figure 5-13).

*Figure 5-13: Welding a group of objects together and then using a 50% Transparency lens can make for an instant shadow effect.*

4. Shift-select both the fish shadow and fish objects, and open the Scale & Mirror roll-up (Alt+F9). Toggle the Horizontal Mirror button on and click Apply To Duplicate. This will flip and copy our fish in one step. Now select the new shadow and move it into the corrected orientation (flipping the fish distorted the shadow.) To make the duplicate fish look more unique, it should be recolored. Ordinarily, this would be a hassle, but not with CorelDRAW! It is pretty easy using a feature introduced in Version 7 called color styles (see Figure 5-14).

*Figure 5-14: Color styles make for easy recoloring of objects.*

5. From the Layout menu, select the Color Styles option. Now with your fish selected, click on the Auto Create Color Styles button (looks like two boxes with chicken-pox!). In the Automatically Create Color Styles dialog, drag the slider over a tad to the right toward Few Parents (see Figure 5-15). The fewer parent colors there are, the easier it is to recolor an object; however, too few colors and CorelDRAW will reduce the number of colors in your image to the point of losing tonal variation.

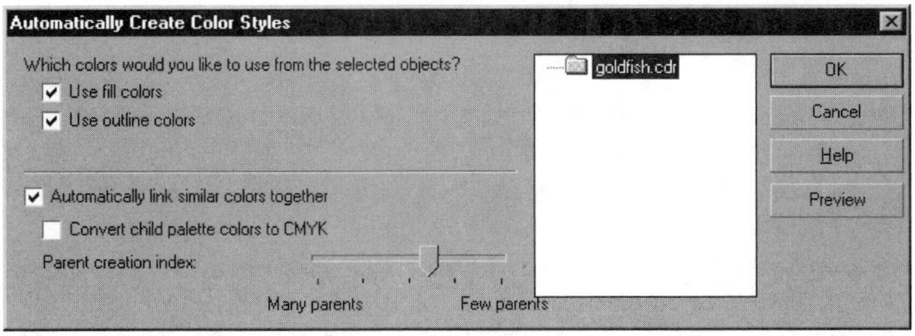

*Figure 5-15: It takes some experimenting with the Parent Creation Index slider in the Automatically Create Color Styles dialog to get the perfect balance.*

6. Click OK to generate the styles, which are visible when you click the + sign next to the filename in the Styles roll-up. Now if you select the parent color of the orange group and then click the Edit Color Style button, you can replace the orange color with any other color of your choice! This is the greatest tool for recoloring CorelDRAW artwork. Choose a much redder orange color and click OK. CorelDRAW will now not only substitute the red for the orange but will also calculate all of the subtle shading colors in the child group (see Figure 5-16).

*Figure 5-16: Replacing the parent color with a new one will regenerate all of the subtle tones in the child colors associated with it. This changes the entire color range of a selected object.*

**TIP**

*If you are having problems with a file that contains active color styles, you may wish to freeze them. I have found that CorelDRAW files that have active color style objects in them can be unstable (especially in version 7). I prefer to freeze the colors and eliminate the color styles. To do this, I save the drawing as a version 5 file, which does not support color styles, so they are eliminated during the save process. From the Save Drawing dialog (File | Save As), change the version to version 5.0 and rename the file so that you will know it is a version 5 copy. You may also want to save the file as a version 7 or 8 to keep the color styles active so you can change them later on.*

I finished up my logo by adding a *Food* text element and breaking up each letter as before. Then, using the Edit | Copy Properties From function, I selected the Fill option and then clicked on one of the fish scales in the word *Gold*. This gave the word the same coloring, but at the same time, its own unique fill. If you want to load and experiment with the Freeze function, this file is in the \Chapt5\ subdirectory on the Companion CD-ROM and is called goldfish.cdr. The scales are in a file called scales.cdr, which you can load and use in your own designs or use to practice using the Lens and Freeze function. In Chapter 30, we walk through converting a flat image such as this into a 3D-looking box object.

## Gorilla

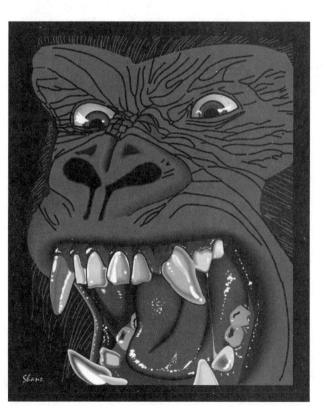

*Figure 5-17: Multistage blends can create the illusion of rounded objects, such as the teeth and eyes in this gorilla graphic.*

Although the image of an enraged primate in Figure 5-17 is one of the first things I ever drew in CorelDRAW, I still like it (it's a pre-caffeine, Monday morning self-portrait, actually). I spent hours on my old slow computer creating this image, which I entered into one of the first CorelDRAW design contests. For my tireless efforts I was rewarded with a spanking new Corel key chain and matching mouse pad. Oh well! The artwork still jumps out at you and gets positive viewer reaction. To emphasize the wet and shiny surfaces of the eyes and mouth, I purposely made the rest of the face kind of flat and dull by comparison. This image started as a quick ink illustration of just the main features of a gorilla's face, which I scanned and traced using the Centerline function. I was originally just going to use the CMX file as a reference and draw everything again freehand in CorelDRAW (the centerline trace of this image resulted in many lines and few closed objects). However, the hair and black outlines in the face are the actual results of that centerline trace.

The technique I like in this piece is the use of multistage blends (as in the fangs) to get a round, interesting blend. Instead of blending just two objects, I blended three to broaden the color range of the blend and add more control. The really wet look is also a basic technique of drawing tiny solid white circles strategically placed to suggest reflection and texture. I won't walk you through this whole design as that would take too long, but I will show you some neat tricks in the eyes and teeth, which you can work into your own monstrosities! Here is how to draw shiny eyes and fangs:

1. Using the Freehand or Bezier tool (your preference), draw the main eye outline. The Bezier tool is great for drawing like this, except that hard edges (as in the eye corners) are difficult. If you create a curve by dragging, the node you create is a smooth one. To get a cusped node, click with no drag to get a straight line. It takes some practice to draw curved shapes with the Bezier tool, and to date I still prefer to draw simple straight lines and then modify the curves using the Shape tool and Node Edit roll-up. This also makes for very simple, low-node count shapes (see Figure 5-18).

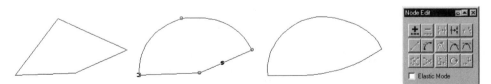

*Figure 5-18: It is often easier to draw straight lines and then use the Shape tool and Node Edit roll-up to create a curved shape, especially one with cusped nodes (as in the corners of the eye shape).*

2. Draw the largest of the eye detail circles first using the Ellipse tool and holding down the Ctrl key to draw a perfect circle. If you make it a habit to draw the largest objects first and the smaller ones later, you will save time restacking the objects. Objects "stack" themselves in the order of creation. So if you draw a small circle and then draw a large one, the larger one will be on top of the smaller. The same is true for duplicates. Select the circle, duplicate it (+ key), and reduce it by dragging a corner sizing handle inward. This duplicate is now on top of the original. Duplicate and downsize once more for the pupil shape. Now from the Arrange menu, open the Intersection roll-up and disable the Other Object Leave Original option. Now one by one, select the eye pieces (largest to smallest again to maintain the correct order), click the Intersect With button, and then click on the main eye shape. This will place your iris and pupil shapes perfectly within the eye. Shade the eye with a black-to-white linear fountain fill from the Fountain Fill dialog (F11), and give the two outside pieces a black fill and the middle piece a dark brown fill (see Figure 5-19).

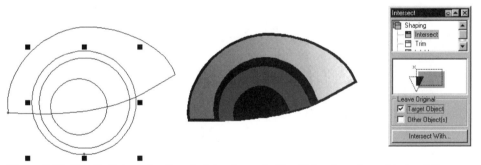

*Figure 5-19: Use the Intersect roll-up to trim shapes to fit within a boundary object and then color the pieces for a realistic eye.*

3. Now select the largest black circle and shift-select the brown one on top of it. Open the Blend roll-up (Ctrl+B), change the number of steps to 5, and click Apply. Select only the top brown control curve, shift-select the small black circle on top of it, and click Apply again. The result is a compound element of three control curves and two blend groups (five total elements). If you change any of the control curves, it will affect all of the elements in the compound element group. With this compound element selected, choose Arrange | Separate, then Arrange | Ungroup All. To make the retina more crisp, delete some of the resulting objects in the

second blend. Use the Freehand tool to draw in some vein lines, following along a suggested curve of the eye, and give them a red outline. Use the Freehand tool to draw objects suggesting reflected light on a wet eyeball. These shapes can be very abstract; just follow again a suggested curve of the eye to make things look more round. Color them solid white for a stark reflection (see Figure 5-20).

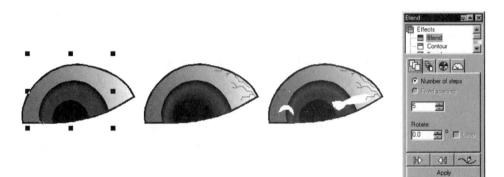

*Figure 5-20: Three objects blended together form a Compound Element. The Freehand tool draws the jagged lines of the veins as well as the abstract reflection pieces.*

4. I used this same double-blend technique on some of the teeth to get a rounded look with a wider color range than a single blend can achieve. On some I just use a traditional blend on top of another object to accent the tooth. The trick to smooth blends is to have the exact same number of nodes in each control curve. To guarantee that both objects have the same number of nodes, it is a good idea to generate the second control shape by duplicating (+) the first. Now use the Pick tool and sizing handles to drag, skew, and resize the duplicate. Also use the Shape tool to sculpt the duplicate shape into its final form manually rather than risk changing the node count (by using the Intersection command, for example). To shade the big fang, a smaller object was drawn inside of the main tooth shape and given a darker orange fill. This was duplicated, and the duplicate was shaded gray and formed with the Shape tool to maintain a like node count. When these two objects are blended (Ctrl+B), the transition is smooth because of the like node orientation and number. The Freehand tool again draws shiny spots, which accent the illusion of wetness and roundness (see Figure 5-21).

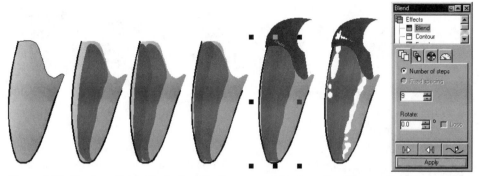

*Figure 5-21: For smooth blends, both control curves need to have the same number of nodes. To ensure this, create one control curve by duplicating another. Use the Shape tool to distort the second control object, but to keep the blends smooth, do not alter the number of nodes.*

**TIP**

*For smooth, predictable blends, both objects need to have the same number of nodes. The status bar displays the number of nodes in the selected object; you can use the Shape tool to add or delete nodes until the numbers are the same. Then, using the Map Nodes feature (found under the Miscellaneous Features tab on the Blend roll-up), you can tell CorelDRAW from which point to start the blend on each target object.*

*Click the Map Nodes button, then click the arrow on the starting node of the first object, next click the arrow on the corresponding node on the end object, and finally click Apply. This helps you control blends that seem to give oddball results otherwise. The easiest way to get predictable results with blends is to use the same shape for all control curves. Duplicate the parent object, which ensures the same node count and orientation, and then manipulate it for the blend. You can warp, twist, downsize, and recolor the duplicate, whatever you wish; and as long as you don't alter the node count, the blend should be smooth and predictable.*

5. Blending original objects to smaller duplicates always produces a nice smooth blend. Accent the round look of these blends with solid white gleam shapes drawn with the Freehand tool. It isn't difficult to achieve a convincing look; it just takes a little time to draw in all of the fine details (see Figure 5-22).

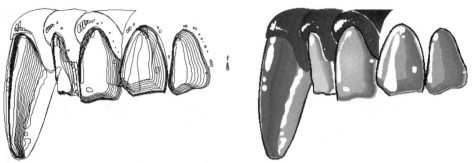

*Figure 5-22: Blending a large object to a smaller duplicate produces a smooth and round look. Add more steps for smoother blends, fewer for a stepped look. Accent with solid white shapes to suggest wet sparkles and highlights. The Wireframe view on the left shows where the blends are.*

This file is called gorilla.cdr and is in the \Chapt5\ subdirectory on the Companion CD-ROM. The live blends have been eliminated (Edit I Select All, Arrange I Separate), leaving only the parent shapes and frozen blend groups. This was done somewhere along the way to speed up the processing of this very complex image. Live blends recalculate constantly, whereas separated blends are simply frozen groups of colored objects. Zoom in on the teeth, delete the interim blend shapes, and experiment with blend steps to create really smooth transitions. I used a minimum number of blend steps when I made this image on my old computer, so upping the number now would result in smoother color transitions!

## Moving On

In this chapter, we addressed some of CorelDRAW's limitations and also how to get around them. Essentially, if you can imagine it, you can create it in CorelDRAW! As powerful as the bitmap and texture pattern fills are, there are many advantages to creating patterns by hand using native CorelDRAW objects (see Chapter 28 for more on patterning). There are times when you just can't get a bitmap or texture fill pattern to behave or output correctly, and that is when handmade patterns excel.

As we have seen, the PowerClip function is also a unique CorelDRAW function that has tons of potential (see Chapter 8 for more examples). Trimming or constraining objects within a curve is a great way to generate very cool-looking type or symbols and is easier and more flexible than pasting within a selection in a paint program (which does not allow you to go back and edit the pieces later). Also, the concept of multistage blends, which we will use in future examples, adds a new dimension to the Blend tool.

In the next chapter, coincidentally, we will focus on a very cool way to use the Blend function to create solid-looking objects. Although this technique was developed to illustrate human organ systems, with a little twist we can use it to build less gutsy designs! So I hope you like sushi, 'cuz were off to snack on some tentacles.

▼ **Beyond f/x**

Although you may not find yourself rendering many scaly or wet objects at the moment, you never know what project will walk through your door! I had to create a "smiling, sunglass, and sombrero wearing" iguana one day, and found myself drawing scales on the beast. So even scale-rendering knowledge may be useful one day! The more generalized concepts, especially the problems with placing patterns in perspective, can be used for any geometric pattern, such as brick walls or dalmation spots. Making things look wet and shiny is also a universal technique to transform a flat company logo into one made of shiny plastic or a puddle of oil. These examples are not meant to be taken literally, but just offer solutions to broader design problems. The multistage blending used to create the realistic, round-looking teeth is a great way to render other tubular objects, like coffee mugs or telephone poles. Probably the most powerful feature in this chapter, at least from an automation perspective, is the Color Styles function. This is a great way to easily recolor any artwork in a controlled and convincing manner. With the Color Styles feature you could create car brochures with only one original graphic, using the Color Styles to give the duplicate cars different paint schemes. It is a really handy tool, and once you master it, you will wonder how you ever got along without it! Now maybe you won't wince as much when a client asks for a total recoloring of their artwork. Hmm. Maybe I'll go back and make the gorilla blue....

# chapter 6

# Tentacles, Tentacles & More Tentacles

I was attending a big CorelDRAW conference in Baltimore when I met a very interesting person by the name of Martin Boso (pronounced BOSS-oh). He is a medical illustrator who uses CorelDRAW to generate the images for medical training films and multimedia applications. He took great delight in showing me his unique techniques and, of course, plenty of raw, icky footage of the insides of people. Ew! Making me squirm became his favorite hobby!

Although I almost never need to illustrate the intricacies of human organ systems, I did walk away with some neat ideas of my own (in addition to an upset stomach!). Instead of using them for veins and intestines, I would use Martin's blending technique for tubes and tentacles!

Blending many objects along a curve can give the illusion of solid objects, such as tentacles or a tube. You start with two objects and then create a new solid-looking object by blending them together. The trick is to use many, and I mean *many*, steps—so many steps that the blend becomes a solid-looking object.

The other vital part of the illusion is the shading of the parent shapes. If you use a solid fill color, you get a solid-looking object in a single color. However, if your parent shapes are shaded correctly with highlight and shadow areas, the blend builds the illusion of dimension. As the shaded objects stack on top of one another, the shaded areas combine to give an amazing look of depth. You will know it is a blend, but your audience will just be mystified as to how you got the effect!

Because the illusion is based upon the Blend function, you have a lot of flexibility. You can leave the blend straight, twist it, rotate it, or use a path for an unlimited number of possibilities!

## Octopus

*Figure 6-1: The tentacle shapes here look remarkably three-dimensional, but they are actually very simple to create. A multiple-step blend along a path creates the illusion of light and shadow with a custom color blend in both control curves.*

Although I loved Martin's technique, it took me a while to find a use for it in my nonmedical world. Veins, intestines, and gooey organs are not exactly a staple in my design diet! However, I find this technique to be more and more useful as time goes by, especially when I combine it with other f/x tricks, like the explosion technique from Chapter 2! (See "Sea Star" later in this chapter.) The key to making a many-step blend along a path seem like a solid object is in the custom color blend in the two control curves. I used the technique for a comic octopus character (see the color section for the finished graphic). Here is how to create a rubbery limb:

1. With the Ellipse tool, draw a circle. Now open the Fountain Fill dialog and create a custom color blend (see Figure 6-2). The trick here is to create a dark bottom, a highlight in the middle, and a darker color on top. For the octopus arm, my custom blend went from black to red to white to magenta. Change the Angle setting to 70 degrees and click OK.

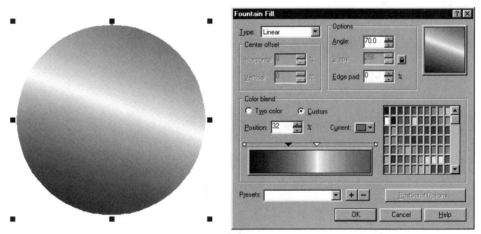

*Figure 6-2: A custom color blend is critical to the success of this effect. The idea is to have shadow, highlight, and then shadow again in the color scheme.*

2. Duplicate the circle (+ key) and reduce it by dragging a corner sizing handle inward with the Pick tool. Use the Bezier tool to draw an *s* curve or any other shape to eventually run the blend along. Now move the two circle objects to the start and finish of the curve and open the Blend roll-up (see Figure 6-3). Change the number of steps to 300 and click Apply.

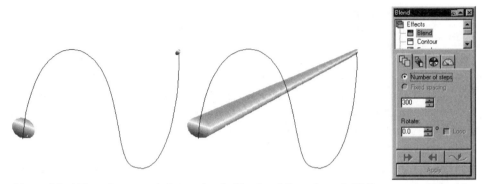

*Figure 6-3: Although a curve is drawn for the blend to follow along, initially you must blend to objects directly.*

3. On the Blend roll-up, click the Path Options button (an arrow pointing toward a squiggly line). Click New Path and then click on the curve you want your objects to blend along (see Figure 6-4). When you click Apply, you will generate a new tentacle!

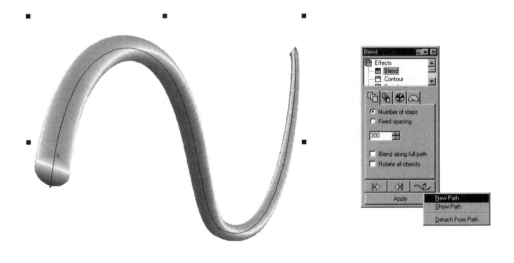

*Figure 6-4: Blending along a path transforms the straight tube into a wiggly tentacle shape.*

4. Select the control curve and right-click on the "no-fill" swatch. That completes your tentacle! To change the orientation of the tentacle, simply change the order of the parent shapes. For example, drag-select the right control curve and send it to the front (Shift+PgUp). The blend will re-draw, changing the way the tentacle looks; instead of looking like it is going away from you, it will look like it's coming toward you (see Figure 6-5). It is essentially all an optical illusion, but it works great!

**TIP** *To ensure that your blends are as smooth as possible, try not to use any outline attributes in your control curves. Blending objects with outlines creates a more perceptible stagger-step than those without.*

*Figure 6-5: Sending a control curve to the front or to the back changes how the blend redraws itself. This makes the tentacle seem to be either going away from you or coming toward you.*

That is basically it! It is a super-simple technique that yields awesome results! As you can imagine, I *love* it! I love anything that is mostly automated but still looks cool. I used this technique to create the octopus.cdr file found in the \Chapt6\ subdirectory on this book's Companion CD-ROM. The same technique repeated eight times produced all of the individual tentacles. The tentacles meet to a simple circle that was given a radial fountain fill for a round body center. I used a thick black outline around everything to give it a more cartoony feel. Here is how to make the thick outline:

1. Once you have all of your tentacles built and connected to a center circle, select all and group (Ctrl+G) the objects.

2. Now duplicate this group (+ key), and left-right-click (click with both buttons, first the left, then the right) on the black onscreen color well to give everything a black outline and fill.

3. Now click on the Fill tool to open the Fill tool flyout. Then click on the 8 Point Outline (Medium) thickness button. You can use this as a shortcut to create common outline widths rather than using the Outline Fill dialog (F12). Now send this fat black group to the back (Shift+PgDn). See Figure 6-6.

*Figure 6-6: Duplicating the entire octopus, giving the duplicate group a fat black outline and fill, and sending it behind the original is a quick way to give blend objects a cartoony outline.*

The background for this image is a Texture Fill called Plankton, which is found in the Samples 7 Texture Library. To fade the ocean background beneath the octopus into darkness, a duplicate black rectangle is placed on top of the plankton and given a fade using the Interactive Transparency tool. The bottom is solid black, fading into the top, which is totally transparent. This technique is a simple way to make something darker, even though technically you are just making the black rectangle on top more transparent.

## Sea Star

**COLOR STUDIO**
*Figure 6-7: Combining the explosion blend technique with the tentacle shading and blending steps can create an interesting variety of sea creatures.*

The octopus image required the creation of eight individual blend groups along eight control curves. It was not that difficult, but I wondered what kind of results could be achieved with a more randomized automation approach, as with the explosion and fireworks examples in Chapter 2. I could not sleep until I created a tentacle explosion, combining the many-step blend technique we just saw with the spinning pinwheel techniques of Chapter 2!

This experimentation session resulted in three major variants: the straight blend, the blend with a 180-degree twist, and finally, a 360-degree spin (seen in Figure 6-7 and also in the color section). In essence, I used the same technique I used in the explosion, except that all objects share the specialized custom color blend to give the illusion of three dimensions, and of course, the number of steps is dramatically increased.

## Straight-Legged Sea Star

I was very excited to try the explosion blend on the tentacle pieces. But as the blend assembled itself on the screen, I was confused—it didn't look like anything. Then slowly, as the shapes stacked up, the straight legs of a creature that looked like a sea urchin began to appear and I was really jazzed!

This is a fun technique; it's more mesmerizing to watch it build in version 7 than in version 8, but the end result is the same. Here is how to generate the straight-legged sea star:

1. Start with a circle filled with the tentacle custom color blend. Reduce this circle, duplicate it many times, and scatter into a circle. This procedure is opposite of the procedure used to create an explosion, where you started with the center pieces, and you will see why in a second.

2. Select all of the objects and group them (Ctrl+G). Now duplicate this group (+ key) and ungroup (Ctrl+U) the objects in this duplicate. Now open the Align and Distribute dialog, enable the Center and Center options, and click OK. This will align the center pieces of the star perfectly. Group these objects again (Ctrl+G), and enlarge the grouped objects by dragging a corner sizing handle outward (see Figure 6-8).

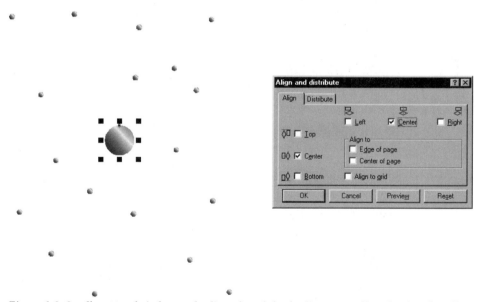

*Figure 6-8: Small scattered circles are duplicated, and the duplicates are aligned using the Align and Distribute dialog box. The group of aligned circles is also enlarged and regrouped in preparation for the blending process.*

**TIP**

*It is easy to use keyboard shortcuts to align objects. For example, Ctrl+A opens the Align and Distribute dialog, and then tapping the appropriate letter on the keyboard will toggle the options. Press C, E, and then the Enter key to center objects both vertically and horizontally. The shortcuts are displayed as underlined letters in the dialog box.*

3. Select the inside circle group and send it to the back (Shift+PgDn). Now shift-select both the inner circle group and the outer one and open the Blend roll-up (Ctrl+B). Change the number of steps to 200 and click Apply. If you don't send your middle group to the back, your star will face away from you (see Figure 6-9).

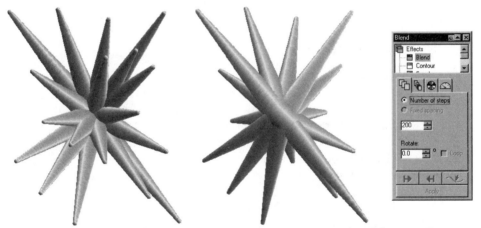

*Figure 6-9: Using a many-step blend between the two groups creates the solid sea star. Reversing the order of the control objects gives the illusion of the arms pointing away from you.*

## Rotated Once

Once the blend for the sea star was created, it was just a matter of twisting the arms around using the Rotate option. Variant 2 results from rotating the sea star 180 degrees. The rotation adds a sense of movement and life to the image.

To spin your star, simply select the blend and change the Rotate value on the Blend roll-up to 180. When you click Apply, the blend will twist itself around 180 degrees. I spun the backward-facing tentacles in the opposite direction using the same 180-degree setting. This is because this rotation number is based upon the objects closest to you in the blend. Because the objects closest to you are reversed in the two examples, I didn't have to reverse the angle of rotation (see Figure 6-10).

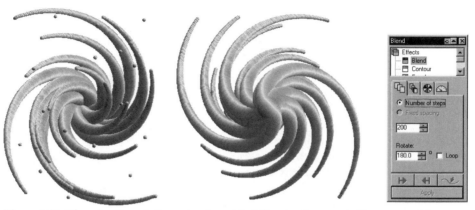

*Figure 6-10: Changing the rotation value from 0 to 180 spins the arms halfway around in a circle.*

## Rotated Twice

You could continue to spin the arms around for the maximum 360 degrees. With this much rotation, you may want to increase the number of steps to 400 to smooth things out (but it would really slow things down!). Spinning the arms 360 degrees starts to transform the free-floating arms into a tighter, almost shell-like object or perhaps a wild-twisting set of dreadlocks!

To spin your star 360 degrees, simply select the blend and change the Rotate value on the Blend roll-up to 360. When you click Apply, the blend will twist itself around 360 degrees, stepping the pieces a little further apart. To combat the stepping, increase the number of steps to 400 and click Apply once more. You may even wish to experiment with the Acceleration parameters because you really don't need the objects so dense in the center; they should be more staggered on the outside end of the blend (see Figure 6-11).

You can watch the blends build in real-time by loading the seastar.cdr file and examining it. The file is in the \Chapt6\ subdirectory on this book's Companion CD-ROM. It is a monster! As soon as it is loaded, choose Simple Wireframe from the View menu and delete all but one live blend area. Then you can switch back to Normal view, select the blend, and open the Blend roll-up (Ctrl+B). Change the angle of rotation, including negative values, to see how it changes the orientation of the tentacles. Also play with the Accelerate objects settings to see how you can actually make the blend smoother without increasing the number of steps. For even more drama, select the inside or outside control shapes and change the blend. Ooooh. Aaaah.

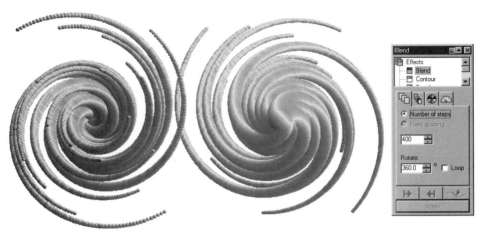

*Figure 6-11: Changing the rotation value from 0 to 360 spins the arms all the way around in a circle. Increasing the number of steps makes the blend smoother.*

## Candles

While trying to work out another design problem, I stumbled on another use for this tentacle technique (well, many uses actually!). There are examples of how to use this technique to create all kinds of objects scattered throughout this book (Tribal objects in Chapter 14, star patterns in Chapter 21, metal trees in Chapter 23, and even robot arms in Chapter 24!). My goal is to suggest that even the most unconventional solution sometimes is the easiest, and best.

This image is created by blending blends. This is technically impossible, as you can not blend a live blend group. "Impossible" isn't in my vocabulary though, so here is how to create the multiple-blend object:

1. Start with an object that you want to build in candles. I used a heart shape from the ZapfDingbats Symbols library. Draw a small circle, and fill it with a red variation of the tentacle fill, with a shadow, highlight, and neutral custom color blend. Duplicate this circle, then use the Blend roll-up (Ctrl+B) to scatter these objects along the heart. Select both circles, and click Apply on the roll-up. Now click the Path button on the roll-up, click New Path, then click on the heart shape. Enable the Blend along full path option, and click Apply. This will place the candle circles all along the heart (Figure 6-12).

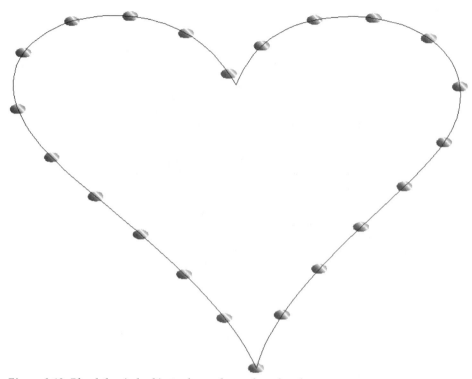

*Figure 6-12: Blend the circle objects along a heart shaped path.*

2. Now select the blend group, and do the dance. This is a little stream of commands that you will be doing a lot in this book, but they go quickly. From the Arrange menu, choose Separate. Then select Arrange | Ungroup All. Now shift-select the heart curve to deselect it from the circle shapes, and Group (Ctrl+G) the objects back together. What this does is disable the live blend, makes all objects individuals, then groups them into one again. This is the step that is necessary so you can blend a blend.

3. Duplicate the group of circles in the heart shape (+ key), and Ungroup (Ctrl+U) the duplicate. Open the Align and distribute dialog (Ctrl+A), enable the horizontal Center option, and click OK. Now all of the circle shapes are lined up in a row. Group this row (Ctrl+G), and drag a corner sizing handle outward while holding the Shift key to enlarge the group a bit. These objects are the candle bases (see Figure 6-13).

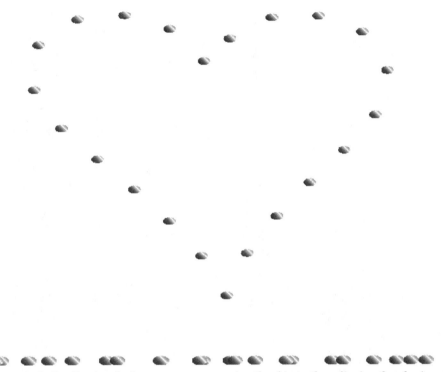

*Figure 6-13: Duplicating the heart group, ungrouping the objects, then aligning them horizontally creates the candle bases.*

4. Select the horizontal group, and send to back (Shift+PgDn). Now shift-select both the horizontal and heart-oriented circle groups, and use the Blend roll-up to blend them together using a 200 step blend. Instant candle arrangement! If the candles look to choppy, increase the number of blend steps. The more steps, the smoother the candles, but the longer it takes to render the scene. Figure 6-14.

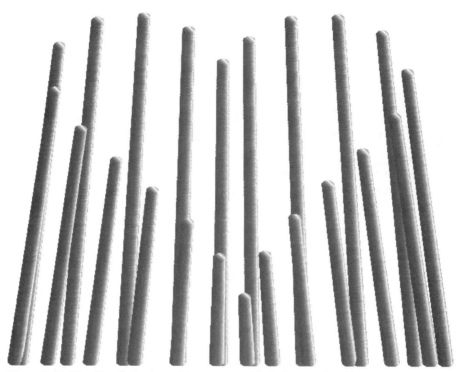

*Figure 6-14: Blending the horizontal base group with the heart-oriented group creates a candle arrangement.*

5. For the flame on top, use the Freehand tool to draw a flame shape. Give this shape a yellow fill, then use the Interactive Transparency tool to fade from solid yellow in the center to clear on the edges. A white circle on top with the same radial transparency setting (solid in center, fade to clear on edges) gives the radiant glow. Drag-select and group these flame objects, and place a duplicate on each candle end (see Figure 6-15).

**TIP** *You can not blend a group of objects that contain any transparency settings. You can, but the duplicate groups created with the blend roll-up will not have any of the Transparency attributes. For this reason, you can't simply use the blend along the heart path to place the flames on the candle ends (unless you don't want any transparency features.*

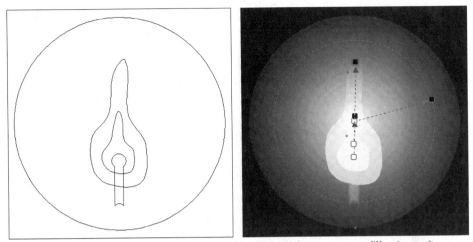

*Figure 6-15: A flame group (in wireframe on left) with radial transparency fills gives soft lighting to the candle ends.*

That's basically it. You can find the finished image in the color studio. You can change the way the candles look by modifying the base or heart groups before you create the blend that connects them. For example, I went back and enlarged the base shapes, and manually arranged them beneath the heart group so the candles were more vertical. This made the candles fatter on the bottom.

The candles were combined with other artwork, including leaves created in Chapter 9 to create an altar-looking thingy that you can see in the color section, or load the heartc.cdr file from the \Chap6\ subdirectory. The hearts along the left side are illustrations done in pastels, scanned from photographs and imported into the scene.

## Moving On

Experimenting with the CorelDRAW functions is the best way to stumble on something new and fun. I have always been more interested in trying to use CorelDRAW in a new and innovative way rather than trying to solve a design problem in another program. You could get some very interesting 3D tentacles using CorelDREAM, but it would take a lot more work and wouldn't be nearly as flexible as a CorelDRAW file is. Besides, who wants to exit CorelDRAW?!

The next chapter again takes ordinary CorelDRAW functions and uses them in extraordinary ways, such as creating dimension with the Extrude function and lighting effects with the Transparency tool. Hey, if you wanted normal or ordinary, you wouldn't have bought this book! So slap another CD in the stereo (dig up the old "Egyptian Lover" dance mix or "Walk Like an Egyptian" by the Bangles!) and let's go make some hieroglyphics!

▼ **Beyond f/x**

These strange tube blends can work into many design projects, many still to come in this book! Martin built a cut-away view of the entire human body using this technique, then using the back-to-front screen refresh of CorelDRAW 7 (8 builds the screen differently), he videotaped the file as it builds on the screen for use in medical training. You can of course use this technique to build any other number of things beyond human organs! Try other shapes, such as stars or polygons, rather than the circles, to create angular and dimensional objects. With fewer steps and the rotation option in the blend roll-up, you can get crazy patterns for use as borders or background shapes. You can create a neon-tube type logo, blending circles along a long, flowing, handwriting path, or many paths, to give a headline text object a unique, 3D look. If you still are stumped, no worries. We use this technique at least five more times in the book, to create everything from spaceships to metal trees!

# chapter 7

# Chiseling Rock & Hieroglyphics

People have been cutting and carving images into stone or wood since the dawn of civilization. Man has always had the urge to make his mark in stone and leave an indelible symbol for all to see. This tradition carries on in the world of graphic art, with everything from the corporate ID to clothing design somehow incorporating this classic theme at one point. CorelDRAW has some neat features, both simple and complex, to help chisel your own niche in the marketplace!

In this chapter we will create chisled and 3D-looking objects, and also dabble with some lighting effects. In the first example, we will use the Extrude function to create stone-carvings, complete with depth and shading. Then, using the rotation option on the Extrude roll-up, we will see how to take an object and spin it in virtual 3D space. Finally, we are going to create a spooky Egyptian tomb, and use the Interactive Transparency tool to add torch-like lighting effects. Grab the pith helmet as we are off on a stoney exposition!

## Shell Medallions

*Figure 7-1: The Bevel function, found in the Extrude roll-up, adds the perfect highlight and shadow shapes to any surface to give it the illusion of depth. When the Bevel function is used in conjunction with a bitmap pattern fill, the results are very realistic.*

The technique of creating a chiseled-in-stone look is just the kind of CorelDRAW magic I love—little effort and big payoff! The results are stunning, to the point where you can stare at the finished piece and swear you were looking at a photograph or an actual stone carving (see Figure 7-1 and the color section). On the even cooler side of the equation, the process is highly automated, with CorelDRAW doing most of the actual hard work of generating shadow and highlight shape. As they say in Southern California when something is really cool, "Stony!"

The illusion works because there is actually more than one extrude group working for us. There is an outer ring group, the actual shell shapes, and a neutral background object. In the case of the cutout shell, which we will look at first, the neutral background shape shows through in the recessed, carved area. In the second example, the beveled shell object rests on the background. Both techniques are very similar: the only thing that sets them apart is one small circle shape, which changes everything! By combining the circle to the shell shapes, you transform the object and in doing so dramatically change the way the Extrude and Bevel functions work on it.

## The Cutout

Here is how to get the cutout look:

1. With the Ellipse tool, draw a perfect circle. Duplicate this circle object (+ key on your keypad) and reduce it by dragging inward on the corner sizing handle while holding down the Shift key. Duplicate the circle again so you end up with a set of three rings. Now shift-select the smallest and largest ring and combine them (Ctrl+L). This should create a solid doughnut shape, with another circle outline on top (see Figure 7-2).

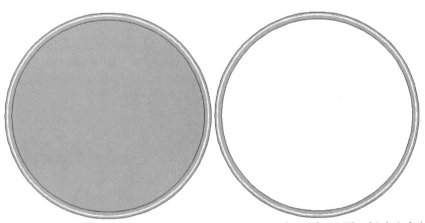

*Figure 7-2: Combining two circles together creates a doughnut shape. The third circle is on top, with a white outline and no fill.*

2. Open the Symbols roll-up (Ctrl+F11), find a shell shape in the Animals 1 font, and drag it onto your desktop. Enlarge and center it (Ctrl+A) within the circle shape. Now select the remaining center circle (the other two are combined into the doughnut), duplicate (+) once more, and enlarge it slightly. Select this ring and the shell and combine them (Ctrl+L). This will punch the shell shape through the circle and is the last step in creating our parent shapes. Now there are three objects: a circle with the shell punched out of it, a simple circle background, and a doughnut ring around everything (see Figure 7-3).

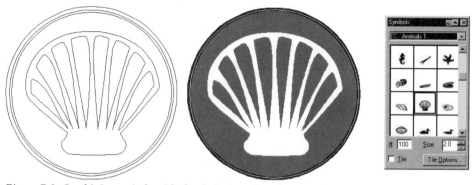

*Figure 7-3: Combining a circle with the shell shape, in effect, punches a shell-shaped hole through it, resulting in a see-through space in the shape of the shell (the Wireframe view is on the left).*

3. Select the outer ring shape and send it to the front (Shift+PgUp) and then select the background circle and send it to the back (Shift+PgDn). Drag-select all of the objects, and from the Fill tool flyout, open the Pattern Fill dialog. I chose a bitmap pattern from the \tiles\stone\large directory. Click the Load button, select the Preview option to view the image tiles, and click Open when finished. Change the Tile option to Large and then click OK. At this point, all of the pieces will blend together in Preview mode (shown in Figure 7-4 with outlines so you can see where each is).

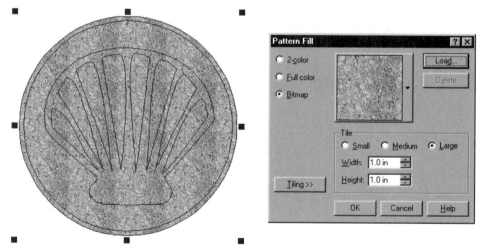

*Figure 7-4: A bitmap pattern fill is the key element to creating the stone texture; however, at this stage, all pieces blend together.*

4. Here is where the fun begins! Work in Wireframe mode to keep things speedy. Select the outer ring object, and open the Extrude roll-up (Ctrl+E). From the Vanishing Point tab, change the Depth value to 5 and set the extrusion's vanishing point attribute to VP Locked to Object. Click Apply, even at this early stage, so that the extrude will build and you can change the vanishing point with the Edit button. Move the vanishing point to the exact center of the circle. Now switch to the Lighting tab and enable one light source at the right-center position. Then click to the Bevel tab and enable the Use Bevel option. Now change the Bevel Depth option to .05 inches and click Apply. This should give our outer piece depth.

**TIP** *For most applications, the default bevel depth is way too big, resulting in total mayhem on the screen. It seems sometimes that even if you change this value initially, it will switch back to the default when you click Apply. To make sure your values sink in, key in the new Bevel Depth value and then click the mouse on the Bevel Angle value box. This should ensure that the new Bevel Depth value is registered. Then click the Apply button.*

5. Select the shell shape and open the Extrude roll-up (Ctrl+E). Move to the Lighting tab and enable one light source at the right-center position. Then click to the Bevel tab, and enable the Use Bevel option. Now change the Bevel Depth value to .05 inches. Enable the Show Bevel Only feature before you click Apply. Because lighting is enabled, the surface of the extrude group becomes slightly darker so CorelDRAW can then calculate highlight and shadow objects (see Figure 7-5).

*Figure 7-5: The Extrude function with a light source and beveling options enabled calculates the highlights and shadows for a chiseled look (the Wireframe view is on left).*

That is it! This process yields great results but is mighty slow to render. You may wish to work in Wireframe mode to speed things along.

**TIP** *To speed up file save times, disable the thumbnail feature. From the Save Drawing dialog (File | Save As), change the Thumbnail option to None. A thumbnail is a nice reference graphic, but CorelDRAW must calculate every single thing in your design to create this tiny image. So if your file has a complex extrude or series of lenses, having this feature enabled will dramatically increase your save time.*

## Inverse

To change from the cutout look to the inverse, with the shell embossed rather than recessed, the changes are minor. First, you need to remove the circle from the shell shape and then reapply the bevel. Here is how to make the shell embossed:

1. If you are using the pieces from the previous example, be sure to save them first with a unique filename. Now, in Simple Wireframe view, select the shell shape and duplicate it (+ key). Drag this shape off to the side. Since you selected only the control curve, your duplicate does not contain the extrude information. With the duplicate selected, break it apart (Ctrl+K), delete the outer circle, and then drag-select and combine (Ctrl+L) the pieces again. This should leave you with just the shell (see Figure 7-6).

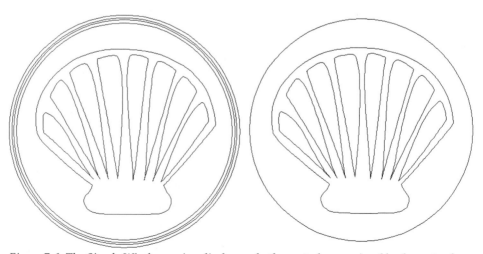

*Figure 7-6: The Simple Wireframe view displays only the control curves in a blend or extrude group. This makes selecting and duplicating an object such as the shell shape easier than in any other view.*

2. Although the bevel function worked fine on this shape in the previous example, we need to modify it slightly in this one. The bottoms of the scallops in the shell object are very pointy. In the previous example, because the circle shape was combined to the shell object, the bevel was inside of the points and everything rendered fine. However, removing the circle changes the cut-away area to the inside of the scallops, reversing the logic of the function. Creating a bevel on the outside of these really sharp points results in some unpredictable and undesirable shapes. To make things work better, you first need to round out the spikes. With the Shape tool, double-click on a point above the ending spikey node and add a node there by clicking on the + button on the Node Edit roll-up (Ctrl+F10). Continue to add points just above both sides of the pointy scallop ends (see Figure 7-7).

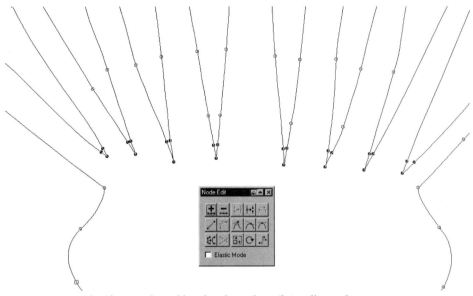

*Figure 7-7: Use the Shape tool to add nodes above the spiky scallop ends.*

**TIP**  *Unlike some bitmap plug-in filter effects (such as Alien Skin's Bevel, from the Eye Candy collection), CorelDRAW only will bevel to the inside of an object. The shell in the first example appears to be beveled on the outside because it has been combined with a larger circle, creating a solid object with the shell shape punched in it. The CorelDRAW bevel always follows along the inside edge of an object. When you remove the outer circle, the inside edge becomes the shell shape again, reversing the logic of the bevel. CorelDRAW always calculates the bevel in the same way; you just alter the logic of the object to get different results (see Figure 7-8).*

*Figure 7-8: The bevel function always creates shapes on the inside of a solid object. Combining the shell shape with a circle punches a clear area in the center, leaving the shell scallops as solids. Removing the circle makes the shell shape solid, with the scallops cut out.*

3. With all of the new nodes in place, drag-select the end nodes and click the Smooth button on the Node Edit roll-up. This will remove the points (but with the new nodes in place). It will not dramatically change the way the object looks (see Figure 7-9). If you smooth the end points without adding the new nodes, the scallop shapes will distort.

4. It's a good idea to also reduce the number of nodes in the object to make the calculations simpler and smoother. With the Shape tool, drag-select all of the nodes and click the Auto Reduce node button on the Node Edit roll-up (see Figure 7-10).

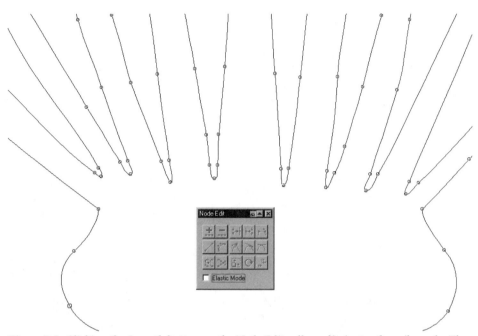

*Figure 7-9: Clicking the Smooth button on the Node Edit roll-up eliminates the spiky ends. The additional nodes keep the shape from distorting during this process.*

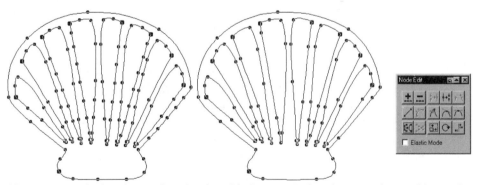

*Figure 7-10: Reducing the number of nodes with the Auto-Reduce feature makes an object easier to extrude, bevel, or blend.*

5. Switch from Simple Wireframe view to Wireframe view. With the shell selected, choose Effects | Copy | Extrude From. Now click on the extrude pieces of the original shell piece. Delete the original shell and position the new one in the center of the medallion. That's it! With the outer circle shape around the shell removed, the extrude group rests on the neutral background and looks embossed (see Figure 7-11).

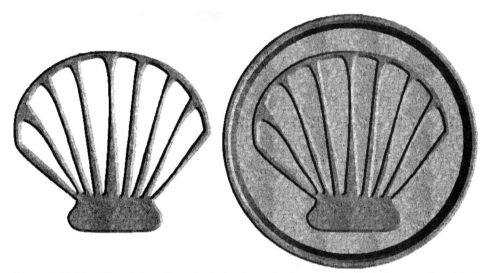

*Figure 7-11: The Effects | Copy flyout includes the option to copy an extrude from another object group. The cutout shape resting on the neutral background object creates the embossed illusion.*

That's all there is to the process for creating embossed or engraved objects. Because these are extrude groups, you can take the whole thing one step further and spin the object in space using the 3D Rotation tool. The next section is an example of just that!

## Twirling Stones

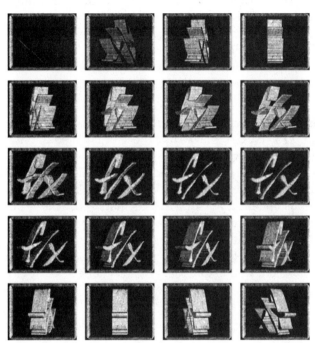

*Figure 7-12: Because an extrude object is infinitely malleable, you can create the illusion of motion. When you increment the 3D Rotation values, the extrude object will appear to spin around.*

The Extrude function is a live setting on a CorelDRAW object. It is a series of settings that recalculate every time you work with that object. At any time you can change the parameters for a new result or even remove the extrude entirely. This flexibility is awesome, as you can always change the texture and orientation of your objects while still maintaining the advantages of vector artwork (as opposed to a 3D modeling package such as CorelDream where you can only output images as bitmaps, which are big and clumsy to work with). This flexibility adds power and potential to your design cycle and can even lend itself to animation projects.

**TIP** *This Extrude roll-up rotation process is a bit heavy on the manual-labor side of the equation to be used for creating low-res onscreen animations such as animated GIFs for the World Wide Web. Other programs (CorelDream 3D, for instance) can create such animation files with significantly less effort.*

This example will show you how you can indefinitely alter an extrude group for the life of your design, either to add built-in flexibility (for a corporate logo that your client wants to see at different angles, for example) or even animation applications. I did assemble this series of twirling objects into an animation (the fxspin.avi file in the \Chapt7\ directory on the Companion CD-ROM and on the CorelDRAW f/x Web site at http://www.corelmag.com/shane/corelfx), but just because I am a masochist, doesn't mean you have to be! Here is how to twirl stone objects in 3D space:

1. To make this process as simple as possible, I wanted to limit the shapes to one. This process of creating frames for an animation just gets too complicated on a stack of images like those in the medallion (but it is not impossible if you are a nut with lots of time on your hands!). I used a simpler text object with a static frame around it. Use the Artistic text tool to set the f/x text on the screen. The font is called Tiger Rag. In my opinion, animations benefit from solid objects that do not move and that serve as a point of reference for those that are moving, so to this end, I drew two rectangles and combined them to create a frame.

   My Web site (where I will use this animation) has a black background, so I made the background solid black. Choose Effects | Copy | Extrude From to copy the extrude and fill values from the shell medallion for the first frame (see Figure 7-13).

**TIP** *If you drag a node on a rectangle with the Shape tool, it will change the corners from harsh 90-degree angles to soft corners.*

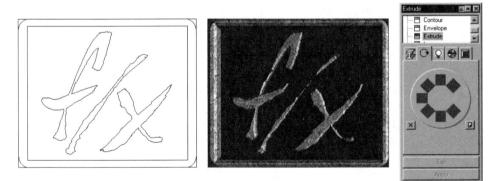

*Figure 7-13: For an animation, a simpler set of objects is easier to manipulate, necessitating only one change per frame export.*

2. Select the center extrude object, and from the 3D Rotation tab on the Extrude roll-up, drag the left-center box to the right slightly. You should see the dotted-line preview box around your object change as you make the move, giving you an idea where your extrude will be. For more precision than the interactive interface affords, open the second page by clicking on the little page button. Now you can key in the rotation values manually. In this example, I increased the second value by 15 each step to create the spinning logo illusion. I also added a second, less intense light source on the left so that my shading would not be solid black; that way, it can be seen against the dark background. Change the values and click Apply (see Figure 7-14).

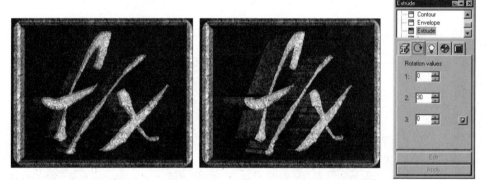

*Figure 7-14: Incrementing the values of the 3D Rotation options in the Extrude roll-up will spin your object in space.*

3. Continue to create frames by incrementing the rotation value and then exporting the scene (Ctrl+H) as a bitmap for assembly into an animation later (Chapter 30 covers this process in detail). You can continue to spin the object around, even until it is backward, with the second rotation value at the maximum of 100 (see Figure 7-15).

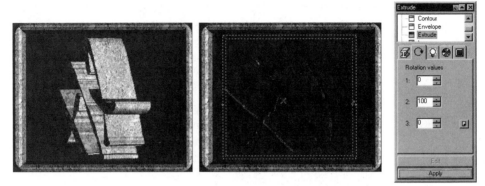

*Figure 7-15: The max value of 100 will spin your object completely around.*

4. With increments from 0 to 100, your object will spin completely around. To spin it back around toward the front continuing in the same rotation axis, you need to increment from –100 back to 0, using only negative numbers (see Figure 7-16).

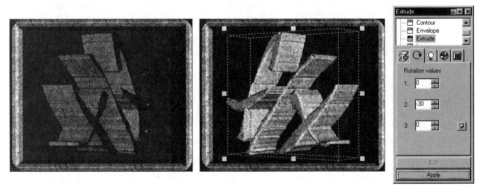

*Figure 7-16: To rotate the object from back to front in the same axis of rotation, you must use the negative number range, from –100 back to 0.*

To simplify the process, you may even wish to start at –100. Decide how many cells you want in your animation and divide by 200 (the total number of available rotation steps) to get your increment value. For example, for a 20-cell animation, you start at –100 and add ten each time (200/20=10) to the rotation value. This will generate a smooth rotation animation.

The file fxspin.cdr in the Chapt7 subdirectory on the Companion CD-ROM is the parent CorelDRAW file from which each scene was generated; the image is also in the color section. Also in that directory is the fxspin.avi file, where you can see the logo moving in the assembled animation. You can load the CorelDRAW file and practice changing the axis of rotation to get a feel for the process before you start an animation sequence of your own. Although in this example we only changed the horizontal rotation value, you could get some wild results by also incrementing the other two rotation values. Again, this is only one example of what you can do with this tool and not the most practical. But hey, you might be as nuts as I am and want to create animations like this too!

## Dark Tomb

*Figure 7-17: A wall of symbol shapes or bricks can be distorted into a dark tomb using the Perspective tool. You can use a black shape on top with a moving transparent hole to light the scene like a dim torch, moving from side to side to reveal the secrets of the dark tomb!*

The Extrude function is a great tool to use to add a lot of depth to an object. The illusion works because CorelDRAW generates highlights and shadows based upon a set light source. Another trick is to use a transparency mask to create the look of a weak light source, in this case a torch, to illuminate a CorelDRAW scene. This example uses the Perspective tool to give flat objects depth and the Interactive Transparency tool to create the "torch-lit" effect. Again the power of CorelDRAW transforms simple shapes into an interesting, flexible graphic. This scene could easily be used to generate a set of animation cells, such as the three that are shown in Figure 7-17 and in the color section.

The hieroglyphics in this image are objects found in the symbol fonts. You will notice I use them a lot, because they are easy to use and also because there are a whole lot to choose from (there is a printed reference included with CorelDRAW). Here is how to use symbol shapes to make your wall of hiero-glyphics:

1. Use the Rectangle tool to draw out the dimensions of your wall. Now open the Symbols roll-up (Ctrl+F11), and open a font of your choice (I used the Space symbols). Simply drag the images out of the library onto your design.

   I arranged the pieces along the wall in three rows, but you can lay them out however you wish (see Figure 7-18).

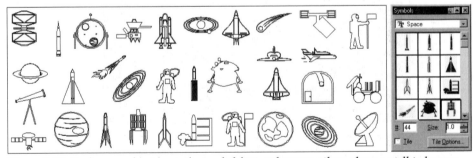

*Figure 7-18: Grab many objects out of a symbol font and arrange them along a wall to become hieroglyphics.*

**TIP** *The objects in the Symbols roll-up may not be to scale in relation to your design when you drag them onto your desktop. You can resize them individually once they are there, or you can change the Size value in the Symbols roll-up itself. This way you can make the objects to scale as you drag them off, which is faster than resizing individually, especially if you are dragging many off at one time.*

2. Drag-select all of the pieces, and combine them (Ctrl+L). This will punch out the symbols in the wall shape. Now give the object a nice sandy-colored fill and no outline. Draw a smaller rectangle behind this wall object and give it a black fill, which will show through the image holes (see Figure 7-19).

*Figure 7-19: Combine all of the objects to create image holes, which let whatever is behind the object shine through. In this example, a solid black object is behind the "holy" wall.*

3. Now we will employ the same technique we used in the impression example in Chapter 6 to get a highlight and shadow effect. Select the front object with the image holes and duplicate it (+ key). Now offset this up and to the right just a hair. The nudge arrow keys are useful for this, but only if you have changed the default nudge setting in the Options | General dialog box (Ctrl+J) to something small (.003 inch, for example). Give this duplicate a solid white fill and send it back one (Ctrl+PgDn). This becomes the gleam shape. I repeated this process to create a duplicate to the left and down and shaded it in a darker sand

color for a shadow shape. This shadow shape is so subtle you may wish to skip it, depending on how zoomed-in your image will be (see Figure 7-20).

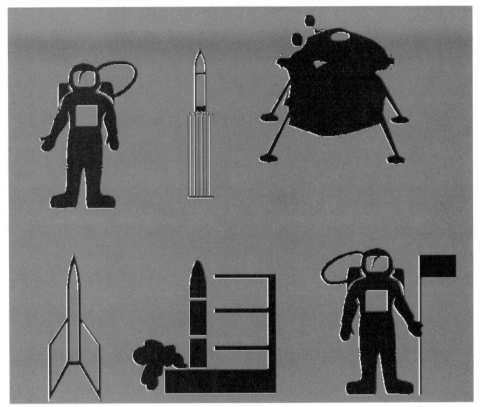

*Figure 7-20: Offset duplicates of the original object to create highlights and shadows for a shallow carved look.*

4. Drag-select all of the objects and group them (Ctrl+G). Now open the Scale & Mirror roll-up (Alt+F9), and with the group selected, depress the Horizontal button and then the Apply to Duplicate button. This will create a mirrored copy of the original wall (see Figure 7-21).

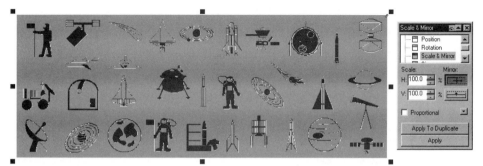

*Figure 7-21: The Scale & Mirror roll-up creates a horizontally mirrored copy of the original.*

5. From the Effects menu, choose Add Perspective. Now with the Shape tool, grab the top right corner and drag down while holding the Ctrl and Shift keys. This will give the wall a single vanishing point perspective (designated by the onscreen *x*). Select the mirrored wall, and from the Effects | Copy submenu, choose Perspective From and click on the distorted wall. This will give both walls the same perspective (see Figure 7-22).

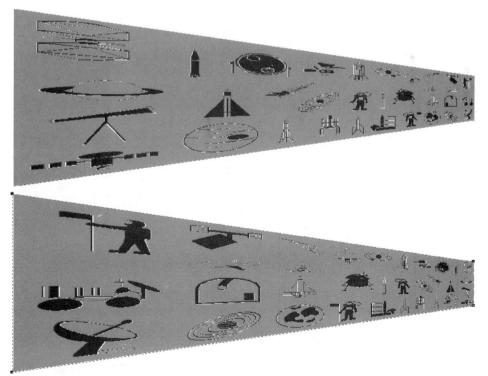

*Figure 7-22: The Perspective function assigns a vanishing point to your group of objects.*

6. Select both walls and reduce them horizontally about 36% by dragging the right-center sizing handle to the left. Now select the bottom wall only and drag the left-center sizing handle to the right while holding down the Ctrl key; this will flip-flop it to create the opposite wall. Position it directly across from the other wall to create the hallway (see Figure 7-23).

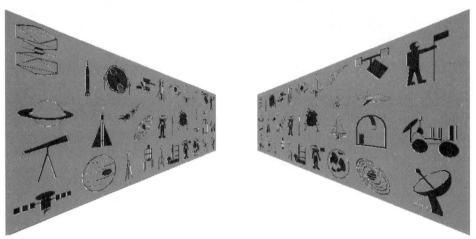

*Figure 7-23: Squish the walls horizontally and then flip the copy to create the basic hallway.*

7. For the ceiling and floor bricks, I followed the same procedure we used in Chapter 7 to create rows of rectangles for a brick wall. These bricks were grouped into one object and again distorted into position using the Perspective function. Drag the top right and left corners down with the Shape tool toward the far doorway to get the object as close as possible to the desired vanishing point; then squish the bricks vertically by dragging the top-center sizing handle down until the floor is in place (see Figure 7-24).

8. Duplicate and flip-flop the floor to create the ceiling. Now draw a rectangle over the entire scene and give it a solid black color. Duplicate it (+ key) and send it to the back (Shift+PgDn). This serves as a black background and also removes any tiny white cracks showing through the distorted floor and ceiling bricks. Now select the top black rectangle and click on the Interactive Transparency tool. On the property bar, change the type to Fountain and click the Radial button. This will illuminate the hallway from the center and fade the fill to darkness at the edges (see Figure 7-25).

*Figure 7-24: A collection of rectangles becomes the floor once they are distorted using the Perspective function.*

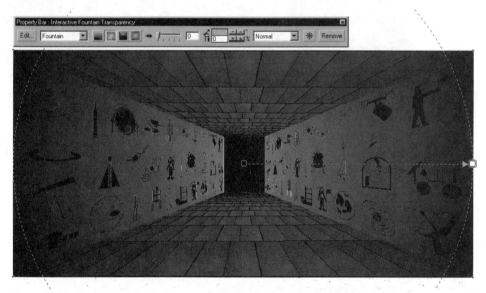

*Figure 7-25: The Interactive Transparency tool creates a round light-to-dark fade in the center of the front black rectangle.*

9. With the Interactive Transparency tool, grab the outer control box at the end of the arrow and drag it toward the center. This point controls where the fade ends—in this case, from 100% transparent to 0% transparent. To move the center point of the transparency sphere, grab and move the center box of the Interactive Transparency heads-up display and drag it wherever you wish. I got the look of dim torchlight by changing the Transparency setting (see Figure 7-26).

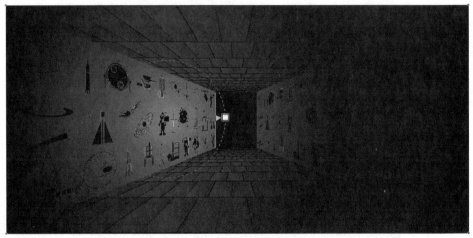

*Figure 7-26: Adjust the settings on the Interactive Fountain Transparency to create the illusion of a dim light source lighting the mysterious hieroglyphics-lined hallway.*

And that's it! Again this CorelDRAW file could easily provide a stack of scenes to assemble into an animation or any other application where you might want to easily change the light source.

This file, called glyphs.cdr in the \Chapt7\ subdirectory on the Companion CD-ROM, is a good one to load and use to dabble with the Interactive Fountain Transparency tool. I think it is fun to watch CorelDRAW recalculate the scene with a new setting, changing the way the light moves in the hallway. You can make it a really small area at the end of the hallway, or you can light up everything that is up close. Experiment and have fun!

## Moving On

In this chapter, we cut and spun objects with the Extrude roll-up, added depth with the Perspective function, and added some trick lighting effects with the Interactive Transparency tool: three more handy weapons for your arsenal.

I keep babbling on about the flexibility of CorelDRAW images because I feel this is where the program is really powerful. The fact that you can constantly tweak objects ad nauseam is just very appealing to me! If you don't like the way something works out the first time, you can tune and massage it until it is just perfect, or you can steal pieces to use in another project. Paint programs just don't have that kind of power, and while virtual reality 3D universes such as CorelDream do, they don't have the output flexibility or bitmap manipulation features that CorelDRAW has.

In the next chapter, we will explore some cool ways to take your images and rip them into pieces! Not only is this a neat technique, it is one of those that is almost impossible to achieve in any other graphics application! Oh mighty CorelDRAW, we worship thee... Now let's go shred, dudes!

▼ **Beyond f/x...**

There are many practical uses for the effects outlined in this chapter. Using the Extrude function is a great way to add depth and shading to any object, such as company logos or mastheads. The animation options work well to bring a logo into a Web page, and then make it sing and dance! The Extrude roll-up's power and flexibility is perfect for "carving" your niche in the Web, with graphics and buttons made of stone. Manipulating the bevel option can also animate your stony buttons, to make them come alive as you click or roll the cursor over them (see Chapter 27 for examples). Using a Transparency effect for mood-lighting is also a great way to change the look of an image, or animate a scene, with little effort. You could design a site-map for your Web Pages that show visited pages as dark rooms, and those still to explore as bright icons. Like Dylan said, "Everybody must get stoned," and with the effects in this chapter, now you can too!

# chapter 8

# Rips, Tears & Pieces

By now I am sure you have seen the ever-popular page curl somewhere in your design-world travels. You can get this effect using the nifty little bitmap plug-in available to you in CorelDRAW and PhotoPaint and is pretty easy to use (Bitmaps | 3D Effects | Page Curl). I like to take the page curl idea and tweak it a bit into shredded rips and tears using CorelDRAW objects, not bitmaps. Call me destructive, but I like images that look as if they have been torn and tattered!

In this chapter we look at several techniques to get a ripped look. The first technique involves using freehand drawing and blending, with some tricks for shading and shadow to create claws ripping through a page. The last two examples use a cool PowerClipping technique unique to CorelDRAW. This process involves creating the illusion of pieces by PowerClipping a bitmap inside a series of combined curve shapes and then breaking them back into individual units. I don't think any other design package at any price can duplicate this process. First we will use the technique to rip a photo in half, then to create an intricate set of interlocking puzzle pieces. If you weren't already getting your 279 bucks worth, this feature should give you that warm fuzzy happy-to-be-a-CorelDRAW-user feeling!

## Claws

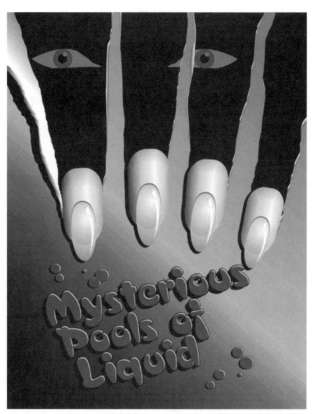

*Figure 8-1: Using a blend between two rough, torn objects creates the tattered edge of claws ripping through this book cover design. For the fingers, use a series of blends to create depth, and duplicate shapes with lenses give the illusion of cast shadows.*

Although the majority of my work seems to be technical writing, I also dabble in short stories and fiction. Many times a story idea is accompanied by an image in my mind for the lead-in graphic or book cover. To get myself in the right mood or to feed my imagination further, I often find myself creating the artwork long before I have finished the story! The graphic in Figure 8-1 is for just such an idea of mine; a contemporary murder/mystery story. Can't you just hear the screams?

With CorelDRAW, as you have seen, you can stack and manipulate images in a logical order. In this way you can have objects in the background subdued, while those in front seem to pop right out at you. Image "stacking" can be invisible or exaggerated, depending on the need (see "Atmospheric Perspective" in Chapter 9 for more on embellishing depth). In this design, the claws pop out, while in the distance, subtly menacing eyes stare at you. Here is how to get this creepy, torn, layered look:

1. The first thing you need is a claw, so draw a rectangle and an oval. Use the Shape tool to round the corners of the rectangle by dragging a corner node inward. Create the main finger shape by welding the oval and smoothed rectangle shape together; then smooth out the resulting shape by deleting nodes with the Shape tool. Make this shape look round with a custom color blend, from black, to dark brown, to tan, and back to dark brown. Duplicate this object (+ key), and reduce it by dragging on the sizing handles with the Pick tool to create a knuckle about two-thirds of the way up the finger. Recolor the custom color blend with a lighter color range, then shift-select both objects and open the Blend roll-up (Ctrl+B). Click Apply to create a 20-step blend between them (see Figure 8-2).

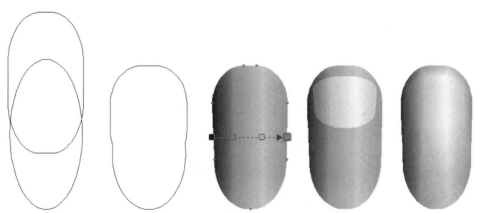

*Figure 8-2: A custom color blend creates a rounded feel to objects welded together to create a finger object. To create more depth and suggest a knuckle, blend the dark original to a lighter copy, and to create images with a broad range of hues, blend objects with color blends.*

2. Draw an oval for the main claw shape, and give it a white-to-tan radial fountain fill. Switch to Simple Wireframe view, and select and duplicate the main finger shape. You must do this because the Intersect function will not work on a blend group, but it works fine on a duplicate of the control curve. Select the nail oval and choose Arrange | Intersect to extract the inside of the claw shape from the finger duplicate. Stretch this inside claw shape and the outside claw shapes vertically to create the

offset fingernail look. I thought this claw looked too pointy on the top, so draw another circle, weld it to the original fingernail, and smooth it with the Shape tool to get a fingernail shape. Duplicate the nail again and offset it up a tad with a dark red fill to create the cuticle. Send it back one layer (Ctrl+PgDn) to place it behind the nail. When working with objects with solid (not transparent) fills, you can just stack them to get highlights and shading effects. Finally, use the Freehand tool to draw reflection shapes and fill them with white along the right edge of the nail (see Figure 8-3).

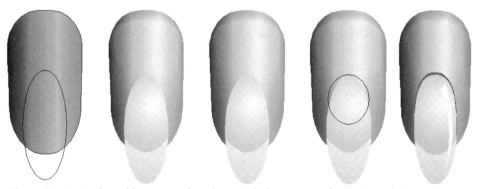

*Figure 8-3: A simple oval becomes a claw shape with the creation of secondary shading objects using the Intersection and Weld functions.*

3. Drag-select all of the claw objects and group them (Ctrl+G). Then duplicate, arrange, and resize the group to create four individual fingers (see Figure 8-4).

4. Draw a bounding box for the limits of the project (in this case a book cover), and then position your fingers in the center toward the top. Using the Freehand tool, now draw a shape with the ripped claw sections in it, and continue around to encircle the entire bounding box. You can be quick and loose, as the more jagged the rips, the better (see Figure 8-5). The shape will be neatly trimmed to within the rectangle later using the Intersection tool anyway, so don't be neat!

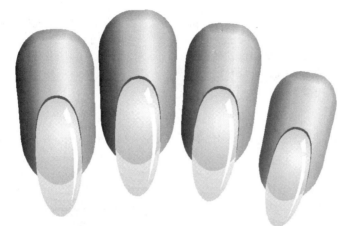

*Figure 8-4: The original finger is duplicated, resized, and arranged to create the other three finger objects.*

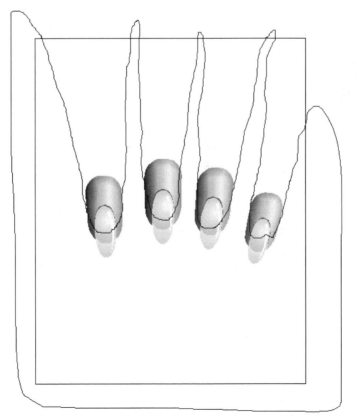

*Figure 8-5: The Freehand tool is used to quickly create a shape for the ripping effect.*

**TIP**

*When drawing a shape with the Freehand tool, if you do not start and stop in the exact same place, it will not be a closed shape. The status bar will not tell you if it is open or closed, but the Property Bar will. If the Auto-Close button is enabled, your object is an open curve. Click the Auto-Close button to connect the end nodes automatically to create a solid shape.*

5. Now draw another shape with the Freehand tool for the folded-over area (see Figure 8-6). I only did this on one of the rips, but you can create folds on any or all of the tears. Again, don't worry about neatness; just draw the shape so it is inside and outside of the rip. The Intersection tool will clean things up for us later. Duplicate this object, move it to the left and down slightly for a shadow effect, and send it back one (Ctrl+PgDn).

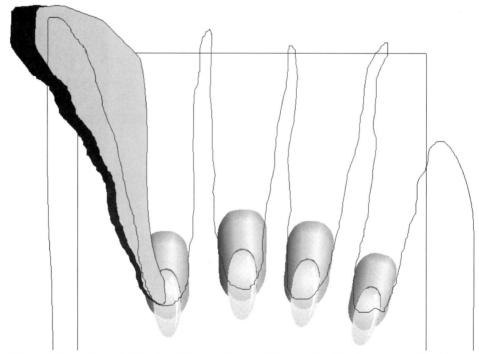

*Figure 8-6: Another set of Freehand-drawn shapes will become the folded-over material and an accompanying shadow.*

6. Duplicate the big main tear shape (+ key), and downsize it vertically around 98 percent of its original size by dragging the top-center sizing handle down. Now drag a center sizing handle inward while holding down the Shift key to squeeze the image so that it is 99 percent smaller horizontally.

   This will offset the duplicate and make it just different enough for an interesting blend variant (see Figure 8-7).

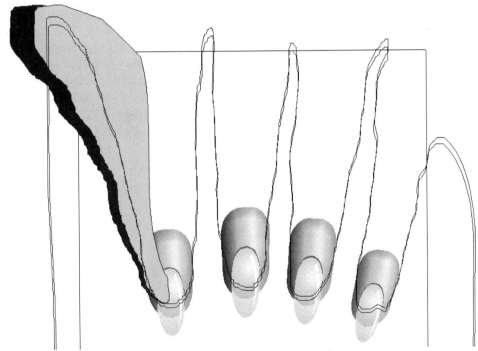

*Figure 8-7: Duplicate and downsize the tear shape to become the front of the rip.*

7. Select the bounding box and open the Intersect roll-up from the Arrange menu. Now deselect the Target Object option, enable the Other Objects option, click the Intersect With button, and then click on the original tear shape. This will trim the tear neatly within the bounding box. Repeat with the smaller tear shape. With the small tear still selected, click on the fold object (shown in gray). Select the small tear and repeat on the other fold shadow object (shown in black). The goal here is first to trim the big tear shapes to the page size and then fit the smaller shapes within the big tear objects. Now all of the pieces are ready for the blending steps (see Figure 8-8).

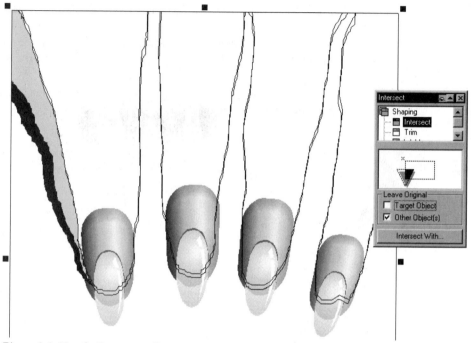

*Figure 8-8: Use the Intersect roll-up to trim down the objects within the bounding box and each other.*

8. Fill the back tear shape with white and the front the color of your choice (I chose green). Shift-select them both, open the Blend roll-up (Ctrl+B), and apply a 10-step blend. Select the front fold object, duplicate it (+ key), drag it down a tad, like 1/8th inch, and send it back one layer (Ctrl+PgDn). Now fill it with dark blue, fill the front object with white, and blend them together also. Finish off by coloring the bounding box black (see Figure 8-9).

9. With such a stark shadow under the fold, I decided the claws needed some shading. Drag-select all of the claw shapes, duplicate them (+ key), and move them off to one side. Now from the Arrange menu, choose Separate | Ungroup All. This will ensure you have nothing but happy separated pieces. Again from the Arrange menu, open the Weld roll-up. Click the Weld To button and then click on any of the shapes. This will merge all of the pieces together into one object, which will be shaded like the last thing you clicked on (see Figure 8-10).

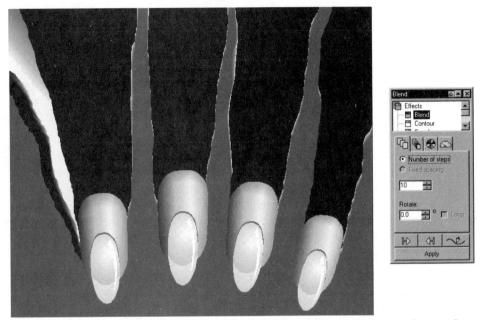

*Figure 8-9: Blending the slightly smaller duplicates from dark to light colors gives the ripped look.*

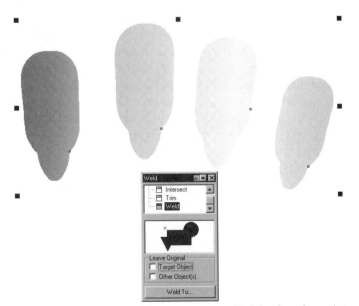

*Figure 8-10. Use the Weld feature to merge all of the claw shapes into one object that will be used as a shadow.*

10. Position the new shadow shape behind the claws and give it a black fill. I decided a flat green for the cover was boring, so I duplicated the top rip object and assigned it a custom color blend. If you don't duplicate this control curve and assign it the custom color blend, CorelDRAW will assign all of the interim blend objects a custom color blend as well, which will really slow down the refresh. It is better to select either the blend and "freeze" it with the Separate command or just duplicate the front object and then assign the fill.

11. I found some eyes in the CorelDRAW clip-art collection and placed them behind the rip and on top of the boundary box. They were just too bright, so I drew a black box over them, and from the Lens roll-up (Alt+F3), assigned a 50% Transparency lens. This subdued the eyes back into the darkness from whence they came! Finally, I imported (Ctrl+I) the blood text from Chapter 3, which is the working title of this project. Hmm, kind of gives me the creeps! Figure 8-11 shows the completed image.

**TIP**

*In order to speed things up, create your design in pieces. If you select a section of your design and then choose File | Save As | Save Drawing | Selected Only, you can save pieces of your complex design to disk independently. Once you have a copy on disk, you can then delete the objects from the live work in progress and free up memory. This is useful for designs that have many complex elements in them. By parking these pieces on disk, you ease the load on your gasping processor because it no longer has to rebuild and recalculate these pieces all of the time. This speeds up your work on the rest of the design by eliminating thumb-twiddling time—you know, the time you spend randomly wiggling your fingers and staring off into space while your machine calculates the effect of your last filter, blend, or whatever on the design. Then, when you have finished all of the pieces, you can import them (Ctrl+I) again into a final file. CorelDRAW retains the original size and position of the image when you save it to disk, so it should drop right back into place when you import it again!*

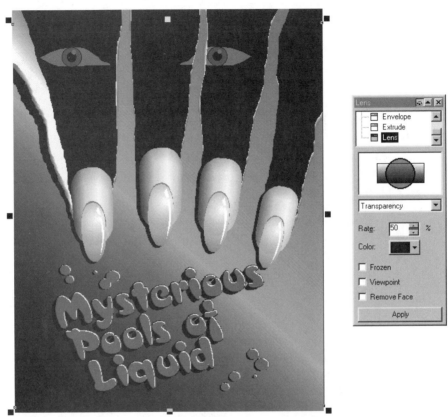

*Figure 8-11: The Transparency lens makes the eyes look like they are further back in the darkness. Importing text created earlier finishes off the cover.*

This book cover is called claws.cdr and is in the \Chapt8\ subdirectory on the Companion CD-ROM. Sorry, but all you get is the cover and not the "who dunnit" resolution to the mystery! I will tell you that the story involves contemporary technology as key clues, including the old star-six-nine phone trick! If I live through these CorelDRAW books, I might get to that one.

## Lost Loves & Torn Photos

*Figure 8-12: The PowerClip function works well to constrain objects, including bitmaps, within other objects. Using a special PowerClip trick, you can then break apart and scatter the pieces. The interesting border shapes around the edge of the design are achieved using a third-party bitmap plug-in effect that ships with CorelDRAW.*

Ripping and shredding up art or photos has a nice, therapeutic feel in the real world. In design, ripping also provokes powerful emotional responses from viewers. The PowerClip function makes tearing the photo in Figure 8-12 in half a breeze. The knife is clip art adorned with blood (Chapter 13), and the background effect is achieved using the Auto F/X Bitmap plug-in filter. Here is how to rip your photo and fray your edges.

1. Draw a rectangle, duplicate it (+ key), and move the copy off to the side for now. With the Freehand tool, draw a shape with a ragged edge covering the right edge of the rectangle. Now, select the rectangle, and from the Arrange menu, open the Trim roll-up. Click the Trim button, and click on the ragged edge shape. This will rip one side of the photo (see Figure 8-13).

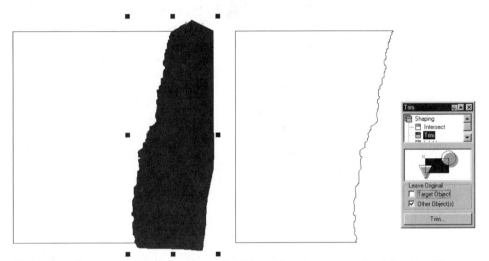

*Figure 8-13: Draw a ragged shape and use the Trim roll-up to cut away the right side of the rectangle.*

2. You should have a torn side and a duplicate rectangle without the tear. To get the tears to match up and yet be different, select the torn side again, duplicate, and tilt by double-clicking to reveal the rotation arrows and dragging the top-center one to the right about two degrees. Position the unmodified rectangle to the right to become the second half of the photo (I stretched my rectangle horizontally a tad). Now select the right rectangle, and trim away the tilted rip from the right rectangle object (enable both Leave Original options as you will use the duplicate rip shape later). Figure 8-14 shows the effect you will get.

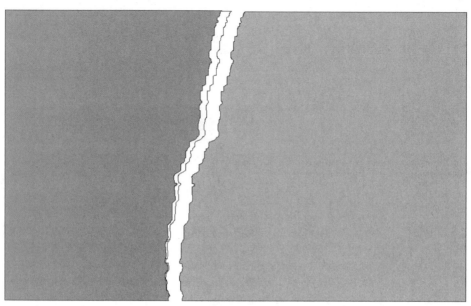

*Figure 8-14: A skewed duplicate of the original rip shape is used to trim away the rip on the right rectangle.*

3. Select the left and right tear shapes and combine them (Ctrl+L). Select the skewed duplicate of the left side, give it a gray or a texture fill (I used the Concrete fill from the Samples 7 Texture Library), and send it to the back (Shift+PgDn). Now all you need is an image! I imported a bitmap from the \photo\couples directory on the CorelDRAW CD. Position the photo over the ripped rectangle, and with the bitmap selected, choose Place Inside Container from the Effects | PowerClip submenu. Now click on the ripped rectangle shape to stuff the photo inside of it (see Figure 8-15).

**TIP** *You can use the default PowerClip setting to center automatically the images when you place them inside of a container. Most of the time, however, you will want to control the positioning manually. To disable this default setting, open the Options dialog (Ctrl+J) and from the Advanced tab, disable the Auto-Center New PowerClip Contents option. This will make your PowerClipping much more predictable.*

*Figure 8-15: The PowerClip function places the photo inside of the ripped curve.*

4. Now you have your image stuck inside of the ripped pieces. If you want
   to separate them, simply select the PowerClip and break it apart
   (Ctrl+K). Now CorelDRAW will explode everything into individual
   pieces, duplicate the bitmap, and place a full copy in each of the broken
   up pieces. However, CorelDRAW will only display the area of each
   bitmap dictated by the object curve. (In this example, there are only two
   pieces, but in the next example we will use this trick to create a puzzle.)
   Now you can select each half of the torn photo and rotate and reposition
   as you wish. Cool huh? See Figure 8-16.

*Figure 8-16: Once a multipiece curve has an image PowerClipped into it, the Break Apart command lets you then manipulate each piece individually. A full copy of the photo is PowerClipped into each piece automatically.*

**TIP** *When you place a bitmap inside a container using the PowerClip function, all of the information is still in the bitmap. CorelDRAW does not shave it down in any way; it just changes the way you see it. When you break apart a PowerClip containing a bitmap, each and every piece contains the entire bitmap. You can move the bitmap within the PowerClip shape with the PowerClip | Edit Contents command.*

Breaking apart the PowerClip is the whole trick to this technique. I then laid out my photo bits with other "clues" for my bloody-knife image. Everything is resting on a wooden butcher block, which is just a rectangle filled with a full-color Bitmap pattern from the \tiles\wood directory on the CorelDRAW clip-art CD. To get the spooky torn edges around the image, you must first convert the entire image to a bitmap and then use a bitmap filter effect. You can do this directly in CorelDRAW or use the filter in CorelPhoto paint, whichever is your preference. I will walk through the process in CorelDRAW. This image, before the conversion and in its native CorelDRAW format, is called mailman.cdr and is in the \Chapt8\ subdirectory on the Companion CD-ROM. If you just want to practice the Auto F/X Photo Edges feature, a smaller version of the image, called fresh.tif, is also in the directory. Here is how to shred the edges of your design:

1. First you need to convert the image to a bitmap. From the Edit menu, choose Select All and then choose Convert to Bitmap from the Bitmap menu. From the Convert to Bitmap dialog, change the Color value to 24 Bit - 16 Million Colors (which is RGB format), enable the Dithered option, set the resolution to 300 dpi (for print, 72 for the Web) and set the Anti-Aliasing option to Super-Sampling (see Figure 8-17). This can create a heck of a big file and take a while, so click OK and take a break!

*Figure 8-17: Use the Convert to Bitmap function from the Bitmap menu to convert vector artwork directly into bitmaps within CorelDRAW.*

2. From the Bitmap menu, choose Plug-Ins. CorelDRAW will now load the aftermarket plug-ins that shipped with the program. It needs to load them before you can use them, so the first time you try, CorelDRAW will just boot you from the menu to load the programs. So from the Bitmap menu, again choose Plug-Ins | Auto F/X | Photo/Graphic Edges. (If you don't see this option, see the tip about the Photo/Graphic Edges 3.0 filter in this section.) A dialog will appear to control the options of this plug-in (see Figure 8-18).

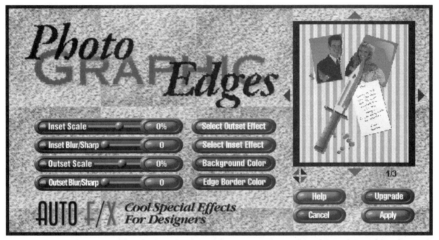

Figure 8-18: The Auto F/X dialog appears when you select Photo/Graphic Edges from the Bitmaps | Plug-Ins submenu. The dialog is how you control the way this plug-in will change your bitmap.

**TIP**    *CorelDRAW 7 ships with a utility, called Auto F/X, which has the Photo/Graphic Edges 3.0 filter in it. However, I have found that more than likely this feature is not automatically installed for you. The option should appear from the Plug-Ins submenu under the Bitmaps menu in CorelDRAW 7. If it does not, then you need to open the Tools | Options dialog (Ctrl+J) and click on the Advanced tab. Under the Plug-in directories area, click the Add button and then browse the hard drive until you find the autofx directory. This should be in the \Corel\Draw70\plugins\ folder. Click on it and click OK to add this set of plug-ins to your CorelDRAW Plug-Ins menu.*

3. Use the printed reference guide in the CorelDRAW clip-art book to locate the exact shape you want to use. There is no "preview" function, so using the book is the only way to go! These edges are located on the CorelDRAW \phot_edg\ directory on the main CD-ROM, which needs to be accessible for this step. Click the Select Outset Effect button, locate an edge that you like, select it, and click Open. Auto F/X will display how the image looks in the preview window. A single Outset effect will give you a jagged edge ending in white. Select a second shape for a shadow, or simply move the Inset Scale slider to create a shadow with the same shape as the first. Experiment with these settings or click the Help button for more information. When finished, click Apply (see Figure 8-19).

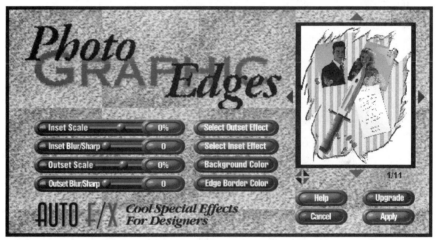

*Figure 8-19: The preview window in the Auto F/X dialog shows you how the options affect your image. Click Apply to change your bitmap.*

Changing from a square to a ragged border was the final step in creating this image, which can be seen in the color section. The downside to this effect is that once you convert your image into a bitmap, you lose the flexibility inherent to a CorelDRAW file. It is always a good idea to save both versions (the CorelDRAW information and the converted bitmap) separately so that you can go back and make changes if you have to. Also, you might find it is faster to export (Ctrl+H) your images from CorelDRAW as bitmaps and then massage them in PhotoPaint, as PhotoPaint is designed solely to work on bitmaps and is faster and more efficient at this task.

## Puzzle Pieces

*Figure 8-20: If you create a complex shape by combining many smaller units into one, you can then PowerClip an image inside of it. Then, when you break apart the PowerClipped object, each little piece will have the corresponding image inside of it.*

The PowerClip/break apart trick has some cool potential, such as the ability to create puzzle pieces. Again, this is one of those tricks I love where the input is minimum, the computer does most of the work, and the results have tons of potential. There is one huge drawback to this technique, however, and that is the files can easily get really big and unmanageable. This is because when you perform the Break Apart command on a multipiece PowerClipped curve, CorelDRAW copies *all* of the image data to each and every piece. So if you have a 10-megabyte image and create a 10-piece puzzle, then technically you have created a 100-megabyte monster! So use an image that is as low res as possible to start out with for your project at hand (this technique is great for onscreen low-res applications that use small bitmaps anyway). Be brave and give it a shot! With memory prices as low as they are, quit your snivelin', slap in another 32 megs, and get serious! Here is how to make the puzzle pieces shown in Figure 8-20:

1. Import (Ctrl+I) a bitmap or any other design into a blank page. The PowerClip function works on vector and bitmap images. Use as small a bitmap as possible and at actual size (massage in PhotoPaint if necessary; 225 dpi is about as low as you can go for print publishing, and RBG is smaller than CMYK). Now with the Freehand and Bezier tools, map out areas of the image that would make good pieces (see Figure 8-21). You don't need to worry about perfection at this point; just make sure each object is solid (use the Auto-Close button on the Property Bar to close up any loose ends). When finished drawing your puzzle pieces, draw a rectangle around the image to serve as a bounding box.

*Figure 8-21: Draw shapes on top of a bitmap to create puzzle pieces. Use the image as a guide while drawing the shapes with the Bezier or Freehand tools.*

2. You may wish to move your bitmap to its own layer and make it invisible at this point. Select the bitmap and open the Layers roll-up. From the top right arrow flyout, choose New. Now from the fly-out, choose Move To and then click on the new layer you just created. Click on the eye icon to toggle off the layer. Now only your pieces are visible (see Figure 8-22).

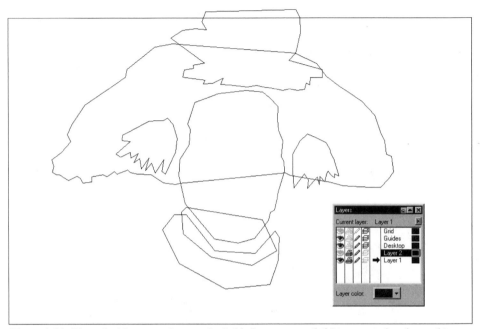

*Figure 8-22: Place the bitmap on its own invisible layer to speed things up and make working on the puzzle pieces easier.*

3. Select one of the puzzle pieces and switch to the Shape tool (see Figure 8-23). Drag-select all of the nodes, and from the Node Edit roll-up (Ctrl+F10), click the Smooth button. This will remove any harsh angles, as die-cut puzzle pieces are usually pretty smooth.

4. Now the trick is to create non-overlapping pieces. This isn't too hard, but it takes a little thinking and creative use of the Trim roll-up. If you select the top piece, for example, and open the Trim roll-up from the Arrange menu, enable only the Other Object option, then click Trim, and finally click on the piece right below it. It takes a little practice to predict the results of the Trim function (I still mess things up!) and get the order of selection right. Keep selecting and trimming until none of your objects overlap (see Figure 8-24).

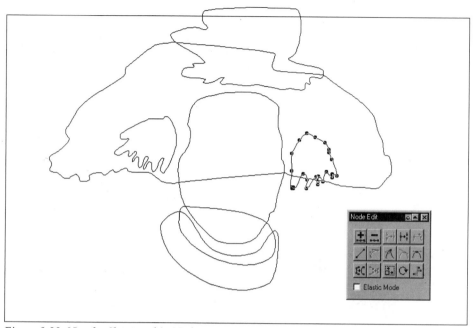

*Figure 8-23: Use the Shape tool in Node edit mode to smooth out the puzzle shapes.*

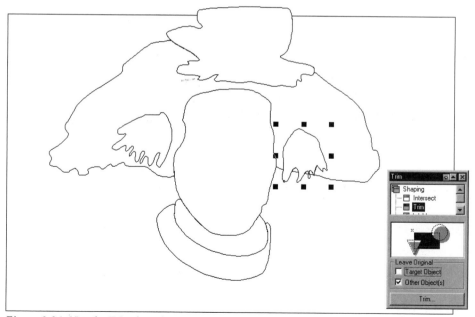

*Figure 8-24: Use the Trim function to create non-overlapping objects.*

5. Once all of the smaller pieces have been trimmed away so as not to overlap, you need to work out the problems of the bounding box, which also must not overlap. This is a little tricky. First, you must use the Intersection function on any pieces sticking outside of the bounding box to trim them down to size. Select the bounding box, open the Intersect roll-up (just click the Intersect section in the Trim roll-up to toggle to the Intersect command), enable Other Object under the Leave Original option, click Intersect With, and then click the top head piece. This will trim the top head piece to within the bounding box. Now, shift-select all of the pieces except the bounding box, toggle to the Trim roll-up, click the Trim button, and then click on the bounding box. This should punch out all areas and essentially result in individual puzzle pieces. I gave these a fountain fill so you could see each piece better (see Figure 8-25).

*Figure 8-25: The Intersect and Trim functions within the Shaping roll-up help create each individual puzzle piece.*

6. We are so close now, you can taste it! Select all of the pieces, including the bounding box, and combine them (Ctrl+L). Now switch to Wireframe view, and also make your bitmap visible again by clicking on the eye icon next to the bitmap layer on the Layers roll-up (Ctrl+F3). Now select the bitmap, and from the Effects | PowerClip submenu, choose Place Inside Container and click on the puzzle curve. Zing! Almost there! Figure 8-26 shows where we are with this step completed.

*Figure 8-26: Use the PowerClip command to place the bitmap within the puzzle shapes.*

7. Now to get puzzle pieces that you can move and rotate individually, simply select the PowerClip and break it apart (Ctrl+K). That's it! You now have a great cyber-puzzle, with which you can do whatever you want (see Figure 8-27).

*Figure 8-27: When you break apart the multipart PowerClip object, each piece can be moved or rotated like pieces of a puzzle.*

Once you have your puzzle in pieces, you can do a lot of things with it. You can, for example, animate the pieces exploding and reassembling themselves or create a cyber-game or even an actual puzzle to cut out and assemble. This file, in the exploded version, can be seen in the color section and can also be found in the \Chapt8\ directory on the Companion CD-ROM, in a file called indipuzl.cdr. If you load the file, select one of the small pieces, and choose the Effects | PowerClip | Extract Contents command, you can see why these files are so big. Notice how the entire original bitmap then pops out of even the tiniest piece! Breaking apart a PowerClip is a great trick, but it does eat up some memory!

## Moving On

In this chapter, we looked at how to rip things up using optical illusions with blends and also how to make pieces with the PowerClip function. There are many uses for the PowerClip/break apart trick, and remember that it is not limited to bitmaps. When you use CorelDRAW objects in your puzzle pieces, the files are not nearly as large! Remember also that you can export a CorelDRAW collection of puzzle pieces as one bitmap and then use a paint program to manipulate the pieces further. I like to do this because it is really easy then to use a filter (such as the Eye Candy Bevel filter) to give the pieces a soft, round, cardboard puzzle look. Like everything in this book, this is just a starting point. Go forth and conquer, my wicked design minions!

In the next section, we look at creating landscapes and other miscellaneous flora and fauna (and I don't mean Flora and Fauna, Tarzan's girlfriends). We will again use the Blend function to create repeating leaves and petals and the PowerClip for evil! Specifically, we will confine a hapless damsel to an eternal flower-petal prison.

▼ **Beyond f/x**

The tearing and ripping effects in this chapter can work into many real-world projects. I have used the technique to play off of typical advertising slogans like "shredding prices" or "cutting costs." You can easily animate the pieces ripping apart for use on the Web or multimedia movies. The puzzle metaphor is also a natural for advertising, making for some very powerful imagery. Taking a group portrait, then pulling people out with the puzzle trick, can add impact to statistics or whatever you can think of ("One person in ten will be effected by violent crime...."). You can create images that build themselves using the puzzle pieces, or start as a whole and explode into oblivion, using the pieces to build an animation. A picture is worth a thousand words they say, and I say even more if you work in some clever CorelDRAW effects!

# chapter 9

# Landscapes, Foliage & Flowers

Landscapes have populated artists' canvases as long as there have been canvases to populate! You could spend hours fleshing out a realistic landscape scene with every tiny detail, but more often than not, the landscape serves as a secondary design element to other foreground elements. The same thing could be said for plants, trees, and flowers. It is essential to have these kinds of design elements at your disposal, and there is a ton of clip art available just for that purpose. Personally, though, if time permits, I like to try to create my own unique landscapes and plant life, because with a few shortcuts, it really isn't that hard, and the results are more satisfying.

In this chapter, we will explore ways to create different landscape looks. First, we explore using landscapes and plants as design elements, either primary or secondary. We will use the Blend roll-up to create basic building blocks for trees and bushes and then use the tool again to arrange these elements in our landscape examples. Also thrown in to break things up is an example of using the Blend function to create and arrange flower petals and how to stuff images inside them with the PowerClip feature. Then, we'll experiment with using blurring and lighting techniques to add the illusion of distance to a scene.

## Landscapes

*Figure 9-1: Simple shapes drawn with the Freehand tool become mountains and clouds in a basic landscape template file. Recoloring the objects can change the locale from plush green plains to harsh brown desert.*

I like to keep a generic landscape template available with basic shapes that I can recolor for the task at hand. A basic collection of land, sky, and horizon elements are useful for many applications, from logo design to generating chrome reflections (Chapter 23 discusses how to use such elements in shiny metal objects). The trick to transforming these basic elements is in the coloring. Here is how to make a basic desert landscape:

1. First, draw a bounding box with the Rectangle tool, with no outline or fill. Now duplicate this (+ key), and drag the bottom-center sizing handle upward a little less than halfway. This will become the sky element. Duplicate this shape (+ key), and drag the top-center sizing handle down, past the center point and back to the bottom line of the boundary

box. The box will flip-flop as you pass the bottom line, but as there is yet no fill, all that happens is that we ensure that we have the exact same horizon line for the sky and the ground shapes! With the boundary in place, use the Freehand tool to draw in some clouds and maybe a set of rolling hills (clouds and hills are pretty common landscape elements, so I included these shapes in this template file). Draw a larger mountain range first; then draw smaller ones on top. If you draw from back to front, you save yourself the steps of rearranging the shapes later. Finally, a circle drawn with the Ellipse tool will become the sun (see Figure 9-2).

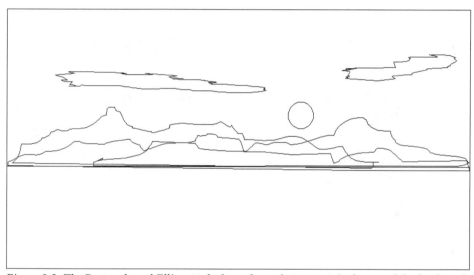

*Figure 9-2: The Rectangle and Ellipse tools draw the perfect geometric shapes, while clouds and mountains are created with the Freehand tool.*

2. To keep things simple, switch to Normal mode and drag and drop colors from the onscreen palette on to the shapes (you can do this in Wireframe view, but you won't see anything happen until you preview or switch to Normal view). This is a very quick and easy way to color objects in CorelDRAW 7 and 8 since you do not need to select them first as in previous versions of the program. Select a blue color from the onscreen palette with the left mouse button, place the pointer over the sky area, and release. Notice that as you move this interactive fill pointer, it will change from a solid box (for a fill) to just a box outline (for the outline color). This is so you can also drag and drop new outline colors as well as fill colors. It is a cool way to work once you get used to it! Drag and drop brown for the land, white for the clouds, and yellow for the sun.

Coloring the mountain range depends on where your light source is. In this case, it is behind the mountains, so the mountain closest to us will be the darkest, with further mountains getting progressively lighter. For high contrast, make the closest mountain shape solid black, with lighter shades of gray as they fade backward (see Figure 9-3).

*Figure 9-3: The drag-and-drop interactive coloring abilities of CorelDRAW 7 and 8 make coloring the landscape shapes a breeze.*

**TIP**   *Remember that the colors shown in the onscreen palette are only a small number of the total available to you. Click on the arrows on the top and bottom of the palette to see more. Also, you can place this palette anywhere you like, just drag and drop it from the right to, say, the bottom (where all versions of CorelDRAW previous to 7 had the palette, and where you may feel the most comfortable with it). Or keep the palette floating over the center of your design, and resize it to reveal all of the available colors. If you are coloring a lot of small objects, it is nice to move the palette closer for drag-and-drop convenience!*

3. The interactive fill tools go beyond solids in these new versions of CorelDRAW. Select the Interactive Fill tool and drag from the bottom of the sky up to the top. This will set up a standard two-color fountain fill

in the default setting. The default is to blend from whatever fill color the object was to solid white. Not exactly a desert sky, but easy enough to remedy. Drag magenta off of the onscreen color well and release it over the bottom box. Hey! Drag and drop works great with the interactive blend! Now drag orange over and release just above magenta. Zing! This is just like adding a color point on a custom color blend using the Fountain Fill. In CorelDRAW there are usually several ways to do the same thing. Continue to drag and drop until your color blend goes from magenta to orange, to yellow, to blue, and finally to black. Now that looks like a desert sky! Figure 9-4 shows the Interactive Fill tool.

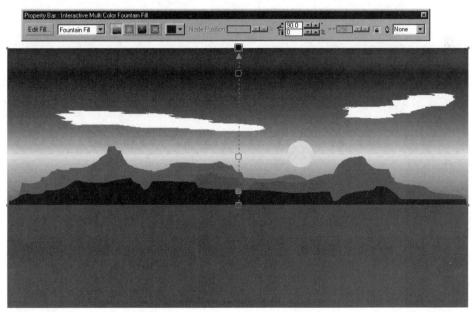

*Figure 9-4: The Interactive Fill tool allows for onscreen creation and manipulation of custom color blends.*

4. Toggle to the Pick tool (tap the spacebar) and select the land object. Toggle back to the Interactive Fill tool (tap the spacebar again) and drag from the top to bottom to create a fountain fill in the land shape. This time the colors go from a light tan in the foreground, to a dark brown on the horizon, and a mid-tone in between. Notice how you can also drag each color point on an interactive fill to change the way things look (see Figure 9-5).

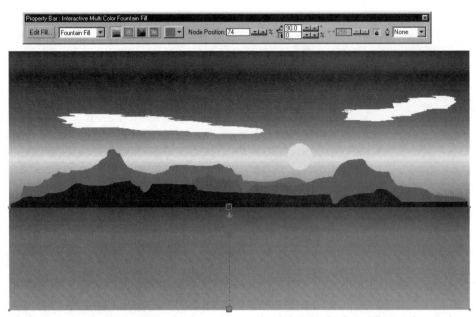

*Figure 9-5: The Interactive Fill tool color points can be slid along the dotted line to change the way the colors blend to create harsh or smoother color transitions.*

**TIP** *Using the spacebar is a handy way to navigate between tools. Tapping the spacebar will toggle between the Pick tool and whatever other tool was last used. This makes selecting and working with objects easier as you switch between tools and cursors. This trick does not work with the Text tool, however, and if you try to use it, you will simply add more spaces to whatever text you are currently editing!*

5. To finish things off, shift-select both cloud shapes, open the Lens roll-up (Alt+F3), choose the Transparency lens at a rate of 50%, and click Apply. This will make our clouds seem fluffy and also automatically recalculate for any sky color scheme we choose.

With all of the pieces in place, it is easy to recolor our landscape objects to suggest a variety of locales and times. Here is how to convert the hot desert sunrise into a cool meadow sunset.

1. To suggest a night/dusk sky, I again used a custom color blend and set it up using the Interactive Fill tool. However, I personally prefer the Fountain Fill dialog when it comes to fine-tuning a custom color blend, so open it to fine-tune the night sky blend (F11). This custom color blend goes from magenta, to cyan, to a 100C100M purple, and then to black. As we saw in Chapter 3, it is a good idea to monitor the color content, especially black, when creating a color blend. Select the black end point on the color blend, click the Current button, and then click the Others button to reveal the Uniform Fill dialog. Here you may wish to add cyan and magenta to the black color so that Corel does not first create a gray transition between them. It just makes for smoother blend effect, and hey, smoother is better! Figure 9-6 shows the Fountain Fill dialog.

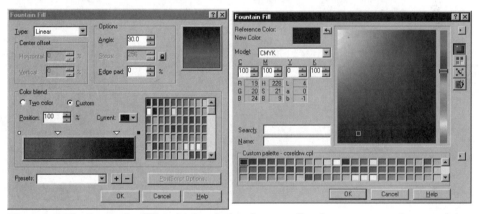

*Figure 9-6: The Interactive Fill tool is handy, but does not allow for one-stop precise control that the Fountain Fill dialog affords.*

**TIP**  *To monitor and adjust the color content of points along a custom color blend that was set up using the Interactive Fill tool, use the Property Bar. When you select a point along the custom blend, the Property Bar will display that color chip. Click on the chip to open a palette of color choices, or click Other to open the Uniform Fill color picker dialog. Now you can add or remove colors to the color point to make the blend smoother. Also, right-clicking on a color-point will remove it from the interactive fill custom color blend.*

2. Change the fill in the land shape from a light green to black with a medium green in between. Again, you may want to fine-tune the colors for a smoother blend. I usually check the color composition of the previous color and then add those colors to my black to get a smooth blend. Change the colors in the mountains from grays to varying hues of green. For the crescent moon, duplicate the sun, and offset the duplicate up and to the right. Then use the Arrange | Trim function to get your moon. Color it white, and you are done! See Figure 9-7.

*Figure 9-7: Changing the color scheme of the landscape shapes dramatically changes the mood and locale. Use the Trim function to change the sun into a crescent moon.*

This is a pretty simple example of landscape coloring, but the results are nice. I like projects that look great but are less *grilling*. These two examples are in the color section. Open the file called landscpe.cdr in the \Chapt9\ subdirectory to see two more color variations and to experiment with the Interactive Fill tools. In the next examples, we will expand upon these basic backgrounds and create more elaborate, finished pieces.

## Read My Palms

COLOR
STUDIO

*Figure 9-8: Palm trees are a popular and fun design theme that you can easily make using the Blend function. Your own unique trees can be used to populate and enhance your landscape images.*

I guess it may be a Southern California thing, but people love palm trees in their artwork here! From automotive accessory businesses to the local hamburger stand, palm trees permeate both the literal and the design landscape. And why not? They are just the thing to add a little exotic flair to any image!

CorelDRAW ships with plenty of tree clip art, and even a few palm tree examples, but I never found anything I really liked. Besides, it is much more fun for me to invent a technique and create something new rather than recycle old stuff. (Good thing too, or this would be one heckuva short book!) I came up with two varieties of tropical-looking trees, broad leafed and spiky leafed. Here is how to make the broad leafed variety:

1. Draw an oval with the Ellipse tool and convert it to curves (Ctrl+Q). Now drag-select all of the nodes, and from the Node Edit roll-up (Ctrl+F10), click the To Line button. This will make the shape a diamond. Now click the To Curve button and select and delete the two center nodes. This will create the basic pointy-leaf shape. Now use the Shape tool on the Bezier control handles of the remaining two nodes to get a more sweeping curve with a fatter center. Draw a rectangle that will be

used to cut the leaf in half and to serve as a guide for drawing the cuts (a leaf like this is really solid, with rips creating the familiar look). Now switch to the Bezier tool, and click straight lines to create a solid object that cuts into the leaf shape. Then select Arrange | Trim to trim away the rectangle and the cut shape, leaving the leaf half. Duplicate the half (+ key), and rotate it 180 degrees by dragging a corner rotation handle with the Pick tool. Position it in place up against the original to create your leaf object. Color to your tastes (I used a light-to-dark-green fountain fill). See Figure 9-9.

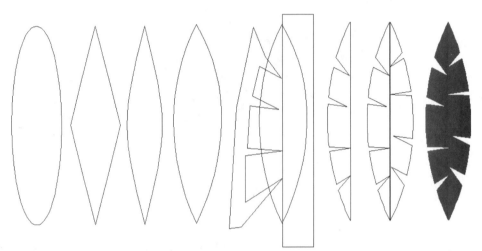

*Figure 9-9: An oval is transformed into a leaf shape, which is given cuts using the Trim tool. To save time, only one half is created, then duplicated, and rotated around 180 degrees. Fountain fills give slight color variation.*

**TIP**

*The Pick tool can move, resize, skew, and rotate your objects. If you double-click on the wireframe, you toggle from the sizing handles to the skew/rotation handles. Dragging a rotation handle spins the object on its axis of rotation (the small double circle that appeared with the rotation arrows). You can drag the axis from the dead center of the object to anywhere else to spin it on a new axis. Also, holding down the Ctrl key as you drag the arrows will constrain your movements to 15-degree increments, which makes quick rotations precise. The default value is 15 degrees, but you can change this to anything else by using the Constrain Angle Value option on the Edit tab of the Options dialog (Ctrl+J). (In V.7, it is under the General tab.)*

2. Use the Freehand tool to draw out a trunk section. Give this a brown-to-gold radial fountain fill. Now duplicate (+ key), downsize, and position the duplicate above the original. Now draw a line with the Bezier tool, with just a slight curve. This will be the path for the blend to follow. Now shift-select both pieces, open the Blend roll-up, and click Apply. Click the Path button, select New Path, and then click on the line you just drew. Enable the Blend Along Full Path option in the Blend roll-up, and click the Apply button again to create a palm tree trunk (see Figure 9-10).

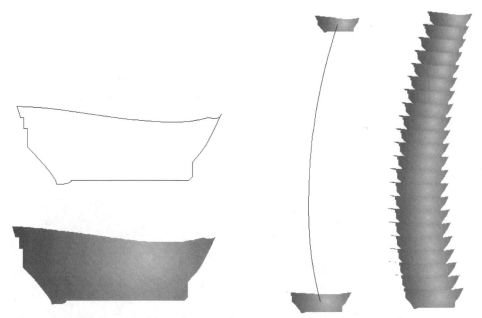

*Figure 9-10: Blending two objects along a path creates a sweeping palm tree trunk. You can make the trunk bow more or less by editing the blend path with the Shape tool.*

3. Now group the leaf halves (Ctrl+G), and distort them using an envelope. You can use the Envelope roll-up (Ctrl+F7) or use the Interactive Envelope tool, which is on the Interactive Blend tool flyout. Change to Single Arc in the Property Bar and drag the top-center node upward while holding down the Ctrl key to create an arched leaf (see Figure 9-11).

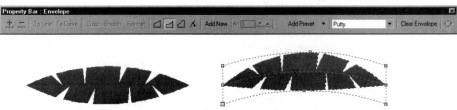

*Figure 9-11: The Interactive Envelope tool makes distorting the leaves into swept arcs easy.*

4. Now one by one, select and arrange the leaves around the top of the trunk. Place a leaf in position, duplicate it (+ key), and rotate the duplicate around. Resize or change the envelope arc in the duplicates to avoid a cloned look (or blend them in a circle with the Blend tool to emphasize a computerized look—it's up to you!). When finished, you can drag-select all of the objects, group them (Ctrl+G), duplicate, and downsize to create a smaller companion tree. To hide the bases, scribble in a grass object, or you could draw some stones or shrubs (see Figure 9-12).

*Figure 9-12: Duplicate and arrange the leaf shapes to create a whole tree. Group and duplicate the tree to create a downsized companion. Rotate or skew the smaller duplicate to offset it slightly.*

5. Now you can use the trees however you like. I grouped them and used them along with the green meadow landscape for a brochure graphic. You can copy (Ctrl+C) and paste (Ctrl+V) the group from one file into another open file; just toggle between windows with Ctrl+Tab. Copy the palm tree group, toggle to the landscape file, and paste. Now duplicate (+ key) and flip horizontally by dragging the left-center control node to the right while holding down the Ctrl key (the Ctrl key constrains the flip to its original size). Position the trees to create a leafy frame (see Figure 9-13).

*Figure 9-13: A pair of the tree duos creates a frame for type or a logo. The landscape artwork serves as a subtle and appropriate backdrop.*

6. Select the Text tool and type out your headline. My "Tropical Paradise" text is set in a font called Pablo LET (Normal). To arrange the letters, use the Shape tool to drag-select the bottom nodes of the word *paradise*, and now drag the letters into a new position. To eliminate the areas where letters overlap each other, first convert the type to curves (Ctrl+Q) and then weld any overlapping pieces together. Finally, select all of the pieces again and then combine them (Ctrl+L). See Figure 9-14.

*Figure 9-14: Use the Shape tool to move a letter or entire word of a text object. The Weld function was used to merge overlapping pieces together.*

7. Select the text (now a curve) and open the Contour roll-up (Ctrl+F9). Change the settings to Outside, .005 in. Offset, 1 Step, and click Apply. This will create an outside shape, but to manipulate it, choose Separate from the Arrange menu, and then ungroup (Ctrl+U). This contour shape was given the Heat Map effect from the Lens roll-up (Alt+F3). The lens reacts to the colors behind it to create a color scheme similar to tempera-ture-sensitive film. In this example, it just creates a nice outline abstract for the text, which is laid on top and given a black fill with a white out-line (see Figure 9-15).

*Figure 9-15: Use the Contour roll-up to generate a unique shape based on the text object. Use the Heat Map option from the Lens roll-up to give this a dynamic fill that reacts subtly to the color scheme behind it.*

That wraps the brochure graphic. I like using original elements as opposed to clip art to avoid that "hey, I recognize that..." syndrome. This wouldn't be an issue if my friends weren't all graphic artists! This file, along with the other example to come, is in the color section and also in the \Chapt9\ subdirectory on the Companion CD-ROM; the file is called horizon.cdr. Feel free to snag the trees or landscapes for your own designs, and I'll be thrilled to one day say, "Hey! I recognize that!"

In this next example we will use the Blend function again not only to build our palm trees, but also arrange them in a vanishing row along a highway. Here is how to create the spiky palm trees and arrange them along a roadway:

1. Start with the leaf shape from the first example. Duplicate (+ key) and reduce horizontally by dragging the right-center sizing handle inward. Now draw a rectangle over half of the "blade" and then use the Trim function to cut it in half. Duplicate the blade and rotate -90 degrees. Use the original leaf shape as a guide, and reduce the blade by dragging the right-center sizing handle to the left. Now select the two blades, open the Blend roll-up (Ctrl+B), change the steps to 10, and click Apply. Now Separate this blend and ungroup it. Using the Shape tool, select the end node of each new blade and drag it out toward the original leaf-shape guide. Finally, these blades were given a dark-to-light-green radial fountain fill from the Fountain Fill dialog (F11). See Figure 9-16.

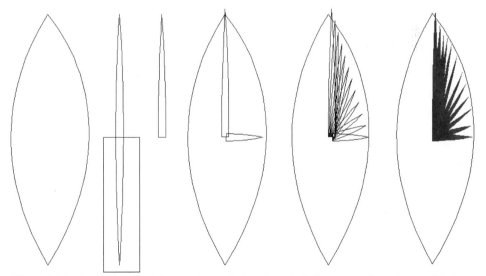

*Figure 9-16: The original leaf shape is downsized and cut in half to create the spiky new blades. Two blades are combined, and then the resulting object is resized to form the curve of a sweeping palm frond.*

**TIP** | *Certain functions will not work on a group of objects (i.e., Extrude). If you generated an object using the Contour function, even if it is a single object, CorelDRAW classifies it as a Group. Use the Arrange | Separate command to "freeze" a Contour group and then ungroup it (Ctrl+U). Now the curve generated by the Contour command can be further manipulated.*

2. Drag-select all of the spikes, and duplicate them (+ key). Then flip them horizontally to create a whole palm end. Select them all, and group (Ctrl+G) them into one object. Now stretch vertically by dragging the bottom-center control node down. With the object selected, toggle to the rotation arrows by clicking again. Drag the axis of rotation bull's-eye down to the bottom, and then duplicate the object (+ key). You want both objects to have this new axis, so when you use the Rotate option on the Blend roll-up, the new pieces will pivot off of this point (see second example in Chapter 17 for more on this feature). Drag-select both objects, open the Blend roll-up (Ctrl+B), set Number of Steps to 10 and Rotate to 360 degrees, and click Apply. There it is, the spiky palm top (see Figure 9-17).

*Figure 9-17: The original half is again duplicated to create the whole leaf object. By using the Rotate feature of the Blend roll-up, and also by changing the axis of rotation, the leaves are spun into a circle configuration.*

**TIP** *You can not perform many functions on a live blend. You will need to Separate a blend group and then group (Ctrl+G) the pieces before you can, for example, use the envelope to distort the group. Also, you can not blend live blends, so in order to create a row of trees using the Blend roll-up, all of the live blends in the tree must be frozen, and all pieces put in one group. Once that is done, the group can be duplicated and blended with another.*

3. With the blend selected, Separate it to freeze it. Then group the pieces (Ctrl+G). Now you can distort it using the Interactive Envelope tool or the Envelope roll-up. Either way, distort the palm group with a single arc just like we did with the earlier leaf example (see Figure 9-18).

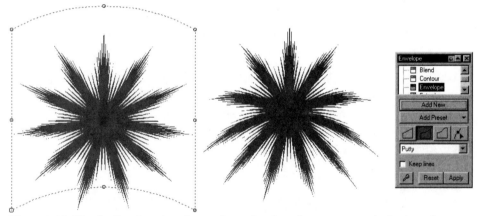

*Figure 9-18: Use the Envelope function again to give the palm group an arched orientation.*

4. Use the trunk piece from the earlier example and blend a long, tall palm tree trunk. With the palm ball stuck on top, you have your tree! Select all of these objects and group them (Ctrl+G).

5. Copy (Ctrl+C) and paste (Ctrl+V) this palm tree into the desert landscape example from earlier. Duplicate the tree again, and downsize it to become a tiny little tree on the horizon. Duplicate these trees to create a frame on both sides of a road, which we will draw in the next step (see Figure 9-19).

*Figure 9-19: The spiky palm trees again serve nicely to augment the desert scene drawn earlier.*

6. Draw a rectangle and open the Envelope roll-up (Ctrl+F7). Add a new straight line envelope; then drag the top-right corner inward while holding down the Shift key to create a pyramid. Click Apply and draw a pointy centerline to complete the road (see Figure 9-20).

*Figure 9-20: An envelope distorts a rectangle to become a vanishing road.*

7. Select the front two trees and select send to front (Shift+PgUp). Now select the right-front tree and the far-right small tree and open the Blend roll-up. Change the number of steps to 4, then open the Accelerations page, slide the Accelerate Objects slider to the left, and click Apply.

The acceleration will make the trees seem to bunch up closer on the horizon, creating the illusion of distance. Select the other two trees and click Apply again on the Blend roll-up. The settings are still the same as they were in the first blend, so they should match up correctly on both sides (see Figure 9-21).

*Figure 9-21: Use the Blend roll-up to create a row of trees on each side of the road. The acceleration option changes the spacing with distance.*

8. The last step is to create shadow shapes. This is a little involved, but sometimes you have to sweat for your effects. First, select and duplicate one of the big trees, move it off to an open area to work, and ungroup the objects (Ctrl+U). Select the palm objects, and again ungroup them (Ctrl+U). Now select the top palm and delete it. (During the blend process, two copies of this leaf were placed on top of each other and will make a Weld function go perquacky!) Drag-select all of the palm leaves, select Arrange | Ungroup All, then use the Convert to Curves (Ctrl+Q) command. Now open the Arrange | Weld roll-up, click Weld To, and then click on one of the leaves. This should merge all of the objects into one curve. Now drag-select the trunk objects, use Arrange | Separate, then Arrange | Ungroup All, and then weld them together. Finally, weld the trunk to the leaf shapes (see Figure 9-22).

*Figure 9-22: Use the Separate command to freeze blends, then Convert to Curves to freeze envelopes, and finally, Ungroup All to break everything into individual pieces. Now the Weld command can be used to merge the objects into one shape.*

9. Now rotate the shadow shape 90 degrees, and then from the Effects menu, choose Add Perspective. With the Shape tool, move the corner points around to place the shadow in a twisted, elongated position for an evening shadow. Freeze the perspective with the Convert to Curves (Ctrl+Q) command (see Figure 9-23).

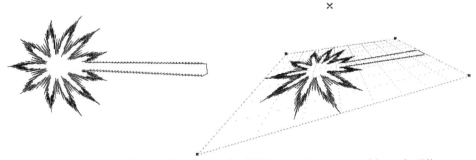

*Figure 9-23: Distort the shadow shape using the Add Perspective command from the Effects menu.*

10. Using the skew and sizing handles, place the shadow on the ground in front of the closest palm tree. Now duplicate it (+ key) and really downsize the duplicate for the far-away shadow. Use the left-center skew arrows to skew this far shadow up. Now open the Blend roll-up (Ctrl+B) and select one of the palm tree blends to change the Blend roll-up settings. Now select both shadow shapes and click Apply. This places the shadows along the same spacing as the trees (see Figure 9-24).

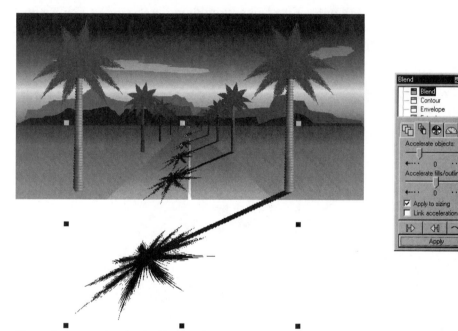

*Figure 9-24: Use the Blend roll-up with the same settings you used for the tree blend to place the shadows along the street.*

11. Arrange and separate (Arrange | Separate) the shadow blend and then use the Arrange | Ungroup All command to manipulate each piece further. Skew and tweak each individual shadow a little, or if you prefer, leave them as they are; you just may be happy with the way the blend looks. You can skew and adjust the front shadow object before you separate the blend to fine-tune the results more if you wish. Each shadow object was given a black fill, no outline, and a 50% Transparency lens (Alt+F3) to finish it off, and the whole process was repeated for the other side. Use the Arrange | Trim function to chop off excess overhanging shadow, or just draw a solid white box over it in case you want to keep the blend active.

That's that! The addition of the shadows really made me like this piece, which may end up as a music CD cover (or not, depending on that fickle force in the universe known as *clients*). This landscape is also in the horizon.cdr file, found in the \Chapt9\ subdirectory on the Companion CD-ROM. In the color section, there are two versions of this image. The top one is exported as a CMYK bitmap directly from the CorelDRAW file without any further modifications. The one below it is the same bitmap, only the Add Noise feature was used; the Add Noise feature is available under the Bitmap menu in CorelDRAW or the Effects menu in PhotoPaint. The Add Noise filter gives your image a grainier look, like air-brushed art on textured paper, and it also helps eliminate *banding* (noticeable color shifts in fountain fills).

## Petal Power

*Figure 9-25: Using the Blend feature to create flower petals creates a nice daisy shape. A bitmap image is duplicated and constrained within the petal shapes using the PowerClip function.*

Landscapes and plants make nice filler backdrops for many applications. However, the repeating elements that make up the leaves or, in this case, flower petals, also make for a nice main theme. In this image, a summer sun becomes a flower, and then each petal has a little fashion pixie trapped inside! The Blend roll-up creates the nice evenly spaced petals, and then the PowerClip function allows us to entrap a bitmap within them. Here is how to make this daisy image:

1. Import an image to clip into the petals. I used an image from the \objects\people directory on the CorelDRAW clip-art CD. With the Freehand tool, draw a horizontal line by clicking and then moving the pointer across the page while holding down the Ctrl key. Now duplicate (+ key) and rotate this line 90 degrees to create a crosshair, which we will use for reference. Select the bitmap of the model and place her at the top center of the vertical crosshair. With the model still selected, click with the Pick tool to reveal the rotation arrows and the axis of rotation. Drag the axis of rotation down until the crosshairs of the target match the reference crosshairs we just drew (see Figure 9-26).

*Figure 9-26: Draw two lines for reference and then change the axis of rotation of the bitmap to be the point where the two lines cross.*

2. With the bitmap selected, open the Scale and Mirror roll-up (Alt+F9) and select Apply To Duplicate. This will flip-flop and copy the bitmap in one step without moving it. Now with the Pick tool, grab and drag the top-left rotation arrow while holding down the Ctrl key to spin the girl around 30 degrees (see Figure 9-27).

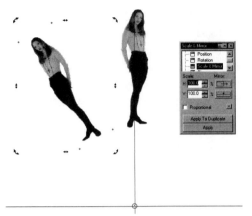

*Figure 9-27: Use the Scale & Mirror roll-up to duplicate and flip the bitmap. Then rotate the duplicate 30 degrees by holding the Ctrl key while dragging a rotation arrow.*

3. Continue to duplicate and rotate the bitmap around, alternating the left- and right-facing models until you complete the circle (see Figure 9-28).

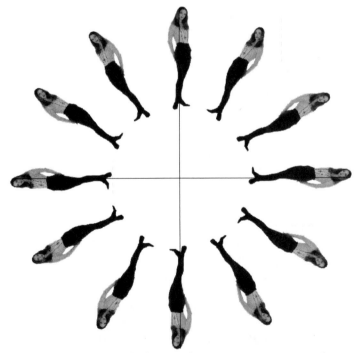

*Figure 9-28: Repeat the duplicate-and-rotate process to create a ring.*

4. Draw an oval around the first bitmap at the top center of the circle. Center it by eye around the girl. Now click again to reveal the rotation arrows and axis and move the axis to the center of our crosshair reference shapes. Now duplicate the oval. Drag-select around both ovals and the bitmap and then shift-click the bitmap to result in the selection of just the two ovals. Open the Blend roll-up (Ctrl+B), change Number of Steps to 11 and Rotate to 360 degrees, and click Apply. This should create a nice set of flower petals, which you can give a white fill (see Figure 9-29).

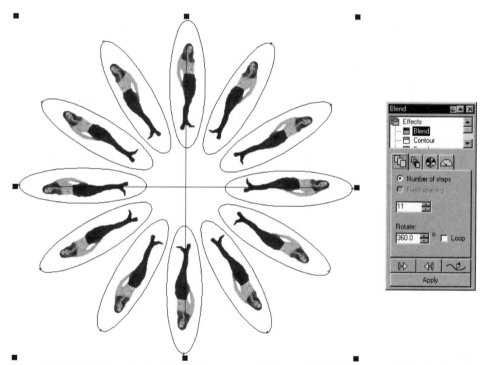

*Figure 9-29: With the axis of rotation the same as the one used for the bitmap, the blended petals are in a shared orientation.*

5. Duplicate the blend (+ key), rotate 15 degrees, and send it to the back (Shift+PgDn). Give these petals a radial fountain fill from baby blue to white, with no outline. Select the front petal group and use the Arrange | Separate command. Then use the Arrange | Ungroup All command. Now select and delete the top petal (which is again a redundant duplicate from the blend process). Then select all of the white petals again and combine them (Ctrl+L). Finally, shift-select all of the bitmap

objects, choose Effects | PowerClip | Place Inside Container, then when the PowerClip arrow appears, click on the combined petal curve. Now all of the little model pixies will be trapped inside of the flower petals (see Figure 9-30).

*Figure 9-30: Combine the petals into one curve and use the PowerClip function to trap the bitmaps inside of the oval shapes.*

6. Draw a circle in the middle of the petals for the sun shape and duplicate it. Then enlarge it just beyond the edge of the petals and send it to the back for a background object. To make a circle look like a rounded sphere, use a radial fountain fill with a custom color blend; use either the

Interactive Fill tool or the Fountain Fill dialog (F11). The flower center is a custom color blend from red to dual-yellow points to white. Move the white spot to the top right to simulate a highlight. Then move the color points along the blend to make the sphere look round. The background circle also has a four-point color blend, from white and white to yellow and yellow. The redundant color points let you adjust the color transition to adjust the fade-away point (see Chapter 17 for more on this). Figure 9-31 shows the process.

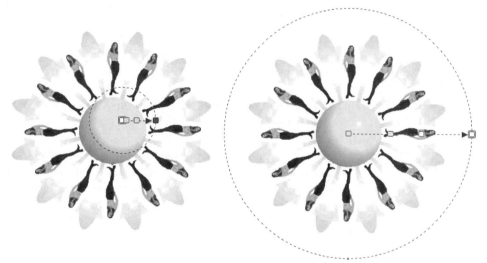

*Figure 9-31: Radial fountain fills with custom color blends (set up via the dialog box, or as shown here, using the Interactive Fill tool) create the round sphere center and a soft yellow background.*

7. I needed some ad copy below this image; I set the ad copy in a nice froofy font called TypoUpright. To get a softer edge, blend the outline of the type to the paper color, in this case white. Select the text and give it a fat outline (.111 inch) and white fill. From the Outline Pen dialog (F12), you should change to the rounded corner to avoid problems. Now duplicate this text again (+ key) and give the object a yellow hairline and fill. Then perform a 20-step blend between them (Ctrl+B). Duplicate just the front control object and give this a no-outline, ice-blue fill. Finito! Figure 9-32 shows the finished text elements.

*Spring Values* *Spring Values* *Spring Values*
*are* *are* *are*
*In Full Bloom* *In Full Bloom* *In Full Bloom*

*Figure 9-32: Blending text with a fat white outline to a duplicate with a yellow hairline creates a soft fade.*

This image is kind of out of character for me, but you never know what projects will wander into your studio! It is a good idea to hang on to any and all art projects on which you work, even if they are only comps that don't get developed, as eventually they can be used in other projects, whether you use the whole project or just part. I try and maintain a stack of laser-printed copies of things I have done, and also a record of their current locations (backup tape, archive, etc.) so that I can refer to it for inspiration or actual source material. In fact, pieces of this image resurface later in another project (Chapter 16) for a totally different look! The finished daisy graphic, called daisy.cdr, is in the \Chapt9\ subdirectory on the Companion CD-ROM. Open this file and see how you can use the Effects | PowerClip | Extract the Contents command on the daisy petals to free the models or how you can manipulate the control points on the color blends to see how that changes things.

## Atmospheric Perspective

*Figure 9-33: In its stock form, this beach scene looks nice, but the illusion of depth is not as pronounced as it can be. In the second image, Transparency lens shapes make the background seem further away (exaggerated to look misty) and the car a little closer, and finally, the woman pops out of the foreground. Using a bitmap Blur filter, the final image simulates depth by blurring the background objects.*

## California Waves

The trick to gaining believable depth is a phenomenon known as *atmospheric perspective*. When you view a landscape naturally, the tiny particles in the air make the far-away objects appear duller, even blurry. On a foggy day, this is really obvious, but even on clear days, atmospheric perspective is at work. In addition to this concept, it is also natural for the eye to focus on one plane at a time. This is why objects far away seem out of focus if you are looking at something close, or why the reverse is true if you are focused on the far-away objects (Chapter 11 has a reverse-focus example). You can duplicate both the atmospheric perspective and blurry images concepts to add forced depth to your artwork. In this section, we will use the CorelDRAW Lens feature, as well as convert the images to bitmaps, so we can then manipulate them further with the Blur filter to give our design atmospheric perspective.

Growing up in both southern California and southern Germany has resulted in a strange mix of cultural values (like mixing an emphasis of being laid back and creative with efficiency and adherence to norms). It also has made me appreciate those things most uniquely Californian, like classic cars and beach sunsets! What could be more classic than a woodie along the So Cal coast? Capturing that unique coloring that light creates shining through a wave is not that difficult using a custom color blend. Also, the frothy cauliflower wave shapes are important to many water-based illustrations.

This image started as an ink illustration of the car, which was scanned and converted into CorelDRAW objects using the OCR/Trace utility (see Chapter 18 for more on this conversion process). When the car was finished, the beach and wave were drawn, combined with a clip-art woman image, and assembled into the California post card. We will build the flat image first and then later add the tricks and illusions to enhance distance. Here is how to trace and color the car (Chapter 18 has more on the OCR/Trace utility and also colorizing these converted images):

1. Start the ORC/Trace application and outline-trace the image using the Accurate settings. (The car illustration is called woodie.tif in the \Chapt9\ subdirectory on the Companion CD-ROM if you want to practice this technique.) Save the vector file, exit OCR/Trace, and start CorelDRAW.

2. In CorelDRAW, import (Ctrl+I) the CMX file into your workspace and ungroup (Ctrl+U) the objects. Now each object can be selected and given an appropriate fill color. In an illustration such as this, there is a large black pad that the smaller objects sit on. For this reason, you will typically not want to give these objects outline attributes. However, the wood grain objects were filled with a light caramel color and also given an outline with a darker version of this color. This just gives the wood grain a more interesting wood look without much additional labor. In a design such as this, realism is not really the goal; what we want is more of a cartoony feel.

3. The process for coloring the car is pretty straightforward. Select an object or group of objects and assign a color, either by clicking an onscreen color well, opening the Uniform Fill dialog (shift+F11), or opening the Fountain Fill dialog (F11). Or you can use the Interactive Fill tool or drag and drop colors onto the objects. There are many ways to colorize objects now in CorelDRAW! Subtle two-color fountain fills, say from red to magenta in the metal car panels, add depth without getting overly complicated. The car was saved with its own filename to import as one group into the beach scene later (see Figure 9-34).

*Figure 9-34: A bitmap is easy to colorize once it is converted to CorelDRAW objects with the OCR/Trace utility.*

All of the main blocks of the sky, ocean, and beach are fountain fills. Although they are easy to create, the trick to convincing the viewer that they are seeing an earth beach sunset and not, say, a Martian one lies in your color choices! This is of course subject to artistic interpretation, but there are some predictable color schemes for the waves and water that we can reproduce here. Here is how to color the evening sky, distant ocean, and cresting wave:

1. Draw a rectangle for the sky and open the Foutain Fill dialog (or use Interactive Fill tool). The sky is simply a rectangle filled with a red-to-magenta-to-yellow custom color blend. With the yellow on the horizon, it looks as though the sun has just set. Draw another rectangle for the far-away ocean and give it a two-color fountain fill from dark to light blue. To get the look that the thickness of the water is changing the wave colors (deep water is deep blue), the wave uses four subtle color variations—we start at the top with a pale green (yellow sunset + blue water = slightly green!), and the mid-point of the fill is a rich blue, which trickles off to light blue and finally ends in a ghostly green for the shallow, frothy surf hitting the sand. The sand itself is just a two-color fountain fill with black added to the foreground color to make it darker. It really isn't hard to set up the custom color blends, and the color choices subtly suggest depth as well as create a vibrant backdrop. In Figure 9-35, the blends from left to right are sky, far-away ocean, wave, and sand.

*Figure 9-35: Use custom color blends to add depth and interest to simple rectangles to colorize the background elements of the beach scene.*

2. Use the Freehand tool to draw a cresting wave shape and give it a white fill. Draw another freehand object where the wave extends above the rectangle and use the Arrange | Weld command to weld it to the original wave rectangle. The frothy foam in the wave is a collection of gray shapes drawn with the Freehand tool and blended to smaller white duplicates. Use the Freehand tool to draw a fluffy-cloud shape. Give this shape a gray fill with no outline. Duplicate it (+ key) and downsize it by dragging a corner sizing handle inward. Give this smaller duplicate a white fill and again no outline (for smoother blends, avoid using outlines if possible). Shift-select both objects and open the Blend roll-up (Ctrl+B). The default setting of 20 steps is plenty for a small blend such as this, so click Apply to make it happen. Repeat this process for the frothy wave areas. You can duplicate and flip-flop the blend groups to save time but avoid a "cloned" look by hand-drawing as many shapes as possible (see Figure 9-36).

*Figure 9-36: Duplicating a fluffy-cloud shape, reducing and recoloring, and finally blending back with the darker parent shape results in a soft foamy blend group. Many of these blend groups form the fluffy-wave shape.*

**TIP** *When using the Blend roll-up, it is important that your starting and ending Control shapes have the same number of nodes. If not, the results of a blend can be kind of strange. To ensure that both objects have the same number of nodes, blend to a smaller, recolored duplicate.*

3. Draw little frothy blend groups along the edge of where the water meets the sand just to avoid a mechanical straight-line look. Use the Freehand tool to draw free-form sea foam and ocean reflection shapes horizontally across the water. For pieces that are near the wave, be sure to follow along an imaginary contour of the wave in a semicircular motion. The foam objects in the foreground have gray-to-white radial fountain fills, while the far-away ocean reflections are solid blue hues (see Figure 9-37).

4. To populate the landscape, import (Ctrl+I) the car file and the model image. The woman in the foreground is a clip-art image from the \clipart\people\misc directory on the CorelDRAW CD-ROM; the image has a cartoony look to match the other components. With everything in place, we get the first of the image's three variants (see Figure 9-38 and the color section).

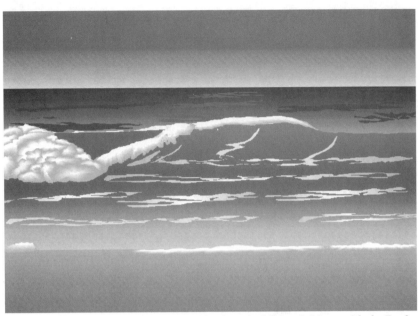

*Figure 9-37: Create foamy objects using blends and additional objects with the Freehand tool to suggest reflections and froth.*

*Figure 9-38: The colorized car illustration on the beach backdrop with the model clip art in the foreground. At this point, only size and orientation suggest depth.*

---

### ▼ Consistency Is the Key to Illusion

When you are trying to create an illusion, any illusion, consistency is important. If you want to suggest depth and use a shadow, a highlight on the wrong side of an object kills the effect. Little things go a long way, such as adding curve to the sea foam in the wave, which reinforces the depth and shadow already suggested with the coloring.

Even though the beach, car, and woman in the final image originated as separate elements, they need to work together as a whole. The shading in the car is consistent with reality, but the model is also lit from the front. This seems reasonable, though, as we are used to viewing artificially lit models in diverse locations to make them stand out. It would be odd, though, if there were two cars with different-facing shadows, for example. Also, it would be strange if the model were obscured with atmosphere, as she is obviously in the foreground in relation to the car. However, she could easily be blurry, if you were trying to emphasize a different point of focus. For example, if the car were the point of focus, the model would be blurry as well as the ocean and sky.

---

To further enhance the depth suggested by the object placement and sizing (giant female torsos rarely loom over full-size automobiles at the beach), use the Transparency lens. You will need a lens object on top of each object to alter the appearance of the objects below. You could simply split this image into the three main elements (background, car, and model) using two lens shapes to obscure the car and background. Use a white fill with varying transparency to create the atmospheric perspective. I used four lens shapes to allow more flexibility for the sky and ocean. How much or little control you need is up to you. Here is how to add more atmosphere to the image:

1. Select the sky, ocean, and sand rectangles (but not the wave) and duplicate them (+ key). The duplicates will become the first three lens shapes, so fill them with white and send them to the front (Shift+PgUp). Stretch just the sand rectangle upward until it meets the top of the wave. Now use the Shape tool to add nodes and match the rectangle contour to that of the wave below. The white froth line helps hide this transition. Open the Lens roll-up (Alt+F3) and choose the Transparency option. The separate objects add more control to the way you can manipulate the atmosphere. In this example, I used very low transparency settings to create a very white, misty image. Use more subtle settings (higher transparency) for less atmospheric interference. Apply a 50 percent transparency rate for the sky lens, an almost opaque 10 percent for the far-away ocean lens, and a very misty 25 percent for the front beach lens (see Figure 9-39).

*Figure 9-39: Three lens objects for the top, middle, and bottom will add misty atmosphere to the beach scene (shown here on top of everything).*

2. Select the car and girl object groups and send them to the front (Shift+PgUp). If you have trouble selecting the objects because the lens objects are in the way, switch to Wireframe view. Now select just the car group, and while holding down the Ctrl key, click on the dark shadow shape to select it. Copy it (Ctrl+C), and paste the new duplicate. This will become the shape we use to add a lens to just the car (see Figure 9-40).

**TIP** *You can select and manipulate objects within a group with the Ctrl key. Then you can edit the properties of the object, including size and location, without ungrouping the pieces. When you are finished, simply press Esc and select the object group as usual.*

3. Break apart (Ctrl+K) the new car outline and delete the window shapes. This will result in a custom-fit shape just over the car. Fill it with white, no-outline, and give it a 75 percent Transparency lens for just a subtle amount of atmosphere. Select the model again, send her to the front (Shift+PgUp), and your image is now looking more like a misty morning than a clear sunset (see Figure 9-41 and also the color section).

*Figure 9-40: A duplicate of the black-pad from the trace objects becomes the lens object when recolored and placed in front.*

*Figure 9-41: The car outline duplicate is given a subtle transparency lens for a softer atmosphere effect. It is sharper than the waves but not as clear as the model, which has not been made to look misted.*

To add an even more dramatic sense of depth, we will have to use the Convert to Bitmap function to take advantage of the blur filter. This kind of image manipulation requires pixels, not vector art, but luckily CorelDRAW can do it all for us! Here is how to make parts of your image blurry to suggest depth:

1. Separate the pieces into three groups: beach, car, and model. Select all of the beach scene objects and from the Bitmap menu, choose Convert to Bitmap. Now set the Color option to 32 bit (CMYK) and Resolution to 300 dpi, enable Super-Sampling, and click OK. Hang tight while the image converts (see Figure 9-42).

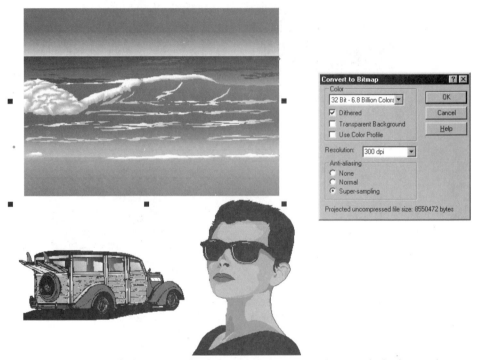

*Figure 9-42: Separate the image into the three main components. Convert the background elements into a bitmap using the Convert to Bitmap function found under the Bitmap menu.*

2. With the new bitmap selected, choose Blur | Gaussian from the Bitmap menu to open the Gaussian Blur dialog. The higher the Radius value here, the blurrier and further away your background will appear. I used a setting of Radius 30 (see Figure 9-43).

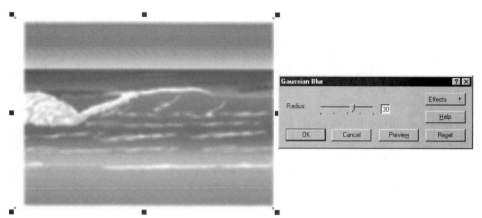

*Figure 9-43: Use the Gaussian Blur feature from the Bitmap menu to make the background seem out of focus.*

3. Select the car object group and open the Convert to Bitmap dialog. Again, pick 32-bit color and set the Resolution option to 300 dpi, except this time enable the Transparent Background option. This will let you move the car over the landscape without a big white box ruining things for everyone! When this is done converting to bitmap, again use the Gaussian Blur feature at a lower setting (try 10) to take the car out of focus.

4. There you have it. The images are not clear but the instructions are! Move the model in front of the other two bitmaps to finish the image (see Figure 9-44 and the color section).

*Figure 9-44: In CorelDRAW, you can apply the Blur filter and still keep the transparent background. Bonus! The CorelDRAW vector clip art is placed in front for maximum pop.*

By converting bits and pieces of your design to bitmaps, you can manipulate them using the Gaussian Blur filter to enhance the illusion of depth. Remember to save a backup copy of the original CorelDRAW artwork before you convert it to bitmaps in case you need to backtrack later. Bitmap conversions are very permanent and potentially inflexible, so work safely.

**CD-ROM**

These images can be loaded off of the Companion CD-ROM from a file called atmosph.cdr in the \Chapt9\ subdirectory (as can the original bitmap image, woodie.tif). Use the bitmap to experiment with OCR/Trace settings to get a feel for what you can do to convert line art into CorelDRAW objects. Select and modify the lens shapes to reduce the atmospheric perspective, and experiment with the Convert to Bitmap feature. The CDR file also contains some tricks I didn't talk about, such as boxes over the windows in the car with Interactive Transparency fills to simulate glass. Hey, I have to give you some reasons to actually load and look at these files!

## Moving On

In this chapter, we used the Blend roll-up again to create the pieces for flowers and leaves. We also saw how you can freeze blends and group objects so that you can create even more duplicates with the Blend function. Also, our friend the PowerClip was once again a handy way to stuff bitmaps inside a curve shape. Finally, we looked at several techniques to give landscapes atmospheric perspective to enhance the feeling of depth and dimension.

In the next chapter we will continue to manipulate bitmaps, in both CorelDRAW and also PhotoPaint, to create unique photo collages. We will "antique" photos to look old and then assemble, blur, and merge them into a potpourri of new imagery. Gather up your snapshots and get the scanner humming—it's time to create some photo collages (Shane-style, of course).

### ▼ Beyond f/x

Landscapes pop up constantly in design. They are such nice, benign backgrounds that add visual interest but do not detract from a logo or other primary design element (like the tropical paradise example in this chapter, or the dinosaur land logo from Chapter 5). We will use the landscapes again in Chapter 23, to give the look of chrome with a suggested reflection of the surrounding environment. Landscapes give a sense of immensity and grandeur to images that otherwise have no sense of scale. Your company logo suddenly seems really big and important when it is dwarfing the trees around it! The illusions of depth, with the blurring techniques or atmospheric perspective, are also great tools to direct the reader's focus. With secondary design elements made to look out of focus or far away, the primary objects pop right out! It's also a great way to draw attention to a single item in a very busy design. (See Chapter 26 for more on this technique.) The natural world is always a great place to start if you are stumped in a design, like in the fashion world example. The geometry and mass-appeal of plants and landscapes should make them a popular addition to your artwork. If not, you need to move to a state where palm-tree adorned logos are all the rage!

## chapter 10
# Photo Collages

Mixing scanned photos into computer designs is a staple of the contemporary art diet. It is an amazingly popular method of creating interesting images. This is because you need little illustration talent to mix photos together, and you can get great-looking graphics without too much effort. In addition, there is a much larger image base for photos than there is for vector-based clip art, with stock photo companies digitizing their inventory and even the Corel corporation offering literally thousands of photos for sale in their photo CD collections.

In a bit of an oxymoronic twist, there is also a trend to "antique" images, making them look old and weathered, and then using oh-so high-tech and modern computer image manipulation techniques to merge these photos together. Ahhh, that great enigmatic era known as the '90s.

In this chapter, we will endeavor to mix the old and new, creating collages of antiqued bitmaps in cool modern ways. In the first example, we will "antique" the images with photo filters and change the borders once using the Auto F/X plug-in filter. In the second example, we exploit the interactive interface of a new CorelDRAW 8 plug-in to paint effects exactly where we want them. Then, we will create a unique hexagon collage by stuffing images into shapes using the PowerClip feature. Finally, we will create a unique collage effect using the flexibility found in black-and-white bitmaps.

## Motorcycle Memories

*Figure 10-1: Bitmaps are easy to import and manipulate within CorelDRAW to create interesting photo montages. The images can be manipulated with filters and also mixed with CorelDRAW objects.*

This collection of motorcycle memories is a typical themed collage, but you could use the same kind of techniques to create catalogs or brochures (I do ride a Yamaha RZ-350, if you are curious). In this example, we'll use bitmap filters to give the bitmaps an old and faded look and also use a great plug-in to create cool border effects. Also introduced in this chapter is the Interactive Drop Shadow tool, which is the easiest way to add realistic shadows to your images.

The bitmaps in this example are right off of the CorelDRAW clip-art CD-ROM, except the woman. Sorry. She is from the Corel Photo CD collection entitled "Women in Vogue." Some lovely young ladies who work at Corel Corporation sent me that CD, as some kind of joke I think, but I find it useful now and again! Here is how to make a neat photo collage in CorelDRAW:

1. First, you will need motorcycle photos. I found three great old classics in the \photos\transportation directory of the Corel clip-art CD. Import (Ctrl+I) the image of your choice.

2. The next step is to size the bitmap to its approximate size in the final collage and convert it into a usable format. Use the Pick tool and sizing

handles to move and size the bitmap into place. Before you can use many of the bitmap filters, your image will need to be in a single-layer RGB format. (If you can not access the filters, it is probably because you need to convert the bitmap first.) To change the bitmap, select it and choose Convert to Bitmap from the Bitmaps menu to open the dialog; then select 24 Bit (RGB), 300 dpi, and Normal Anti-Aliasing (bitmaps are already anti-aliased).

3. With the image at the desired size, resolution, and color depth, it is time to play with filters. From the Bitmaps menu, choose Plug-Ins I PhotoLab I CSI PhotoFilter. This filter dialog lets you change the colors in your photo to a variety of different looks, including old and faded color schemes. Select Afternoon Tea from the preset listing and click OK. This gives the photo an old and faded Kodachrome-from-the-'70s look (see Figure 10-2).

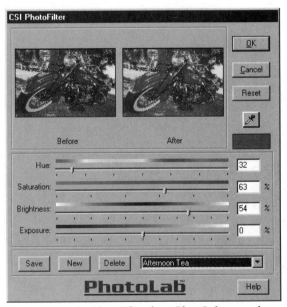

*Figure 10-2: The PhotoFilter from PhotoLab can make your photos look old and faded.*

4. Now to get the interesting non-square edge effect, we return again to the Auto F/X Photo Edges filter (introduced in Chapter 8). From the Bitmap menu, select Plug-Ins I Auto F/X I Photo/Graphic Edges 3.0 to open the dialog. Make sure that the appropriate CorelDRAW CD is in your reader to access the edges.

**TIP**  *If for some reason you get an error that says, "Photo/Graphic Edges works with rectangular mask selections only," when opening the Auto F/X dialog, don't go postal. This happens sometimes, even if your image appears to all the world to be a rectangle. Just use the Rectangle tool to draw a rectangle that is just a hair smaller than your image, with no outline or fill. Now select the bitmap, switch to Wireframe view, and use the PowerClip feature to constrain the bitmap inside of the new rectangle shape. This will ensure that the object is rectangular as far as the Auto F/X plug-in is concerned. Now use the Convert to Bitmap dialog from the Bitmaps menu to make this a true rectangular bitmap, and you are back in business!*

5. From the Photo Graphic Edges dialog, click the Select Outset Effect button (see Figure 10-3). Use the printed reference to the Photo Edges in the Corel clip-art book (that fat thing only slightly bigger than the manual). Choose an edge to your liking and click Open. Now in the preview window you can see what your altered image looks like.

*Figure 10-3: Use the Auto F/X filter to give your image a creative edge.*

**TIP**  *If you want to increase the size of your bitmap so that less of it is cut away with the Photo Edges effect, use the Inflate Bitmap command. This will add area around the bitmap just like increasing the paper size in PhotoPaint. If you are using CorelDRAW 7, simply draw a larger rectangle around your image, with no outline or fill. Then shift-select both rectangle and bitmap, and use the Convert to Bitmap command to merge the two into a larger bitmap with more image area on the edges so you will have some breathing room when working with the edge filters.*

6. To add images that look like floating snapshots, you will need to import more bitmaps! The motorcycle is from the same directory as before, and the woman is from the "Women in Vogue" Corel photo CD. Use the Pick tool to size and position your bitmap.

7. From the Bitmaps menu, choose Plug-Ins | PhotoLab | CSI GradTone. This is another great filter to give your images unique and antique color schemes. Choose the Old Gold setting and click OK. This converts all the colors into a black and gold/brown scheme. See my Web site samples (index.htm) in the \Chapt27\ subdirectory on the Companion CD-ROM for another use of this filter.

8. Once the image is converted into the new color scheme, draw a box around it with the Rectangle tool. Fill it white and place it behind and centered to the image. Old-style photos always seem to have a white border, so this shape will serve as the border (see Figure 10-4). Also, this rectangle will facilitate drop shadows later.

*Figure 10-4: The CSI GradTone filter from PhotoLab with the Old Gold setting creates a antique-looking image. Drawing a rectangle around the photo (in Wireframe on left) creates a white border.*

9. Now shift-select both the rectangle and the photo, and move them into position over the other image. Toggle between the sizing and rotation arrows by clicking on the selection, and rotate the image –10 degrees. Select just the white rectangle and then grab the Interactive Drop Shadow tool (located in the Interactive Blend flyout). Now with the Drop Shadow tool, drag down and to the left to create a shadow box. You will see the outline of where the shadow will be, so release when it is where you wish. Change the values on the Property Bar to control the feathering and the opacity of the shadow. You can also change the color, but usually you will want to keep the shadow color black (but you could use this tool to create a reflection in water, where a white shadow would make sense). The closer an object is to the surface below, the darker and crisper the shadow is. So adjust these settings to make the photo float at a height that you like (see Figure 10-5). Repeat the process with any other photos you want to drop onto your collage.

*Figure 10-5: The Interactive Drop Shadow tool is a fast and easy way to create realistic and transparent shadows in your artwork.*

**CD-ROM**

This image can be seen in the color section and found in the \Chapt10\ subdirectory on the Companion CD-ROM in a file called cycles.cdr. Load the file to experiment with the drop shadows or the bitmaps themselves. I also recommend loading a smaller version of your favorite bitmap so you can experiment using the different preset settings for the PhotoLab plug-in filters. It is always much faster to experiment on a small bitmap than to try and see all of the options on a full-sized monster!

▼ **Motorcycle Gangs**

The image and the file in this "Motorcycle Memories" section also contain the image from the "Hell's Registration" example, as I was trying to save some money on film. My service bureau charges by the sheet, not by megabyte, so if I can cram more than one job onto a page (called *ganging*), I can save some money. For a four-color process job, that can be quite a savings, with film prices around $15–$30 bucks a sheet! Ganging two jobs together like this and then cutting the film apart myself also cuts my cost in half and doubles my profit on one of the jobs (since I charge both clients for film). The printer doesn't care if the film is perfectly rectangular as long as it has the correct registration marks and color markings. So "gang" up your artwork and with the money you save, you can buy all of your friends this book!

## Golden Years

COLOR STUDIO

*Figure 10-6: Using effects filters available in both CorelDRAW and PhotoPaint, images are given antiqued and golden tones and also stylized with brush-style filters.*

Because computer-assembled photo collages are made up of bitmaps, you can go a step further and also alter the images themselves. This is a task usually reserved to PhotoPaint, but with the bitmap filters built into CorelDRAW, you have quite a few options at your fingertips. For the most part, the bitmap filters and plug-in effects change the entire image (like we saw with the PhotoLab filters). However, there are a few exceptions that use unique user interfaces that let you manipulate select areas within a bitmap, such as the new Squizz filter used in this example (see Figure 10-6). Although PhotoPaint may allow for more flexibility in manipulating bitmaps, CorelDRAW offers features and flexibility unavailable in any other program. When you combine features such as stuffing an image inside a shape with the PowerClip function and then use an Interactive Transparency effect on that object, you can end up with amazing images. The bonus with CorelDRAW collages is that you can easily fine-tune effects such as the transparencies until you get exactly what you want.

▼ **Don't Forget the Net**

When I was wrapping-up this dreamy collage, I wanted some nice gooshy poetry to place into the montage. Not in a particularly romantic mood at 2:00 AM when I was finishing this off, I logged on to the trusty Internet and did a quick search. Ahhh, the benefits of technology! The lyrics from an old Eurythmics song fit perfectly and are, in fact, quite moving.

▼ **Choosing Between CorelDRAW & PhotoPaint**

The addition of bitmap-editing features within CorelDRAW means that you do not have to use PhotoPaint as much as you used to. This is fine with me, as flip-flopping between applications always slows things down anyway. The problem with the bitmap effects in CorelDRAW, however, is that you are usually limited to filters that affect the bitmap as a whole. You can not create a selection, as you can in PhotoPaint, to limit the area you want to change. For some effects, you have no choice but to modify the bitmap in PhotoPaint—if you wanted to blur the background around the girl in the "Golden Years" example while leaving her in focus (see Figure 10-7).

However, there is a new plug-in in version 8, Squizz, that uses a unique interface that allows you to paint the effect within the dialog box, giving you more flexibility in some cases. Again, it is really a matter of preference and the needs at hand that will dictate whether or not you should use PhotoPaint for bitmap effects. While the "Golden Years" example will limit the changes to what you can do within CorelDRAW, don't forget that you can always Export a bitmap from CorelDRAW, open and manipulate it in PhotoPaint, and then import it again back into CorelDRAW.

*Figure 10-7: The effects filters in CorelDRAW do not allow you to isolate a section of the image, as you can in PhotoPaint. Here, for example, the girl has been isolated in PhotoPaint so only the background is selected for modification with the Blur filter.*

This kind of image, where you have different shots of the same subject and with text over the image with de-emphasized areas, is a popular design technique (think *car brochure*). Chapter 16 also has some great techniques for this style of design. This is a simple example with just two images, but you could easily expand the technique to include many more. Here is how to get a dreamy collage using CorelDRAW and plug-in bitmap effects:

1. Import the closeup of the subject, in this case, another model off of the "Women in Vogue" photo CD. (There seems to be a pattern here….) Once again, the PhotoLab CSI GradTone filter, using the Old Gold setting, modifies the bitmap so that it looks antiqued and less flashy.

2. To get the image to fade into the background, use the Interactive Transparency tool. Drag from the model's nose down and to the right and to the corner. On the Property Bar, change to the Square Fountain transparency by clicking the rightmost Fountain Fill option button. Now the image fades from a clear center to an opaque edge, which is, of course, exactly opposite of what we need! So drag white from the onscreen color well and drop it over the black center Interactive Transparency fill point,

and then drag black and drop it on to the original white point. This will reverse the logic of the transparency fill and create the mood we want (see Figure 10-8).

*Figure 10-8: The Interactive Transparency tool, using the Square Fountain option, creates a diamond-shaped transparency to fade out the edges of the photo.*

3. Now use the Freehand tool to draw a shape around the head and body of the model to isolate it from the background. Give the object no fill or outline attribute, and from the Wireframe View, select the bitmap and stuff it inside the shape with the PowerClip command (see Figure 10-9).

4. Import another bitmap of the subject, this time a full-body shot. Again, use the PhotoLab Old Gold routine to get the same color scheme for the new bitmap. Position the close-up over the other image so that the pieces mix and fade harmoniously (things like belly buttons protruding through foreheads can be distracting, for example). At this point, you might want to set any other elements into place in the design, such as the text, so you can fine-tune placement to your exacting tastes (see Figure 10-10). Once the images are merged into one bitmap, moving things around becomes impossible. Also be sure to save a backup copy of the file while everything is still in pieces so, in case you do have to move things, you can repeat the process from this point, and you won't have to start all over again.

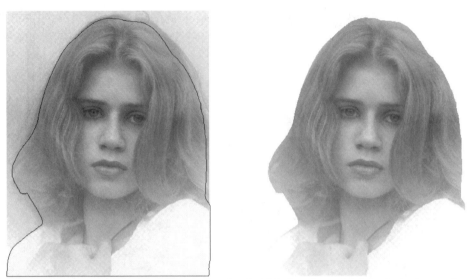

*Figure 10-9: A shape drawn with the Freehand tool will isolate the model from the background in the bitmap. Using the PowerClip feature, the image is isolated to the shape.*

*Figure 10-10: Use the Old Gold PhotoLab filter to give all the images the same antiqued look; then dummy up the image by putting all of the pieces in place.*

5. Select just the main background figure and use the Inflate Bitmap feature from the Bitmaps menu to add a white border around the image. (If you are using CorelDRAW 7, draw a white rectangle around the bitmap, send it behind, select both the rectangle and the bitmap, and then use the Convert to Bitmap dialog to create a new bitmap with a white border.) From Bitmaps | Plug-Ins | HSoft, select Squizz. This bitmap filter lets you twist, distort, and fuzz out your image in strange ways. The big attraction is the interface, which lets you brush-on the effect to just the areas that you want. Click the Brush option on the opening screen to enter the Squizz Interactive Brush dialog. Drag the circle around the background of the photo to give it a melted, warped look. Change to a smaller brush size if you want to get in close but not affect the girl. Click Apply when finished (see Figure 10-11).

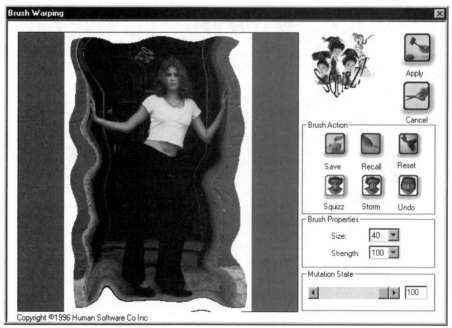

*Figure 10-11: Use the Squizz filter from HSoft in the Brush Warping mode to distort the background.*

6. Now select both the close-up PowerClip and the background image and open the Convert to Bitmap dialog from the Bitmap menu. Change the Color values to 24 Bit (RGB), and Dithered, 300 DPI and enable Normal Anti-Aliasing before clicking OK. This will merge the two bitmaps into one composite image so we can further manipulate them.

7. When the conversion is complete, choose Bitmaps | Plug-Ins | Hsoft | Squizz again. Choose the Brush option, but this time switch the Brush Action mode to Storm. This mode is like a big pixel version of the Gaussian blur. Drag the big brush around the edge to fuzz the border and then change to a smaller size to blur the areas where the photos overlap to eliminate any hard edges (see Figure 10-12).

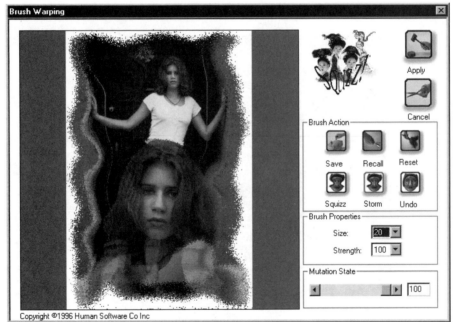

*Figure 10-12: Use the Squizz filter in the Storm mode to blur the edges.*

8. Arrange your text on top and you are done! To make the paragraph text easier to read, assign a heavier dark outline (.023 inch), but enable the Behind Fill option from the Outline Pen dialog (F12). I used a dreamy font called ShelleyAllegro for the poetic verse.

**CD-ROM**   This image can be seen in the color section or loaded as a file called sarah.cdr from the \Chapt10\ subdirectory on the Companion CD-ROM. By the way, Sarah is no one I know, just the name of the model off of the Corel Photo CD collection. Although this image was created entirely within CorelDRAW, you could also get some great results by bringing PhotoPaint into the mix. It is nice to be able to limit the areas of an effect, such as a blur, with the options in PhotoPaint. The Squizz interface is a nice compromise to enable controlled changes on a bitmap within CorelDRAW, though. Load the file and mess with the Squizz features, including the Grid instead of the Brush option. This feature is great for more precise warpings, which sounds strange, but they are useful at times, especially to create more nightmarish images! Check out Figure 10-13 and you'll see what I mean.

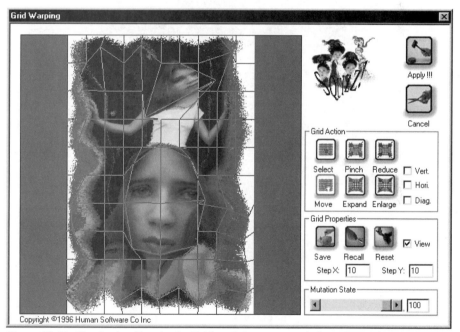

*Figure 10-13: The Squizz filter in the Grid mode lets you precisely grab and drag grid points to warp your images.*

## Careers in Beekeeping

**COLOR STUDIO**

*Figure 10-14: You can use the PowerClip function to constrain images within any shape, including nonconnected ones as in this beehive honeycomb, for many unique design possibilities.*

I am an image pirate. Avast ye scurvy dogs, prepare to be pilfered! Case in point: I saw a magazine table of contents a while back with a similar beehive design theme of images broken into the compartments of a honeycomb. I immediately sketched my own idea into the cover of the magazine I had just bought (the magazine I was copying the idea from otherwise didn't interest me) as the store clerk gave me strange looks. People look at me funny all of the time, so I am used to it. I told him I was with the secret "Art Police" and went on my way.

The PowerClip function is a mighty powerful feature in CorelDRAW. With it you can stuff images into all kinds of strange shapes and positions. The nice thing is that the target shapes need not be solid and can be made up of many disembodied parts, such as honeycomb blocks. This really opens the doors to some neat design opportunities that are otherwise a pain in the booty to create in other programs! Here is how to create an image montage using the CorelDRAW PowerClip function:

1. First of all, we need a honeycomb. Right-click over the Polygon tool to change the properties to a six-sided polygon. Click OK and then create a perfect hexagon by holding the Ctrl key as you drag the Polygon tool. With the Pick tool, drag the hexagon to the right; then before you release the left mouse button, click and release the right mouse button. This will place a duplicate of the honeycomb in position. Since this duplicate was put into place in what CorelDRAW considers one step, you can repeat the process with Ctrl+R. Cool huh? Press Ctrl+R again eight or so times to create a row of honeycombs.

2. Drag-select the whole row of hexagons and duplicate them (+ key). Arrange the duplicate row below and to the left of the original to create the honeycomb mesh. The lower row should line up so that the top center of the hexagons point to the space between the hexagons above it (see Figure 10-15).

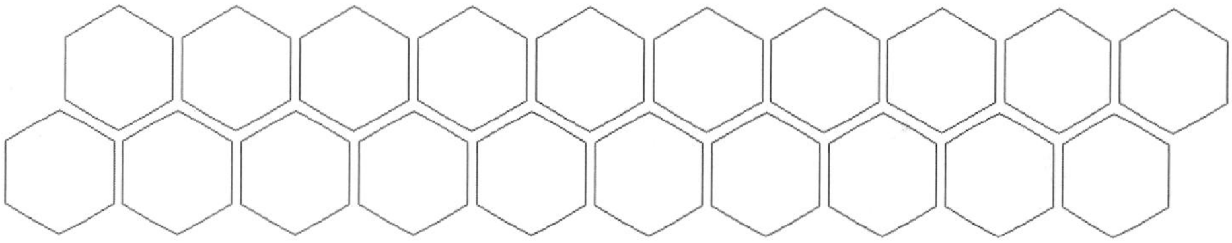

*Figure 10-15: The Polygon tool creates a perfect hexagon, which is duplicated and arranged to create a honeycomb pattern.*

3. Select both rows of honeycombs, drag them down, and then use the right mouse duplicate trick to place another two rows beneath the originals. Use the Ctrl+R shortcut to create a whole page of honeycombs. Draw a rectangle around the honeycombs, choose Select All from the Edit menu, and combine (Ctrl+L) all the pieces into one curve. Use the Pick tool to skew the top of the curve just a hair to the right to make the image less square (see Figure 10-16).

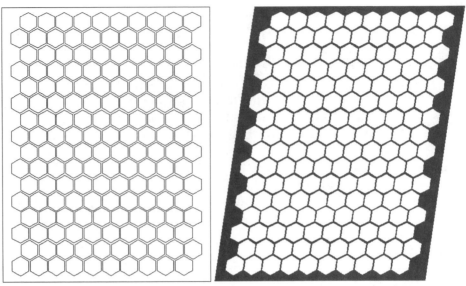

*Figure 10-16: Draw a box around the hexagons and then combine all of the objects into one curve to create a solid object with hexagon holes in it. You can then fill the image and skew it (on right).*

4. Import a bitmap that you want to stuff inside some of the honeycombs and place it in position behind the honeycomb object. Duplicate the big honeycomb object and break it apart (Ctrl+K). Now with all of the pieces still selected, deselect the hexagons that are in the areas in which you want to stuff the photo by holding down the Shift key and clicking on them. Then delete the rest, leaving a pattern of hexagons over the photo (see Figure 10-17).

5. Drag-select just the loose hexagons over the bitmap and combine (Ctrl+L) them into one curve. Now select your bitmap, choose PowerClip | Place Inside Container from the Effects menu, and click on the new smaller hexagon curve. This will stuff the bitmap inside the hexagons, creating an interesting image/pattern (see Figure 10-18). Tell me this doesn't kick butt over trying to get a similar look in a paint program!

*Figure 10-17: A duplicate of the main honeycomb curve is broken apart so that a pattern of hexagons can be placed over an imported photo.*

*Figure 10-18: Use the PowerClip command to stuff the bitmap image inside of the smaller hexagon curve.*

6. Repeat this process as many times as you wish with as many images as needed. I wanted to have several images stuffed in this way and still leave room for a big bitmap in the background behind the honeycomb (see Figure 10-19).

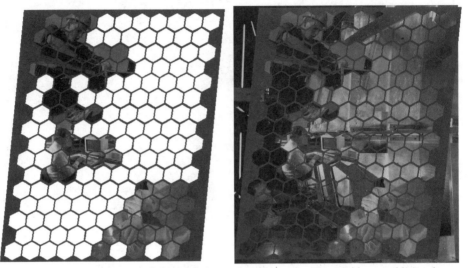

*Figure 10-19: With images stuffed into their own hexagons, there is room for an additional background image to show through the remaining honeycombs.*

7. With the Shape tool, grab the top-left node of the honeycomb curve and drag it to the left to square-off that side. Repeat the process for the bottom-right node so we have a nice rectangular book cover. Use a custom color blend linear fountain fill to give the front honeycomb a metallic look. The blend should go from black to white to black to white and so on.

8. Set the book cover Artistic Text over a neutral area that doesn't cover up any of the people in the bitmaps. I used a font called OakMyopic from Garage Fonts and I right-justified it. Use the Contour roll-up (Ctrl+F9) to create a single-step outside contour at a .1 inch offset. This will be a base for the text to rest on. Select the Contour group, and choose Separate from the Arrange menu. Now select just the new contour group and ungroup it (Ctrl+U). Select the honeycomb shape and save a duplicate

with the File | Save As command, enabling the Selected Only option. You need to keep an unmodified copy of the honeycomb in case you need to change the book title later because the next step will corrupt it.

**TIP**

*If you don't leave yourself digital tidbits along the way, then if you make a mistake or have to make changes (and tell me clients don't make constant, mindless, annoying changes!), you will have to start all over. It is better to keep copies of major items or changes on disk as you work. Before you convert text to curves, for example, you should save the original to disk in case you need to make changes later on. Pieces like the book title in the "Honeycomb" example are likely to change, and since the text changes another design element, in this case, the honeycomb, it is a good idea to save these items to disk before you permanently alter them.*

*Another good scheme is to save "in progress" files as you go, such as Cover1.cdr, Cover2.cdr, and so on. In case your system crashes and corrupts the file you are working on, you'll have an older backup. Disk storage is very cheap compared to your sanity! This scheme only costs a little hard disk space and a few extra wait moments in your workday, but you will thank yourself later if you have a trail of tidbits for reference should you need to go back and make unexpected changes.*

*If you take control of backups yourself, disable CorelDRAW's backup scheme. If you are making backup copies of the file you are working on as you work, there is no need to make yet another backup with the Make Backup On Save option enabled. From the Options menu (Ctrl+J), on the Advanced page, disable Make Backup On Save. This will cut your save time in half, but you must remember then to take responsibility of this process yourself and make copies of your work as you go. While on the Advanced page, disable the Auto-Backup function. In my experience, this feature will just make you crazy as your system locks up every 10 minutes to create the auto-backup. Do these things yourself and save time in the process!*

9. Position the text with the contour on the cover where you want it. Give the text a heavy .113 black outline, with the Behind-Fill option enabled, and a light/dark blue custom color blend. Now select the contour shape, and merge it with the honeycomb using the Weld command. Duplicate the honeycomb, nudge it down and to the right a tiny bit, fill it with black, and send it back one. This will give the honeycomb some substance, like it is cut out of a thin sheet of metal (see Figure 10-20).

*Figure 10-20: The Contour roll-up creates a base for the text to rest on, which is merged to the honeycomb with the Weld command. A duplicate of the honeycomb shape in black is set behind and offset to the original to add a hint of depth.*

10. Duplicate the honeycomb again, give it a black fill, and offset it much more dramatically behind, down, and to the right of the original. Give this duplicate a 50% Transparency lens to create a neat drop-shadow effect. To make the image-filled PowerClipped honeycombs also appear to be casting shadows, use the Shape tool. Drag the nodes of the honeycomb shadow curve so that they create shadows behind the image-filled honeycombs. Just move the nodes so that they create more shadow where you can see. It doesn't need to be perfect; you just want to create the illusion that there are cast shadows everywhere (see Figure 10-21).

*Figure 10-21: To cast shadows in honeycombs that are not solid but contain PowerClipped images, use the Shape tool to drag nodes on the shadow curve. Dragging the nodes behind the image makes the shadow look solid.*

The shadow was a finishing touch that made the front pop out and gave the piece more depth. Again, you could experiment with different shadow options, including the Interactive Drop Shadow tool, but you would have to prepare a more accurate parent shape first. I just faked the drop shadow behind the image-filled hexagons by node-editing the shadow curve. If you use the Drop Shadow tool, you will need first to alter a copy of the honeycomb so that it is solid behind the image-filled hexagons so the shadow will look right. Use the Weld command to fill open hexagons with shapes drawn with the Bezier tool.

This image is in the color section and also found in the honycomb.cdr file in the \Chapt10\ subdirectory on the Companion CD-ROM. Open this file and see how the images fit into the honeycombs. You can edit or extract the PowerClip contents and use the honeycomb pieces for your own designs. Since I practice what I preach, there is a file called hexagons.cdr for you that is a duplicate of the honeycomb curve before I welded the text to it. Aren't I a nice guy? Now you can just snag that for your own designs!

## Hell's Registration

*Figure 10-22: Because you can change the fill and outline attributes to any color, even clear, black-and-white bitmaps can be manipulated in CorelDRAW to create some strange images.*

Right in line with the anachronistic low-tech look is the trend to create images that are blurry or out of registration. The "Sarah" example was an exercise in making things blurry and dreamy, while this one is an interesting graphic that looks like a printing mistake.

CorelDRAW may not be the first program you think of for bitmap manipulation, but there are some very cool techniques that are unique to it. One-bit bitmaps (black and white) are very powerful in CorelDRAW; you can change the outline and fill attributes to anything or remove them entirely for clear effects. This allows you to do things like colorize a scan of an ink illustration (see Chapter 18), create electricity and sparks (check out Chapter 21), and also stack multiple copies of the same bitmap, as in this example. Stacking copies of single-bit bitmaps is an easy way to create highlight and shadow shapes, just like you do with CorelDRAW objects by offsetting and recoloring the duplicates. In this example, the duplicates are colored with the four process colors, creating an illusion of a print out of alignment or a psychedelic photo collage. Here is how to create registration tricks using black-and-white bitmaps in CorelDRAW:

1. Load your image into CorelDRAW. From the Bitmaps menu, choose 2D Effects | Edge Detect. This will create an interesting variant of the image, in an almost line-art style. The default settings on the dialog are fine, so just click OK (see Figure 10-23).

2. With the bitmap selected, open the Convert to Bitmap dialog from the Bitmaps menu. Set the Color values to Black and White, Dithered, and 300 DPI Resolution. This will reduce the image to just little black dots on a white field (see Figure 10-24).

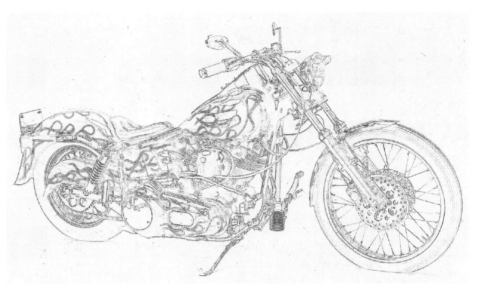

*Figure 10-23: The Edge Detect bitmap effect transforms a color bitmap into black outlines.*

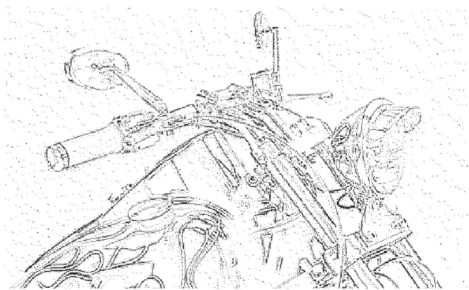

*Figure 10-24: Converting the image to a black-and-white bitmap reduces the image to uniform dots on a white field (enlarged to show detail).*

**TIP** *For more control when converting an object to a black-and-white bitmap, choose Convert To | Black and White (1-bit) from the Bitmaps menu. This dialog gives you some more options for black-and-white bitmaps than the Convert to Bitmap dialog does. You can change the type of conversion method and even create halftone screens just like in PhotoPaint.*

3. Now that the image is a 1-bit bitmap, you can assign any color to replace black and also make the white clear. Left-click on the no-fill onscreen color well to remove the white background so you'll end up with black dots on a clear sheet. Now right-click on cyan to make the image blue. Duplicate the bitmap, and offset the duplicate slightly by nudging it up and to the left. Right-click on magenta for this duplicate. Duplicate and nudge again, only use yellow as this last color. This finishes off the freaky effect (see Figure 10-25).

*Figure 10-25: You can assign a 1-bit bitmap any outline color and change the fill to nothing to create a clear background. Duplicating, offsetting, and recoloring creates ghostly images.*

**TIP** *For more options, click and hold the left mouse button over the desired onscreen color well. This will cause a palette to pop up filled with related shades and tints. Now just right- or left-click on the desired color to change the fill or outline attribute of the selected object. For even more subtle coloring changes, use the Ctrl key. When you hold down the Ctrl key and click on an onscreen color well, 10 percent of that color will be added to the selected object. You can change the outline or fill value by right- or left-clicking while you hold down the Ctrl key. This is a great way to mix colors without ever opening up the more complicated color picker dialogs.*

That is really all there is to it. You can use this technique, especially the Edge Detect, for many things. This would be a great way to use the image in the foreground as a subdued and unique background design (see Chapter 16 for more on this). This art is ganged up with the previous example in the color section and also in the cycles.cdr file on the Companion CD-ROM.

## Moving On

In this chapter we looked at creating interesting photo montages mixing a variety of technologies and techniques. Using CorelDRAW, we created drop shadows, manipulated bitmaps, added captions, and even created neat collages with the PowerClip function. With the bitmap plug-ins, we used filters to make photos look old and faded, and even warped and fuzzed. All in all, I think we looked at some very cool techniques, which should come in handy in your virtual studio to create all kinds of projects. You probably won't use these examples verbatim (unless you happen to be designing a "Career" book cover or assembling your own "motorcycle memories" pages), but the techniques will prove to be useful, I guarantee. Unless of course you happen to be the only computer artist in the world not using scanned photos.

This chapter concludes the "Ancient Creations" section, where I tried to focus on effects found in the natural and old world. Of course, there were contemporary examples thrown in there, but dang it, I tried to limit the topics to natural phenomena and old school looks!

In the next section, we look at contemporary design themes and trends. The techniques to create popular looks that made you think, "Hey, man, I wanna do that," will now be revealed to you. Those cool type effects you see in ads, weird futuristic looks, and even hard-core tattoo and branding designs are all coming up in the chapters ahead. Try not to faint from the heady rush of excitement as we blast into the present in the next section! So sit your Gen-X butt down, grab a half-caf, nonfat mocha cappuccino, adjust your carpal tunnel support pad, and let's get ready to rumble!

▼ **Beyond f/x**

Finding creative ways to mix and match photos is the bread and butter of commercial designers. Catalogs, advertisements, brochures, flyers, even Web sites often boil down to simple photo montages. Break things up with interesting border effects, or use the power and flexibility of a CorelDRAW layout to stack the images right on top of each other. Because each object can be constrained within a custom shape using the PowerClip feature or given a transparent background with the Bitmap Color Mask, you can easily modify the layout through the life of the design (see Chapters 19 and 22 for more on the PowerClip feature and the Bitmap Color Mask). With the addition of layers to PhotoPaint, this isn't as critical as it once was, but with all of the other design elements coming together in CorelDRAW, you might as well create the bitmap effects there as well.

In addition to being primary design elements, bitmap collages also make interesting backgrounds, or even abstract patterns for other unique applications. For a unique gift idea, instead of making one of those hideous hand-cut photo collages, create a digital montage instead. Scan and assemble the photos in the computer and then output the composite image at a service bureau on a high-end color printer. This will cost about the same as having duplicate photos made, is easier than hand-cutting out all of those pieces, and you can use incredible computer tricks to merge the images into one beautiful composite. If you gang two of the images on one landscape tabloid sheet, you can create two 8 1/2- X 11-inch collages. Cut these out, frame 'em, and make your grandmas happy!

# chapter 11

# Graffiti, Stressed Type & Bullet Holes

Until now, we have been dealing with re-creating effects that occur in nature. These themes are a popular and essential part of your design toolbox. This next section introduces themes that are more on a contemporary, man-made level, and because this is my book, we will also take a look at themes from the fringe element. I find there is much to be learned from artists far from the mainstream and even from the underground design scene, even though these disciplines, if you will, are often scoffed at by traditionalists.

In this chapter, we will just touch on several interesting type effects from the edge and the underground. First we will use the Contour function to achieve a flashy, graffiti look that you might find sprayed on a local urban surface, complete with a spray of random bullet holes. Then, we will explore two popular type effects created with the Interactive Transparency tool and also look at the blur effects from the Bitmap menu. All these examples will help get you out of any humdrum art slump and add some danger to your designs!

## You Write? _____

*Figure 11-1: You can use the Contour feature to add multiple outlines to a shape and, with the addition of a bright color scheme, create a graffiti look. You can use the pieces as is or use the Interactive Transparency tool to let the texture of the surface below show through.*

While promoting my own line of apparel, Slimy Dog Grafix, I made acquaintance with many interesting (and often frightening) characters. Hard-core, ex-con, gangbanger graffiti and tattoo artists were getting into clothing, and designs from the street were evolving into street wear. One company was promoting their apparel with a small bottle on a necklace. Inside the bottle were all kinds of different spray tips for aerosol paint cans. I thought that was pretty cool and tried to score myself a set! Don't get me wrong. I am not condoning tagging or graffiti; I hate to see anything vandalized. However, I find that the techniques are noteworthy, and I even support designated graffiti areas (such as organized murals or The Pit in Venice Beach). Personally, I love to grab a handful of spray cans and go nuts! I set up big sheets of plywood and have graffiti parties. Once I had a house with an empty, nonfunctioning swimming pool that we converted into a basketball court/skateboard park, and we covered it in graffiti. I guess I am just a controlled vandal, a.k.a. artist-at-large.

▼ **Art on the Street**

*Tagging* is a practice in which graffiti artists mark their territory with a special icon, their nickname, or a combination of both. More often than not, a tagger is not affiliated with a gang but just a frustrated inner-city youth seeking attention or recognition. Taggers greet one another with "You write?" to announce their status and verify that they are speaking to fellow taggers. They then compare techniques and styles as well as ambitious or dangerous *tags*. It is a subculture all of its own.

Although I have not personally heard of anyone designing a tag or graffiti mural in CorelDRAW, anything is possible! You could easily design an entire wall at full size (Layout | Page Setup, set the Paper option to Custom, and then key in any dimensions), and then use the Tiling feature (Print | Options | Layout | Print Tiled Pages) to output the image at actual size to create stencils, masks, or any full-size reference. Many sign companies will use a CorelDRAW file to generate masks that you can lay down and then spray paint to get a crisp image. Usually this high-end process is reserved for expensive custom car paint jobs, but hey, who knows?

Since I imagine it is more valuable for you to re-create the look of graffiti and not actually design spray-paint graffiti projects, I will focus on the former. In this section, we will create type that has the flashy look of painted graffiti, including the texture of the wall it is on. Here is how to vandalize a virtual wall:

1. Use the Artistic Text tool to set your headline. For my *CorelDRAW* text, I used a font called Dancin LET, but you can use this technique on anything. Open the Contour roll-up (Ctrl+F9), set the option to Outside, set the Offset value to .05 inches, set the Steps value to 2, then click Apply. This will create the shapes needed for the multiple outline effect (see Figure 11-2).

*Figure 11-2: The Contour effect creates additional shapes with Offset and Steps variables.*

2. With the contour group selected, choose Separate | Arrange | Ungroup All from the Arrange menu. This will give you three separate curve shapes, which you can color white, black, and red (from the outside in) and then stack to create a cool look. I found that there were some contour goobers from the contour calculations resulting from the small shapes inside of the counters (like the little dot inside the *o*, for example). This also made for too much detail for a spray-painted image! To fine-tune each contour shape, select the curve, break it apart (Ctrl+K), and then delete all the objects except the main outline. Now when these images are stacked, they have a bold but simple look (see Figure 11-3).

*Figure 11-3: You can use the shapes that result from the Contour command or eliminate any counters for just a fat outline.*

3. To add a gleam to the text, select the smallest inside text curve and duplicate it. Nudge the duplicate up and to the right and give it a white fill
and white hairline. Now send it back one (Ctrl+PgDn) so that the original covers all but a sliver, resulting in a gleam. Draw a rectangular wall
behind the text and use the Texture Fill option to give it the look of
stucco. From the Texture Fill dialog (open from the Fill tool flyout),
change the Texture Library to Samples 7, select Concrete from the Texture list, and then click OK (see Figure 11-4).

*Figure 11-4: Offset a duplicate to create a gleam highlight. Use the Texture Fill dialog to give a
rectangle a concrete fill.*

**TIP**    *For crisper images in your high-end projects that contain texture fills, be sure to up
the Bitmap Resolution and Texture Size Limit values from the Texture Options
dialog. In the Texture Fill dialog, click the Options button to open the Texture
Options dialog box and then increase both options to maximum values. This will
make the texture fill usable for printed applications (the default setting of 120 dpi is
just too low). Remember now that these values act as multipliers when calculating
the bitmap that makes up a texture fill, so your file size will also increase dramatically when you increase these values. To help save disk space with this now huge
file, use the advanced settings from the Save Drawing dialog (File | Save As). Click
the Advanced button to open the Advanced Settings dialog and then enable the
Rebuild Textures When Opening the File option. Now CorelDRAW will just save
the settings associated with texture fills and recalculate them when you open the
file rather than save the entire huge bitmap to disk.*

4. Use the Artistic Text tool to set more type. For the *8*, I used a font called
MarkerFeltWide, which has a fat, hand-drawn look to it; for some reason,
I flipped it horizontally. Give the text a fat black .111-inch outline and
enable the Behind Fill option from the Outline Pen dialog (F12). Give this
text a radial fountain fill from white to blue using the dialog (F11) or the
Interactive Fill tool. Use the Freehand tool to draw shapes that will

become abstract reflections of the surrounding landscape, making the object look chromy (see Chapter 23 for more on chrome). After you draw the abstract shapes, use the Intersection command to trim down the blobs so they are within the main text shape (see Figure 11-5).

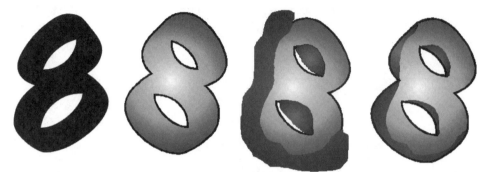

*Figure 11-5: A plain text element is transformed into a chromy one with a radial fountain fill and objects meant to look like reflected landscape. The Intersection function trims the freehand shapes within the text shape.*

5. Move the cursor over the Polygon tool on the toolbar, right-click, and choose the Properties option. Enable the Polygon as Star option, change the Number Of Points/Sides value to 4, and up the Sharpness slider to 75. This makes for a nice cartoony sparkle. Click OK and drag the Polygon tool to create the sparkle shape. Then use the Pick tool to position the sparkles on the top-right edges of the chromed letters (see Figure 11-6).

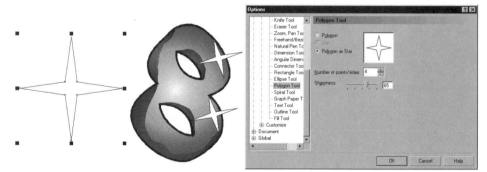

*Figure 11-6: The Polygon tool creates all kinds of stars; they can have from three to five hundred points.*

6. For the *FX* text, I used the Bezier tool to hand-draw my own type. Select the Bezier tool and click from point to point to draw a big funky *F* and then a fresh *X*. Now select both objects, and group them (Ctrl+G). Give the group a fat black .222-inch Outline, and from the Outline Pen dialog (F12), select the round Corners option. Use the Interactive Fill tool to create a yellow-to-magenta linear fountain fill, only with a harsh transition in the center (make the start and end points close together). Finally, duplicate the group and assign no-fill and a thinner .092 white outline. This thin-on-fat outline technique is an alternative to the Contour effect, with similar results (see Figure 11-7).

*Figure 11-7: A fat black outline underneath a thinner white one creates a multiple outline look similar to what the Contour roll-up can create, only in fewer steps. The Interactive Fill tool sets up a linear fountain fill, and by moving the points close together, creates a fast color transition (the same as adjusting the edge pad value in the Fountain Fill dialog does).*

7. Arrange your pieces on the rectangular wall to complete the graffiti. The next step is to riddle it with bullet holes! First, draw a rough circle with the Freehand tool. Now switch to the Interactive Fill tool and drag from the top right to the bottom left. Click on the Conical button on the Property Bar. This will give the shading of an indentation. Now, use the Ellipse tool to draw a circle in the center and give it a medium gray fill. Duplicate the circle (+ key), offset the duplicate to the top and right, give it a solid black fill, and send it back one (Ctrl+PgDn). This is the hole shadow (an indentation is shaded in reverse compared to how extruded objects are shaded). Now select the original circle, duplicate again, and move the duplicate to the bottom and left. Shade it white, and send it back one to create a gleam. Select all of the bullet-hole objects, and Group them (Ctrl+G). See Figure 11-8.

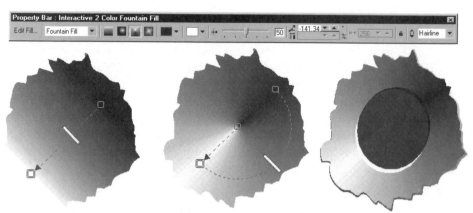

Figure 11-8: The Interactive Fill tool creates a fountain fill across the bullet-hole shape. Clicking the Conical button changes the fill type, which provides convincing shading when teamed with a circle group.

8. Arrange your bullet-hole group on one end of the mural, duplicate it, and place the duplicate on the other end. Now shift-select both and open the Blend roll-up (Ctrl+B). Reduce the number of steps to five and tab to the Acceleration page. Here you can change the scatter of your bullets by dragging the Accelerate Objects slider to the right or left. Click Apply to let loose a spray of bullets (see Figure 11-9).

Figure 11-9. The Accelerate Objects option gives a staggered look to the bullet-hole blend.

9. That finishes off the main graphic, but I wanted to add texture to make the image look more like graffiti. Select the rectangle with the texture fill and duplicate it (+ key). Now send it to the front (Shift+PgUp). Select the Interactive Transparency tool, and change the transparency type from None to Texture on the Property Bar. Drag the Starting Transparency and Ending Transparency sliders to adjust how much texture you want in your letters. As you can see in Figure 11-10, I chose 61.

*Figure 11-10: Use the Interactive Transparency tool and the Property Bar to adjust the opacity of the texture-filled box in front of the artwork to make it look like the art is painted on a wall.*

You will need to move the bullet-hole blend to the front (Shift+PgUp) to move them on top of the texture and keep them crisp. That's it! The results of this exercise can be seen in the color section as well as in the file called bulhole.cdr in the \Chapt11\ subdirectory on the Companion CD-ROM. Load the file and fiddle with the Acceleration settings on the bullet-hole blend. Also, it is important to note the difference in how the Interactive Transparency tool Property Bar sliders work on a texture fill compared to the other types (Uniform, Fountain Fill, etc.). Open the file, select the semi-opaque texture object, and then select the Interactive Transparency tool. Now move the Starting and Ending Transparency sliders on the Property Bar and see how each affects how the image looks. You may wish to eliminate the original texture-filled background shape so you can see exactly what the changes do. (Since the background and the front semi-transparent object have the same fill, some changes won't be immediately obvious unless you delete the background object.) Have fun, you cyber-vandal!

## Blurry Type

*Figure 11-11: If you convert text to bitmaps with the Transparent Background option, you can use plug-in filters while retaining a see-through look. This allows you to blur and stack images for strange results.*

In a strange trend, many artists are creating images that are actually difficult to read and purposely out of focus. As more and more design is computer generated, there seems to be a backlash with images that strive to look anything but. Artists strive for a non-computer-generated feel with images that are purposely out of focus and designed to look out of registration, poorly photocopied, or scratchy. The irony of course is that computers just make these images easier to create!

Using the bitmap functions that we explored in Chapter 9, we will now reverse the blurry in the distance logic and create images in the foreground that are out of focus. This reverse-logic brings emphasis to a background image, which is in sharp focus. It is a popular design look, made easy with CorelDRAW. Here is how to fuzz your type:

1. Use the Artistic Text tool to set your type. This technique will work on any font (I used a freaky one called MonkeyCaughtStealing from Garage fonts). Arrange your type on the page in the size and position you desire. This technique involves converting the type into bitmaps, so you need to spend some time working out the layout because after the pieces are converted, resizing them can result in low-resolution images (which are bad, bad, bad). Import an interesting background image to help you lay out everything to your liking before we proceed. I used an image off of the Masters 1 CorelDRAW photo CD. Corel has literally hundreds of useful photo collections to choose from on CD format. Import the image and arrange the text in a way that balances the image, keeping the area of focus open for later emphasis (see Figure 11-12).

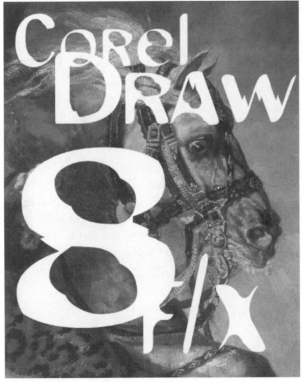

*Figure 11-12: Import your background image and arrange your type pieces. Once the type is converted into bitmaps, you will not be able to enlarge them without losing resolution, so take some time to work out the layout.*

2. Draw a rectangle, with no outline or fill, around each text element. This becomes a logical bounding box for the bitmap conversion step. If you do not provide a boundary, CorelDRAW will use the object size to calculate the bitmap size. This is fine, except that we need some breathing room beyond the edges of the text so we can use the Blur filter. If you don't provide a bounding box and use the Blur filter, the effect will end abruptly at the edges and look strange. (In CorelDRAW 8, you can use the Inflate Bitmap option to create this breathing room instead of drawing a bounding box). See Figure 11-13.

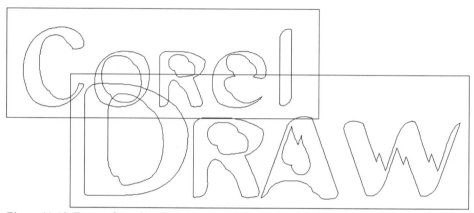

*Figure 11-13: Draw a bounding box around each text element to define the limits of the bitmap. This extra area lets you use the effects filters with room to spare.*

3. Select a text element and its bounding box, and from the Bitmap menu, choose Convert to Bitmap. In the Convert to Bitmap dialog, change the Color to 256 shades of gray (or one of the color options if your text is in color), enable Dithering, and give it a Transparent Background. Set the Resolution value to 300 dpi, enable the Super-Sampling option, and click OK. After a few seconds, your image will be transformed into a bitmap (see Figure 11-14).

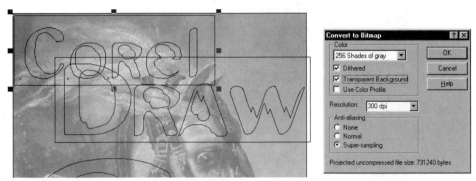

*Figure 11-14: Use the Convert to Bitmap feature with the Transparent Background feature enabled to pixelize the vector art.*

4. With the bitmap selected, select Gaussian from the Bitmap | Blur submenu. In the Gaussian Blur dialog, drag the Radius slider to the right. The farther you drag, the more out of focus the type will be (see Figure 11-15).

*Figure 11-15: Use the Gaussian Blur dialog to make your type seem fuzzy and out of focus. The more blur, the less in focus it will seem.*

5. Repeat this process for each text element, varying the degree of fuzziness for each word to create the illusion of words scattered near and far. Images up close should have less blur than those far away. The concept of near and far is a bit blurry itself, however, as the background that is the farthest will also be the clearest! Experiment with the technique to get words at varied levels of focus (see Figure 11-16).

*Figure 11-16: Scatter the words dimensionally by using different levels of the Gaussian Blur function.*

6. To give the image a darker feel, add a solid black rectangle over everything and give it a radial fountain fill transparency. Draw the rectangle and fill it black by clicking on the black onscreen color well, then select the Interactive Transparency tool and drag from the center out toward the edge. Now change from Linear Fountain to Radial on the Property Bar. Drag the outside control node to create the mood and shading to your liking (see Figure 11-17).

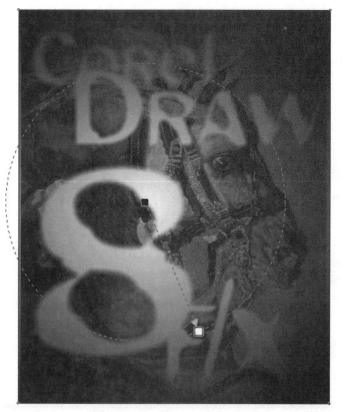

*Figure 11-17: A solid black rectangle becomes mood lighting when the Interactive Transparency tool transforms it into a radial fountain.*

7. Arrange the text elements in front of or behind the transparent black block to highlight or shade the text.

The final result can be viewed in the color section and is also on the Companion CD-ROM in the \Chapt11\ subdirectory—the file is called blurry.cdr. The CorelDRAW file has all of the elements converted to bitmaps, save the last rectangle with the lens. This technique of blurring bitmaps and using the Transparent Background option lets you get results that other poor slobs are killing themselves to achieve by using complex multilayered bitmap manipulation in PhotoPaint or Photoshop. Ha! We Corel artisans know better, and we ain't tellin'!

## Subdued Type

*Figure 11-18: Using the Interactive Transparency tool, you can de-emphasize text and make it more subtle. The Contour function creates additional shapes, which can be shaded with opposing fills for a wispy yet shiny look.*

This style again falls in the category of reverse design psychology. Instead of de-emphasizing the text elements by making them blurry and out of focus, they are made more subtle using the Interactive Transparency tool. Also, a dual-outline look again is achieved with the Contour effect. However, there are additional steps that must be taken to prepare the pieces because of their transparent nature. Here is how to make your text transparent.

1. This time the text elements will remain CorelDRAW objects throughout the life of the project so you can continue to fine-tune the layout forever. Still, as the Contour will be frozen, it will not redraw itself if you enlarge or reduce the parent objects and will not then be uniform in relation to the other contour shapes. So arrange your pieces in a layout with which you can be happy. Import (Ctrl+I) a background image and resize it to fit your page. I once again used an image from the Corel Masters 1 photo CD. The image was too small, so I drew a black rectangle behind it at my desired pages size to create a black border into which my text could fall off. Set the type with the Artistic Text tool (I used a font called Serb on the top and Papyrus on the bottom), fill it with neutral color such as pale yellow, and assign it no outline (see Figure 11-19).

*Figure 11-19: Arrange your text elements over a background image.*

**TIP**

*Is it live? When you work within CorelDRAW, there are many effects that stay alive and recalculate often during the life of your design. Blend groups, for example, will redraw themselves should you change the size, location, or any other attribute of one of the parent shapes. The same live characteristics can be observed with extrude groups, lens effects, contour groups, and even polygons, ellipses, and rectangles. If you attempt to node-edit a live rectangle with the Shape tool, you will only be able to round the corners until you convert it to curves (Ctrl+Q). When you resize a live contour group, it will recalculate the image using the original settings, which will result in a new image with effects out of proportion compared to the parent shapes. If you can, it is a good idea to freeze live Corel effects. This not only will avoid resizing problems, but will also speed up screen refresh. Frozen effects are simple objects, where "live" effects are dynamic, recalculating, rebuilding, reshading groups of complex objects. Use the Separate feature to freeze blends, extrudes, or contours. Use the Frozen option on the Lens roll-up to freeze those effects, and use the Convert to Curves command to freeze envelopes, perspectives, deformations, polygons, rectangles, and ellipses.*

2. Select one of the bottom text elements and click on the Interactive Transparency tool. Now drag from the side you want to be solid to the side you want to disappear into oblivion. The control points on the Interactive Transparency line control where the fill is completely solid and where it fades to complete transparency. You can drag these points to start and end inside or even way outside of your objects to get all kinds of transparency transitions (see Figure 11-20).

*Figure 11-20: Use the Interactive Transparency tool to create wispy text effects. Drag the control points to change where the text fades into nothingness.*

3. Drag-select the top text pieces and copy (Ctrl+C) them (we need a copy later on). Select one of the top text elements and open the Contour roll-up (Ctrl+F9). Now enable the Outside option, change the Offset to .03 inches, decrease Steps to 1, and then click Apply. Repeat this process with the same settings on the other two text elements (see Figure 11-21).

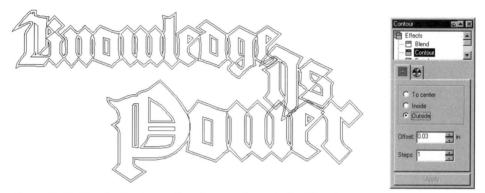

*Figure 11-21: Use the Contour roll-up to generate a set of outline shapes.*

4. Now drag-select all of these text elements and choose Separate | Arrange | Ungroup All from the Arrange menu. Drag-select the two curves that make up each word and combine them (Ctrl+L). This will punch out the inner curve from the outer, resulting in a solid outline shape. Repeat this on the other text objects. Paste (Ctrl+V) the original text objects and send them to the back (Shift+PgDn). Now you have two sets of shapes, the inside originals and the outside contour (see Figure 11-22).

*Figure 11-22: Combine the contour shape with the original to get an outline object with a hollow center (shown in black). The original objects (in gray) can then shine through.*

5. Now give all of the pieces the same pale yellow fill and no outline. Select one of the outside contours and with the Interactive Transparency tool, drag from the top of the shape down. This will create a fade from solid yellow on top to transparent on the bottom. Repeat this process on all three outline pieces (see Figure 11-23).

*Figure 11-23: Use the Interactive Transparency tool to fade the fill color in the outside pieces from solid yellow on top to transparent at the bottom.*

6. The inside shapes will get the exact opposite fill. Select an inside shape, and with the Interactive Transparency tool, drag from the bottom up. Repeat for the other pieces (see Figure 11-24). That's it!

*Figure 11-24: Use the Interactive Transparency tool again, only this time reversing the fade-out logic to fade from transparent to solid in the inside pieces, to finish the effect.*

**CD-ROM** The end results can be seen in the color section and also in the trans.cdr file found in the \Chapt11\ subdirectory on the Companion CD-ROM. You may wish to load the file and experiment with the Interactive Transparency fills in real-time by moving the control points and watching everything rebuild. I had some display problems in CorelDRAW 7 with these opposing transparency fills, but they went away in CorelDRAW 8. If you have a problem with the Interactive Transparency tool, select the fill and click the Freeze button on the Property Bar. That should fix any strange rendering anomalies.

## Moving On

In this chapter, we used the Contour effect several times to create additional outlines for our text elements. We also used the Transparency functions to add texture or remove emphasis from our text. The blur effect also came to our aid to fuzz out our text. All of these techniques are useful and certainly not limited to the previous examples.

In the next chapter, we again will look at some strange ways to use CorelDRAW, both in the real world and in the fringe design realm. Ready for some pain? We're heading into the world of flash sheets and tattoo parlors!

▼ **Beyond f/x**

The graffiti and type effects in this chapter are a great way to modernize your designs. Okay, admittedly not every project is screaming for a graffiti look, but multiple outlines and added texture are useful effects for many applications, such as logo design or interesting product layouts (a catalog with the products painted on a stucco wall instead of laying on a page, for example). The blurry and faded examples are also pretty easy to create in CorelDRAW, making these new design ideas accessible without all of the tedium that other programs require.

Using blurry type is a neat way to get a message across subtly without losing focus in the design. People are attracted to the extraordinary, and this kind of reverse-logic image, with the foreground blurry and background in focus, catches the eye in an almost subconscious way. It's like when you print the mirror image of a photo. Things look right at first, but somehow you know something isn't right, so you keep staring at the image until you consciously figure out the visual trick. You can combine this technique with another blurry concept, the speed blur (outlined in Chapter 26), for even more focus-changing tricks. For a more sophisticated audience, use subtle tricks that gain attention with a whisper, not a scream!

# chapter 12

# Tattoos & Other Body Art

With tattoos and a devil-may-care attitude all the rage these days, it only makes sense to work the look into your designs. The whole edgy-but-cartoony look of a tattoos makes it the perfect candidate for CorelDRAW artwork. The flexibility of a computer-aided design package really shines through with a topic like tattoos. CorelDRAW can do everything; with it you can create designs that have the look and attitude of tattoos for all kinds of commercial applications, stick those designs on people in a virtual sense, and create artwork for use in actual tattooing applications.

In this chapter, we will explore this broad topic and how CorelDRAW fits into the mix. In the first example, we will create an image of a very creepy skull graphic, much like these dark tattoo images, and then give this artwork a traditional blue and "stippled" monochrome tattoo look. Then we will see how the tattoo style fits into modern design examples, such as packaging or advertising. Next, we will use some transparency tricks to apply tattoo artwork to a model photo. Finally, we will discuss how specialized computer-aided design techniques can be used to solve some age-old tattooing problems. Park the hog; it's time to get serious!

## Scary Skulls

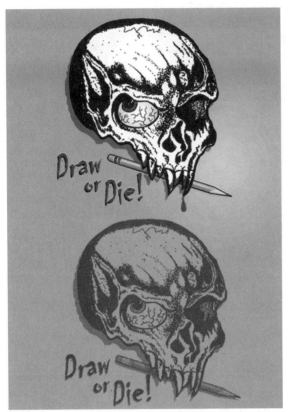

*Figure 12-1: CorelDRAW is the perfect place to transform an ink illustration into a scary tattoo-like image and also take it a step further for a monochrome "stippled" tattoo look.*

Tattoos and tattoo artists have always fascinated me, and the imagery is more useful than you might think. Some of my more spooky clients, who have some very strange design parameters indeed, want designs that incorporate either tattoos or something that resembles them. Even the most tame customer will no doubt hit you up for a Halloween flyer, and suddenly even "Grandma's Kitchenware Shop" has creepy skulls and spiders in its ads!

The nice thing about the second half of this next technique is that you can also take virtually any color image and, with a few modifications, convert it into a dithered old-school tattoo-like image. This kind of artwork translates very well into black-and-white applications (since it is basically a black-and-white bitmap) as well as other applications when you want a more graphic tattoo-like image or when you are limited to just a few colors. You could do a one-color flyer using the tattoo effect to dither the artwork and then print the image in blue on tan or flesh-colored paper. Tricks like this cost no more than printing black on white paper, are much more interesting, and leave a lasting impression (excuse the pun).

## Full-Color Horror

In this first example, I scanned an ink illustration I had done of a scary skull that was very much influenced by a tattoo I had seen. (If you think the skull is scary, you should have seen the dude it was on!) Like I have said many times, don't limit your artistic influences to the obvious. Go out and buy some weird magazines, just to get some ideas. At the very worst, you can just use them as a "things not to do" reference! Here is how to create a full-color tattoo:

**CD-ROM**

1. Import (Ctrl+I) a black-and-white scan of your ink artwork (the file is called skulleye.tif in the \Chapt12\ subdirectory on the Companion CD-ROM, or see the sidebar "My Favorite Thing" for tips on searching clip art for skulls). In CorelDRAW, you can control the fill and outline value of black-and-white (1-bit) bitmaps, so you can change from the original two colors to any other, or in this case, change the white fill value to "nothing" by left-clicking on the no-fill color well. With the bitmap still selected, open the Object Manager *docker* from the Layout menu (used to be the Layer Manager roll-up in V.7 and works essentially in the same way). Now click the arrow button located at the top right of the Object Manager docker to open the fly-out, and select New Layer. This will create Layer 2, which I named Skull so I would remember it was for the bitmap. With the skull bitmap selected, select Move To Layer from the Object Manager flyout and click on the newly created layer name, Skull. Now click on the pencil icon next to the layer name to disable any editing. Point and click on Layer 1 to make it the current layer, so you can now begin to colorize the bitmap (see Figure 12-2). If you forget to change to a layer that isn't locked, CorelDRAW will remind you when you try to create something new.

▼ **My Favorite Thing**

Because I am a consummate computer geek, I like to attend the local computer fair now and then (check your newspaper and I am sure you can find one near you soon). These events are amazing to me, with literally hundreds of vendors all hawking the latest computer technology in an Arabian fruit bazaar atmosphere. You see people haggling, trading, arguing—with booths and tables filled to overflowing with technology. You can find amazing deals on everything from books to hard disks, with slightly older technology at incredible bargains. It was here I found my favorite thing: a 4-disk CD-ROM changer for $35. Yes, *$35!* Why was it so cheap? Well, it is only a 4x reader, and with current technology up to like 24x, it is painfully anachronistic to most people. But in the desktop design world, who really cares? I only use my CD-ROM drives to read clip art and photo CDs anyway, so 4x is fine.

I stuff all of my clip-art CDs into the thing and then use Windows Explorer's Find feature to search for an image by name (i.e., Skul*.*). The difference from a single-drive search is that I change the Look In option to My Computer. When I click the Find Now button, the system searches each and every disk in my system, including all of the CDs in the changer, for the files I want. It takes a few minutes, but, man, I love it! (Even if you don't have a CD Changer, the Explorer Find feature is a great way to locate images on the disk.) All those files obediently reveal their otherwise encrypted location, just waiting to be harvested for my latest design feast! Not to mention I almost never swap out clip-art CDs anymore; I just click on the drive and it swaps it for me. Trust me, for $35, you cannot begin to understand how I love this thing. Find one; buy one; you will love it.

2. With the bitmap locked onto its own layer, it's easy to draw shapes and colorize it with the Freehand tool. Drag along the perimeter of the skull shape with the Freehand tool keeping the line within the thick, black outline of the bitmap and circling all the way around to create a pad for the entire skull. If you are like me, a victim of caffeine, you will need to go back and use the Shape tool to node-edit the line within the skull perimeter! Give this big pad a radial fountain from pale yellow to white to look like old bone. Use the Freehand tool to draw shapes for the teeth and fill them white. On top of the teeth, create smaller objects in red for blood. Create the shape to color the main part of the eye and then create one to color the smaller iris. Create and fill shapes for any part of the skull you want to have color (see Figure 12-3).

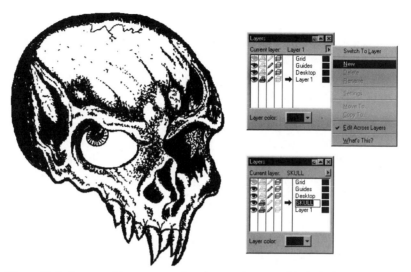

*Figure 12-2: Import a bitmap, move it to its own layer, and lock the layer to prevent accidental moving of the bitmap.*

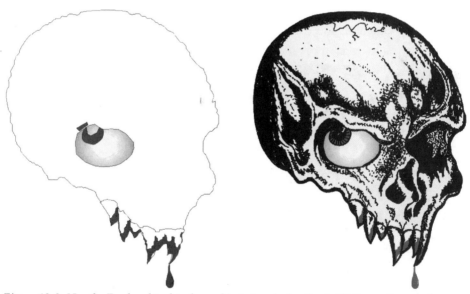

*Figure 12-3: Use the Freehand tool to draw objects to colorize the skull bitmap. Because the bitmap is on its own layer and locked, you draw on it, but the pieces are actually below it. The objects (shown on the left without the bitmap on top and with outlines for demonstration only) are filled with an appropriate color, no outline, so that when the bitmap is placed on top, it creates the finished artwork.*

**TIP**

*It is easy to drag and drop colors on top of objects to recolor the fill or outline without ungrouping or even selecting them. This shortcut is limited to solid colors off of the onscreen palette, which is kind of limiting. (I hate limits, and I am also lazy—what a dilemma.) The solution is to quickly draw another shape, like a circle, and fill it with any fill or outline that you want to give to the object stuck in the group. Now select your fill object and drag using the right mouse button. When you release over the target object, a menu pops up from which you can choose to copy the outline, fill, or both. Oh yeah! I use this trick to recolor things like buttons that are object groups buried within other object groups and would be a hassle to ungroup and manipulate normally. It may sound strange, but try it; you will find it's a great shortcut!*

3. Zoom in on the eye and use the Freehand tool to draw some nice veins. Start from the edge of the eye and work a squiggly line inward, remembering to follow the imaginary contour of the eyeball. Branch more veins off from the main trunk like branches from a tree. If you were really detail oriented, the veins would get smaller the further away from the main trunk they are, but hey, who has that kind of time? Open the Outline Pen dialog (F12) and give your veins a .013-inch outline width, red color, and rounded corners (see Figure 12-4).

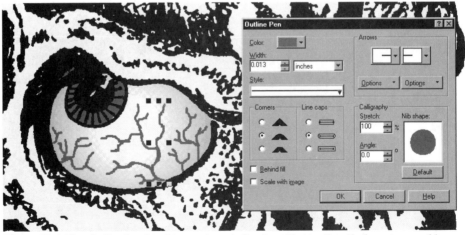

*Figure 12-4: Use the Freehand tool to create eyeball veins. Change the nib shape to round by changing to rounded corners in the Outline Pen dialog box.*

4. You can add any details or type to your tattoo to personalize it to your taste. I imported a pencil from the \clipart\office\supplies directory on the CorelDRAW CD-ROM. To get a fat outline for the pencil, group (Ctrl+G) all of the pieces (if they aren't already), duplicate (+ key), and send the duplicate back one (Ctrl+PgDn). Open the Outline Pen dialog (F12), change the color to black, set the width to something big like .1 inches, change to rounded corners, and click OK. This will give everything in the pencil group this fat outline, but since it is behind the original, only the outline around the perimeter will appear. It makes for a little redundant processing for poor old CorelDRAW, but it is a heck of a lot easier than trying to find all of the pieces manually and give them a thick outline (see Figure 12-5).

*Figure 12-5: To create a fat outline for the clip-art pencil, it is duplicated and the duplicate group is given a heavy black outline. This makes it look strange, but when it is placed behind the original, the result is a nice fat outline.*

5. Use the Artistic Text tool to set type. Remember that you can use the Shape tool to drag the letters around to get the spacing you want. I used a font called Chiller LET in red and then created a highlight and a gleam by offsetting duplicates (just like we have a million times before). To get a drop shadow behind the skull and pencil, duplicate all but the bitmap pieces, move down and to the left, use the Send To Back (Shift+PgDn) option, and give them a gray fill, no outline. Or you could use the CorelDRAW 8 Interactive Drop Shadow feature, located on the Interactive Blend tool flyout. I wanted a crisp shadow, but the Drop Shadow feature is cool too. If you want to use this feature, create a simplified set of shapes first. Select all the skull pieces, duplicate them, and move the duplicates off to the side. Delete all but the main skull shape and pencil. Get an outline-only shape for the pencil group by first ungrouping (Ctrl+U) and then using the Weld function to merge all the shapes into one. Now shift-select the skull and pencil outline shapes and combine them into one curve (shadows work better on single objects). Give your shape a solid white fill, no outline, and create your drop shadow by

dragging on it with the Interactive Drop Shadow tool. Change the feathering and opacity settings on the Property bar to your tastes (see Figure 12-6).

*Figure 12-6. For the CorelDRAW 8 Drop Shadow function, first start with simplified shapes and then use the Interactive Drop Shadow tool to drag out a drop shadow.*

To stay in line with the tattoo theme, draw a dark flesh-colored rectangle behind the artwork. (This is also a handy way to preview a tattoo in its natural setting. Scan your own arm if you want to see how a color scheme works with your skin tone.) Check out how this looks in the color section, where I used my own pasty arm as a reference. Hmm. Not bad.

## Monochrome Mandibles

I always thought that tattoos were limited to that dark, bluish-greenish ink that I always saw on bikers and veterans. Although today's technology allows for virtually any color to be a part of a tattoo (even white!), many people like me still think of those old images when they think tattoo. For this reason, you might want to play up the old-school look and take advantage of these archetypes. It also makes for interesting one-color designs, like I already said. To take the color skull image (or any other) and create the old-time tattoo look, you can take advantage of CorelDRAW's flexible Export function or Convert to Bitmap functions. Here is how to make your tattoo art look retro-monochrome:

1. First, you should simplify the artwork. Think *exaggerated*. Eliminate wishy-washy midtones, as in the eyeball and teeth details. Red will go almost black in a monochrome scheme, but it will look terrible. So make

all red objects black, or delete them all together. During the Export process, midtones will be dithered, which means broken into dots to make them look like shades of gray. To eliminate excessive dithering, make the fountain fills in the eye and skull solid white (see Figure 12-7). The pencil is a bit to detailed for this process, but I left it in so you can see how much dithering effects detailed objects.

---

▼ **Why Dots?**

In the old days, instead of changing colors for shading, the artist only had a single color of ink for a tattoo and would use little dots to simulate shading, a process called *stippling*. The closer or farther apart the dots were, the lighter or darker the shades of gray were.

---

*Figure 12-7: Simplify the artwork for the monochrome look to avoid excess dithering.*

2. Open the Export (Ctrl+H) dialog and change the Save as Type setting to
   TIFF Bitmap. Name your file as desired and click Export. From the
   Bitmap Export dialog, change the color to black and white and enable the
   Dithered option. Now you can make the image more or less chunky by
   changing the resolution; 75 dpi makes for a really grainy image but has a
   convincing hand-stippled look of an old tattoo. Import (Ctrl+I) the resulting bitmap back into CorelDRAW (see Figure 12-8).

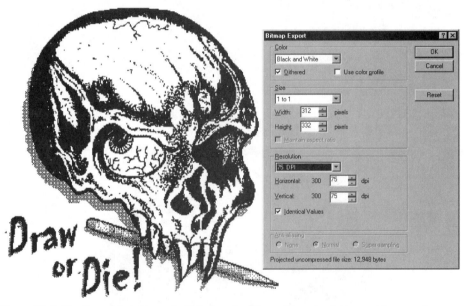

*Figure 12-8: The Export function set at black and white and low resolution creates a grainy,
stippled-looking graphic.*

3. Now you can choose any color to give the black-and-white bitmap an
   old-time tattoo look. Remove any fill by left-clicking the no-fill color
   well. Then change the black to something with a more retro ink color,
   like Storm Blue. Now you can place the image on a skin-colored background.

You can see this monochrome image in the color section to get a feel for the
stippling feel. For more control during this process, use the features of the
Convert to Black and White dialog rather than the Export function.

**TIP** *Instead of using the limited dithering of CorelDRAW's Convert to Bitmap option, use the advanced features of the Convert to Black and White dialog. First, don't convert your image to a black-and-white bitmap; instead, give it 256 levels of gray at a higher resolution (300 dpi) using the Convert to Bitmap dialog under the Bitmap menu. Then, from the Convert flyout (again from the Bitmap menu), choose Black and White. Now you have more halftone options on the Convert to Black and White dialog. Choose the Error Diffusion option for a more randomized, hand-drawn look than the CorelDRAW Export Dithering option creates. Or, use the Line Art option to specify a mechanical newsprint-style dot pattern. For a more grainy image, use the Image | Resample option to lower the resolution of the grayscale bitmap and then use the Convert To command to get your stippling. There are many options to take your artwork back in time!*

## Working Tats

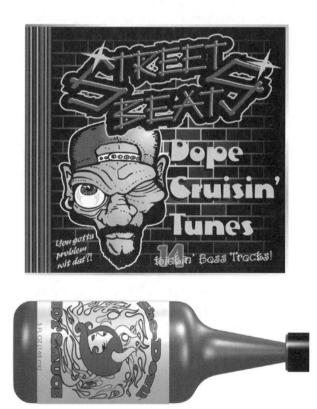

*Figure 12-9: Images born as tattoos can find new life as commercial artwork, as seen in these packaging designs.*

With the addition of computers to my design studio, much of my art is now in digital format. I am used to leafing through sketch books, art drawers, and magazines, so to me, a hard disk just doesn't have any traditional, tangible feedback. To remind me and my bad brain of artwork that exists digitally, I try to always create some sort of hard-copy printout that down the road I will stumble across and be inspired to use. I am notoriously bad at organizing artwork and have been known to lose things. I have lost precious original illustrations and been forced to locate a digital backup copy on some old backup tape somewhere (the drive that is handily still available, but only functions from DOS—ick!).

Anyway, my point here is that today's studio is a hodgepodge of traditional media thrown into the digital mix, with many possible results. You can use bitmap and vector artwork in the same image, or if you prefer, you can use the Corel OCR-Trace program to convert the artwork into vector format. With tattoo art all the rage, more and more projects are using these kinds of images. I have found myself using artwork inspired by tattoos in some very normal designs. These pieces are sometimes all vector, scans of illustrations, or both. It really doesn't matter where you start, you can always get where you need to go using CorelDRAW tricks. The next section will show you how to use bitmap and vector images to create tattoo inspired logos.

## Devil Girl

Even the most idiosyncratic artwork sometimes can get recycled into other art projects! This also works for tattoo-type icons and images. I had drawn this devil girl years ago (see Figure 12-10), and at one point it was even a T-shirt for an underground clothing line sold on Melrose Boulevard in Hollywood. Although the origins were kind of hard core, this image was perfect for another, more mainstream application. With my typical bad luck, I could not find any of the original artwork when I needed it! What I did find was a CorelDRAW file that had a grainy black-and-white scan of the image in a brochure, which was a good enough place to start! Here is how to transform an old bitmap image into a contemporary product label:

1. The she-devil image was perfect for the label project I was working on, so I dug up the old file and opened it. If you start with a scan from another CorelDRAW file, select it, copy the image (Ctrl+C), and start a new image (Ctrl+N). Now you can paste (Ctrl+V) the bitmap into the empty

work space and you are ready to start fresh. Use the same technique to lock the bitmap and create shapes for coloring we used in the skull example. Create separate shapes to color the face and eyes differently, even if in this example they end up both white anyway (you may change your mind later for another project). This is a three-color logo (red, black, and yellow) printed on white, so limit your color selections to that color scheme (see Figure 12-10).

Black
Red
White

*Figure 12-10: Even a grainy bitmap can be used for tattoo-type art. A simple black outline benefits from CorelDRAW objects to color, and add missing detail, such as the shape of the right horn.*

2. Import (Ctrl+I) the goddess.cdr image from the \Chapt2\ subdirectory on the Companion CD-ROM and steal a set of flames. Delete the rest of the goddess image, which will leave you with just a flame group. Now select the Color Styles option from the Layout menu and reduce the number of colors from many to just yellow and red (this process is outlined in Chapter 5). Change the blue color to Style2 and all of the child colors to solid red. This will result in an acceptable flame group without the huge hassle of editing the pieces manually to eliminate the blue outline (see Figure 12-11).

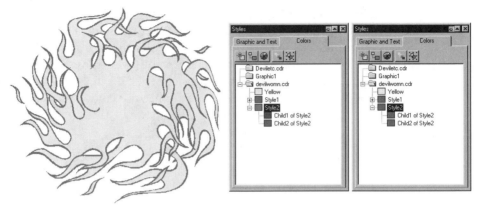

*Figure 12-11: All your artwork, in whole or just parts, is up for grabs for other projects! Here flames from an earlier image are imported and recolored using the Color Styles option.*

3. Place the devil girl in the flames to finish the tattoo image. To add emphasis without adding an additional color, duplicate (+ key) the frame group, send it back one (Ctrl+PgDn), and give the duplicate group a fat white (or black) outline like we gave the pencil in the first example. This will add some pop to the image. Again, as in the first example, you can create a monochrome stippled look with the export feature (see Figure 12-12).

*Figure 12-12: Combine the elements to finish the central image. Use the fat outline on a duplicate trick to give the flames a dark frame. The Export function can also convert this image into a monochrome, stippled-looking graphic.*

4. Use the Artistic Text tool to transform the type in the tattoo into something more mainstream, in this case a logo for a hot sauce bottle. Draw a circle and then move the Artistic Text tool over it to automatically set the text to the curve as you type. I used a font called LatinWidD (Latin Wide) that just seemed perfect for this application. A red-filled copy of the text with a thin yellow outline is sitting on a duplicate given a really fat black outline for the double-outline look (see Figure 12-13).

*Figure 12-13: Arranging appropriate text elements transforms the tattoo instantly from pop art to product logo!*

5. To create a sticker for placement on an object in CorelDream, export the label artwork as an RBG bitmap using the BMP file format. Then in CorelDream you can assign the bitmap as a shader and paint a shape with it. This process is outlined in Chapter 30.

The completed logo, stuck onto a virtual bottle, can be seen in the color section. This and the next example are in the cooltats.cdr file, found in the \Chapt12\ subdirectory on the Companion CD-ROM. If you load it, you can see how the bitmap merges seamlessly with the CorelDRAW objects despite the resolution being a bit too low. This logo is still in the early stages where a low-res images works fine for comps and mock-ups like the 3D bottle created in CorelDream. If this project takes off and I can't find the original artwork, I may have to redraw the girl and drop in a crisp new scan. Dang, I need a better filing system!

## One Eye

This example features another weird image that I drew. The inspiration came from a freaky vampire tattoo I had once seen. Instead of drawing shapes manually, I used the Corel OCR-Trace to convert the artwork. This makes colorizing easy, as we have seen in several examples now. Here is how to take an OCR-Trace image and make it into a color image for a tattoo-inspired record label:

1. In CorelTrace, convert the bitmap (called buddy2.tif in the \Chapt12\ subdirectory on the Companion CD-ROM) to an outline trace using the Accurate trace settings. Save the image to disk. In CorelDRAW, import (Ctrl+I) the image and ungroup (Ctrl+U) the pieces. Now select all of the white objects and give them an appropriate color. Use a radial fountain from gold to sand for the skin areas to give a slight range of highlights. Continue until all of the white pieces (except the eye and the hat fastener) are colored (see Figure 12-14).

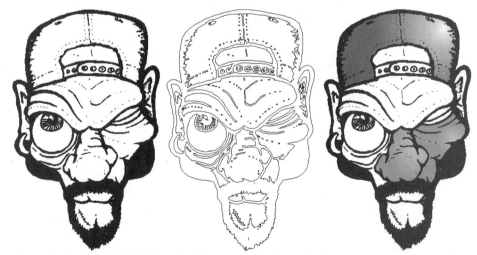

*Figure 12-14: A Corel OCR-Trace Outline trace image is a collection of colored shapes on a big black pad (the wireframe is shown in the center). Select the pieces and color them to bring the image to life.*

2. Once you have finished coloring the trace objects, you can add your own. Set text using the Artistic Text tool (I used a font called Bang LET on the hat), tweak it slightly with an envelope, and give it a really fat black fill and outline (.111 inches). Duplicate (+ key) the text and give the duplicate a less-fat yellow outline and fill (.05 inches). Duplicate the text again, and this time use a thin black fill and outline (.021 inches) to create the double outline for the text. Select the fat black pad (click the base of the beard), duplicate (+ key), send it back one (Ctrl+PgDn), and give this duplicate a fat .103 yellow outline. Duplicate and send it back one again, with this final duplicate having a fat .222-inch black outline. Now your tattoo image has a freaky fat multiple-outline look (see Figure 12-15).

*Figure 12-15: Add text and multiple-outline effects to finish off the tattoo part of your image.*

3. Once again, text elements will transform the image into a functional commercial art project! Set artistic text for the headline (I used a font called Tag LET, which seemed appropriate for the graffiti look I was after, as a tag is a personal grafitti icon). Convert the text to curves so you can break it apart. The right-hand *s* is a duplicate of the left, flipped horizontally and vertically. Use the techniques outlined in Chapter 11 to get a multiple outline using the Contour roll-up to finish the grafitti-izing of the logo.

4. Draw a rectangle the size of a CD and open the Pattern Fill dialog to create a brick background. From the Pattern Fill dialog, select the Full Color option and then click on the preview window to reveal other tiles. Scroll down until you find the brick wall and click on it. Then click OK to fill the rectangle with the bricks.

5. Arrange your logo and face character on the CD cover. Add any other text elements you need, choosing fonts that stick to the street beat theme.

6. To get a more moody background than just the bright bricks afford, use a transparency effect to darken things like we did in Chapter 11. Duplicate the bricks shape and fill it solid black. Now click on the Interactive Transparency tool and change the parameters in the Property Bar without ever actually clicking on the target object. Change the type to Fountain and then click on the Radial Fountain Transparency button. The default settings should get you just what you want (see Figure 12-16).

*Figure 12-16: A radial fountain transparency darkens the background bitmap pattern and makes the foreground objects stand out better.*

**CD-ROM**    This image is in the color section and also in the cooltats.cdr file in the \Chap12\ subdirectory on the Companion CD-ROM. Open the file and see the difference between images that contain bitmaps and those generated from OCR-Traced pieces. It doesn't really matter where you begin; with a little effort and some CorelDRAW magic, you can mold any artwork into your dream image.

## Skin Art

*Figure 12-17: Using transparency tricks, you can stick a tattoo on anything and anyone!*

Yes, my job is to stick virtual tattoos on various and sundry body parts of hapless digital people. Man, my life is weird sometimes. The technique in this next section has some interesting potential. You could, for example, create a "try-before-you-buy" image to see how a tattoo looks on you or a friend before you have it done (or use the art to try and talk someone out of it!). Other uses are in advertising, where it seems all the rage to stick corporate logos on models and call it an ad. Save some poor model the grief and create the artwork digitally (as I did in Figure 12-17). Here is how to apply a digital tattoo.

1. First, find some appropriate artwork for the tattoo (there are a ton of great images available in the CorelDRAW clip-art library; see the sidebar "Clip-Art Chaos"). I used a Slimy Dog logo I had handy, and also stole the wings logo from Chapter 26 (neat trick, huh, stealing from the

future?). These two images are based on tattoos I have seen. (The Slimy Dog head is a parody of a very popular old hot rod racing tattoo. Perhaps you recognize it?) Import the images into CorelDRAW along with an image of the lucky recipient. Photo-CDs are much easier to work with than real people, particularly when you're trying to tattoo them.

### ▼ Clip-Art Chaos

My buddy showed up one day with a spanking new wolf tattoo on his arm. It caught my eye because it was a piece of CorelDRAW clip art (see Figure 12-18). Clip art is a very handy resource, with tons of images just begging to be a part of your tattoo project. However, there are a few hidden pitfalls when using this resource. Clip art often will not resize correctly, especially if there are any heavy line weights used. This is because unless the original artist chose the Scale With Image option from the Outline Pen dialog (F12), the lines will not enlarge or reduce proportionately when you change the size of the image. This is beyond annoying, but don't despair, your crazy Uncle Shane has yet another way to fix the artwork!

Select the offending clip art at its original size and open the Export dialog (Ctrl+H). Now change the Save As Type setting to Encapsulated PostScript (EPS). This is a vector format, similar to the native CorelDRAW format. Now click the Export button, and on the EPS Export options page, be sure that the Include Header option is *disabled*. Click OK to export the image. When finished, open the Import dialog (Ctrl+I) and change the Files of Type setting to PostScript Interpreted. Now choose Import Text as Curves option and sit tight while CorelDRAW imports and fixes your artwork!

Now the lines have all been set to Scale With Image, so you can enlarge and reduce to your heart's content. The downside to this technique is that if the clip art has features like fountain fills that translate poorly, the fixed file can be very complex. You need to decide if it is worth fixing by hand or manually or just giving up and using something else.

*Figure 12-18: The CorelDRAW clip-art library is filled with images and icons perfect for that tattoo look. Resizing clip art can cause problems if line weights are not set to Scale With Image.*

2. Group your images and place them about where you want them. The dog head is a colorized bitmap, so find a spot that is pretty flat, as you can't alter it with an envelope. Draw a rectangle around the tattoo, with no outline or fill. Then drag-select all of the pieces, including the boundary rectangle, and use the Convert to Bitmap dialog to transform the group of objects into a single pixel-based entity. Set to the desired color and dithering, but the critical feature is the Transparent Background option, which should be enabled to keep the tattoo free-floating.

3. With the objects transformed into a single bitmap, it is easy to create the look of a tattoo using a transparency effect. Select the bitmap and click on the Interactive Transparency tool. Now change the transparency type on the Property Bar to uniform and drag the slider until the starting transparency is at 40%. This setting lets enough of the background color and detail show through to mute the bitmap and look darn close to a real tattoo (see Figure 12-19).

*Figure 12-19: Changing the bitmap from a solid object (left) to one with a 40% uniform transparency creates convincing skin art.*

4. You can twist and distort vector-based images such as the wings logo to fit on top of any strange body contour. To get the logo to fit on the model's shoulder, distort the image with the Envelope tool. Remember, you can click the Add New button on the roll-up to manipulate an object with more than one envelope in multiple stages. That way you can start with a single-arc envelope and then move on to more controlled tweaking with an unconstrained envelope (see Figure 12-20).

*Figure 12-20: Use the Envelope tool to distort vector artwork so it will fit correctly on the target body part.*

5. Now again draw a no-fill, no-outline rectangle around the wings artwork and convert it to a bitmap with the transparent background like before.

6. Use the Interactive Transparency tool as before, only this time use the Linear Fountain Fill option. Drag the tool across the length of the bitmap from left to right to assign the direction of the fountain fill. This will assign the standard 100% solid to 100% transparent fill setting. You can

control the opacity of the transparency fill with color points. White is 100% solid and black 100% clear, so by dragging different shades of gray from the onscreen color wells and dropping them onto the fill, you can change how the image looks. For example, drag and drop 50% black to each end point for a uniform 50% transparency. Now drag and drop 20% gray to the center, which makes the bitmap more opaque in the center (80% opaque, 20% transparent) and fade to more transparent at each edge. This makes the tattoo image seem darker as it reacts to the darker skin tone on the arm and is more convincing than a uniform transparency (see Figure 12-21).

*Figure 12-21: Modifying the Opacity setting on the a Linear Fountain fill Transparency makes a bitmap more clear on the edges and blend more naturally to the skin tones below.*

It's really a simple technique, and the results are quite convincing! See for yourself in the color section, or load up the tatgirl.cdr file from the \Chapt12\ subdirectory on the Companion CD-ROM and see firsthand what's going on. In the file you can see another Slimy Dog logo (like Jimmy Durante says, "I got a million of 'em!") that has been distorted with the enveloping tools to look like it's part of the hat. It's pretty easy to modify artwork to get it to merge into a real image (see the next chapter for even more fun). The beauty of this procedure is that, unlike tattoos, it isn't permanent and is pretty painless!

## Anklets & Bracelets

In addition to the many uses in design for artwork that looks like tattoos, you can also obviously design your own tattoo in CorelDRAW. With all of the clip art and fonts and the ability to place text in all kinds of configurations, tattoo artists drool at the kind of power that CorelDRAW affords!

Computer-aided tattoo design is actually very smart. You can experiment with color and size, and you can fine-tune your image before going under the needle. Indeed, because tattoos are essentially permanent, you should probably work hard to create an image that you really (and I mean *really*) love. Computer-designed tattoos are pretty obvious use of CorelDRAW. What wasn't so obvious was a technique I came up with to solve a long-time problem with tattooing: images that should connect around your arm or leg, but don't.

I thought I would head down to a local tattoo parlor and see what I could learn. I brought along the never-ending horizontal patterns from Chapter 28, figuring I could wow the artists with some computer-generated patterns that you could custom-fit to any size arm. Wrong. Much to my disappointment, continuous patterns are basically a tattooing nightmare because people are not round. Everyone's limbs are shaped differently, and it is impossible to create flat artwork that will fit the contours of the body and wrap around and start and stop in the same spot. Or so they say. I refused to believe it. Somehow I kept hacking away at the problem, and I awoke one night with the typical "Eureka!" Here's how to create a custom tattoo image that will wrap around the target limb perfectly:

1. First of all, you have to take a marker and draw a line on your arm or leg or wherever you want the connecting tattoo to be. Draw this line carefully so it is straight, or have someone help you draw it. Try to draw it straight so that even as your body contour goes in, out, up, and down, the line will connect to itself again.

2. Grab some wax paper and wrap it around the line you just drew. Keep the paper as flat as you can and tape it in place. Now copy the line from your leg on to the wax paper, making sure you clearly mark a reference start/stop point that you can match up again on your leg. When you pull the paper off and lay if flat, you will have a very strange line that is a custom fit to that specific body part (see Figure 12-22).

*Figure 12-22: Copy a line drawn on your arm or leg to a piece of wax paper. When you lay the wax paper flat, you will get a distinctive line (this is Shane's ankle).*

3. Start CorelDRAW with a fresh new page. Now set the zoom factor at 1:1 and tape the wax-paper line on to your monitor. Use the Bezier tool to re-create the hand-drawn line in CorelDRAW, including the start/stop points.

4. Using this line as a guide, you can now generate any pattern you wish to fit seamlessly around your limbs! You know how long the artwork has to be because of the beginning and end points, and you also know the exact strange shape it needs to be in. I used a pattern of skulls and bones blended along the reference line to create a custom piece of artwork that fits perfectly around my ankle to create a seamless tattoo (see Figure 12-23).

*Figure 12-23: Using the reference line transferred into CorelDRAW, any pattern can be custom-fit to the individual for a never-ending circular design.*

**CD-ROM**   This file is called skulslev.cdr and is in the \Chapt12\ subdirectory on the Companion CD-ROM. It's a strange technique that admittedly will appeal to a tiny select few, but it does help illustrate how sometimes even the strangest design task can be solved with a little unconventional creativity and the built-in versatility of CorelDRAW.

## Moving On

In this chapter, we looked at many ways to get a tattoo look in your designs. We also saw how to take images and make them virtual tattoos that adorn any image or digital person. And we took a quick glance at designing artwork for actual tattoos.

In the next chapter, we will continue to explore unconventional uses for CorelDRAW by examining how to pierce and brand in virtual land. Sound crazy? Jump into the next chapter and you'll see what I mean.

▼ **Beyond f/x**

Tattoo artwork may not seem practical immediately, but more and more, the style is gaining in popularity. It's not just a specific look but a kind of homage to carefree, kitschy pop culture, with cheesy lounge lizards, fuzzy dice, and dash of nightlife hedonism. Images and icons from this genre, like dice, eight balls, and martini glasses, are popping up everywhere, especially in the music industry. As a designer, you should embrace this kind of icon-based cult, as the images are very easy to work with and to reproduce in print and on screen.

Tattoos can instantly change the mood and tone of an ad from ordinary to edgy. They also change the impression one has of the people in your designs. Add a tattoo (or piercings, as outlined in the next chapter), and you can even make Martha Stewart look dangerous, wild, and likely to blow smoke in your face! Tattoo art works well in logos for fringe corporations, such as those involved in alternative clothing or music. They also can find their ways into more mainstream logos, like we saw with the salsa label, depending on the product and the targeted demographic.

It's great fun to take a product that isn't especially exciting and create a campy brochure or ad using a seedy nightlife theme. Just like on *Sesame Street*, "one of these things is not like the other" is an awesome concept to draw attention to a product; an element is so out of place you can't help but react (a baby playing pool in a seedy bar, grandma and friends smoking cigars and playing poker, Hell's Angels having a tea party, and so on). The art is fun, the images are bold, and there is an ample supply at hand for you to use. Now if only a design trend would come along that utilized a bunch of skull illustrations; then I would be set!

# chapter 13

# Piercing & Branding: Not Just for Livestock Anymore

Like tattoos, the art behind branding and piercing lends itself to contemporary computer art design themes, without any painful side effects! As I did in the tattoo chapter, I will take a tertiary look at using CorelDRAW to design actual body artwork using some advanced techniques that again solve some age-old problems unique to the genre. Body modification—it's not just for *National Geographic* anymore.

In the first example, we will look at how natural the unique, shiny, and geometric piercing paraphernalia fits into artwork as interesting design elements. Then we will take some of those pieces and pierce and recolor a photo to transform a traditional model into an alterna-model (you know, like the people working down at the espresso bar). Finally, we will see how to brand an image into another digital victim, using a combination of bitmap and transparency effects, for the purpose of creating a unique advertisement. Then, we will take a quick glimpse into generating artwork for real branding and scarification, only because there are some interesting design parameters that CorelDRAW is ready to conquer and because giving everyone the willies makes me laugh!

## Pierce Me

**COLOR STUDIO**

*Figure 13-1: Although it is pointless to use a computer to design piercing layouts, the hardware makes for interesting design elements.*

A huge trend at the moment is body piercing. One of my best friends has at last count fourteen piercings. I always ask him how he gets through airports—he just smiles and waggles the bolt in his tongue at me. That must make eating difficult. But I digress. Unlike tattoos or branding, there is very little need to sit down and design a piercing scheme on the computer. That would be a huge waste of time and technology! However, the implements themselves make very interesting secondary design elements (see Figure 13-1). In fact, I used some piercing hardware in the latest update of the Slimy Dog T-shirt logo. We will talk more about shiny metallic objects in Chapter 23, so here we will just discuss rendering these surgical steel implements of torture!

## Rounded Studs

Many piercing bolts have rounded ends, and once you create one, you can use it in many places. Here is how to create chrome bolts with rounded chrome ends:

1. First draw a rectangle and open the Fountain Fill dialog (F11); these objects are so small that it is difficult to use the Interactive Fountain fill to generate a custom color blend, so I prefer to use the Fountain Fill dialog. The key to the chrome look in what is essentially a black-and-white color scheme is to suggest a reflected landscape in shades of gray. In the Fountain Fill dialog, set the Color Blend option to Custom, starting with white and ending with 50 percent black. Now add a black color point in the dead center, and right next to it, add a white one. Two color points close together like this make for a harsh transition and, in this case, simulate a reflected horizon. To the right of this white color point, add another white one, which will make the sky brighter longer before fading into gray. Change the Angle value to 90 degrees and click OK (see Figure 13-2). This simple custom color blend was used to color virtually all of the chrome elements from this point on!

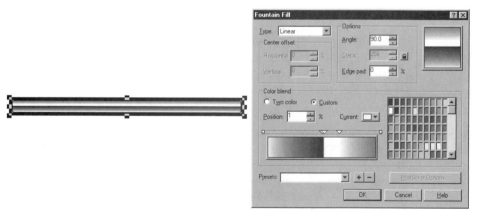

*Figure 13-2: Create a metallic look with a custom color blend.*

2. Use the Ellipse tool to draw a perfect circle at one end of the chrome bar. Hold down the Ctrl key to draw a perfect circle. Duplicate (+ key) the circle and move the duplicate to the other end. Shift-select both objects, and from the Edit menu, choose Copy Properties From. Now select Fill, click OK, and then click on the bar shape to steal the fills for the circles. Open the Fountain Fill dialog, change the Type value to Radial and the

Vertical value in the Center Offset section to 40 (or drag the center upward in the preview window). Click OK and this will bend the horizon and make the circles look round (see Figure 13-3).

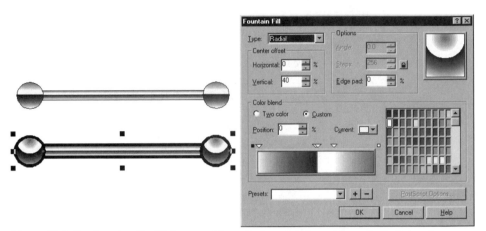

*Figure 13-3: By changing the fill borrowed from the bar piece from Linear to Radial and offsetting the center, the circles transform into chrome balls.*

To turn these into the mouse dumbbells you see poking through the eyebrows of hard-core piercing fans, simply draw rectangles at the ends instead of circles. Use the Shape tool to round the corners of the rectangles to the desired pointiness, and use the same custom color blend to make them chrome (see Figure 13-4).

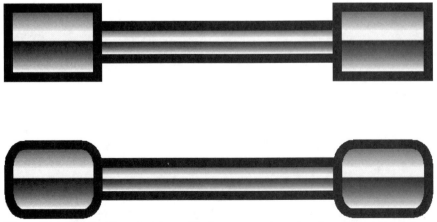

*Figure 13-4: Use the Shape tool to modify the corners of a rectangle and create smooth corners.*

## The Infamous Ring

If you haven't seen one of these, in someone's nose or elsewhere, then you live in a hole or don't frequent coffeehouses much! Here is how to make the curved ring with rounded ends:

1. Use the Ellipse tool to draw a perfect circle. Duplicate the circle and downsize it by dragging a corner sizing handle inward while holding down the Shift key to pull in all corners simultaneously. Select both circle shapes and combine them (Ctrl+L). Give this shape a radial fountain fill from 30% black to white. Use the Bezier tool to quickly draw a shape to open up the end of the ring. Now select the new object, choose Trim from the Arrange menu, click the Trim button, and then click on the ring shape. This will cut away the shape, leaving an open-ended ring (see Figure 13-5).

*Figure 13-5: Two circles are combined to create a solid ring shape. A shape drawn with the Bezier tool serves as a cutting template to trim away an area and leave the ring open.*

2. Use the Freehand tool to draw shapes to represent the reflected landscape. A curved metallic object like this reflects things in a very abstract way, so just take a guess at how things might look. Give these objects a radial fountain fill from black to 20 percent black for a subtle shading effect. Now use the Intersect roll-up from the Arrange menu to trim the shapes to inside the ring (see Figure 13-6). This creates objects within the ring shape that look like reflections of the surrounding environment.

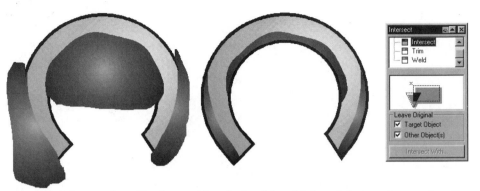

*Figure 13-6: Draw reflected landscape objects by hand for odd-shaped chrome pieces such as the ring. Use the Intersect roll-up to trim down the shapes to create objects on the inside of the ring.*

3. Position two of the rounded balls from the first example on the ends of the ring. Use additional circle shapes to get round white highlights. Draw a perfect circle with the Ellipse tool and duplicate it. Offset the duplicate to the right and down, and use the Trim function to create a rounded gleam object. Place the highlights on the ring to make it look more dazzling. To make the ring look like it is going through the paper, draw a white rectangle at the top center of the ring, and use an envelope (Ctrl+F7 or the Interactive Enveloping tool) to curve in the vertical edges. A custom color blend on this shape adds to the illusion (see Figure 13-7).

*Figure 13-7: Use circle shapes to generate gleam objects by trimming one from another. A white rectangle with an envelope makes the paper look pierced.*

These pieces of piercing hardware can be worked into your current art projects, especially for those clients wanting a little hard-core edge! The Blend function gives you a great way to scatter duplicates of the objects to create interesting patterns (see Figure 13-8).

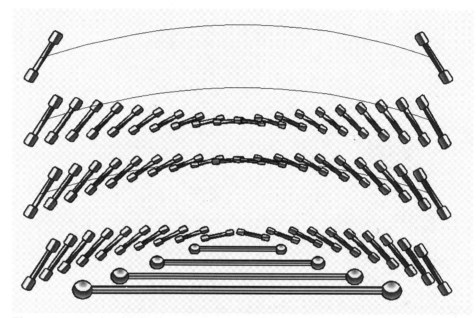

*Figure 13-8: Use the Blend roll-up to create interesting patterns out of the piercing hardware for use in your artwork.*

Another idea is to stretch the hardware to pierce through artwork as interesting design elements or as vehicles to divert and direct attention in a design to something else. In the color section, and also in the pierceme.cdr file in the \Chapt13\ subdirectory on the Companion CD-ROM, you can see how I used these piercing bits to create interesting patterns and also how I worked them into a corporate logo. The pattern looks very much like the display case at a piercing parlor I was in, with a lovely purple-haired girl trying to convince me to purchase some of the hardware. Hmm. Sorry, I'll stick to virtual piercing for now, which leads us into the next section!

## Metal Makeover

*Figure 13-9: Using the PowerClip function, you can pierce your favorite model, and then using options in PhotoPaint, you can even change the color of her hair and lipstick for a total virtual makeover!*

Sometimes you just have to use your powers for evil, as this graphic shows! The poor woman in Figure 13-9, another of the Women in Vogue models, will be so less than thrilled when she sees what I have done to her beautiful photo! This kind of image manipulation, surprisingly easy, makes you really wonder about those supermarket tabloid images. If you see the first lady with green hair and piercings, you probably shouldn't panic; just chalk it up to digital manipulation! Here is how to pierce and recolor a photograph:

1. Start with a scan of the intended victim and the pieces of piercing hardware from the last section (steal them out of the pierceme.cdr file to save time). Copy each piece of hardware into the new file and move into position over the area that you want to pierce.

2. First, to add a touch more realism, duplicate the object and use the Weld function to create a solid curve to use as a drop shadow element. The Interactive Drop shadow tool won't work for this, as it will just make a flat shadow that won't follow the contours of the face. Create a shadow shape and twist and distort it into shape so that it looks correct—in this case, drooping down the bridge of the nose. Little optical illusions like this just sell the effect even more. Remember that much of the image will be hidden, so just worry about creating a convincing look for the area that will actually show (see Figure 13-10).

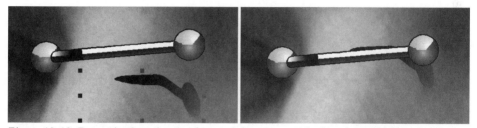

*Figure 13-10: Put a piercing piece in place and then create a shadow shape to add to the illusion of reality.*

3. Now with the Bezier or Freehand tool, create a shape that will hide the pieces where they are supposed to be inside of the face (yikes—got the willies again...). What you are doing is drawing a shape to outline the area that will be exposed; anything outside of the shape will be hidden. Where the hardware enters the skin, make it look rounded, and follow the contour of the bridge of the nose on the other side (see Figure 13-11).

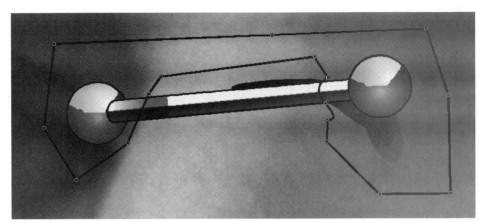

*Figure 13-11: Draw a shape to define the visible area of the piercing pieces.*

4. Now remove any outline or fill value from your shape, select all of the piercing pieces (including the shadows), and stuff everything into the shape with the PowerClip function (see Figure 13-12). Ouch! She's pierced!

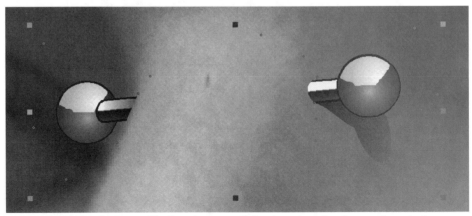

*Figure 13-12: Use the PowerClip function to stuff the pieces into the shape and create the piercing illusion.*

You can select and duplicate the PowerClip to create multiple pierces in the same area like I did for the nose. Repeat the process with the other piercing pieces to fill a face full of metal! This file is called face.cdr and is in the \Chapt13\ subdirectory on the Companion CD-ROM. Open it up to see how the PowerClips work to get the illusion started. For more realism than you can get in CorelDRAW alone, export the image as a bitmap and manipulate the file in PhotoPaint. The CorelDRAW objects just look a tad too crisp against the fuzzy photo. To make things look more natural, use the lasso or the irregular mask tool to select an area around the piercing artwork and make it look more natural with the Effects | Blur | Soften filter.

While you are still in PhotoPaint, tweak the colors in things like hair and lipstick. Double-click on the Paintbrush to open the Tool Settings dialog and then change the Paint option to Color. This will let you paint in a new color while still retaining the highlights and shading for a remarkably convincing effect! Sometimes this job can be really fun!

## Branded a Loser

*Figure 13-13: With the Envelope function and a few bitmap tricks, any object or person can be branded with a logo or slogan.*

While working with all of this branding artwork, it of course occurred to me that it was much more likely that the average sane person would simply want the *look* of a brand and not actually go under the iron themselves. Personally, I rely on accidental contact with stationary objects at speed as my method of choice for creating scar tissue (I call these incidents *accidents*). Anyway, here is how to use lenses and some other tricks to create a branded image:

1. Once again, find a clip-art volunteer for your branding antics. The bald guy in Figure 13-13 came off of the CorelDRAW clip-art CD, from the \photos\people directory. You can strike gold on that CD—this image was perfect for the project at hand!

2. Create your brand, keeping things fairly simplistic and in black and white. Real-world brands (like those used by cowboys) are simple designs fashioned out of bent metal. Technically, the images should be constructed like neon tubing, with a continuous, sweeping curve that creates letters that look like handwriting. For the sake of legibility and artistic license, I used a bold font with boxy serifs called Stymie. Draw two rectangles around the text, using the Shape tool to smooth the corners, and then combine everything into one curve. Place and size the brand where you want it.

3. Just like in the tattoo example from the previous chapter, you can use the Envelope function to distort the object to better fit the target body part (see Figure 13-14). In this case, the Envelope function, in the single arc mode, was perfect to give the artwork the right tweaks to fit right on the shiny dome of our digital model!

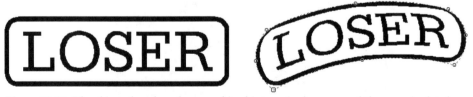

*Figure 13-14: The objects for a brand are combined into a single curve and then manipulated with the Envelope feature to distort the artwork to fit the contour of the target body part.*

4. At this stage, you can follow the same procedure you used in the tattoo technique in the last chapter, but I wanted something more gristly. Draw a box around the brand curve with no outline or fill. This will be our boundary box and also define the transparent background area for the next step. Select the brand curve and the boundary box, and from the

Bitmap menu, choose Convert to Bitmap. Now change the Color values to 254 shades of gray, 300 DPI resolution, and Transparent Background. Click OK to convert the vector art into a bitmap.

5. To get a fuzzier brand, choose Blur | Gaussian from the Bitmaps menu, and then bump the radius to your taste to fuzz the edges. Click OK to transform the bitmap. Notice that the background is still nice and transparent. CorelDRAW is your friend!

6. If you want a chunky look, use the Convert to Bitmap function to change the grayscale bitmap into a dithered, black-and-white bitmap, just like we did to get the monochrome tattoo look in the last chapter (see Figure 13-15). Make sure you *disable* the Transparent Background feature when you convert to the black-and-white bitmap; simply click the left mouse button on the no-fill onscreen color well to regain the transparent background.

*Figure 13-15: Using the Gaussian Blur filter, you can soften the edges of the brand or convert the image to a dithered black-and-white bitmap for a more gristly look.*

The results of this brand strike can be seen in the color section and in the loser.cdr in the \Chapt13\ directory on the Companion CD-ROM. I was going to add smoke and steam like in the hot image from Chapter 2, but it made things too busy. I like the simplicity of this image and a traditional split of the page. (Statistically, people prefer images that are weighted visually more on top, with the 60/40 split being the most effective way to lay out a page. See the first example in Chapter 19 for more.) With CorelDRAW's design power, I think it is easy to lose sight and overwork an image (as you saw in my piercing patterns example). Just remember these little hints (even if I sometimes forget): "More is not better," and "Just because it is cheap or free doesn't mean you need it." I tell my dad that last one all of the time, like when he brings home broken lawnmowers and things that sane people have thrown away. Now if I could only follow my own advice...

## Branding Anyone?

Along with tattooing, other body-implementation techniques, such as piercing and scarring, are on the rise. All fine and well, you think (or if you are like me, you think "OW!"), but what does this have to do with CorelDRAW? Well, you can design simple to complex designs for scarification just like you can for tattoos.

OK, I admit that only a few of you will actually use CorelDRAW to design a brand. So this section will be brief!

### Single-Shape Patterns

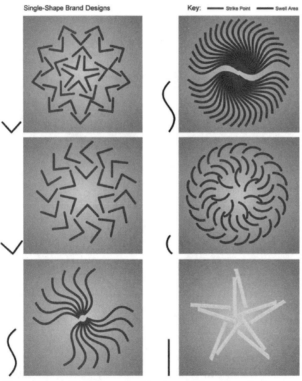

*Figure 13-16: Branding graphics have interesting design parameters. First of all, the image will expand beyond the original brand shape, from 200–400 times, depending on a person's skin type. You need to account for this swell area so you don't design a bad brand that can result in tissue death.*

Branding is the strangest thing I have ever designed for, and I have designed some pretty strange things in my day (women's underwear for example!). I have to say, I am not the least bit excited about having someone push a red-hot piece of surgical steel into me, but the design challenge is very unique. Custom brands are created by bending a sheet of metal into a unique shape by hand, and then one by one, striking the skin to create a pattern or design. The design is worked out ahead of time on a piece of paper, and the brands are bent to match the shapes needed. The paper image is traced on a carbonlike paper, and the image is then rubbed onto the skin of the proud recipient and used as a guide for each brand. The difficult part is creating a symmetrical or even-spaced pattern by hand using the simple shapes available in traditional branding. This, my friends, is where CorelDRAW comes into the picture, with computer-generated precision in creating patterns and even-spaced objects. Here is how to use the Blend function to create a pattern using a single object:

1. First, draw two lines in a crosshair for reference like we did for the daisy blend in Chapter 9. Now create a simplistic *V* brand shape with three clicks of the Bezier tool. Position the brand at the top center of the crosshair reference line. Double-click on the shape with the Pick tool to reveal the rotation arrows and the axis of rotation. Drag the axis to the center of the cross-hair and then duplicate (+ key) the shape. Drag-select both objects and open the Blend roll-up (Ctrl+B). Now change the number of steps to 8 and the Rotate value to 360 and click Apply. This will spin the duplicates around in a perfect circle, all perfectly spaced (see Figure 13-17).

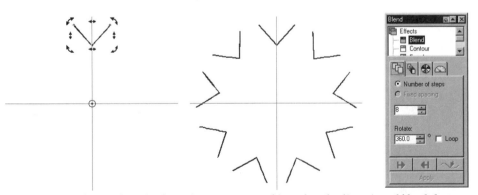

*Figure 13-17: Change the axis of rotation on a parent object; then duplicate it and blend the two using the Rotation feature of the Blend roll-up.*

2. Select and duplicate the control curve and move it down to the bottom of the center crosshair. Again change the axis of rotation to the center of the crosshair shape, and duplicate (+ key) the object. Now once again shift-select the objects and apply the 8-step, 360-degree blend (see Figure 13-18).

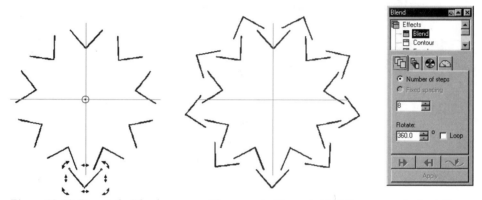

*Figure 13-18: Repeat the Blend process with a new starting point but the same axis of rotation for additional pattern shapes.*

3. Repeat this process a total of four times, each time moving the brand object but using the same axis of rotation. The final two blends both use four steps, but with the wedge pointing in opposite directions (see Figure 13-19).

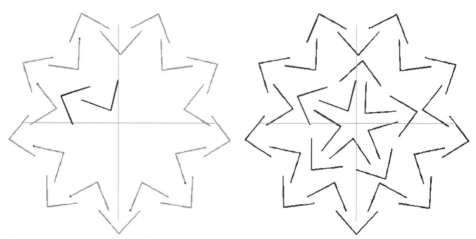

*Figure 13-19: Use the Blend function two more times with half the number of steps to create the inside shapes. The starting points for the last two blends are shown on the left, and the finished blends are shown on the right.*

4. Drag-select all of the pieces in your brand, duplicate (+ key) them, and send them to the back (Shift+PgDn). To get an idea of how the flesh will expand, assign a line weight several times that of the original. This is a process you'll learn with experience and also changes with each person, so just a good guess to estimate the swell area is the best you can do (see Figure 13-20).

*Figure 13-20: A thick-lined duplicate, shown here in gray, suggests how a brand will swell and eventually look.*

5. One problem with brands is that if during the first week of swelling, a part of the image becomes closed off, the skin there can lose its blood supply and die. This is bad. To avoid problems, parts of the design may be done at a second branding session several weeks later. So some pieces of your brand may be earmarked for a future session and left off of the primary branding artwork. The final artwork should be a crisp black-and-white image with a thin line to show the precise strike area and a dotted line to differentiate strikes for the second branding session, if any (see Figure 13-21).

*Figure 13-21: To avoid closing off sections of skin during the swelling process, pieces are left off for a second branding session in several weeks after the first has healed properly.*

The results of this patterning exercise can be seen in the file called smallbrnd.cdr in the \Chapt13\ subdirectory of the Companion CD-ROM. There are also other examples of essentially the same process, each one using a different simplistic shape to come up with a interesting design for branding. In the file bigbrand.cdr, objects are blended along a diamond shape for a different look. You can create unlimited variants using this simple technique. (For more on this type of design, see the "Spirograph" section of Chapter 17.) In the smallbrnd.cdr file, I tried to colorize the objects like a real brand. As everyone's skin pigment is different and reacts to the branding process differently, there is not a unique coloring scheme that is readily reconcilable as a brand. The kind of brand most people think of in terms of design or for use in an advertisement we saw in the previous section. Okay, you can relax now. We are through with the torture!

## Moving On

In this chapter we looked at how to incorporate the strange but unique look of piercing and branding into modern art applications. We saw how to use the piercing pieces and brands as design elements and also how to augment photos to give models pierces and brands. We also took a quick and frightening look at how to use CorelDRAW to design actual brands, again solving some odd design problems and revealing just how amazingly versatile CorelDRAW really is!

In the next chapter, we will continue to explore the sharp and potentially painful, only I promise to no longer give you the willies with talk of tattooing, branding, and scarring! The next chapter is full of dangerous sharp and pointy objects (like barbed wire and knives), but from here on out we limit the use to printed or onscreen graphics. So stop clenching your muscles and clear your mind of searing flesh and unholy pain, as the only way the graphics in the next chapter can hurt you is if you get a paper cut or drop the mouse on your foot! Let loose a sigh of relief and let's go.

▼ **Beyond f/x**

Once again we have a chapter full of really strange art and bizarre techniques. Although rooted in ancient cultures, these ideas are more contemporary than ever. The piercing hardware and tribal-looking art are right at home in my own logo design, and I am guessing you can find similar uses for these techniques. Imagine how freaky you could make a Web site look using metallic rings "piercing" the page as the navigation buttons. Branding also lends itself to many applications, like taking a company logo and "branding" people, cars, or even the traditional branding victim, livestock, with the image. Like my advertisement example, branding has interesting meanings that can be worked into an advertising campaign. So does piercing, with contemporary valentines just begging for a play on the "you pierce my heart" theme. If you still can't think of anything, perhaps you could find some work by contacting Pierce Bronson...

# chapter 14

# Barbed Wire & Other Pointy Things

Barbed wire and spiky shapes are popular in the tattoo community, and they also make for interesting design elements. As the alternative becomes more and more mainstream, even the most conservative design studios may find themselves searching for appropriate art elements for a client looking for a more hard-core image. These kinds of design elements look great, and they are extremely flexible and easy to create.

In this chapter, we will use the Blend function to create round wire and pointy tips, and we'll use the new CorelDRAW 8 Distortion tool to spike objects. We'll also find new solutions for images once rendered with the now-defunct PowerLine function. And we'll touch on metallic-shading concepts (elaborated on in Chapter 23) to colorize some dangerous oriental throwing stars. All in all, we'll have a fine selection of prickly and pointy things from which to choose!

## Danger Wire

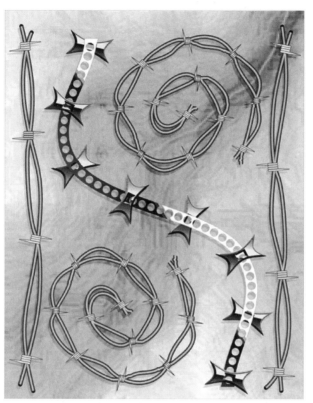

*Figure 14-1: Barbed and razor wire are flexible and popular, and have many uses in design.*

## Barbed Wire

For some reason, barbed wire just really appeals to me. It just suggests "danger" or "beware" and works right into designs for a more hard-core crowd. This market continues to grow, however, as things like cruiser bikes and gangster rap enter the mainstream. If nothing else, it makes for an interesting diversion from other, boring, border elements! Here is how to lay some barbed wire:

1. Use the Bezier tool to draw a sweeping horizontal line with soft waves in it. Now draw another line in an opposite sweeping motion and on top of this one to create the wire shape. Try to crisscross the lines at a distance that's close to uniform, as this is how real barbed wire works. You can

create barbed wire in virtually any shape or configuration, but this small piece of horizontal wire is a good place to start. Shift-select both lines and combine (Ctrl-L) them (see Figure 14-2).

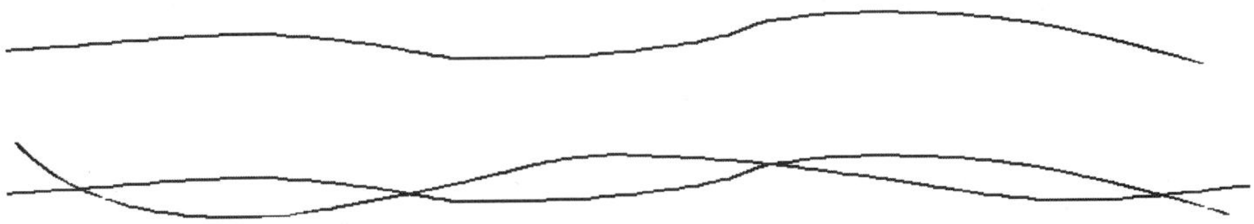

*Figure 14-2: Use the Bezier tool to create two overlapping lines in the shape of your choice.*

2. Select the wire shape and give it a fat black .111-inch outline. Now duplicate it and give the duplicate a thin white hairline outline. Drag-select both stacked pieces and open the Blend roll-up (Ctrl+B). Click Apply to blend the two pieces into a round wire shape. Notice that the objects do not look like two separate wires at the points where they cross, and that is because we combined the lines into one shape. If you want individual wires, don't combine them (see Figure 14-3).

*Figure 14-3: Blend a fat black line into a thin white one to create a rounded wire.*

3. Draw a rectangle and round out the ends by dragging a corner node with the Shape tool. Duplicate (+ key) this shape and convert it to curves (Ctrl+Q). With the Shape tool, drag the bottom center node down. Now drag-select all of the nodes in the lower half of the object, and from the Node Edit roll-up (Ctrl+F10), click the To Line button. This will make a spiky end on one of the twisted wire shapes. Now duplicate the original object two more times and the spike one more time. Arrange the objects to look like the twisted, spiked barbed wire hub. Drag-select all of the objects and open the Fountain Fill dialog (F11). Create a linear custom color blend with a white center and black edges to suggest a shaded round cylinder. Click OK to finish the barb (see Figure 14-4).

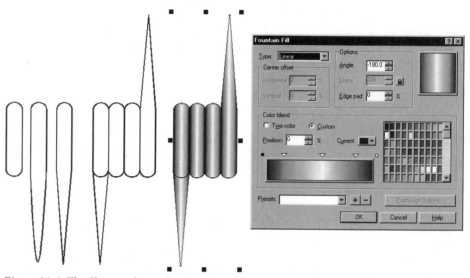

*Figure 14-4: The Shape tool transforms a rectangle into a rounded wire object and then into a sharp barb. Finally, a custom color blend gives the shapes a round appearance.*

4. Drag-select and group (Ctrl+G) the barb shapes. Duplicate the barb group and place the duplicates at each point where your wire blend crisscrosses. Double-click on the barb group to reveal the rotation arrows and spin each barb slightly to orient it to the wires below (see Figure 14-5).

*Figure 14-5: Place the barb groups at the points where the wires crisscross to finish the look.*

You can create barbed wire in virtually any shape. Here is how to create a barbed spiral:

1. Click and hold the Polygon tool to open the flyout; then select the Spiral tool. Drag the Spiral tool onscreen to create a spiral (right-click over the spiral tool to change the properties). Now place a barb group at each end of the spiral, shift-select both, and open the Blend roll-up. Blend the barbs along the path to space them out evenly (see Figure 14-6).

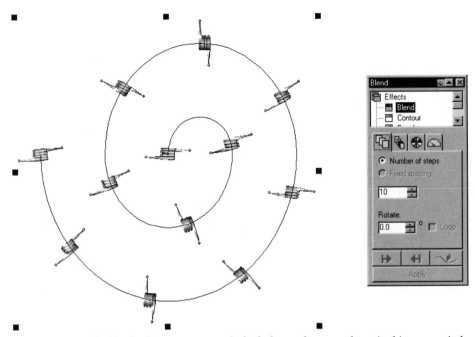

*Figure 14-6: Use the Blend roll-up to space out the barb shapes along any shape, in this case a spiral.*

2. Use the Freehand tool to draw in the wire shapes, crisscrossing at each barb point. Use the Shape tool to auto-reduce the nodes and to smooth out and clean up the lines (see Figure 14-7).

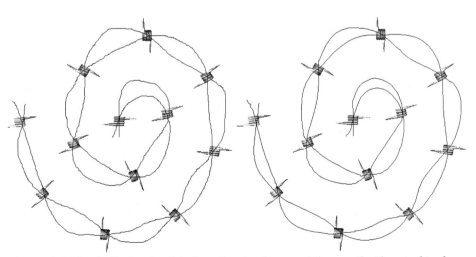

*Figure 14-7: Use the Freehand tool to draw the wire shapes and then use the Shape tool to clean up the freehand-drawn lines. The blend-spaced barbs act as guidelines for drawing the wire.*

3. Now duplicate and blend the wire shapes as before. Send wires to the back (Shift+PgDn) and you are done!

## Razor Wire

Razor wire is usually a solid strand of metallic tape stamped with a razor shape every few inches. This is kind of bland, so I created a more spacey-looking razor wire with more defined individual razors welded to the tape. Here is how to make my idealized razor wire:

1. Draw a rectangle, duplicate it, and downsize the duplicate. On the large original, add a straight line envelope from the Envelope roll-up (Ctrl+F7). With the Shape tool, drag the top-center node of the envelope inward while holding down both the Ctrl and Shift keys. This will move all of the center nodes inward simultaneously, creating a star shape. Click Apply to distort the shape (see Figure 14-8).

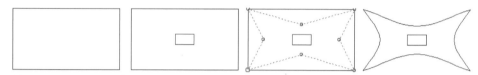

*Figure 14-8: A rectangle becomes a razor blade with the help of a straight line envelope.*

2. Shift-select both objects and combine (Ctrl+L) them. Now borrow the custom color blend from the piercing pieces in the previous chapter or create a new one with the same color scheme (see Figure 14-9).

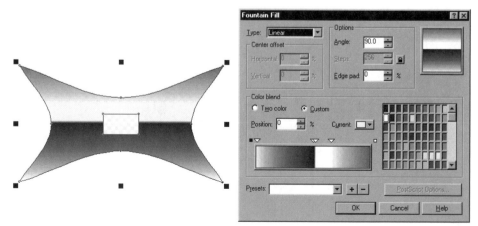

*Figure 14-9: Use a custom color blend to give the razor piece a metallic look.*

3. To give the razor a beveled edge, use the Extrude roll-up (Ctrl+E). From the Lighting page, enable a light source at the top right. From the Bevel page, enable the Use Bevel option and also check the Show Bevel Only check box. Now change the Bevel depth to .05 inches and click Apply. Because the default option on the Fill Color page is Use Object Fill, the resulting pieces all have the custom color blend of the original, only shaded according to the light source setting. The result is a polished-looking razor (see Figure 14-10).

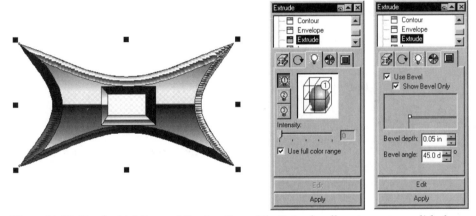

*Figure 14-10: Use the Lighting and Bevel options of the Extrude roll-up to create a polished razor object.*

4. Separate the extrude group and then group the objects. Draw a smooth *s* shape with the Bezier tool. Select and duplicate (+) the razor group and place a duplicate at each end of the *s* curve. Select both, open the Blend roll-up, and blend the two objects along the curve (see Figure 14-11).

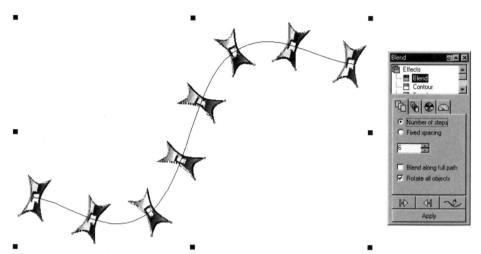

*Figure 14-11: Use the Blend roll-up to spread razors along any curve, in this case, an s shape drawn with the Bezier tool.*

5. Draw a small circle shape in one of the parent razor groups. Duplicate it and move the duplicate to the razor shape at the far end of the blend. Now create a many-stepped blend along the same path as the razor shape (see Figure 14-12).

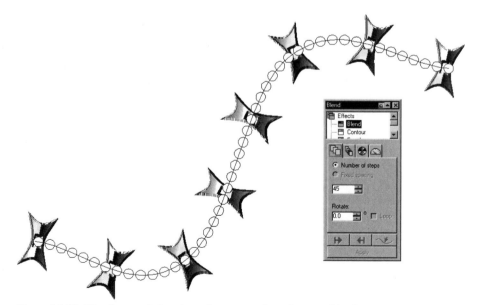

*Figure 14-12: Blend some circles along the same path as the razor blend.*

6. Select the circle blend, use the Arrange I Separate option, and then use the Arrange I Ungroup All option. Zoom in, and while holding down the Shift key, click on the blend path to delete it. Now combine (Ctrl+L) all of the circle objects into one curve. Select the blend curve again and duplicate it (it is still the control curve for the razor shapes). With a free curve selected, open the Contour roll-up. Now create a single-step outside contour with an offset to be just larger than the circle shapes (see Figure 14-13).

*Figure 14-13: Use the Contour roll-up to create a long snaking rectangle just larger than the circle shapes (shown here in Wireframe view).*

7. Select the contour and use the Arrange I Separate, and then Arrange I Ungroup All commands to separate the objects. Now select just the contour shape, shift-select the circle shapes, and combine (Ctrl+L) them. This will create the winding metal tape used to connect the prickly razor objects. Use the Copy Properties From (Ctrl+Shift+A) option from the Edit menu to copy the fill from one of the razors to the connecting ribbon. To alternate the razors front/back, first select the blend and free each razor object from the blend with the Arrange I Separate and Ungroup (Ctrl+U) commands. Now shift-select every other razor shape, then bring them to the front (Shift+PgUp). See Figure 14-14.

*Figure 14-14: Combine the Contour shape made from the control curve with the blend of circles on the same curve to create a winding metal tape to connect the razor objects.*

These barbed wire examples can be seen in the color section or in the file called barbed.cdr found in the \Chapt14\ subdirectory on the Companion CD-ROM. Now all you have to do is create your own wire or metal tape shapes, steal one of the barbs or razors from the CD-ROM, and you are ready to run danger-wire around anything you desire.

## Tribes & Knives

*Figure 14-15: S curves are combined into tribal-looking design shapes that have complex patterns in which only a few unique pieces are used. The dimensional pieces are created with the same technique as the tentacles in Chapter 6; the only difference is the addition of a second Blend function. The clip-art knife is adorned with fresh blood to create a creepy mood.*

Although it may be a bit of a stretch, the abstract, almost tribal-looking shapes in Figure 14-15 fit into the pointy theme. The PowerLine function is now gone (weep, moan), but there are still several ways to get these kinds of shapes. First, I'll cover a rather dull method of combining line pairs; then I'll describe an exciting use of the tentacle blend technique from Chapter 6. This technique lets you create multistage blends that in this case taper off into nice pointy ends on two sides. Also found here, rather mysteriously and suspiciously, is a knife covered in blood! Yikes! The Intersection function is used to create this incriminating item.

## Tribal Vines

If you want to create a very intricate design using these intricate shapes, I highly recommend that you use an earlier version of CorelDRAW that supports the PowerLine function. This feature makes it really easy—first you draw a sweeping line, and then you apply the scallop shape as a Wedge option from the PowerLine roll-up. PowerLine vines allow for smoother curves and more automation. The Natural Pen tool, which replaces PowerLines, sucks pond water unless you have a steady hand and a pressure-sensitive graphics tablet. I have neither, so I open CorelDRAW 5, make my PowerLines, and then import them into the latest version of CorelDRAW to take advantage of the new features. However, since not everyone has CorelDRAW 5, here is how to make sweeping vines without PowerLines:

1. First of all, we need some nice symmetrical waves in a line. Draw a straight line with the Bezier tool (hold the Ctrl key to constrain to a perfect horizontal line). Now switch to the Shape tool, drag-select the two nodes on the line, and open the Node Edit roll-up (Ctrl+F10) or use the Shape tool options on the Property Bar. Click the Add Nodes button to add a node exactly at the midpoint between the two. Click the Add Node button again and then click it once more to create a line with nine nodes on it. Select every other node (hold down the Shift key and click a node) and then drag the last node selected upward. This creates a sawtooth curve. Drag-select all of the nodes and then click the To Curve option on either the Node Edit roll-up or the Property Bar. Next click the Symmetrical button. This will change the waves in the line from pointy to perfectly smooth. Drag-select all of the nodes and click the Add Nodes button one last time (see Figure 14-16).

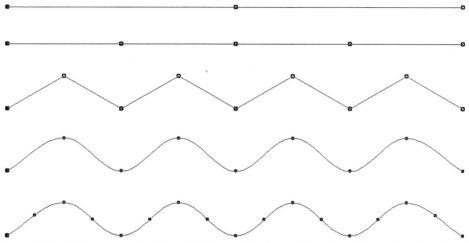

*Figure 14-16: The Shape tool adds perfectly spaced nodes to a line; the nodes can then be selected and moved to form a sawtooth pattern. These spikes are made into nice waves with the To Curve and Symmetrical options.*

2. We add nodes in the last step to facilitate breaking up the line into three shapes. With the Shape tool, select the starting and ending points along the line for the unique vine shapes that you want. Then click the Break Curve button on the Property Bar or roll-up to separate the selected nodes. Now break apart (Ctrl+K) the line into five separate shapes. Select and delete the extra pieces on each end, leaving three curve shapes (see Figure 14-17).

*Figure 14-17: Use the Break Curve option to separate nodes. Use the Break Apart command to separate the broken curve into individual objects.*

3. Drag-select and duplicate the three line shapes and move the duplicates down. Drag-select the line pairs, and one by one, combine them (Ctrl+L). With the Shape tool, drag-select the end nodes of the combined line pairs and click the Join Two Nodes button. Repeat this to join all of the ends on the line pairs (see Figure 14-18).

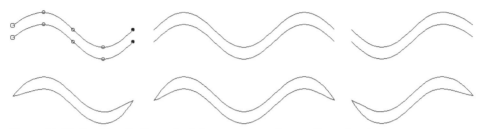

*Figure 14-18: Combine the line pairs into one curve and merge the end nodes.*

4. Finally, fine-tune the shapes into the smooth sweeping vine curves that we want. Use the Shape tool to eliminate nodes in order to reduce the curves down to their simplest form; in other words, with the smoothest curves. This takes a bit of manual massaging, but the results are just what we are looking for. Give the final shapes a black fill and red .023-inch outline (see Figure 14-19).

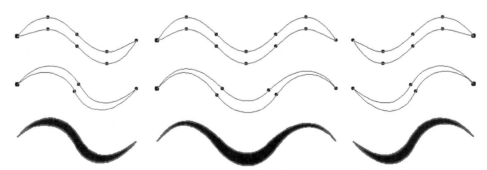

*Figure 14-19: Use the Shape tool to fine-tune the vine objects into sweeping, fluid curves.*

5. These three shapes (really only two, as the left is a mirror of the right) are duplicated and arranged to create the design. Select the *S* vine and open the Scale & Mirror roll-up (Ctrl+F9). Click the Horizontal Mirror button and then click the Apply to Duplicate button. This will create a pattern shape that you can use throughout a design (see Figure 14-20).

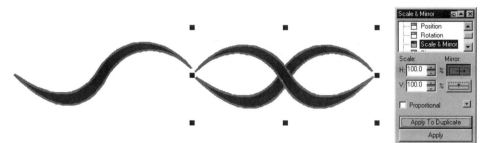

Figure 14-20: The Scale & Mirror roll-up duplicates and flips objects in one step.

6. Duplicate, flip, and arrange the objects to create a border in sections. Once you finish a corner, you can duplicate and flip-flop it for the other corner. Once you finish the top, you can duplicate and flip it for the bottom. It is quick and easy to turn a simple shape into a cool pattern and turn the pattern into a border (see Figure 14-21).

Figure 14-21: Duplicate groups of the objects to create an intricate pattern.

In no time, you can finish a border design with just these two basic shapes. Use the Send to Front (Shift+PgUp) command to vary how the shapes interact and also to break up the mirrored look in the final image. The finished border can be seen in the color section and also in the file called tribal.cdr in the \Chapt14\ subdirectory on the Companion CD-ROM. The image includes rounded vines and the bloody knife, which we will now also examine.

CD-ROM

## Techno Tribal

I really hate having to node-edit a shape to look smooth like we did in the previous example. It is tedious, and without the perfection of computer calculation, it is subject to human error and strange shapes. In my quest to find an automated technique to replace that lost with PowerLines, I came across this variant for 3D-looking vine shapes. I used the tentacle shading from Chapter 6 and a two-stage blend technique. Here is how to grow this vine:

1. Start with one of the nice symmetrical S-shaped lines. Now draw a circle in the center of the line and fill it with a custom color blend in the style outlined in Chapter 6. Give it no outline. Duplicate (+ key) the circle and downsize the duplicate until it is almost an invisible, tiny dot. Move this tiny dot to the far left end of the curve. Duplicate this small circle again and move to the right end of the curve (see Figure 14-22).

*Figure 14-22: A circle filled with a custom color blend is duplicated and downsized to become tiny points on the end of a curvy line.*

2. Select the center circle and bring To Front (Shift+PgUp). Now select the right small circle and bring To Front as well (Shift+PgUp). This places the pieces in the correct orientation for the blending process. Select the left small circle, shift-select the center circle, open the Blend roll-up, and click Apply. (This 20-step blend is totally wrong, but you have to get the blend started in order to assign a path.) Click the Path button on the Blend roll-up and then click on the S curve. Change the number of steps to 200 and click Apply again (see Figure 14-23).

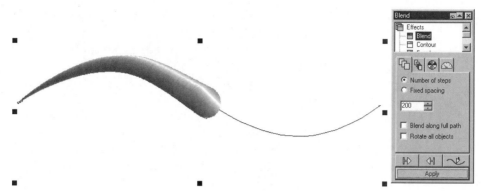

*Figure 14-23: Use the Blend Along Full Path feature, as is shown in the figure.*

3. Now select the center circle again (which is now a control curve in the first blend) and shift-select the small circle on the right. Click Apply on the Blend roll-up and then click the Path button, the New Path button, the control curve, and then Apply once more. That's it, you have a 3D vine (see Figure 14-24).

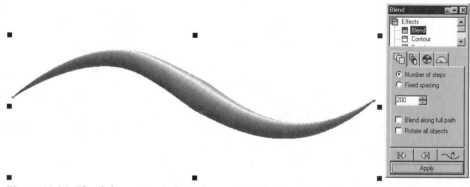

*Figure 14-24: Blend the center circle to the small duplicate on the other end to finish off the vine shape.*

**TIP** *Blend objects, especially those with many steps, are difficult to work with in the Normal and even the Wireframe views. In the Simple Wireframe view, however, only the parent shapes and control paths are shown. This makes selecting a control curve and changing its attributes (such as size or color) much easier.*

4. Select the vine blend and open the Scale & Mirror roll-up again (Alt+F9). Enable the Horizontal Mirror option and click Apply to Duplicate to create a flip-flopped version of the original. This looks okay, but it can result in flip-flopping the gleam and shadow effects too (here things still look pretty close; see Figure 14-25). For an interesting variant, recolor the front blend with the same settings as the back blend. With the duplicate still selected, choose Copy Properties From from the Edit menu and then borrow the fill from the original blend. This will make the shadows and highlights correct, with a reverse build order (the object closest to you in the original is on the right; in the duplicate, it is on the left.)

*Figure 14-25: Flip-flopping the original with the Scale & Mirror roll-up also flips and reverses the blend order. Both objects are given the same fill with the Copy Properties From option, but with reversed blend-orders they look different (on right).*

Duplicate and arrange these two compound blend shapes as before to make an interesting border pattern. Instead of a custom color blend, you could also just use a solid color to get a flat vine look. Use the fat-outline trick from Chapter 6 if you want a colored outline (see Figure 14-26).

*Figure 14-26: Instead of using the custom color blends to add depth, you can use the blend trick to create traditionally colored vines.*

## Bloody Knife

I used this image in the boyfriend piece back in Chapter 8, and I promised to explain it, so here it is! It's really just clip art with a few of my own special tweaks and additions. Here is how to make the clip-art knife bloody:

1. Open the bayonet.cdr file found in the \clipart\weapons\directory on the CorelDRAW clip-art CD-ROM. With all the objects selected, choose Ungroup All from the Arrange menu so you can work with the individual pieces in the clip art. Now with the Freehand tool, draw a blob shape, which will become the blood stain on the blade.

2. With the blob shape selected, open the Intersect roll-up from the Arrange menu. Click Intersect With and then click the blade object on the knife. This will stain the blade with blood when you color it red.

3. To make clip art seem more lifelike, remove black outlines from the objects. Simply select an outlined object and then right-click the onscreen no fill well. This looks more convincing because real-life objects are almost never really outlined. Add any gleams or wet-looking details to the blood to finish off the knife. I also added a drop shadow by using a simplified version of the knife objects and blending a gray copy to a white one (see Figure 14-27).

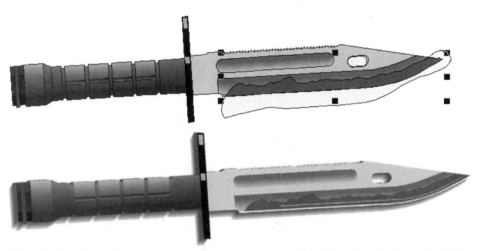

*Figure 14-27: Use the Intersection command to constrain a blob of blood within the knife blade. Remove outlines to add realism and add gleams and a shadow for depth.*

These last three samples are grouped together in the same tribal.cdr file, found in the \Chapt14\ subdirectory on the Companion CD. Load and examine this file if you have any questions on how things were assembled. Be forewarned that this file with the many 3D vine objects (each contains 404 objects) takes a while to load and render. Experiment with the blended vine shapes, and try the technique on other, more complex control curves. Also go beg the Corel corporation to return the PowerLines.

## Ninja Stars

*Figure 14-28: All kinds of dangerous-looking throwing stars can be made using CorelDRAW's versatile rendering options.*

I think every kid who took metal shop in school ended up making a dangerous but simplified version of the metal throwing star, made famous by cheesy Kung-Fu movies. With CorelDRAW, you can make even more varieties of these stars, from traditional to totally fantastical! You can use prefab objects off of the Symbols roll-up, design interesting variants using the Polygon tool, or just plain go nuts with the Interactive Distortion tool! Here is how to make some dangerous ninja stars.

1. The easiest way to create a star shape is to use one that already exists! Open the Symbols *docker* (Ctrl+F11) and select the Stars1 Symbols Library. Use the elevator arrows to scroll down until you find the shape you like; then drag it to the desktop. This library contains a shape that is very much like a traditional throwing star (on the right in Figure 14-29) as well as other suitable star shapes.

*Figure 14-29: Use the Symbols roll-up to find shapes for the throwing stars.*

2. Duplicate and downsize the first star shape and combine it with the original to create a cutout in the center. Now apply the reflected horizon custom color blend borrowed from the razor wire to give the pieces a shiny metallic look.

3. You can use the Bevel function from the Extrude roll-up to give a shiny sharp edge to these stars in the same way we created the razor wire. Since you already know that trick, let's try another one to add an edge. First, select a star shape and open the Contour roll-up (Ctrl+F9). Enable the Inside option, change the Offset value to .04 and the Step value to 1, and click Apply. This will create an inside bevel with the same fill as the parent shape (see Figure 14-30).

*Figure 14-30: Use the Contour roll-up to create an inside set of shapes for new shading options.*

4. To separate all of the objects, use the Arrange | Separate command on the contour groups and then select the outside, original objects. To create an interesting abstract reflection in the back shape, create a new custom color blend from the Fountain Fill dialog (F11). Use a light-to-dark repeat pattern and then change the angle to 128 degrees. Click OK to fill the back shape (see Figure 14-31).

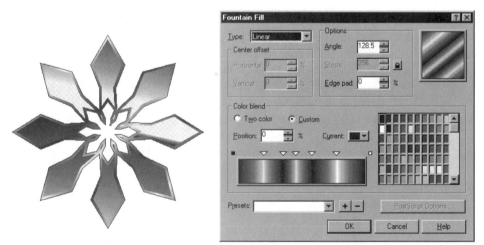

*Figure 14-31: Fill the back shape with a custom color blend to suggest random reflections and highlights.*

That's it! You can use the Contour roll-up to create some interesting metallic looks, which we will explore in more detail in Chapter 23. The rest of the star shapes in this chapter use the contour effect along with the custom color blend to create the look of different metals. The different color schemes can be seen in the ninja.cdr file found in the \Chapt14\ subdirectory on the Companion CD-ROM, and also in the color section of this book. Open the file and examine the different colors used to create the white, yellow, pink, and bluish metal varieties. Now let's look at more star options.

The Polygon tool and the Blend function can also create unique star shapes. Here's how:

1. Select the Polygon tool and change the options on the Property Bar to draw stars. Click the Polygon/Star button to toggle between the two options and change the number of points to your liking (I used six). Drag to create a star. If the center of the star is open, you need to enable the Polygon as Star option, which is available from the Options menu (Ctrl+J) under the Toolbox tab. Once this option is set, you can create a broad range of star shapes by using the Sharpness setting on the Toolbox page or the Shape tool to drag an inside point of the star outward or inward. To change the look even more, use the Shape tool to drag a point of the star in other directions, which will move all the other points in unison (see Figure 14-32).

*Figure 14-32: Use the Polygon tool to create star shapes. Modify the star shapes further with the Shape tool.*

**TIP** *To quickly get to the options dialog for a desired tool, use the right mouse button. Right-click over the tool and choose the Properties option from the pop-up menu. You can then change the options for that specific tool and click OK to enable them immediately.*

2. For another even more dangerous star shape, use the Blend roll-up. First, draw a circle with the Ellipse tool. Duplicate it and move the duplicate down. Now use the Trim function from the Arrange menu to create a moon-sliver shape. This will become a sharp blade in the star object. Double-click on the blade to reveal the axis of rotation and move the axis down and to the right. Duplicate this blade, drag-select both, and open the Blend roll-up. Now change the Rotation value to 360 and the Number of Steps value to 6 and click OK (see Figure 14-33). Wow, that looks pretty dangerous!

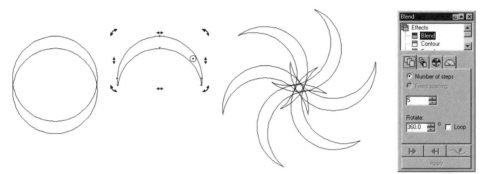

Figure 14-33: Use the Trim function to create a blade from circle shapes. Then use the Blend roll-up to spin the blades into a star.

3. With the blend shape selected, separate everything with the Arrange | Separate and Arrange | Ungroup All commands. Now select and delete one of the control curves, which are stacked on top of each other and will not weld correctly if you don't delete one of them. Drag-select all of the pieces, and weld them into one. With the pieces as one object, you can use the contour and custom color blend scheme to create a shiny metallic look for these stars as well (see Figure 14-34).

*Figure 14-34: Weld the blend pieces into one object and use the Contour roll-up and custom color blends as before to color the objects with a metallic sheen.*

The final method for creating sharp objects involves the new CorelDRAW 8 Interactive Distortion tool. Here is how to use this function to create scary sharp star objects:

1. Draw a perfect circle using the Ellipse tool. Select the Distortion tool and drag from the center of the circle out. This will enable a distortion for the object. Now click the Push and Pull Effect button on the Property Bar and change Distortion Amplitude value to –53. This should result in a clover leaf object (see Figure 14-35).

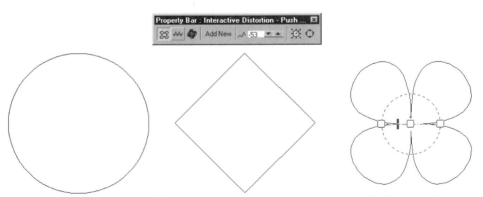

*Figure 14-35: The Interactive Distortion tool changes a circle into a clover leaf by using the push and pull effect.*

2. Duplicate (+ key) the clover leaf object and set it aside for a future step. Now select the original and select the Distortion tool again. Click the Convert to Curves button on the Property bar. Now increase the Zipper Distortion Amplitude and Zipper Distortion Frequency values (or experiment with the interactive slider) to create a very unique spiky object (see Figure 14-36).

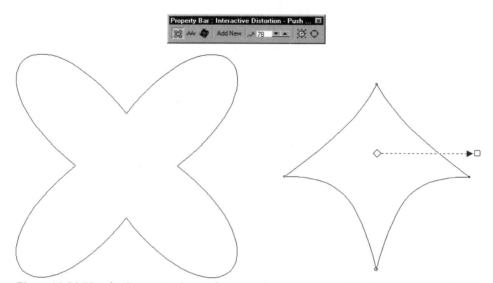

*Figure 14-36: Use the Convert to Curves button to freeze a current distortion so you can then assign a new one.*

3. Select the duplicate of the clover leaf object and again click the Convert to Curves option on the Property Bar. Now toggle to the Zipper effect and change the Amplitude and Frequency values (or play with the interactive slider again) to create any number of toothed objects. Experiment with the option buttons on the Property Bar, especially the Smooth Distortion and Local Distortion buttons (see Figure 14-37).

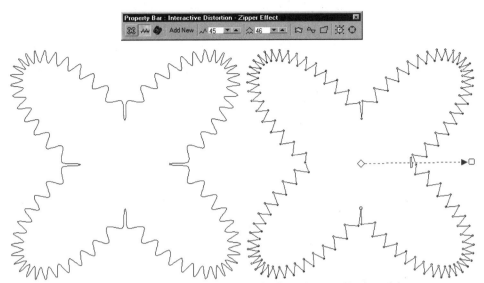

*Figure 14-37: The Zipper Distortion tool places teeth of varying amplitude and frequency around your object.*

4. Select the objects and convert them to curves (Ctrl+Q). Now you can node-edit the objects with the Shape tool to add or modify the spikes. When you are happy with the shape, you can use the same contour and custom color blend technique from the previous section to give them a metallic look.

The two zipper-star shapes we just created with the Distortion tool are also in the ninja.cdr file, however the distortions have been frozen with the Convert to Curves option. You will have to create your own live distortion object in order to play with the settings on the Property Bar. This tool is a bit unpredictable, especially when you use the interactive interface instead of keying in values on the Property Bar. It takes a little experimenting to get to a point where the results don't seem totally random.

## Moving On

In this chapter, we covered a lot of ground exploring sharp pointy objects. Starting with barbed and razor wire, moving on to tribal vine shapes, and finishing with dangerous throwing stars, we explored many ways to create nasty pointy things. I introduced the techniques in this chapter to open your eyes to some of the many ways you can trick and finagle your way to the desired result. Sometimes you have to make the best of what you have, as with the blend trick to replace PowerLines. In other cases, new features such as the Distortion tool open new doors and offer intriguing possibilities. Whatever the case, just don't hesitate to mix and match ideas and experiment with the tools at hand. For example, not only can you use the Bevel function to give a ninja star the same metallic look you gave the razor wire, but you can also spin it around using the 3D Rotation page on the Blend roll-up. The potential is only limited by your imagination.

In the next chapter, we will develop the techniques introduced in the barbed/razor wire section even further. Using the Blend function, we will create chains, ropes, and other patterns. It is amazing what you can do with just a few simple shapes, and the next chapter will further convince you of this! So prepare yourself for some digital bondage as we explore chains and ropes.

### ▼ Beyond f/x

Pointy objects and sharp things can give a design a dark, edgy mood. As a framing element, barbed and razor wire is perfect for ads for products like motorcycle components, leather goods, or alternative music. You can even create a spoof ad with these hard-core graphics for decidedly soft-core products or create tension between really sharp and dangerous objects and delicate, fragile ones (razors and balloons, barbed wire and babies). It's hard to ignore the uneasy feeling of impending disaster with one of these mismatches; they work great in advertising to get and hold attention. Of course, telephone calls from angry mothers might be a nasty side effect, but as they say in show business: There is no such thing as bad publicity.

Pointy objects and sharp things can also make interesting button shapes or page dividers for a dangerous Web design. Spinning razor-star buttons would be interesting and original, and not difficult to animate. (If you do rotate a star for an animation, reset the fill so the horizon line stays level. This makes for a more convincing metallic-reflection illusion.)

Logos and promotional graphics for companies can also benefit from the occasional danger theme to gain the edge over the competition. You really have a lot of options here; just be careful not to cut yourself on all those pointy things, and make sure your tetanus shots are up to date!

# chapter 15

# Chains, Ropes & Links

In the last chapter we used the Blend roll-up to space barbs and razors evenly along a curve. In this chapter, we will use the same idea, but we'll increase the number of steps to create a connecting row of objects. This technique is useful in the creation of custom chain or rope shapes. The great thing about this technique is that there are few limitations to the shape of the curve that you can run the chain or rope links along, resulting in a variety of handy applications. You could easily create a signature or any other unique shape in chain or rope (see Figure 15-1).

Rope and chain make great borders, but they aren't limited to that purpose. The CorelDRAW clip-art disk has plenty of pieces of rope and even chain in ordinary round or rectangular configurations, so it is our task to come up with a solution for any strange shape that you can imagine. This is made possible with the Blend roll-up and the ability to blend along a curve. The computer-accurate spacing makes things like connecting chain links possible, but the same procedure could work with any shape or image (you could just as easily connect a series of plastic monkeys!). These kinds of designs were just too tedious to do by hand, but with a little computer assistance, heck, anything is possible!

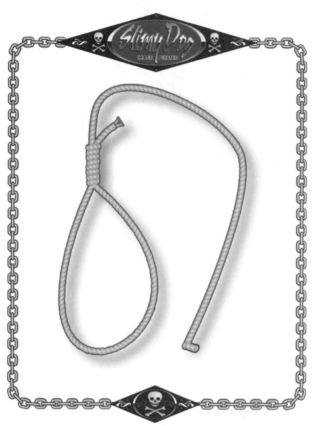

*Figure 15-1: Blending objects along a path can result in chains or rope in virtually any shape imaginable.*

## Chains

Chains are one of those design elements that pop up here and there, in everything from nautical images to dog leashes. From an artistic perspective, they are an interesting and flexible design element. You can use them as a primary element, as a secondary border design, and with ads riddled with "weak link" slogans; sooner or later you will find yourself looking to hook up with some links. Here is how to create a row of connected chain links along virtually any path:

1. Simplified chains are made up of two variations of links: those viewed from the top and those viewed from the side. Use the Rectangle tool to draw a link shape, rounding the corners with the Shape tool. Give this

object a fat black .075-inch outline and no fill. Duplicate the shape (+ key), and give the duplicate a thin white hairline. Drag-select the two, open the Blend roll-up (Ctrl+B), and click Apply to create a round-looking link object. Repeat the process for the side link, only with a single line. Be sure to enable the rounded line caps from the Outline Pen dialog (F12) to create the hot dog shape (see Figure 15-2).

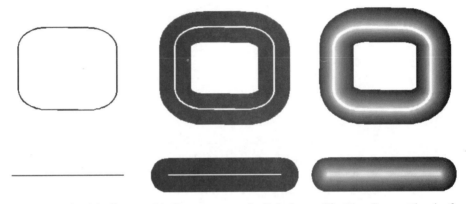

*Figure 15-2: Blend fat lines to thin lines to create the link shapes. The Line Caps setting in the Outline Pen dialog changes the ends of heavy line shapes from pointy to square, or in this case, round.*

2. Once you have created your link shapes, you need to freeze the blends in them. You can not blend blends, but you can blend benign groups of objects. Select a link blend, choose Arrange I Separate, then choose Arrange I Ungroup All, and then group (Ctrl+G) everything again. This will disable the blends and allow you to blend the link shapes.

3. Now draw a shape that you would like to run the links along. You can use any shape, but for this example we will use a squiggly line (closed shapes are okay, but one set of links will need to have a duplicate of the closed shape broken open to work right). Once you have the main shape, place a duplicate of the top link on each end. Now duplicate the shape, and move it below the original. Set a duplicate of the side links at each end of the curve, only move them in so they align correctly with the top links. Now with the Shape tool, double-click on the blend curve object at the mid-point of the side links to add a node on each end; then delete the original end nodes. This will shorten the control curve for the side links one half of the link length on each end, which makes the blending process work right (see Figure 15-3).

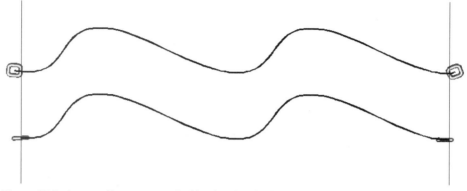

*Figure 15-3: A curvy line serves as the blend path, which needs to be slightly shorter for the second set of links.*

4. Shift-select the two top links, open the Blend roll-up, and click Apply. Now click the New Path button, click on the curvy shape, enable the Rotate All Objects option, and then click Apply again. Repeat the process for the side links, decreasing the number of steps by two (see Figure 15-4).

5. Now align the two blend groups to finish up the chain. If things don't align just right, increase or decrease the steps in each blend until they do. You may need to select the control links in each blend and move or rotate them to get things to line up right. Typically, the smaller blend (in this case the side links) use one less step then the larger link blend. It takes a little tweaking, but since CorelDRAW is doing all the work when you add or delete steps in the blend, you can't really complain! Figure 15-5 shows the results of this step.

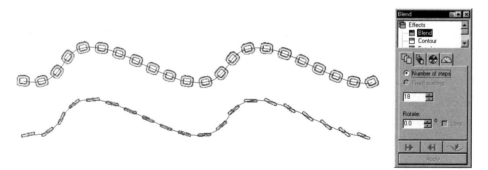

*Figure 15-4: Use the Blend roll-up and the New Path option to place the duplicates along the desired path.*

*Figure 15-5: Align the top and side link blends to result in a unique chain shape following the contour of your choice.*

6. If some of the links just don't look right, you can arrange and separate the blend (choose Arrange | Separate) and then ungroup (Ctrl+U) the objects to manually fine-tune them. This process is not as painful as it sounds, as each line is usually in the right place or real close, so you only need to move or rotate a few to get things right.

That's about it! I used the links as a border around the page of a promotional flyer, which can be seen in the color section and also in the file pirates.cdr in the \Chapt15\ subdirectory on the Companion CD-ROM. I had a lot of these pages printed, like a stack of letterhead, at a reasonable cost. I then run the paper through the laser printer to create the few announcements, ads, signs, flyers, newsletters, or whatever as I need them. The laser-printed text blends in well with the black and red border design, which adds visual interest and a professional look because that part is printed on a high-quality press. Additionally, this is much cheaper and easier than designing a two-color flyer each time I need one.

## Rope a Dope

I was sitting in a restaurant, having a nice dinner conversation when I looked up and saw a guy with a nautical logo on his shirt. I turned to my date and said "Hey, I can make rope!" I then started drawing on my arm, trying to explain the process of blending a shape along any path to build the image. She of course had no idea what I was talking about and just thought I was nuts! Here is how to blend an object along a path to create rope:

1. Draw a rectangle, and then cap it off with an oval on each end. Use the Weld feature from the Arrange menu to merge the three objects into one. Now squash the object vertically, and expand horizontally by dragging the center sizing handles with the Pick tool. Finally, double-click on the object to reveal the rotation and skew arrows. Drag the bottom center skew arrows to the right to create the repeating twine shape (see Figure 15-6).

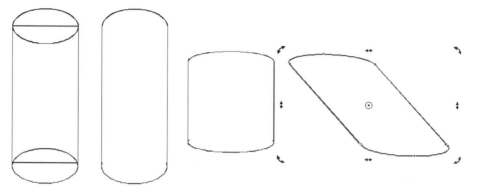

*Figure 15-6: The Weld function changes simple shapes into the rope sausage, which when squashed and skewed, is ready for the blending steps.*

2. Give the twine object a radial fountain fill from a light color to a darker one to help make the object look rounder. To test if the shape will work for a rope blend, duplicate the twine object and move it horizontally across from the original. Now shift-select both, open the Blend roll-up (Ctrl+B), and apply a blend to connect the shapes. You may need to experiment with the number of steps or move the control curves slightly to get the pieces to fit together, but you get the idea (see Figure 15-7).

*Figure 15-7: Blend the two objects together to get an idea of how the rope pieces fit together. A radial fountain fill adds to the effect.*

3. For the rope pieces, you can use any shape as a blend path to run the rope along. The effect works well but tends to fall flat if your blend path has sharp curves or transitions. So keep the curves smooth and you should have no problems. Use the New Path button on the Blend roll-up to run the rope pieces along any curve (see Figure 15-8).

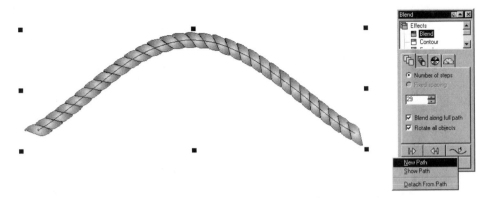

*Figure 15-8: Use the New Path function on the Blend roll-up to run rope along any curve you wish.*

4. The blend works great, but you need a way to cap it off and finish the rope look. Draw a rectangle and then distort it with the Envelope function to create a bent piece of twine. Now duplicate, flip the duplicate, and move it the distance of the rope piece horizontally to the right. Blend the two together to create other frayed ends, then choose Arrange | Separate | Arrange | Ungroup All, and then combine (Ctrl+L) the shapes into one curve. Move a copy of the rope twine shape beneath the frayed objects. Then use the Shape tool to node-edit the object and essentially cut it in half. Take the half-twine shape and choose Arrange | Weld to connect it to the frayed pieces. Draw a rectangle across the point where the frays meet the twin piece, and round the edges to represent that little piece of cord used to keep ropes from completely unraveling. For added contrast, you can draw a black shape behind the frayed pieces, as I did, or leave them open and airy (see Figure 15-9).

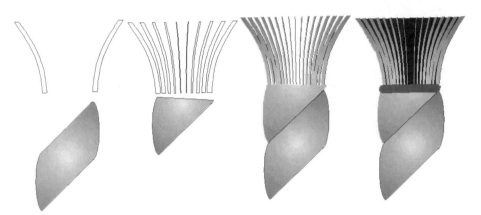

*Figure 15-9: Cut a twine shape in half and weld it to a curve made from blended strands to create an end cap for the rope blend.*

5. Position the end cap group at each open end of the rope to finish it off. The same end cap will work on both ends of the rope blend (see Figure 15-10).

*Figure 15-10: Use the end caps to finish off the rope pieces.*

This technique will let you create sweeping rope in any size or shape. We still need to work out how to finish off the ends, otherwise our rope will not look right. You can do this with knots or other end-caps. Here is how to make the noose:

1. Use the Bezier tool to first draw a line in the shape of a hangman's noose. Now place the rope pieces on each end of this curve, and use the curve as the blend path to connect them with a 200-step blend. Enable the Blend Along Full Path and the Rotate All Objects options on the Blend roll-up. You may need to add or reduce the number of steps to get the rope to build correctly (see Figure 15-11).

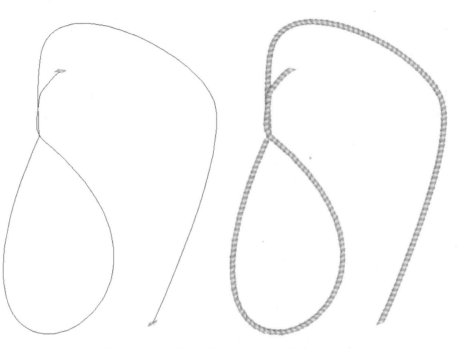

*Figure 15-11: Create a blend along a "noose" path to create the hangman's rope.*

2. Add the end caps to the rope to give it a nice finished look.

3. For the knot, you need to create a half-loop piece to cap off each end. Start with the standard shape, and use the Shape tool to select and delete the top-right nodes. Then fix the resulting curve so that it creates a nice rounded end for the rope loops. Duplicate and flip-flop this end for both sides, and group the objects. Now you can place the noose-knot group in place and create the rest of the knots by duplicating and arranging the duplicates (see Figure 15-12).

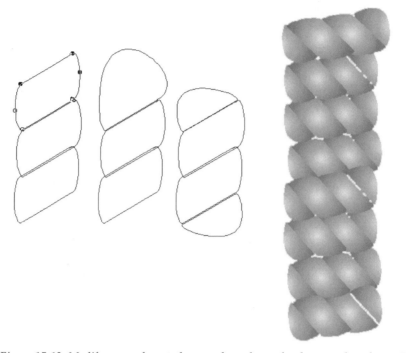

*Figure 15-12: Modify a rope shape to become the end caps for the noose-knot loops. Duplicate and arrange these loops to create the signature hangman's knot.*

4. To get a nice outline, drag-select all of the noose pieces, group them, and then duplicate the group. Send the duplicate group behind the original, and give it a fat, dark .053 outline and fill color. This will outline the rope without adding an outline to every object in the group, which would be too busy.

5. With the outline group still selected, use the Dropshadow command from the Effects menu in CorelDRAW 8 to add even more depth (see Figure 15-13).

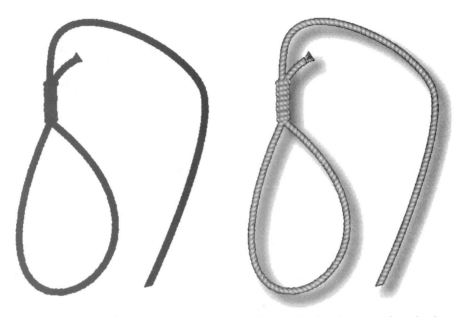

*Figure 15-13: A fat-lined duplicate creates a nice outline and is also the parent shape for the drop-shadow.*

Now you can entwine anything, anywhere, like some crazed Zorro character! This technique works well with big sweeping curves, but like the chain blends, may need to be arranged, separated, ungrouped (Ctrl+U), and massaged to make all the twines look okay. There are sections in the hangman's noose, in my pirates.cdr image for example, that look kind of rough if you zoom in and examine it closely. I left these in so you can see what kinds of problems to watch out for.

## Moving On

This was a short and sweet chapter focusing on the Blend function and how to use it to create chain links and rope objects. Generally speaking, the quick techniques covered here will work fine, but occasionally you may need to alter them slightly. For example, if you are creating a round rope object, you should make the inside of the twine object slightly smaller with the Envelope function so that the blended objects fit together more smoothly.

In the next chapter, we will ignore the Blend function entirely and focus on how to circumvent a common design problem, which is how to make a single image more interesting. The solution kind of breaks my "more is not necessarily better" rule, but in this case, it offers a fun solution and dizzying possibilities. Rub your eyes and break out the Visine—it's time to get into double vision!

▼ **Beyond f/x**

Chains and ropes are great ways to lay out a page. Because now you are not limited to any particular size or shape for your linked graphic, your rope or chain can serpentine around and through the page as you wish. This serves not only to break up the page into smaller chunks, but also to direct the eye of the viewer to different parts of the design. Chains or rope also offer interesting associations, from Western motifs and nautical designs to creepier, darker subjects. Since you can run the links along any path, you can use hand-writing style lettering to create words with a connected path, then run the links along it. This makes for cool thematic logos or promotional graphics ("Western days," "jailhouse rock," etc.). Blending along a path is always a great way to get proportionately spaced object duplicates, like saw-teeth, gears, or rivets. Just don't give your clients just enough rope to hang themselves (or maybe you should!).

# chapter 16
# Double Vision

Multiple images are pretty common these days; you'll see them in all sorts of media, including television, print ads, and Web sites. I have seen things like award shows where the host stands in front of a wall of TVs with a live-feed image close-up of the host's face on the monitors, or catalogs with a close-up of a product and its full-view as a subdued background. Web sites use this strategy a lot to get an interesting image out of essentially one picture.

In this chapter, we will look at ways to work multiple images into your artwork. This design style is a great way to add visual interest to an otherwise limited graphic. If you have ever had to try to make something from nothing, or had to stretch some customer-supplied artwork a little further than you wanted, then you will find these techniques of interest.

First, we will take a single illustration of a female jester and duplicate the image for both an interesting subdued background graphic and the main focus of the design. Second, we will use the powerful export features of CorelDRAW to create a bitmap background image, which can be made larger and in different colors than the original characters in the foreground. Finally, we will create a flower-like pattern with duplicates of the same model bitmap and surround that with a chaotic pattern made from resized and recolored duplicates of the headline text. We will see how even images and objects that are alike can be made to look very different, resulting in some very interesting design possibilities!

## Jokers Wild

*Figure 16-1: Using one image in the foreground and a muted version of the same image in the background adds depth and interest without having to build entirely new pieces.*

This jester-girl image is from a T-shirt and other items commemorating the fifth anniversary of our design studio, nicknamed the "Dog House" because that is where Slimy Dog was whelped years before. I had scanned the ink illustration to work out some other design issues and ended up creating this double-vision layout by combining duplicates of the image in the foreground and background.

This is a great example of how you can milk a design for more than its original purpose. This image is really tall and thin, which was perfect for the T-shirt design for which it was made, but it has strange dimensions for standard print applications. By using the objects in a background image, the image was fattened up, and even though the original image is still tall and skinny, the overall page is more balanced. Often the pieces are lying right in front of you and all you need to do is assemble them creatively to get what you are looking for! Here is how to combine images into a foreground/background double-vision orientation:

1. For the background design, I used a playing card image that flip-flops the jester-girl, using a reverse-coloring scheme on each side. First, import the black-and-white scan of the image. (This file is on the Companion CD in the \Chapt16\ subdirectory and is called girlnbox.tif. In the same directory is jestrgal.cdr, which is the finished playing card graphic if you want to cheat and skip ahead!) Then, using the techniques outlined in Chapter 18, add shapes to color the transparent bitmap.

2. Draw a rectangle about twice as wide and as tall as the jester-girl. Curve the corners with the Shape tool to create a playing card outline. Duplicate the card and divide the card duplicate in half by adding two nodes at the center of the top and bottom lines with the Shape tool and then deleting the rest on one side. (Or draw another rectangle and use the Intersection tool to get the other half. Whatever works!) Use the Artistic Text tool to name your playing card, in this case, the Joker. I used a traditional-looking serif font called PalmSprings. Select the bitmap and shapes that make up the jester image, as well as the text, and then duplicate them. (Before you do anything else, you should make a copy of the jester bitmap and pieces for later on. Use the File | Save As | Save Selected Only command to place a copy of the jester-girl on disk.) Now rotate them 180 degrees and place them on the other side for the playing card arrangement. Change the coloring scheme so that everything that was white on the left is red on the right and vice versa (see Figure 16-2).

CD-ROM

*Figure 16-2: Draw shapes with the Freehand tool to add color to a black-and-white bitmap. Create a playing card by duplicating and rotating the image 180 degrees. Changing the color scheme for each half makes the card brighter and more interesting.*

3. Choose Edit | Select All and rotate to get away from a straight head-on view. Duplicate the big card shape, move the duplicate down and to the left, fill it with black with no outline, and use the Send to Back (Shift+PgDn) command. Duplicate this object again, move it even more to the left and down, fill it white, and again use the Send to Back (Shift+PgDn) command. Shift-select the black copy, open the Blend roll-up (Ctrl+B), and click Apply to create a dark-to-light shadow blend. (Another option is to use the new Drop Shadow command from the Effects menu.) When the tweaks are finished, use the Convert To Bitmap function from the Bitmap menu to convert the image into a bitmap.

   Set the Color options to 256 Shades Of Gray and Dithered, set Resolution to 300 dpi, and set the Anti-Aliasing option to Super-Sampling. Click OK to convert the image (see Figure 16-3).

**TIP** *Remember that the conversion process is permanent, so be sure to save a copy of the file in both the before- and after-conversion formats.*

**TIP** *If you don't want to use any bitmap effects on your background image, you can use the Tinted Grayscale lens to mute the background objects and make them gray without converting them into a bitmap at all.*

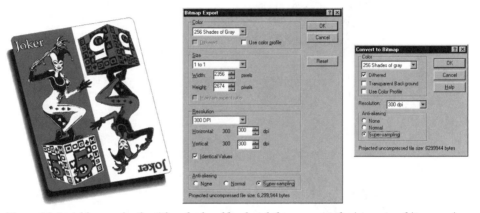

*Figure 16-3: Add some depth with a shadow blend and then convert the image to a bitmap using the CorelDRAW Bitmap menu.*

4. To mute the image more, draw a rectangle over everything and fill it white. Now open the Lens roll-up (Alt+F3) and use the Transparency option at a rate of 50% to create a soft image for the background. Save this file for use as the background later (see Figure 16-4).

5. For the main image, I used a full-color version of the jester-girl. This image is the same as the ones used in the playing card file, only more shapes were added to add more color. (Open [Ctrl+O] the copy of the jester-girl with the coloring pieces saved to disk in step 2 to save time making the full-color version.) To make the object stand out even more, the whole object was given a fat yellow outline (see Figure 16-5).

*Figure 16-4: Use a white rectangle with a 50% Transparency lens to mute the image for the background.*

*Figure 16-5: The ink-illustration bitmap was colorized using many shapes behind it to create an interesting and colorful image for the foreground.*

6. All that is left is to arrange the crisp color image over the background image. Change to more or less transparency on the white box to mute or emphasize the background. For an interesting variant, use the Blur options from the Bitmap menu in CorelDRAW to lower the detail in the bitmap and make the foreground image pop even more.

This image can be seen in the color section and is called jokers.cdr in the \Chapt16\ subdirectory on the Companion CD-ROM. Load the file and experiment for yourself with changing the Transparency value or blurring the bitmap like the atmospheric perspective examples in Chapter 9. For a really freaky look, use the 2D Effects | Swirl option from the Bitmap menu on the background image to give it a nightmarish feel.

Using a little creativity, I got to milk this illustration one more time, despite its odd proportions! I know you are thinking about which of your own designs could go another round using this technique, much to my delight. I'm so proud to make you a design recycler weenie like myself.

**TIP**

*To convert CorelDRAW objects into bitmaps, you can either use the Export (Ctrl+H) dialog or use the Convert to Bitmap command from the Bitmap menu. I have tested both methods and found that it takes almost exactly the same amount of time for each conversion to take place.*

*The Export feature is nice because it creates a file that you can then load and massage in PhotoPaint if you want to perform many changes or fine-tuning while also retaining the original CorelDRAW file intact. The Convert to Bitmap option, however, is super convenient, but unless you then export the image again, it limits the tweaks to within CorelDRAW. In some cases, the Convert to Bitmap option is better, depending on the kind and types of changes you want to make on the bitmap. You need to remember to save the original file before you use the Convert to Bitmap option, as once you convert your objects to a bitmap, you can't go back to the vector data unless you have a backup file. It is a matter of personal taste, but like many things in CorelDRAW, there is more than one way to skin the proverbial cat.*

## Skull Angels

*Figure 16-6: Once you have a double-vision file set up with the Corel objects in front of a bitmap reproduction in the background, you can subdue the background (left) or get chaotic results with other lenses such as Invert (right).*

I was content with the muted grayscale background like that in the previous jester-girl example and was on my way to creating a similar image with another illustration using virtually the same technique when curiosity got the best of me! Instead of muting the grayscale image with a Transparency lens, it is just as easy to recolor it using other Lens options. This can dramatically change the mood of the image, in this case making things more nightmarish and chaotic, which is, of course, perfect! Once again this is a great design vehicle to get more mileage out of your artwork. Again, we are taking a single image, and through nothing more than creative duplication and manipulation, making it much more unique and interesting than the original design alone. What was once limited subject matter now has almost an unlimited number of potential variants. What could be better than getting something for nothing? Here is how to use the double-vision technique with dramatic chaotic results:

1. This image started as a file I had created a while back in which I colorized ink illustrations I had drawn of an angel, skulls, and little

demons. I have sort of a clip-art library of things I have drawn, scanned, and then colorized using CorelDRAW, which I can mix and match into many twisted images (ah, the power of CorelDRAW used for evil...). The angel illustration has a strange history, and if you look in the hair and folds of cloth, you will find eerie faces and skulls looking back at you. Anyway, for this double-vision exercise, I had no choice but to use the Export (Ctrl+H) dialog to produce the grayscale background bitmap, as I needed to change the bitmap properties beyond what is convenient in CorelDRAW. Open the Export dialog (Ctrl+H), change the Save As Type option to TIFF Bitmap, assign a unique filename, and click the Export button. Now on the Bitmap Export dialog, change the Color option to 256 Shades of Gray, the Size option to 1 to 1, and the Resolution to 300 dpi and enable the Super-Sampling option under Anti-Aliasing for the smoothest graphic possible. Click OK to create the bitmap (see Figure 16-7).

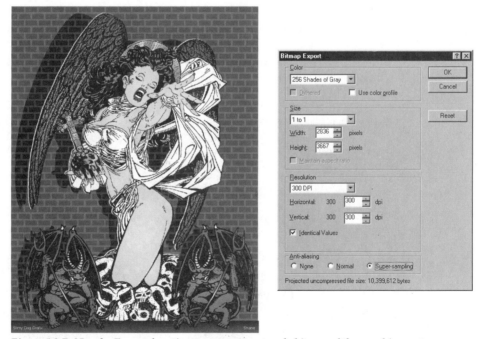

*Figure 16-7: Use the Export function to create a grayscale bitmap of the angel image to use as a backdrop in the same file later.*

2. Open the grayscale bitmap in PhotoPaint and use the Rectangle Mask tool in the Normal mode to drag-select an area to crop and on which to "zoom in." From the Image menu, choose Crop and then choose To Mask

from the flyout. This will trim down the bitmap to just the selected area. Now, under the Image menu, open the Resample dialog. If the dimensions of the cropped bitmap are too small to be the background of your image, you can lower the Resolution values a bit until the physical dimensions of the bitmap are what you need. For offset printing with a halftone screen at 133 lines per inch, you can dip down into the 225-dots-per-inch resolution range before you start to degrade noticeably your bitmap. (More is usually better when it comes to resolution; however, anything over 300 dpi typically is overkill for color or grayscale.) Change these values as needed, click OK, save the bitmap, and exit PhotoPaint.

3. Back in CorelDRAW with the original angel file loaded, now import (Ctrl+I) the cropped bitmap for the background. CorelDRAW 8 lets you assign the top-left coordinate of the imported image, so move the pointer to the top left of the page and click the mouse button to import (if you drag the mouse, you can also assign the size of the imported object in relation to the rest of the page, but in this case we want the image full size). Arrange the bitmap so it is behind the original, creating a powerful double-vision image. Downsize the original pieces rather than enlarge the bitmap in the background, as downsizing does not degrade image resolution, but enlarging bitmaps does (see Figure 16-8).

*Figure 16-8: Crop down the bitmap in PhotoPaint to create a zoomed-in backdrop when the bitmap is combined with the original file back in CorelDRAW.*

4. Now, just as before, draw a white rectangle over the background bitmap but behind the other image pieces. Open the Lens roll-up (Alt+F3), and for the muted look, choose the Transparency option. For a freaky, night-marish look, choose instead the Custom Color Map option. Change to the Forward Rainbow option, change the From and To colors to solid magenta, and click Apply (see Figure 16-9). Ooh, freaky, dude!

*Figure 16-9: Instead of using the Transparency lens to mute the background, use the Custom Color Map option to change the background bitmap into a strange nightmarish backdrop.*

5. For even more variety, with the Lens object selected, change the fill value from white to magenta. That is wild. Now change the fill value to cyan. That is just sick! Try yellow. Wow! Fiery heat. Experiment until you find a look you like (see Figure 16-10).

*Figure 16-10: Changing the fill color value of the shape containing the Custom Color Map lens dramatically changes the look of the background.*

A composite of images resulting from different Lens settings can be seen in the color section, while the angel.cdr file in the \Chapt16\ subdirectory on the Companion CD-ROM contains the original pieces. Load the file and experiment with the Lens option to get an entirely different background look. Some of the settings I tried are Heat Map, Tinted Grayscale, and Color Limit. For really strange results, change the Palette rotation value with the Heat Map lens. Just too weird! I used this technique to create animation cells for an on-screen movie. The AVI file, angels.avi, is also in the \Chapt16\ subdirectory if you want to enter my nightmare.

## World of Weirdness

**COLOR STUDIO**

*Figure 16-11: Multiple copies of the text elements, enlarged and using outline-only shading, add a chaotic sense of energy to this image. The Bitmap Color Mask lets the model bitmaps float freely, avoiding the boxy look of bitmaps without clear backgrounds.*

While working on the daisy fashion ad back in Chapter 9, I imagined the models standing on a planet surrounded by buzzing text elements instead of a flower. Okay, so maybe I had too many double espressos that day, but that was the image that popped into my mind! When I look at the finished version of this art, I can see the text buzzing around like in a hyper ESPN 2 commercial! In fact, it is easy to animate these kinds of text elements, and we will in Chapter 29.

Anyway, to free the models from their square bitmap prisons, we use the magic of the Bitmap Color Mask, which allows you to use just the image area of a photo without the background. Again, this design technique takes a limited subject matter and makes it very alive and interesting using duplicates. Here is how to create the free-floating models and the noisy double-vision text elements:

1. Using the techniques outlined in Chapter 9, the model bitmaps were arranged around a sphere and in front of a circle filled with a custom color blend. The custom color blend, set with the Interactive Fill tool or the Fountain Fill dialog (F11), goes from black to cyan to magenta to yellow. The redundant black points along the color blend are to control how and where the circle fades to black. Since this object rests on a black background, without the extra points for the black, the transition is harsh and noticeable (see Figure 16-12).

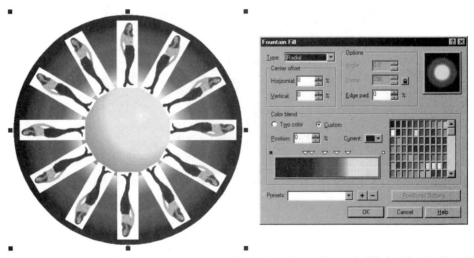

*Figure 16-12: Arrange the bitmaps around a sphere and in front of a circle filled with a brilliant custom color blend.*

2. Select a bitmap object and open the Bitmap Color Mask roll-up from the Bitmap menu. Now click on the little eyedropper button and then click on the white background of the bitmap. Click Apply to remove the background and make the model float freely. Adjust the Tolerance setting on the Bitmap Color Mask roll-up to combat little white dots resulting from anti-aliasing within the bitmap. Repeat this process for all of the bitmap objects (see Figure 16-13).

*Figure 16-13: The Bitmap Color Mask roll-up lets you assign colors to mask out (in this case the white background), leaving the images to float freely.*

### ▼ Cloning vs. Copying

Instead of duplicating objects, such as the bitmap of the model in this example, use the Clone option from the Edit menu instead. The advantage of a clone over a duplicate is that anything you do to change the original (like, for example, apply a Bitmap Color Mask) will automatically be reflected in the clones. This is a handy trick to speed up changes in like objects within an image file.

To avoid hopping when you clone, that is, having the clones appear in the same place as the original (like when you press the + key to duplicate), change the Duplicate placement and nudge values in the General page of the Options dialog (Ctrl+J). Now you can clone your bitmap and use the clones to create the image in essentially the same way you would when working with normal duplicates. The difference is that anything you do to the parent will also happen to the clones. Happy cloning!

3. I wanted the models to be standing on the earth instead of just a sphere. Import (Ctrl+I) a bitmap of the earth from the \Objects\misc\ directory on the CorelDRAW clip-art CD. Arrange the globe behind the models, and use the PowerClip | Place Inside Container option from the Effects menu to get the globe bitmap inside of the sphere. Now the models are standing on the earth (see Figure 16-14).

*Figure 16-14: Import a bitmap of the earth and then constrain it within the sphere on which the models were standing with the PowerClip function. Now they are standing on the earth.*

4. Draw a black rectangle the size of the page and send it to the back (Shift+PgDn). Use the Artistic Text tool to set text elements around the background. I used a font called Swis721 BlkEx BT, with a gray-to-white radial fountain fill. Once all of the text is in place, shift-select all of the pieces, duplicate them (+ key), and use the Send Back One (Ctrl+PgDn) command. Now enlarge the duplicate text shapes by dragging a corner sizing handle outward while holding down the Shift key. Give the duplicates no fill and a .023 magenta outline. Now one by one arrange the word duplicates randomly around the originals (see Figure 16-15).

5. Repeat the duplicate-and-scatter process two more times, each time choosing a different outline color. Scatter and enlarge these text objects even more for a totally random size and placement look. Don't worry if the text elements hang off the edge of the page boundary in your efforts to achieve the perfect balance of chaos (see Figure 16-16).

*Figure 16-15: Set the main text elements on the screen and duplicate them; then enlarge, recolor, and scatter the duplicates.*

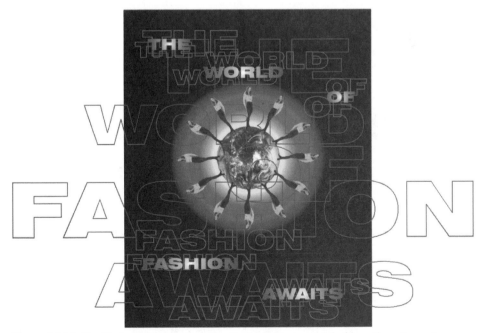

*Figure 16-16: Duplicate, enlarge and scatter the text objects a total of four times to create a really chaotic, energy-filled image.*

6. Select All from the Edit menu and then hold down the Shift key and click on the black background box. From the Effects menu, choose PowerClip and then Place Inside Container. Now click on the black background box to stuff everything inside of the page limits. We'll call that controlled chaos.

The results of this mayhem can be seen in the color section and also can be found in the world.cdr file, which is residing in the \Chapt16\ subdirectory on the Companion CD-ROM. If you want to play with this image, you will first need to use the Extract Contents command from the PowerClip flyout under the Effects menu. Then you can see firsthand how the Bitmap Color Mask works and the way the custom color blend in the background circle is controlled with the multiple same-color nodes. Check the Corel f/x Web site (http://www.corelmag.com/shane/corelfx) and Chapter 29 for examples of using the double-vision background and text effects in animated examples.

## Moving On

In this chapter, we explored ways to expand the uses of a single piece of art from just a boring solo flight into a total visual barrage. Using duplicates, the original artwork became interesting background material and other design elements to flesh out and augment an otherwise potentially dull or inappropriate graphic. This technique is more than practical, as any designer is often called upon to make something mundane look totally exciting. (From our studio came such wonderful design challenges as making bronzed turds—no joke!—look interesting!)

This style of multiple imagery is very useful for making portraits of people or products more interesting, and at the same time, highlighting the object in question. "Hindsight is 20-20," they say, and many past projects have popped into mind that could have benefited from this unique but interesting style. I'll catch them next time around!

Using a Lens object to change the way things behind it look is another technique that has a lot of potential and is almost exclusive to CorelDRAW. From the obvious and predictable use of the Transparency lens to lighten or darken objects to the seemingly bright and random results with the Custom Color Map, there is plenty of room for experimentation. These lenses also provide a great way to add color to a grayscale image that you would otherwise have to leave gray. Of course, I love lenses because they do so much with so very little actual work! How else could you take a low-quality black-and-white image brought to you by a client and actually use it in a color brochure? And CorelDRAW effects will save you someday, guaranteed!

From double-vision we move on now to even more bizarre tricks to play with your eyeballs. With the CorelDRAW rendering engines doing all the work, it is easy to create dizzying artwork reminiscent of the '60s psychedelic movement. So throw in a Hendrix CD, plug in the lava lamp, and grab those rose-colored glasses, 'cuz we are getting into the groove, baby!

▼ **Beyond f/x**

Double-vision techniques such as these are a great short-cut or trick to make a little bit of artwork go a long way. Oftentimes you are faced with a situation where you have little original source material, but plenty of space to fill. This technique lets you get away with using the same image in both the background, and as the primary image in the foreground. Even if you have other options, it is a great trick and looks nice. It also double-emphasizes the subject, but not in a harsh or even obvious way, which is a great sales and marketing tool. Product catalogs, brochures, and other support materials can benefit from the foreground/background treatment of the same subject. If you have the materials available, the same subject, only from two different angles, is also a great use of the double-vision technique. Multiple copies of the same text is also a very popular design theme. With a master set of text in place to get the message across, you are free to experiment with duplicates of the same words. Enlarging, fading, blurring (see Chapter 11 for ideas) the duplicates adds visual interest and subtle emphasis, without having to worry about legibility or content, because the original text is still in place. This is especially true with animation, as you can have the duplicate text flying around to create a unique and attention-gaining graphic. The possibilities are quite literally dizzying—you don't need bifocals to take advantage of double-vision!

# chapter 17

# Psychedelic Mind Trips & Other Eye Candy

In today's chaotic climate, getting your audience's attention and pulling them into your design is harder than ever. With millions of bits of information bombarding your potential reader from other sources, your printed art, with nothing but visual tricks, must somehow stand up and scream "read me!" It is no easy task, but not impossible, to create art that is interesting enough to accomplish this. We have already covered many great techniques that are anything but boring.

One great attention-getting device borrows from techniques that originated during the psychedelic '60s, techniques that use high-contrast coloring and dizzying patterns to create bright and, above all, interesting graphics that are impossible to ignore. The look isn't always appropriate, but when it is, it's as subtle as a car crash, with the same attention-gaining effect.

In this chapter, we will look at different ways to create attention-grabbing graphics using a variety of dazzling techniques. In the first example, we use techniques to create images reminiscent of the Spirograph, a Gen-X toy that created patterns with mathematical blending of colored lines that is as likely to please now as it did back then. In the second example, we again use the Blend function, only this time to create multiple-outline shapes that, when combined, create dizzying patterns of light and dark colors. Then we look at how this technique can be custom-tailored to any shape making it an ideal base for an advertisement. Next, we borrow from a popular pop graphic to create a crisp but loud circular graphic using custom color blends. Finally, we will look at some of CorelDRAW's bitmap effects filters and how they can transform ordinary artwork into the eye-frying variety with just a few clicks. Hope you are not prone to motion sickness.

# Spirograph

**COLOR STUDIO**

*Figure 17-1: Using both the Rotate and Rainbow options from the Blend roll-up, a simple line is transformed into images reminiscent of the Spirograph toy of yore.*

As a kid, I would spend hours with my collection of plastic gears, ink pens, pushpins, and cardboard that made up the Spirograph toy set. These tools, in the hands of the patient and masochistic, would produce amazing and colorful designs based on repeating geometric patterns.

Fast-forward to today, and you can create strange Spirograph-style images much easier in CorelDRAW (see Figure 17-1). Instead of plastic gears, the Blend roll-up works nicely to render wonderfully complex images without fear of losing little pushpins in the carpet to be found by an angry mom when vacuuming. These images are easy to create, and they are interesting patterns guaranteed to get some attention. Without fail, they result in "Hey, remember the Spirograph?" conversations! Designs like this make cool border shapes and backgrounds; they can even be animated for a pulsing eye-grabbing banner on a Web site. Here is how to use the Blend roll-up to create Spirograph patterns:

1. This technique is so cool and yet so simple. First draw a curve-shaped line with two clicks of the Bezier tool and fine-tune it with the Shape tool if necessary. Now double-click on the curve with the Pick tool and drag the axis of rotation down and to the right (see Figure 17-2).

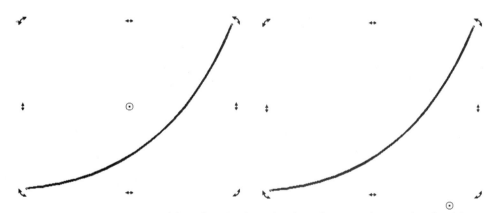

*Figure 17-2: Draw a curve and drag the axis of rotation from the center down and to the right.*

2. Duplicate (+ key) the line, drag-select both duplicates, and open the Blend roll-up (Ctrl+B). Change the number of steps to 100 and the Rotate value to 360 and then click Apply (see Figure 17-3). Told you this was easy!

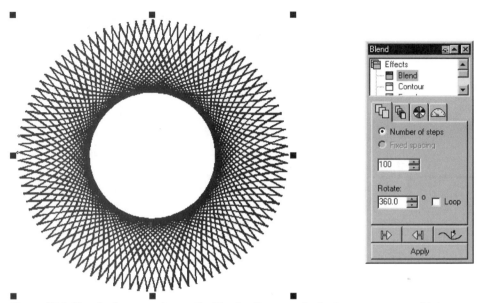

*Figure 17-3: Use the Rotate option on the Blend roll-up to spin the two curves around into an intricate pattern.*

3. To add color to your blend, first change from a black outline fill to an-other color, like yellow. With the blend group selected, simply right-click on the onscreen color well. Now your blend should recalculate in all yellow, which is pretty bland. No worries; just open the Colors page on the Blend roll-up and click the Clockwise Path button, which will color the blend shapes in all shades of the rainbow (see Figure 17-4).

**TIP** *Black and white are not on the color wheel, so if your blend objects use these colors for fills or outlines, the rainbow option on the Colors page of the Blend roll-up won't do anything! Control curves need to have colors off of this color wheel for the rainbow option to work.*

4. We already have a wild image, but no, we want more, *more!* In order to use this blend group in future blends, you need to first freeze it. Select the blend group, separate it, and then group (Ctrl+G) the pieces. With the group selected, choose the Add Perspective option from the Effects menu. This will add the illusion of depth and distort the design nicely.

Use the Shape tool to drag a corner node inward while holding both the Shift and Ctrl keys. This will move both corners inward simultaneously, resulting in the deformation that we are after (see Figure 17-5).

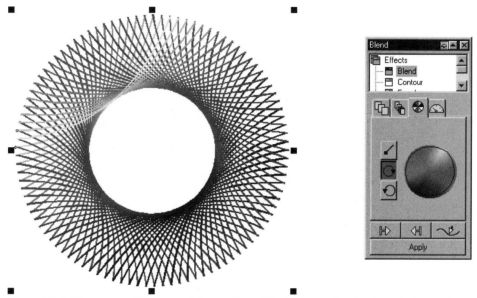

*Figure 17-4: Choose one of the two rainbow options (Clockwise or Counterclockwise) from the Colors page on the Blend roll-up to add the full range of color to a blend group.*

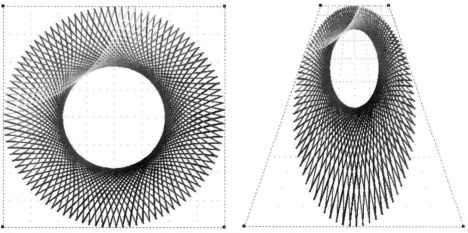

*Figure 17-5: Use the Perspective tool to distort the circle pattern.*

5. With the Pick tool, double-click on the object and drag the axis of rotation up. Duplicate this object, drag-select both, and open the Blend roll-up (see Figure 17-6).

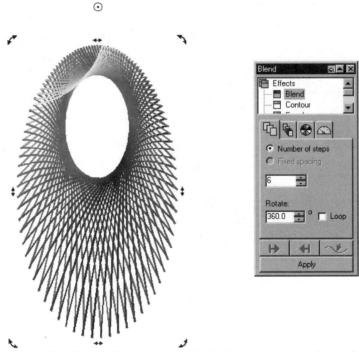

*Figure 17-6: Change the group's axis of rotation in preparation for another blend.*

6. In the Blend roll-up, change the number of steps to six and rotate to 360 again. Now, depending on where you dragged the axis of rotation in step 5, you will create any number of strange flower shapes. (The flower in the opening graphic is made from the same pieces, just with a different axis of rotation). See Figure 17-7.

# VENTANA *COLOR* STUDIO

**Free! BONUS**

**THE ADVENTURE CONTINUES!**

**WOW! 96 AMAZING PAGES**

## INCREDIBLE EFFECTS THAT ARE OUT OF THIS WORLD!

CorelDRAW objects can be stacked in front of and behind each other to add a sense of depth. A wispy look can be created with the Interactive Transparency tool. (Chapter 2)

Layering objects lets you stack images on top of each other, allowing you to animate flames behind a colorized illustration. (Chapter 2)

Blending two circle groups results in an explosion effect, which can be modified using the Acceleration options from the Blend roll-up. (Chapter 2)

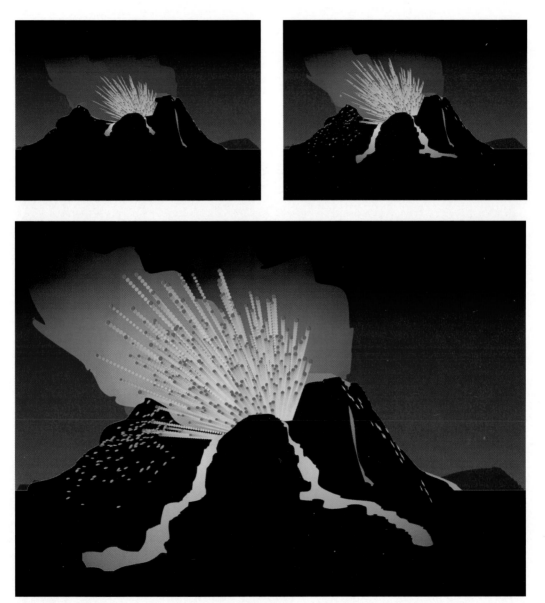

Using the same blend technique as the Explosion, you can create the hot magma of an erupting volcano. To create the eruption, simply enlarge the bend group, which recalculates to the new size and creates the effect. (Chapter 2)

Modifying the parameters of the explosion from the Blend roll-up instantly transforms bursts into spinning, flaming pin-wheels. (Chapter 2)

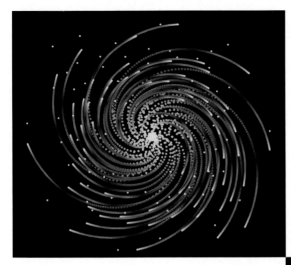

You can get virtually every color of the rainbow in your blend by giving both the inner and outer Control Groups the same fill color and using the Rainbow option on the Blend roll-up. Click Color tab, then click either the Clockwise or Counterclockwise (shown) button.

If you choose a color on the opposite side of the color wheel for each Control group (in this case yellow and cyan), you can then decide which piece of the rainbow to use by clicking either the Clockwise (shown) or Counterclockwise button.

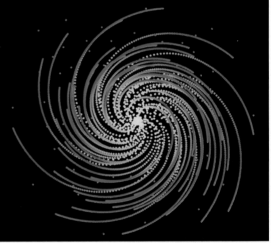

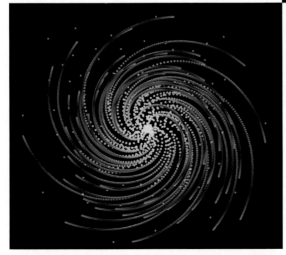

One little button can dramatically change the look of your blend! Here the Counterclockwise button makes use of the other half of the rainbow, providing a colorful alternative to the Clockwise option. (Chapter 2)

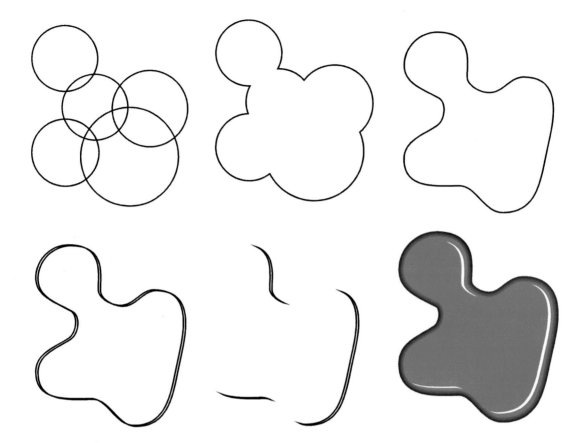

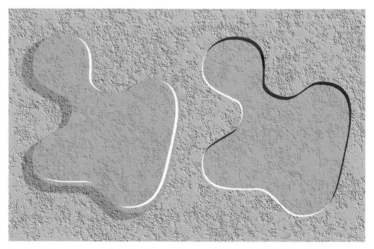

Basic shapes are merged together with the Weld tool, then given highlight and shadow shapes to look like water droplets or a recessed puddle. (Chapter 3)

The gleam and shadow objects created with copies of the original using the Trim roll-up can transform any object, including text, into wet-looking droplets. Changing the transparency of the fill, the contrast of the shadow elements, and varying the background texture, you can create a convincing look for many different materials. (Chapter 3)

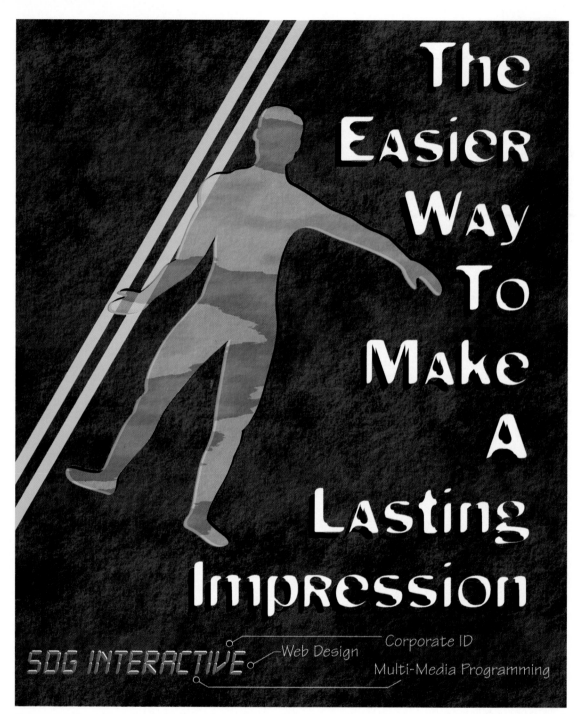

The Easier Way To Make A Lasting Impression

SDG INTERACTIVE

Web Design
Corporate ID
Multi-Media Programming

Reversing the gleam and shadow shape logic of water on the surface creates liquid in a recessed puddle. A Texture Fill can also be given transparent qualities with the Interactive Transparency tool to suggest clear water and also reflect clouds from above. (Chapter 3)

CorelDRAW lets you combine hand-drawn images with native objects. A black and white scan can have a transparent background, which makes it possible to colorize the image with CorelDRAW objects. (Chapter 3)

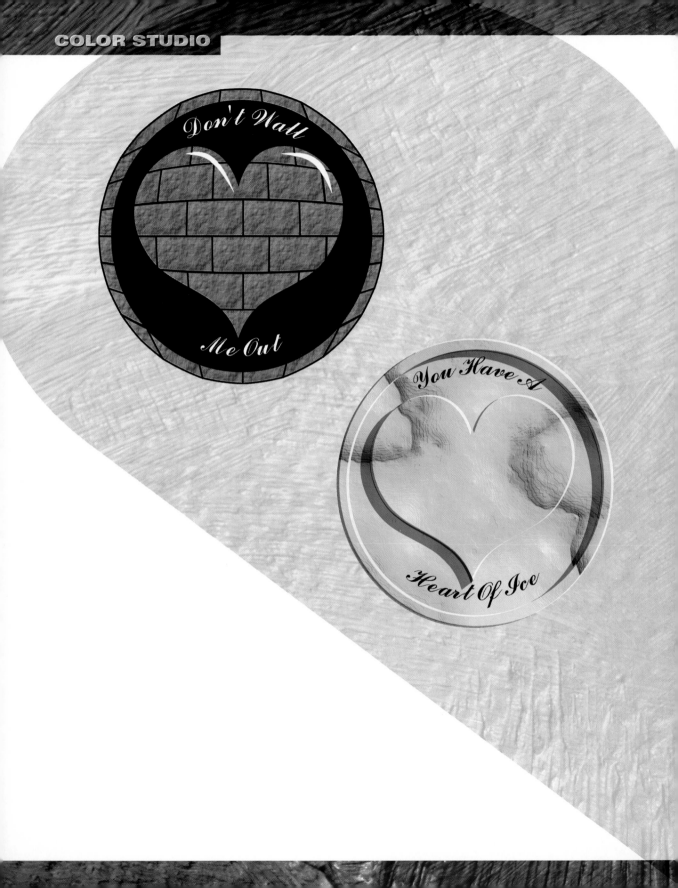

There is a wide variety of fill options in CorelDRAW, including bitmap-type fills. Texture Fills are CorelDRAW generated bitmaps using a specialized texture engine. You can change the style, colors and density to create a huge variety of fill options. Also available are full-color bitmap pattern tiles which, although not nearly as flexible as Texture Fills, make for even more realistic fill options. (Chapter 4)

Using essentially the same explosion technique from Chapter 2, snowflake shapes are scattered into a randomized pattern using the Blend roll-up. (Chapter 4)

The Extrude roll-up will not only add depth and shading to your objects, but also create a chiseled look with the Bevel function. This feature adds a great deal of depth and interest to an otherwise flat object. (Chapter 4)

Although Textures and Pattern Fills look great and add a lot of depth and color to your CorelDRAW objects with little effort, they are not especially flexible. If you attempt to rotate, or in this case, use the Perspective tool on an object, you will find that the fill does not reflect the change. This limitation can be circumvented using CorelDRAW native objects and a little creativity. (Chapter 5)

Shane

A blend is a great way to merge two objects together, graduating color and shape between two control curves. A control curve can be associated with more than one blend, to add more depth and realism to a design. (Chapter 5)

The Lens function can be used not only to distort objects, but with the Freeze feature enabled, also constrain them within a shape. The Color Styles feature allows you to easily substitute colors in a selection, making, for example, recoloring clip-art an easy task. (Chapter 5)

The tentacle shapes here look remarkably three-dimensional but are actually very simple to create. A many step blend along a path creates the illusion of light and shadow with a Custom Color Blend in both control curves. (Chapter 6)

Combining the explosion blend technique with the tentacle shading and blending steps can create an interesting variety of sea creatures. (Chapter 6)

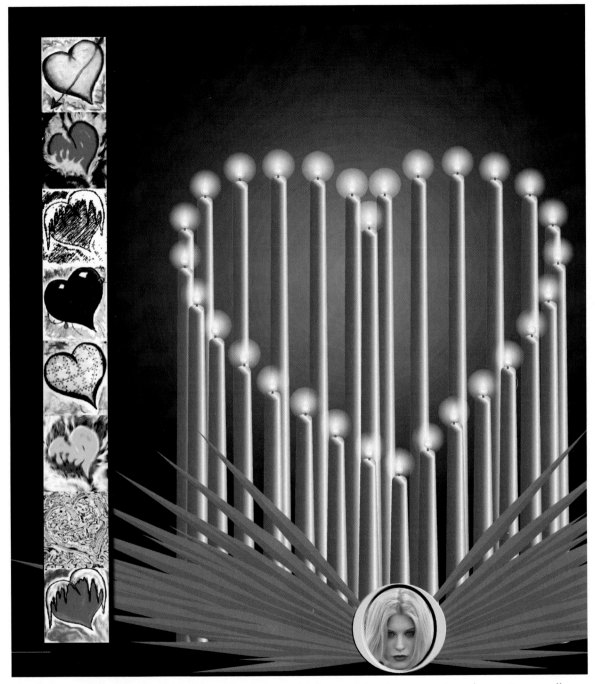

Blending objects along a path, then using another high-step blend, can create a decorative candle arrangement. (Chapter 6)

Carving and shaping stone never became easier than in CorelDRAW. The Bevel feature, found in the Extrude roll-up, adds the the perfect highlight and shadow shapes to give any surface the illusion of depth. When used in conjunction with a Bitmap Pattern fill, the results are very realistic. (Chapter 7)

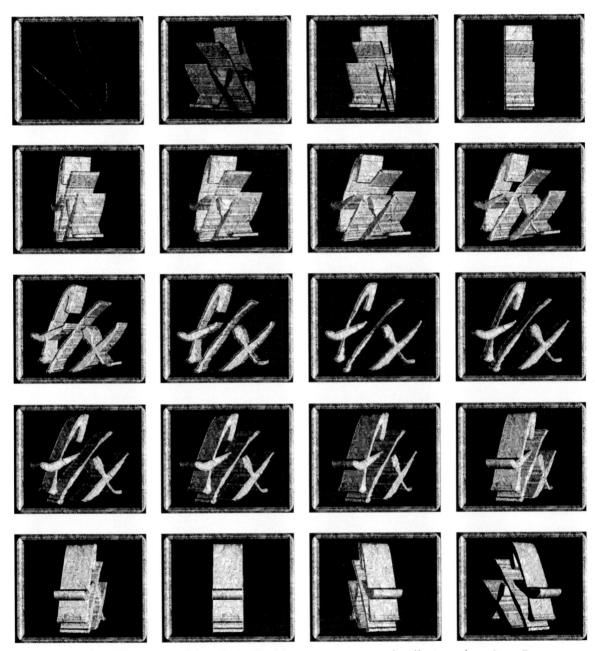

Because an Extrude object is infinitely malleable, you can create the illusion of motion. By incrementing the 3D Rotation values the Extrude object will appear to spin around. (Chapter 7)

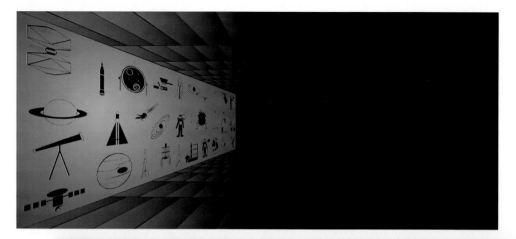

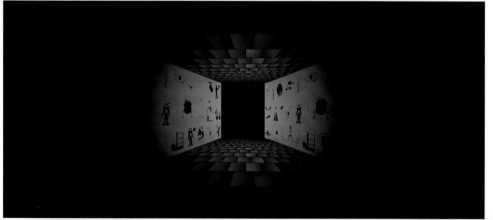

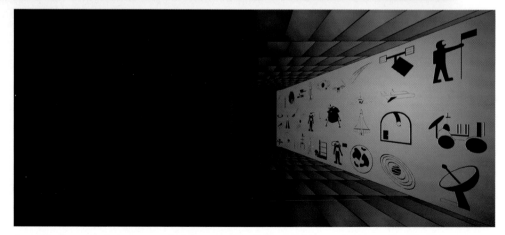

A wall of symbol shapes or bricks can be distorted into a dark tomb using the Perspective tool. Using a black shape on top with a moving transparent hole can light the scene like a dim torch, moving from side to side to reveal the secrets of the dark tomb. (Chapter 7)

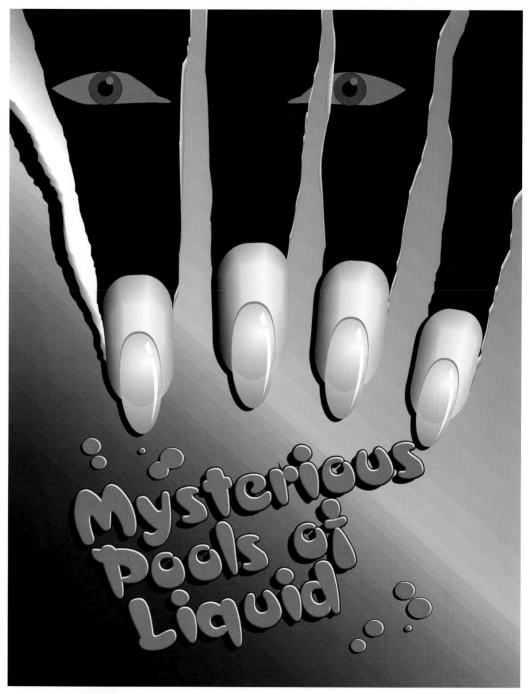

Using a blend between two rough, torn objects creates the tattered edge of claws ripping through this book cover design. The fingers use a series of blends to create depth. Duplicate shapes with Lenses give the illusion of cast shadows. (Chapter 8)

The PowerClip function works well to constrain objects within a curve, including bitmaps. Using a special PowerClip trick, you can then break apart and scatter the pieces. (Chapter 8)

If you create a complex shape
made up of many smaller units, and
combine them into one, you can then PowerClip
an image iside of it.  Then, when you Break Apart
the PowerClipped curve, each little piece will have
the corresponding image inside of it, making it easy
to create a puzzle.
(Chapter 8)

Simple shapes drawn with the Freehand tool become mountains and clouds in a basic landscape template file. Recoloring the objects can change the local from plush green plains to harsh brown desert. (Chapter 9)

Palm trees are a popular and fun design theme. Using CorelDRAW's Blend function you can easily make the pieces for your own unique trees, which can be used to populate and enhance your landscape images. The middle image has been converted to a bitmap, using the Add Noise filter to create a grainier look. (Chapter 9)

The PowerClip function works well to constrain objects within a curve, including bitmaps. Using the Blend feature to create flower petals creates a nice daisy shape, which duplicates of a bitmap image are then PowerClipped into. (Chapter 9)

Spring Values
are
In Full Bloom

In its stock form, this beach scene looks nice, but the illusion of depth is not as pronounced as it could be. In the second image, Transparency Lens shapes make the background seem further away (exaggerated to look misty), the car a little closer, and finally, the woman direct in the foreground. Using a bitmap Blur filter, the final image simulates depth by blurring the background objects. (Chapter 9)

Bitmaps are easy to import and manipulate within CorelDRAW to create interesting photo montages. The Interactive Drop Shadow tool makes adding shadow effects a snap. (Chapter 10)

Cool tears flow upon my pillow.
And I'm freezing blue with misery.
You know that I never meant to hurt you
But something always gets right in the way.

So I'll fill this bedrom full of mystery.
Hang our last conclusions on the wall.
And if this empty building starts to get to me
Please remember that it just might be your fault.

Better to have lost in love
Than never to have loved at all...

Using effects filters
available in both
CorelDRAW and
PhotoPaint, images
are given antiqued
and golden tones,
and also stylized with
brush-style filters.
(Chapter 10)

So the fated lovers turn to enemies
And all their hidden feelings start to show.
And I never though that boy
Could mean so much to me.
And now it seems I'll have to let you go...

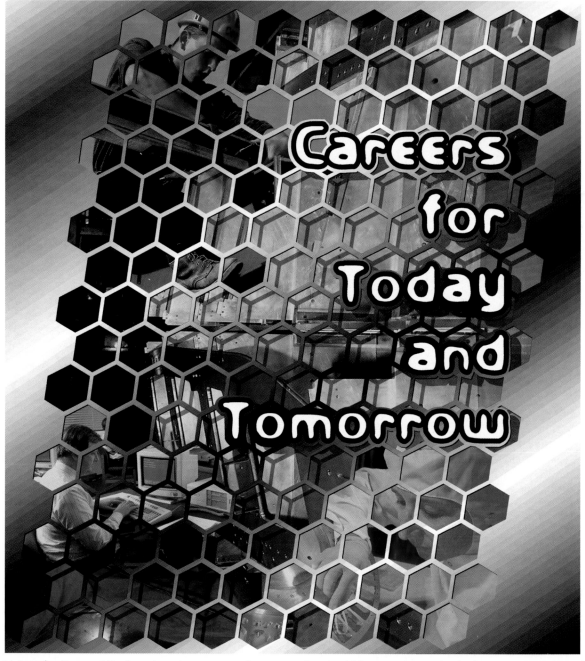

Using the PowerClip function, images can be constrained within any shape, including non-connected ones as in this beehive honeycomb, for many unique design possibilities. (Chapter 10)

Using the Contour feature, you can add multiple outlines to a shape, and with a bright color scheme, create a graffiti look. You can use the pieces as-is, or let the texture of the surface below show through using the Interactive Transparency tool. Random sprays of bullets result from use of the Acceleration option from the Blend roll-up. (Chapter 11)

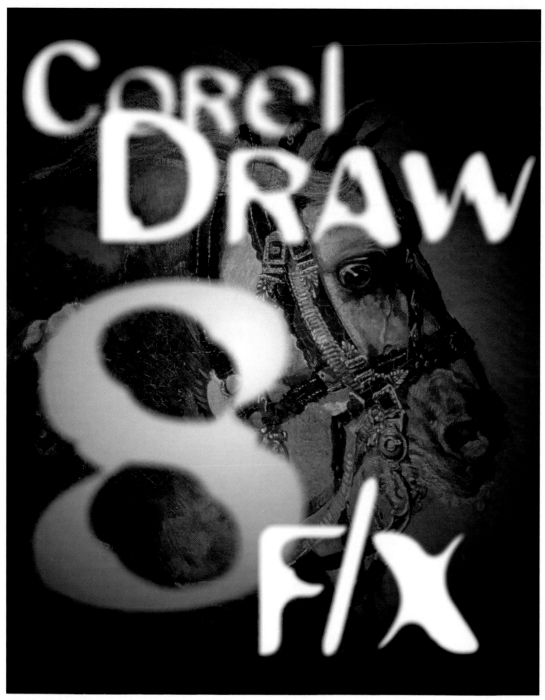

Converting text to bitmaps using the Transparent Background option lets you use plug-in filters while retaining a see-though look. This allows you to blur and stack images for strange results. (Chapter 11)

Using the Interactive Transparency tool you can de-emphasize text and make it more subtle. The Contour function creates additional shapes, which can be shaded with opposing fills, for a wispy yet shiny look. (Chapter 11)

The CorelDRAW clip-art library is full of images screaming to be a part of your next virtual tattoo. (Chapter 12)

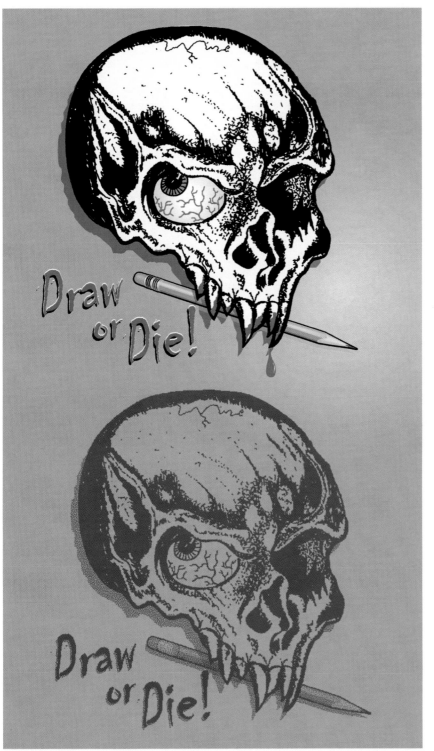

CorelDRAW can be used to create a color reference for a tattoo artist, a wild design for an ad or product label, or converted into a stippled monochrome image for an old-school tattoo look. (Chapter 12)

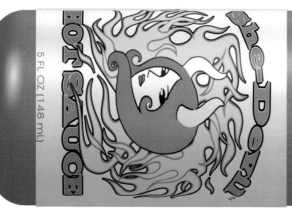

Tattoo imagery can be worked into all kinds of contemporary designs, including product labels. (Chapter 12)

Using a bitmap with a transparent background, you can stamp a brand on anyone's noggin! (Chapter 13)

Piercing parephenallia, with its hard edges, intersting geometric shapes and shiny metal coloring, can make for an interesting addition to contemporize a design. (Chapter 13)

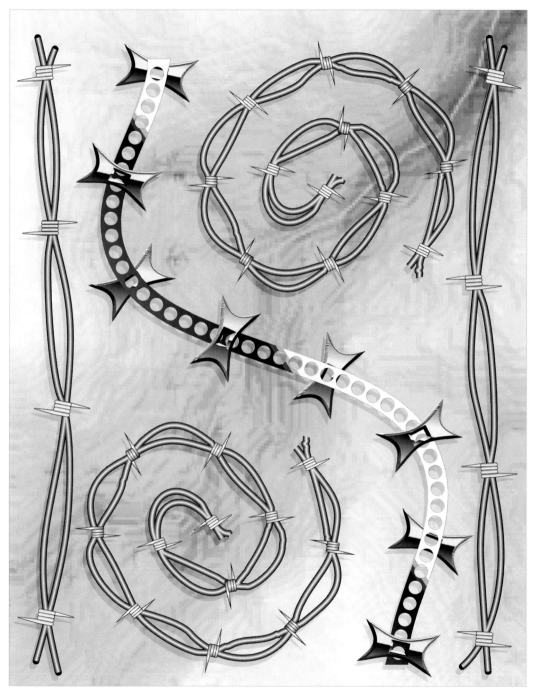

Flexible and popular, barbed and razor wire has many uses in design. Add a sense of danger or a rough-and-tough feel with a string of wire in any size or shape. (Chapter 14)

"S" curves are combined into tribal-looking design shapes, with complex patterns possible using only a few unique pieces. The dimensional pieces use the same technique as the tentacles, only with the addition of a Split Blend function. The clip-art knife is adorned with fresh blood to create a creepy mood. (Chapter 14)

All kinds of dangerous looking throwing stars can be made using CorelDRAW's versatile options. (Chapter 14)

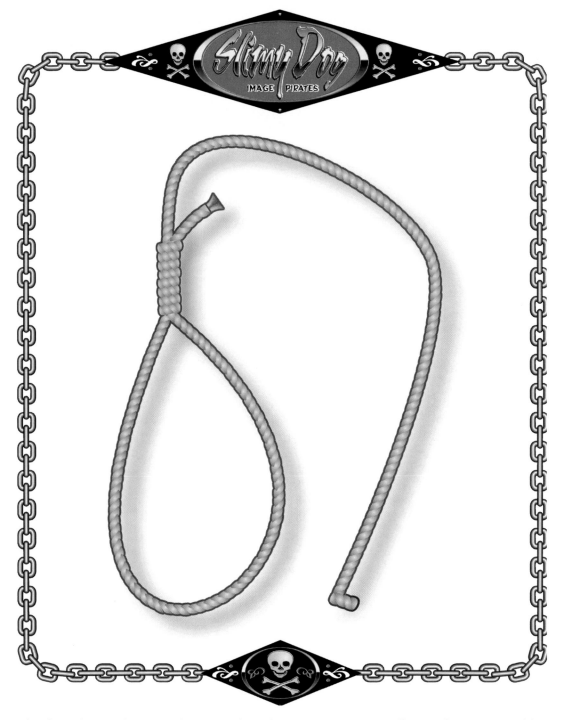

Blending objects along a path can result in chains or rope in virtually any shape imaginable. (Chapter 15)

Play your cards right and join us for our fifth year anniversary party at the Dog House. You never know what might pop up!

Using the same image in the foreground, and a muted version in the background, adds depth without having to generate entirely new pieces. (Chapter 16)

Once you have a double-vision file set up with the Corel objects in front of a bitmap reproduction in the background, you can get cool variants using the Lens roll-up. (Chapter 16)

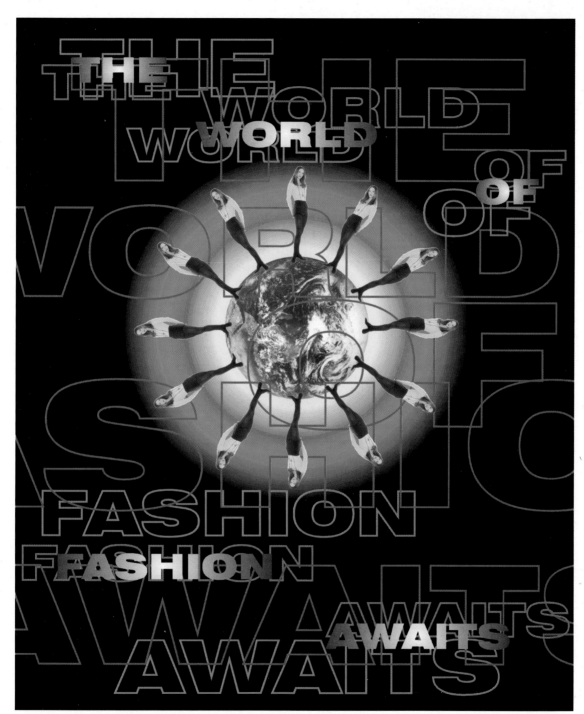

Multiple copies of the text elements, enlarged and using outline-only shading, add a chaotic sense of energy to this image. The Bitmap color mask lets the model bitmaps float freely, avoiding the boxy look of bitmaps without clear backgrounds. (Chapter 16)

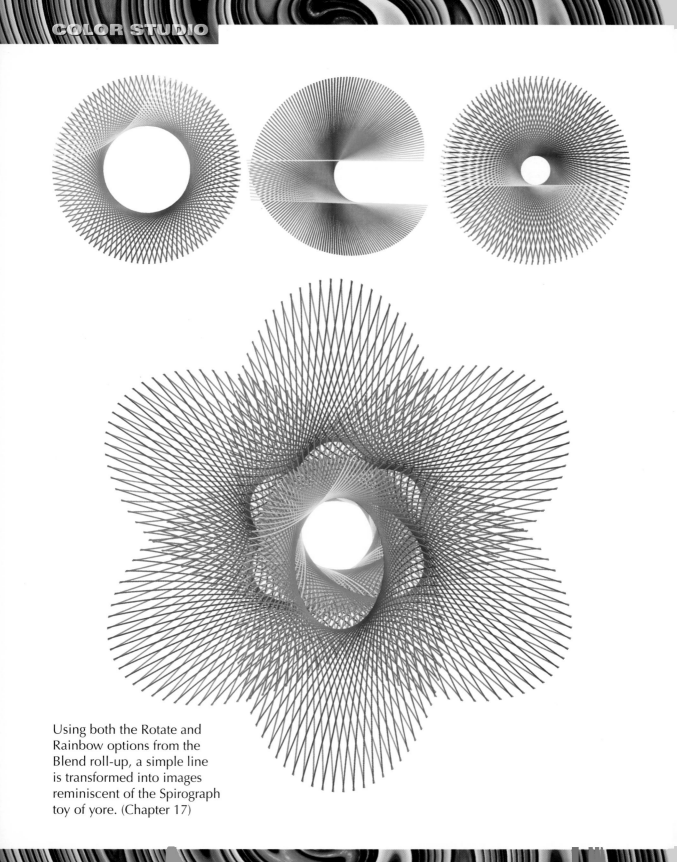

Using both the Rotate and Rainbow options from the Blend roll-up, a simple line is transformed into images reminiscent of the Spirograph toy of yore. (Chapter 17)

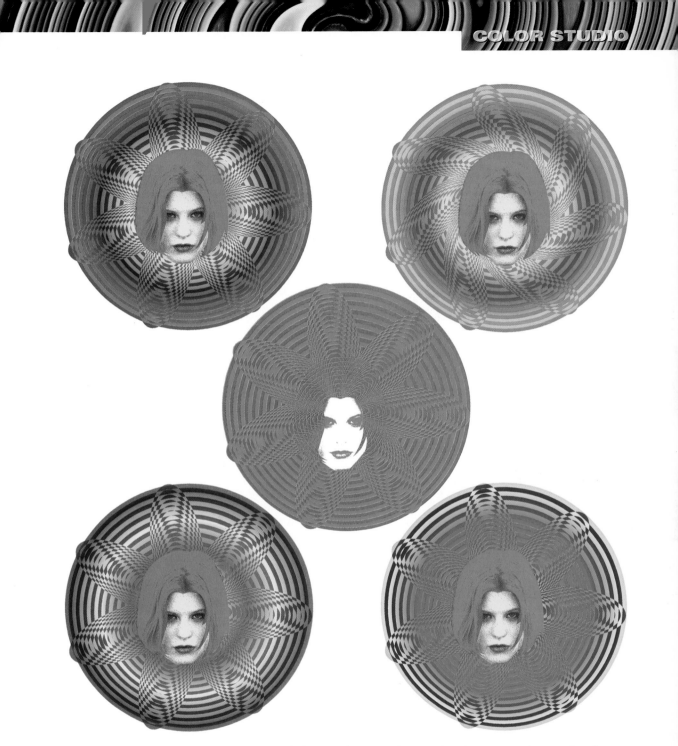

Using the Blend roll-up to create ringed shapes, then combining the shapes together, makes for some very strange psychedelic objects! To make the image even more dizzying, the Rainbow option from the Fountain Fill dialog adds an explosion of colors. (Chapter 17)

The dizzying psychedelic pattern can be custom-tailored to any shape, making it an ideal attention-getting vehicle for advertising designs. (Chapter 17)

This image imitates a popular detergent box. The bright happy logo was created using the Interactive Fill tool. (Chapter 17)

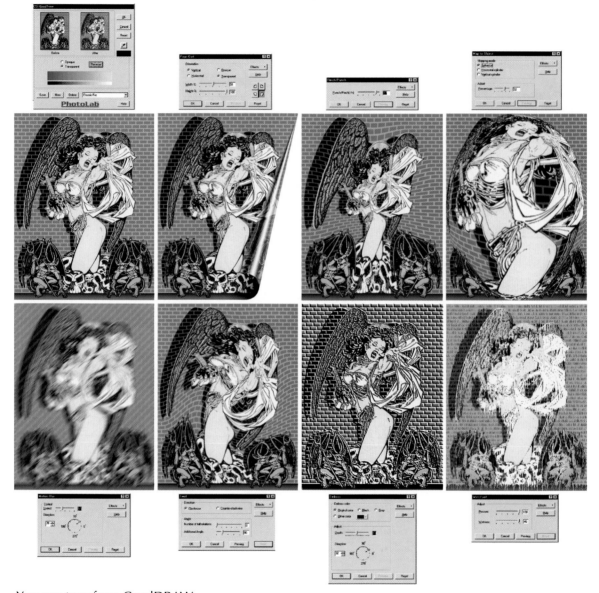

You can transform CorelDRAW
objects into bitmaps, then use a
wide range of filter effects on
them to get results not possible
with conventional CorelDRAW
effects. (Chapter 17)

Combining hand-drawn artwork colorized in CorelDRAW with computer-aided effects creates an image that's impossible to produce by hand or computer alone. (Chapter 18)

Top: If you can draw stick figures, you can create comic characters in CorelDRAW. Simple shapes are transformed into animated actors for a fun cartoony look. Bottom: Using the Frozen option on a lens lets you capture and distort your cyber-comics with a blob of cyber-silly putty. (Chapter 18)

Hand-drawn images are placed in a computer-generated scene, which has been converted to a bitmap so filter effects can give it a rough, hand-drawn look. (Chapter 18)

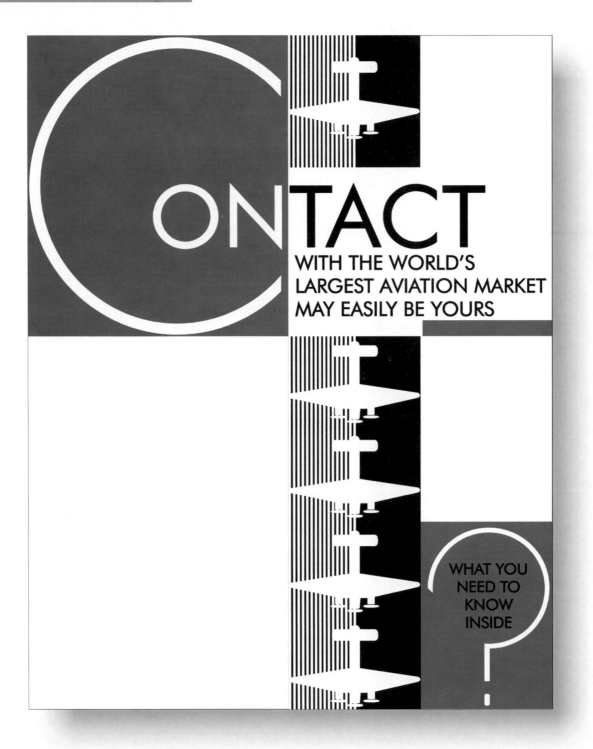

Modern artists can learn from the past to create simple, cost-efficient designs that are interesting and professional. (Chapter 19)

In addition to kitschy design and funky fonts, the choice of colors really screams retro. (Chapter 19)

Even a simple-looking design can benefit from high-end tricks! The TV image is a PowerClip behind a static line blend, the design elements are symbols, and the "FX" logo was created with the Combine function. (Chapter 19)

CREATE MAGIC WITH CORELDRAW

FX CHANNEL

Tune In!

CorelDraw 8 f/x. Now playing.
(Check local listings)

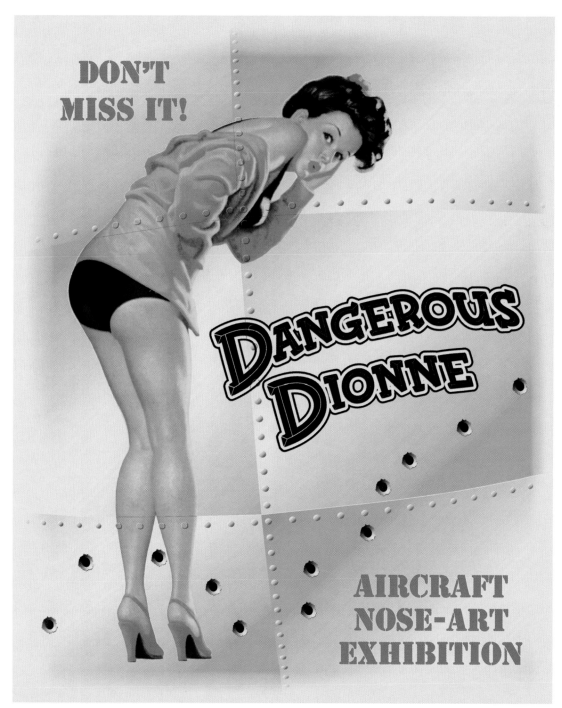

A pinup on a riveted airplane hull makes for a unique WWII poster. The Bitmap transparency mask makes the background on the pinup girl transparent, while lenses create the highlight and shadow effects in the rivets. (Chapter 19)

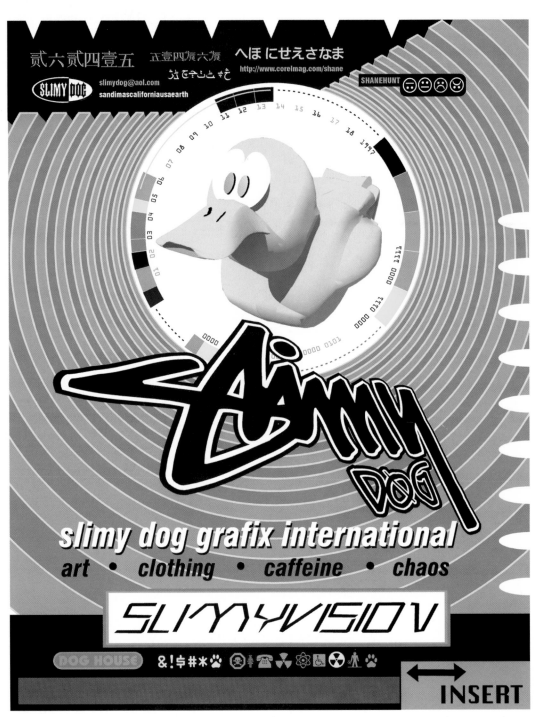

Mixing text, vector, and 3D artwork into one design creates a contemporary barrage of visual information. (Chapter 20)

This image mixes ink drawings with a plethora of CorelDRAW effects such as the new Interactive Distortion tool, with the Twister option enabled. (Chapter 20)

A bitmap is encased in glass by creating a wooden frame with the Extrude roll-up, and then using the Interactive Transparency tool to create glass. (Chapter 20)

Space scenes lend themselves to computer aided design. The computer makes short work of populating an empty sky with stars, planets, comets, and other miscellaneous debris. (Chapter 21)

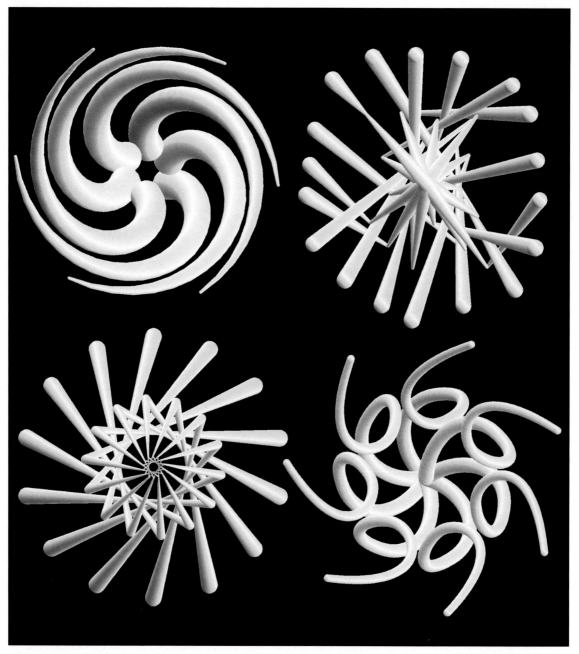

Objects blended using techniques from Chapter 6 can be further manipulated to create stars, patterns, and space stations. (Chapter 21)

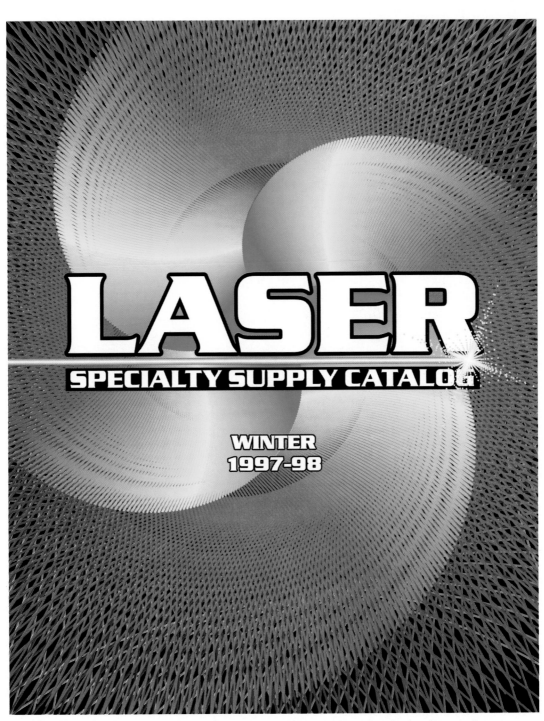

The Blend function creates not only the round laser beam but also the background pattern, and even the exploding sparkle. (Chapter 21)

Adding energy sparkles to a laser beam using a Bitmap blur effect adds glowing energy to the ray o' destruction. (Chapter 21)

Old-time images can be worked into contemporary designs by using PhotoPaint to clean up the images, and CorelDRAW to merge all of the design elements. (Chapter 22)

The clone brush in PhotoPaint lets you erase existing text from a magazine cover and then add texture to text and other details created in CorelDRAW. (Chapter 22)

Electricity sparks create an interesting glow behind objects, pulling them away from the background. (Chapter 22)

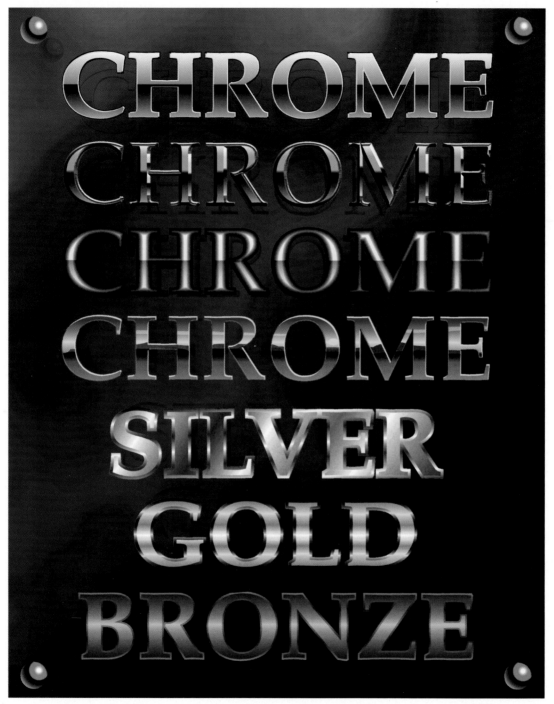

Using Custom Color blends, PowerClipped objects, the Extrude function, and the Contour roll-up, a convincing metallic look is achieved without much effort in CorelDRAW. (Chapter 23)

Using a bitmap rendered from CorelDRAW, you can achieve a variety of effects in
PhotoPaint, depending upon the choice of landscape bitmap. (Chapter 23)

Using a complex Custom Color blend, the tentacle technique from Chapter 6 renders objects which appear to be dimensional and metallic. (Chapter 23)

Simple jointed limbs and other dynamic elements can be changed in CorelDRAW to animate a robot character. (Chapter 24)

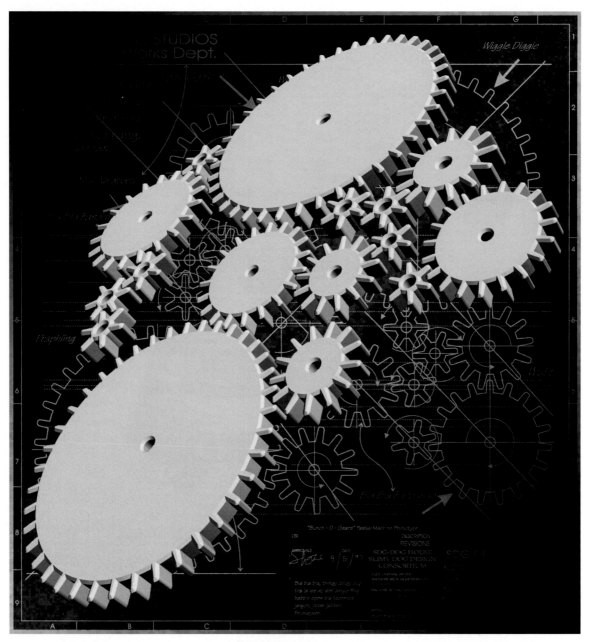

The Blend roll-up and the Weld command make gear shapes in any size. These objects can be used for the background blueprint image or made into three-dimensional objects with the Extrude roll-up. (Chapter 24)

Gears are an interesting design element suggesting motion or machinery. When combined into a single curve, the Extrude function creates the depth with shadows and highlights, and also a shared vanishing point. (Chapter 24)

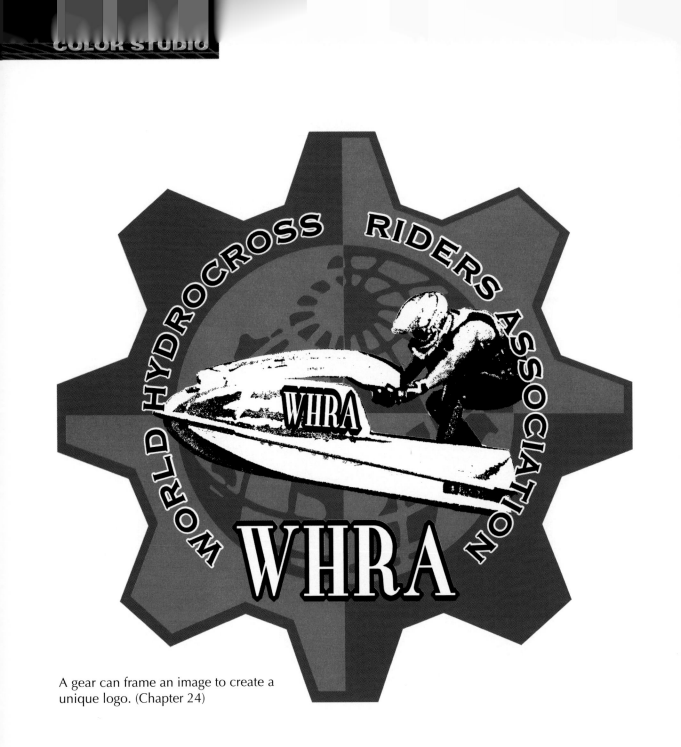

A gear can frame an image to create a unique logo. (Chapter 24)

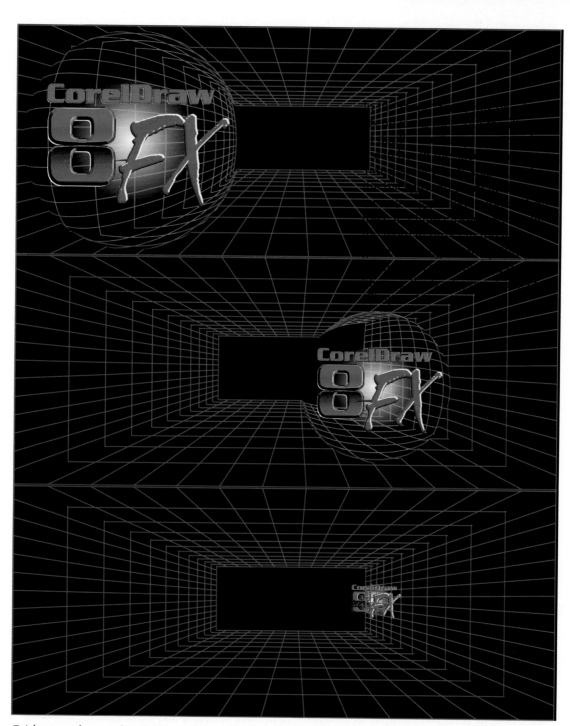

Grids manufactured with the Grids tool are made to look three-dimensional with the Perspective tool. A circle with the Fisheye Lens appears to bend the light as it floats by. (Chapter 25)

Blending a spiraled set of spokes to a smaller duplicate results in an impressive light show. Changing some of the blend parameters creates colorful black holes. (Chapter 25)

# PHYSICS
## An Introduction

Combining the grid and light show elements creates a bright and interesting book cover. (Chapter 25)

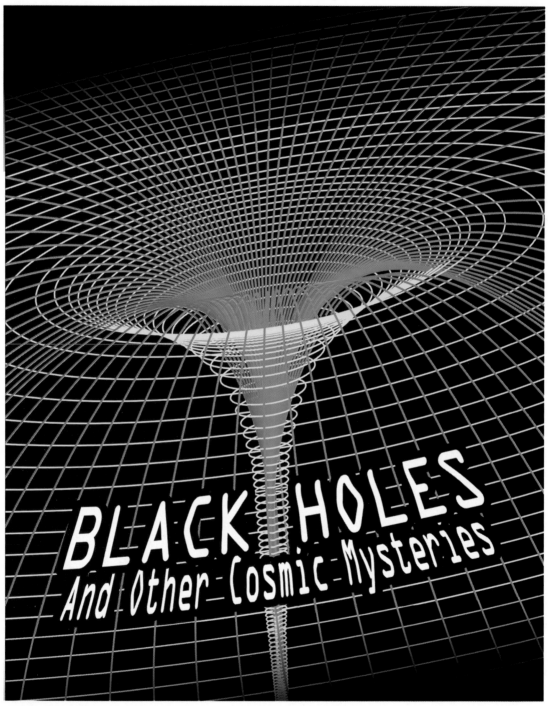

Bend space to your will by applying the Blend roll-up to grid lines. (Chapter 25)

Top and center: Using the Blend roll-up, you can suggest movement by blending either the object outline or the entire image. Bottom: With a bitmap of the image, you can use motion blur effects to create some zip and zoom. (Chapter 26)

Using the Interactive Transparency tool, a jet speeds by leaving clear vapor trails. (Chapter 26)

Add a sense of speed to a background created in CorelDRAW by converting the image to a bitmap, then applying the motion blur effect. (Chapter 26)

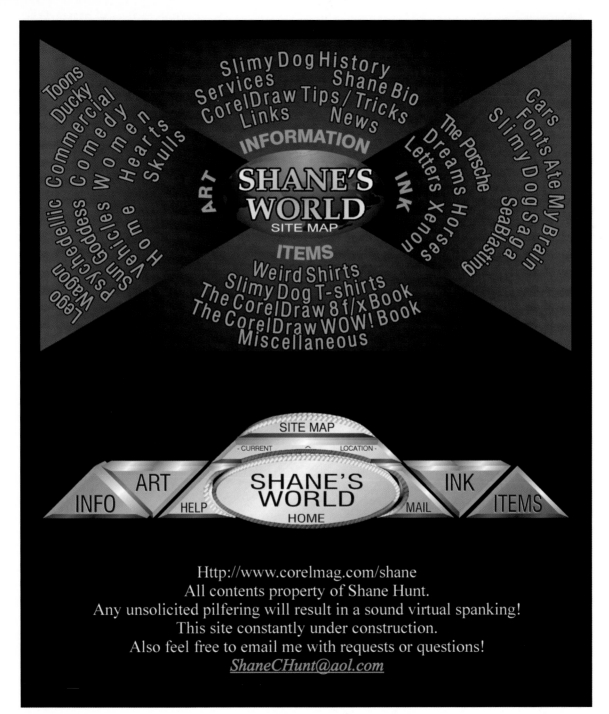

CorelDRAW can be used to create image maps for Web sites. (Chapter 27)

Plan out the whole look of your Web page using CorelDRAW—then generate Web-friendly graphics directly from the file. (Chapter 27)

Top: Using the clone feature of CorelDRAW, you can create an endlessly repeating pattern of geometric objects (a *tessellation*). Bottom: Tiling a star creates an interesting background for a Web site or an advertisement. (Chapter 28)

It's easy to plan out repeating designs in CorelDRAW. (Chapter 28)

You can create tiles for seamless background images with the PowerClip feature.
(Chapter 28)

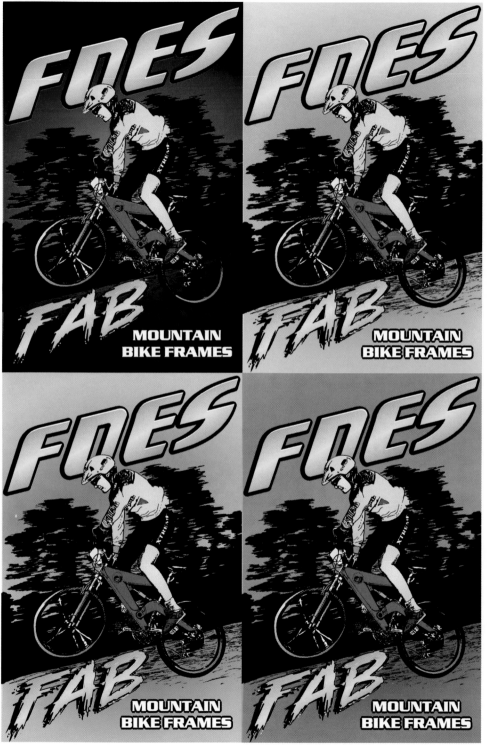

Using a lens to alter the background of an illustration animates a static image. (Chapter 29)

"Gelatin" letters can be created using a blend, and then jiggled by selecting and moving the top control curve. (Chapter 29)

Skewing flat artwork can help you visualize a finished 3D product. (Chapter 30)

Using CorelDRAW to create the sides of the box and the inlaid marble bitmap image, you can assemble an ornate jewelry box in CorelDream. (Chapter 30)

Objects created in CorelDRAW get depth and dimension when imported into CorelDream.
(Chapter 30)

# CAN YOU DRAW "LITTLE CHIRPY"?

## THEN YOU ARE READY FOR AN EXCITING CAREER AS A COMMERCIAL ARTIST!

### LEARN EVERYTHING YOU NEED TO KNOW TO START YOUR NEW CAREER FROM

## Crazy Uncle Shane's
(CORRESPONDENCE)
## Academy Of Design

*"Easy financing available!"*

Name: ............................................................
Address: ........................................................
City: .......................................... State: ................... ZIP: ...............

Mail this form, along with your "Little Chirpy" illustration and a check or money order for a gazillion dollars to: Crazy Uncle Shane's Academy of Design:  123 Big Sucker Lane, Ubintook, California,  00834-02134

---

# LEARN THE SECRETS THAT PROFESSIONAL MUSCLEMEN USE TO BUILD UP THEIR BODIES IN JUST 90 SECONDS A DAY!

ORDER NOW!
**1-800-STEROID**

*Mike Marvelous*

Almost like a miracle - this latest Amazing Motionless Exercise discovery - MIKE MARVELOUS' SCIENTIFIC ISOMETRICS - will give you fantastic strength with muscles Of steel without Sweat or Strain! Powerful arms, magnificently-powerful chest, powerful shoulders, strong stomach muscles and legs that will seldom tire!  No Apparatus or Exercisers - your body is your own Gymnasium!  This Secret System develops muscular strength 3 times faster than conventional methods!

---

## BE TALLER

If you wish to know the facts about HEIGHT INCREASE, send $1 for details to TALL-UP. Dept. U-Bshort, 410 Slouch St., SmallVille, Ohio 43645

## KARATE

Learn-At-Home-Course

So your wimpy comic-reading butt won't get beat up every day for the rest of your life!

FREE!

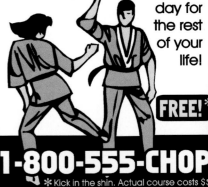

# 1-800-555-CHOP

✳ Kick in the shin. Actual course costs $

*Figure 17-7: The Blend roll-up spins the duplicates around the altered axis of rotation, resulting in a flower design.*

That's all there is to it. This is one of my favorite tricks because the results are so stunning with very little effort involved. Some of my experiments can be seen in the color section and in the spiro.cdr file found in the \Chapt17\ subdirectory on the Companion CD-ROM. This is one file I highly recommend you open; I dabbled for a long time with this technique, with curved and straight lines resulting in way too many variations to walk through! The technique is so simple, though, that if you look at the blends, you will immediately see how things work. Use the Simple Wireframe option under the View menu to see just the control curves. Then double-click with the Pick tool to see the axis of rotation for each piece—change it and see how the blends change. It's fun, and it beats the heck out of those little plastic gears!

## Psycho Women

*Figure 17-8: Using the Blend roll-up to create ringed shapes and then combining the shapes together makes for some very strange psychedelic objects! To make the image even more dizzying, the Rainbow option from the Fountain Fill dialog adds an explosion of colors.*

Although the fundamental guidelines for design always lean toward maximizing comprehension and making images easy to view, I can't help but want to go in the opposite direction. I love to create images that are just downright dizzying to view. With CorelDRAW, I can now take things one more step and also animate these images to create an art piece that nearly causes vertigo. The trick is to use the Blend function to create ringed objects. Then by combining these shapes, absolute chaos results! If this style of artwork doesn't grab your audiences' attention, they're either blind or dead. Here is how to make psychedelic images:

1. Draw a large perfect circle and duplicate it (+ key). Downsize the duplicate by dragging a corner sizing handle inward with the Pick tool while holding down the Shift key. Now select both circles and open the Blend roll-up (Ctrl+B). Change to 21 steps and click Apply. Separate everything

with the Arrange | Separate and the Arrange | Ungroup All commands, and finally, combine (Ctrl+L) the objects. Give the object a black fill to see the rings you have created (see Figure 17-9).

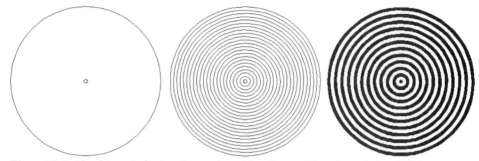

*Figure 17-9: Blend two circles together and combine the resulting shapes into solid rings.*

2. Now already you are in business to create some dizzying designs! Duplicate the ring shape and move it to the right. This looks pretty crazy already, but for some real chaos, select the two shapes and combine them (Ctrl+L). See Figure 17-10.

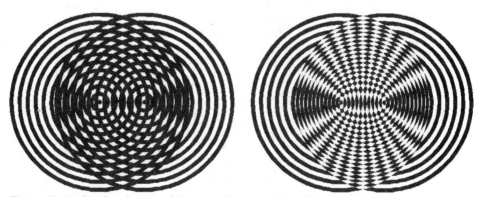

*Figure 17-10: Overlap the rings for a neat effect, or combine them for real chaos.*

3. To get the flower, I combined the circle ring shape with another ring shape made into a petal configuration. First, draw an ellipse, and using the now familiar change-axis-and-blend routine, create a flower shape. Now separate the blend, then ungroup all to free the pieces, and delete the extra petal shape. Select all of the petals and weld them into one object. Duplicate and downsize this object, and just like you did with the

circle, blend the two objects into a set of rings. Separate the blend and combine the rings into one object (see Figure 17-11).

*Figure 17-11: Create a flower shape with a blend and weld the petals into one curve. This curve is blended to a downsized duplicate, which in turn becomes another ring shape.*

4. Arrange the flower ring shape in the center of the original ring shape. If you combine (Ctrl+L) the two, you get a real dizzying image (see Figure 17-12).

*Figure 17-12: Align and combine the flower and rings shapes to create a dizzying pattern.*

5. Select the new freaky shape and open the Fountain Fill dialog (F11). Change the Type setting to Radial and then make the From and To colors both the same yellow. Finally, click either the Clockwise or the Counter-clockwise button to fill the object with a rainbow color scheme (see Figure 17-13).

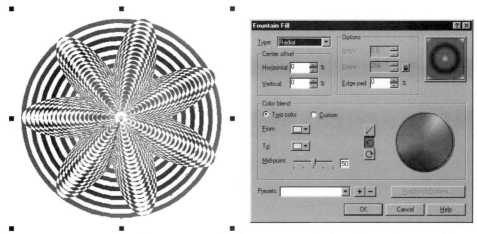

*Figure 17-13: You can use the Fountain Fill dialog to create a rainbow fill shape by using like colors in the From and To selections and then clicking one of the Rainbow Rotation buttons.*

6. Draw a circle and send it behind the flower curve object. Now fill this circle with yet another rainbow, only start the rainbow at a different point by setting the From and To colors to cyan. Click OK to get a really trippy, colorful image (see Figure 17-14).

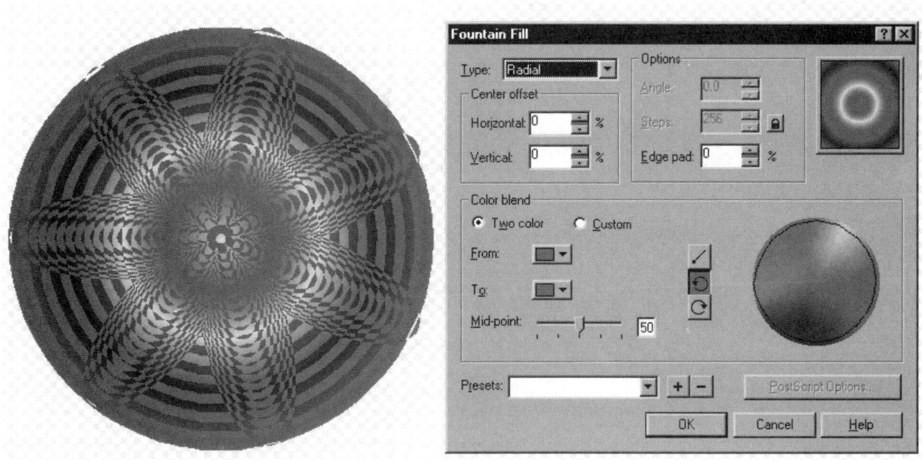

*Figure 17-14: A rainbow-filled circle shape behind the flower curve object makes for even more color.*

That's like, all, man. With a rainbow filling both the curve and the background shape, you get a barrage of color. This would make for an interesting tile graphic adorning, say, a flashback newsletter, with one of the flowers on each side of the masthead. Brilliant color always gets attention, and this image has plenty of coloring options. You can see the different color options in the color section and also in the amys.cdr file found in the \Chapt17\ subdirectory on the Companion CD-ROM. The file is named after the model I used to adorn the center of the flower shape, found on the Women in Vogue Corel Professional photo CD. "Psycho-Amy," then, refers to this image and not to "Amy the project editor"—maybe not. =)

Also check out the amy1.avi animation found in the \Chapt17\ subdirectory on the Companion CD-ROM. I created this dizzying movie by advancing the rainbows in the flower curve and background circle. To advance the rainbow, open the Fountain Fill dialog and change from the current From and To colors to the next colors in the color wheel. For example, to advance the clockwise rainbow in the yellow From and To fountain fill, change to the next color that is counterclockwise in the color wheel, which is magenta. From magenta, advance to cyan, and so on to make the rainbows appear to pulse when you animate the frames.

## Psycho Text

Although the trend during the psychedelic movement was to render images almost unreadable, you can create interesting and even legible text elements using similar techniques. Here is how to make some groovalicious headline text:

1. Use the Artistic Text tool to set some text. I used a font called BellBottom Wide. Arrange the text inside one of the circle ring curves and squish the ring shape to fit the text better (see Figure 17-15).

*Figure 17-15: Mix a text element in with the circle ring shape.*

2. If you combine the text and the rings, you get a very ghostly, unreadable message (on left). If you first duplicate the text object and then combine the duplicate with the circle rings, you can shade the original text to

make it stand out against the ring shape. Because the ring shape also contains the text, there is a neat positive/negative look to the coloring where the two objects overlap (see Figure 17-16).

*Figure 17-16: Duplicate the text and combine the duplicate with the ring shape. Use the original text object to add a contrasting shading element, making the text easier to read.*

3. For a different kind of eye candy, use the Contour roll-up (Ctrl+F9) to create the rings around an object. Then use the Separate, Ungroup All, and Combine (Ctrl+L) commands to first separate all of the objects, and then combine them to create a funkadelic text item (see Figure 17-17).

*Figure 17-17: Use the Contour roll-up to create the shapes needed to create the color rings around text or any other odd-shaped object.*

The high contrast that these ringed shapes create makes your eyes buzz, but in a good way! For even more color, use a heavy outline with the Behind Fill option enabled from the Outline Pen dialog (F12). Select colors that bounce (like red and blue) or complementary colors for more friendly reading. Still not convinced how this is worked into commercial applications? Read on brothers and sisters.

## Tripping Adtastic

*Figure 17-18: You can use any shape, including those custom fit to a specific application, to generate the pieces for the dazzling psychedelic effect.*

It's the summer of love, man, with peace, happiness, joy, and the best deals in town on cellular phones. Come on down! Even something as blasé as a phone suddenly looks darn interesting when it is at the center of this eye-grabbing pattern in Figure 17-18. It's created with essentially the same technique we used in the previous section, except that the phone itself provides the shape for the blend—just a little more effort, but with a bigger and much more useful payoff! Here is how to use the psychedelic blend technique with a custom shape:

1. Import the image to which you wish to draw attention. I found the phone on the CorelDRAW clip-art CD, in the \objects\bus-equi (business equipment) directory. The nice thing about the images in the objects directory is that they are free floating with transparent backgrounds, so you can stick them anywhere.

2. Use the Bezier tool to click along the edge of the phone from point to point, creating a simple straight-line outline of the phone. Then go back with the Shape tool and smooth out the edges for a smoother curve.

3. Shrink the phone outline until it is really small, then duplicate it, and enlarge the duplicate to the edge of your page. Now select both and create a 10-step blend between them (see Figure 17-19).

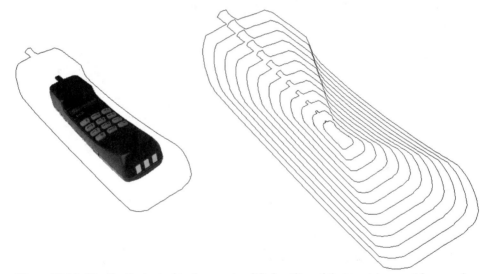

*Figure 17-19: Use the Bezier tool to draw a simplified outline of the target image. A large and small duplicate of the outline are blended together to get things started.*

4. Now as before, kill the blend, ungroup the objects, and combine the pieces into a single curve (see Figure 17-20). Things are already getting interesting!

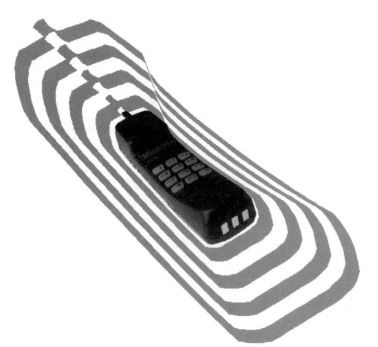

*Figure 17-20: Separating the pieces in the blend and then combining them into one curve creates the fill/open pattern unique to this effect.*

5. For an even more interesting effect, add a sunburst to draw the eye to the center of the graphic. Start with a perfect circle that extends beyond the edges of your page and then use the Shape tool to transform the circle into just a sliver.

6. Duplicate this sliver, select both copies, and use the Rotation option on the Blend roll-up to create the sunburst with a 30-step blend. Use the Separate and Ungroup All commands to break up the blend into individual pieces. Then select and delete the extra sliver object from the blend step and combine the rest into a single sun ray curve. (If you forget to delete the extra sliver, one of your rays will be inversed-out leaving an open space as the two stacked shapes cross-cancel each other out when you perform the combine step). See Figure 17-21.

7. Place the sunburst so that its center is at the center of the phone to ensure that all eyes are drawn there. Then select both the sun ray and the phone curve graphic from step 4 and combine them (see Figure 17-22). Bang, right between the eyes! This technique could sell ice to Eskimos.

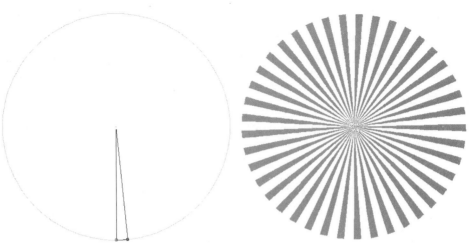

*Figure 17-21: Use the Shape tool to modify a circle into a sliver and then blend two copies of the shape into a sunburst image.*

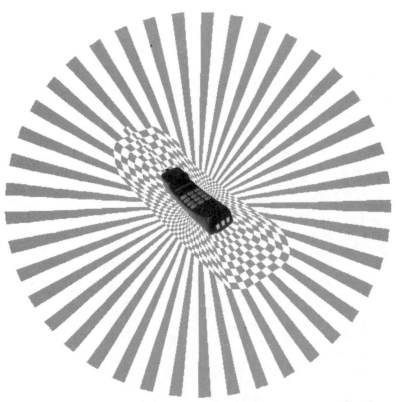

*Figure 17-22: Combine the sunburst with the phone curve to create a dizzying pattern.*

8. Use the PowerClip function to stuff all of the pieces neatly into the page limit, add some text, and call it a day!

The image is exploding in the color section and also in the phone.cdr file found in the \Chapt17\ subdirectory on the Companion CD-ROM. If you want to manipulate the pieces in this file, remember you have to extract the contents from the PowerClip. You can select the sunburst curve, break it apart, delete the phone pieces, and steal the spokes for your own designs. Images like this that just suck your eye to the center are perfect for drawing attention to objects that just fail to excite on their own. As another bonus, the high-contrast and effective attention-getting design is perfect for low or no color print applications. The graphic in the color section would be just as effective printed only in yellow and black (the phone does have some other colors in it, but they are not critical to the success of the design). You have to remember that back in the '60s when this kind of graphic was in its heyday, printing technology was low tech, so simple one- and two-color designs were very popular and also more cost effective. You can exploit these savings today as well. Frugality is not an anachronistic concept!

## Funky Fresh

*Figure 17-23: Bouncing hard and loud, this image borrows from a popular detergent box for a bright, happy logo using the Interactive Fill tool.*

Although not a part of the '60s design movement, there has been a recent trend to incorporate images from the past into a high-tech feel of the present. This logo, which looks like a Tide detergent box, has found its way into many contemporary applications, including my own! It is one of those graphics that you can see from across the room, and it always gets noticed. Here is how to incorporate that triple-exploding look into your own design:

1. Draw a perfect circle and select the Interactive Fill tool. Now drag in the circle to start a fountain fill. Click the Radial button on the Property Bar to change the type of fountain fill and then drag yellow to the center color point and red to the outside point (the little slider in the middle controls the midpoint setting). This makes a nice smooth blend, but we need a harsher transition. Drag and drop another yellow point along the blend line and also drag out another red one. Now by sliding the points along the line, you change the way the blend works and looks. It takes a bit of finesse to move the points around and get the desired results (see Figure 17-24).

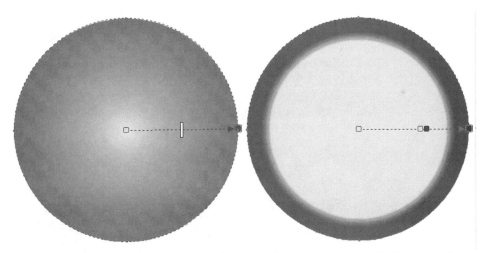

*Figure 17-24: Use additional redundant color points along a custom color blend to change how and when the colors blend together.*

2. Duplicate the circle shape (+ key) and downsize the duplicate about 79 percent by dragging a corner sizing handle inward while holding down the Shift key. Duplicate this circle again (+ key) and downsize it about 70 percent. This places the circles in the right orientation with about the right shading, but it's really not quite on the money yet. Use the Interactive Fill tool to move the points along each custom color blend to correct the fill for each downsized circle shape (see Figure 17-25).

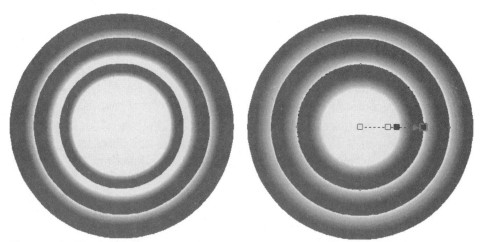

*Figure 17-25: Duplicating and downsizing the circle creates the other color rings, but things don't look right until each color blend is tuned with the Interactive Fill tool.*

3. Draw a rectangle the size of the page, fill it with the same red as the circle blends, and send it to the back (Shift+PgDn). Now all that remains is to set some text. Use the Artistic Text tool to set some fat verbiage (I used a font called Swis721 Blk BT). Skew the text from its standard layout into something interesting and give it a fat .153-inch black outline. Duplicate the text (+ key) and give the duplicate a thinner .111-inch white outline. This will make for a thin black outline around the heavy white one, which will make the main text stand out more (see Figure 17-26).

*Figure 17-26: Stack a thinner white-outlined copy of the text on a fatter black-outlined version to result in the multiple outline look.*

4. Use the Artistic Text tool again to set the smaller copy. I used the same font I used for the title, only smaller. Break up the text into smaller chunks so you can more easily manipulate each word, or even each letter. Give the text a white fill, and from the Outline Pen dialog (F12), give it a fat .111-inch black outline. Enable the Behind Fill option and change to the squared-off corner option (see Figure 17-27).

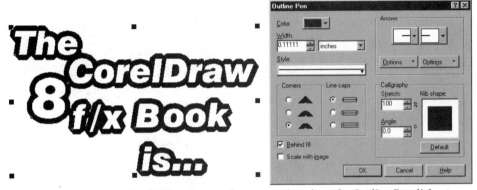

*Figure 17-27: Use the Behind Fill and squared corner options from the Outline Pen dialog to make other text stand out.*

5. Skew the text objects at the same time so they all have the same slant even though they are individual objects. With the Shape tool, select an individual letter or shift-select to select more than one letter within a word object. Now you can drag the node to move just the selected letter without moving the rest of the word. If you double-click on a selected node (or nodes) on a text object with the Shape tool, it will open the Format Text dialog. Any changes you make, such as size or even a new font entirely, will only be made to the selected letters. In this way, you can enlarge just the first letter in these individual text elements (see Figure 17-28).

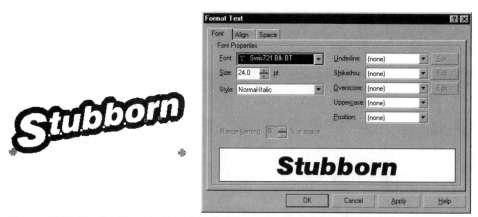

*Figure 17-28: Use the Shape tool to select and change the font attributes of a single letter.*

**TIP**

*With the Shape tool, you can select individual letters within a text element, be it an Artistic or even Paragraph text item. Once you have selected a letter, or shift-selected several, you can then change the font attributes on the selected letters by double-clicking the node to open the Format Text dialog. Okay, fine—you knew that. But in the same way you can also change the outline and fill attributes of individual letters within a word or paragraph. Select the letters with the Shape tool by clicking on their associated node; then change the outline or fill like you would for any other object. Pretty slick, no? If you select the entire word or paragraph with the Pick tool and change things, all of the pieces will change, even those you singled out with the Shape tool.*

6. Arrange the text elements in a scattered yet readable layout over the triple blend.

Funky fresh, my friends! Once again, a bright and colorful image without even the hint of an aneurysm.

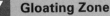

**Gloating Zone**

What you may not realize is what a pain it is to try to control the blends in the background circles in any application other than CorelDRAW. The ease of use and fine-tuneability of the Interactive Fill tool make short order of a task others slave over.

Should you gloat? Of course! Torment those poor slobs still clinging to their design-specific computers and high-priced software with a cheery smile and a wave as you head out to do something fun while they labor painfully into the overtime zone to create their effects.

## Dizzying Possibilities

*Figure 17-29: You can transform CorelDRAW objects into bitmaps and use a wide range of filter effects on them to get eye-popping results otherwise impossible with conventional CorelDRAW effects.*

In the last chapter, we talked about how you can change the look of a bitmap within CorelDRAW by placing a lens object over it, which is a flexible way to experiment with different looks; a lens doesn't modify a bitmap, only the way you see it. This is an important concept in projects such as this one where we will physically change the bitmap itself using the filter effects under the CorelDRAW bitmap menu. The point of this exercise is to take an image you have finished in all different directions without much effort. You can get an incredible amount of variety with these built-in bitmap effects filters and just a few mouse clicks. This type of layout, with many variations of the same theme, is good for presenting a bunch of design ideas to a fussy client. They get a dizzying array of variety, and they are happily dazzled with options. What they don't know (and it will be our little secret) is that CorelDRAW did most of the work! Here is how to change a bitmap object in CorelDRAW using filter effects:

1. Start with any garden-variety bitmap, or use the Convert to Bitmap function from the Bitmap menu in CorelDRAW. It is noteworthy to mention that many filters only work on RGB images and not CMYK images. This is common, as it is much simpler to work with three variables than four. If you use the Convert to Bitmap feature within CorelDRAW, just make sure to set the Color option to 24 Bit - 16 Million rather than 32 bit, which is CMYK. I used the pieces from the angle.cdr file in Chapter 16 and converted them to an RGB bitmap within CorelDRAW.

2. Duplicate the bitmap, or better yet, save it (File | Save As) with a unique filename. This is a good habit to get into, as once you convert a bitmap, there is only one level of undo as the default. You can change this value to more in the Options dialog (Ctrl+J), but each undo level hogs huge amounts of memory. I recommend multiple file saves, which uses disk space but leaves more memory free.

**TIP**

*To save time when you experiment with Bitmap plug-in effects, first try everything on a much smaller bitmap. Full-page bitmaps are huge and calculations for effects take forever. If you are just looking for something cool to do, to speed things up, first use a smaller thumbnail of your image. Create the thumbnail by either choosing a smaller resolution from the Export dialog or downsizing the full-size bitmap with the Resample dialog in PhotoPaint. When you find a combination of filter effects that you like, then go back and perform the same sequence on the full-size bitmap.*

3. With your bitmap selected, choose Plug-Ins from the Bitmap menu. If things seem to freeze and then nothing happens, it is because CorelDRAW is loading the files needed. Don't panic; just choose Plug-Ins again from the Bitmap menu, and the second time, they will all behave nicely! (If you still don't have any plug-in options, open the Options menu (Ctrl+J), and from the Workspace | Plug-Ins options page, you can select and load the ones you want.) From the Plug-Ins submenu, choose PhotoLab. From the PhotoLab submenu, choose GradTone. What this filter does is add or replace colors based on the luminance of the image. You can set the colors manually by selecting any color on the screen with the eyedropper, placing the color on the blend bar, and reviewing the results in the Before and After windows. To get your feet wet, I suggest you just use one of the handy presets (Old Gold gives a great antique look, for example). For this image, I picked Electric Fire and then clicked OK to transform my bitmap (see Figure 17-30). See the color section for the results.

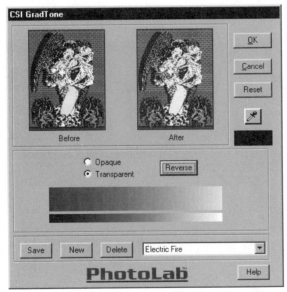

*Figure 17-30: The PhotoLab CSI GradTone filter adds or replaces colors based on the luminance of the image.*

4. Save this image with a unique filename. I used this recolored image for the remaining examples, always saving the results with a new filename and reloading the original to try a new filter. Remember that you do have that one level of undo working for you, so if your results are not what you expected while you are experimenting with bitmap filters, just undo them (Ctrl+Z) to jump back to the image as it was before you applied the filter. Select your bitmap again and from the Bitmap menu, choose 3D Effects; then choose Page Curl from the submenu. This dialog lets you create the look of paper curling up on the corner of your choice; you can set it by clicking one of the four buttons with the paper curl icons on them. By dragging the Width and Height sliders, you can set how wide and tall the curl will be in relation to the bitmap. Make your choices and click OK (see Figure 17-31).

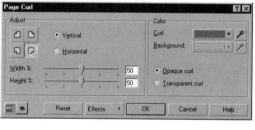

*Figure 17-31: The Page Curl filter rolls a corner of the paper over part of the bitmap.*

**TIP**  *The Preview button on the filter dialogs lets you see the effect before you commit to it with the OK button. This feature is nice, but kind of misleading. If you click Preview, like what you see, and then click OK, CorelDRAW calculates the filter twice, so it just took you twice as long to change your bitmap. If you think you are close with the settings, just go ahead and click OK. Then you will only have to wait for CorelDRAW to calculate the change once. If you don't like the results, you can always use the Undo function (Ctrl+Z) and try the filter again, but chances are you will be happy with the results and only have to wait for one calculate cycle.*

5. Select the original bitmap, and from the 3D Effects submenu, choose Map to Object. What this filter does is create the illusion that the bitmap is being wrapped around the surface of a 3D object, such as a sphere or cylinder. Select the Spherical Mapping mode and adjust the Percentage to 32 (the preview window gives you an idea of how warped the image will be). Click OK to make the bitmap look round (see Figure 17-32).

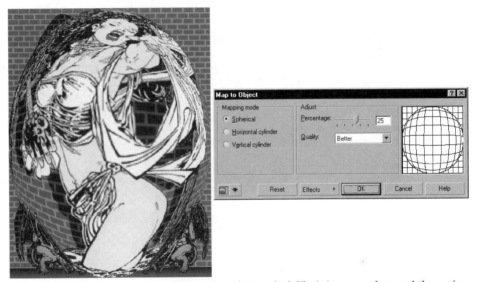

*Figure 17-32: The Map to Object filter makes a bitmap look like it is wrapped around the surface of a 3D object, such as a sphere, for example.*

6. Select the original bitmap, and from the 2D Effects submenu, choose Swirl. This filter rotates the bitmap like it is in a whirlpool. Select the Clockwise Direction option, set the Additional Degrees slider to 90, and click OK. This will twirl the bitmap (see Figure 17–33).

7. Select the original bitmap, and from the 2D Effects submenu, choose Wet Paint. This adds drips and drops to the image, which either makes it look like wet paint or melting wax, depending on your point of view! For lots of drama, crank the Percent slider up to 100 and the Wetness slider to 45 and click OK. Figure 17-34.

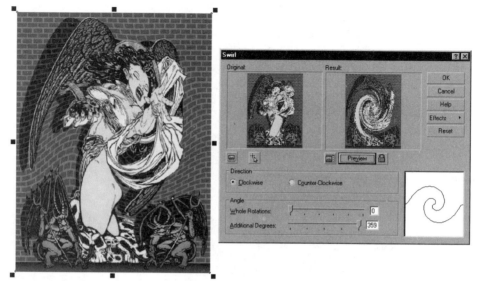

*Figure 17-33: The Swirl filter twirls the image like a whirlpool.*

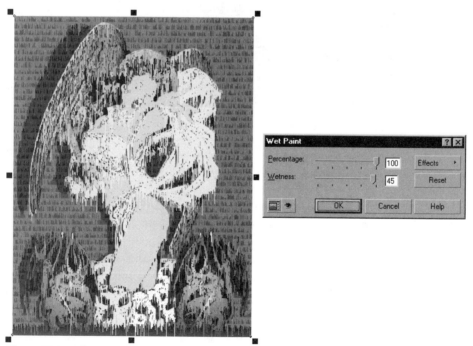

*Figure 17-34: The Wet Paint filter makes bitmaps look like they are dripping with fresh paint.*

8. Select the original bitmap, and from the 3D Effects submenu, choose Pinch Punch. This filter makes the bitmap look as though it is pushed out or pulled in from the center. If you drag to the right, you set a *pinch* (pulled toward center), and if you drag to the left, a *punch* (pushed out from center). Drag to the right, and click OK (see Figure 17-35).

*Figure 17-35: The Pinch Punch filter pushes or pulls the image from the center.*

9. Select the original bitmap, and from the Blur submenu, choose the Motion blur option. This filter creates the illusion of movement or the look of moving a camera when you snap a photo. Click the edge of the dial to set the direction of the blurring and move the Distance slider to set the level of intensity. A higher Distance value makes for a more dramatic blur. Set the value and click OK (see Figure 17-36).

10. Select the original bitmap, and from the 3D Effects submenu, choose Emboss. This filter creates a three-dimensional relief effect, as if the paper itself were pressed into an image. For a more obvious effect, increase the Depth slider to 10 and keep the light source to a common top-right configuration with the default Direction setting of 45. Click OK to add some weird depth to the image (see Figure 17-37).

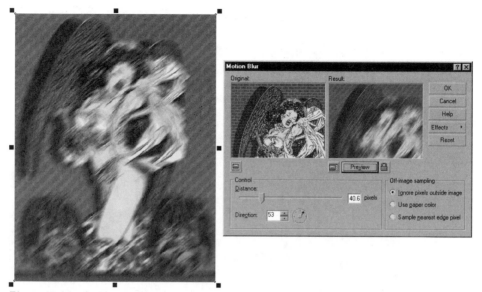

*Figure 17-36: The Motion Blur filter gives you a shaky camera hand or the illusion that your images are in motion.*

*Figure 17-37: The Emboss filter adds a three-dimensional relief effect.*

I could go on and on, but I think you get the idea. I use this trick for those high-dollar clients who want to feel like I am really busting my butt for them, even though in the long run they end up going with something predictable and probably boring. I am sure you know the personality I am talking about. Sometimes you have to dazzle the client just to sell the design itself, long before it even has a chance to work on the general public. It's all part of the dog and pony show that is the world of advertising design! You can see the results in the color section, or you can open the file called angstep.cdr in the \Chapt17\ subdirectory on the Companion CD-ROM. The CorelDRAW file is exactly like the image in the color section, so you may want to create your own bitmap to experiment with. Happy filtering! Hmmm, speaking of filters, time to make some coffee.

**CD-ROM**

## Moving On

In this chapter, we looked at creating bright, chaotic, even nightmarish-looking designs using CorelDRAW functions and bitmap filters. We again saw how the Blend roll-up can be used to create all kinds of shapes, including the simple, the mechanical, and the downright dizzying! We also saw how the Contour roll-up can be used to create shapes for vibrating options.

With these techniques, there are so many possible outcomes and variants available. It's important not to lose sight of the project you are working on as a whole by focusing on a single technique. No design will be made or destroyed using a single effect outlined in this book. These are just options and ideas to give your designs more potential. You need to balance effects to achieve the goals of your specific design. For example, if you use a wild effect like those in this chapter excessively, your design will lose impact. You can't emphasize *everything!* Like I said before, more is not better!

The examples in this section were extreme and used many bright colors. You can use the same kinds of techniques to get much more subtle images for more conservative designs. Throw a white box over the image with a transparency lens to mute the colors nicely for almost any application.

In the next chapter, we are going to look at how to use CorelDRAW to create comic book heroes and heroines. We will examine how to use the program to colorize ink drawings and also see how anyone can create fun and interesting cartoon characters right in CorelDRAW. Hey, I understand that not everyone is an illustrator, but I refuse to believe that you don't possess the talent necessary to create amazing artwork with CorelDRAW. You have hung in there so far, either because you have some talent or you are some huge masochist! In either case, it's time to get into the funny pages.

### ▼ Beyond f/x

Explosive, bright designs such as these help draw attention because of high contrast, both within the designs themselves and in a broader sense. Things naturally stand out when they are different, so for a market that is normally sedate, a bright, fun graphic might work really well. However, these images might actually just look boring and ordinary in a demographic that is already suffering a glut of visual noise. So research your market so you know if the design is right for it or if it is inappropriate because of the shock value.

Almost anything can benefit from a bit of eye-blasting imagery now and then. A graphic using these techniques could draw attention to new products in an ad or new pages in a Web site. The techniques work equally well as primary design elements or as secondary pieces like borders or edge designs. Promotional materials, such as stickers, T-shirts (see Figure 17-38), or buttons, can push the design limits and benefit greatly from a violently interesting graphic that won't go unnoticed. Perhaps you could take the idea too far, though. Is a dizzying billboard that literally stops traffic a bad design? Hmmm.

*Figure 17-38: Even a simple two-color promotional T-shirt design becomes a bright and interesting image using techniques from this chapter. When it is printed in black and neon orange, you can't miss it!*

# chapter 18
# Comic Book Heroes

There is nothing more Americana than the Sunday comic strip. These colorful and fun images have made their way out of the comic strips and into virtually every other type of media. From Roy Lichtenstein's fine art renderings of comic-style images to television commercials featuring animated cartoon characters, this style of art continues to grow in popularity.

CorelDRAW offers a flexible digital workspace that will appeal to both computer-based and pen-and-ink artists for creating stunning comic-book-style artwork. In fact, there are more and more commercially successful comic strip artists using the computer as their media of choice because of the design flexibility and, of course, those thousands of nifty fonts for the thought balloons.

For computer artists, CorelDRAW allows for easy creation of characters with the ability to use common shapes augmented by the flexibility of fill options. For traditional pen-and-ink artists, CorelDRAW offers tools for colorizing hand-drawn sketches and for creating complex scenes for those characters ranging from impressionistic to high tech. The modern virtual studio of CorelDRAW offers more flexibility than the traditional tools, allowing an artist to change and experiment with different scenes, colors, and poses quickly and easily. Art boards are out, my friend. Grab an accelerated, high-res video board with about 4 megs of RAM instead!

This chapter will show you how to create comic-book-type characters and scenes using CorelDRAW. I'll start by demonstrating how to create and color simple cartoon characters and a background for them quickly and completely in CorelDRAW. This is a comparatively simple skill that you can use to liven up all sorts of designs with minimal effort. Next, I'll show you how to use CorelDRAW to colorize hand-drawn and scanned artwork, and I'll not only show you how to create a scene for it, but I'll also demonstrate one of many techniques for making that scene look hand-drawn so that it matches the artwork. Finally, I'll take you through a more complex example of colorizing hand-drawn artwork and creating a dynamic high-tech scene around it. This example will make use of several techniques covered earlier in the book, most notably blends and repeating images.

I will show you how to colorize hand-drawn and scanned artwork, how to build characters entirely within the program using simple shapes, and also how to mix and match both kinds of artwork into one scene. CorelDRAW really works well for cartooning and this style of artwork, so this will be a fun chapter!

## Game Over

*Figure 18-1: If you can draw stick figures, you can create comic characters in CorelDRAW! Simple shapes transform into animated actors for a fun cartoony look.*

I am amazed at how people always claim to have no artistic skills. "I can only draw stick figures," people tell me when I show them some art piece I am working on, like it's an excuse as to why they don't draw or paint. I don't buy this. You don't have to be dripping with talent to be a good artist; you just have to learn how to use the tools that you have and be patient enough to work out any design problems that arise.

Take me, for example. Personally, I think I am a lousy artist when compared to my gifted associates. What my artist friends can render in one simple step takes me hours to sketch out in pencil and then ink up as line art. This is where CorelDRAW becomes the perfect creative medium for me. What I lack in talent I make up for in creativity and tenacity. I don't have to be able to draw a straight line or perfect circle—CorelDRAW does it for me. If I am not happy with the way a design is laid out, I can easily resize, rearrange, re-everything in CorelDRAW. It may take me a little longer, but with a little effort I can get the results I want. I am guessing you can too.

With very simple shapes you can create some very fun comic characters. Even the most gifted artists start with simple shapes and move on from there. The same techniques apply to creating comic characters, where you can be as simple or complex as you wish. In any case, even if you just stick with the simplest of shapes, you can get some pretty fun and animated characters with just a little effort. Here is how to make fun comic characters using only CorelDRAW objects:

1. With the Ellipse tool, draw a circle for the head. Then use the tool again to draw an oval for an eye. You can freehand draw the other eye, but I like to keep things symmetrical by duplicating objects (+ key) and then moving the duplicates into place using the Pick tool. Remember, you can always toggle between the Pick tool and the active tool by tapping the spacebar. Switch to the Bezier tool and click to create a pyramid-like object for the torso. If you don't start and stop in the same place, the object will be an open curve. Click the Auto Close button to convert open curves into solid objects.

2. Continue to use the Bezier tool to click around and make a skirt shape. Then create some pointy triangles for the legs. It's easy, huh? Now create the left and right arms, which require a little more attention. Finally, use the Ellipse tool to draw in other details, such as ear pieces (see Figure 18-2).

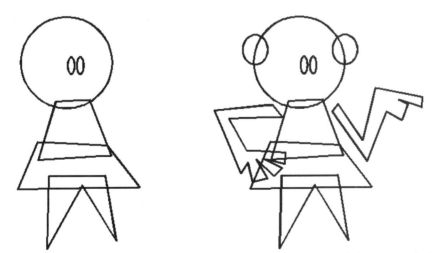

*Figure 18-2: The Ellipse tool draws great circles, while the Bezier tool draws straight-lined objects easy with single clicks from point to point.*

3. Draw more circles to fill in details like the shoulders and big poofy hair. To speed things up and keep everything symmetrical, duplicate like object shapes (such as ears, hair, etc.) and flip-flop the duplicate horizontally by dragging a left-center sizing handle to the right while holding down the Ctrl key. You should now start to see the girl figure emerge from the simple shapes (see Figure 18-3).

*Figure 18-3: Duplicate and flip-flop objects to speed things along and keep the like object pairs symmetrical.*

4. Now our figure looks very much like a stick person, or robot, which is fine, but I like my cartoons more gooey. With the Shape tool, select an object such as an arm or leg, drag-select all of the nodes, and then open the Node Edit roll-up (Ctrl+F10). Now click the Convert Line to Curve button and then the Make Node Smooth button. This will convert the straight and pointy objects into mooshy sausages (see Figure 18-4).

*Figure 18-4: Use the Node Edit roll-up to convert the lines to curves and smooth out the nodes.*

5. Fine-tune the objects with the Shape tool. Some pieces, like the feet, need to have the nodes changed back to cusp so you can make them pointy again. You can get carried away, as I do, massaging the pieces until you get them just right. Now you can start to fill the pieces with colors and arrange them in front and behind each other to make the girl come to life (see Figure 18-5).

*Figure 18-5: The Shape tool makes fine-tuning the objects to get the exact lines and curves easy. Assign outline and fill colors to change the wireframe objects into solid objects.*

6. To add pieces such as the hair and the socks, don't try to draw objects that fit together because that takes too long. Draw a simple object with the Freehand tool and then use the Intersect roll-up from the Arrange Menu to create a new object where the two overlap. This way you can quickly create custom-fit pieces for many details (see Figure 18-6).

*Figure 18-6: Use the Intersection command to create new shapes where objects overlap for such things as socks and hair.*

7. Add small details such as circles for gleam shapes and fingernails. For the boy, first I used the Freehand tool to draw the pieces and then cleaned things up using the Shape tool and the Node Edit roll-up. Which tool you are more comfortable working with will depend on how adept you are at using the mouse. My Freehand mouse shapes look darned pathetic until I cleaned them up with the Shape tool! Once again, big simple shapes, such as the circles, will trim down nicely to become hair and other objects using the Intersection tool (see Figure 18-7).

*Figure 18-7: Instead of the straight-line shapes created with the Bezier tool, try drawing objects with the Freehand tool. The Shape tool can clean up even the most clumsy shapes into what you want.*

8. Color and stack the pieces like you did with the girl. For the pants, open the Pattern Fill dialog from the Fill flyout, choose the 2-color checker pattern, and then change the front color to red and the tile to medium. Click OK to fill (see Figure 18-8).

*Figure 18-8: The 2-Color pattern fill provides some fun cartoony fill options.*

Characters in themselves are not very interesting; they need to be in a scene. For these simple characters, I thought a video-game-type scenario would work well. Here is how to create an abstract high-tech scene for simple comic characters:

1. Use the Rectangle tool to draw a horizontal rectangle and then use the Shape tool to round the corners. Now duplicate this object many times and arrange the duplicates randomly, varying the height and width of each copy. Fill some of the objects and leave others with no fill and a heavy .40-inch outline. For an interesting look, I used three shades of blue for all of the outline and fill attributes. When you use the same color for a fill in one object and the outline in another, the point where they overlap disappears. Mix and match your background to taste using three similar tones right off of the onscreen palette to make things easy. If the colors are too strong, as I decided my blues were, simply draw a white rectangle over them and use the Lens roll-up (Alt+F3) to soften them with a Transparency lens (see Figure 18-9).

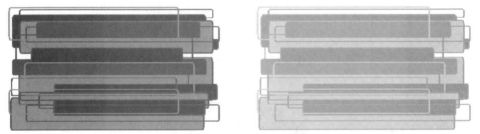

*Figure 18-9: A hodgepodge of rectangle shapes becomes the background elements. Use a white box with a Transparency lens to soften the colors to taste without the hassle of recoloring the objects manually.*

2. Draw another curved-corner rectangle to serve as stage for your characters and place them in the scene. For other action elements, I used star shapes from the Symbols roll-up. Open the Symbols roll-up (Ctrl+F11), switch to Stars1, and drag stars to your liking onto the scene. Color the stars with the same colors used in the background shapes (see Figure 18-10).

*Figure 18-10: Use the Symbols roll-up to add other design elements to your scene.*

3. Throw in a smattering of text and other little tidbits to finish off the design. The Blend roll-up was used to blend a white circle to a black one for the collection of shapes to the left of the main text. The main text is a font called BauHaus, with a black fill and heavy .111 outline and the Behind fill option enabled from the Outline Pen dialog (F12). The digital readout (seen in the final graphic in the color section) is a font called LCD, which is one of my favorites!

See? I told you that anyone who can draw stick figures possesses the talent necessary to create interesting computer art! Look through popular gaming and techie publications and you will see all kinds of artwork done in much the same way. My spin on the style can be seen in the color section, and if you are really hurting and can't draw these guys for yourself, the file is called gameover.cdr and is in the \Chapt18\ subdirectory on the Companion CD-ROM.

## Silly Putty

*Figure 18-11: Using the Freeze option on the Lens roll-up lets you capture an image like Silly Putty, and just like the real thing, you can twist and distort the picture using the Envelope tool.*

With your virtual comic strip coming to life, what could be more appropriate than to tweak it with some virtual Silly Putty? Silly Putty is that toy from way back (still available however, now in other colors and even with glitter!) that not only bounces around like a super-ball, but also had the unique ability to capture the printed images from the Sunday comics. Once the image was stuck in reverse to your Silly Putty blob, you could then twist and distort the image to create funny images. (It was the low-tech answer to today's MetaTools's Goo program!) Since it is my job to create strange things, I decided a computerized Silly Putty experience was in order! Here is how to capture an image and distort it in the computer:

1. First, open an image on which you want to use your Virtual Silly Putty (VSP). I should point out that you can Freeze any image, including bitmaps, using the Frozen option on the Lens roll-up, however only vector objects will distort correctly during the Enveloping steps. I used the comic characters from the previous exercise, but you can use any image, including clip-art. Draw an oval over your artwork, and for the Silly Putty look, color it faded pink (M-20, Y-20). Now open the Lens roll-up (Alt+F3), set the type to Transparency, rate at 50%, and click Apply.

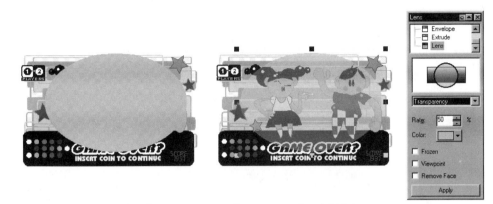

*Figure 18-12: An oval with a Transparency Lens creates the pinkish image.*

2. Now enable the Frozen option on the Lens roll-up, and click Apply. Now instead of just changing the way the artwork below the Lens looks, CorelDRAW will create new objects to look like the Lens effect. This process is complex (in this example there are 970 objects in the Frozen Lens Group), so it may take a while to compute. When finished, you will have a group of objects in addition to the originals, with the new group shaded like the Lens effect. See Figure 18-13.

*Figure 18-13: The Frozen feature of the Lens roll-up creates new objects to mimic the way the objects below the Lens effect appeared. You then can move and manipulate these objects.*

3. To distort the object, use the Interactive Envelope tool to twist and tweak like stretching the putty. Or use the Envelope roll-up (Ctrl+F7) to Add a New Unconstrained Envelope, with the Putty setting, and click Apply to distort. See Figure 18-14.

*Figure 18-14: Tweak and twist your virtual Silly Putty image with the Envelope feature.*

**TIP** *If you are experiencing difficulty outputting a file, it may be because it has many active lenses. Lenses and other CorelDRAW functions are not PostScript-based, and therefore may crash the processor when you try to use too many of them (CorelDRAW has to convert lenses into things PostScript will understand). The Frozen feature will avoid this problem, as the active lens is removed, and replaced by ordinary CorelDRAW objects (albeit many of them!). Keep in mind that just like converting Text to Curves, freezing a lens kills the flexibility, like replacing a pink glass lens with a photo of the image made with the pink glass lens. So you may wish to make a backup copy of any file in which you are thinking of freezing the lenses. If you still have problems outputting a file after you have frozen the Lenses, you can always resort to exporting the image as a CMYK bitmap, which virtually anyone anywhere can output for you!*

4. Use the Freehand tool to draw a blob around the distorted image, and color it dark brown. Duplicate the blob, and downsize by dragging in the corner sizing handles while holding down the Shift key. Color the duplicate the same faded pink as before, shift-select the brown blob, open the Blend roll-up (Ctrl+B), and click Apply. This will create a rounded-edge and finish up the silly putty look! You can also create highlight and shadow objects, in the same way as in Chapter 3. See Figure 18-15.

*Figure 18-15: A dark blob blended to a smaller, lighter copy becomes a flattened piece of Silly Putty, with our captured and distorted image on it.*

That finishes up the Silly Putty image, viewable in the color section and also in a file called sillyput.cdr in the \Chapt18\ subdirectory on the CD-ROM. If you look, I flip-flopped the final image so that, like real Silly Putty, the image captured would be the mirrored image of the original. Also, if you look closely, you will notice that the checkerboard pattern in the boys pants do not distort. This is because it is a Two-Color pattern fill, which is essentially a bitmap. I told you that bitmaps won't distort! If you want a pattern like this to distort along with everything else, use the Tips in Chapter 8 to convert the bitmap pattern into a vector image (the Export as EPS trick), then you can go through the Enveloping process again and the pattern will distort as well.

## Hydrant Hound

*Figure 18-16: Hand-drawn images are placed in a computer generated scene, which has been converted to a bitmap so filter effects can render it to look more rough and hand-drawn.*

This little hound dog and hydrant in Figure 18-16 just popped into existence one day, and even became part of my novelty T-shirt line. I am not rich and famous, so I guess I was the only one who thought that a graphic of a dog who pees on a hydrant was a great way to adorn your body. Oh well! I got to re-cycle the artwork a few times anyway, so it all worked out in the end.

The great thing about computers is that you can create artwork that doesn't look so computer generated. With today's design landscape suffering from a glut of computer-generated artwork, the hand-drawn look is getting mighty popular, and very marketable. In this scene, with the cartoon characters having rough shaded areas, I used a bitmap filter to change the CorelDRAW background elements into a matching hand-colored-looking element. Here is how to convert vector pieces into smudgy hand-drawn artwork:

1. Draw a rectangle for the page limit of your design. Now Import (Ctrl+I) the black-and-white scans of the dog and hydrant illustrations. Remember that in CorelDRAW 8 you can select multiple files to import, designate their import location by clicking the pointer on the page (this is the top left corner of the bitmap), and also designate their size by dragging to create a box. This is an extremely handy feature, especially when you are zoomed way in, and want to import something. In versions previous to 8, a file always imported to the center of the page, which could be distracting. Place your characters where you want them on the page, and use the Bezier tool to map out the dynamics of the scene. I created a vanishing point above and behind the comic characters on the horizon line. Using this point as a reference, draw lines to aid in drawing a fence, sidewalk, street, and building. See Figure 18-17.

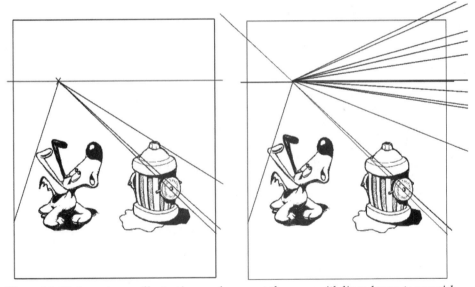

*Figure 18-17: Import your illustrations and map out the scene with lines drawn to a vanishing point.*

2. Using the lines as a guide, use the Bezier tool to draw a triangle shape for the sidewalk. Use the Interactive Fill tool to create a white to dark fill to create the illusion of distance (that danged atmospheric perspective thing again!). Now duplicate the triangle (+ key), and grab the bottom left node with the Shape tool. Now drag the node up and to the right until it

aligns with another one of the guidelines you drew. Because this shape is a duplicate of the sidewalk, the shared-edge is exactly aligned. Neat trick, huh? Use this duplicate and node-drag flip-flop trick to create three pieces; the main sidewalk, the street, and far off sidewalk. Shade the pieces using Linear Fountain fills to get an illusion of distance. See Figure 18-18.

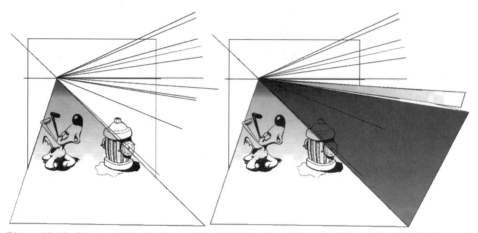

*Figure 18-18: Create a triangle shape using the Bezier tool. Dragging the nodes of a duplicate of this shape creates the other filled areas, while ensuring that shared lines are perfectly aligned.*

3. Draw shapes with the Freehand tool to add color, or in the case of the dog, simply keep him white. Don't worry too much about coloring inside of the lines, as a little out of register color just makes things look more hand-drawn and less computer-perfect! Drag-select and group all of the coloring objects along with the reference bitmap so that you can easily move and arrange the characters later in the scene. See Figure 18-19.

*Figure 18-19: Use the Freehand tool to create shapes to color the bitmap objects.*

4. Continue to work on the scene to add in details for the background. The sky is a Texture fill called Clouds, Midday, found in the Samples Texture Library. Use the Bezier tool to draw rectangles, for the building and window shapes. The windows also have the same cloud texture fill. For the fence on the left, draw a rectangle using the Bezier tool and following the reference lines, for the board closest to you. Now duplicate the board, downsize it using the sizing handles, and position the tiny duplicate way off in the distance. Select the two boards, open the Blend roll-up (Ctrl+B), and create the fence by blending the two together using only enough steps to create boards next to and not on top of each other. If the blend does not look right, experiment with different numbers of steps, and also the Accelerate objects option (see Figure 18-20).

*Figure 18-20: Use the Bezier tool to draw straight-line objects such as the building and windows, using the lines drawn earlier for reference. Blending two boards becomes a fence image.*

5. Select and delete all of the hand-drawn guidelines. Select the two comic characters, and select File I Save As. Enable the Selected Only option, click OK, then delete the saved characters from the scene. We need the background only for the next steps, and cutting the pieces to the clip-

board is risky, as any other copy or cut will erase them. I prefer to save things to disk. A lot. Like every few minutes. Call me jumpy, but I have just lost too much information over the years to system crashes and power failures! Anyway, with the characters and guidelines out of the way, Edit | Select All, then shift-click on the border rectangle to deselect it. Now, from the Effects | PowerClip submenu, choose Place Inside Container, then click on the border rectangle again. This should constrain the pieces nicely to the page size. With the PowerClip selected, open the Convert to Bitmap dialog from the Bitmap menu. Although most offset printing requires a 300 dpi CMYK image, for this technique, set the Color value to 24 bit (RGB) and the Resolution value to 75 dpi. Click OK to convert the bitmap (be sure to first save a backup copy of these pieces). See Figure 18-21.

*Figure 18-21: Constrain all of the objects to the page size by PowerClipping them into a rectangle. Then use the Convert to Bitmap function to create a malleable pixel-based graphic.*

6. Select the bitmap, and from the Bitmap Plug-Ins submenu, choose Fancy, then Alchemy. This is a neat filter set that can create some really cool brush effects, and I recommend you spend some time dabbling with these settings. For this example, change the Saved Style to Vortex Mosaic and click OK. This will give the bitmap a hand-dabbled look, and because we set the resolution so low, the effect is big and rough, and more cartoonish (see Figure 18-22).

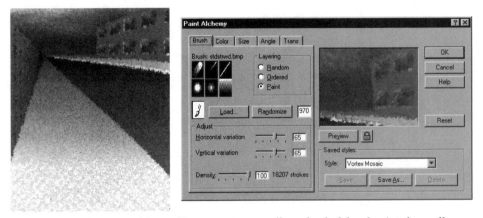

*Figure 18-22: The Paint Alchemy filter creates many effects that look hand-painted as well as other bizarre effects.*

7. Import (Ctrl+I) your comic characters on to the now painterly scene. To change the lighting and draw attention to the center, draw a black rectangle over the background, but behind the comic characters, and give it a radial interactive transparency fill. Text elements, using the now familiar highlight and fat multiple outline effects, finish off the poster. I used a font called MarkerFeltWide (see Figure 18-23).

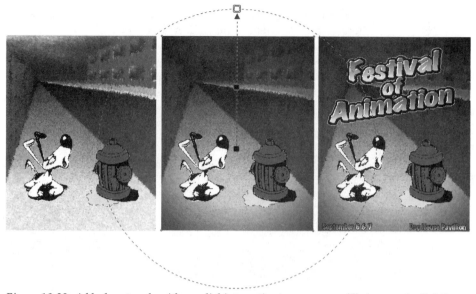

*Figure 18-23: A black rectangle with a radial interactive transparency fill changes the lighting and draws emphasis to the center.*

*Depending on your service bureau and other variables, your CorelDRAW file may not process correctly to output for film. Things like lenses, which translate poorly into PostScript, can cause problems (especially if you stack effects one on top of another!). To remove any headaches, simply export your images as 300 dpi, CMYK TIF files. This file type will process painlessly, even across computer platforms. This book, for example, had all of the text and images created on the PC using CorelDRAW, but it was assembled and output from a Macintosh (a pretty common phenomenon in the publishing/graphics world). To avoid problems, all of the images have been translated into CMYK TIFs. The downside to this is some image degradation, which is usually unintelligible to all but the most trained eye.*

My finished poster can be seen in the color section, and loaded from the \Chapt18\ subdirectory on the Companion CD-ROM as toons.cdr. There are other, more realistic hand-drawn type filters available from other vendors, which will work even better to create this anti-computer look. Adobe Gallery Effects, for example, offers a very wide variety of artistic tweaks, and will work with CorelDRAW and PhotoPaint. Don't forget to experiment also with the same filter on bitmaps with different resolutions. High-resolution images sometimes just are not grungy enough to appear hand drawn.

## Sword of Beauty

*Figure 18-24: Combining hand-drawn images with computer-aided design techniques results in images impossible to create using manual or digital techniques alone.*

For a long time now (yes, even before it became trendy!), I have been a fan of Japanese animation. This choppy style does not appeal to everyone, but for me, it hits home. Even as a kid, as much as I loved the classic Warner Brothers cartoons, my allegiance was for Japanese animated classics like Speed Racer and Simba.

The image in Figure 18-19 is really a combination of my many favorite Japanese animated female characters. I love this image, and I have placed this poor girl in many chaotic scenes, including a series of paintings in my living room. In this comic scene, she seems to be under surveillance, as if she is invading the secret lair of the evil dark lord, Dr. Von ClickenDrag, who our heroine must stop from taking over the world!

Okay, so my imagination runs a bit wild at times! The point is, even a wild design concept can come to life much easier in CorelDRAW than by using traditional techniques alone. In fact, the computer expands the design horizons further, and the artist is able to exploit the technology itself. For example, using screen captures and other computer-specific design elements creates new design potential that simply does not exist elsewhere. Here is how to create a fun comic scene combining hand-drawn and computer-generated elements:

**CD-ROM**

1. Once you have a scan of your illustration, open Corel OCR-Trace, and open (Ctrl+O) the bitmap. (This image is saved as beauty.tif in the \Chapt18\ subdirectory on the Companion CD-ROM if you want to practice this technique. The finished trace, beauty.cmx, is also there.) From the OCR-Trace menu, choose Trace Settings and change the Present settings to Accurate. Click Close, and then again from the OCR-Trace menu, choose By Outline from the Perform Trace submenu. This will convert the image from bitmap into usable CorelDRAW objects. When finished, choose File | Save | Vector and then exit (see Figure 18-25).

*Figure 18-25: The CorelOCR-Trace utility converts bitmap artwork into CorelDRAW objects.*

**TIP**   *Photocopy your ink illustrations before you scan them. I sketch out an image first in pencil (which looks like hell, full of smudges and eraser marks!), then place a sheet of Duralene (a semi-opaque plastic illustration material) on top, and trace the pencil image with an ink pen. This results in a nice crisp image, but Duralene does not scan well (at least not on my scanner) because it is only semi-opaque. Your results may vary, but I find making a photo-copy of hand-drawn images, then scanning the paper copy, results in crisper images and consequently better scans. The better the scan, the better Corel OCR-Trace will work.*

2. Now start CorelDRAW and Open (Ctrl+O) the CMX file. The image is made up of small objects on top of a black pad. The first step is to select any areas that need to be "knocked through" (such as the space between the head and hand), then shift-select the big black pad object (just click on the solid black hair or any outside outline) and combine the objects (Ctrl+L). I shift-selected the area where you can see through the sword, under the left arm, between the right arm and head, and also beneath the right pony tail, and combined them with the outside outline object. (See Figure 18-26.)

*Figure 18-26: Once converted into a CorelDRAW file, you can manipulate an illustration like any other object. Combine the areas that should be knocked through with the main outline object.*

3. Time to color! Colorizing Corel traced images is so easy now in CorelDRAW 7 and 8. Drag colors right off of the onscreen color palette and release them over the areas you want to color. This is faster than selecting an object and then clicking on a color well. To speed things along even more, move the onscreen palette right to where you are coloring. To move the palette, click next to a color well and drag on to the desktop. Now you can size and position the palette to make drag-and-drop coloring a cinch! See Figure 18-27.

*Figure 18-27: Use the drag-and-drop coloring feature to add color quickly to the trace objects. Move the palette closer to speed things up even more.*

**TIP**
*If you have a collection of colors that you like to use more than others, you can create your own custom palette. This feature is a pain in any other version, but CorelDRAW 8 finally makes this happen! From the Tools menu, you can choose New Palette from Selection, or New Palette from Document. From the Edit menu, choose Select All | Objects, then from the Tools menu, select the new Palette from Selection option. Name the custom palette, and click Save to generate it. This only creates the palette, so to use it, from the View menu, choose Color Palette | Load Palette. This will display and dock the available palettes on the right of the screen, and clicking on a different name will activate that palette. A custom palette makes it easy to color a series of cartoon panels all alike. Or if you have several people working on the same project, and want them all to use the same colors, you can create and include a custom color palette along with any other template files and guidelines.*

4. Because all of the small shapes rest on a big black filled object, you can select it and give it a fat outline, with the Behind Fill option enabled in the Outline Pen dialog (F12) to help isolate our heroine from a busy background. When you have finished coloring the character, drag-select all of the pieces and group (Ctrl+G) them so you can easily position and size the girl in the scene.

**TIP** *Drag-and-drop coloring works even on objects already within a group. Unlike clicking a color well with a group of objects selected, when you drag and drop color, only the object directly beneath it will receive the color, not all of the objects in the group. Remember too that you can always hold down the Ctrl key and select an object within a group.*

5. For the computer-monitor graphics within the scene I imagined, I needed a screen capture of our heroine. This is a cakewalk in Win95, or you can use the Capture utility program that also ships with Corel. To capture the current screen, hold down the Alt key and then press the Print Screen key. This will copy the current screen information to the clipboard. Now simply paste (Ctrl+V) the contents of the clipboard into your CorelDRAW image (see Figure 18-28).

*Figure 18-28: Use the Windows screen capture keys (Alt+Print Screen) to capture the current screen image.*

**TIP**

*Customize your CorelDRAW screen to your own tastes. You will notice that I have removed the Standard toolbar and also the rulers from the screen. I like to use as much screen space as possible and hate to take up valuable real estate with idiot buttons. (Do I really need a button for Print and Save when I can use keyboard shortcuts or even just move another centimeter to the File menu? No, of course not!) I even close the Property Bar, preferring roll-ups and dialogs, but that is just me. Use the options under the View menu to change how your screen looks, especially from the Toolbars... dialog. You can also set the Win95 bottom taskbar to disappear as well. Right-click on a blank area of the bar and choose Properties. Then from the Taskbar Options tab, enable the Auto Hide option to salvage another piece of monitor real-estate!*

6. Within CorelDRAW, you can crop down the screen capture using the Shape tool. Drag-select two nodes on any side and then drag the side to crop the image, holding down the Ctrl key to constrain movement to one plane (you can create odd-shaped crops as well if you wish). Crop away all of the extra bits leaving only the girl. Now duplicate the bitmap (+ key) and crop down the girl to zoom in on her face. Downsize the bitmap for the full-body shot to be the same size as the head shot by dragging the sizing handles with the Pick tool. When all bitmaps are at the desired size, use the Convert to Bitmap command from the Bitmap menu to adjust to the correct size and also to convert to grayscale. If you skip this step, CorelDRAW retains all of the information in the bitmaps, including what was hidden during the cropping process. When you convert the image to bitmap, the object is frozen, with only the visible bitmap in the conversion process. Converting the objects to bitmap keeps you from carrying around excess image baggage that you don't need (see Figure 18-29).

*Figure 18-29: Crop, downsize, and adjust the screen capture to fit in a square. Use the Convert to Bitmap function to make it grayscale.*

7. To create a frame, draw two rectangles, round the corners on the outside shape, and combine (Ctrl+L) the two together. Now arrange the bitmaps from the screen captures inside of the frames and add detail elements such as text. I used the font called LCD to add on-screen notations. For a third monitor, duplicate the full-body shot, and alter it with the Edge Detect filter from the Bitmap, 2D Effects fly-out. Arrange the three monitors vertically (see Figure 18-30).

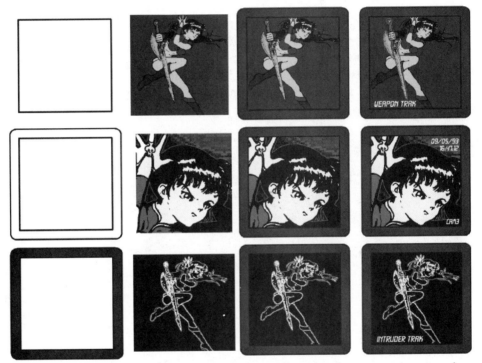

*Figure 18-30: Create a frame with the rectangle shape and arrange the screen captures to make our heroine look like she is under surveillance.*

8. For the target shapes in the background, first draw two circles and blend them together with a two-step blend (Ctrl+B). Draw lines for crosshairs, and add text to designate values for the rings. Drag-select the entire bunch, separate the blend, ungroup all of the pieces, and then combine them (Ctrl+L). Now use the skew arrows to distort the target (see Figure 18-31).

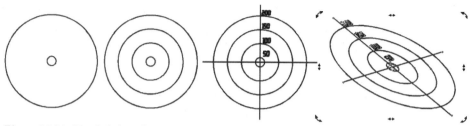

*Figure 18-31: Blended rings become a target object with the addition of cross-hairs and text.*

9. Select the target curve and give it a magenta outline with no fill. Duplicate it (+ key), move the duplicate down, and color it cyan. Now shift-select both and apply a two-step blend using the Rainbow function on the Colors page to automatically color the interim objects (see Figure 18-32).

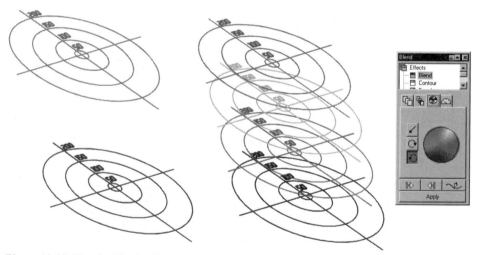

*Figure 18-32: Use the Blend roll-up to duplicate and color the target shapes.*

10. The little crosshair grid is simply an *x* blended to a duplicate across the page. When you freeze this blend (Arrange | Separate), you can blend it again to a duplicate on the other side of the page. I also used this method to create the grid of squares. You can also use the Graph Paper tool, located in the Polygon Tool flyout, to make grids on the page. Right-click

to open the Properties dialog for the Graph Paper tool and key in the number of cells for how wide and high you want the grid to be. Then click-drag to create a Graph Paper object (see Figure 18-33).

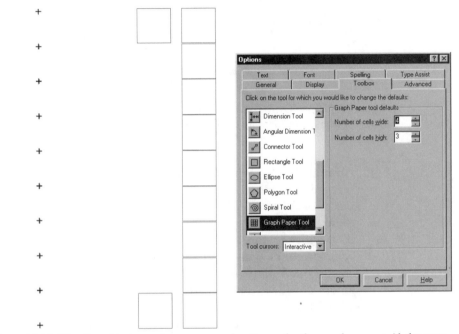

*Figure 18-33: Blending objects creates even-spaced patterns, for the x and square grid elements. You can also use the Graph Paper tool to create grids.*

11. While working on this project, I really wanted some sort of Japanese writing on it. I called my friend in San Francisco, and she faxed me the characters, which I digitized directly using a fax-modem. I used the Corel OCR-Trace utility to trace the objects (which spell out Sword of Beauty) but was unhappy with how thin they were. By using a fat .055-inch outline, I got the width I wanted (see Figure 18-34).

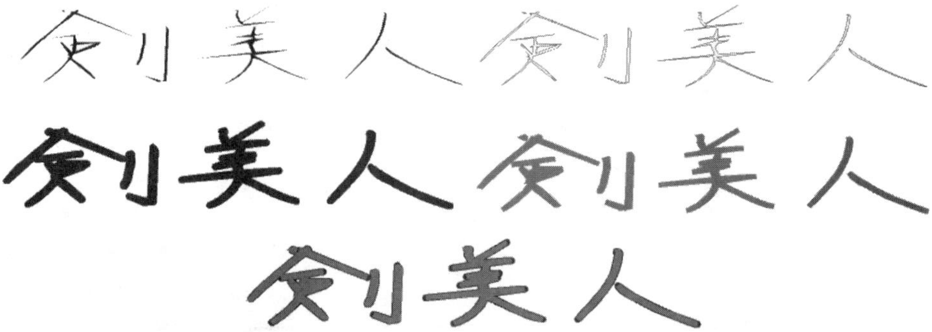

剣美人 剣美人

剣美人 剣美人

剣美人

*Figure 18-34: CorelOCR/Trace can convert images from any source, including fax/modems. The thin characters were beefed up with a heavy line weight.*

12. Arrange the character and other design elements to create a busy image that creates a mood of urgency and excitement. Layer objects, such as pieces of the grid, in front of and behind the main character shape to add more depth. Draw a rectangle for the page limit, send it to the back (and fill it with a texture fill called banded malachite). Change the mineral colors from the default greens to dark blue, pink, and blue again. This creates interesting visual noise in the background. Depending on the amount of chaos desired, you can also add more elements to the scene. I added straight dotted lines. You can make any outline a dotted line by changing the Style option in the Outline Pen dialog (F12). See Figure 18-35.

This finished poster can be seen in the color section or can be loaded from a file called sword.cdr in the \Chapt18\ subdirectory on the Companion CD-ROM. There is so much going on in this image that would have just been too tedious to draw by hand, and yet, because the main character started as an ink illustration, the image still retains a real cartoon feel. More and more I find myself mixing and matching mediums to create the images in my mind. The girl graphic was also available as a T-shirt for a spell, and so I silk-screened the image onto big vinyl stickers, which I used to create a series of mixed-media paintings. In this collage series, our hapless heroine leaps through all kinds of strange things, such as a laser-beam-like grid made by illuminating fluorescent fishing line with light bulbs! And for the ultimate in mixed media, I output this image as you see it from the computer on a high-end color printer and mixed in flashing lights and a tiny little chirping sound board.

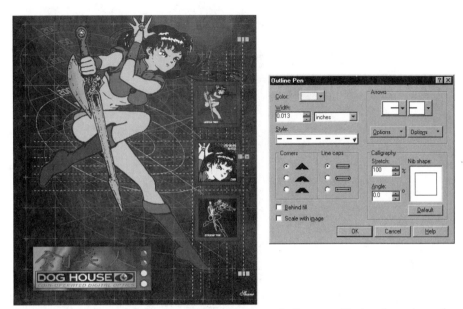

*Figure 18-35: Assemble the pieces and character to create the scene. Design elements can have dotted lines instead of just solid, using the Style option on the Outline.*

## Moving On

In this chapter we looked at mixing traditional ink illustrations with CorelDRAW objects. We saw how to color the illustrations by drawing objects by and with the Freehand tool, or by converting them into Corel objects using the CorelOCR/Trace utility. For all you non-illustrators, we also looked at creating creatures and characters entirely within CorelDRAW, using simple shapes and geometric objects.

The great thing about assembling comic scenes in CorelDRAW is that you are then able to go on beyond the static printed page right into action-media. Because you can move and manipulate the characters within the scenes, you are only a heart-beat away from animating them! If you took the time to create multiple poses for the same character, you could then go right into the animation mode. In fact this new kind of computer-animation is gaining in popularity, with a series already airing on cable. Hmm, perhaps I should start working to computerize my own comic strip concept—"The Adventures of Slimy Dog and Slippery Weasel." I think I just talked myself into it. What do you think of my comic heroes, shown in Figure 18-36?

*Figure 18-36: The future adventures of Slimy Dog and Slippery Weasel will be a CorelDRAW-based comic strip.*

In the next chapter we will continue to explore animated options and uses for CorelDRAW. In keeping with the low-tech/high-tech theme, we will endeavor to create designs and images reminiscent of the middle-half of this century. Contemporary design tools like CorelDRAW make creating crisp and visually engaging designs a snap, even for anachronistic images. So, crawl into your bomb-shelter, grab a TV dinner, and get ready for a 50's flashback!

▼ **Beyond f/x**

The potential is endless for a computer-based comic strip. A black-and-white strip could be colorized (or vice versa) and the text converted into different typestyles, or even other languages. The same images for print can migrate into animations and Web sites or pop up on merchandise, you name it. Beyond comic strips, the techniques for colorizing hand-drawn illustrations lends itself to many applications. You could use a hand-drawn illustration as the basis of an advertisement, using the same kind of coloring techniques from this chapter to avoid a cookie-cutter computer generated look. Using screen-captures to create additional artwork for a design is also a great way to milk more out of your design day without adding much effort. A background pattern based upon a screen capture, or a piece of a screen capture, adds a unique look to your design without adding much effort, as seen in Figure 18-37.

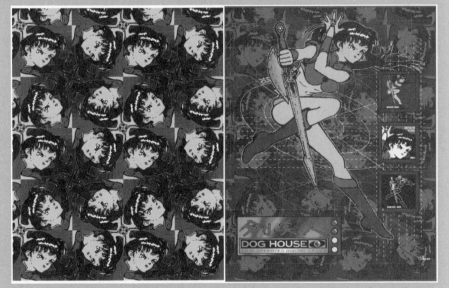

*Figure 18-37: A screen-capture image is cropped down, and made into an interesting background pattern.*

# chapter 19
# Fifties Flashback

Back when life was simpler, before computers, before eight versions of CorelDRAW (eek, that is a long time ago!), designs were also simpler. Because everything was more difficult to do, often requiring physical cutting and pasting, art had a clean-cut look to it. Designs were thought out way in advance, and many more interim steps were involved to make sure the end result was perfect. The less-is-more lesson here is worth looking into, though, as in our digital age of visual noise and information overload, simplicity seems darn appealing.

Too much art these days is created with an artist's "see what I can do" ego rather than by just trying to solve the design problems for the project at hand. There is also a question of appropriateness; not every piece of art needs to be dripping with technical complexity. Use your technical ability to create good designs faster, and use the extra time doing something else, like, uh..., well I can't remember, but something other than working on the computer!

In this chapter, we will create simple but visually engaging pieces with a retro look to them (and not just limited to the '50s, but I liked how that sounded). In the first example, we will see how a simple, two-color design using classic and clean page layout can produce an interesting and professional-looking design that's right at home in the modern world. Then, continuing with the theme, a simple layout is brought to life and given a retro look with select shape, font, and color choices. After that, we switch on the idiot box to work the American pastime into another flashback image; we'll use the PowerClip function and other tricks to put an image on TV. Finally, we capture the spirit of a '40s pinup, launching scans of images from the past into the present in the form of digital stock. The technology of the future works well to create images from the past!

## Contact _____

*Figure 19-1: Modern artists can learn from the past and create simple, cost-efficient designs that are interesting and professional.*

I am a huge fan of the history of art and graphic design. There is so much to learn from the past, and if nothing else, books on the subject serve as great sources of inspiration. Many times I have been stumped trying to come up with some new look or design twist only to find the art history archives were the catalyst necessary to ignite my creativity. If you have not already taken some time to peruse through books on the topics of art and graphic design history, I recommend you do so.

The image in Figure 19-1 has a simple and clean layout, which takes advantage of a commodity many people lose sight of: white space. In design, there is an adage: "It's not always what's there, but what isn't there that's important." To keep costs down, you are often limited to one or two colors. Use the white color of the paper as a third color option, creating interesting patterns and making use of the negative space in a positive way. The white creates nice areas of contrast and rest where the eye can linger away from visual noise. It is such a natural tendency to try and cram as much as possible into a design, but you will find that less is more, and it's also very effective.

### What Isn't There

My favorite example of the importance of what *isn't* there is a story that also involves airplane silhouettes. During World War II, the British were searching for ways to reduce their losses and got mighty creative in the process. After each mission, an artist would come out and inspect a returning airplane for bullet holes and flak damage. They would mark the damaged areas of the plane on a sheet of cellophane that had a diagram of the plane on it. Then they would stack up sheets from many different damaged planes until a pattern began to emerge for that model of aircraft. There were distinct areas of light and dark that created a pattern of damage that was common to the returning aircraft. They took this graphic to the aircraft factories and added armor and reinforcement to the planes on the areas in the diagrams where the markings *weren't*. This is because the blank areas on the diagrams were where the planes that *didn't* make it back were hit. Pretty clever, eh? What's *not* there can be mighty important!

Here is how to use contemporary tools to create a clean two-color design:

1. Use the rectangle tool to draw out a box the size of your paper and then open the Scale & Mirror roll-up (Alt+F9). Change the Horizontal value to 50% and click Apply to Duplicate. This will create a rectangle that is half the width of the original. Click Apply to Duplicate again to create a shape one quarter as wide as the page. Shift-select all of these shapes and use the Align and Distribute dialog (or just the single key shortcuts in CorelDRAW 8) to align the elements to the right. Now select the full-size rectangle, and on the Scale & Mirror roll-up, change the Vertical value to 50%, change the Horizontal value back to 100%, and click Apply to Duplicate. With the new duplicate selected, change the Vertical value to 80% and again click Apply to Duplicate. Shift-select these objects and align them to the top. This will divide the page into neat and orderly sections (see Figure 19-2).

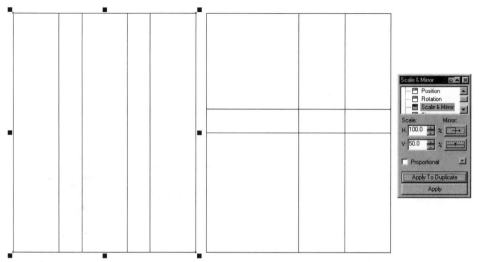

*Figure 19-2: The Scale & Mirror roll-up divides the page object horizontally and vertically to create an orderly page layout design. The Align and Distribute dialog aligns the pieces to one another.*

2. Select the one-quarter page vertical block and fill it black. Now flip-flop it by dragging the right-center control handle left while holding down the Ctrl key. Next duplicate the shape (+ key), squeeze it horizontally until it is just a thin line, and fill it white. Shift-select the thin box and the one-quarter page object and align them to the vertical Center (hit the "C" key). Now duplicate the thin white line, shift-select the one-quarter page object again, and align it to the Left (hit the "L" key). Finally, select both thin rectangles and blend (Ctrl+B) them together to produce a perfectly spaced pattern on half of the one-quarter page black object (see Figure 19-3).

3. Open the Symbols docker (Ctrl+F11), select the Transportation Symbols Library, scroll down until you find a plane to your liking, and drag it onto the desktop. Now flip the plane vertically, fill it white with no outline, and move the plane to the bottom of the page. Shift-select the one-quarter page shape and align the plane to its vertical center. Duplicate the plane and drag the duplicate up the page while holding down the Ctrl key to keep it aligned with the original. Shift-select both planes and create a 5-step blend to create a row of evenly spaced flyers (see Figure 19-4).

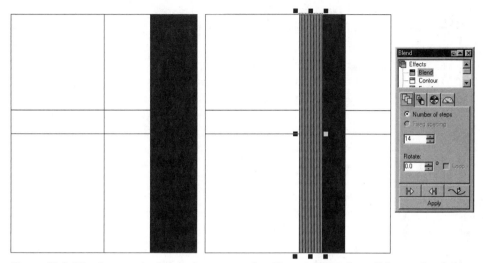

*Figure 19-3: Use the new single-key shortcuts or the Align and Distribute dialog to place white lines in the center of and on the left of the black shape; then blend them together.*

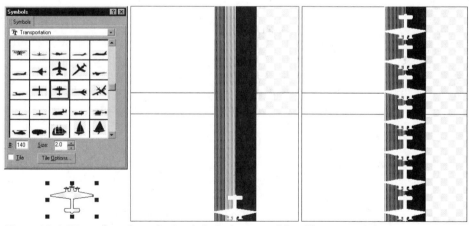

*Figure 19-4: Use a plane from the Symbols docker as a white silhouette and then create an evenly spaced row of them using the Blend roll-up.*

4. Select and color the sections of the design in white and green. Green is a nice, neutral color that has universal appeal. (For a cooler look, you could substitute light blue, and for hotter, orange or red.) If this job were destined to go to press at your local print shop, you would want to use a

spot color for the green. From the View menu, choose Pantone Matching System colors from the Color Palette submenu to switch to a spot color theme. Each spot color outputs as a single plate when you create color-separated film to give to your printer. Duplicate the guideline shapes and reduce with the Scale & Mirror to produce proportional copies of the guideline shapes. You may need to change the order in which the objects are stacked. The Arrange | Order | In Front Of and Arrange | Order | Behind commands make stacking easy. Use the Align and Distribute dialog or the keyboard short-cuts to keep all objects perfectly aligned.

**TIP**

*Understand the parameters of a job before you begin to build the artwork. For a two-color job such as this example, it is idiotic to use a CMYK color, as it will result in additional film and higher printing charges. Use a spot color from the Pantone Matching System instead, which will create only one color plate on output. Because this book does not use spot color (it uses CMYK), I chose Grass Green, which is a CMYK color choice off of the onscreen palette. In the real world, I would have chosen Pantone 3288 CV as the fill color and produced exactly the artwork that my printer needs (two separate color plates).*

5. Draw a perfect circle in the top-left box of the page and align it to the top and left in relation to the box. Duplicate the circle, downsize it by dragging a corner handle inward while holding down the Ctrl key, shift-select the original circle, and combine (Ctrl+L) the two. To trim away the right side, draw a rectangle over the trim area and use the Trim function to create a big letter *C*. Set the rest of the letters using the Artistic Text tool. I used a classic-looking font called Futura Bk (see Figure 19-5).

6. To make the *ON* white, simply shift-select the two letters using the Shape tool and then click on the white onscreen color well. The question mark is made up of the same shape as the big *C*, just downsized and rotated with two white bars to create a *?* object. Okay, I did modernize the look a bit with the addition of a drop shadow! Select the original full-size rectangle and use the new CorelDRAW 8 drop shadow feature. Grab the Interactive Drop Shadow tool (from the Interactive Blend tool flyout) and drag down and to the right to create the default drop shadow. You can change the parameters, such as Feathering and Opacity values, on the Property Bar (see Figure 19-6).

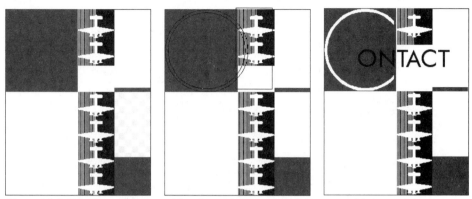

*Figure 19-5: Divide up the page with color and shapes and then create a big letter C from a perfect circle to stay with the clean geometric look of the design.*

*Figure 19-6: Use like shapes when possible to save time; the C can become a ?. The new CorelDRAW 8 Interactive Drop Shadow tool gives you a quick and easy way to add convincing depth to an object.*

Well, this image is perhaps not as exciting as some we have walked through, but I think it is important to also address simple design strategies. The finished piece can be seen in the color section and can be found in the \Chapt19\ subdirectory on the Companion CD-ROM, in a file called contact.cdr. I like this graphic because it starts first with layout, in which the page is divided into neat quadrants, and then adds pieces to enhance visual interest. By nature, humans like to divide and conquer, and subconsciously, that is still how we digest visual information. Neat and tidy sections are appealing, and that is why you will find that most good design has pages that are divided into easy-to-digest chunks. Take a clue from the past and don't over-design a project!

## Avocados, Plums & Carrots

*Figure 19-7: In addition to kitschy design and funky fonts, the right choice of colors really screams retro-funky.*

In the '90s, there is this strange mix of the previous four decades, especially in areas like art and fashion. Today's trends borrow heavily from the past but simultaneously mix in pieces of the present. There is nothing like seeing a kid in bell-bottoms playing with a Game Boy to mess with your head! Or how about oldies music on CD?

Getting a retro look means sticking to the formula of the times. Older graphics use lower-tech printing and design methods, which help define the look. Simple geometric shapes, natural colors (avocado green, carrot orange, plum purple, banana yellow, etc.), and fonts from the same era all add up to a blast-from-the-past look. These designs are all the rage again, as people appreciate not only the look, but the simplicity at all levels of production.

### ▼ Color Consistency

Matching onscreen colors to their printed counterparts has always been a problem. In CorelDRAW 8, a color-corrected display is the default, with the onscreen images very closely representing their printed values. The Corel Color Manager utility will help you fine-tune your equipment to provide the best onscreen color representation possible. I work with the color correction enabled, so I see an image on my screen that is close to the CMYK printed equivalent. If you are working on Web graphics, however, you may be surprised if you work with CMYK color correction while creating RGB graphics! So set your screen for the task at hand. In CorelDRAW 8, open the Options menu (Ctrl+J), and on the Global|Color Management options page, you can turn the Calibrate Colors for Display on or off (default is on). In CorelDRAW 7, choose your poison from the Color Correction submenu under the View menu.

Here is how to capture that groovelicious look:

1. Draw a rectangle and fill it with a lovely avocado green. To create colors that aren't on the onscreen palette, open the Uniform Fill dialog (Shift+F11). Click on a green color well to get started and then drag the selector in the preview window to change the CMYK values. I use a color reference swatch book, which tells me the CMYK values I need in order to get certain colors in printing. This is a handy item, especially when trying to convert spot colors into CMYK (CorelDRAW now does this automatically and fairly accurately, but I like to double-check). For the green, the values are C-47, M-0, Y-88, and K-0. Now draw an oval with the Ellipse tool and fill it with a what's-up-doc orange (C-0, M-60, Y-100, K-0).

**TIP** *If you are really serious about calibrating color, forget the gadgets, gizmos, and companion software; just do the math. There are so many variables (including heat, color of your clothing, time of day, etc.) that change the way onscreen colors look, that the chances of ever calibrating your monitor are nil. What you can do is monitor the color mixes in your artwork and compare the mathematical values to a trustworthy printed reference. Use a printed swatch book to pick colors and then key in the CMYK values for that color. Now it really doesn't matter how it looks on screen; the printed result should be what you keyed in, or close.*

*Make sure your printed reference is new, not faded, and from a reputable source. Compare the final printed version and take notes on how the color varies in your own printing experience so you can adjust the colors the next time. Differences in output machines, printing presses, and so on all alter the outcome, so you have to track what happens so you will know how to fix things. If jobs you send to your local print shop always look blue, you need to adjust the levels of cyan in your artwork. If things look green, you may need to increase the magenta level (green is yellow and cyan, so what's left? Magenta!). Unfortunately there is no plug-in replacement or upgrade available for good ol' real-world experience!*

2. With the Artistic Text tool, set your ad copy on the page. I used a font called Balloon for the top text and AdLib for the lower text. Use the Shape tool to shift-select the nodes of the first letters of the top text. Now double-click on one of the nodes to open the Format Text dialog and add 10 to the value in the Size box. Click OK to enlarge just these selected letters. With the Shape tool again, select the second text element and drag the bottom-left arrow up to change the line spacing. This will make less space between the words vertically. Now with the Shape tool, drag the letters so that they are not all aligned along the baseline, to make them seem more excited and happy to see you! Give these words a fat, white .333-inch outline and enable the Behind Fill option from the Outline Pen dialog (F12). See Figure 19-8.

3. Open the Symbols docker (Ctrl+F11; in V.7, it's called the Symbols rollup) and locate the Stars1 Library. Now scroll down until you find the star that looks like a kid's jack (a little metal star with rounded ends on the points) and drag it onto the desktop. Give it a plum/pink fill (C-5, M-75, Y-0, K-0) with a .029-inch yellow outline, with the Behind Fill outline option enabled from the Outline Pen dialog (F12). Duplicate and arrange a whole bunch of these guys, enlarging or reducing the duplicates as you go to create a random-looking barrage of those nonslip shower flowers (see Figure 19-9).

*Figure 19- 8: Use the Uniform Fill dialog to choose any funky color. Artistic Text is manipulated with the Shape tool to change line spacing, size, and placement of the individual letters or the entire word.*

*Figure 19-9: Use the Symbols docker to find the perfect star icon to duplicate and scatter around your page.*

4. For the final element, I wanted a starburst kind of shape. You could use the Interactive Deformation tool's Zipper mode to distort an oval into this object or use the Polygon tool as I did. Right-click over the Polygon tool; then click on Properties to open the tool's Options dialog. Enable the Polygon as Star option, change the Number of Points/Sides value to 44, and drag the Sharpness slider until you get the look you are after. Click OK and drag the Polygon tool onto the desktop to draw the object. (Remember that the Shape tool is useful for fine-tuning a polygon object if necessary.) Fill this funky polygon with cyan and call it a day! The colors in this piece are very low contrast for a mellow design, which is interesting because when I converted the screen captures to grayscale, some of the colors (the green and the orange) turned into the same 40% black. Trippy, dude. I modified the images for the grayscale graphics here (see Figure 19-10).

*Figure 19-10: Use the Polygon tool to create a circular burst behind the text.*

**CD-ROM**   This image can be viewed in the color section and also retrieved from the \Chapt19\ subdirectory on the Companion CD-ROM (the file is called 50sad.cdr). The burst in the file is a curve, so the Shape tool won't perform the same way it would if it was still an active polygon. Open the Polygon tool settings, draw a star, and see then how the Shape tool changes things. Remember that you can drag the outside points as well as the inside points with the Shape tool.

## Classic TV

*Figure 19-11: Even a simple-looking design can benefit from high-end tricks! The TV image is a bitmap and static lines stuffed into a screen shape with the PowerClip feature, the design elements are symbols, and the FX logo was created with the Combine function.*

Part of putting any contemporary project together is working out the peripheral details. Corresponding Web sites, brochures, mailers, postcards, you name it, all start to pop up on your job board. The fun thing is combining the past with the present. For example, a Web site design could benefit from the clean, quirky styling of a retro look incorporated with modern twists such as animation or interactive buttons.

This design is just such a project, where a printed image will work into an onscreen Web experience (see Figure 19-11). I decided a television is a good way to swap images for an animation, in a campy classic TV kind of spoof, to add motion and interest to a Web page. You can create a series of images for the screen and swap them to create animation cells, to make your television change channels. For the Web, you would want to slice the image into three separate GIFs, so just the center is animated, to cut down load time and file size. (See my example in Chapter 27.)

We'll walk through the process of putting the first image into a screenshape and making that image look like it's appearing on an old 1950s vintage TV. We'll also create a background that combines retro coloring and modern objects. We'll even throw in some modernistic text effects:

1. Draw a TV screen by creating a rectangle and curving the corners with the Shape tool. Import an image for your screen (I used a photo from \photos\entertain directory on the CorelDRAW clip-art CD). Select the photo, and align it to your screen. From the Effects menu, choose PowerClip | Place Inside Container and then click on the screen. Since you will be stuffing this image into a different screen object later, again using the PowerClip function, this step is just to help you visualize the screen and aid in the layout of the TV graphic (see Figure 19-12).

*Figure 19-12: Put anything into the TV screen with the PowerClip function.*

2. To create scan lines or static, use the Blend roll-up to create a row of straight lines across the screen. For snow, increase the number of blend steps, but in the Outline Pen dialog (F12), change the line style to dotted. Add any text or other tidbits to your screen, drag-select everything, and convert it to a bitmap. I used a grayscale setting, but you could also set it to RGB and then use the plug-ins from the Bitmap menu to give a washed-out, old color-TV feel to the graphic. (From the Bitmaps menu, select the Plug-Ins | PhotoLab | PhotoFilter, with the Afternoon Tea setting to get a look just like my uncle's old TV set!) Convert the bitmap to either Grayscale or RGB, and click OK (see Figure 19-13).

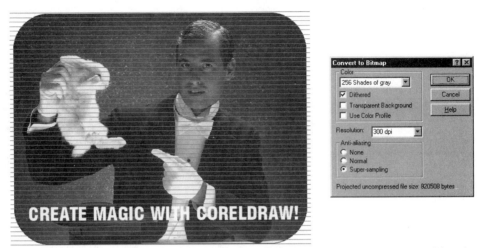

*Figure 19-13: Use the Convert to Bitmap command to transform your pieces into a pixel-based image. Then use the Bitmap filters to add noise or change the colors of your image.*

3. Now we need a TV! I did a file search on the CorelDRAW clip-art CD for **tv\*.\*** to see what was out there. I find this is faster than thumbing through the reference book, although I always have the book close at hand. The search gave me 11 choices, and I picked one from the \clipart\home\electron directory on the CorelDRAW clip-art CD. Import (Ctrl+I) the TV and use the Ungroup (Ctrl+U) function. Now take the image that you want, and using the left skew arrows, tilt it into position. Switch to Wireframe view and PowerClip the bitmap into the clip-art TV screen shape. Hey look, your art is on TV! For a final touch, add a white rectangle with curved corners to the top of the screen and use the Interactive Transparency tool to turn the solid box into a subtle gleam (see Figure 19-14).

Figure 19-14: The image is PowerClipped into a clip-art TV screen and then given a highlight by applying an Interactive Transparency lens to a solid white box.

4. Position your TV in the center of the page. Now draw two kidney-shaped blobs. You can use the Bezier tool, or start with a curved-corner rectangle and convert it to curves (Ctrl+Q). Use the Shape tool to delete all but two of the nodes for a relaxed, sweeping blob (see Figure 19-15).

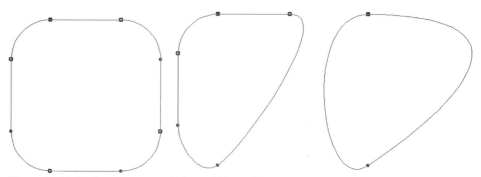

Figure 19-15: Node-edit a rectangle into a kidney shape.

5. Duplicate and flip-flop the blob and arrange the original and the duplicate behind the TV shape. Fill one with a light chalky yellow (Y-60) and the other with a pale green (C-47, Y-88). For more design elements, open the Symbols docker (Ctrl+F11). I used objects from the Electronics Symbols Library for a high-tech but interesting abstract pattern (see Figure 19-16). Drag off the symbols and color them ice blue (C-40).

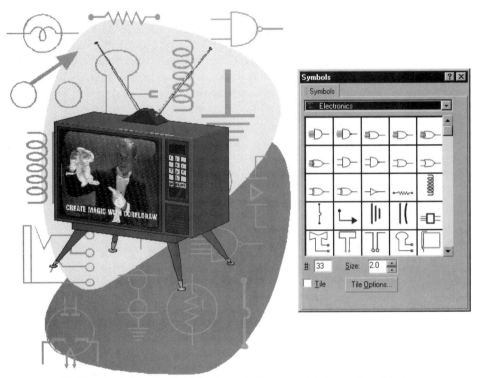

*Figure 19-16: Use the Symbols Library to decorate the page with interesting objects.*

6. The FX Channel logo, with its reversed-out areas, is actually easy to create using the CorelDRAW Combine command. First, draw a perfect square; then set the text elements using the Artistic Text tool. Use the Shape tool to align the letters to the upper left and lower right corners inside the box. Now select the box and duplicate it twice. Move one duplicate up and to the left and use the Trim command to create a flopped over *L* shape. Select the other box duplicate and drag the top-left corner inward to downsize it so that the area of the box that passes through the *F* is about as thick as the flopped over *L* shape passing through the *X*. Convert this box to curves (Ctrl+Q) and use the Shape tool to delete the bottom-right node and create a triangle. Now drag-select all three objects and combine them (Ctrl+L). This will create an inverse color scheme where the objects overlap. Keep in mind that these white areas are open, and anything below this image will show through the holes. To prevent this, draw a white box behind the *FX* curve that is large enough to accommodate the rotated *Channel* text (see Figure 19-17).

*Figure 19-17: Create three objects that, when combined, create an interesting logo with an alternating black/white pattern. This object must be set on a white pad to prevent anything beneath it from shining through the white areas, which are actually now knocked out.*

This image can be viewed in the color section, in the classictv.cdr file in the \Chapt19\ subdirectory on the Companion CD-ROM, and eventually as an animation on the Corel f/x Web site. I usually disable the Auto-Center PowerClip Contents option from the Edit page in the Options dialog (Ctrl+J), but to make a series of animation cells using the television, leave it enabled. Then you can select a bitmap and stuff it into the TV screen frame using the PowerClip function, and it will automatically center in the same step. You can then select the TV objects and export them as a single GIF for use in an animated stack to change the channels. Chapter 29 discusses animation more thoroughly.

## Pinup Posters

*Figure 19-18: Adding rivets and other details changes a classic pinup image from a third-party clip-art collection into a convincing piece of aircraft nose-art.*

I love this image. It has such a classic look, and thanks to modern imaging tricks, it even looks yellowed from age! Sometimes I mix so many modern tricks with classic art that I feel like I could stop time.

This image uses a derivative of the retro formula to achieve the desired look (see Figure 19-18). Instead of symbol shapes, a pinup illustration from the era provides the first piece of the puzzle. The pinup girl alone provides a date reference for the image, with a classic '40s-era pose, hairstyle, clothing, and illustration style. The font is from a new collection of old-style fonts from House Industries (who wouldn't give me the fonts for the Companion CD-ROM, even when I begged!); it looks like the hand-lettered style used to personalize aircraft bombers during World War II. For the all-important coloring portion of the formula, the entire image was altered using a bitmap filter. Here is how to create an old pinup graphic:

1. First, locate an appropriate pinup girl graphic. Time Tunnel, a unique supplier of digital images, was gracious enough to provide us with a sample collection of their images, including their brand-new Pinups collection. Start PhotoPaint and load the file called pinup1.jpg, located in the \timetunl\ directory on the Companion CD-ROM. This is a great-looking image with the signature style of '40s pinups.

2. We need to prepare the bitmap in PhotoPaint for use in CorelDRAW. You should take control of your images and make sure they are the correct size and color depth in PhotoPaint before importing them into CorelDRAW. This will save you some headaches later. First, make sure the size and resolution is correct, which you can monitor from the Resample dialog. From the Image menu, open the Resample dialog and make sure the resolution is 300 dpi and the dimensions are what you want. Click OK to close the dialog. Then convert the image to CMYK for printing or RGB for onscreen applications. From the Image menu again, choose Convert To and then select the desired color depth. For this example, we'll use CMYK color.

3. Next we need to remove the busy background to use the Bitmap Color Mask back in CorelDRAW. You could paint away the background using a neutral color like white, but I thought of a different approach for this graphic. The background is cyan, but we don't really need cyan anywhere in this graphic, so we can remove it and solve our background problem. From the Image menu, choose Adjust | Level Equalization. Change to the Cyan channel in the Equalize section and drag the right Output Range arrow all the way to the left. Click OK to modify the image. This will remove the blue from the background, leaving only a faint yellow tint. You can get rid of this yellow by increasing the Brightness and Contrast from the Brightness-Contrast-Intensity dialog (Ctrl+B). Save the bitmap and exit PhotoPaint (see Figure 19-19).

4. Start CorelDRAW and start a new page. This pinup girl needed to be stuck on the side of an airplane, reminiscent of World War II nose-art. To simulate a plane, create riveted metal sheets. Draw a rectangle, and from the Fountain Fill dialog, fill it with the Cylinder-Grey 02 preset. This has a nice metallic look to it. Angle it at –45 degrees.

*Figure 19-19: Use the Level Equalization dialog in PhotoPaint to remove the blue background pattern. Then increase the brightness and contrast from the Brightness-Contrast-Intensity dialog.*

5. Draw a circle in each corner of the rectangle and fill them with the same metallic custom color blend as the rectangle to make them look like rivets. Now select the two top circles and use a 15-step blend to create a row of rivets. Repeat the same blend for all of the corner rivets to create a blend group of rivets all around the edge of the object (see Figure 19-20).

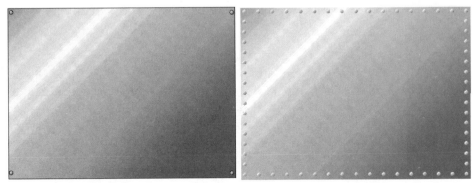

*Figure 19-20: A rectangle with a preset fountain fill becomes a riveted metal sheet when four circles create rivet rows with the help of the Blend roll-up.*

3. Duplicate and arrange the riveted panel to create a large wall of metal sheeting. To get away from the cloned look, select every alternate sheet and reverse the angle of the fountain fill from –45 to 135 degrees. This will create a more flowing coloring scheme. Then select all of the shapes and rotate them 5 degrees to avoid a grid feel.

4. Draw a rectangle over the sheets the size of your page. Then, using the Lens roll-up, apply a Fish Eye lens to distort the sheets so they look like an aircraft fuselage. A rate of 50% gives a slight distortion that is perfect for this application. Enable the Frozen option to end up with a collection of pieces that are distorted and trimmed down to the desired page size. You can then delete or save the original panels to disk. I thought there were too many rivets, so I whipped out my artistic license and deleted a bunch (see Figure 19-21).

*Figure 19-21: Modify the fountain fills to create areas of light and dark. Use the Fish Eye lens to distort the objects slightly for the look of a rounded plane fuselage.*

5. Import the pinup girl bitmap and use the Bitmap Color Mask to render the background of the bitmap transparent. From the Bitmap menu, open the Bitmap Color Mask dialog, click on the eyedropper tool, and then click on the white area in the pinup bitmap. Now bump the Tolerance value up to 24% and click Apply. This should leave just the image of the pinup on the side of the airplane!

6. To get the look of raised rivets (another artistic leap, as airplane rivets are really flush and flat), use the same techniques you used in Chapter 3 to add a highlight and gleam to each rivet. It isn't hard. First select all of the desired rivets in the Wireframe mode and combine them into one curve. Then duplicate the curve, offset it down and to the right, and use the Trim function to get the shadow shapes. Repeat the process, moving the duplicate to the top and left, to get the highlight shapes. The shadow shapes are filled black, the highlights are filled white, and all are given a 50% Transparency Lens (see Figure 19-22).

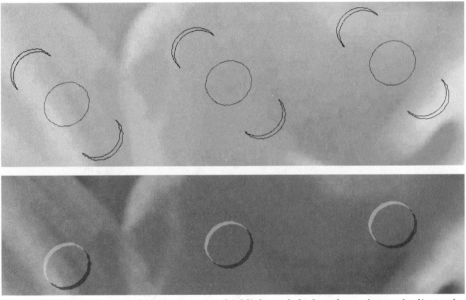

*Figure 19-22: Use the Trim function to create highlight and shadow shapes from a duplicate of the rivets (top, in Wireframe view). When given a 50% Transparency lens, the rivets look round and shiny (bottom).*

7. Set your text to name the plane. Pilots were very superstitious and also sentimental and would name their planes after sweethearts back home. Use artistic text and then modify the text with an envelope to give it a curved look. I used a font called Fink from House Industries. Using the Behind Fill option from the Outline Pen dialog (F12), give the text a really fat .133-inch black outline, duplicate it, and give the duplicate a thinner .083-inch white outline. This will give the text the double-outline look (see Figure 19-23).

*Figure 19-23: Use a retro-looking font distorted with an envelope and given the double-outline effect to name the plane.*

8. Swipe the bullet holes from Chapter 11 to add a sense of danger to the graphic. To get the image to fade away to white, use transparency fountain fills on white rectangles. Draw white rectangles over each edge and use the Interactive Transparency tool to drag from the outside inward to get the fade-away look (see Figure 19-24).

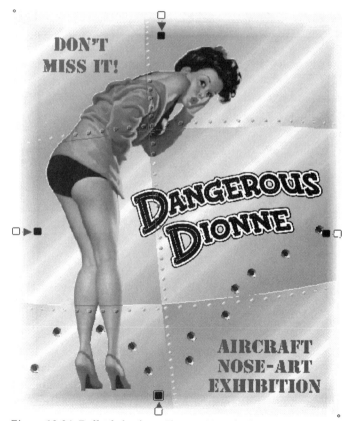

*Figure 19-24: Bullet holes from Chapter 11 and white rectangles with transparency fountain fills finish off the graphic.*

The final image can be seen in the color section and can be loaded from the file called pinup.cdr found in the \Chapt19\ subdirectory on the Companion CD-ROM. I was very pleased with the coloring of the original CorelDRAW file, but after experimenting with filters in PhotoPaint, I went ahead and ran the image through the PhotoLab PhotoFilter. The Afternoon Tea setting gave the bitmap the perfect faded look I wanted. Just when you think you have the perfect image, you can still go a step further. The problem is knowing when to stop. Usually a nasty deadline makes that decision for me!

## Moving On

In this chapter, we looked at ways to exploit the modern conveniences of CorelDRAW to create designs that look like they are from past decades. We also looked at how to achieve the modern retro look by combining old design ideas with more modern ones. And we proved that you can create artwork that is really fun and engaging without losing its simplicity.

In the next chapter, we blast from the past into the present and then beyond. We will see how the simplicity of computer-aided design is resulting in a new type of techno imagery. Using the automation features in CorelDRAW and borrowing images from CorelDream, this new style is seemingly haphazard and busy, but in the end becomes a balanced, workable design. Lose those poodle skirts, watch a copy of *Blade Runner*, and get ready for some digital entropy!

### ▼ Beyond f/x

In what I am calling a reaction *against* the computer design revolution, more and more designs are embracing a retro or low-tech look. This is great news for everyone, as old-school images are easy on the eyes, simple to build, and usually a breeze to output and print.

Everything from annual reports to advertising campaigns can benefit from the simple but eye-catching look of the past. Using existing stock images, like the pinup girl, adds a sense of nostalgia to artwork without adding hardly any effort on your part. In fact, you can "stand on the shoulders of giants," as the saying goes, and "steal" amazing artwork from the ever-growing archives and use them as your own. What a cool deal, especially with trends the way they are. Why not use those images and start your own line of nostalgic silk ties, or promotional posters, or whatever you can dream up. I am a huge fan of the retro look and will be working it into every design opportunity I can! The beauty of using this kind of artwork is that it is really hard for things to go wrong. There are few color-correction hassles, and if the colors look kind of funky, just call it an effect and pretend you did it on purpose!

# chapter 20

# Digital Entropy & Media Madness

I am always fascinated by how new inventions can dramatically change our lives. Snowboards, a seemingly low-tech invention, have changed the entire ski industry, and imagine trying to live without a microwave (how did previous generations make popcorn, anyway?).

The same kind of dramatic mutation can be seen in the world of design. Computers and design power that was once limited to an elite few is now resting comfortably in the hands of millions. Design techniques that used to be slow and laborious now happen with a few mouse clicks. Even more frightening, the invention of virtual reality has artists producing objects and landscapes out of thin air, manufacturing realities like gods creating universes.

Out of this evolving mass of techno-hysteria comes new kinds of designs that mix all types of media. Traditional cultural art is being incorporated into digital canvases with very cool results. On the other end of the spectrum, new designs mixing in text, vector, bitmap, and 3D information are popping up, with a unique sense of balance mixed into the mayhem. What was once alternative is now mainstream, opening up new doors and breaking down barriers for designers. "No rules" is the new rule, and this is an exciting time for artists!

In this chapter we will look at new kinds of technology collages, combining text, vector, bitmap, and 3D information into one. The first example explores combining flat vector art with 3D objects, exploiting the new 3D Metafile format that lets you import and manipulate CorelDream objects directly in CorelDRAW. Then, we will mix hand-drawn illustrations with a hellish background made with the help of the new Twister option on the Interactive Distortion tool. Finally, we will mix high- and low-tech technologies to paste hand-drawn illustrations onto a laser-printed graphic and then scan the image to incorporate into a digital picture frame. It's a chaotic hodgepodge barrage of mixed media that is just part of another day in the world of the contemporary computer artist!

## Ducky

*Figure 20-1: Mixing text, vector, and even 3D artwork into one design creates a contemporary barrage of visual information.*

As cultural influences mix in the new world order, new styles continually evolve and emerge. The image in Figure 20-1, which seemingly has no purpose or direction, is heavily influenced by artwork I have seen from Japan in techie publications. The rich art history and quirky graphic style of Japan serve as a great source of inspiration. What kills me about Japanese design is the insistence of using English names and phrases, which are often out of context or in an odd usage (Dew Dew and Chocolate Colon candy bars, for example!). With that in mind, Slimy Dog Grafix, my T-shirt company, looks right at home.

This image mixes text and symbols into a interesting albeit bizarre image. International ads usually have text in many languages, including Arabic and Chinese symbols. I just used pieces from the corresponding Symbol fonts, and I hope I didn't build words or phrases that are offensive in my random assembled symbol collections. (If so, I apologize profusely.) In any case, this is a fun graphic that incorporates vector art, text placed along curves, and "live" 3D objects linked via Metafiles. This new feature adds tremendous power and flexibility when incorporating 3D files into your CorelDRAW designs. Here is how to mix vector and 3D images into one design:

1. First of all, you must convert a CorelDream file into a file format that is more flexible. On the CorelDRAW clip-art CD there is a directory called 3Dmodels, which has tons of objects from which to choose, so there is bound to be something you like. I found the rubber ducky in the \3dmodels\home subdirectory. In CorelDream, open the 3D model file, which will appear in a box on the screen. You don't have to know CorelDream to pull this off (I am a Dream novice, for sure). With your duck on the screen, choose Export from the File menu. Change the Save As type to 3DMF file (means 3D Metafile), enter the filename, and click Save. That's it. Exit the complex and intimidating world of CorelDream and return to the comfy confines of CorelDRAW!

**TIP** *For more on CorelDream (which is essentially the same as Ray Dream), check out* Ray Dream 5 f/x, *also from Ventana.*

2. In CorelDRAW, import (Ctrl+I) the 3DMF file, changing the file Type to 3D Model to display it. You will see our pal in the default view, in this case from the top right; you'll also see the 3D Toolbox and Property Bar set to 3D model options (see Figure 20-2).

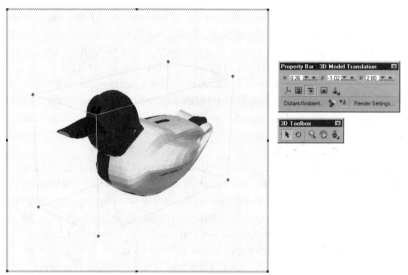

*Figure 20-2: A 3D Metafile can be manipulated in CorelDRAW with the 3D Toolbox and the Property Bar.*

3. Use the magnifying glass to zoom in on the ducky by dragging to the left or up (dragging down or to the right zooms out). Click on the 3D Rotate tool, which will surround the object with a ring in each axis. Dragging a ring will spin the object around in that plane. This interface lets you easily spin the ducky around to face you (see Figure 20-3).

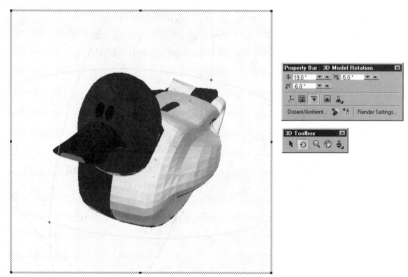

*Figure 20-3: Use the 3D Rotate interface to spin the duck around.*

4. In addition to the position and size of the 3D object, you can also control light and shadow effects if the default Ambient lighting doesn't appeal to you. Click on the Distant/Ambient button on the Property Bar with the ducky selected. Change the type to Spot and then press the + button to add a spotlight. Now you can enable shading and even change the color of the light. Illuminate the figure to your tastes and click OK when finished. You can then manipulate the spotlight within the mini-3D scene using the movement and rotation tools in the 3D Toolbox window. Figure 20-4 shows how the ducky ended up after my manipulation of the 3D interface within CorelDRAW.

*Figure 20-4: Use the Property Bar's many 3D features, including lighting, shading, and rendering options, to get the highlights and shadows just the way you want them on your 3DMF object.*

5. When finished, click on a blank area of the desktop with the Pick tool to exit the 3D editing mode. 3D objects like this are like bitmaps with clear backgrounds, so you can add CorelDRAW objects on top of or underneath

them with no sweat! (If you are using CorelDRAW 7, you will have to set up the scene in CorelDream, render the bitmap, and then import the bitmap into CorelDRAW.)

6. With your duck in place, draw a perfect circle around him. Duplicate and enlarge the circle and move it down off-center. Now shift-select both circles and blend (Ctrl+B) them together in 20 steps using the Accelerate Objects option to make the circles closer together at the center (see Figure 20-5).

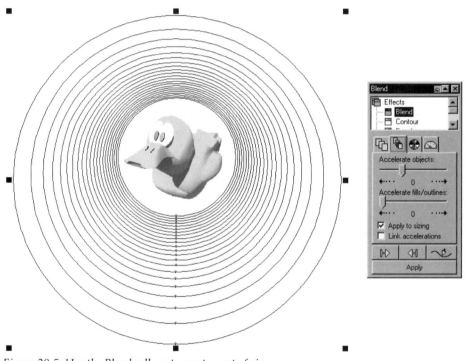

*Figure 20-5: Use the Blend roll-up to create a set of rings.*

7. Separate the ring blend. Use the Ungroup All function and then the Combine (Ctrl+L) function to create solid ring shapes. Use the Rectangle tool to draw a rectangle for the page limit. For some strange reason I wanted to hack off the top left sections of the rings, so draw a trim shape using the Bezier tool. With the Trim shape selected, open the Trim roll-up, click Trim, then click on the rings. See Figure 20-6.

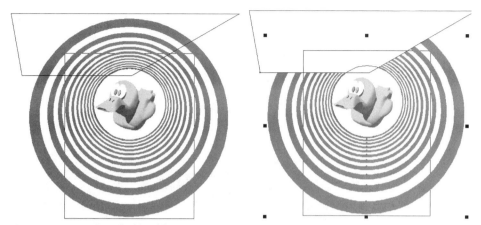

*Figure 20-6: Freezing the blend lets you combine the circles into a multi-ring shape. The odd shape across the top (on left) is used to cut away a section of the rings using the Trim command (on right).*

8. Give the ring objects an orange fill and no outline. Open the Extrude roll-up (Ctrl+E), and add depth with the default effect, only change the Solid fill option on the Fill Color page to a burnt orange. Click Apply to build the new shapes (see Figure 20-7).

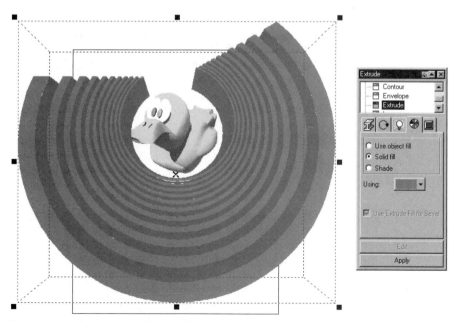

*Figure 20-7: The Extrude roll-up adds depth shapes, but with a Solid fill color assigned, no shading results.*

9. Separate the extrude and give the front rings a pink .023-inch outline (part of this look is created by using many colors from a very similar palette, in this case, light and dark tones of orange). Fill the page rectangle with black and bring the duck to the front (Shift+PgUp). Now draw some more circles behind the duck and you have the basic page layout finished (see Figure 20-8).

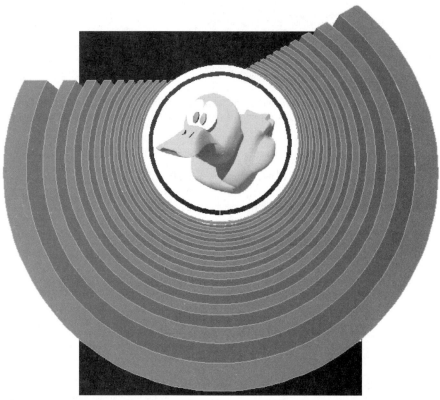

*Figure 20-8: Arrange the elements on the page and separate the extrude elements so you can give only the front objects an outline.*

10. The shapes around the duck are pizza slices with a white circle on top to hide a large portion of them and to make the objects look like arced rectangles. Draw a circle and then use the Shape tool to drag the node to the right, on the *inside* of the circle, to create a pizza slice. Duplicate and color the pizza slices in the same orange tones, throwing in a black one here and there for contrast. To create the solid and dotted arcs, use the Shape tool to drag a circle node on the *outside*, which creates an arc line (see Figure 20-9).

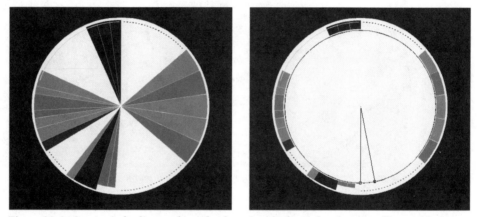

*Figure 20-9: Create circle slices and arcs by dragging the control node on an ellipse with the Shape tool.*

11. Some text in the circle area looks interesting. Draw a circle and then switch to the Artistic Text tool. Drag the pointer over the circle and it will change from crosshairs into a bracket shape. When the pointer is over the circle and a bracket, click, and when you type, the letters will be centered on the top of the circle. Cool! Or, you can type the text out, shift-select both the text and the circle, and from the text menu, open the Fit Text to Path. Now you can change the placement of the text with the options on the Property Bar, so you can place the text on the bottom, on the inside, on the outside, and even choose different letter orientation (see Figure 20-10).

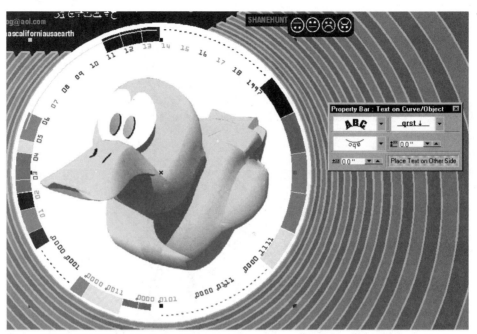

*Figure 20-10: The Fit Text to Path roll-up gives you many options for arranging text along a curve, or in this case, a circle.*

12. To add the busy array of images, open the Symbols docker (Ctrl+F11). Drag and arrange a mixed jumble of pieces to create that international-communication look. Use characters from Japanese, Korean, and Arabic alphabets to get a real global village feel.

The rest of the design is pretty straightforward. I arranged all kinds of symbols and text around the page to make for a busy but interesting ad design. The even-spaced cutouts along the edge and top of the card are just two white shapes blended together. The big logo in the center is a scanned image of a marker-drawn word, converted to vector artwork using CorelTrace, then skewed with the Perspective tool. When finished, all of the pieces were constrained into the page rectangle using the PowerClip function.

You can trip on this image in the color section or in the ducky.cdr file nestled in the \Chapt20\ subdirectory on the Companion CD-ROM. Due to technical and legal hassles (I can not redistribute unaltered Corel clip art, which is what a 3DMF file essentially is), the ducky image in this file is just a bitmap. You can open your own copy of CorelDream and create a new 3DMF file to experiment on in CorelDRAW using the 3D functions. To check out the CorelDRAW file, remember you will have to use the PowerClip | Extract Contents function to see anything!

## 4th Dimension

*Figure 20-11: Mixing hand-drawn ink images with a plethora of CorelDRAW effects, including texture fills, a lens, and the new Interactive Distortion tool with the Twister option, creates a nightmarish vortex into the unknown.*

I think it is safe to say that Norman Rockwell wasn't exactly a big influence on my artistic style. If you guessed Salvador Dali, Robert Williams, Hans Rudi Giger, Edvard Munch, Albrecht Deurer, or Hieronymus Bosch, you would be much more on the mark! I draw inspiration from all kinds of artwork, sometimes as a spoof, often just as a starting point. For example, the last image in this section, Ghouls Under Glass, is a spoof based on a 15th-century engraving by Martin Schongauer, entitled *The Temptation of St. Anthony*, in which the hapless soul is accosted by all forms of nasty little monsters! Also, the Skull Angel graphic from Chapter 16 was influenced by a sculpture by Gian Lorenzo Bernini, *The Ecstasy of St. Theresa*.

The nightmarish vision in Figure 20-11 is another example of mixing classic gargoyle-type images with computer-generated effects. It is also a mixture of low-tech, hand-drawn images brought to life within CorelDRAWS's high-tech, automated, digital canvas. The background is the result of mixing the Twister effect and a texture fill, while a lens alters the image within the chain portal. It is the kind of art that would be too tedious to render by hand, but by mixing in scanned ink images, it maintains a traditional cartoonish feel while still exploiting the high-tech computer effects (see Chapter 18 for more). Here is how to mix technologies to create whirling vortex scenes:

1. The centerpiece is a mixture of techniques we have already covered and artwork from my archives (which with the purchase of this book are essentially now your archives as well). The chain portal can be created with the techniques outlined in Chapter 15, blending link objects around a circle. The gargoyle guards are the same ones found in the Skull Angel image, only now they are gray. They are a group of objects made up of a black-and-white bitmap colorized with shapes. For this design, only the main gargoyle body was recolored. You have got to love CorelDRAW for this kind of simplicity! With the Ctrl key depressed, click on the main fill object within the group and select it all by its lonesome. Now open the Fountain Fill dialog and assign a new body color scheme to the gargoyle (see Figure 20-12).

*Figure 20-12: The Ctrl key lets you select a single object within a group so that you can manipulate it without first ungrouping or otherwise affecting the other objects.*

**TIP** *If you are having trouble selecting CorelDRAW objects behind a bitmap (even in Wireframe view), you need to disable the Treat Objects as Filled option. Right-click over the Pick tool, then choose properties. From the Pick tool options dialog, disable the Treat All Objsts as Filled option. The Pick tool defaults to Treat All Objects as Filled, which is really annoying! Disable this option to get more functionality out of the Wireframe view.*

2. With the Pick tool, click on a blank area to deselect the subgroup object and then select the gargoyle group. Duplicate it and flip-flop by dragging the left-center control node right while holding down the Ctrl key. Arrange the gargoyles on either side of the chain gate. I am the king of image swiping! I grabbed the f/x logo from Chapter 25 and plunked it into the center of the chains. Use the technique from the Ninja Stars example (Chapter 14) to recolor the *CorelDRAW* and *8* using a red and yellow color scheme to match the future background (see Figure 20-13).

*Figure 20-13: Bits and pieces come together to create a new image.*

3. With the CorelDRAW clip-art book open to the "Crests" section, I spotted a file with some nifty design nuggets waiting to be mined! Import a file with cool knife objects from the \clipart\crests\misc directory off of the CorelDRAW clip-art CD. Ungroup the objects and delete all but the pointy pieces. Now arrange these objects like rays of the sun around the chain circle, duplicating any objects that you need to finish the pattern. Use a white-to-cyan fountain fill to create a random reflection in the pieces. Create one side and then duplicate and flip for the other (see Figure 20-14).

*Figure 20-14: Pieces from a clip-art crest are recolored and arranged to use in the new image.*

4. The bat is an illustration that I created just for this image, so it isn't all borrowed or stolen! This image was scanned and colorized just like every other black-and-white bitmap in this book (by now you must notice a trend in my design style!). There is one notable difference. Because the wings need to be behind the chains and the head in front, there are actually two bitmaps in the image. The second bitmap had the areas behind the chains painted away in PhotoPaint using a white brush. (To keep the task within CorelDRAW, you could create a shape for the head, PowerClip the whole pieces into it, and then place the PowerClip in front of the chain.) The bat is made up of a coloring object and the original whole bitmap is behind the chain. On top of the chain are the pieces to colorize the face and then the bitmap with the areas painted away, resulting in the back/front illusion (see Figure 20-15).

*Figure 20-15: Since you can't bend objects, a duplicate of the bat bitmap, with areas painted away, is in front of the chb6ê objects, while the original is behind.*

5. Now it is time to create the spinning vortex shape. First, draw a perfect circle with the Ellipse tool. Now with the Shape tool, create a thin pizza slice by dragging the nodes on the circle to the inside of the circle. With the Pick tool, first convert the object to curves (Ctrl+Q) and then change the axis of rotation to the top-center of the object. Duplicate the shape, shift-select both, and open the Blend roll-up. Change the Rotate value to 360 and click Apply to create a spinning wheel (see Figure 20-16).

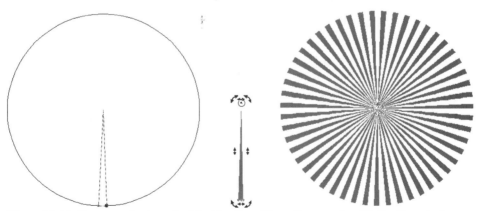

*Figure 20-16: Create a spinning wheel by blending ellipse slivers made with the Shape tool.*

6. Now separate the blend and then use the Ungroup All function. Locate the original two sliver objects and delete the redundant one. Also randomly delete every fourth spoke or so to create open areas in the vortex. Drag-select all of the remaining spinning wheel objects and combine them (Ctrl+L). Now select the Interactive Distortion tool from the Interactive Blend tool flyout. On the Property Bar, click the Twister Distortion button, key in 350 for the Additional Degrees, and stand back. Unleash the beast! Finally, convert the vortex to curves (Ctrl +Q). See Figure 20-17.

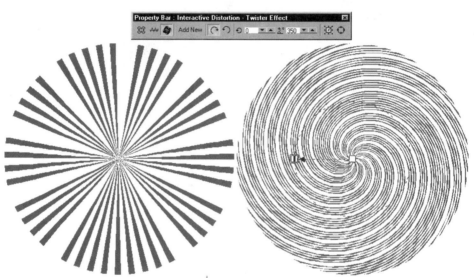

*Figure 20-17: The Twister option on the Interactive Distortion tool Property Bar spins the object into a vortex illusion.*

7. Fill the vortex shape with a custom color blend using the Interactive Fill tool; use an alternating yellow-red pattern. Then use the Intersect roll-up to trim the vortex shape down to fit within the desired page size (see Figure 20-18).

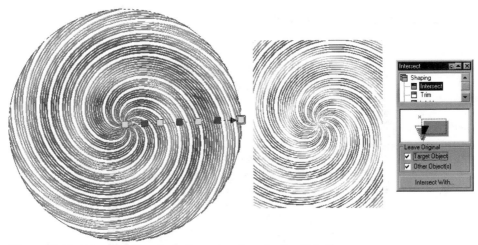

*Figure 20-18: Color and trim down the vortex shape to fit within the page.*

8. Arrange the new vortex shape and page frame behind the ghoul gate. Use a yellow outline on the vortex object to make it stand out more and fill the page frame with a texture fill. From the Fill Tool flyout, open the Texture Fill dialog and change the Texture Library to Styles. Browse the list until you find Mineral, Cloudy 2 Colors. Select it, change the mineral colors from brown and cream to purple and yellow, and click OK. (For abstract backgrounds, you can leave the default Texture Fill values, but to avoid chunky images, increase the values found in the Texture Options dialog, opened by clicking the Options button.) To change the mood in the area inside the chain, draw a circle behind the gate and in front of the background and use the Lens roll-up (Alt+F3) to change things. I used a straightforward Transparency lens, filled purple and given a 50 percent transparency rate. You could make things even crazier with another Lens choice, like Invert or Heat Map.

**CD-ROM**   This image, in its dizzying brilliance, can be seen in the color section and can be found in the \Chapt20\ subdirectory on the Companion CD-ROM; the file is called 4thdimen.cdr. Load the file and practice selecting an object in a group and recoloring the gargoyles. Try changing the Lens shape to make the area inside the chains more or less wild. Also, you can dramatically change the mood by recoloring the vortex shape and the background rectangle. Go nuts and use the pieces to realize your own twisted visions! That's the advantage of mixing old-art in a new computerized environment: unlimited potential!

## Ghouls Under Glass

*Figure 20-19: A bitmap of an ink illustration is made to look like it is encased in glass by creating a wooden frame with the Extrude roll-up and then using the Interactive Transparency tool to create glass.*

As I mentioned earlier, the illustration in Figure 20-19 is based upon on a 15th-century engraving by Martin Schongauer, entitled *The Temptation of St. Anthony*. It is a good example of working with high- and low-tech design techniques, starting with a working backward tactic (see the "Working Backward" sidebar). There is absolutely no rule that says you must use the computer for everything, and sometimes the old manual techniques simply work better, or perhaps faster, for you. Don't fall into the "I must use the computer" design trap. Do whatever it takes, however you want, to get your results. That's my ruthless creativity philosophy, and it often translates to taking the path of least resistance, which I am sure you can appreciate!

### ▼ Working Backward

The logo in Figure 20-19 is a good example of how I often work in circles. Sometimes I find myself creating pieces for a pen-and-ink drawing in CorelDRAW, where things like type are very easy to manipulate. The logo in this image was constructed in CorelDRAW, tweaked and distorted using the Envelope function, and then given depth with the Extrude roll-up. This is much easier than trying to draw these pieces by hand. I then output the artwork as a laser print at actual size and cut and pasted the other ink illustrations on to them. It is a strange mix of high-tech/low-tech, I know, but I prefer working with tangible materials like paper and ink whenever I can! The jester girl image back in Chapter 16 was also done in this way, with the box fashioned in CorelDRAW (using the perspective function) and printed, cut, and pasted to the girl illustration. If the printed graphic is too perfect to match up with the other hand-drawn objects, I'll trace it in ink to make it look right, using the printout for reference, or I'll redraw lines or add hand-drawn shading. Assembling the pieces for an ink illustration in the computer also helps with things like perfect circles and laying out type. If you ever create artwork for a tattoo in CorelDRAW, for example, the artist will retrace everything by hand in the classic tattoo tradition to transfer the image to your skin for reference. It's a trick not unlike one used by product illustrators before computers came around, where they would enlarge a photo of their subject on a photocopier and then trace the main features of the photocopy to get the perspective and logo type right. Whatever it takes, don't hesitate to mix and match old and new technologies to get what you need! Figure 20-20 shows how the hand-drawn pieces fit to the laser-printed logo.

*Figure 20-20: CorelDRAW tricks and shortcuts are used to render a logo (seen on left in wireframe), which is laser-printed. The printout is then cut apart and pasted to other ink illustrations to create a final composite.*

For this image, I combined a logo generated in CorelDRAW with a bunch of hand-drawn ghoul illustrations. Rather than try to assemble all of the pieces in the computer (which would require scanning and importing seven illustrations!), the easier solution seemed to be simply laser-printing the CorelDRAW logo and sticking the illustrations to it. This way I could rotate and position my ghouls around the logo much faster and easier than in PhotoPaint. Then, when I had a composite with which I was happy, I digitized the image with only one scan. Easy! Then it was easy to import the single bitmap into CorelDRAW so I could enshrine my ghouls in a glass frame, like an arty ink illustration on fancy paper. Stick to the appropriate technology for the task at hand, even if it is paper and glue! Reserve computer time for effects that are impossible or impractical to achieve in the real world, such as the glass and frame in this example. Here is how to go about creating the frame, glass, and paper effects:

**CD-ROM**

1. Draw a rectangle for the paper, and import your black-and-white scan on top of it (this image is called ghouls.tif and can be found in the \Chapt20\ subdirectory on the Companion CD-ROM). Open the Pattern Fill dialog, select Bitmap, and then click Load to find a nice fancy paper graphic. There are many samples in the \tiles\paper\large directory on the CorelDRAW clip-art CD. Find a tile you like by scrolling through the examples using the Preview option to see the images, then click Open when you are done, and then click Load to fill your paper. Make sure your black-and-white bitmap is set to No Fill so that the background is transparent and the paper color will shine through.

2. Duplicate the paper rectangle twice and reduce one of the duplicates to create the inside of a picture frame. Now shift-select the smaller frame shape and the larger original and combine (Ctrl+L) them to create a solid frame. Again open the Pattern Fill dialog, and this time load a bitmap tile that looks like wood from the \tiles\wppd\large directory on the CorelDRAW clip-art CD (see Figure 20-21).

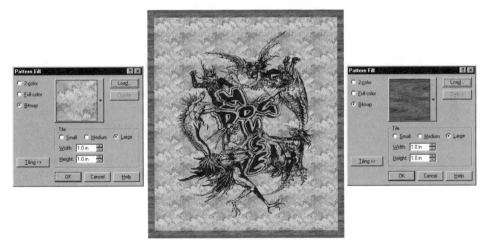

*Figure 20-21: Bitmap pattern fills provide the "fancy" paper coloring as well as the nice wood frame texture.*

3. Select the wood frame and open the Extrude roll-up (Ctrl-E). Move the crosshairs to the center of the frame, change the depth to 10, and then click on the Lighting page. Add a light source to the top right at 100% intensity and another at the bottom right with 50% intensity. This creates a nice illusion of depth without having just a bunch of solid black boxes. Finally, click on the Bevel page, click Use Bevel, and change the bevel depth to .1. Click Apply to build your wooden frame (see Figure 20-22).

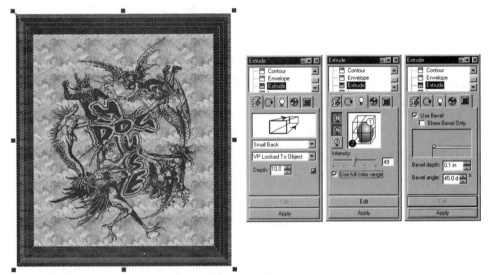

*Figure 20-22: Use the Extrude roll-up options to build a shaded, wooden frame group.*

4. For a glass object, draw a rectangle inside of the frame over the artwork and give it a white fill. Now grab the Interactive Transparency tool and click-drag from way outside of the object on the top-right corner to just outside the bottom-left corner. This places the starting point of the Inter-active Transparency well outside the glass object, but that is a good thing. The starting point is solid white, so by moving it way outside the glass rectangle, the transparency is well into its clear range by the time it passes through the glass. This makes for a soft but obvious highlight at the top right, fading into total transparency at the bottom left (see Figure 20-23).

*Figure 20-23: Starting an interactive transparency outside of the object increases the amount of transparency inside the object.*

To finish off the image I added a few white hairline scratches and also a drop shadow using the Interactive Drop Shadow tool from the Interactive Blend tool fly-out. This picture is hanging in the color gallery and is also in the ghouls.cdr file in the \Chapt20\ subdirectory on the Companion CD-ROM. Load it and see how you can change the bitmap fill in the frame to any other tile to create other coloring varieties. I love live extrudes that rebuild everything automatically. Also, you might want to diddle with the Interactive Transparency tool on the glass to understand how that is working to create a glossy and see-through look.

## Moving On

In this chapter, we explored the ever-evolving world of contemporary design. We looked at completely computer-generated artwork, which used text, vector, and even 3D images crammed into one canvas. We saw again how to work hand-drawn images into awesome CorelDRAW scenes, and we even saw a way to work backward using computer printouts with hand-drawn pieces for good ol' paste-up work.

Working in today's fast-paced world means managing the chaos of clashing technologies. Don't fight it—work with it! Traditional art and design philosophies, techniques, and tools should be a natural part of your modern art studio. There are times when you will have to mix media, and CorelDRAW will let you pull it off brilliantly!

The sky, as they say, is the limit, and that is, in fact, where we are headed in the next chapter. Stars, comets, and other celestial bodies (but no females!) will be the topic of discussion. As irony would have it, the topic is lofty, but the chapter is rather down-to-earth, covering some cool but simplistic effects that won't put your brain in orbit while you're trying to reproduce them. Get set, space cadets, as we blast off to the stars....

▼ **Beyond f/x**

Mixing media is hardly a new concept. More than likely you already have had to face the challenge of taking existing artwork and somehow digitizing it. Scanning existing logos and using the bitmap as a reference to create a new version in CorelDRAW is how I spent many a day in my design career. And this media-conversion process continues, as hand-drawn logos are converted to vector artwork in CorelDRAW and then taken even further with the likes of CorelDream 3D rendering packages (see Chapter 30 for more on this).

Using traditional tools to aid in computer design also helps give your pieces a very unique look. For example, setting type in CorelDRAW for a logo and then laser-printing it to use as a reference to draw it by hand again will totally disguise the computer-generated origins, even if you scan it and bring it back into your computerized design jobs. Or scan textures from around the house, such as leaves, fabric, your face, whatever, for use as interesting bitmap patterns fills or abstract backgrounds. In today's design climate, there are no rules, and mixing technologies just makes you look more skilled and your art more contemporary.

chapter **21**

# Space Debris, Laser Blasts & Sparks

Outer space is one of those themes that seems to enter almost every design realm. There are people who specialize in rendering nothing but fanciful space landscapes using the latest in 3D modeling. Back in the world of two-dimensional design, the great black vacuum does make for a nice backdrop for many design applications. Of course, there are also times when you just want to get spacey and boldly go where no man has gone before....

As a kid, I used to draw elaborate space scenes, and my room was covered wall to wall with images from the cosmos (one of my friends' dad worked at Jet Propulsion Laboratories in nearby Pasadena). In school, my Pee Chee folders were covered with spaceships and star battles, and to this day, I can bust out a pretty good X-wing. The sad thing is that my rendering skills basically peaked then, and now I leave spaceship creation to the geniuses using 3D technology or the millions of behind-the-scene artists pumping out those piles of handy clip art.

In this chapter, we will examine ways to create star fields, planets, and other miscellaneous flotsam and jetsam found in the cosmos. In the first example, we will create a space scene using the Interactive Transparency tool for the planets and the Blend roll-up for comets, and we'll expand on the tentacle technique to create spacey objects. From there we continue to tweak the building with the Blend technique to create starships and space stations. Then we will add some lethal capability to a satellite with a unique laser beam made from a blend and a dithered bitmap. And we will finish off with another laser light show, again using blends, but also taking advantage of the rotation options. 10, 9, 8... Blast off!

## Project: U.F.I.C.I.S. (Unidentified Flying Ice Crystal in Space)

*Figure 21-1: Space scenes are a popular design theme and lend themselves to computer-aided design. The computer makes short work of populating an empty sky with stars, planets, comets, and other miscellaneous debris.*

When I first started thinking about space projects, I spaced out. I drew a total blank. I grew up in a room full of space photos, *Star Wars* posters, and NASA literature, and suddenly I could not think of a thing. I am just going to chalk that up to the nasty cold medication I was on, as the next day my head was littered with space debris.

The advantage of using a computer for this kind of work is in the duplicating process. An image like this has very few unique elements but many duplicates. Even if a duplicate is not identical to the original, the changes are typically only to size and coloring choices. Here is how to quickly fill a dark sky with interesting cosmic objects:

1. Start with a big black rectangle the size of the page. Now draw a tiny little circle with no outline and fill it with Powder Blue from the onscreen palette. Grab this little sucker and move to a new spot, only before you release the left mouse button, depress the right. Now you have moved and duplicated the star in one step. If you then repeat (Ctrl+R) this action, you can make a row of evenly spaced stars. Stars are not that neat and tidy, so duplicate and arrange the stars by hand. Vary the size of the duplicates until you make a little group of stars. Drag-select the group and use the move/duplicate trick to fill up the sky quickly. Spin the duplicate group around once in awhile to avoid a cookie-cutter patterned look. Then go back and move, add, or delete stars in sections so that there is no discernible pattern to your stars (see Figure 21-2).

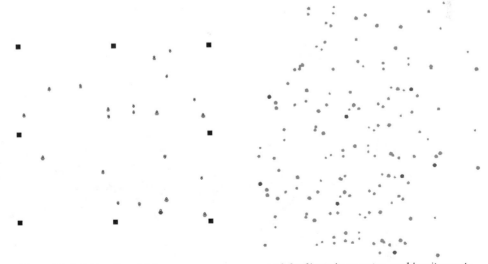

*Figure 21-2: Using the right mouse, you can move and duplicate in one step, making it easy to fill the sky with stars.*

2. For shooting stars, start with a star shape and duplicate it. Move the duplicate to the area from which you want the shooting star to be coming, give the circle a black fill, and reduce it in size slightly. Shift-select both circles and apply a 100-step blend (Ctrl+B) to create the shooting star. The star appears to fade away because the second circle is the same color as the background (see Figure 21-3).

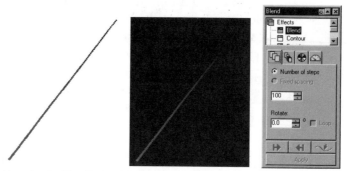

*Figure 21-3: Create a shooting star by blending a star to a black duplicate.*

3. For the slightly larger stars, there are two ways of thinking: blends or fountain fills. Blending a larger black circle to the powder blue color makes for a smooth transition into the background. Fountain fills need a little more effort to get them to blend away nicely and not look like flat plates in space! Use the Interactive Fill tool to create a custom color blend to fill a circle, dragging the black outside point back into the object so the blend is more abrupt and solid black by the time it gets to the edge of the circle. For a cool variant, try a square fountain fill and rotate it 45 degrees for a star shape (see Figure 21-4).

*Figure 21-4: Blend a star to a larger, black duplicate to create a rounded object. Fill a circle with a custom color blend to create the look of a round planet or sparkly star.*

4. Use the Blend roll-up to create a comet. First, draw a circle and convert it to curves (Ctrl+Q). Now drag the center-right node to the right. Then drag-select the remaining nodes, open the Node Edit roll-up (Ctrl+F10), and click the Add Node button. Select and delete all but the three nodes necessary to create the unique sweeping shape. Duplicate the shape and downsize it to create a midpoint, and duplicate and downsize to create the tiny little nugget of ice that is the actual comet. Color these objects black, blue, and white. Then, using the Blend roll-up, first shift-select the black and blue objects and click Apply to create a 20-step blend between them, and then select the blue and white objects and repeat the blend. This will create a compound element of two blends for a smooth three-color transition (see Figure 21-5).

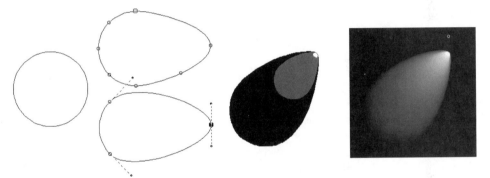

*Figure 21-5. A three-stage blend of the egg shape creates a comet and tail.*

5. For the earth object, I found a nice starting point in the \clipart\space\ planets directory on the CorelDRAW clip-art CD. The file I picked had a nice earth, but the coloring was too flat and the other unwanted elements needed to be deleted. Import (Ctrl+I) the image, and then ungroup the objects. Now delete everything except the continent shapes and the ocean circle. Shift-select all of the continents and combine them (Ctrl+L). Use the Interactive Fill tool to create a custom color blend radial fountain fill from a light green to dark green to black. Place the light green starting point closest to an imagined light source and drag the ending black node to a point where the objects look round and shaded. Select the ocean circle, and using the same Interactive Fill technique, create a color blend from light blue to dark blue to black. Place the light blue starting point in the same orientation with the light source and adjust the ending black node again to make the planet look round (see Figure 21-6).

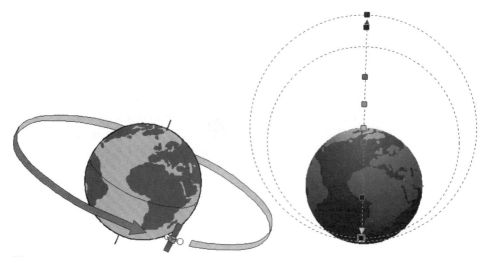

*Figure 21-6. Use the Interactive Fill tool to transform flat clip art into a round planet.*

6. I started to draw shapes and use custom color blends to make my planets, but that was too laborious. Instead, I created the planet-maker shape (which is a Radial Transparency lens from clear to black) that you can drop on any circle to make it look round. Draw a perfect circle and fill it with shapes or a texture fill (the Above the Earth texture fill in the Samples 7 Texture Library seems appropriate). Duplicate the original planet shape and fill the duplicate black. Now with the Interactive Transparency tool, drag from a spot closest to the light source to a spot away from it. The default is a linear fill, so change to radial. Now you need to reverse the logic of the fill, so drag black from the onscreen palette and drop it on the white point on the blend; then drag white and drop it on to the original black point. This will make the radial transparency black to clear. Move the point of clear to where you want the most color from below to shine through, like a highlight, and drag the far point to fade to black in a circular fashion to complete the planet (see Figure 21-7).

7. The mysterious giant ice crystal is actually our friend the sea star from way back in Chapter 6, only now it has a new color scheme. This object, as you recall, is made with high-step blends of groups of circle objects to create the tentacles. In this example, the shading of the circles has been adjusted from the brown tones to the powder blue, but retaining the white highlight and black shadow area in the custom color blend. Notice the orientation of the color blend is such that the shadow is away from the imagined light source, which is at the top of this image (see Figure 21-8). See Chapter 6 for step-by step instructions on how to create such objects.

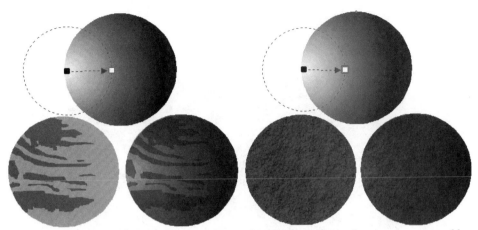

*Figure 21-7: Use the Interactive Transparency tool with a radial fountain transparency to add shading and roundness to any circle object below it.*

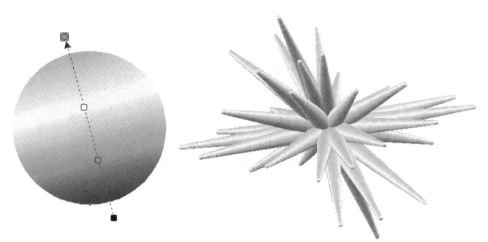

*Figure 21-8: Change the custom color blend of the sea star object to create an icy crystal in space.*

The finished universe can be found in the color section and the space.cdr file in the \Chapt21\ subdirectory on the Companion CD-ROM. If you open the file, be prepared to wait a spell for the ice crystal to build. The results look cool, but the high-step blends are painfully slow to render. Feel free to steal bits from my starry sky to use in your own, or create different-looking space debris. Also, take a peek at the next section to see how to add a laser beam to the mix and blow some things to kingdom come.

## Stars or Starships?

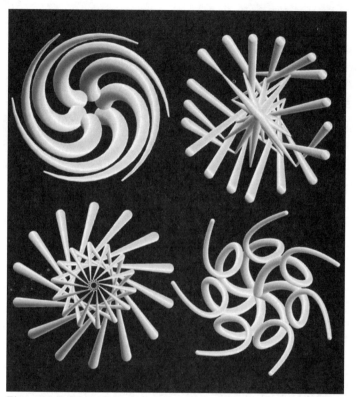

*Figure 21-9: Objects blended using techniques from Chapter 6 can be further manipulated to create stars, crystal creatures, and space stations.*

The space theme can involve some far-out images and techniques. The crystal creature in the first tutorial demonstrates that Martin Boso's blend techniques can create space creatures as well as undersea ones (and blood vessels and intestines, the technique's original use). I'm going to expand further on this versatile technique here and show you how to use it to create a spinning star, a more random-looking crystalline creature, and an ultra-tech space station. The beauty here is that these are easy images to create even though they look very involved. I'll walk through each example individually so you can understand what is happening and also offer some special patented Professor Shane tweaks you will need to make all the pieces look right in the end.

## Spinning Space Station

This beauty kind of looks like the sea star in Chapter 6, but it is really different in many ways. That example is the result of a single-blend step that uses the rotation option, where this one uses multiple steps. It is a little more work, but it is much, much more flexible! Here is how to make the spinning star:

1. For this trick, I will need an ordinary curved line.... Why thank you, my dear! Use the Bezier tool to draw a nice curving line. Now draw a circle on the bottom end of the twisted line and use the now famous custom color blend scheme (dark, neutral, highlight, neutral) to shade the object.

2. Duplicate the circle, move it to the far end of the twisted line, and downsize it dramatically. Now shift-select both objects and open the Blend roll-up (Ctrl+B). Create a 125-step blend along the twisted path to create a horn shape (see Figure 21-10).

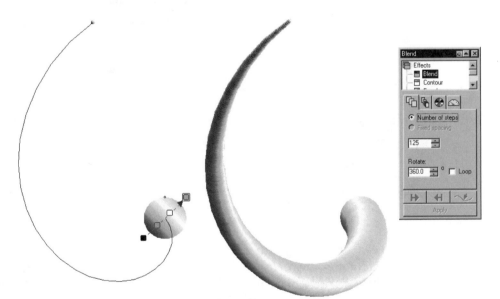

*Figure 21-10: Use a high-step blend along a path to create a horn object.*

3. Select the blend group, and separate everything with the Arrange | Separate, Arrange | Ungroup All, commands, and then group (Ctrl+G) them again. You have to do this little cha-cha menu dance because you can not blend a blend, but you can blend the tarnation out of any benign group, no matter how many objects are in it. Select the

group and double-click to change the axis of rotation from the center to just above the big end of the horn. (Where you place this little guy will dramatically change the way things look, so take a mental note of where you placed it and how things turn out.) With the axis changed, now duplicate the group (+ key), drag-select both objects, and open the Blend roll up (Ctrl+B). Change the number of steps to something reasonable like 5 and set Rotate value to 360 degrees (see Figure 21-11). A click of the Apply button will draw your star! (Check to see that object acceleration is not enabled, or enable it to see some strange variants.)

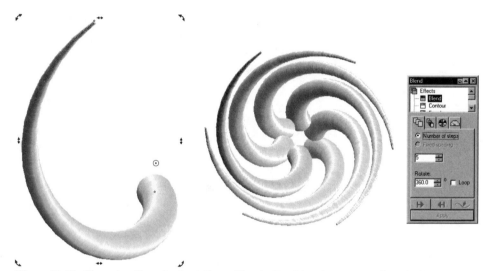

*Figure 21-11: Changing the axis of rotation will spin the object into a star when the Rotate value is set to 360 on the Blend roll-up.*

You can get so many outrageous variations on this theme it is nauseating! You could, for example, use the tribal blend from Chapter 14 with the thin, thick, thin tube look to create a different kind of horn or, as in the star4.cdr file, blend the circles along a spiraled line instead of just a curvy line. These stars are in the color section, natch, and this example is called star1.cdr in the \Chapt21\ subdirectory on the Companion CD-ROM. Load and compare star1.cdr with star4.cdr, and you will see that the only difference is that the blend path in the first step is twisted. This stuff is easy and fun, don't you think?

## Pandemonium!

I like this image because it is so dang random. Instead of using a controlled, mathematical type of blend, I randomly scattered the objects in each blend group manually. During the blend process the objects seek out their original parents, with just crazy results. Here is how to get blend chaos:

1. Start with that same old circle, with the dark, neutral, highlight, neutral custom color blend. Now duplicate and arrange 18 of these guys in a circle and group them. Select all 18, duplicate, and downsize the duplicates dramatically. Ungroup the duplicate group and randomly scatter these little dudes on the inside of the original circle. When you are finished scattering, shift-select these pieces again, group once more, and send them to the back.

2. Select the original big group again and duplicate it. Ungroup the objects in the duplicate group, but do not deselect them. Now align the objects Center to Center from the Align & Distribute Dialog (or just press the "E" and "C" keys in CorelDRAW 8). Once they are aligned, group the objects for the blend to assemble correctly, and send To Front. This will create what looks like a single circle in the dead center but is really a stack of 18 objects (see Figure 21-12).

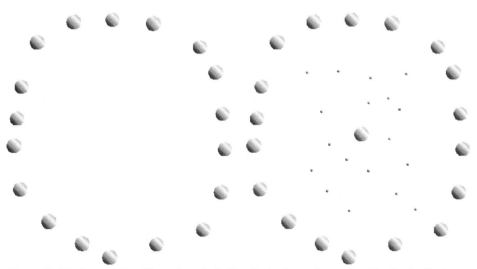

*Figure 21-12: Arrange the ellipses in a circle. Duplicate, downsize, and scatter the duplicates, and finally, create a perfect stacked group in the center.*

3. The magic of blends is that when you duplicate a group of objects—
CorelDRAW remembers which object is the parent for each duplicate.
During the blending process, the parents and the children hook up again,
in this case with wild results. Shift-select the outer ring group and the
smaller inside circles and blend them together with 200 steps, no rotation. You will see that no matter how strangely scattered the objects (like
penguins on a busy beach), parent and child hook up again! Switch to
Simple Wireframe view so you can select the small inner circle group and
then the center stack and blend them together (see Figure 21-13). Switch
back to Normal view to see the chaos ensue.

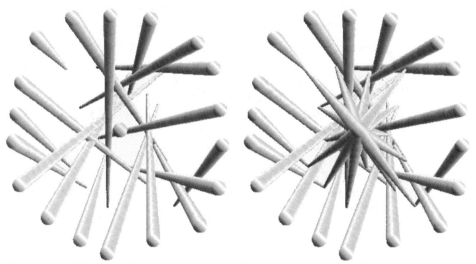

*Figure 21-13: Blend the circle groups to create a chaotic weave as each duplicate seeks out its
parent shape.*

This was one of those accidental discoveries that just made me go, "Whoa!"
You may not be as easily amazed as I am, but if you are, open the stars2.cdr
file in the \Chapt21\ subdirectory on the Companion CD-ROM and take a
gander at this mess firsthand. It's mighty spooky how each duplicate remembers where it came from.

## Controlled Chaos

This star (bottom left in Figure 21-9) looks so nice and evenly calculated, it has an eerie "technology beyond our own" feel. Here is how to get the evenly spaced star shape:

1. Start again with our pal the (dark, neutral, highlight, neutral) filled circle and duplicate it twice (press the + key twice). Take one of the duplicates and set if off to the side for now. Blend these two guys along a larger circle path to create an even distribution around an ellipse. Do the dance (Arrange | Separate, Arrange | Ungroup All) and then delete the extra redundant circle hiding behind the first control curve. Drag-select all of these, and group them.

2. Duplicate this group, and downsize. Now, to put the family ties power into effect, select the inside ring of circles and rotate it 90 degrees. Duplicate this ring again and downsize dramatically for a small circle in the center (see Figure 21-14).

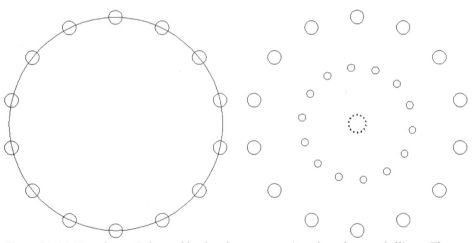

*Figure 21-14: Use a large circle as a blend path to create a ring of evenly spaced ellipses. Then duplicate and downsize twice, rotating the middle group 90 degrees.*

3. In the Simple Wireframe view, shift-select the outer and middle ring sets and blend them together with 200 steps. Then shift-select the middle and center ring sets and blend those also with 200 steps. Back in Normal view, after a brief moment for your processor to catch its breath, you should see a cool 3D space station thing (see Figure 21-15).

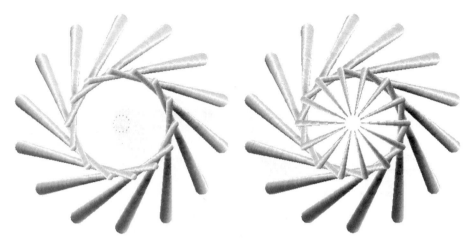

*Figure 21-15: Blending the circles together creates the star. Because the middle ring set duplicate was rotated in relation to the original, there is a twist effect during the blend process.*

4. There is one problem (or not, depending on your point of view). When we rotated the middle ring set, we also rotated the custom color blend in those circles. With the color scheme rotated, the shadow and highlight colors are in the wrong place. To fix things, just select the Compound Object, then steal the correct fill with the Copy Properties From dialog. From the Copy Properties dialog (Ctrl+Shift+A), enable the Fill option, click OK, then click on that circle I had you set aside in step 1. That should fix things.

This image, stars3.cdr in the \Chapt21\ subdirectory on the Companion CD-ROM, should provide you with hours of amusement. Select each ring set and rotate it to see how the new blend rebuilds. Don't worry, after a few days someone will come looking for you and pry your frozen eyes away from the screen long enough for you to gain control again.

## Killer Satellites

*Figure 21-16: Add energy sparkles to a laser beam using a bitmap blur effect to add glowing energy to the ray o' destruction.*

Well, now I am starting to detect the influence of those *Star Wars* posters. Here is a killer satellite, blasting some evil thing into smithereens (see Figure 21-16). The laser beam is the result of blending a fat magenta line to a thin yellow one. The static sparkles are created using essentially the same technique that we fuzzed the "Loser" brand with back in Chapter 13, only now with the addition of bright colors. Here is how to create a fuzzy laser beam:

1. This is a great scene, but quick to build. The stars were stone-cold ripped-off from the first example in this chapter, and the explosion was lifted from Chapter 2. The satellite and Space Command logo are images from the \clipart\space archives off of the CorelDRAW clip-art CD. Arrange the pieces on the page to your taste.

▼ **Shortcuts**

Hey, time is money. If you would rather start from scratch every time, feel free. I would rather take shortcuts and spend more quality time in the sandbox at the local park with my two-year-old niece. If you create artwork for a living, or would like to, you have got to learn to be efficient or you will end up spending too much time on each piece and not making any money. Your clients have no idea how you create these images, and don't give them any clues either. Never work in front of your clients. They will just get the impression that what you do is quick and easy, and they won't want to pay top dollar for your services. They are paying for your talent, and being efficient should mean more time for you, not less pay from them. Shortcuts such as using clip art or borrowing from previous work just makes your job easier. The satellite in this image would take a long time to work out, but you don't have to, so cash in on someone else's labor.

2. Draw a straight line from the radar dish at the top of the satellite to the center of the explosion and give it a .052 inch magenta outline. Duplicate and give the duplicate a yellow hairline. Select both objects and blend them together to create a laser beam.

**TIP**  *When you work with two lines directly on top of one another, it is difficult to select the bottom line. To make your life easier, use the Tab key to change the currently selected object, or Shift+Tab to select in the opposite direction (the direction is determined by the order of creation, so the Tab key moves backward, from the newest object back toward the oldest, and Shift+Tab moves from the oldest toward the newest). So for the laser blend example, with the top line selected, press the Tab key to select the older original line beneath it. Then it is easy to Shift-select the top line and then blend the two together. See, yet another reason why you should feel good about buying this book.*

3. Ungroup the pieces in the satellite and arrange them so that the pieces in the dish are in front of the laser blast. Draw a blast shape with the Freehand tool and give it a yellow fill with an interactive transparency fill that fades to black (see Figure 21-17).

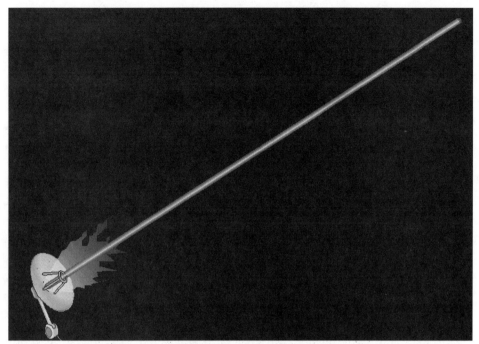

*Figure 21-17: Blended lines create a laser beam, and a freehand-drawn shape with a linear transparency fountain fill becomes an energetic blast shape.*

4. Select the laser blend, duplicate it, and place the duplicate off to the side. Change the outline color to black, and convert the object to a grayscale bitmap. Now instead of first drawing a bounding box like we did with the loser conversion, we will use the CorelDRAW 8 Inflate Bitmap command to create the extra space needed for the Gaussian Blur step to come (CorelDRAW 7 users will still have to use a bounding box for this step). Select the newly created bitmap, and from the Bitmap menu, choose Inflate Bitmap | Manually Inflate Bitmap. Change the Inflate By values to 110% and click OK to add area (like enlarging the paper or canvas size in a paint program). See Figure 21-18.

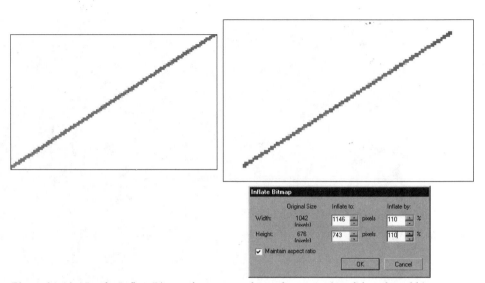

*Figure 21-18: Use the Inflate Bitmap feature to enlarge the paper size of the selected bitmap to create image area for the effects steps to come.*

5. With the new grayscale bitmap selected, use the Gaussian Blur effect to fuzz the line. Now again open the Convert to Bitmap dialog, only this time select Black and White, Dithered, and 300 dpi. Click OK to create the laser static (see Figure 21-19).

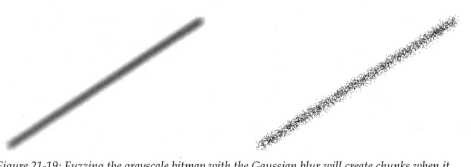

*Figure 21-19: Fuzzing the grayscale bitmap with the Gaussian blur will create chunks when it is converted back to a black-and-white bitmap.*

6. Give the bitmap a yellow outline color and no fill to keep the background transparent. Then place the bitmap under the original laser to create a randomized, sparkling, glow effect (see Figure 21-20).

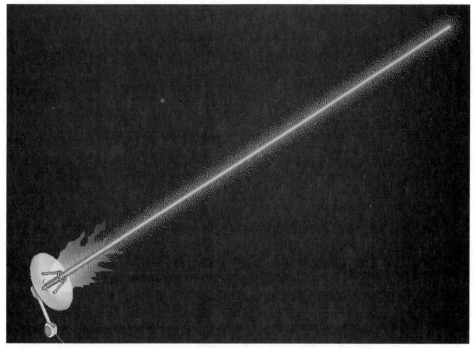

*Figure 21-20: Arranging the black-and-white bitmap, now with a yellow outline color and no fill, creates a glow around the laser.*

7. To customize the satellite and make it a more dynamic part of the scene, add reflections of the explosion in surfaces facing it. Select the shape that makes up the side of the satellite facing the explosion. Now duplicate it and give it a solid yellow fill. Use the Interactive Transparency tool to fade the yellow across, moving the start point outside of the object so just a soft yellow glow remains. Repeat the process on all surfaces facing the explosion (see Figure 21-21).

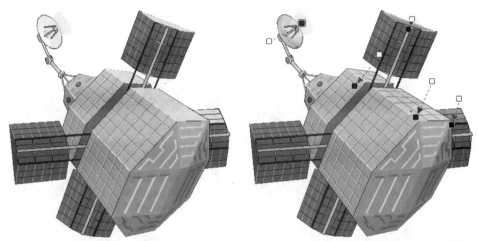

*Figure 21-21: Duplicate surfaces facing the explosion and give them a yellow reflection with the Interactive Transparency tool.*

8. Set text for your logo using the Artistic Text tool. I used a font called CopprplGoth (Copperplate Gothic). Use the Shape tool to select, enlarge, and move the 2. Then create a single-step contour shape outside of the text objects. Separate the contour and fill the objects with a fountain fill preset called Cylinder-02. Open the Fountain Fill dialog (F11) and click the down arrow next to the Presets window until you locate the fill of your choice. Preset fills are great time-savers, especially multicolored custom color blends. Both text and contour have the same fill, only the back contour has the fill set at a 45-degree angle (see Figure 21-22).

*Figure 21-22: Use the Fountain Fill presets to add quickly a ton of color to any object.*

9. Duplicate and offset a copy of the text object for a highlight, and again for a shadow element, and send them behind the original text. This adds a little contrast and pop to the central word object.

Kaboom! Catch the action in the color section or in the spcelazr.cdr file in the \Chapt21\ subdirectory on the now-smokin' Companion CD-ROM. If you haven't already, feel free to use the images and objects on the CD-ROM in your own work. Part of the bonus of buying this book is all the free artwork on the CD-ROM that you can pilfer and call your own. Hey, I know the score. You shelled out the cash for this book, and I appreciate it. That is why I have included even my precious ink illustrations on the CD-ROM, because I want you to be stoked with your purchase and get a bonus you can't find on those other lame-o CorelDRAW books. Aren't you glad I am so ruthless?

## Laser Specialties

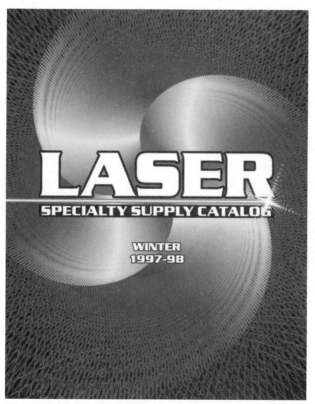

*Figure 21-23: The Blend function creates not only the round laser beam, but also the background pattern and even the exploding sparkle.*

Often associated with space scenes, laser beams also make interesting design elements by themselves. You can emphasize them with the blend technique and dithered bitmap, as in the previous example, or you can leave the lines just a crisp single color and blend them to create a dazzling light show. In this example, the busy colors of the background are a result of a blend of simple outlines, while the laser in the center uses the fat-to-thin-line blend technique. The laser acts as a baseline for the text to rest on, and the blast offers a point of visual interest to draw attention to the text, no easy task in this busy sea of laser light! As they say in the laser industry, "Avoid looking into bright light with your remaining eye." Here is how to create a laser beam and sparkle effects:

1. Draw a straight line with the Bezier tool; the line can be created with only a click at the start and a click at the end. Give this line a fat .08-inch magenta outline. Now duplicate it (+ key) and make the duplicate a white hairline. Drag-select both and blend (Ctrl+B) them together (see Figure 21-24). No sweat.

*Figure 21-24: Blend a fat pink line to a thin white one to create a rounded laser beam.*

2. The sparkle is created in essentially the same way that the star patterns were created earlier in this chapter, only use a star shape instead of a circle for the blend path. Open the Symbols roll-up (Ctrl+F11), choose the Stars1 collection, locate #71, and drag it onto the desktop. This little shape plays a big role in this design! Now draw a tiny little circle and duplicate it. Select both, fill them yellow, and open the Blend roll-up. Create a 50-step blend along the full path using the star shape as the path (see Figure 21-25).

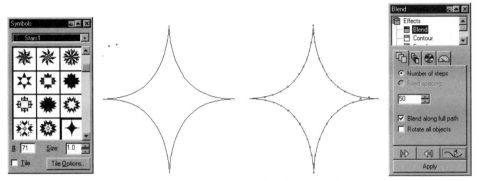

*Figure 21-25: A star becomes the blend path for a series of little circles.*

3. Select the blend and separate the pieces with the Arrange | Separate and Arrange | Ungroup All commands, then Group the circles (but not the control star shape). Now duplicate the circles, ungroup them, and then align them center to center. This will make them look like a small dot, which is actually a stack of 52 circles. Color the center stack white and align the circles in the center of the star shape.

4. Shift-select both circle groups and blend them together with 15 or so steps. To give a tighter cluster of objects in the center of the blend, drag the Acceleration slider to the right. Pow! You have the star burst (see Figure 21-26).

*Figure 21-26: The Blend roll-up creates a burst by blending the two circle groups together. The Accelerate Objects slider changes the blend to cluster objects closer to the center.*

5. For the background image, you will need the same star shape that you used for the burst. Rotate the star –45 degrees and enlarge it to way beyond the size of your page. Now duplicate it and reduce the duplicate to just a small dot in the center of the page. Shift-select them both and give them a .022 inch cyan outline (or as thick or thin as you wish).

6. Open the Blend roll-up and apply a 300-step blend with rotation set to 360 degrees. From the Colors page on the Blend roll-up, enable one of the Rainbow buttons (see Figure 21-27). Better than a laser light show, and no parking hassles.

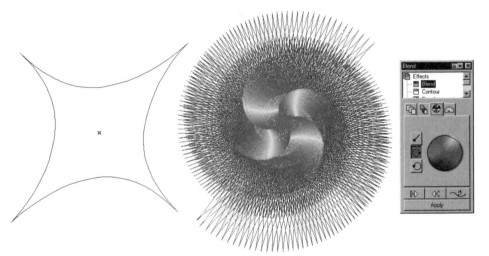

*Figure 21-27: The Blend roll-up, with 360 degrees rotation and the Rainbow functions enabled, creates a laser light show blend between the two star shapes.*

That's the whole process! Add a black rectangle the size of your page, then select all, and PowerClip everything into it. Add your text, if any (I used a font called Serpentine), and call it a day. The light show starts in the color section and also in the lasers.cdr file found in the \Chapt21\ subdirectory on the Companion CD-ROM. Open the file and play with the laser blend for your own personal light show! For even more rotation, select either the outside or inside control curve and spin it manually. Remember all the pieces are stuffed into a rectangle with the PowerClip function, so in order to manipulate the pieces you need first to use the PowerClip | Extract Contents command.

## Moving On

This chapter was full of miscellaneous space-related objects. We made comets, stars (shooting and stationary), and planets in several flavors. Once again we saw how those tentacles from Chapter 6 could create patterns and stars. (There is only one more derivative of this technique left in the book, I promise!) Then we made fat and thin lasers with the Blend roll-up, even spinning them for a light show, and added sparks with a dithered bitmap technique.

 Space is such a hot topic at the moment, with the anniversary of the Roswell invasion, re-releases of the *Star Wars* films, NASA activity, you name it. You can hardly walk down the street without seeing some space-related icon or graphic. With that in mind, I also included a file, aliens.cdr, in the \Chapt21\ subdirectory on the Companion CD-ROM for my own take on the alien invasion! This image, as seen in Figure 21-28, takes the popular alien-head image and works it into my puppy paw Slimy Dog logo (the paw is on everything I own; it's even plastered all over the puppy-mobile). You can work the space theme into just about anything and exploit a popular trend in your designs.

*Figure 21-28: The space theme is worked into the traditional Slimy Dog Grafix puppy paw logo using alien heads to create the paw pads.*

In the next chapter, we will exploit some of the ideas from this one (such as the bitmap sparks technique) to help us get a campy pulp feel of sci-fi publications from the first part of this century. Using original and stock images of antique magazine covers, you can get very cool results with PhotoPaint and CorelDRAW tricks. No need to read under the covers with a flashlight; this pulp fiction is okay out in the open!

▼ **Beyond f/x**

Laser lights and space scenes remain a steady and popular design theme. With so many news items these days involving space exploration and with sci-fi films all the rage, it is a good idea to space out. My very first business card was my company logo drifting through space, and it remains one of the most popular I have ever done.

Space backgrounds, light grids, and laser blasts are great for organizing a product catalog, especially for a high-tech client. (I had a client that sold lasers. The layout was begging for stars and planets!) Advertising projects can bank on "out of this world deals," "take off to savings," and other cosmic design themes. A Web site could easily have a "welcome to my universe" theme, using space objects as icons or buttons and directing attention and action with laser blasts. Still doubting the appeal of space? Check out the Ventana Color Studio in the center of the book or the first two examples in the next chapter.

# chapter 22
# Pulp Vision

There was such an emphasis on the future in what is now the past, the combination makes for great contemporary artwork. People were just as wacky about alien invasions back in the 30's and 40's as they are today, and with Rosewell, New Mexico, appearing in daily headlines, why not bank on the trend and add a little sci-fi pulp to your daily design diet?

Using a comic-book style for commercial artwork is not only unique, it can also be very easy. Working with the volumes of stock images available it is quick and easy to create a piece of art that not only works great to draw attention, but also is usually easy to reproduce. The bold, graphic nature of illustrations coupled with the simplistic use of type almost guarantee good results in any media.

In this chapter we will look at exploiting the campy pulp fiction styles of yore in modern design applications. In the first example, we will take a sci-fi image from the first half of the century and make it feel right at home in a modern computer ad. Then, we will manipulate an old comic book magazine cover, painting away the existing copy using the clone tool in PhotoPaint. Finally, we will generate that signature pulp look using an original ink illustration and other tricks.

## Computer Bugs Attack! _____

*Figure 22-1: Old-time images can be worked into contemporary designs with great success, using PhotoPaint to clean up the images and CorelDRAW to merge all of the design elements.*

I have always been a fan of space and comics, and have an eclectic collection that includes such great titles of *True Alien Stories* and the like. (What wonderful drivel to fill a young boys head with, to keep him looking into the skies in fear!) When I discovered that Time Tunnel (the company that also supplied the pin-up girls from Chapter 19) had a "Sci-Fi Pulps" collection, I had to have it! (Samples from this collection are also included in the \timetunl\ directory on the CD-ROM.) This collection is a great source of the kind of campy, girl-in-distress, Buck Rogers art that I so love!

When I get to mix business with pleasure, so to speak, is when I love my job. I have some very cool clients who on occasion let me cut loose and do something different. This works to our mutual benefit, as when I like what I am working on I put more effort and time into the project without charging more, and the client gets great eye-catching art that usually generates sales, and everyone is happy. This technique borrows heavily from the tried and true Wall Street ad formula—interesting photo+(bold text/catchy slogan)=mass appeal+^sales+repeat business. If you flip through any high-end publication you won't find a lot of amazing CorelDRAW illustrations (unless it's a computer art mag, of course). What you will find is the ad formula at work. So why not make it work for you?

The beauty of the formula is that as a contemporary digital artist you can also draw from volumes of amazing images, such as the "Sci-Fi Pulp" collection, already digitized and also royalty free. In the old days, if you used stock photography, you would have to pay a fee every time it ran, and a hefty price tag up front (we once plunked down $10,000 dollars for a one-year contract on an image the client insisted they had to have!). Now for a measly $99 bucks you can score an image CD with no usage limitations or additional fees. A little image massaging in PhotoPaint, text and layout in CorelDRAW, and even the non-illustrator can make money in the ad game.

I like to try and keep the original look and feel of a period piece as much as I can when using it for a contemporary design. Something is lost if you get too flashy with modern techniques or contemporary fonts. You don't have to be dead on, but if you shoot for close to the original, or incorporate popular techniques of the period (such as having characters block out part of the title, as in this example), things look better. If you can nail the original spirit of the design in your makeover, the result is almost like an optical illusion, where your viewer at first thinks they are looking at an antique image. The surprise is things like Web addresses and fax numbers that bring the image into the nineties! Here is how to use a classic stock image in a modern application:

1. Find an image from the archives that suits your application. Don't try to stretch the reader's imagination too much with images that don't match the ad copy in any way. This can be kind of hard, but I found a workable image in the Time Tunnel collection of this very mechanical looking monster thing attacking the obligatory damsel, with our hero space-boy coming to the rescue. I've often imagined my computer as an unruly beast, so I decided the image would work. This image has the cryptic title fu-05_50.jpg and is in the \timetunl\ subdirectory on the CD-ROM.

2. Load the image at the largest size available into PhotoPaint for manipulation (the more image data the better). (The Time Tunnel images are already at 300 dpi, but some PhotoCD's give you a size option when you load. Use the Poster option when you are given an option, which is the largest.) We need to paint away the existing type so we can add in our

own, and there are other issues you need to address in PhotoPaint to make the image right. First of all, most PhotoCD images are not set up for print applications. (Kodak developed PhotoCD technology originally for onscreen applications). We need to convert the image from the on-screen version to something we can use for print (obviously the parameters are different if you are doing Web-only graphics). From the Image menu, select Resample. The Resample dialog shows the current stats on the selected bitmap. Check out those dimensions (of the bitmap, not the damsel!). Many times these PhotoCD images will have huge physical dimensions (Width:22 inches, Height: 32 inches, and low 72 dpi resolution). Not exactly useful. To fix this, enable the Maintain Original Size option on the Resample dialog, then key in the desired resolution, in this case, 300 dpi. Now, with the denser dots, the physical dimensions reflect the size that is appropriate for offset printing, down in the 7 x 10 areas. Change the physical settings of your bitmap to what you need, and click OK. (Get into the habit of taking control of these kinds of bitmap details and you will have fewer surprises. This dialog is also available in CorelDRAW under the Bitmap menu.) Now your image is the correct size.

3. Image collections often are in RGB format, which is again onscreen technology. For the kind of control we need to build this image correctly in CorelDRAW, we need CMYK. The reason being that if we want to match up background objects seamlessly they all need the exact same fill. RGB will translate into CMYK automatically from CorelDRAW, but we have no way to guarantee that new objects will translate the same as the bitmap. Eliminate the guesswork and convert the image to CMYK now. From the Image menu, select Convert to | CMYK (32-bit). Now the image is at the correct size, and color depth for offset printing. Save the image to disk, only use a non-lossy compression (JPEG will lose info to save space). I use the TIFF format, using LZW compression to save space.

4. At this point you can start manipulating the image for your application. You may wish to adjust the contrast or brightness, or even one of the CMYK levels (like we did with the pin-up to remove the background cyan). I bumped the brightness and contrast just a hair, because I like high-contrast images.

## ▼ Rule the Printer

If you work in a controlled environment, where you use the same service bureau, the same printer time after time, you can control your artwork to get better results. For example, if in the printing process your images become dark, you can brighten them up in PhotoPaint using the Brightness-Contrast-Intensity dialog (Ctrl+B). If this doesn't fix the problem, open up the dot patterns in your half-tones by using a looser line screen. A typical printing line screen is 133 (this book uses a tight 155 in the color sections). Drop the line screen to say 100 if printing on less than optimum paper or a press that leaves a lot of ink (newspapers, for example, typically use a loose 85 lpi to compensate for their printing process and paper). The same process can be used to fix color problems as well. If your images consistently seem to yellow, or any other combination of colors, you can tweak the levels of each CMYK color individually from the Level Equalization dialog (Ctrl+E). Select the desired color channel from the Equalize window, then drag the sliders to increase or decrease the value. Use the Preview window to check your progress. You can use the same process to color correct before going to print. Generate a match-print or high-end color proof, and you can adjust the levels of the images to correct for almost anything. Take control of your printing projects, and you will be much happier with the results.

5. Now use the eye-dropper tool to sample the background color. Try in several places to make sure you don't sample some strange color mix. I found my image to have a background color of 79% yellow. Write this down somewhere. Left-mouse click the eyedropper to select the underlying color as your paint color. Now use the paint tool to replace any of the text with just blank yellow area. Try to get in close to the areas that you know you will crop later with a bitmap color mask, and paint the yellow color right up to the edge. A smooth yellow line around the characters heads will allow for better results later in CorelDRAW. Use the selection tool to crop the image down to just above the figure's heads, save it to disk, and exit PhotoPaint. (See Figure 22-2.)

*Figure 22-2: An image from the Time Tunnel Sci-Fi Pulps (left) is the starting point for the design. The bitmap is manipulated in PhotoPaint so it is the right size and color depth. The paintbrush tool is used to paint away any existing text.*

6. Open CorelDRAW and import the bitmap. Now draw a rectangle behind the bitmap at the desired ad size, and fill it with the exact value that you noted when you eye-dropped the background back in step 5, which was 79% Yellow. When you take the time to control the color values, it is easy to use the technology in your favor. Now when printed no one will ever know where the original bitmap ends, and your box begins (see Figure 22-3).

*Figure 22-3: Drawing a box behind the bitmap (on left in wireframe) will create a seamless background if you fill it with the same CMYK value as the bitmap.*

7. Now start to lay out your text elements. I imported a thumbnail of the original and placed it next to my artwork to refer to as I worked. This made matching fonts on my system to those used in the original period piece easier. Back when CorelDRAW 3 shipped with exactly 256 fonts I probably could have found the fonts used in the original artwork in two seconds, but in today's font-fat design environment I can never seem to locate what I want! Grrr! (See last example for more on font phobias.) Use the Artistic Text tool to set your type on the page. I used a font called Faktos for the headlines, which is similar but not exact to the original. (Sorry Charlie, I don't have time to dig through each one of the tens of thousands of fonts I have in the studio. If the job is for Spielberg, and he wants to foot the bill for dead on, then fine. Otherwise, everyone else gets close.) The other font is called Futura, which has a clean, simple, and retro look to it despite its oxymoronic name! Use a simple flat color scheme in life with the original (fountain fills are a no-no if you want a period look).

8. To bring the characters in front of the headlines, first select the bitmap and bring to front. Then from the Bitmap menu select the Bitmap Color Mask option to open the dialog of the same name. Now click on the eye-dropper (a tool not often seen here in CorelDRAW!). Then click on the yellow neutral background of the bitmap. To aviod spots where we missed painting, or that are slightly deviant to the 79% yellow fill, up the Tolerance a tad to 17%. This will also soften the edges a bit where the characters meet the background, by cutting into those anti-alias pixels that surround them. Click Apply and the background should disappear, leaving only the characters on top of the text. The extra effort during the painting stages back in PhotoPaint will pay off now with a clean cutaway of the characters from the background. (See Figure 22-4.)

*Figure 22-4: The Bitmap Color Mask renders the background transparent, leaving the characters to lie on top of other design elements.*

The cyber-battle rages in the color section, and also in the file called upgrade.cdr lurking in the \Chapt22\ subdirectory. Load the file and see how tweaking the Tolerance value effects the bitmap. At some point too great a value will make other yellow areas also transparent, but too little and you may not get the clean cut-out effect you are after. A uniform solid background in your color bitmap makes for much more flexibility than one that is busy or filled with other art, as we will see in the next example. With a solid background color that can go transparent with the Bitmap Color Mask you can change the background color to anything, or nothing at all. (See Figure 22-5.)

*Figure 22-5: A bitmap with a transparent background can be given new backgrounds within CorelDRAW, for infinite variety.*

## Thrilling Invasions

*Figure 22-6: The clone brush in PhotoPaint lets you erase existing text from a magazine cover and then add texture to text and other details added in CorelDRAW.*

Don't you just love how past predictions of how the future, well now actually, were at times so silly? My favorite section at Disneyland has always been "Tomorrowland" with all those fantastical inventions that were supposed to revolutionize our lives. Two-way wrist radios, indeed! What wild imaginations they all, uh, hang on. My pager is beeping and there is a fax coming through....

OK so we are living in what forty years ago would seem like a very bizarre age. Machines that talk, cell-phones that fit in your pocket, the whole technology-based society thing. For my money, though, I will take the more stylish aerodynamic art-deco vehicles of the 20's & 30's than this trend to make cars all look like amoebas!

To that end, I appreciate the more idealized reality that these old graphics offer of the future and technology. Using these old images, which seem to range in quality from crisp to crappy, can be quite a challenge. Poor image quality, page texture, rips, tears, and other visual noise add to the problem. On top of everything else, images such as the magazine covers are often cluttered with text or other design items that you need to remove. With the original artwork often long since lost, there is no choice but to make due with what you have.

Luckily, there are tools in today's modern bitmap editing packages that are designed to help retouch photos and make bad art good again! Here is how to use PhotoPaint to touch up an old magazine cover so that you can add your own text:

1. Once again, a fine Time Tunnel image was the starting point for this project. Of course, as luck would have it the image I wanted to use was in need of much touch up before it would be usable for what I had in mind. >>sigh<< Well, it makes for a good tutorial anyway. Start PhotoPaint, and from the \timetunl\ directory open the file called tw_06-51.jpg and you will see what I mean. The image is really dark, has strange stains on the girls face, her skin is blue, and there is a bunch of text in the bottom right corner where we want our headline to be. Well, we'll just have to fix that....

2. With the image loaded in PhotoPaint, once again check the size in the Resample menu, and also covert it to CMYK. Adjust the Brightness/Contrast to make the image a little more vibrant, but unfortunately that isn't going to fix everything. Zoom into the face and you can see some nasty things happened to this poor woman over time. Use the lasso to select just the offending areas in her face, then open the Level Equalization dialog (Ctrl+E). Change the Channel to Cyan, and then drag the bottom right Output Range Compression slider to the left. This will reduce the cyan in the selected area, which is exactly what is needed to remove the blues from the girl (see Figure 22-7).

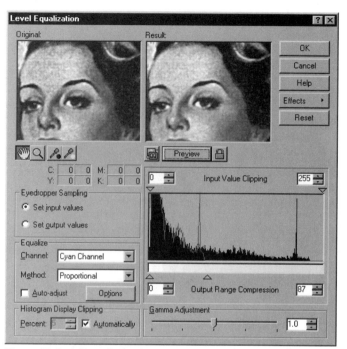

*Figure 22-7: Adjust the levels to remove unwanted colors from sections of the bitmap to clean up the image.*

3. Repeat the process to remove unwanted colors from different areas of the bitmap. Make your selections along existing lines, such as the edge of the elbow and the rocket, to avoid any obvious color shifts. To remove the spot in her face, use the Levels trick and reduce the black in the stain. Poof. Gone. For some reason there is just a lot of unwanted cyan all over this girl's left side. When you edit it out, it stops looking so smurf-like. Then, just to be annoying, her right shoulder has too much magenta in it, from some cosmic tanning salon accident no doubt, who knows. Use the levels trick to bring all her body parts back into the skin-tone range and suddenly things are looking much better (see Figure 22-8).

4. Now comes the lovely hassle of removing the existing text. Zoom in to the text then grab the clone tool. What this does is let you paint using another section of the image as the source material. Move the cursor to an uncluttered area on the red dress. Now set the reference point (a set of crosshairs) with the a click of the right mouse button. Move the brush now over a similar area that has offensive, unwanted text on it. Now drag to paint away the text, with the clone image designated by the cross hairs painting over where you drag your brush. With an image such as

this, with so many random grains in the scan, there is no other way to paint away sections of the graphic without looking strangely smooth. It takes a little practice, but you can make almost anything disappear by painting over it with the clone tool (see Figure 22-9).

*Figure 22-8: Select and adjust levels to remove spots and unwanted color from areas of the image, such as the skin tones. Removing all the extra blue from the model makes her stand out better.*

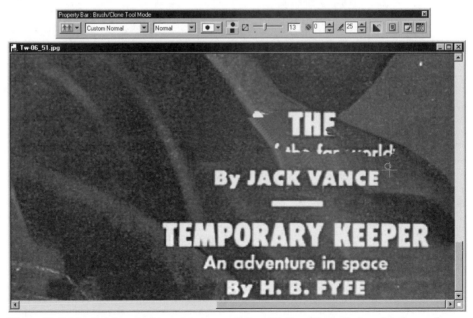

*Figure 22-9: Use the clone tool to paint away existing details with similarly colored areas from other parts of the image.*

5. Keep painting over details with the clone tool until all of the old text is gone. Use existing details from other parts of the image; the left fold, for example, was cloned to replace the center fold that had text over it. You don't have to be perfect, or try and match the old image verbatim. We only need something close, as our own headlines will obscure the details and any imperfections we leave behind. It isn't really that difficult to end up with a workable image, and it is kind of mind-boggling when you finish to see just how believable it is (makes you think about a career with the tabloids!) When finished with the touch up, save the file and exit PhotoPaint. (See Figure 22-10.)

*Figure 22-10: The clone tool removes the unwanted text (inset), and lets you paint an abstract fold of drapes in its place.*

6. With the original text gone, we are free to add our own headlines back in CorelDRAW. Again I tried to use a font and layout similar to the original, which again turned out to be Futura Md BT (Bold). Text was added in a very low-tech way to full color images back when these images were

originally made, using manually typeset words and photographic techniques. For this reason, the text is simple, bold, and often one color.
Graphic art included additions like boxes or lines easily cut into the film
manually. Feeling spoiled? You should! Art like this originally took hours
to paint by hand, and then quite a bit of additional effort to go from
painting to printing press, with much labor in-between.

7. To get the Corel logo on the round earth, use the Fish Eye lens. Draw a
   box around the original logo, then use the Fish Eye lens at a rate of 75%
   to get the desired roundness. To transform the pieces themselves, and not
   just how they look, enable the Frozen option on the Lens roll-up (see
   Figure 22-11).

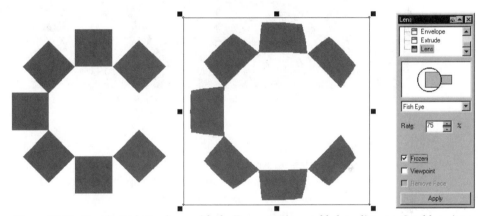

*Figure 22-11: Use the Fish Eye lens, with the Frozen option enabled, to distort a Corel logo into
a round configuration.*

8. To maintain the graininess of the bitmap, you can't just paste the logos
   into place. It is hard to get a convincing look in CorelDRAW alone, but
   we will be back in PhotoPaint later to fix things anyway. Drop the logo
   on the globe, and use the Color Add lens, with the color set to red, to get
   the see-through but vibrant logo in the globe. Trim away the shape in areas
   that should be obscured, by the glove for example. (See Figure 22-12.)

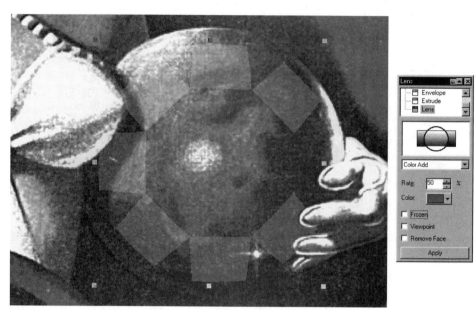

*Figure 22-12: Use the Color Add lens to add the logo to the globe.*

9. To get the logos on the rocket ships, use the Interactive Transparency tool. With the solid red logo in place, change the Type to Uniform, then change the rate to 15 and Transparency Operation to Add. This setting was more convincing than the Normal setting. Again, we will fine-tune this look back in PhotoPaint.

10. Export your image at the full-size and at the color depth for the final application. My image was going to print (the one in the color section), so I output it as a 300 dpi, CMYK bitmap. Close CorelDRAW and open the file again in PhotoPaint.

11. Select the yellow text with the Color Mask dialog, located under the Mask menu. Click on the eyedropper in the dialog box, then click on the yellow text. Click OK to select the yellow text.

12. The color mask also selected some other random yellow spots. Open the Mask/Object property by right-mouse clicking over the tool then enabling the Mask/Object option. From this menu bar change the subtractive mask mode, and then draw boxes over the random yellow selections, leaving only the desired text selected.

13. Zoom in on the text, and from the Effects menu, select the Noise | Add Noise option. From the Add Noise dialog you can give a hint of noise to make the new text seem more at home on this old and grainy image. (See Figure 22–13.)

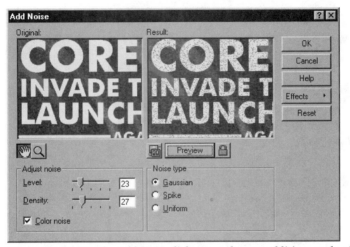

*Figure 22-13: Use the Add Noise dialog to make new additions to the old graphic seem weathered as well.*

14. To make the logos seem more at home, select the area around them with the lasso and use the Smooth setting from the Blur option found under the Effects menu. If the images look too smooth, then you get things grainy again with the Add Noise like you used on the text.

This image can be seen in the color section, or loaded as the spacegrl.cdr file found in the \Chapt22\ sector of the CD-ROM universe. I waffled back and forth with this image, at times laughing hysterically at the original *Thrilling Wonder Stories* magazine title, and then the next moment thinking I might come up with a different title. Well, I didn't come up with a title that made me laugh like the original, but I went ahead and painted out the headline anyway. It is called spacegrl.tif and I stuck it back in the \timetunl\ directory on the CD-ROM. If you come up with a better title, let me know (see Figure 22-14).

*Figure 22-14: The original stock image with all remnants of the cover removed, waiting your own custom application!*

## Fonts Ate My Brain

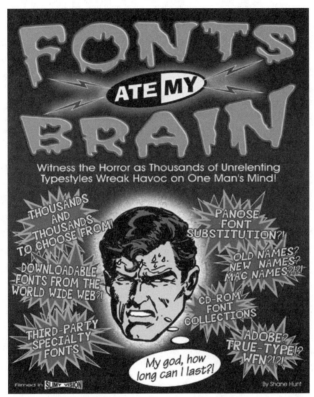

*Figure 22-15: Electricity sparks can add an interesting glow behind objects to draw interest to them, and to pull them away from the background.*

This image was supposed to accompany an article I did ranting and raving about a big font fiasco in an earlier CorelDRAW version upgrade. When CorelDRAW first hit the market, they used copy-cat fonts, which looked similar to Adobe PostScript fonts, but without having to license them (like "Brooklyn" instead of "Bookman"). Well, somewhere along the line, the copy-cat fonts were replaced by the real ones, and I ended up with both versions on my poor choking computer, and I just went nuts. While Corel magazine didn't print my rant, I still love this artwork, and fits in nicely with our pulp theme!

▼ **Font Hell**

Back when all of this lunacy started, with CorelDRAW 1, you got a much, much smaller box. It had a handful of 5 1/4" floppy disks, a smattering of clip art, a VHS training tape, and a bunch of fonts. Well, it seemed like a bunch of fonts, but compared to today's giant box-o-draw goodies, with a handful of *CDs*, it doesn't seem like that many at all! Ah, those simple bygone days of CorelDRAW 1 & 2. (Even Corel 3 had only 256 fonts total, with a handy chart to stick on the wall to find them all!) How is it back then I had only a quarter of the fonts, yet I always found exactly what I wanted, and now, with thousands and thousands to choose from, I am never satisfied? Power corrupts, I suppose. Fonts also eat up system resources big time. If you ever want to commit computer suicide, install all of the fonts that come on those shiny CorelDRAW CD's! Forget about it! You will never recover your system again! (The sad but true tale of a total Corel geek like myself that actually decided to try it one day!) Actually, as a rule of thumb, you should try to have fewer than 400 fonts actually installed on your machine at any given time. This seems like a paltry few, but any more than that and Windows chugs, taking longer to boot up and run any application that uses fonts. (Hmm. Reality check—that would be all of the programs you use.) The best way to keep your font choices wide open while still minimizing the number of installed live fonts which are system hounds, is to use a font management application. As I recall, didn't CorelDRAW 8 ship with one? Why yes it did, my f/x book reader. It is called *Bitstream Font Navigator 3.0*. This program offers a quick and easy way to find and install fonts, organize fonts into manageable groups, and view and print font samples. It beats the heck out of the Win95 font management tools. If you are trying to glean more performance out of your system, limit the number of fonts installed. Then use a program like Font Navigator to keep your font options open. Wow. The best of both worlds. How often does that happen?

Here is how to get a campy graphic with electric sparks, a Saturday afternoon matinee horror marquee headline, and exploding type balloons:

1. Duplicate the objects that you want to create a fuzzy background for, and drag them off to the side to make working on them easier. Now assign a black fill and outline for these objects. To control the area occupied by the sparks, use a thicker or thinner outline. A thicker outline will result in a more dramatic, wider spark area. Draw a bounding box (or use the Inflate Bitmap feature later, your preference—drawing a box is easier I think) the size that you want your bitmap to be, with no outline or fill. Now select all the objects, and from the Bitmap menu, convert to a grayscale bitmap (see Figure 22-16).

*Figure 22-16: Color all objects black, then convert to a grayscale bitmap.*

2. Now fuzz the grayscale bitmap with the Gaussian blur effect. The more blur, the larger the area of your sparks. It takes a little practice to predict the appropriate line-weight and level of Gaussian blur, but this is easy to experiment with. Once the blur is finished, convert the grayscale bitmap into a black-and-white bitmap. For bigger chunks, use a lower DPI setting, like 200 or 150 instead of 300. Give the black-and-white bitmap a yellow outline, no fill, and arrange behind the original objects to create a glowing effect (see Figure 22-17).

*Figure 22-17: The grayscale is converted to a black-and-white bitmap, to make it chunky, colored, and arranged behind the original objects to complete the effect.*

3. You can use this effect on any group of objects, even those that contain bitmaps, such as the colorized comic face in this graphic. Select the objects that make up the face, duplicate, and move off to the side. Now, you don't want to give the bitmap a fill attribute, because that will make it a solid black box! So hold down the shift key and click on the face bitmap to deselect it, then give the remaining objects a black outline and fill. Draw the boundary box, and repeat the Convert to Grayscale, Gaussian blur steps as before (see Figure 22-18).

*Figure 22-18: Anything can be fuzzed, even object groups containing bitmaps.*

4. Convert the bitmap to black and white to create the electricity as before, and assign a magenta outline, no fill. For a twist, enlarge the bitmap 120%. Now duplicate the bitmap, and reduce it 90% and change the outline to yellow. Duplicate and reduce again, with the small center having a white outline. This way you can create electric bursts, much like the explosion blends, except you can't use the Blend roll-up on bitmaps, so you have to create the interim steps by hand (see Figure 22-19).

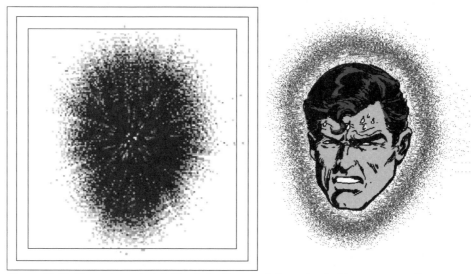

*Figure 22-19: To create an electric blend, duplicate and downsize the bitmaps manually, changing the outline color each time (shown in wireframe on the left). You can create glow with color changes this way behind your original objects.*

5. The slimy headline fonts were given the familiar highlight-shadow treatments with pieces generated with the Trim function (as introduced in Chapter 3). There is one difference here, and that is the addition of a blend to give the letters a fatter look. Start with the artistic text in place (I used a font called Horror). Tweak each word with the Envelope tool, so it is a bit curved, and gets smaller or larger on one end. Arrange the text, and then to speed things up, shift-select and Combine the two elements together (so you don't have to repeat the process for each text object). Now with the Shape tool drag-select all of the nodes in the text curve, and use the Auto-Reduce button on the Node Edit dialog (Ctrl+F10) to simplify the object. For complex blends, simple is better (faster). (See Figure 22-20.)

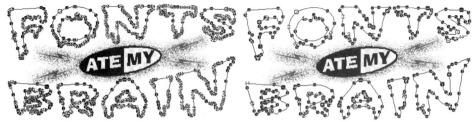

*Figure 22-20: Modify the artistic text with the Envelope feature, then combine the two, and use the Auto-Reduce function to reduce the node count.*

6. Give the object a fat black .111 inch outline, and black fill. Now duplicate and arrange the duplicate just up and to the right. Give the duplicate a green hairline and fill. Now blend these two objects together, and you have your fat text. For more depth, add the highlight and shadow shapes, created with the Chapter 3 techniques (see Figure 22-21).

*Figure 22-21: Blending a fat outlined object to a thin offset duplicate on top, creates the illusion of depth, making for chubby text.*

Witness the cerebral carnage in the color section, and in the fonts.cdr file nestled in the \Chapt22\ subdirectory. Open the file and create a blended electricity blur by duplicating and downsizing the black-and-white bitmap behind the comic face. It's not as automated as using the Blend roll-up on vector objects, but with a little effort you can get some cool exploding effects this way.

The balloons around the words are symbols from a font called, well, Balloons. Use the Shape tool to move around the spikes in each balloon duplicate to make it look unique.

Using the Bitmap menu to create low-res, chunky sparks is a quick and easy way to get a very unique effect. Manually blending a bitmap can expand the concept into explosions or bursts. Don't hesitate to experiment by mix and matching effects in this book, or other CorelDRAW effects. For example, instead of using a Guassian blur, create a white to black blend in CorelDRAW, then convert it to a black-and-white bitmap to get some nifty variants (see Figure 22-22).

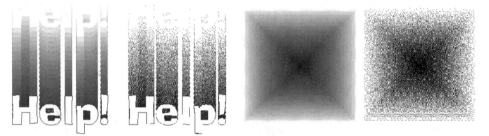

*Figure 22-22: Start with CorelDRAW objects instead of a grayscale bitmap, and then convert to a dithered, black-and-white bitmap.*

## Moving On

In this chapter we looked at using images from the past in contemporary designs. We modified the available artwork so we could add our own text and tailor the designs for our own needs. We also saw how we could start from scratch to create a graphic in a similar vein.

With retro all the rage in everything from movies to music, once again you can ride the current trends using resources from the past to fatten your bank account in the future! It's nice if history repeats itself after the statue of limitations is up, with all those tasty image archives from the first half of our century just waiting to be plundered! The images are striking and unique, and dare I say, pretty easy to use—almost makes you feel guilty for charging so much. Nah!

In the next chapter we will look at creating shiny metallic objects in CorelDRAW and also Corel PhotoPaint. You can get an amazing amount of depth and realism in CorelDRAW, but for that all-convincing, liquid metal look, you need to do some bitmap massaging. Grab the smock and welding goggles, the "Never Dull" polish, and some SOS pads, 'cuz we're off to metal shop!

▼ **Beyond f/x**

Even if you don't see an immediate need for Buck Rogers graphics in your world, keep the magic ad formula in mind. The same technique of adding a catchy slogan to a unique image or enhanced photo can get you through almost any advertising challenge. (Check out the "loser" graphic from Chapter 13. Perfect example. Not too hard to do, very catchy, everybody happy. Except the dude with the branded noggin', of course.)

Other uses for the retro-pulp look are almost unlimited in today's graphic climate. You could to a whole spacy Web site, with heros and heroines on every page, and perhaps even throw in the robot from Chapter 24. Specialty graphics, such as album covers or even alternative apparel will gobble up images based on Time Tunnel graphics, I guarantee! You can add personalized headlines and make fun color birthday cards right off of your office printer for your friends and family (use the New from Template option and let the Template Wizard find a card for you, then add your own graphics). Be a hit at the next Trekkie convention with your own line of retro placemats. The sky is the limit! Up up and away!

# chapter 23

# Shiny Metal Objects

There is probably no other effect that holds more allure than shiny metal. Every graphic artist, from air-brush to virtual reality, has had the task of making something look shiny and metallic. To date I have received more inquiries that read "How did you make those shiny metal objects on your Web site?" than any other. To ignore this topic would be a crime, and no doubt would result in a barrage of hate mail.

The problem with rendering metallic objects is that the look is achieved by reflecting the surrounding landscape. In a flat work space like CorelDRAW, there is nothing to reflect. So you must trick the eye into thinking it sees reflections in otherwise flat objects.

In this chapter we will look at creating shiny metallic looking objects using many tricks to create interesting reflections. First, we will examine several techniques, using custom color blends, PowerClipped landscapes, and also the Contour tool to create a wide variety of metallic surfaces directly in CorelDRAW. Then we will combine the powers of PhotoPaint to render the subtle reflections and shadows of a metallic medallion, and also show how to use the techniques to make any shape, or even text, share this highly reflected look. And finally, we once again tweak the tentacle blending technique to render shiny metallic trees, introducing the Split function on the Blend roll-up.

## Words of Steel

*Figure 23-1: Using custom color blends, PowerClipped objects, the Extrude function, and the Contour roll-up, a convincing metallic look can be achieved without much effort within CorelDRAW.*

Chrome and shiny metals are the graphic art equivalent to chili: everyone likes and wants it, and each designer has their own secret recipe. You can find all kinds of chrome styles, from simple and abstract, to insanely detailed images of twisted and distorted landscapes. It's a buyer's market.

The same variety in the real world (pencil, pen, pastel, airbrush) is now available in the digital arena with 3D modeling, bitmap-editors, and also vector applications. 3D modeling takes a very literal approach to rendering metals by using ray-tracing algorithms to calculate imaginary light beams bouncing around and back into your eye (see the last image in the color section for an example). Bitmap editors such as PhotoPaint let you get strange chromy results using filters and plug-ins. And, of course, there are plenty of options right here in CorelDRAW!

CorelDRAW chrome is based solely on illusion. We have to use the built-in effects to create reflections of objects and light sources that do not really exist. Don't sweat it, it isn't hard, and we'll even get the program to do most of the work for us. There are many ways to get the look we are after so we will work from top to bottom, walking through each example on the opening graphic (and of course, also in the color section). Here is how to make text objects look metallic:

1. Set your text using the Artistic Text tool. For all of the examples I used a font called PalmSprings (Bold). The first example is one of the easiest, and one of the quickest! First, give the text a black fill, and a thickish .048 black outline. Now duplicate the text, and remove the outline from the duplicate. This front piece will be on top, so it needs a fill to simulate a reflected horizon. Not a problem! Using either the Interactive Fill tool or the Fountain Fill dialog, create a custom color blend that goes from lime green, to black, to blue, to white. Drag the black and blue color points close together, so that they create a stark horizon line. Using the Interactive Fill tool, you will drag the blue point basically on top of the black, so that there is a hard line in the center of the blend. (See Figure 23-2.)

*Figure 23-2: A custom color blend, with the two center points dragged close together, produce a stark horizon line for the chrome effect.*

2. Duplicate the text, give it a white fill, send it back one, and nudge it up and to the right .009 inches. (I set my nudge values very low, to .003 inch, then tap the arrow keys to make these kinds of small moves easy.) Duplicate the top text again, send back one, and nudge down and to the left .009 inches. Give this duplicate a mid-tone, like Powder Blue. Done. Instant chrome with a gazillion uses. (See Figure 23-3.)

*Figure 23-3: A duplicate offset slightly behind the front text object becomes a highlight and shadow element.*

3. The next technique is simple also, with a very cool-looking result! Start as before, with the Artistic Text element. Use the custom color blend from the first example, only change the starting color from green to tan, and add another white point on the end, so you can drag the white sky area more into the blue. Remove any outline attribute. Now open the Extrude roll-up, enable a single light source at the top right on the Lighting page, then open the Bevel page. Enable the Use Bevel and Show Bevel Only options, then set the Bevel depth to .045, and click Apply. Whirrrr. Bzzz. Clang. Ding! More instant chrome to write home about! (See Figure 23-4.)

*Figure 23-4: The Bevel function, with a light-source enabled, creates an interesting chrome variant using the Extrude roll-up.*

4. The next example combines a contour group and a Transparency lens. First, start with your Artistic Text, fill it black, and remove any outline. Then open the Contour roll-up (Ctrl+F9), enable the Inside option, change the Offset to .01, and increase the number of steps to 7. Now flip to the Colors page, and change the fill color to white. Now click Apply to generate a round-looking text element, which is a neat trick to remember on its own. (See Figure 23-5.)

*Figure 23-5: The Contour roll-up, with a small Offset value, different Fill color, and Inside option, creates a rounded-text look.*

5. Duplicate the text with the custom color blend from the first example and grab the Interactive Transparency tool. You can not give an object with a custom color blend a Transparency lens, but you can get the same effect by changing the Transparency Type on the Property Bar to Uniform, then changing the Transparency Level with the slider. The higher the value, the more transparent the object will be. Set the slider to 75. (See Figure 23-6.)

Figure 23-6: The Interactive Transparency function can make a custom color blend semi-opaque.

6. Now stack the semi-clear custom color blend on top of the contour group. This gives the rounded text just the hint of a reflection for another chrome variant. (See Figure 23-7.)

Figure 23-7: Stack the clear custom color blend and the contour group to create a different variety of metal shading.

7. For the next example, steal one of the simple landscape files from Chapter 9. Then, squeeze it down horizontally to fit behind a copy of the original Artistic Text, no fill, with a black outline. Duplicate the text object and set it off to the side. Then select the landscape group, and PowerClip it into the original text. (See Figure 23-8.)

Figure 23-8: PowerClip a landscape group or bitmap into the text to become the reflected horizon.

8. Use the duplicate to create shapes for highlight and shadow objects, as described in Chapter 3. Place these on top of the PowerClip, and give light and neutral tones to add more depth to the letters. (See Figure 23-9.)

*Figure 23-9: Use the original text to create highlight and shading objects using the Trim function.*

9. The last three examples use a technique similar to the throwing stars from Chapter 14. Start with your text selected, and open the Contour roll-up. Change the options to Outside, Offset .04 inch, 1 Step, and click Apply. Now Separate the contour group, and select both objects. Assign a custom color blend from black to white to gray to white to gray to white to black. Now select only the front shape, and change the gray and black points to lighter gray points. Drag the fills around so the back one creates highlights almost horizontally across, while the front object has the highlights at almost 45 degree angles. When they are stacked up, they look convincingly like silver or brushed aluminum. (See Figure 23-10.)

**TIP** *If you think creating custom color blends are a drag, use the presets found in the Fountain Fill dialog. There are a great assortment of pre-made custom color blends, including many that will work great for creating the coloring necessary for shiny metal objects. Click the down-arrow next to the presets box to view the list, then scroll down until you find something that you like. Cylinder-Gold 07, for example, is the perfect fill alternative for the Gold object in this section.*

10. The Gold and the Bronze are created in the same way, only with unique custom color blends. Create the contour, then first give both objects the same blend. That way you can match up the gleam points, but just change the colors for the front or back object. The gold uses a black to yellow to black to yellow to black to yellow to black custom color blend in the back. On top, all of the black color points are made brown, and the center yellow point is made white. To keep the golden look, a yellow point is added to each side of the white point, so it is just a bright highlight without changing the yellow coloring scheme. When stacked, the two fills compliment each other perfectly. (See Figure 23-11.)

*Figure 23-10: Use custom color blends to create a series of highlights and shadows, then offset them differently for the front and back shape to make it look shiny in the end.*

*Figure 23-11: A dark version of essentially the same custom color blend assures that the highlight points will meet up in the front object.*

11. The Bronze has fewer highlights, and more brown than the gold text. The back goes from tan to brown to tan to brown to tan. The front from brown to gold to tan to brown. Not dramatic, but when stacked looks good. (See Figure 23-12.)

*Figure 23-12: Bronze is not as shiny as gold, and has more brown in it.*

To make it appear that these objects are floating above a shiny slab of marble, they were grouped, duplicated, and downsized. This smaller group was placed behind a texture-filled rectangle, with the marble looking fill. This was then given a Uniform Transparency of 10%, the same way the text shape was earlier. With such a small amount of transparency, a ghosty reflection shows through. This image can be seen in the color section, and also in the metals.cdr file located in the \Chapt23\ subdirectory on the CD-ROM. If you load the file I recommend you first select and delete both the marble-filled rectangle and the down-sized reflection group, because these objects take forever to render. Once these are out of the way, take a look at the custom color blends, or steal them for your own metallic creations. Also of note are the little chrome balls, which are just circles filled with a radial fountain fill, custom color blend.

# Chrome Medallion

*Figure 23-13: Using a combination of effects in PhotoPaint on a bitmap rendered from CorelDRAW, you can create a shiny metallic look, with many possibilities, depending upon the choice of landscape bitmap used.*

Chrome is a tricky subject, because it is a substance that has no color. It, like a mirror, reflects all that surrounds it, and derives its personality in its entirety from the reflected environment. Like I mentioned earlier, I am always asked how I made the shiny metal graphics on my Web site. Well, the easiest way for an object to reflect an environment is for it to reside in an environment to reflect! To that end I usually create metallic and shiny objects in a 3D application such as CorelDream or TrueSpace by Caligari using pieces created in CorelDRAW. The flat pieces from CorelDRAW are made into three-dimensional objects in cyberspace, then given a mirrored surface to reflect the virtual landscape. (This technique is covered in Chapter 30.)

If you are reluctant to enter the virtual world of three dimensions and CorelDream (as am I!), you can create some really nifty shiny chrome using CorelDRAW in conjunction with Corel PhotoPaint. I hate to bring PhotoPaint into the picture, but you need pixels to make subtle reflections. In this section we will use the effects filters available in PhotoPaint to give an image metallic highlights and reflections. PhotoPaint also has the advantage of allowing you to select just certain areas of your bitmap (and even save and load these selections), where in CorelDRAW you are limited to applying a bitmap filter effect only on an entire bitmap. However, we still start in CorelDRAW because that program is so much easier to generate logos in, especially with things like text that is fitted to a curve. Think of this as a digital shop class, with a grisly old guy in a gray smock shouting "Use the right tool for the job!" Here is how to make chrome using CorelDRAW and PhotoPaint:

## ▼ Magazine on the Scene

I learned this technique from an article by David Huss, a fellow contributor to *Corel Magazine,* and the definitive expert on Corel PhotoPaint. If you haven't already (everyone who registers their copy of CorelDRAW will automatically receive a free issue), you should really consider subscribing to this great magazine. In addition to my brilliant monthly column (humble, aren't I?), there are outstanding articles by other industry leaders and the Corel elite. In addition to CorelDRAW, the magazine covers all the other Corel products, but focuses on the graphics suite (Draw, Paint, and Dream). For more info, check out their Web site at http://www.corelmag.com.

1. In CorelDRAW, fashion a logo in black and white that will become a bitmap template for the chrome effect in PhotoPaint. The areas that are black will reflect the landscape determined by your choice of bitmap later. For this logo, a globe from the GeographicSymbols font in the Symbols roll-up became the centerpiece, with Artistic Text fit to a curve around it. Use heavy outlines to create more black area in the logo. (See Figure 23-14.)

*Figure 23-14: A logo is designed in CorelDRAW, using symbols and type fit to a curve (wireframe on left). Heavy outlines create more black area, which will be filled with the reflected chrome images in PhotoPaint.*

2. Draw a bounding box around the logo, with no outline or fill, at a memorable size (like exactly 5.5 inches). (We will need to Resample bitmaps in PhotoPaint to these dimensions later.) Drag-select all of the pieces in the logo, and open the Export dialog (Ctrl+H). If you have more objects in your document than the selected logo group, be sure to enable the Selected Only option on the Export dialog. Give your bitmap a unique name, and click Export. Now from the Bitmap Export dialog, change the Color to RGB (16 million), Size 1 to 1, Resolution 300 dpi, and Anti-Aliasing at Normal. Click OK to generate the bitmap. When finished, exit CorelDRAW (to free up all of your system resources), and start PhotoPaint.

3. Open the bitmap created in step two, and from the Mask menu, open the Color Mask dialog. Now use the hand in the preview window to drag some of the image into view, then with the eyedropper tool, click on a black spot. Click on OK to select all of the black are in the bitmap. (See Figure 23-15.)

*Figure 23-15: Use the Color Mask dialog from the Mask menu to select all of the black area. You can then save the mask to disk, and load it later.*

4. With all the black now selected, from the Mask menu choose Save | Save to Disk. Give the file a name like mask, and change the Save As Type to Corel PhotoPaint Image (CPT) before clicking the Save button. We will need this mask later on.

5. With the black areas still selected, from the Effects | 3D Effects submenu, pick Emboss. Change the depth value to 10, then click OK. (See Figure 23-16.)

*Figure 23-16: The Emboss effects filter creates a highlight, shadow, and mid-tone area.*

6. Now Invert the mask (Ctrl+I), and from the Effects | Fancy submenu, pick Glass. Change the Style to Lens, and click OK. Remove the Mask (Ctrl+D), and from the Gamma dialog (Image | Adjust | Gamma), change the value to 2 and click OK (this lightens up the image). Save this image to disk to use as the reference file for the Displacement step to come, then you can close its window. (See Figure 23-17.)

*Figure 23-17: The Glass effect modifies the image more, expanding on the effects started with the Emboss filter.*

7. Find a bitmap that you want to use as a surrounding landscape. I found a lovely image on the Corel Professional Photos "Sunsets Around the World" CD-ROM. Open the image, but then use the Image l Resample dialog to change the physical size of the bitmap to match the size of the medallion bitmap you generated from CorelDRAW. If you don't match up the sizes, the Displacement map won't fit right in the image. Don't worry if you have to increase the resolution or if the file looks a bit grainy, it will work fine (see Figure 23-18).

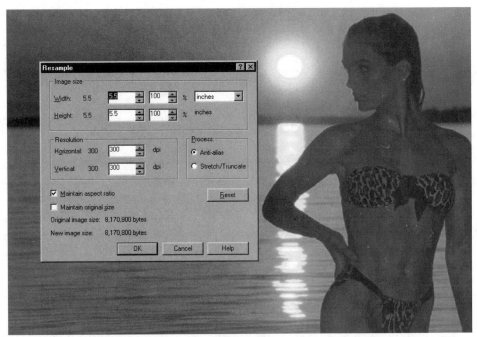

*Figure 23-18: Use the Resample dialog from the Image menu to adjust the physical dimensions of the desired bitmap.*

**TIP**  *Images to go. If you haven't already, you should check out the amazing collection of images available from Corel corporation on CD-ROM. They have a photo-disk on almost every conceivable topic, from women to wombats! Or, if you don't want to purchase an entire CD, you can buy the images one at a time. If you log into the Corel commerce Web site, you can search the image banks and locate the exact graphic you want, purchase, and download it immediately! The prices are reasonable, and you can't beat the convenience or instantaneous gratification!*

8. With your environment bitmap now changed to the correct size, remove any Masks (Ctrl+D). Now from the Effects | 2D Effects submenu, choose Displace. Click the Load button, and find the file you saved in step 6, and click OK. Change the Horizontal and Vertical settings to 10 and 100 respectively, and then click OK. Hey there, looking pretty chromy! At this point it looks like the logo is pressing through the bitmap, distorting it as it does. This alone could work into some weird, very subtle effects, but I leave that up to you. (See Figure 23-19.)

*Figure 23-19: The Displace effects filter, using the file created in step 6, twists and pulls the bitmap around as if the logo were pushing through it.*

9. Now from the Mask | Load submenu, Load From Disk the mask you saved long ago in the first step. Invert the Mask (Ctrl+I), and open the Effects | 3D Effects | The Boss dialog. Set the Style to the Wet preset, then click OK. This will add a few more highlights and shadows to your image. (I like the way this image looks, almost more than the correct finished results after the next step!) (See Figure 23-20.)

*Figure 23-20: Using the mask created earlier and loaded from disk as a guide, a Wet filter creates more highlights and shadows on the image.*

10. With the mask still inverted, change the paper color to black (double-click on the paper color well to open the Paper Color dialog), then Cut (Ctrl+X) the mask away to reveal the new paper color. This will remove the image from all but the area that originally was black (in the CorelDRAW logo), and replace it with the reflected/distorted bitmap, for a mirrored-chrome look. (See Figure 20-21.)

*Figure 20-21: With the mask inverted, you can delete the extra image area, and replace it with a flat color.*

When I finished I found that my bitmap had dark areas which made the text hard to read, so I went back and repeated the displacement filter steps on a different bitmap until I was satisfied with the results. Because the displacement map and saved mask will work on any image (at the correct resampled size that is), it is easy to experiment with different images until you are happy. Hey, what's the point of using the computer if you can't be fickle? I went through the same steps five times, each time using a different bitmap off of the CorelDRAW photos CD-ROM. The results can be seen in the color section, and also in the world.cdr file found in the \Chapt23\ subdirectory on the CD-ROM. If you want to really start from scratch, the original CorelDRAW file is also there, called world1.cdr.

## More Chrome

In addition to working with existing bitmaps, you can use this same technique on pieces created entirely within CorelDRAW, to create your own customized chrome objects. Here is how to use the technique to create chrome letters:

1. Use the Artistic Text tool to set your type, and fill it black. Then draw a box around and centered to the text, with no fill or outline, to define the dimensions of the bitmap. Duplicate this box, and using the custom color blend technique from earlier in the chapter, create a chrome sky/horizon coloring scheme (see Figure 20-22).

*Figure 20-22: A text object and a chrome landscape object are prepared in CorelDRAW for export (wireframe shown on left).*

2. Drag select just the text and bounding box, and Export (Ctrl+H) as the logo bitmap. Repeat the Export for the chrome-filled box. Both objects are now bitmaps, with the same physical dimensions. Exit CorelDRAW and open PhotoPaint.

3. Repeat the process as before, substituting the small word bitmap for the large black logo file, and the horizon-filled box for the reflected landscape bitmap. You can get some great results using the CorelDRAW chrome custom color blends to modify any object, especially text. (See Figure 23-23.)

*Figure 23-23: The PhotoPaint process can use any bitmaps, including CorelDRAW generated images, for the reflected/distorted landscape images in the chromed objects, such as text.*

## Golden Forest

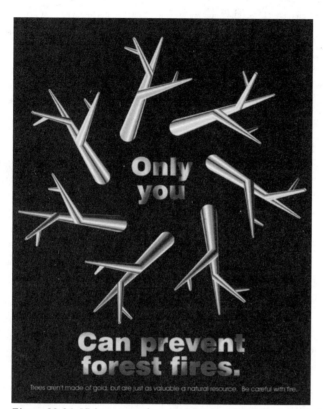

**COLOR STUDIO**

*Figure 23-24: Using a complex custom color blend, the tentacle technique can render objects which appear to be dimensional and metallic.*

I love this high-step blend technique, as you know. And you probably also have noticed by now that I have a nasty habit of fiddling with a technique for hours on end. (Don't worry, I still have a life, I just haven't watched TV since "Baretta" was a hit! Is "Huggy Bear" still considered cool?)

This technique is essentially the same as the Chapter 21 stars, with two major exceptions. The first is a much more complicated custom color blend, and the other is the addition of the Split option from the Blend roll-up, which allows you to use any object within a blend group as a control curve for another blend. The custom color blend gives not only the sense of dimension as in previous examples, but also the abstract reflections of light and dark that all metals have. Again it's all just an illusion, as there really is nothing to literally reflect, so we create it with abstract coloring. Here is how to grow a metallic forest:

1. Use the Ellipse tool to draw a circle, then open the Fountain Fill dialog to create the complicated custom color blend. I prefer the Fountain Fill dialog to the Interactive Fill tool because you can easily manipulate the control points in the custom color blend, even if you are zoomed way out from the object. With the Interactive Fill tool, on the other hand, you need to be right on the object to see everything, and even then, sometimes the points are hard to differentiate. Don't get me wrong, I love the Interactive Fill tool for many reasons and use it all the time, I just prefer the dialog for some things. The color blend looks chaotic, but it is essentially the same as the now familiar color blend for such objects, only with the addition of another shadow and highlight beam. (Open the file called treefill.cdr in the \Chapt23\ subdirectory, which contains the circle-shape with this obnoxious color blend already in place!) Add the color points along the color blend preview ribbon to create this new, enhanced fill for a more metallic look. (See Figure 23-25.)

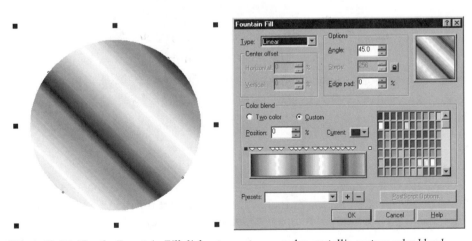

*Figure 23-25: Use the Fountain Fill dialog to create a complex, metallic custom color blend.*

2. Duplicate the circle, downsize it, and move it above the original about 3 inches. Now shift-select both circles, and create a 200 step blend between them using the Blend roll-up (Ctrl+B). Now select the small end control curve, and duplicate it. Move this duplicate over to the right, at a point where you want to end another branch. Now select the original blend, and from the Blend roll-up Miscellaneous options page, click the Split button. With the arrow, click about half-way up the gold tree. This will create and select a new Control Curve. Shift-select the floating circle, and click Apply on the Blend roll-up to create a branch. (See Figure 23-26.)

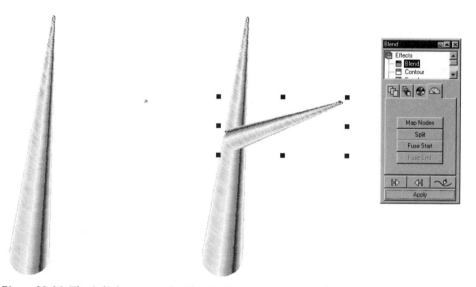

*Figure 23-26: The Split button on the Blend roll-up lets you use any piece of another blend as a control curve for a new split.*

3. Select and duplicate the end control curve again, and move into position for another branch. When you select the blend now, it is a Compound Object, so in order to select the subblend, hold down the Ctrl key and then click on the branch blend. Now you can repeat the Split command, and blend to the floating circle, creating yet another branch. You can repeat this process as many times as you like, creating a metallic tree with many branches. To create branches going away from you, send the duplicate circle to back before blending to the split control curve (see Figure 23-27).

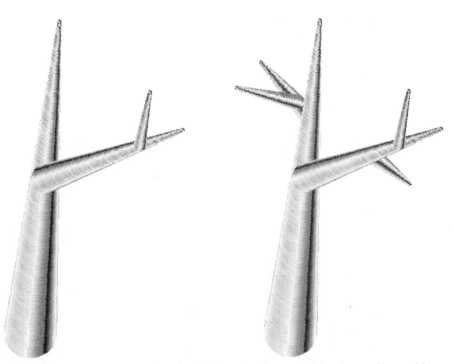

*Figure 23-27: A blend can be selected and split many times, resulting in tree shapes with many branches, and sub-branches.*

4. Repeat the split process until you have a tree shape you are happy with. To create the ring o' trees blend, you will first need to disable all of the blends in the gold tree group. Select the Compound Object, then Separate, Ungroup All, then Group (Ctrl+G). Now the tree is just a group of circles (a whole bunch of circles!). You can then go crazy using the stars technique from Chapter 21, or just duplicate and arrange the trees in a circle shape. When finished, to get the correct coloring in the rotated tree groups, you will have to use the Edit | Copy Properties From command to copy the fill from a tree that wasn't rotated. This last step makes all the objects look like they are in the same orientation, with the blend redrawing each tree in a unique way.

This metal grove can be seen in the color section, and in the file called forest.cdr in the \Chapt23\ subdirectory on the golden CD-ROM. The blends in the trees have been separated so I could blend the trees in a 360 degree circle, so you will have to create your own blends to practice the split feature. Use the treefill.cdr file as a starting point, then duplicate and blend this circle shape to create your own trees. Hey, these metal trees are the kind that Smokey won't have to worry about!

## Moving On

In this chapter we looked at how to create metallic looking objects in CorelDRAW, and also with the help of PhotoPaint. Like many effects, there are many ways to skin this proverbial cat, with the techniques here balancing payoff with ease of use. custom color blends, PowerClipped images, Extrudes and the Contour effects all look good, are relatively easy, and retain the flexibility inherent to all CorelDRAW vector images. Throwing PhotoPaint into the mix just adds to the possibilities, with more subtle highlights and shadows available with bitmap filters. For even more amazing metallic effects, unlock the powers of CorelDream, which has the ability to do ray-tracing, which allows for the reflective qualities of metals to actually show the surrounding objects. (See *Ray Dream 5 f/x* from Ventana for more on these techniques.) Heck, these programs are bundled for free with CorelDRAW, so milk them for all they're worth!

In the next chapter we will exploit some of these metallic looks in the creation of robots and gears. The robot images introduce a concept of modular design, where you build an object in malleable groups, which in turn creates other objects or cells for animation. Grab the oil can and ignore the cries of Danger, Will Robinson, it's time to get mechanical.

▼ **Beyond f/x**

There are endless uses for metallic effects. Everything from Web buttons to logo-updates can benefit from the shiny look. The metal trees effect, with the split function, could be used to blend circles of like sizes to build solid metal pipes for abstract patterns or page borders. Chroming is one of those universally appreciated techniques, and if you have a client that can't decide what they want to do with their company logo, toss a liquid metal version their way. Somewhere in between the "oohs" and "aahs" there will be a "go with it!"

# chapter 24
# Robots & Gears

Before desktop publishing, computers were used more for their number-crunching abilities than for making pretty pictures. With the ability to perform such complex computations, architects and draftsmen were quick to exploit the power. CAD (Computer Aided Design) programs emerged and are still a powerful force in the engineering world. Back in the world of images, we can use the flexibility of a computer program like CorelDRAW to not only create the look of CAD and high-tech drawings, but to bring them to life as well.

In this chapter, we will use the design flexibility of CorelDRAW to create mechanical-looking illustrations. Gears and machines can work well as secondary design elements, or even as a layout strategy. In the first example, we take advantage of the computer's ability to recalculate blends in order to animate the limbs of a robot character. Then we use the Blend and Weld functions to create gears, which can be used as flat objects or given depth and shading with the Extrude roll-up. Next, we take these gears and use them in a design to add structure and focus, and in the next example, the gear shape works to frame a logo design. Finally, we look at how to create belts and pulleys, which work in conjunction with or as a replacement for gears as unique design elements. There are so many looks you can get, only your needs and preferences will decide where CorelDRAW will take you. Grease the wheels and turn on your imagination machine!

## Brian the BrainBot

*Figure 24-1: Creating simple jointed limbs and other changeable objects can lead to all kinds of animation and emotion in a robot character.*

"How to you come up with this stuff?" is something I hear a lot, usually followed with something like, "Do you do drugs?" For the record, I have never experimented with drugs. I have the occasional Caesar (a Canadian drink made from Vodka and Clamato juice, with a dash of pepper), cigar, and of course, my daily ration of coffee, which seems to work just fine for me. Who knows, maybe I was dropped on my head as a kid.

All I know is that ideas and images just pop into my head, sometimes useful, sometimes totally random and ridiculous! I was looking for a robot avatar idea to use as a guide in an educational multimedia program for kids when Brian the BrainBot was born (see Figure 24-1). I needed something interesting enough to hold a kid's attention, but also simple enough to animate. This character works well, as you can change many things to create the illusion of animation. His eyes can move, the electricity sparks can turn different colors, the lights can flash, the message screen can change, and of course, the arms and fingers can move.

When designing a character for this kind of project, you want to find a balance between flexible and too complicated. Even with just a few items to change per cell, it gets mind-boggling when you set out to animate a character like this. I even switched techniques along the way to make things easier (see the sidebar "Simplify").

When you're working on Robots and other mechanical creations, you can take advantage of the computerized medium to cut corners and speed things along. For example, all of the objects on the left side of this robot are mirrored duplicates of the pieces on the right, which cuts your design time in half. With modular art objects like the limbs, you can also easily reposition them to create different poses. You could also duplicate the whole robot, creating an army of invading beasts, and move arms or change other details to make each duplicate unique. With a CAD (that's CorelDRAW Aided Design!) you have many options.

Here is how to make Brian the BrainBot with movable limbs:

1. For the brains of this robot character, I used, er, brains! From the CorelDRAW clip-art CD, import (Ctrl+I) a nice, squishy, pink brain from the \medical\organs\ directory. Draw a metal plate over half of the front exposed brain area using the Bezier tool and give it a shiny metallic fill with the Cylinder-Grey 02 custom color blend preset found in the Fountain Fill dialog. Duplicate the metal plate shape and downsize it. Now use the smaller duplicate (with fill and outline removed) as the reference path to blend rivets along and bolt the plate into the brain (the rivets are simply circles with black-to-white radial fountain fills and the center offset to create a gleam). Duplicate and flip the plate and rivets shape for a symmetrical look. Now draw more fountain circles around the brain for sensors and use the Freehand tool to draw wires connecting them to the plates. If you draw a fat line and then blend it with a skinny one on top, you can create rounded "wires," just like the lasers from Chapter 21 (see Figure 24-2).

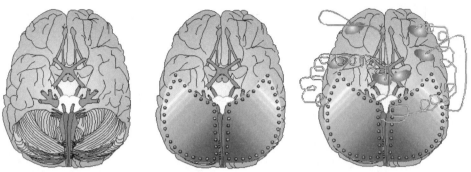

*Figure 24-2: A clip-art brain is wired with sensors and metal plates.*

2. Draw a base with the Rectangle tool to rest the brain on and use the Bezier tool to draw the pointy supports. Give these a black fill and duplicate them. Downsize the duplicate using the Shape tool and fill it with white. Blend it with the original, and it creates a rounded, pointy brain support. Duplicate the support to create a total of four, downsizing two for the distant pair. Fill circles with custom color radial fountain fills for eyes. Draw rectangles connected with spheres for articulators, on which the eyes will rest. Draw ovals with the Ellipse tool for the glass dome shape and the beehive ear electrodes. To make the bottom of the glass dome flat, draw a rectangle and use the Trim function to quickly cut away a uniform base. Place all of the objects behind the glass dome shape except the eyes. Give the dome a semi-opaque look with the Interactive Transparency tool. If you click on the tool, and instead of dragging on the object, change the parameters in the Property Bar, you can assign a uniform transparency much like the Lens roll-up. To heighten the glass look, draw a reflection shape with the Bezier tool and fill it white (see Figure 24-3).

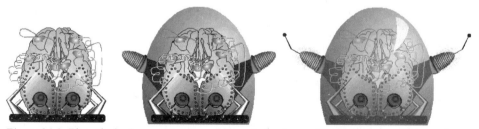

*Figure 24-3: Place the brain on a stand, level it, and give it eyes. Then place everything under glass, which is an egg-shaped object with a 50% uniform transparency.*

3. Create another rectangle to rest the head shape on and make it look cylindrical with the Cylinder-Green 03 fountain fill preset (are you getting the hints about saving time yet?). Then create another rectangle and finally, a third rectangle, which you make into a double parallelogram with an envelope. Give each of these objects the look of a cylinder with one of the cylinder fountain fill presets. Draw circles for the shoulder, elbow, and hand and use a custom color radial fountain fill to make them look round (load the file brainbot.cdr from the \Chapt24\ subdirectory on the Companion CD-ROM to see all of the custom color blends). Use the same technique to create round casters underneath the robot for him to roll around on. Use the Graph paper tool to create a grid for the speaker grill, then stuff that into an oval shape using the PowerClip function.

4. Now draw a circle on the left-center of the shoulder shape, and give it the tentacle custom color blend fill, with a shadow, highlight, and neutral shade of blue. (Remember when we created the metal trees in Chapter 23 and how I said that was going to be the last time we used the tentacle technique? I lied.) Duplicate this shape and move it to the center of the elbow circle. Duplicate again for another elbow shape (we can't use the Split function because one blend needs to be behind and the other in front of the elbow) and then once more for the hand. These four shapes will connect with blends to create the arm. Duplicate and reduce the shape three more times for each finger (see Figure 24-4).

*Figure 24-4: Simple geometric shapes, given life with fountain fills, stack up to become the body of the robot. Control curves are put into place to create the arms and fingers in the blend steps to come.*

5. Now select the small circles in the shoulder and elbow and connect them with a 40-step blend. Repeat this process to create the other arm section and also the fingers. Arrange the objects with the blend groups so that they start in front of a joint, like the shoulder, and end behind the next joint, such as the elbow. This will create an arm group, which you can duplicate and flip-flop for the other side. To make all of the gleams and shadows alike, use the right mouse button to copy the fill properties from the left arm pieces to the right (see the tip). See Figure 24-5.

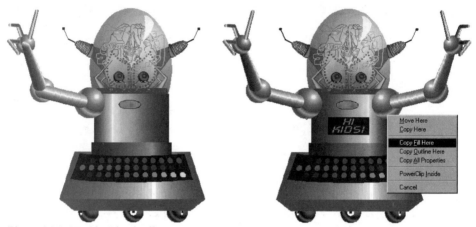

*Figure 24-5: Use the Blend roll-up to connect the small circles into solid arm shapes. Arrange the blend groups and the joints to create a dimensional arm and then duplicate them for the other side. Use the right mouse button to copy attributes from the left to the right.*

**TIP**    *To copy the outline or fill attributes of one object to another, use the right mouse button. Select an object that has the fill or outline you want with the right mouse button and then drag over the target object and release. A menu will appear, and you can choose to copy the fill, outline, or both to the underlying object. The double-knockdown, super bonus is that the target object can even be a part of another group. This is a great way to recolor an object within a group without affecting the other objects. Is CorelDRAW cool or what?*

## ▼ Simplify

The truth is I didn't plan on using the tentacle blend technique again (see step 4). In fact, if you look at the other files in the \Chapt24\ subdirectory, you will find brainbt2.cdr through brainbt4.cdr use rectangles in place of the circle blends for the arms. This turned out to be a big pain, however, when I went to animate this character. Using the circle/blend method made things really easy, as you can just select the control curves in Simple Wireframe view and move them around, and the arms will rebuild themselves automatically! Select and move the control curves around to place the other arm in a different position and repeat the process for the fingers (see Figure 24-6). See how easy the blends rebuild? You forgive me for lying yet?

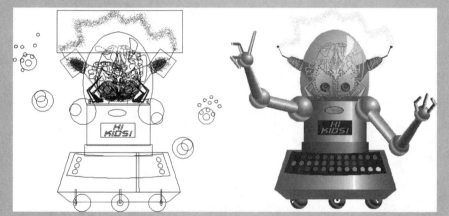

*Figure 24-6: The control curves can be selected and moved in the Simple Wireframe view (shown on left), and the limbs will automatically rebuild themselves thanks to the live blend groups (right).*

6. Use the bitmap-fuzz technique to create a row of ions connecting the ear electrodes and also to create static behind these objects. For a quick refresher, draw a thick black line between the two electrodes and then convert this into a grayscale bitmap. Inflate the bitmap to enlarge the image area, then use the Gaussian Blur bitmap filter to fuzz the line, and then get the desired pixelation by converting to a dithered black-and-white bitmap. For the animations, this static was flip-flopped and given a new color to help designate the desired emotional state of the robot.

7. For additional little bits of animation, add blends of circles for rows of lights. The great part about these blends is that you can drag and drop a new color on any of the control curves to change the interim light colors.

These simple circles also help show emotion and mood for each frame. (If you were animating a multimedia character, this section could be its own film loop, with the circles advancing like lights for each cell.) The addition of a little screen to speak words, using a font called LCD, finishes off the robot companion.

This file is called brainbot.cdr in the \Chapt24\ subdirectory on the Companion CD-ROM and the images can be seen in the color section. The color section graphic shows some of the different poses possible, and each is available on the Companion CD-ROM as its own file (brainbt2.cdr, brainbt3.cdr, and brainbt4.cdr). The numbered files were created before the blended limbs, but I included them so you can see how much easier it is to use the blend scheme for limbs. Open the brainbot.cdr file to see how the custom color blends give the circles depth and also to move the limbs around and see them rebuild for yourself. Heck, who knows, maybe Brian the BrainBot will be the next Barney!

## Geared for Success

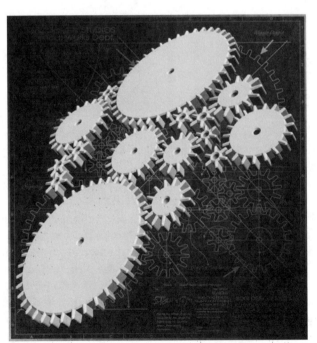

*Figure 24-7: The Blend roll-up and the Weld command make gear shapes in any size. These objects can be used for the background blueprint image or made into three-dimensional objects with the magic of the Extrude roll-up.*

Everything I needed to know about mechanical engineering I learned from Legos! I still have quite an impressive collection of these plastic wonder-bits, from which I fashion all kinds of strange things in my spare time.

▼ **Replacing Air With Salad Oil—Don't**

I once made this remote-controlled, fully suspended, all-wheel drive thing out of Legos that had a very interesting hydraulic steering system. Well, it wasn't designed to be hydraulic, but the pneumatic system just wasn't working to my standards, so I filled everything with salad oil. This worked and was awesome, until of course the added torque of the hydraulic pressure exploded everything into a big, sticky mess.

The Lego parts that always won my favor were the gears. Even now, I tend to still be fascinated with gears and find they make great design elements. They are interesting geometric shapes, are visually interesting, easy to render, and have a great deal of connotative meaning in our society (precision, constancy, high technology, and so on). They are also easy to animate and pop up in places like my sample Web site (see Chapter 27). Gears serve as all kinds of visual vehicles in art, from primary to secondary design elements. In the next three tutorials, we will see how to create gears and how to use them in artwork.

## Gears, Gears Everywhere

CorelDRAW is an awesome tool for creating images that are geometric and also mechanical in nature. The Blend roll-up creates such nice and even-spaced duplicates, it is a natural for things like rivets, bolts, and even the teeth in a gear. Once you create your basic gear shape, you can use it as a 2D design element or take things further with the Extrude roll-up. Here is how to create gears of any size and then make the shapes look three-dimensional:

1. Start with a rectangle and round the edges with the Shape tool. Now use the Envelope function to squeeze the top closer together. (Duplicate this gear tooth and set it aside for later.) Now change the axis of rotation, duplicate, and use 360 degrees of rotation to blend the object into a star shape. Vary the number of steps to get even spacing so that other gears could mesh in theory (see Figure 24-8).

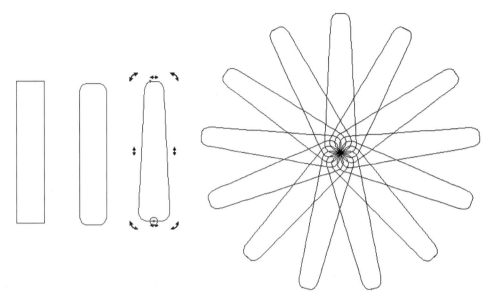

*Figure 24-8: Use the Shape and Envelope tools to modify a rectangle into a gear tooth and then use the Blend roll-up to create a star shape.*

2. Now use the Separate and Ungroup All functions to separate everything back into individual objects so you can select and delete the one extra and redundant gear object. Then drag-select all of the gear objects and weld them into one shape (see Figure 24-9). Yippee! A giant asterisk!

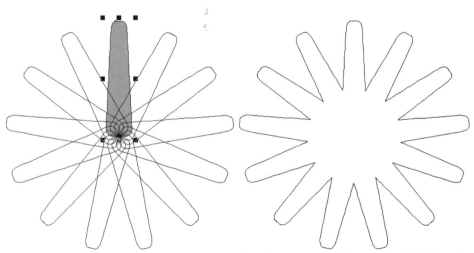

*Figure 24-9: All of the blend objects are separated, and the extra gear shape (in gray) is deleted. Then all of the objects can be merged into one using the Weld command.*

3. Draw a perfect circle and center it to the star shape using the Align & Distribute dialog (Ctrl+A). Now use the Weld command again to merge the circle to the star shape and finish the gear (see Figure 24-10).

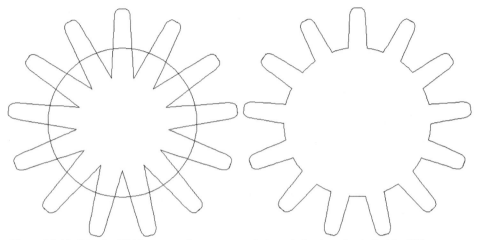

*Figure 24-10: Use the Weld command to merge a circle and star in order to finish off the gear.*

4. Duplicate the gear shape and arrange the duplicates so that they mesh nicely together. When you have the gears in the configuration you like, shift-select them all and combine them into one curve (Ctrl+L). With all of the gears combined into one curve, it is easy to then use the Extrude roll-up to add depth, a bevel, shadows, and highlights and even to rotate them in 3D space! Open the Extrude roll-up (Ctrl+E), set the depth and orientation to your taste, and enable a light source and also a bevel before you click Apply (see Figure 24-11).

*Figure 24-11: The Extrude roll-up converts a gear curve (top) into a set of dimensional objects with shading and even a bevel.*

**CD-ROM**

That is essentially all you need to do to create any kind of gear shapes. This example is in the color section and also in the \Chapt24\ subdirectory on the Companion CD-ROM (called gears.cdr). I used the gear shapes as flat and extruded design elements. By changing the axis of rotation on the original gear tooth before you go through the blend process, you can create gears of all shapes and sizes. Use the same tooth shape each time to ensure that they will all mesh together (see Figure 24-12).

The rest of the gears.cdr file is pretty basic, just a bit tedious. I set up the gear duplicates as I wanted for the extrude but kept a flat copy in white outline for a blueprint look. (If you load the file, the objects are on their own layers (named gears and blueprint), so open the Object Manager from the Layout menu to make a layer invisible so that the focus is on the other.) To get a technical feel, use dotted lines to denote the dimensions of objects and call out details with arrows and text. I used a font called Technical (handy, huh?). Here is a neat trick I used to get the shading I wanted. First, give all the objects no fills and white outlines on a typical blue background. Then to antique the image, lay a rectangle over the entire blueprint and fill it with a texture fill called Above the Earth from the Samples 7 Texture Library. Change the colors to shades of brown and click OK. Now select the Interactive Transparency tool, but don't click on the object; instead, just change the parameters in the Property Bar. Choose the Uniform option with a Transparency Rate of 50%. This will give the image a nice weathered look (see Figure 24-13).

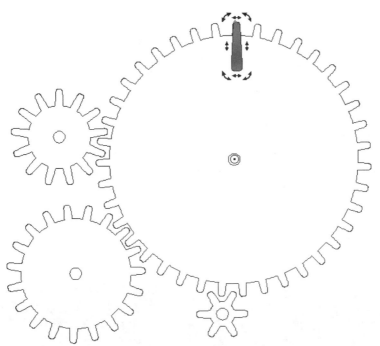

*Figure 24-12: Use the same tooth object (gray) for all the gears so they mesh together. Change the axis of rotation for each to create larger or smaller gears.*

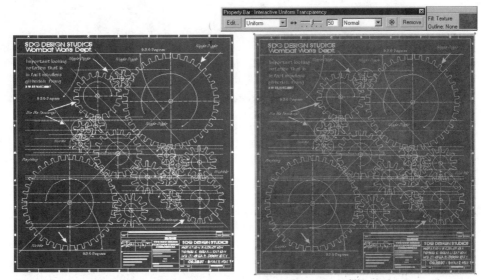

*Figure 24-13: Add a 50% transparency to a rectangle with a texture fill to create an antique look (right) for the objects below (left).*

For even more shading, use a solid black object on top of the previous Transparency texture effect. Duplicate the texture fill rectangle and fill it solid black. Now with the Interactive Transparency tool, drag from the top left to the bottom right. This sets up a nice lighting from dark to light as the transparency moves from solid black to totally clear. But wait, there's more. You can use the Interactive Fill tool to change the opacity of an interactive transparency in the same way you add colors to a custom color blend using the Interactive Fill tool. In a transparency color blend, though, you only use black, white, and shades of gray. Black is 100 percent clear, white is 100 percent opaque, and the shade of gray is the amount of transparency (60% gray is clearer than 40% gray), no matter what the actual fill color of the object is. For this example, I wanted the center to be bright and the corners darker. Drag black from the onscreen color well to a midpoint on the line. Now drag white to both ends of the interactive transparency (see Figure 24-14). Oooh, aaah.

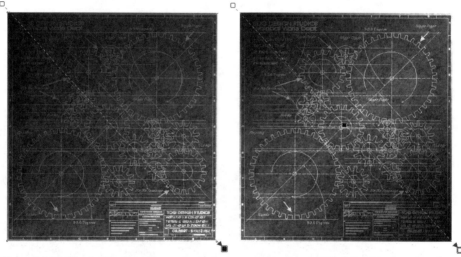

*Figure 24-14: The Interactive Transparency tool can create dramatic lighting by changing the amount and areas of transparency on a solid black rectangle.*

**TIP**  *Stacking lenses and other CorelDRAW effects can result in an image that is mathematically very complex. This complexity can result in problems, especially when you go to output the image for printing purposes. For onscreen uses, such as multimedia or the Web, this is not an issue (as you can always do a screen capture), but when outputting to PostScript image setters, it can be. To circumvent any imaging problems, use the Export command to create a composite bitmap of complex artwork. A CMYK TIF image is a bulletproof file format that is supported across all platforms and will output (or "rip", Raster Image Process) without any problems. Even files that are a nightmare to print will almost without fail generate a nice TIF (which will process nicely) without any glitches. In fact, all of the images in the color section of this book were done in this way to circumvent any problems. With the artwork being generated on PCs in California, and the book being assembled on Macs in North Carolina, generating CMYK bitmaps for the images was the only way to ensure hassle-free processing!*

With the background in place, it is just a matter of dropping the extruded gears into place. One problem to note is that combining all of the gears into one curve shape can result in an object too complex to extrude. I resolved this problem by splitting up the gears equally into two curve shapes. After the first one was extruded, the second was matched up using the Copy Extrude option from the Effects menu. The end result is an image that retains the flexibility of a CorelDRAW file, while at the same time incorporating the look and depth of a 3D image. Check the color section for the end result and also load the file to handle things firsthand.

## The Imagination Machine

*Figure 24-15: Gears can become an interesting design element that suggest motion or machinery. When all of the gear shapes are combined into a single object, the Extrude function creates the depth with shadows and highlights and also a shared vanishing point.*

Ever find something you created a long time ago and say to yourself, "What was I thinking?" The image in Figure 24-15 (well, only pieces of it now) was something I submitted to the Corel International Design contest many moons ago, and gee whiz, it didn't win anything. When I first opened the file, I was so aghast at some of the amateurish techniques that I immediately closed it again, too embarrassed to look. Many weeks later, I remembered that the image used gears, so I opened it again for potential inclusion in this chapter. I liked the layout, but spent so much time fixing the artwork, I probably would have been better off starting from scratch!

Gears work well in advertising or other commercial artwork on both a visual and connotative level. Here the grease on the wheels and the imagination machine concepts are reinforced by the gears. This machine would of course produce nothing but noise and maybe some static if you could turn it on, but the laws of mechanical engineering don't apply here! As an interesting visual vehicle, it rolls along just fine.

As in the previous example, the gears are created using the Blend roll-up and Weld function. They look a little different in this example because the objects have been given big cutout areas in the gear centers for a more stylized and less realistic look. The electric static is created using the exact process as outlined in Chapter 22, and the metallic fills are from the last chapter. (Pretty soon I won't even have to explain anything; I'll just point you back to chapters we have already covered!) There are of course some new techniques worth mentioning, so read on. Here is how to work gears into your design scheme:

1. Just as before, create your gears by blending a common tooth object in a circle. Combine another big circle to the large gear and two smaller circles to the little gears. The double ring inside for the smaller gears creates a cutout with a floating solid center. Shift-select all of the gears and combine them (Ctrl+L). Use the Cylinder-Gold 07 fountain fill preset to give them a nice metallic look (see Figure 24-16).

*Figure 24-16: A pair of teeth objects are blended in a 360-degree spin to create gears of any size. Add and combine circle shapes to the gears to create cutout areas when the objects are filled (right).*

2. Select the combined gear curve, remove any outline, and open the Extrude roll-up (Ctrl+E). Now set the desired depth, enable a single light source to the top right, and also use a .025 bevel. Click Apply to build your gears with the shared vanishing point and lighting attributes (see Figure 24-17).

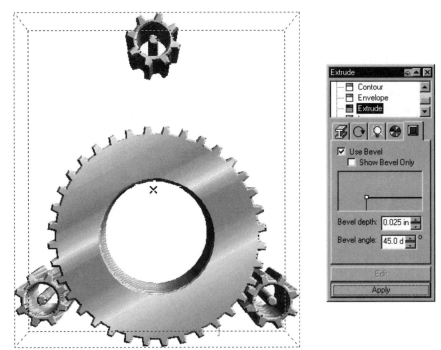

*Figure 24-17: The Extrude roll-up provides depth, highlight, shadow, and even a beveled edge.*

3. Use the Fit Text to Path function to place artistic text along another circle within the main gear. I used a font called CopprplGoth (or Copperplate Gothic). Duplicate and offset a white copy down and to the left behind the original black to create a gleam shape.

4. Draw a triangle. An easy way to do this is to draw a square, and rotate it 45 degrees. Then convert it to curves (Ctrl+Q) and use the Shape tool to select and delete the bottom node. Use the Pick tool to stretch the triangle vertically. Duplicate and downsize the triangle, shift-select the original, and combine the two. This will create a triangular cutout in the center of the large triangle. Now fill the object with a bitmap pattern fill, such as something from the \tiles\metal\large directory on the CorelDRAW CD. Use the Copy Extrude From feature from the Effects menu to add depth and shading to this object (see Figure 24-18).

*Figure 24-18: A square becomes a triangle when a node is deleted. Combine two triangles together to create another cutout object, which is given a bitmap pattern fill and the same extrusion as the gear curve.*

5. In each corner, a screw head fastener seems to hold the object to the background. I love to put little rivets, screws, and bolts around to add a touch of visual interest and high-tech feel to a design. And they are so simple to create, I must say. Draw a circle and give it a gray fill. Duplicate the circle, downsize it a tad, move it up and to the right of the center, and give it a white fill. When you use the Blend roll-up on these two shapes, a round rivet will result. This technique lets you get rounder looking objects than a radial fountain fill. To make the rivet into a screw head, draw a gray rectangle for the slot and then draw another black one for the shadow within the slot (see Figure 24-19).

*Figure 24-19: A circle blend becomes a rivet or screw head. For the screw, solid rectangles become the slot and any shadow within it (Wireframe view on left).*

6. A rectangle resting on the two small gears frames an extruded text element. The trick here is to use a simple gray fill for the extrusion to create the shadows, highlights, and bevel and then go back and give just the face the sky/horizon fill from Chapter 23. To do this, perform the extrude on the text as normal and then separate the extrude objects. Now select just the face pieces and fill them. The end result is beveled and extruded text, but without the chaos that extruding an object filled with the sky/horizon scheme creates (see Figure 24-20).

*Figure 24-20: Use the Extrude function on a neutral gray shape to create simple shadow and highlight shapes. Separate the extrude group to select and shade just the face with a chrome fill for a less-busy result than you would get by simply extruding the shape with the chrome fill initially.*

The bitmap earth and eye were made into a composite in PhotoPaint some time ago, although if I had to do it again, I would simply stuff the eye bitmap into a triangle shape with the PowerClip function and save some grief (hey, wisdom comes with experience!). The lightening bolts are given the static buzz from Chapter 22, and a similar technique was used to generate the fuzzy edge around the image border. Here is how to get the border:

1. Draw a black box the size you want your border to be. Duplicate it and fill the duplicate white. Now downsize and center the white duplicate. Use the Blend roll-up to create interim steps between the black and white boxes.

2. With the blend selected, choose Convert to Bitmap from the Bitmap menu. Change the Color option to black and white, enable the Dithered feature, and change the Resolution value to determine how chunky you

want the bits to be. The lower the resolution, the grainier the result. I set the Resolution to 200. Click OK to convert the image into a bitmap.

3. Now position the fuzzy frame over your bitmap. Left-click on the no-fill onscreen color well to make the bitmap background transparent. (You cannot skip this step if you enable the Transparent Background option in the Convert to Bitmap dialog. Technically, the white of this black and white image is not background during the conversion, so it will be solid white after the Convert to Bitmap step no matter what you do.) With the bitmap now black and clear, you can arrange it to obscure the edges of the background bitmap (see Figure 24-21).

*Figure 24-21: Blend a small white rectangle to a larger black one behind it to create a frame object. When you convert this blend to a dithered black-and-white bitmap, you create a unique fuzzy frame.*

That's all of the real magic behind this piece. All of my secrets are basically now yours (and a huge portion of my personal artwork to boot!), so for the remainder of the book, it will be mighty difficult to wow you, I'm sure. You can see this piece in the color section or load the imagine.cdr file in the \Chapt24\ subdirectory on the Companion CD to look at things firsthand. Make a mental note that there are handy little screw heads in this file, which you can load and steal for your own designs later on.

## WHRA

*Figure 24-22: To create a unique logo, use a gear symbol shape to frame an image.*

I am a big fan of jet ski racing and have been for a long time. Slimy Dog Grafix had many great clients in the personal watercraft world, so when a new fledgling riders' organization was starting, I was more than happy to be involved. To give the group a boost, I offered to create the artwork for free and produce the shirts at a big discount. I had to work all night to meet the deadline, didn't so much as get a thank you, and had to hunt down payment for six months to cover my expenses. Nice, huh? Big surprise: this organization flopped as well.

In any case, this design is a good example of how a gear shape can be used in a more abstract way in a design. Gears have a rounded, but at the same time, angular feel; a gear has a nice geometric shape for framing an image or using as a base for a company logo. Here is how to use a gear as an interesting frame element:

1. This gear shape was not made by hand but swiped right out of the Symbols Science Library. The symbol has two gears with hollow centers. To delete all but the outside curve, break apart (Ctrl+K) the shape and eliminate the unwanted pieces. The globe was scanned and converted to

vector artwork using OCR-Trace from supplied art, but you could use a globe shape found in the GeographicSymbols Symbol Library. Center the globe within the gear (see Figure 24-23).

*Figure 24-23: Use symbol shapes for the gears and globe to map out the beginnings of a logo.*

2. Duplicate the gear shape and isolate a quarter of it. You could use the Shape tool to delete all but the nodes of the corner section, or you could draw a square enclosing the quarter section and use the Intersection command to isolate the piece you need. Duplicate the quarter section and flip-flop it horizontally and vertically to create a quarter section at the opposite side. Shift-select both of these and combine them into one curve. Now duplicate again, flip horizontally, and combine this section with the globe shape. When you combine the gear sections to the globe artwork, the pieces within the gears are reversed-out (see Figure 24-24).

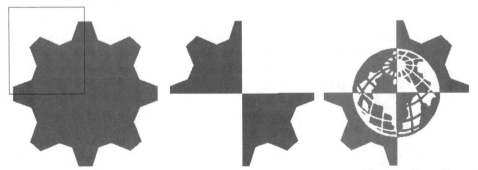

*Figure 24-24: Use the Intersection command to isolate a quarter section of the gear. Since this shape is symmetrical, you can flip-flop the pieces to create opposing halves and combine one half to the globe shape.*

3. Select both halves and use the Align & Distribute dialog (Ctrl+A) to center horizontally and vertically. Now position these new pieces over the original gear shape, which has been given a fat .222 purple outline and purple fill. This will fill the cutout globe shapes in the pink section with purple, finishing off the dynamic of this design (see Figure 24-25).

*Figure 24-25: Align the two symmetrical halves to produce a whole, with the globe image in the center. Place these on top of a fat-outlined original to finish off the design.*

The jet-skier image is a black-and-white bitmap with a solid white shape drawn beneath it. The text around the logo is that CopprplGoth font again, while the WHRA logo is done in the New Yorker font.

This image (and bad memory) can be seen in the color section and also in the whra.cdr file found in the \Chapt24\ subdirectory on the Companion CD-ROM. I fully expect you to load and swipe the gear/globe objects because they are just begging to be used in another logo! Or just snag the globe by breaking apart the gear curve to which it is stuck, selecting only the globe bits, and combining them back into one usable object. Do what you like! The point of this book is not just to fill your head with ideas, but also to fill your hard disk with usable art! Go forth, and prosper.

## Belts & Pulleys

*Figure 24-26: Like gears, belts and pulleys make interesting mechanical additions to a design to add a sense of motion and high-tech edge. The pieces can also work to unify a logo or act as a border element.*

In the same way you create gears, you can also create belts and pulleys. It is sometimes useful as a design element to connect objects with a belt or other visual vehicle to guide the reader's eyes around the page. Belts and pulleys also share the same kind of high-tech and mechanical connotations that gears do, but they are not as obtrusive or harsh as all those toothy gears. It is also difficult to create a border with gears that isn't too busy, but a border is a perfect application for the belts and pulleys. This same type of graphic works for the printing industry as well. Big printing presses that print newspapers and other big publications print on to giant rolls of paper that weave through many rollers, just like the belts and pulleys. For the printing-press look, add more depth to the rollers and pulleys, and decrease the thickness to look more like thin paper instead of a thick belt. Here is how to connect pulleys with a belt:

1. Start with a circle and blend two other little circles along it. Now as before, separate and blend all of the pieces into a grooved pulley shape (see Figure 24-27).

*Figure 24-27: Use the Blend roll-up to scatter circles along a round path; then merge them into a pulley shape using the Weld command.*

2. Use the Polygon tool to create a six-sided shape and then center it with the outside circle. Now combine the two (Ctrl+L) to finish off the hollow-centered pulley. Arrange any duplicates that you wish; then once again add depth with the Extrude roll-up (see Figure 24-28).

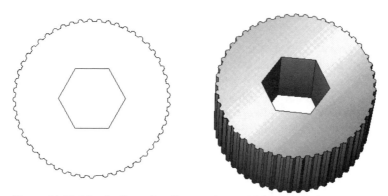

*Figure 24-28: Use the Extrude roll-up again to add depth and shading to the pulley wheel.*

3. Like you did with the gears, you can duplicate and arrange the pulley circle and then combine them into one curve. Use the Extrude roll-up again to add depth and shading to the curve. Draw a shape with the Bezier tool to connect the pulleys with a belt (see Figure 24-29).

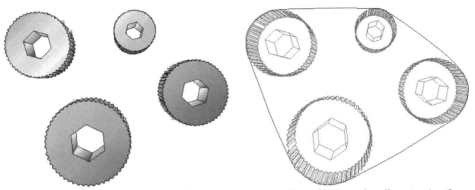

*Figure 24-29: Combine all pulley circles into one curve and use the Extrude roll-up to give them all depth and shading and a shared vanishing point. Use the Bezier tool to draw a belt to connect the pieces.*

4. Again, use the Blend roll-up to scatter two small circles along the path to create teeth in the belt (see Figure 24-30).

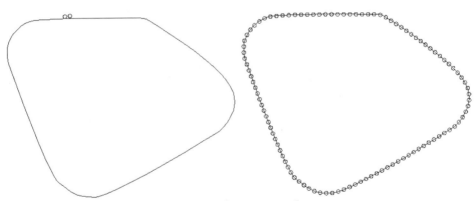

*Figure 24-30: Blend circles along the belt path to create teeth.*

5. Just as before, separate all of the circles in the blend so you can then combine them into one shape. Then use the Contour roll-up (or duplicate and downsize, depending on how complex the belt shape is) to create a second shape for the belt. Combine the inside and outside belt curves into one object and use the Trim command to cut out the teeth, using the circle blend curve as the template (see Figure 24-31).

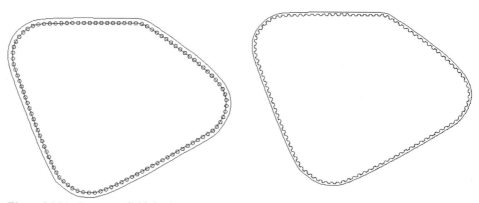

*Figure 24-31: Create a solid belt object using the Contour roll-up; then cut out the teeth with the Trim command.*

6. Now position the belt shape behind the pulleys, and choose Effects | Copy | Extrude From to steal the settings used on the pulley shapes on the belt curve. This will give everything the same depth, lighting, and vanishing point to create a convincing image. To speed things up or for an interesting variant (or to circumvent the teeth in the pulleys not exactly matching up to the belt problem), you can use the same technique on smooth objects (see Figure 24-32).

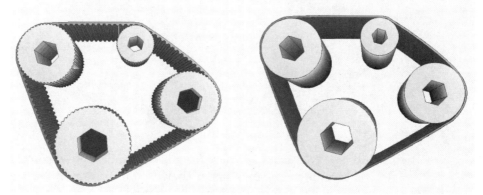

*Figure 24-32: By copying the extrude settings from the pulleys to the belt, all of the objects have the correct depth, shading, and vanishing point settings.*

There you have it. You can place gears and pulleys in, around, and through your next design!

## Moving On

In this chapter, we saw how to create robotics and mechanical-looking designs. The robot image used symmetry to cut design time in half and tricks to make moving and animating the limbs easy. The gear sections showed how to create gears of any size and shape by blending a tooth object. We also saw how to add depth to the gears using the Extrude roll-up and how they can be used as interesting design elements in their flat state, in three dimensions, and even as a frame element.

In the next chapter, we will be using grids and lines, rather than the Extrude roll-up, to create dimension. The great thing about the human mind is how easily it is fooled, and we will endeavor to trick readers into seeing depth and dimension where there is in fact none. So let's leave robots (except maybe Maximilian, who was the evil villain robot from the Disney *Black Hole* flick) and machines behind for now and head into the mysteries of grids and black holes.

▼ **Beyond f/x**

Gears, mechanical elements, and modular designs have a ton of design potential. From logos to animations, there are many uses for these art elements. In fact, we will be animating gears in Chapter 29 to enhance a Web site design created in Chapter 27.

The pulleys can pull a belt through a design, guiding the reader and directing attention throughout a publication. Gears add that sense of action and mechanical feel that are right at home in the corporate logos of many industries. Animated gears (as in my Web page demo) also make interesting button elements, adding a sense of danger. It is against your better judgment to stick your fingers (or in this case, the cursor) into the intermeshing and rotating gears, so it is kind of a reverse psychology design trick. Since the virtual experience is safe, you can create all kinds of moving, dangerous, sharp machines for your viewers to interact with. Using modular design tricks, or the blending techniques we used with the robot arms, your Web machines can easily be animated and come to life when you click on them.

In advertising, you can play off of the mechanical nature of these graphics with tag lines like "Put us to work," or "Working to bring you the best deals," or "Geared for success," or any of a gazillion phrases. Now get in gear and get to work!

# chapter 25

# Grids, Black Holes & Bending Light

In the vein of idealized reality, it is often advantageous to simplify your designs even further by using grids and lines to suggest depth and substance. Sometimes there is little option but to include a man-made object to create a dimensional environment in a universe that has little definition, such as a grid to give the vast blackness of space tangible dimensions. Grids and lines are excellent visual vehicles to create a dimensional universe that the reader can comprehend and explore.

In this chapter, we will create universes using the powerful illusions created with grids and lines. Using the mathematical accuracy afforded by CorelDRAW's functions, it is easy to create perfectly spaced lines that suggest depth and substance. First, we will use the Graph Paper tool to create grids of all sizes and shapes, then we'll add depth with the Perspective function, and finally, we'll add some special effects with a light-bending lens. Next we will create a spinning light show with the Blend roll-up using the rainbow coloring options and object acceleration features. We will then add the illusion of depth to create a multicolored black hole or tunnel into another dimension. We will combine the techniques of the grid and light show and work them into a practical design example. Finally, we will create evenly spaced patterns with the Blend roll-up and use some low-tech design tricks to create a high-tech image of a black hole appearing to bend rays of light. This chapter uses our powers of imagination to fill in the blanks, with images that trick the eyeballs and scream, "Neat-o," full-volume into your voice mail.

## Grids in Space

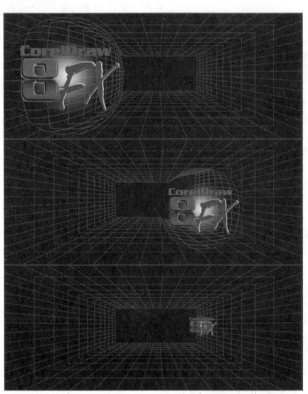

*Figure 25-1: The Graph Paper tool easily manufactures nice grids, which are made to look three-dimensional with the Perspective tool. A circle with the Fisheye lens appears to bend the light as it floats by.*

Believe it or not, this was the first graphic I created for this book (see Figure 25-1). Before I signed any contracts or made any deals, I spent a few days just brainstorming, trying to put my finger on the pulse of what a CorelDRAW f/x book would be about. This image went together so easily, and the results were so cool, I made it into an animation and sent it to the publisher. Within a week we not only were a go for the project, but we had hammered out the table of contents which in turn became this book in your hands! (The file is called grids.avi in the \Chapt25\ subdirectory on the Companion CD-ROM if you want to see it.) It is just the kind of cool, but not insanely difficult, type of effect I was after.

Grids provide a great way to tie images together in a design. They can add depth when placed in perspective and structure when left flat, and they can even suggest shapes when distorted (see the final example in this section). Grids can also bring about other designs, such as art that looks like video games or menacing target-acquisition-type displays for fictitious weaponry (like in the sword girl from Chapter 18). Grids and simple line art hearken back to simpler times, when computer graphics were not as insane as they are today. My favorite video game (Battlezone by Atari. I have had the full-size, coin-operated arcade classic since I was 18!) uses simple vector graphics and grids to build a three-dimensional world. This same kind of imagery, where you just suggest objects and space, can be more dramatic than photos of the real thing.

▼ **Instant Invoices**

I am telling you, if you are ever stumped on a design, start with a grid and go from there. At the ad agency, we used to have a generic formula for generic clients, and it worked every time. Set a row of type in a brush font, set it on top of another row in a sans-serif font, then float them both over a grid. Bang. Instant graphic, happy client, job done. Works every time (see Figure 25-2).

123  Nowhere Lane, Somewhere, CA 912345        Phone: (909) 555-1212

*Figure 25-2: Grids make for a universal design element to add interest to almost any design.*

Here's how to use the Graph Paper tool to create grids and then give them depth with the Perspective function:

1. Right-click over the Graph Paper tool icon on the toolbar to open its Properties dialog (the Graph Paper tool is on the same flyout as the Polygon and Spiral tools). Change both the Number of Cells High and

Number of Cells Wide values to 12 and then click OK. Now drag the Graph Paper tool to create the grid, holding the Ctrl key down to create a perfect square (see Figure 25-3).

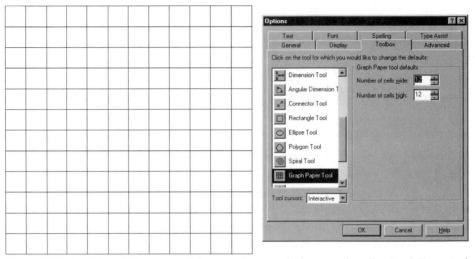

*Figure 25-3: A setting of 12 across and down creates a grid when you drag the Graph Paper tool on the desktop.*

2. With the grid selected (the grid is nothing more than a group of identical rectangle duplicates, by the way, in case you want to ungroup and manipulate the objects), choose Add Perspective from the Effects menu. Now with the Shape tool, drag the top-right node inward while holding down both the Shift and the Ctrl keys, which will bring the opposite node in as well. Release when finished to place the grid in the distance, just like we created the tile floor in Chapter 7. Then use the Pick tool to drag the top-center sizing node down while holding down the Shift key to squash the grid vertically (see Figure 25-4).

3. Duplicate the grid and flip it vertically by grabbing the bottom-center sizing handle and dragging upward while holding down the Ctrl key. This will create two planes that disappear at the same horizon line, which is a quick and convincing way to add depth to a design (see Figure 25-5).

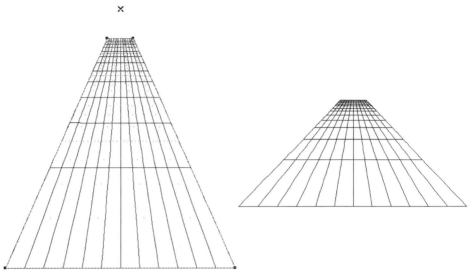

*Figure 25-4: The Perspective tool places the grid in what appears to be a 3D orientation, and reducing its size vertically makes it look less stretched out.*

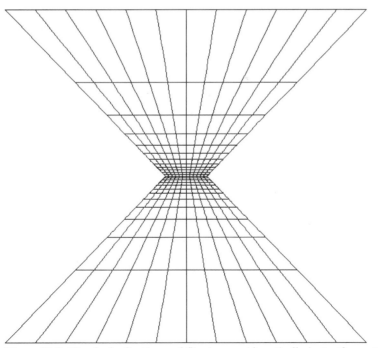

*Figure 25-5: Simply duplicating and flipping a grid vertically instantly creates an illusion of depth.*

4. It is a little tricky to get all of the lines to match up to get a grid box, but it's not impossible. (First, delete the vertically flipped duplicate from step 3. I just wanted to show you how easy it is to get 3D with a grid!) Start with the bottom grid element and duplicate it, but this time rotate it –90 degrees. Now shift-select both grids, and with the Align & Distribute dialog (Ctrl+A), align it to the bottom left corner. Now select the left grid, and using the Pick tool, align it perfectly to the original by resizing horizontally and vertically (see Figure 25-6).

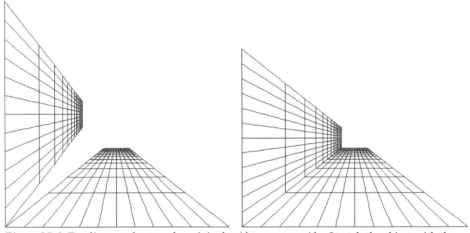

*Figure 25-6: Duplicate and rotate the original grid to create a side. Stretch the object with the Pick tool and align the side up with the bottom grid.*

5. With the left-hand side in place, shift-select both grid groups and duplicate. Now spin the duplicate around –180 degrees by dragging a corner rotation arrow while holding down the Ctrl key. Because the axis of rotation is where it needs to be for a rectangle, all of the pieces will line up to create a perfect grid (see Figure 25-7).

6. Select all of the grid elements and group them (Ctrl+G). I gave my grid a thin .015-inch magenta outline and no fill. (Remember that these are actually rectangles for which you can also assign a fill attribute, such as a radial fountain fill, for a totally different kind of look. See Figure 25-8.) Place the grid on a solid black rectangle to suggest the bleakness of space.

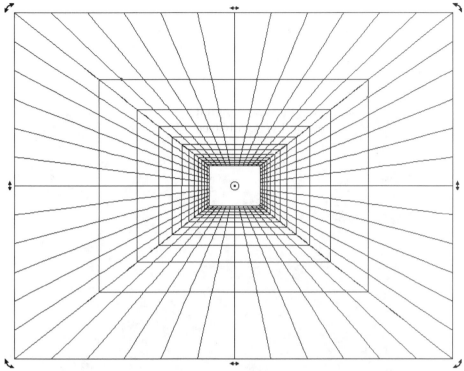

*Figure 25-7: Duplicating and spinning the left and bottom around 180 degrees results in the right and top side of a grid tunnel.*

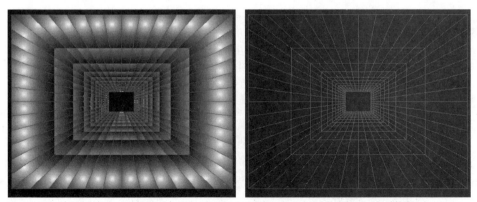

*Figure 25-8: The grid groups are rectangles and can be given a radial fountain fill for a patterned look (on left) or no fill (on right) to emphasize the outline-grid look.*

7. Because the grid is made up of vector objects, it is the perfect design element to tweak with the Fish Eye lens. Draw a circle, open the Lens roll-up (Alt+F3), change to Fish Eye, make sure the rate is at 100%, and then click Apply. This will distort the lines behind the circle to make it look as if the circle were a glass orb (see Figure 25-9).

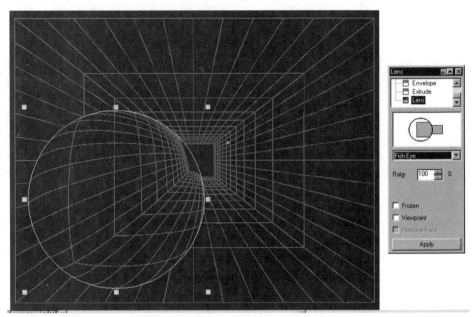

*Figure 25-9: The Fish Eye lens distorts the lines behind it to make a circle appear to be a solid glass orb.*

8. Because a lens does not change any of the objects underneath it (it only changes the way they appear), you can move the circle around to make it look as if it is dancing through the grid tunnel. To emphasize the glass ball theme, duplicate the circle and give the duplicate no outline and a black-to-white radial fountain fill. Then with the Interactive Transparency tool, create a radial fountain fill. Once again you will have to reverse the logic of the fill by dragging black onto the white point and white on to the black point. Drag the control points on the interactive transparency fill to create a convincing gleam. Select both circles and group them; then you can move the orb anywhere and the lenses will redraw each time to create the new illusion (see Figure 25-10).

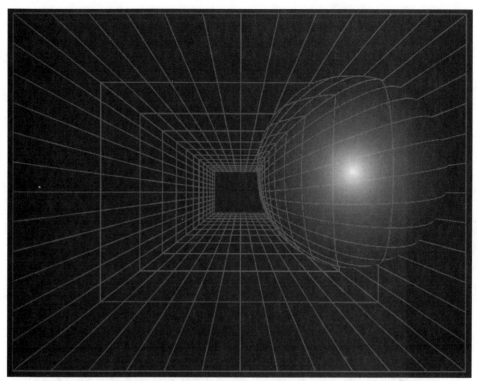

*Figure 25-10: A radial fountain fill transparency on a black-to-white radial-fountain-filled circle emphasizes the glass orb illusion, adding a highlight to the center of the ball.*

That's really all there is to it! Instant grids, automatically redrawing lens effects—heck, what more could you ask for? This file, in various stages of animation, can be seen in the color section, in the grids.cdr file found in the \Chapt25\ subdirectory on the Companion CD-ROM, and also in an animation, grids.avi, found there as well. This is a great example of how a good-looking, versatile graphic need not be incredibly difficult to create. Also, because of the nature of lenses, you can move around and resize the orb at will, and CorelDRAW will dutifully re-create the appropriate illusions for you each time.

## Black Hole Light Show

*Figure 25-11: Blend a spiraled set of spokes to a smaller duplicate to result in an impressive light show. Change some of the blend parameters to create colorful black holes.*

I would like to take this opportunity to thank you for buying this book. Not that the money and all that is so important, but if it were not for this book project, I wouldn't have learned so many handy tricks either! It was during a moment of experimentation—trying to perfect a look for the black hole section of this chapter—that I discovered this very cool technique. Who says you can't teach an old dog new tricks? Bow wow wow, yippee yo, yippee yay.

This brilliant, colorful design (see the color section for the full impact) is another one of those really fun and easy techniques. It is actually a simple blend between two shapes, but those two shapes are key to this design. Unlike other blends, this one starts with a distorted spoked curve that, when blended to a reduced duplicate, creates a very unique design. Depending on how tight or loose (lower rotation and fewer steps) you make the blend, you can get a solid mass or a gridlike design. When you offset and reduce the center control curve (in the bottom two examples in Figure 25-11 and in the color section), the blend builds as a spiral that is sucking down into the center, which could become a black hole variant.

Here is how to create spinning light show blends:

1. First, we will steal an idea from Chapter 20, which is to use the Twister Distortion tool. But instead of pizza slices like we made in Chapter 20, create a blend of straight lines. Draw a straight-up-and-down line and then change its axis of rotation to the bottom center of the line. Now duplicate it and blend the two lines together with 360 degrees of rotation and 26 steps. Separate the blend and delete the extra control curve. Then shift-select all of the lines and combine them (Ctrl+L) into one curve.

2. Select the Interactive Distortion tool from the Interactive Blend tool flyout. On the Property Bar, click the Twister Distortion button, key in 350 for the angle of rotation, and watch the fur fly. Convert this new line vortex to curves (Ctrl +Q). See Figure 25-12.

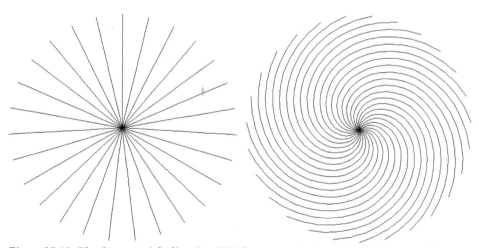

*Figure 25-12: Blend two straight lines in a 360-degree rotation to create a spoke curve. Then use the Twister mode of the Distortion tool to change the image into a spiraling vortex illusion.*

3. Give this curve a .023-inch yellow outline and duplicate it. Downsize the duplicate until it is about 30 percent smaller than the original. Shift-select both objects and open the Blend roll-up. Now change the number of steps to 75 and set the Rotation to 360 degrees again; then enable one of the rainbow options. Click Apply to watch the show begin (see Figure 25-13).

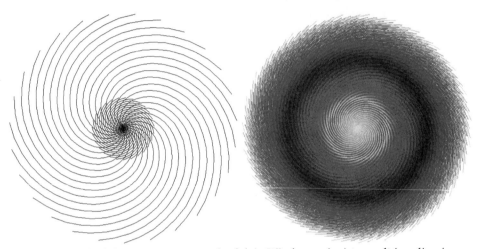

*Figure 25-13: Blend the two vortex curves (on left in Wireframe view) to result in a dizzying color show by enabling the rainbow option in the Blend roll-up.*

4. For even more dizzying variety, experiment with the Accelerate Objects slider on the Blend roll up. Drag the slider to the left to get the results found in Figure 25-11 and the color section. With a different coloring scheme, this object could become a very nice stylized sun image (see Figure 25-14).

5. For a different variant, downsize and move the center vortex curve. Then select the big curve and change the Outline Color value to cyan. Now increase the number of steps to 125 but reduce the rotation to 180 degrees. When you click Apply this time, you will get an image that could be a cornucopia of light, or even a stylized black hole (see Figure 25-15).

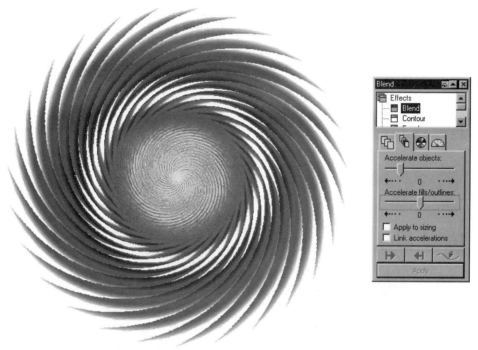

*Figure 25-14: The Accelerate Objects slider on the Blend roll-up creates the spiky sun shape.*

*Figure 25-15: Change the size and location of the center control curve, increase the number of steps, and reduce the rotation to 180 degrees to produce a different result.*

These light shows are on fire in the color section and in a file called lightshw.cdr in the \Chapt25\ subdirectory on the Companion CD-ROM. Load the file and tweak the blend parameters yourself to see how changing the rotation values and the number of steps can dramatically change things. Also, change the colors of the control curves and see how different color choices change the Rainbow options on the colors page on the Blend roll-up.

"These are sure pretty, but what the heck would I use them for?" you ask. Well, read on!

## Physics

*Figure 25-16: Combine the grid and light show elements together to create a bright and interesting book cover.*

This book cover design uses (surprise, surprise) the light-show twirls from the last section and, yes, the multipurpose, all-season, multilingual, nonstick grid. To suggest depth, we once again turn to the trusty Perspective function, and we also take advantage of the computer medium to almost effortlessly duplicate and mirror the image. The impact of the final image again defies the simplicity using the power and automation of CorelDRAW. Here's how to combine the twirly blends with a grid for an artistic but spacy design:

1. Use the Graph Paper tool to create a grid as before and again distort it with the Perspective tool. Use the Pick tool to drag the top-center sizing handle as before to squash the grid vertically.

2. Create (or better yet, just borrow) the light show blend from the previous example. Before you can alter the object with the Perspective tool, however, you must disable the live blend. Use the Arrange | Separate, Arrange | Ungroup All, Group (Ctrl+G) command routine to kill the blend and end up with a group of some 127 objects that will accept a perspective.

3. With the colorful swirl group selected, choose Copy | Perspective From from the Effects menu and click on the grid shape. This will place the black-hole light show in the same perspective as the grid, making for a more convincing graphic with all the elements sharing a like orientation (see Figure 25-17).

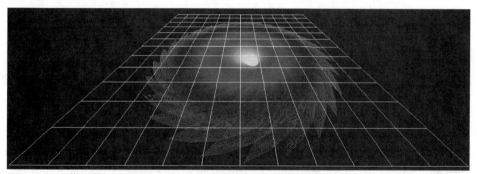

*Figure 25-17: The Perspective tool places a grid in the desired 3D-like orientation; then the same perspective is copied to the black hole swirl object group.*

4. Now select both the swirl and the grid and duplicate them. Flip them vertically by dragging the bottom-center sizing handle upward with the Pick tool while holding down the Ctrl key. Who said design has to be hard? Use tricks to your advantage to increase your profits. As you get better, it will continually take less time for you to finish a job, so don't charge by the hour, but by the design. Unless of course your client insists on helping, or whines incessantly, or is indecisive, or has you make idiotic changes right up until the deadline. Then charge by the *minute*!

5. To get the arrow spinning both behind and in front of the objects, use duplicates of the same curve. Start by drawing an oval with the Ellipse tool; then duplicate it. Now use the Shape tool to drag the control nodes of the ellipse around (on the outside of the ellipse) to create the curve for the area in front of everything. Then use the Shape tool on the other copy to drag the nodes of that ellipse around to create the curve that will be behind everything and that also will match up with the other curve. Place each curve in position and use the Arrange I Order I In Front Of or Arrange I Order I Behind command to place the arrows correctly with the image stack. Select the front arc, open the Outline Pen dialog, and assign an arrow for the start of the curve (see Figure 25-18).

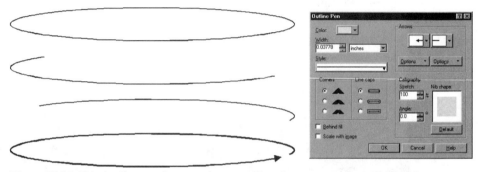

*Figure 25-18: Use the Shape tool to transform an ellipse into a graceful arc. Repeat the process on a duplicate behind the objects to create the illusion of an arc behind and in front of the grids. Assign an arrowhead end from the Outline Pen dialog.*

That's the whole she-bang, or in this case, big bang. The text is a font called Swis721, which has a crisp boldness to it. This image is in the color section, and the corresponding file, physics.cdr, is in the \Chapt25\ subdirectory on the Companion CD.

I love designs like this, which to me seem simple yet visually engaging. When I show other people this artwork, simple never enters into their minds, as they are just dazzled by the image. That is a good thing, sort of the wizard-behind-the-curtain kind of illusion. Keep in mind it is the results that are important, not the process. Even if a design is very easy to create, never let on that it is, especially to clients. Only you will know what actually goes into a job, and a client will just be annoyed if you let on how easy the job was. Even the most generous person wants to feel like his or her job was special and that you worked hard on it. The goal in commercial design is for your artwork to look incredible and unique and be quick and easy to create; no one will be the wiser. This is one career where practice does in fact make perfect!

I love book cover designs. I think I will just retire and do nothing but scholastic book covers. Problem is, eventually I couldn't resist the urge to put in hidden graphics or messages for students to find as they while away the hours sitting in class! On second thought, I had better steer clear of those projects.

## Black Holes

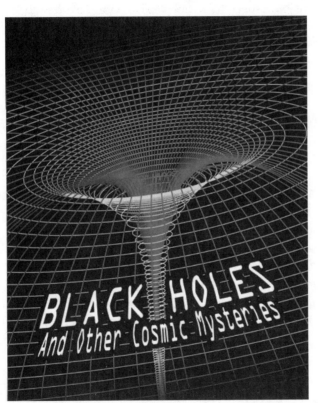

*Figure 25-19: The Blend roll-up can create the illusion of space by using lines to represent bending space and light.*

I am so thrilled with this image (see Figure 25-19), you have no idea. Why, you ask? Well, because it was the eventual solution to my black hole design problem, which is, how do you draw something that is in essence nothing and is so dense that even light can not escape? I spent many a moment staring off into space (uh, figuratively, not literally) and trying to come up with some kind of interesting and unique solution (some attempts went into the old Win95

Recycle Bin, but I did include a file on the Companion CD-ROM, called blckhol2.cdr, which was another interesting result of the experimenting that went into this project).

This image is a series of lines and circles blended together to create the bending of space and light that might take place around a black hole. I came up with the idea when I blended two ovals together with the Acceleration option enabled. This created a suggested funnel shape, made from the stacked wireframe circles. Like we have seen, grids give you a great way to suggest depth and dimension, especially to entities that don't exude those properties on their own (like the blackness of space or bottomless oceans). With grids on my mind, and the subject being black holes (which occur in the blackness of space), it was a natural to marry the two ideas into one, where a grid suggests both depth and dimension and also the shape of the black hole. The design also lent itself to bending light, which is also associated with black holes. It is a great graphic to illustrate an entity that is very enigmatic from a design per-spective in that it is literally a black hole, so dense even light can not escape. It isn't the only solution to this design problem, but as they say, "I may not know much about art, but I know what I like!" The best part of this design is that the majority of the work is pretty easy, although there is a section of mundane manual labor that I simply could not get around. Here is how to blend lines to create a 3D black hole grid:

1. Start with an oval drawn with the Ellipse tool and use the Skew arrows to tilt it up the right-hand side. Now duplicate the oval, move the dupli-cate down, and reduce it.

2. With the objects still selected, open the Blend roll-up. Switch to the Acceleration page and drag the Accelerate Objects slider way over to the left. Click Apply to create a black hole funnel (see Figure 25-20).

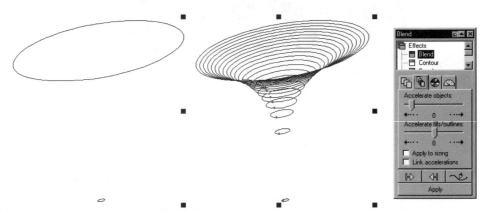

*Figure 25-20: Use the Blend roll-up with the Accelerate objects option to create a funnel-like illusion.*

3. Select the funnel blend and perform the familiar separation dance (Arrange | Separate, Arrange | Ungroup All). The first blend created the funnel part perfectly, but it also resulted in some gaps with far-apart ovals. With the objects all separated into individual ovals, you can select the oval on each end of a gap and fill them in with the Blend roll-up. Be sure to disable acceleration for these in-between blends. Vary the number of steps (sometimes only 1 or 2) to keep the spacing about even for all the blends to create a long-neck funnel out of ovals (see Figure 25-21).

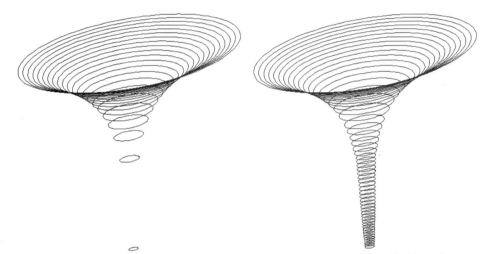

*Figure 25-21: The original blend pieces are broken up so that the gaps can be filled in with even more blends.*

4. Draw a rectangle to represent the page frame so you can begin to position the funnel object. Select and duplicate the largest funnel oval and enlarge it some 630%. Position this huge circle so that the top is closer to the top of the funnel than the bottom is. Now shift-select the huge circle and the largest funnel circle and use the Blend roll-up again to create a 22-step between them. You may need to fiddle with the number of steps to get evenly spaced circular rings. Select all of these grid rings, group them and give them a yellow outline and no fill (see Figure 25-22).

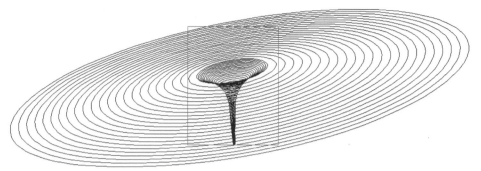

*Figure 25-22: The Blend roll-up creates rings between the funnel and a huge circle enlarged way beyond the page size.*

5. With the Bezier tool, draw lines along an imagined X- and Y-axis with the ends sucked into the black hole. Use the Shape tool to simplify the lines and to ensure that each line is made up of only three nodes. You don't need more than three nodes for a line like this, one at each end and another about midway down the funnel. You need the same number of nodes in all of the lines to ensure that the blends work smoothly in the next step. The top-right and bottom-left lines are magenta, and the other two cyan. All have a line weight of .013 inches (see Figure 25-23).

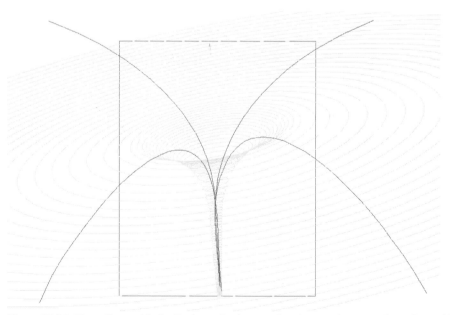

*Figure 25-23: Draw lines with the Bezier tool criss-crossing the page in an x orientation, with the ends sucked into the black hole.*

6. Select the two top lines and open the Blend roll-up. Make sure that there is no acceleration or rainbow effects enabled on the Blend roll-up, change the number of steps to 22, and click Apply. Then select the top-right and lower-right lines and perform the same blend. Repeat with the top-left and lower-left lines. Finally, the bottom two lines should also have the blend applied to them. If you build the blends in this order, the bottom blend objects will be on top of the others, which is what you want. Now our beams of light are being sucked into one spot. (For most projects, you could probably could get away with stopping here, but being a masochist/perfectionist, I had to continue to get an even more convincing illusion.) See Figure 25-24.

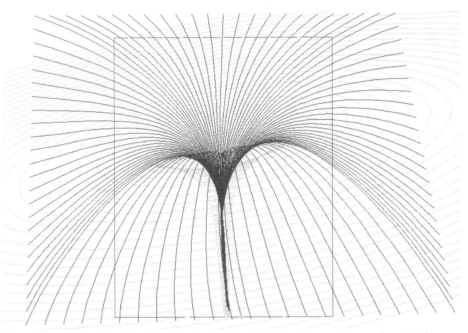

*Figure 25-24: Blend the lines to create the illusion of light and space being sucked into the black hole.*

7. Houston, we have a problem. (Or should I say Ottawa, since that is where CorelDRAW is from!) The illusion begins to break down because the front light beam blend needs part of the lines to go into the vortex and the other half to lie on top. This presents a nasty problem that we've

seen before, where an object needs to be both in front and behind another. Well, as we know, we can not bend CorelDRAW objects, so we need to fool the eye manually. We need to create three pieces to make the illusion work. From back to front, we need the cyan-magenta light beams being sucked into the vortex, then a half-copy of the vortex itself to place on top of the objects inside it. Finally, we need the light beam blend on top of the grid, bending into the vortex (see Figure 25-25). For an accurate 3D illusion to work, the blend elements need to be broken up so they can be stacked in front of and behind each other to create the illusion of bending light and space.

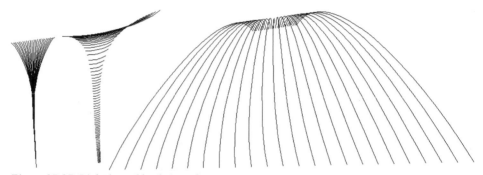

*Figure 25-25: Light beam blends into the vortex.*

8. Splitting up the front line blends is pretty easy. In the Simple Wireframe view, select the left and right lines and duplicate them. This will allow you to work with just the two lines and not all of the other associated blend objects. Now just at the point where the lines enter the vortex, add a node with the Shape tool by clicking the Add Node button on the Node Edit dialog (Ctrl+F10), then click the Break Curve button, and finally, separate the lines into two pieces with the Break Apart (Ctrl+K) command. Repeat this process with the right side so you get four curves; two small ones on the inside of the funnel, and two on top and outside the funnel (see Figure 25-26).

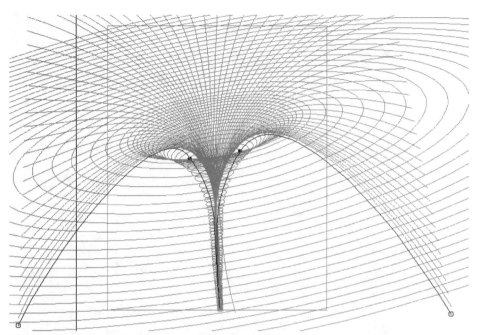

*Figure 25-26: To create blends that are on top of and behind the funnel, the control curves need to be broken in two.*

9. Now select the two small lines inside the funnel and create a 22-step blend between them. Repeat the same 22-step blend on the outside line pair. Fill the background rectangle with black. Things are falling into place, but we still need some way to make the bending light look like it is inside the funnel. With this front set of light beams as two separate groups, we can do it with the addition of one more set of lines (see Figure 25-27).

*Figure 25-27: With the four lines blended, the image is as before, only now it has two blend groups instead of one; the top group can be brought forward in the final steps to literally rest above the other lines.*

10. This, unfortunately, is the most tedious of the steps. I tried to make it easy, but there is no shortcut. It isn't hard, just repetitious. Select all of the small to large circles that make up the funnel and copy (Ctrl+C) them. Create a new document (Ctrl+N), and paste the circles (Ctrl+V) into it. CorelDRAW will paste the objects in the same place on the page that you made the copy so you can easily manipulate the duplicates here on a fresh page and then copy and paste them back into the main document later.

    With all the circles still selected, the first thing you should do is use the Convert To Curves (Ctrl+Q) command to eliminate any live ellipses so you can freely node-edit the curves. Then, and here is the annoying part, you have to go in and manually eliminate half of each of the ellipses. This seems hard at first, but in a few moments I found I had a rhythm going and the whole process took less than 10 minutes. Select a single target ellipse; then with the Shape tool, add a node on the right of the front of the ellipse. Click the Break Curve button on the Node Edit roll-up (or Property Bar) on this new node and then select and delete the node and the others that make up the back side of the ellipse. You need to repeat this process, which removes the backs of the ellipses without altering the arcs of the curves, on all of the ovals in the funnel. This will result in a stack of curves that align perfectly to the original whole circles but can be rested on top of the light beams inside of the funnel and also behind the beams on top of the funnel (see Figure 25-28).

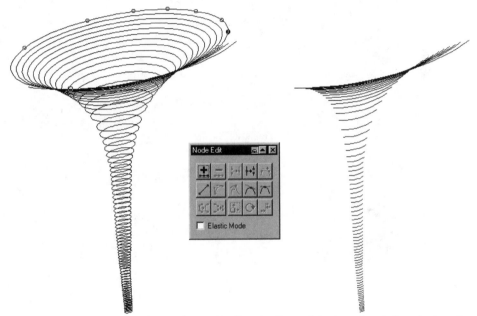

*Figure 25-28: The Shape tool is used to node-edit a duplicate of the funnel ovals in order to cut away the backs. This leaves a stack of curves for just the fronts; the curves will obscure the light beams inside of the funnel, correcting the illusion.*

11. Select all of the stacked sliced ovals, group them, and then copy them. Now switch back to the original art file, and paste (Ctrl+V) the stack into place. Use the Arrange | Order | Behind command, then click on the front light beam blend. This will place the stack in front of the beams being sucked into the vortex but behind those that are still reaching across the top toward the black hole. The end result has the eye fooled into seeing bending light in three dimensions (see Figure 25-29).

*Figure 25-29: Place the oval halves in front of the beams inside the vortex to make them look inside the black hole. With the second light beam in front of everything, the illusion of the beams being sucked into the vortex is complete.*

12. Artistic text elements, distorted with an envelope, appear to also be under the influence of the forces of the black hole. The font is called OCR-A (which is an original Optical Character Recognition font, back before OCR technology could read all fonts). To limit the objects to within the page, all of the pieces were selected and stuffed inside the black page rectangle with the PowerClip command.

This image can be seen in the color section or loaded off of the Companion CD-ROM out of the \Chapt25\ subdirectory. The file is called blckhole.cdr and is just waiting for you to pick apart! You will have to select the PowerClip and then Extract Contents to work with the pieces. (It's Chapter 25, and I'm sure by now you know what's up. I just say it for those people who insist on reading the end of books first!)

## Moving On

In this chapter, we created a lot of eye-popping artwork using ordinary lines. We used the Graph Paper tool to create simple grids, which we tweaked and twisted into new configurations, and then the Blend roll-up was once more called upon to perform its magic. The even spacing that the Blend function affords can create very interesting gridlike elements as well, as we saw in the last example.

Grids and line-based artwork has a myriad of uses. We saw how flashy color patterns and fancy grid work became book cover designs, but by no means are they limited to this use. Grids and line art are just too versatile to ignore. If you haven't already, you will find that there are many times when a simple grid can jazz up a boring logo or page layout, or even aid as an organizational tool. (Whenever you can divide a full-page image into smaller, more easily digested chunks, you will make it more appealing to your audience.)

In the next chapter, we will continue on the theme of illusions, only this time we'll add the concept of speed and motion. Once again we will trick the eye into seeing motion that isn't there (unless you happen to fling the book past your face). Fasten your seat belts, we are going to move into the fast lane, hit the gas, and taste some speed!

### ▼ Beyond f/x

Grids and vector-type graphics can work into many design applications. As I said earlier, you can create interesting and fantastical computer screens for video games or graphics where you want to suggest some sort of automated target tracking or what have you. (Remember the weapon systems on the *Millennium Falcon* from *Star Wars*? A grid!) The funnel grid can be used to suggest twisters, or you could work in a drop at the tip of the funnel to represent a digital version of a water droplet hitting a puddle (it has that unique shape of the inverted funnel). Grids work out well to organize information for easy consumption, like a hierarchy chart for data. Or map out sales territories with a grid over a map. Or create a Web navigation scheme where each page is part of a grid and visited pages go black. The uses are endless, as grids are such a design staple. Remember the grid design formula if you want to appease a generic, waffling client. Brush script over Eurobold, hovering over a grid. If that doesn't do it, toss in a drop shadow and a few palm trees!

# chapter 26
# Speedy Things

These days, with multimedia and the World Wide Web, designs are able to be much more than simple static images. Animations, jumping and dancing icons, sounds, music, streaming video, you name it, make the modern electronic design experience very energetic and interactive. A side effect of this new media avalanche is that it also raises the bar for traditional print applications. No longer is the playing field level, with the flat, two-dimensional page directly competing with all kinds of other media for the reader's attention. Somehow, your printed pages must gain and hold a viewer's attention without the benefit of sound or animation. It's downright unfair!

In this chapter, we level the playing field by looking at a few techniques to get your images to pop off of the page and look like they are moving and alive. In the first example, I use three variations of the same theme to suggest motion in a racing buggy by using the Blend roll-up and a bitmap blur effect. In the second example, a jet fighter is given speed trails with the Interactive Transparency tool to make it speed across the page. Finally, a combination of effects is used to create a blurry background for a speeding motorcycle. It's a fast ride guaranteed to blur your vision, but you can handle it!

## Bouncing Buggies

*Figure 26-1: Using the Blend roll-up, you can suggest movement by blending either just the object outline or the entire image (top and center). With a bitmap of the image, you can exploit the motion blur effects to create some zip and zoom (bottom).*

The graphic in Figure 26-1 is from a piece I was going to use to illustrate an article I wrote about racing remote-controlled model cars. (Believe it or not, I actually can write about things other than CorelDRAW!) The magazine I was working for sent me a car to build and review. Well, I ended up smashing the test car into a gazillion little bits when it crashed in the empty swimming pool, which really annoyed my contacts at that magazine and quickly ended my career as a model car journalist.

Getting an image to look like it is moving isn't really that difficult. Using comic-strip-like motion trail images, both straight and strewn along a path to suggest rotation, and blurring a duplicate of the image are universally understood ways of showing motion. In the next sections, we will look at a few tricks to add motion to my bouncing buggy illustration. Each technique suggests a different kind of motion and speed, so you will have to choose the one that is right for your fast designs.

## Green Ghost

One way to suggest motion is to leave a ghostly trail of color behind the speeding object. Like the effect it creates, this trick is also a quick and easy blend. The primary object is blended to a duplicate, which has been placed to the back and behind, and filled with the background color. The blend fades the original into the duplicate, which is the same color as the background, so it appears to fade away altogether. Here is how to make a fade-out effect from the buggy to the background:

1. The buggy started as an ink illustration, which I converted into vector artwork using the Corel OCR-Trace utility. The CMX trace file was imported into CorelDRAW where it was easy to colorize the pieces. This kind of file is a lot of smaller objects resting on a big black shape. By selecting the smaller objects and combining some of them (such as all of the pieces that make up the main body), you can assign a fountain fill that flows across the entire car body. If you don't select and combine these individual objects and fill them with fountain fills, they will not line up correctly (see Figure 26-2).

*Figure 26-2: An ink illustration is converted into CorelDRAW objects using the OCR-Trace utility. Once imported into CorelDRAW, the pieces can be selected and given outline and fill attributes. Combining several objects that make up one thing (like the car body back, which is separated from the front by a big spring), will make patterns and fills line up.*

▼ **Road Maps for Painters**

One thing that I have used illustrations such as this buggy for is to work out color and graphics schemes for the real world. You don't need much more than a simple line drawing of a car, motorcycle, jet ski, you name it, to work out really cool graphics schemes.

You can then give this road map to the people who actually paint the graphics onto the vehicles for them to use as a reference. Or you can take it one step further and design the graphics to scale and then use the artwork to create the actual masks used when painting. Most computerized sign companies will also cut paint masks for you right from your CorelDRAW files, using big sheets of masking tape material instead of vinyl. If paint isn't your style, you can also find places that will print full-color, sun- and weather-proof images on vinyl for stickers of all sizes, again right from your CorelDRAW files. A dull-looking vehicle is simply unacceptable.

2. Because an image like this one is a bunch of smaller objects on a big black outline, it is easy to select and duplicate the outline. Duplicate the big black outline pad, give it a solid white outline with no fill, and move it up and to the right. This is the point that your speed blur will fade to solid white. Send this white outline to the back (Shift+PgDn). See Figure 26-3.

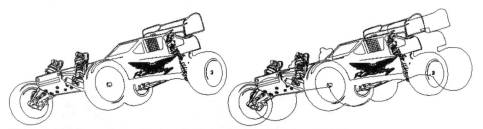

*Figure 26-3: A trace image is a bunch of small objects on a big outline curve (shown here in Wireframe view). Select and duplicate the outline shape and move it behind and in back of the original for the blur effect.*

3. Shift-select both the new white outline object and the original black outline object and open the Blend roll-up. Click Apply to create a 20-step blend between the two and create a black-to-white speed-blur effect. For control over the beginning and end colors in the blend, select the black control curve and duplicate it. Now you have the black outline on top of the black control curve. Press the Tab key to select the next youngest object (the duplicate is the newest object, with the original behind it being next in line). With the control curve selected, change the fill to any color, such as the green that I chose for the color page (see Figure 26-4).

*Figure 26-4: Blending the black outline curve to a duplicate in white creates a stark motion blur. Duplicating the control curve allows you to change the colors in the blend to soften the speed blur.*

This is a quick and easy way to get your objects moving.

## Motion Steps

To offer up a path of travel, you can blend an all-white copy of the buggy along a path. This not only shows motion, but where the buggy has been and a direction of travel. Here is how to do it:

1. Start with a colorized version of your buggy, drag-select all of the pieces in it, and group them. Duplicate the group and give the duplicate a white fill and outline by clicking both the left and right mouse button over the white onscreen color well. This will fill all of the objects within the group with white and change the outlines, if any, to white as well. Move the duplicate to where you want the speed blur to fade out entirely and rotate the buggy in a upward angle.

2. Now draw a line with the Bezier tool to show a range of motion. Shift-select both the colorized and white-only buggy groups and prepare them for blending by choosing the Arrange | Order | Reverse Order command (we need the colorized version in front). See Figure 26-5.

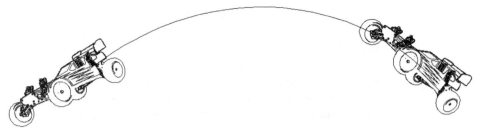

*Figure 26-5: A colorized buggy (on the right, in Wireframe view) and an all-white copy (on left) will be blended along the curve to show a range of motion.*

3. Open the Blend roll-up and create a blend along the path. Vary the number of steps to as few or as many as you wish. Be sure to enable the Blend Along Full Path option, and if you like, try the Rotate All Objects option as well (see Figure 26-6).

*Figure 26-6: Blend the buggies along the path to create a trail of image duplicates.*

4. To make all of the blended objects more ghostly white, use the Accelerate Fills/Outlines slider on the Blend roll-up. Dragging to the left makes the duplicates favor the white end of the blend, so they all become more pale (see Figure 26-7).

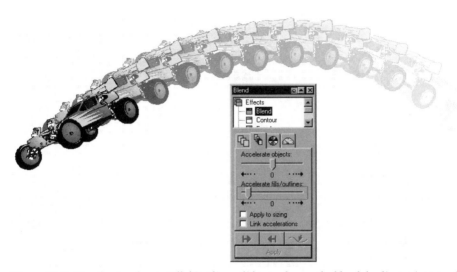

*Figure 26-7: Use the Accelerate Fills/Outlines slider to change the blend duplicates into a paler set of objects.*

That's all it takes to give your objects a trail of motion that indicates rotated movement (as opposed to simple linear movement). Vary the number of steps for many or few ghostly images.

## Transparent & Blurry

This last technique uses a duplicate of the buggy to create a bitmap, and from there, a motion blur. Like the first example, it leaves a ghostly trace where the buggy has been. This time, however, the entire subdued image is in the speed blur. Here is how to get blurry eyed:

1. Select your buggy group again and draw a rectangle around it. Give the rectangle no outline or fill attributes, as its function is to provide a transparent background for the bitmap. Shift-select the outline rectangle and the buggy shape and duplicate them. Move the duplicate to the side and convert the image to a bitmap from the Bitmap menu. Choose whatever color depth and resolution is appropriate for your project (72 dpi RGB for onscreen, 300 dpi CMYK for print) and make sure the Transparent Background option is enabled before you click OK (see Figure 26-8).

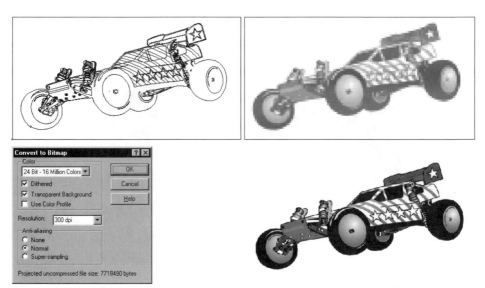

*Figure 26-8: Use the Convert to Bitmap option to convert the vector art into a bitmap. The top row (in Wireframe view) shows the no-fill, no-outline rectangle used to assign the area for the transparent background.*

**TIP**

When you use the Convert to Bitmap function's transparent background option, the transparent background remains that way through any and all of the bitmap effects you apply to the object, so only the image itself shows through. So why is this cool? Because you don't have to worry about certain colors being see-through the way you do with the bitmap color mask.

If you had created a bitmap with a white background and then used a bitmap color mask to make the background transparent, whoops, the stars and stripes would be transparent as well. While this could be a cool effect, it's generally not what you'll be shooting for.

2. Select the bitmap, and from the Bitmaps menu, choose Blur | Motion. Now crank the Distance value up to 50 and change the direction to hit your object head on. Click OK to fuzz the image (see Figure 26-9).

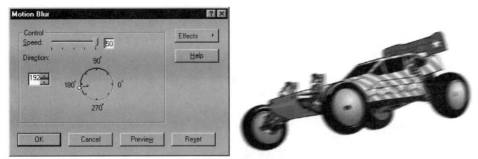

*Figure 26-9: Use the Motion Blur bitmap filter to add a speed-blur effect to the bitmap.*

3. You can repeat the Motion Blur filter as many times as you wish to really get the image super fuzzy. To add white to the bitmap and consequently soften the image, when you have the Motion Blur dialog open, click the Effects button, then choose the Color Adjustment I Brightness-Contrast-Intensity menu option. From the dialog, increase the Brightness value to make the image lighter and change the other values if you so desire, using the Preview button (looks like an eyeball) to get a look at how the changes affect the image. When you are satisfied with the changes, click OK (see Figure 26-10).

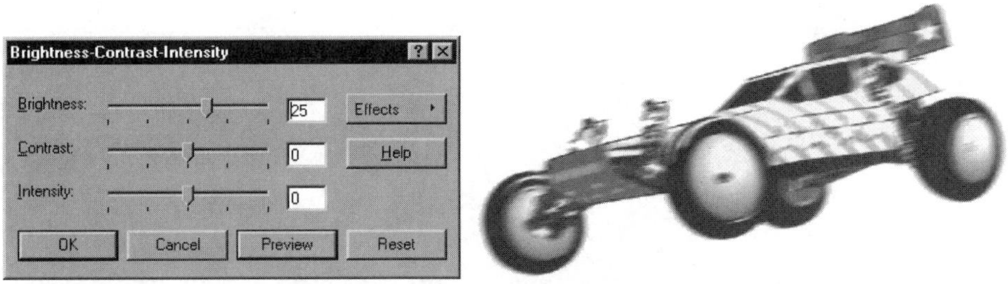

*Figure 26-10: Use the Brightness-Contrast-Intensity dialog (available from the other bitmap filter dialogs by clicking the Effects button) to lighten the blurred bitmap to become a background image.*

4. Now place the original buggy objects on top of the bitmap to contrast the light, fuzzy blur with the crisp, high-contrast vector objects. Remember that the bitmap background is transparent, so you can place objects behind the racing buggy, such as this checkerboard, to add depth to the design. In addition to depth, you will have people scratching their heads wondering how you blurred a vector image (see Figure 26-11).

*Figure 26-11: Stack the bitmap and original artwork on top of other background elements to exploit the transparent background of the bitmaps.*

For even more versatility, instead of using the brightness/contrast on your background blur bitmap, use an interactive transparency to give it a semi-opaque look. Use the Uniform mode or a fountain fill for different looks (see Figure 26-12).

*Figure 26-12: Use the Interactive Transparency tool instead of modifying the brightness setting on the bitmap to get a softer background image.*

Adding speed or motion to an image might not immediately seem very practical, but there are many uses for the process. For example, the blending technique is a great way to add both depth and a sense of energy to a logo. To see what I mean, examine Figure 26-13. Here the front logo group is blended to a smaller all-white duplicate. The results are much more interesting than the original logo alone.

*Figure 26-13: Using the speed blur technique of blending a logo group to a smaller, all-white duplicate makes for a more interesting image.*

That's enough of the bouncing buggies. The race continues in the color section and in a file called rccars.cdr, pitting in the \Chapt26\ subdirectory on the Companion CD-ROM. Open the file and experiment with the blend steps and the acceleration options for the live blends in the racing logo and bouncing buggies. The logo is especially interesting to toy with. A few changes in the acceleration options and you get a totally different set of results!

## Jet Trails

*Figure 26-14: Using the Interactive Transparency tool, a jet is given a sense of speed by leaving clear vapor trails in its path.*

Motion trails are great for adding a sense of speed and motion to an object, as we just saw. The buggy examples, however, did not have a busy background to contend with, which poses some new problems. You will want to create a sense of motion that is appropriate and also transparent so that background details still shine through. This is a great use of the Interactive Transparency tool.

Adding *movles* (pronounced moo-vels) to a picture is a device commonly used in the comics to suggest motion. Movles are lines showing where an object has come from and the speed that it was traveling, as seen in Figure 26-15.

*Figure 26-15: Movles are lines that suggest motion and direction, often used in comic strips to suggest action.*

This same kind of technique can be given more finesse in CorelDRAW using the Interactive Transparency tool to create subtle but convincing vapor trails for a screaming jet, or any other object you want to give motion to. You could use the same technique, for example, on an arrow showing how to put pieces together in an instruction booklet or installation guide. Motion effects pop up in many design projects. Transparency effects hint at motion without distracting too much from the overall design. Here is how to make a jet scream across the sky:

1. Once again, I turned to the versatile art archives of the CorelDRAW clip-art CD. Import a cool plane from the \clipart\aircraft\jets\ subdirectory. To give the entire plane a fat outline, group all of the plane objects, duplicate them, and give the duplicate a fat .05-inch black outline. Enable the round corner option from the Outline Pen dialog, and then send this fat outline group behind the original objects. This is an old line-art illustration trick that I still like to use to isolate images from the background (see Figure 26-16).

*Figure 26-16: A clip-art jet is given the fat-outline treatment by assigning a heavy outline to a duplicate group of the objects sent behind the originals.*

 **The Corel Balloon**

For some reason, I have always wanted to do a graphic showing some evil nasty thing happening to the Corel balloon, despite how much I love the people at Corel Corporation. They even gave me a ride in that infernal thing over Las Vegas during the big COMDEX computer convention. Boy was that a surreal moment. Nothing like entrusting your life to wicker!

Anyway, I couldn't resist the parody, so here I am in a jet shooting down that little wimpy balloon (see Figure 26-14 and the color section). CorelDRAW needs a more hard-core symbol anyway, in my opinion. I'll take a vehicle that screams across the sky breaking the sound barrier while armed to the teeth over a drifting gas bag any day! But that's just me.

Why a balloon, anyway? What's the scoop? Well, what I learned while floating over Las Vegas is that the balloon logo is homage to the city of Ottawa, Canada, location of Corel's corporate headquarters. Apparently, Ottawa hosts a world-famous hot air balloon gathering every year. Ottawa is so proud of this event that the city tries to have hot air balloons painting the skies year-round. Yes, even in the dead of winter.

2. Draw a rectangle the size of the desired page and send it to the back. Use a texture fill called Aerial Clouds from the Samples Library to fill the rectangle. Position and rotate your jet fighter pieces into place in the center of the sky rectangle and arrange any other graphical elements key to the design. Use guidelines to help align the objects, especially text elements, so all pieces line up perfectly. This kind of alignment may not be amazingly obvious in a busy design such as this, but subconsciously, your eye finds these guidelines to organize and help digest a complex image. Set up guidelines off of the wing tips and other elements to set the stage for drawing the speed blurs (see Figure 26-17).

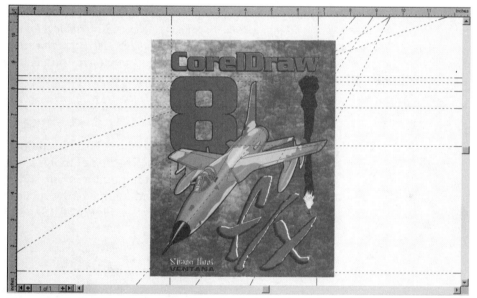

*Figure 26-17: Guidelines help align objects in a design and are also useful to set up vanishing points or help block up art before it is drawn.*

**TIP** *If you're happy with your texture fill selection but want to see just a slightly different variant, use the Preview button in the Texture Fill dialog. When you click this button (without having made any other changes), CorelDRAW will use a random number generator for the variables available to that texture to produce a different variant of the original. Keep clicking the Preview button until you find a combination that best suits your needs, or tweak the number values manually until you get just what you want. We aim to please here on Planet Corel.*

**TIP**
*Although I really don't use guidelines too much, the Guidelines feature can be useful. From the View menu, enable the Rulers option. Now to create a nonprinting, onscreen-only guideline, simply place your pointer in either the top or left ruler and drag it onto the desk top. If you drag from the top down, you will have a horizontal guideline, and from the left, a vertical one.*

*You can drag these over your work space to help align objects manually, or if you enable the Snap to Guidelines feature from the Layout menu, objects will "stick" to the nearest guideline as you move them. To create angled guidelines, drag off a guideline as usual and then click on it. Now rotation arrows will appear, as well as the familiar axis of rotation. (In CorelDRAW 7, the arrows change when you move from the dotted line to the solid ends of the guideline, so you can slant them.) Now drag the rotation arrows to spin the guideline. If you need a specific angle or location for a guideline, use the Guidelines Setup dialog, found under the Layout menu, or double-click on a specific guideline. Here you can set the exact location and angle for each guideline and also remove them again individually, or make them all go away with the Clear All button.*

*Corel giveth, and Corel taketh away.*

3. Use the Bezier tool to draw straight-line shapes for the trailing edges you want to have vapor trails coming off of. The Bezier tool is great for this kind of work, as you need only click from point to point to draw a straight-lined object. Try to draw the ending line of the curve in the same angle as the edge wing it is paired with (see Figure 26-18).

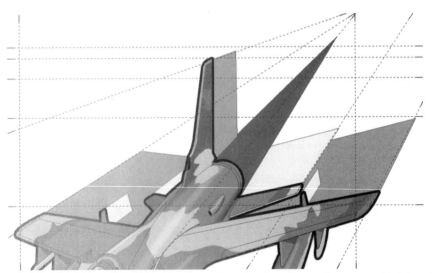

*Figure 26-18: Use the Bezier tool to draw objects for the vapor trails coming off of the wings.*

4. Fill all of the vapor trail shapes white and then select the Interactive Transparency tool. Now one by one, drag the tool along each vapor object to give it a white-to-clear fade. Start at the point where the object butts against the wing, then drag out toward the sky. You will have to experiment with the placement of the clear point on the transparency fountain fill to make the fade look correct for each wing. Straight up or straight across sometimes seems to work better than following the flight path. Experiment to find the angle that looks best (see Figure 26-19).

*Figure 26-19. The Interactive Transparency tool gives the solid objects the white-to-clear fountain fills that create the vapor trail look.*

5. More power, Scotty! For an afterburner flame, use a compound blend element. Use the Bezier or Freehand tool to draw a flame object shooting in the correct flight path. Give this object no outline and a cyan fill. Duplicate and downsize this flame shape for a midpoint and give the duplicate a magenta fill. Duplicate and downsize one more time, for the hot spot, and make this smallest duplicate yellow. Now select the cyan and magenta shapes and use the Blend roll-up to create the 20-step pink-to-blue color transition. From the Simple Wireframe view, select the magenta and then the small yellow shape and use the Blend roll-up again to create the 20-step yellow to magenta color transition. Flame on! See Figure 26-20.

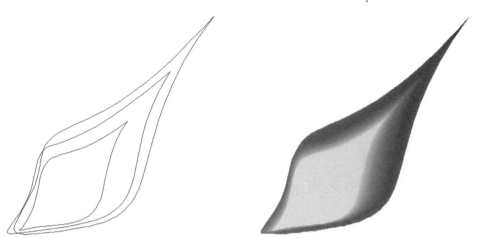

*Figure 26-20: Blend three flame shapes (on left in Wireframe view) to create the afterburner discharge.*

The jet screeches across the sky in the color section and in a file called jetcover.cdr in the \Chapt26\ subdirectory on the Companion CD-ROM. If you open the file, you can check out the vapor trails yourself or dissect any of the other artwork pieces. By now you must recognize the metallic and shading effects from previous chapters, so I won't bore you with those details. For the aircraft nose art, I stole the Slimy Dog tattoo from Chapter 12 and used the rotation arrows and the sizing and skew handles to put the bitmap in place. It's amazing how much you can get accomplished with just the Pick tool.

The nature of your design will dictate the kind of motion effect you need. For simple motion, try a movle or a fade into the background blend like we did with the first buggy. Or you may want more steps to indicate motion and position—if you were making a diagram or instruction book, for example. The transparency tricks add the action more subtly, which may also make things look too fast. It sometimes takes a few tries to get what you like. The buggy blend along a path had me staring at the screen for quite a while, as I kept changing the number of steps from higher to lower numbers. If you can't make up your mind, it is a good idea to close the file and work on something else for a while. You start to lose perspective when you work on something too long, but if you come back later, things are much clearer.

## North Pole Racing

**COLOR STUDIO**

*Figure 26-21: Creating a background in CorelDRAW, then converting the image to a bitmap, allows you to add a sense of speed with the motion blur bitmap effect.*

The previous examples deal with using design techniques to suggest motion. This tutorial looks at a technique that mimics the results a photographer gets when they take pictures of speeding objects. So in a sense, this may be the most real technique, even though again it is just an optical illusion.

A speed blur is a great way to make Santa's racing motorcycle look fast. Santa's racing team?! Well, every year I try and come up with an interesting holiday card, and at one time most of our clients were in the motor-sports market, so this card was a big hit (see Figure 26-21).

This image is typical of photos you will see of race vehicles on the move. The photographer, in an attempt to keep the vehicle in focus, will move the camera along with the subject as they shoot the photo. The effect is that the subject stays in focus, but the surrounding images are fuzzy. Replicating the real or natural world in design is a sure-fire way to make an image more believable, even if it is complete fantasy. There are many other uses for this technique beyond suggesting speed. This is a good design vehicle to isolate and emphasize a person from a crowd or other background noise or to use anywhere else you want to draw attention to a crisp object surrounded by a sea of fuzziness. Here is how to take an object and make it look like it is moving by blurring the background:

1. In typical Shane fashion this image once again started as an ink drawing. I didn't convert it the illustration with the OCR-Trace utility but rather just drew objects underneath the bitmap with the Freehand and Bezier tool to color it, as we have seen before in Chapter 18. See Figure 26-22.

*Figure 26-22: An ink illustration is scanned and then colorized by drawing objects beneath it in CorelDRAW. When the black bitmap is laid on top (right), the image appears to be full color.*

2. The next step is to make the image racy by adding numbers and sponsor logos. As Santa's race effort is fictitious, I had to invent a bunch of potential companies that would logically stand behind the great bearded one. This was not a problem and made for a very amusing afternoon! Using our formula for logos (serif font over sans-serif, or brush over block type, etc.) and the impressive CorelDRAW font collection, it wasn't long before I had a collection of appropriate logos.

**TIP** *If you ever want to take an ordinary vehicle and make it look racy, just stick a big number on it and then plaster it with sponsor logos; suddenly you are trackside!*

3. Group the objects in a logo and use the Pick tool to position, size, and rotate the object. To get the upward curve in a logo, use a single-arc envelope. Use the envelope on the logo group before you rotate it. It is easier to get a simple arc with your image horizontally oriented than at an angle. Plaster the rider and the motorcycle with the logos and you're off. I'm telling you, you could make a bowl of fruit look racy with the number and logos technique! See Figure 26-23.

*Figure 26-23: Use CorelDRAW's huge font library to invent racing logos, then stick them all over the rider and motorcycle to give it a racy look.*

4. Draw a box behind your rider at the desired page limit size. Then use a texture fill or any pattern to create an abstract background. Pick something that has strong enough light and dark areas to make the blur effect interesting (I used the Aerial clouds texture fill from the Samples Library). Now select all of the motorcycle rider objects, group them, and duplicate them. Move the duplicate on top of the bitmap background. You don't want to forget to make a duplicate of the original CorelDRAW motorcycle objects, as once again we will be converting them into a bitmap.

5. Select the motorcycle and background object, and from the Bitmaps menu, choose Convert to Bitmap. (For my project, my goal was a two-color design, black and red.) Two-color projects are cheap to print but look so much nicer than just black alone. For this reason, though, I needed the background to be grayscale. Your project may be different, and you may want a full-color background; it's up to you. From the Convert to Bitmap dialog, select the desired color depth and click OK (see Figure 26-24).

*Figure 26-24: The motorcycle and background are merged into one using the Convert to Bitmap dialog.*

6. From the Bitmaps menu, choose Blur | Motion to open the Motion Blur dialog. Crank the Distance variable up to around 50 and set the Direction of the blur coming at the rider (0 degrees). Click OK. Increase the Distance value if you wish to get a really exaggerated speed-blur look (see Figure 26-25).

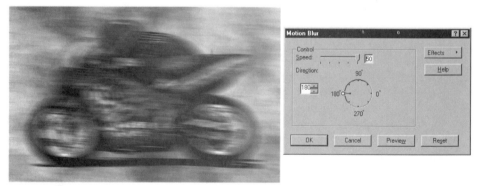

*Figure 26-25: A high Distance value set from the Motion Blur dialog create an exaggerated sense of speed.*

7. Drop the original crisp and colorized version of the motorcyclist back onto the background and you are finished.

The race is on in the color section and in the santa.cdr file found in the \Chapt26\ subdirectory on the Companion CD-ROM. If you open the file, you can see how the motorcycle objects rest on the blurred bitmap. Delete the background bitmap and repeat the steps to come up with your own fuzzy background image. Try a street scene or other bitmap for a unique look for your racing vehicles. Using the transparent background technique from the buggies example, you can also place fuzzy objects in front of the motorcyclist to really get a cool look full of depth and action (see Figure 26-26).

*Figure 26-26: Use the Transparent background technique to place blurry objects in front of the crisp motorcycle to add depth as well as motion to a scene.*

## Moving On

In this chapter, we looked at many ways to get motion in your static designs. Using blurring, duplicating, and transparency techniques, your objects were given life, depth, and the energy to shoot across the page. Better get a paperweight to hold 'em down!

In the next chapter, we will look at how different CorelDRAW images not only can suggest movement, but also make it happen. Using pieces generated in CorelDRAW, buttons and screens come to life in your Web and other onscreen applications. So warm up your browser and clean your mouse balls because we are going to whack some buttons and design some screens.

### ▼ Beyond f/x

As I've mentioned throughout the chapter, there are all kinds of uses for this design technique. In advertising, a catch phrase or call to action can also literally be active if you use techniques to suggest movement and have the words jump out at you. Guides or instruction books can use the multiple subdued images along a path to show how things fit together or come apart. An object can be pulled out of a busy background for emphasis, or a character placed in a blurry landscape, with blurry nightmarish characters in front of and behind the subject.

Of course, the obvious uses in motor-sport logos or images also spring to mind. Speed has many connotations that you can exploit, in promotional materials or anywhere. Concepts like "Speeding Into the Future" or "The Company That Is on the Move" can work into appropriately speedy graphics. How many times have you heard the words *fast* or *furious* or *high-paced* used in the world of business? Now you can create graphics that are synonymous with those concepts! Hurry! Urgent! Get going!

# chapter 27

# Buttons & Screens

If by now your artwork has not evolved to include multimedia and Web page development, it is just a matter of time before it will. Whereas the huge multimedia hype of a few years back hasn't quite panned out as anticipated, the influence of the World Wide Web has. Everyone and his brother-in-law (literally—my brother-in-law has a Web development company) is making Web pages these days, with a level of ability that varies from professional to pathetic. I am no exception, with my own handful of obligatory Web sites under my cyber-belt. The nice thing is you already have the tools and ability to explore this medium; you just have to take on the challenge!

The advantages to developing onscreen projects with CorelDRAW are many. For starters, you get all of the obvious benefits of endless versatility, countless effects, and color options at your fingertips. CorelDRAW objects, as we have seen in many examples, are ready for animation, and with PhotoPaint and CorelDream in the graphics bundle, you are armed for bear! Basically the whole enchilada, including all of the effects in this book, can work their way into your multimedia projects.

There are incredibly strong advantages to using CorelDRAW for multimedia and Web development beyond the obvious graphics factor. CorelDRAW images are vector based, which means that graphics designed for a low-res onscreen application, such as a Web site, can migrate directly into other high-res peripheral support material, such as advertising and printed promotion.

With the never-ending versatility of CorelDRAW artwork, your original efforts in the planning stages (hierarchy charts, dummy pages, site plan, story boards, etc.) become the groundwork for the actual images. Why enter that text twice? A font change, new fill color, a unique background, and suddenly your comps are fleshed out into the real deal. Recycle, exploit, divide, and conquer!

In this chapter we will look at creating graphics useful for Web sites and multimedia applications. The first section deals with creating multiple images for a custom control panel to animate buttons for "at rest," "roll-over," and "depressed" states. Then we look to exploit some of the built-in Web features of CorelDRAW to build and maintain that constantly changing headache lurking on the Web—the site map. Then, we will design actual Web pages using CorelDRAW to work out the look of the whole experience first and then breaking up the images into Web-friendly little chunks. This chapter has additional support files on the Companion CD-ROM, so slap that baby in the drive and let's go!

## Sit, Roll Over, Lie Down

*Figure 27-1: CorelDRAW objects are perfect for creating multistate buttons. On the left we have the buttons at rest, in the center the buttons each light up as the mouse travels over them, and finally, the buttons flatten out when pressed with a mouse click.*

These days, buttons are more prolific on the Web than coffee houses are in Seattle. The whole GUI interface things thrives on buttons, with your entire work day filled with pointing and clicking on those little buggers. What surprises me is that, for the most part, buttons and user interfaces look like they were added at the last minute with little or no creativity involved in their layout or construction. I am far from your super Webmeister, but I at least try to make interesting button shapes and navigation panels.

If you plan ahead and know what you need before you even start thinking about graphics, you will be much better off. In this example, I figured out all of the buttons I would want on the control panel way ahead of time (see Figure 27-10). Then, I created an interface that had all of the buttons, with the primary buttons larger than secondary options. In CorelDRAW it is easy to create custom button designs based on your exact needs at hand, and the result will be a unique interface that is much more interesting than those rectangles everyone else is using. Once you have the basic interface in place, it is easy to create graphics for multiple button states. Instead of just lying there, your buttons can be very animated. They can change colors when the pointer is moved on top of them (called a *roll over*), when they are clicked on (*mouseDown*), and also when they are released (*mouseUp*). Even if you are not creating images for onscreen applications, faux interfaces and buttons make interesting design elements for print applications. Here is how to design and build a custom user interface and create graphics for all of the button states:

1. First you need to establish the number and type of buttons needed in your control panel. I needed a total of six buttons, with two of them as large arrows for "next" and "back" navigation. I chose an up/down configuration to facilitate a round-center area that would later be filled with an animation. The oval center mapped out the look of the control panel, although the same basic scheme would work for a left/right orientation of the buttons. Use the Ellipse tool to draw out an oval. Then use the Rectangle tool to draw a perfect square centered to the oval. Duplicate the square and enlarge it slightly. Use the Shape tool to round out the corners on the larger rectangle. Select the smaller rectangle and rotate it –45 degrees like a diamond. These three shapes will generate all of the buttons for our custom interface (see Figure 27-2).

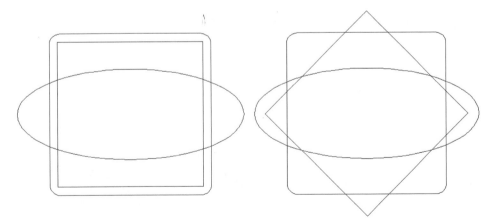

*Figure 27-2: Two simple squares and an oval are all that is needed to create a custom button interface.*

2. Select the oval shape, open the Trim roll-up from the Arrange menu, and enable only the Other Objects Leave Original option. Click Trim and then click on the round-corner square. This will cut the oval away from the center of that shape. Now select the diamond, click Trim again, and once more click on the round-corner curve. Select the round-corner curve and create four individual buttons with the Break Apart command. Now select the oval again, click Trim, and then click on the diamond. This will create the up and down arrows after you use the Break Apart command to separate the shape into two curves. Fill all these buttons with a neutral gray color (see Figure 27-3).

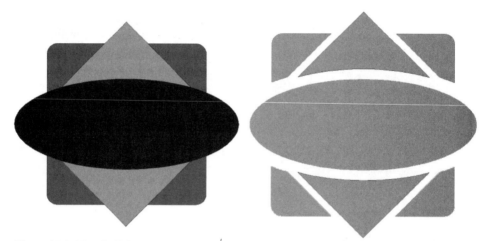

*Figure 27-3: Use the Trim command on the shapes to create three separate curves (on left). Use the Break Apart command on each curve to create the individual buttons (on right).*

3. Open the Extrude roll-up and use the bevel page to add depth to the button shapes. Repeat the same bevel for all of the objects in the group. Then add Artistic Text elements to label each button. I used a font called BankGothic. When finished, duplicate the entire button group and set it aside. Now to freeze the bevel groups, use the Arrange I Separate command. Then follow with the Arrange I Ungroup All command so that all of the pieces can be individually manipulated. This was done so that the top pieces of the beveled buttons could be given an interesting custom

color blend to look more like shiny metal. The oval object was exported as an Adobe Illustrator file for use in CorelDream. I used the 3D program to create the cells for an animation that plays continuously inside the navigation panel. (See Chapter 30 for more on working with CorelDream.) The center panel oval could also be a great place for a message board that changes to tell you what each button does as you roll it over. My program was so simple I didn't need a pop-up help screen, but you might (see Figure 27-4).

*Figure 27-4: The button shapes are given depth with an extrude bevel; then the faces are filled with a custom color blend to look shiny.*

4. This first group of buttons with the black text were each individually selected and exported for the "buttons at rest" graphic. Select and change the black text to red-filled, yellow-outlined text elements. These again were individually selected and exported for the "roll-over state" button graphics.

5. Select the duplicate button group with the live bevels from step 3. Now change the bevel depth from deep to very shallow on each button shape. Also change the text to some other color, like blue. These buttons when individually selected and exported will become the "down-buttons" graphic (see Figure 27-5).

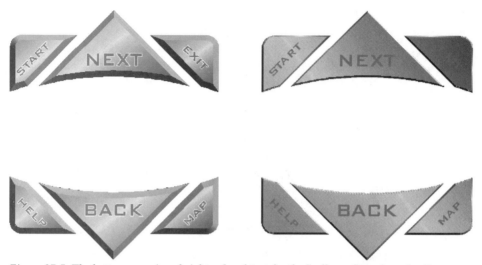

*Figure 27-5: The buttons are given bright-colored text for the "roll-over" group; a duplicate set is given shallow bevels for the pressed button group.*

Each button graphic was imported into Macromedia Director as its own cast member. The "at rest" group was laid out on the page with the animation oval in the center completing the console. The Lingo script swaps out each button graphic depending on the state and location of the mouse. If the mouse rolls over a button, the program swaps the existing graphic with the "roll-over" art. If the button is depressed, the art is again swapped out, this time with the "button-down" art. You can also get the same action on a Web site using JavaScript or aftermarket Java programming tools. My Web site (http://www.corelmag.com/shane) uses a roll-over JavaScript to change the button graphics when you move the cursor over them. I did this with the help of a program called Mousetrap, which is available online from Sausage Inc. (at www.sausage.com). I love the Sausage mini-programs, which work great and are easy to use, and because their company name makes Slimy Dog seem less ridiculous.

**CD-ROM**

You can watch the button action work firsthand by starting the doggone.exe program, nestled in the \Chapt27\ subdirectory of the Companion CD-ROM. With the program running, click on the spinning globe to initiate the introduction sequence. After the introduction (which you can skip by clicking on the slow-scrolling text), the control panel will appear with the buttons made in this exercise. They will just sit there until you move the mouse over them, and then they spring to life. Click on the Next button to move to the next screen and notice how the button changes to the "down" graphic when you do. This is a pretty common example of button action, which you can expand on to create your own cool interface.

You could easily elaborate on the buttons; you could spin or what not when you click them, or you could even create an animation for the "at rest" panel to entice your viewer to click a certain button. The potential is really unlimited. The native button pieces are in a file called buttons.cdr, also located in the \Chapt27\ directory. This file also contains the custom interface from the next example. These were made in exactly the same way, starting with simple shapes and then creating custom shapes using the Trim function, and finally adding depth and shading with the Extrude roll-up. Much more interesting than a row of rectangles!

## Out-of-Site Map

*Figure 27-6: Setting up a living document such as a Web site map in CorelDRAW is the easiest way to maintain the graphic as well as generate the associated image map needed for Web navigation.*

Color me fickle, but I can never seem to be satisfied with my Web site. After a while I end up hating what I have and can't rest until it meets my criteria of the moment. Currently I am working on a total redo, calling for the Internet equivalent of a Web site mulligan. My old site was built as an experiment years ago to help me get acquainted with HTML and is by no means up to my current demanding standards.

One big problem with Web sites in general is that by nature they are always changing. Where this really becomes a hassle is with pages like site maps, which are a practical and popular addition to a Web experience but a big pain to implement and a bigger one to maintain. With the built-in Web features that CorelDRAW now possesses, this task is no longer as nightmarish as it once was. Using the Internet Objects toolbar, you can associate a URL with every CorelDRAW object right in your design and then generate both the graphic and the image map directly from the CDR file. With an ever-changing entity like a site map, this is a gift from the cyber-gods! Here is how to set up a graphic with URL associations in CorelDRAW:

1. Again, the nature of your project will dictate how this graphic looks. My site is broken up into four major areas, so the graphic needed to reflect that organization visually. The graphic needed to incorporate a lot of text elements, be flexible for adding and deleting objects, and not be too big. My site map is pretty simple, with triangles dividing a big rectangle into four sections. Each section has the title of a page fit to a set of circular paths that repeat through the graphic and serve as a guide for the text objects. Use the Fit Text to Path option from the Text menu to put the text objects into place. If you want to move them free of the curve and assign the text an individual Internet address, use the Arrange | Separate command (see Figure 27-7).

2. Select a text element to which you wish to assign a URL. From the View menu, select Toolbars to open the Toolbars dialog. Select the Internet Objects toolbox and click OK.

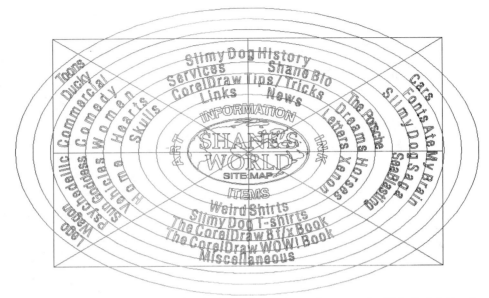

*Figure 27-7: A graphic with an individual text element for each page on the Web site is laid out using circles as a guide.*

3. Now you can enter a link for the selected object in the Location (URL) box. (Where Version 8 has an Internet Bookmark option, Version 7 has an Alternate Text box for each object. This is nice for single images, but is not practical for multiple hot-spot bitmaps such as this example, as the alternate text is what flashes on the screen as an image is loading. This is handy as a memo pad for each object and also embeds the memo harmlessly in the HTML code.) The default setting of Use Object Shape to Define Hotspot is fine, so after you enter your URL for the object, press the Enter key. Repeat this process to define a URL for every object in your site map. If you are linking to a local file in the same subdirectory as the site map file, you need only define the target name, such as slimy.htm. If you are linking to another site, you will need to include the entire URL, such as http://www.corelmag.com/shane/slimy.htm to make the links work correctly (see Figure 27-8).

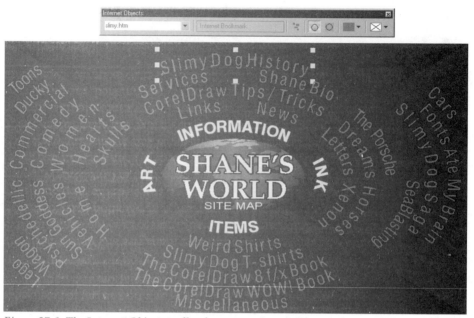

*Figure 27-8: The Internet Objects toolbar lets you assign a URL and alternate text to each object in your CorelDRAW file.*

4. Once you have assigned a URL to each link object, you are ready to create the bitmap and the HTML file (use the Show Internet Objects button on the Internet Objects toolbar to check that all objects have been assigned a URL). From the File menu, choose Publish to Internet. Choose Single Image from the Publish to Internet wizard screen and then click Next. Select the target folders (CorelDRAW 8 creates a separate folder called \images for the bitmaps, which you will also have to upload to your remote host), then click Next again. From the next window, pick either JPEG or GIF. GIF used to be more universally acceptable and is still the only format that supports multiple frame animations, but it is your choice. GIF images allow you to assign a transparent background, while JPEG images can compress to smaller sizes and allow for more colors. Make your choice and click Next. From the next screen, choose the filename of the HTML file you are creating and then click Finish to make it all happen. (If you are like me and you think that wizards are annoying and condescending, from the initial Publish to Internet window, click the Use Internet Dialog button to open the Publish to Internet dialog.)

**TIP**
*Version 7 can do the same thing, only the procedure is slightly different. After you choose Publish to Internet from the File menu, change the Save as Type setting to Corel Image Map (HTM) and name the file as you desire. Click Export to continue and open the HTML Image Map Export dialog. Here you have your choice of bitmap, either GIF or JPEG (see related sidebar for more info). Make your choice and click OK to open the Bitmap Export dialog. For GIF images (the most universal), you should set the Color setting to 256, enable the Dithered option, set Size to 1 to 1 and Resolution at 72 dpi, and enable the Super-Sampling Anti-Aliasing option. Super-sampling is more critical with low-res images such as this exported at actual size. Click OK and take a breather while CorelDRAW does some major work for you!*

## ▼ GIFs or JPEGs

Creating images for the Web also means choosing between these two file formats for your bitmap images. GIF images are limited to 256 colors (although dithering can simulate colors beyond the 256 palette), while JPEG files can be in the millions of colors. It used to be that you had to address the least common denominator with building a Web site, which is a screen size of 640 x 480 and a color depth of 256 colors. With technology changing so fast, the bar has been raised a bit to larger screen sizes and bigger palettes, but the old rule remains if you want to guarantee that your site can be viewed by all. The GIF format, although limited in color depth, also supports multi-cell animation, where JPEG images do not. Since I use so many animations, and I don't find the 256 color palette an insurmountable restriction, I use the GIF format almost exclusively. For nicer images (it really makes a difference with photos, for example), the JPEG format is better and also takes advantage of file-compression technology. When you save a JPEG, you have the option to change the "quality factor." Lower quality means smaller files but also degrades the image (keep a copy of the high-quality original before you start experimenting with the quality factor option in case you need to start over!). If you use this format, find a happy medium between small file size and high quality. (The CorelDRAW 8 JPEG Export dialog lets you preview the results of the compression before you execute the export, which is nice.) If you use the CorelDRAW 8 Publish To Internet wizard, the default action is to export bitmaps greater than 256 colors in the JPEG rather than the GIF format. Remember, you can mix and match both formats within one Web page, although, as in my example, if you build a big graphic in pieces and then assemble it with a table, you will want to stick to the same file format within that connecting graphic.

**TIP**

*You can also use the CorelDRAW Internet Objects/Image mapping technique to assign multiple hot spots on a single CorelDRAW object, such as a big bitmap. Import your bitmap and then draw shapes over areas you want to connect to links as hot spots. Assign URL information to these objects as before, only don't give them any outline or fill attributes. Now these are "invisible" areas over the bitmap, but when you create the image map and GIF for the Web, they will be live and act as links. Nifty deal. This is just as easy as using one of those image map utilities, but the bonus is that you can also mix and match other CorelDRAW images and Internet associations along with the bitmap to get some really custom results.*

5. What the Publish to Internet | Single Image feature does is create two files: the bitmap and an HTML file that has the image map information in it. You can open the file directly with your browser or use a text editor to drop the image map text section into your own HTML file. Text elements make for some very complex coding to define the hot spots, but no matter, it is all automated! See Figure 27-9.

```
<HTML>
<HEAD>
<TITLE>E:\fxbook\chapt30\sitemap2.htm</TITLE>
</HEAD>
<BODY>
<IMG SRC = "sitemap2.jpg" USEMAP = "#sitemap2.jpg" BORDER = 0>
</BODY></HTML>
<MAP NAME = "sitemap2.jpg">
<AREA SHAPE= POLYGON HREF="tshirt1.htm" COORDS="252, 197, 252, 196, 253, 196, 253, 197, 252, 197, 253, 208, 252, 199, 254, 199, 255, 208, 253, 208, ">
<AREA SHAPE= POLYGON HREF="tshirt1.htm" COORDS="210, 197, 210, 196, 211, 196, 211, 198, 210, 197, 208, 208, 210, 199, 211, 199, 210, 208, 208, 208, ">
<AREA SHAPE= POLYGON HREF="tshirt1.htm" COORDS="186, 204, 187, 191, 188, 192, 188, 202, 192, 193, 194, 193, 193, 204, 198, 194, 199, 194, 194, 206, 192, 206, 193, 195, 188, 204, 186, 204">
<AREA SHAPE= RECT HREF="tshirt1.htm" COORDS="184, 191, 278, 210">
<AREA SHAPE= POLYGON HREF="tshirt1.htm" COORDS="252, 197, 252, 196, 253, 196, 253, 197, 252, 197, 253, 208, 252, 199, 254, 199, 255, 208, 253, 208, ">
<AREA SHAPE= POLYGON HREF="tshirt1.htm" COORDS="210, 197, 210, 196, 211, 196, 211, 198, 210, 197, 208, 208, 210, 199, 211, 199, 210, 208, 208, 208, ">
<AREA SHAPE= POLYGON HREF="tshirt1.htm" COORDS="186, 204, 187, 191, 188, 192, 188, 202, 192, 193, 194, 193, 193, 204, 198, 194, 199, 194, 194, 206, 192, 206, 193, 195, 188, 204, 186, 204">
<AREA SHAPE= RECT HREF="tshirt0.htm" COORDS="226, 268, 227, 255">
<AREA SHAPE= POLYGON HREF="tshirt0.htm" COORDS="220, 268, 221, 255, 222, 255, 222, 268, 220, 268">
<AREA SHAPE= POLYGON HREF="tshirt0.htm" COORDS="188, 254, 189, 252, 190, 253, 190, 254, 188, 254, 187, 265, 188, 256, 190, 256, 188, 265, 187, 265, ">
<AREA SHAPE= POLYGON HREF="tshirt0.htm" COORDS="181, 264, 183, 252, 178, 264, 177, 263, 176, 251, 174, 263, 173, 263, 175, 250, 177, 251, 178, 262, 183, 252, 185, 252, 183, 264, 181, 264">
<AREA SHAPE= RECT HREF="tshirt0.htm" COORDS="172, 250, 285, 268">
<AREA SHAPE= RECT HREF="tshirt0.htm" COORDS="226, 268, 227, 255">
<AREA SHAPE= POLYGON HREF="tshirt0.htm" COORDS="220, 268, 221, 255, 222, 255, 222, 268, 220, 268">
<AREA SHAPE= POLYGON HREF="tshirt0.htm" COORDS="188, 254, 189, 252, 190, 253, 190, 254, 188, 254, 187, 265, 188, 256, 190, 256, 188, 265, 187, 265, ">
<AREA SHAPE= POLYGON HREF="tshirt0.htm" COORDS="181, 264, 183, 252, 178, 264, 177, 263, 176, 251, 174, 263, 173, 263, 175, 250, 177, 251, 178, 262, 183, 252, 185, 252, 183, 264, 181, 264">
<AREA SHAPE= POLYGON HREF="tshirt4.htm" COORDS="274, 210, 274, 208, 275, 208, 276, 209, 274, 210, 277, 220, 275, 211, 276, 211, 278, 220, 277, 220, ">
<AREA SHAPE= POLYGON HREF="tshirt4.htm" COORDS="250, 220, 249, 219, 253, 218, 254, 220, 250, 220">
<AREA SHAPE= POLYGON HREF="tshirt4.htm" COORDS="244, 225, 243, 213, 240, 214, 240, 212, 247, 212, 247, 213, 244, 213, 245, 225, 244, 225">
<AREA SHAPE= POLYGON HREF="tshirt4.htm" COORDS="179, 208, 179, 206, 181, 206, 180, 208, 179, 208, 176, 218, 179, 209, 180, 209, 178, 219, 176, 218, ">
<AREA SHAPE= POLYGON HREF="tshirt4.htm" COORDS="171, 217, 175, 205, 176, 205, 172, 217, 171, 217">
<AREA SHAPE= RECT HREF="tshirt4.htm" COORDS="160, 202, 300, 228">
<AREA SHAPE= POLYGON HREF="tshirt4.htm" COORDS="274, 210, 274, 208, 275, 208, 276, 209, 274, 210, 277, 220, 275, 211, 276, 211, 278, 220, 277, 220, ">
<AREA SHAPE= POLYGON HREF="tshirt4.htm" COORDS="250, 220, 249, 219, 253, 218, 254, 220, 250, 220">
<AREA SHAPE= POLYGON HREF="tshirt4.htm" COORDS="244, 225, 243, 213, 240, 214, 240, 212, 247, 212, 247, 213, 244, 213, 245, 225, 244, 225">
<AREA SHAPE= POLYGON HREF="tshirt4.htm" COORDS="179, 208, 179, 206, 181, 206, 180, 208, 179, 208, 176, 218, 179, 209, 180, 209, 178, 219, 176, 218, ">
<AREA SHAPE= POLYGON HREF="tshirt4.htm" COORDS="171, 217, 175, 205, 176, 205, 172, 217, 171, 217">
<AREA SHAPE= POLYGON HREF="http://www.corelmag.com/shane/corelfx/" COORDS="319, 224, 314, 212, 315, 212, 318, 218, 319, 213, 321, 212, 320, 217, 325, 221, 323, 222, 319, 218, 319, 220,
320, 223, 319, 224">
<AREA SHAPE= POLYGON HREF="http://www.corelmag.com/shane/corelfx/" COORDS="277, 236, 279, 230, 276, 226, 277, 226, 280, 229, 281, 225, 282, 225, 281, 230, 284, 234, 283, 235, 280, 231,
279, 235, 277, 236">
<AREA SHAPE= POLYGON HREF="http://www.corelmag.com/shane/corelfx/" COORDS="274, 223, 272, 238, 271, 238, 273, 223, 274, 223">
<AREA SHAPE= POLYGON HREF="http://www.corelmag.com/shane/corelfx/" COORDS="240, 240, 237, 230, 238, 230, 240, 238, 241, 230, 243, 230, 245, 238, 246, 230, 247, 230, 246, 239, 244, 239,
242, 232, 241, 240, 240, 240">
<AREA SHAPE= POLYGON HREF="http://www.corelmag.com/shane/corelfx/" COORDS="205, 239, 206, 226, 208, 226, 206, 239, 205, 239">
<AREA SHAPE= POLYGON HREF="http://www.corelmag.com/shane/corelfx/" COORDS="140, 222, 145, 212, 142, 211, 142, 210, 149, 213, 149, 214, 146, 213, 141, 223, 140, 222">
<AREA SHAPE= RECT HREF="http://www.corelmag.com/shane/corelfx/" COORDS="137, 210, 325, 240">
```

*Figure 27-9: CorelDRAW creates both the bitmap and the HTML coding defining the image-mapped hot spots. You can use the file as a stand-alone page on your Web site or copy and paste the text into your own HTML code to take advantage of the complex image-mapping programming.*

The page layout plan for the site map can be seen in the color section and also loaded from the sitemap.cdr file in the \Chapt27\ subdirectory on the Companion CD-ROM. If you load the CorelDRAW file, you can click on an object and see the corresponding link. You can practice by adding links to the custom button interface below the site map, which does not have links yet associated with the graphic in this file. You can then use the Selected Only option to create an image map and bitmap for just the button section of the file if you wish. Also in the \Chapt27\ subdirectory is the sitemap.htm file, which you can open with your browser and test to see how it works. The file is designed to work on my Web site, so only the links with complete URLs in them (such as the book titles in the Items section or the "Shane's World" logo) will actually launch you anywhere, assuming of course you are logged on to the Net and ready to surf! The built-in Internet features are a powerful addition to CorelDRAW, and you can accomplish a lot using this power.

## Web Site From Hell

*Figure 27-10: CorelDRAW makes it easy to plan out the whole look of a Web-page; you can generate the Web-friendly graphics and any other support graphics you may need directly from the file.*

Designing for the World wide Web is the new challenge for the contemporary artist. CorelDRAW offers many features to help you create a powerful Web experience, and it also offers the flexibility to deal with some of the limitations and challenges unique to the medium. No other design forum has issues like download speed or median hardware, which can make designing for the Web very frustrating! Suddenly demographics also include modem speed, monitor size, and display capacities. It's a barrage of technical concerns enough to make a right-brainer cry.

This section will deviate from the step-by-step formula in order to focus on Web-specific tips and tricks. I used these techniques to create the Web page design in Figure 27-10, in the color section, and also in the files on the Companion CD-ROM (open the index.htm file found in the \Chapt27\ directory with your browser). Web design is such a huge topic in itself, with volumes already written on the subject. Here I will just hit you with a few of my own favorite insights on the topic and some CorelDRAW-specific tips and tricks.

**CD-ROM**

## Webbing in CorelDRAW

There are many advantages to designing a Web page layout in CorelDRAW. The flexibility and techniques available to you for printed projects are just as available (if not more) for projects that will end up on the Web. The Web even allows you to take your graphics further, with the addition of animation, sound, and interaction. Your CorelDRAW Web-page design can migrate effortlessly to printed materials at the correct resolution for cross-promotion projects. In addition to that, as we saw with the site map example, CorelDRAW allows you to easily build and maintain a constantly changing page, combining the powerful graphic features of the program with Webbing power. The new Publish to Internet features in CorelDRAW 8 offer powerful HTML translation (including tables) to get WYSIWYG porting direct from your CorelDRAW files right to the Web. And for the truly masochistic, Barista technology will also translate your CorelDRAW file into Java-based code.

CorelDRAW's Web-publishing features are nice and are handy as support tools; however, I highly recommend you use a specifically Web-oriented package to build and maintain your Web sites. CorelDRAW should be your primary source of graphics, but by no means your primary Web building and maintenance tool, as the power just isn't there. Corel's Barista technology, for example, which uses JavaScript to build your CorelDRAW files on the Web, is much slower than simply building and downloading the pages traditionally, and Barista pages look like hell. The HTML publishing features in CorelDRAW 8, with its tables, layers, and styles support, are very impressive, but a page doth not a Web site make! A Web site typically needs more than just pretty text and pictures; it also needs animations, forms for viewer input, e-mail support, and other high-end capability. In addition, a single change on one page can have an impact on many pages on a site; other purpose-built, Web-site-specific software packages are designed to manage link changes and CorelDRAW simply isn't. With all of the links, graphics, and other issues, it is just not the smartest solution anymore to build a Web site page by page. Rather, you should compose a site as a whole using Web-specific software. Microsoft FrontPage, Adobe PageMill, Netscape Communicator Gold, and of course, Corel's own WebMaster Suite are all much better products for real-world Webbing. These programs not only allow for painless Web page creation, they also offer flexibility and power (such as data entry forms, Java applets, e-mail options, etc.) that you won't find in the focused CorelDRAW graphics suite. CorelDRAW is for graphics creation, and at that it excels (which is why CorelDRAW 5 is included in Corel's Web.Master Suite). Use CorelDRAW's powerful graphics tools to enhance your Web site, but exploit true Web-building power elsewhere.

That's just my two bits on the topic, and anything is possible. It is perfectly feasible to build a nice site with nothing more than CorelDRAW. Heck, most of my first Web site was built using CorelDRAW for the graphics and Notepad to do the HTML coding! If you are looking to throw a few pages together for a personal site, then CorelDRAW will be all you need. If, however, you find your business now includes building and managing complex Web sites, get an additional Web management program.

## Making Pages

Although you may wish to build and manage a site with other software, CorelDRAW is still an invaluable addition to the Web designing experience. The advantage of an object-based design application like CorelDRAW is that you can use the same pieces through all stages of the Web building process. For example, you can create a basic flowchart in CorelDRAW, laying out the entire Web site design in a logical hierarchy. Then you can use the same pieces to start mocking up the pages themselves and eventually work those comps objects into the actual artwork. The basic text and shape elements from the mock-ups and planning stages can easily work into the final artwork, serving as a base to expand and get crazy on. When finished, the pages can also undergo unlimited changes and, like the site map example, even generate the necessary Web-specific code if necessary.

I suggest mocking up the entire Web site, page by page, first in CorelDRAW. This helps you to work out design problems and other Web-specific issues. (Remember too that Web design is both horizontally biased (screens are wider than tall, unlike printed pages) and also vertically enhanced (you can scroll down indefinitely). Working with the screen set at the actual resolution and color depth of your target audience also helps you create a more appropriate design (see the related tip). The advantage to first creating the pages in CorelDRAW as opposed to a Web-builder program is that you can design whole-page artwork instead of slapping in buttons and graphics haphazardly as you go along. The whole-page design can then be broken into smaller pieces and assembled back into one solid graphic using an HTML table. Breaking up an otherwise solid graphic like this lets you create animations for sections of the page and also lets you take advantage of speedy-download tricks. If you use common graphics in more than one page, they need only be downloaded once, speeding things along. Figure 27-11 shows how the top of my full-page graphic is broken up into four sections. The right sections change with each page, while the left two pieces are common to all. These left two pieces were also made into animated GIFs to add motion to the site; they only need to be downloaded once and are common elements on every page.

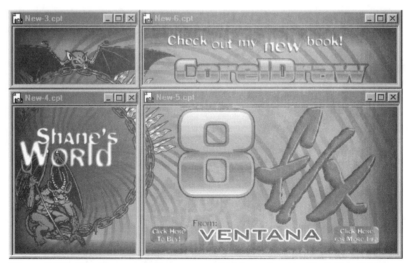

*Figure 27-11: Breaking up a full-page graphic (shown here in PhotoPaint) lets you add animation to sections of the page. With an HTML table, the pieces fit together seamlessly on a Web site.*

Another bandwidth-saving trick is to use a horizontally repeating graphics for page breaks. The chain page-break graphic on my test site is actually just one small bitmap that is tiled four times across the page (see Figure 27-12). Once loaded, the graphic can be used as many times as you like without increasing future download time. (Creating these kinds of repeating graphics is explained at length in the next chapter.)

*Figure 27-12: Using a single bitmap (top) that can be tiled across indefinitely (bottom), you increase your design capabilities without increasing download time.*

**TIP** *Theft prevention is another reason to design your site using the full-page approach, where individual graphics are on top of a signature background and they all fit together like a puzzle. The background behind the buttons on the demo site connects to the background in the top graphics, subtly creating a whole-page feel (See "Closure" in Chapter 29) while also keeping them from floating free. Free-floating Web graphics are easier to pilfer and work into other designs; just a few paint strokes are all that is needed to customize them for the image thief. A background makes this much more difficult to do because, for one thing, it would be impractical to paint it away. The background will look wrong on another site but perfect on yours! This is not a huge issue, but when you invest a lot of time into, say, a unique animation for your Web site, you don't want to have it ripped off!*

**TIP** *Set up your monitor to preview your Web site at actual size. A pitfall for many designers is that they forget to design for their target audience and really miss the mark. Most computer artists have much larger screens and more computer capability than their target demographic and design to their own system and not the end user's. To set up your display for the most common screen size and color depth, use the Win95 Display Properties dialog. From the Win95 desktop, click on My Computer and then click on the Control Panel. Now click on the Display icon to open the dialog, and from the Settings tab, you can change to a more appropriate screen size—640 x 480 with a color palette of 256 colors is still considered the "least common denominator"; however, you should assess your target audience and set your screen accordingly. Back in CorelDRAW, set your zoom factor to 1:1 and you are on the money!*

## Web Graphics

Creating images for the World Wide Web is so much easier than creating them for print applications. For one thing, the graphics needed are at screen resolution, which is a low 72 dpi. The palette typically is also a meager 256 colors, which makes for small files that are easy to create and manipulate. It is one of the few design tasks where the old WYSIWYG (What You See Is What You Get) acronym is actually true! The low resolution nature of Web graphics also ensures that they won't be stolen for publishing purposes, but keep in mind that all graphics are essentially up for grabs once posted on the Net. (This isn't an issue if you use the full-page design approach I mentioned earlier!)

Once you have your graphics and page for your Web site laid out in CorelDRAW, you can either select them individually or export them as a whole (as bitmaps to use with your Web-builder program to assemble your site). Or you can use the built-in Win95 screen-capture capabilities to generate the bitmaps (see related tip). Of course, you can also export the page as HTML code using the Publish to Internet features; it is up to you and your Web needs.

**TIP** *Screen captures offer a very quick solution to getting images for your Web site. It is not the only way, just the fastest! You can always export the images as bitmaps, but why waste the processing time? If the image is already on the screen, it is at the correct resolution for your Web site and any other onscreen applications you might have. First, select the Zoom tool, and from the Property Bar, choose 1:1 (if you are using the traditional Zoom flyout, just select that option there). This will show the images at actual size, which is perfect for your Web site. Then from the View menu, choose Enhanced to get the best possible onscreen representation of your image. Use the arrows and elevators at the edge of your work space to center your image. When you have a entire section displayed, press the Alt and Print Screen keys simultaneously to create a screen capture. The image will be copied to the clipboard. Open Corel PhotoPaint, and from the Edit menu, choose Paste | As New Document. Now you have the image in PhotoPaint! With the image in PhotoPaint, the first thing you need to do is trim away the rest of the screen capture. Draw a normal selection around your image and choose Crop | To Mask from the Image menu. This will trim your image down to size. Now you can manipulate the image further with filters or effects, convert to GIF or JPEG, and even create an animation. I used the PhotoLab GradTone filter to convert the full-color image into gold tones and then used the Image | Convert To | Paletted command to select a color depth appropriate for a GIF graphic on the Web (my page includes GIF animations, so I am forced to use this format). From the Convert to Paletted Image dialog, select Adaptive and Ordered Dither. (From the Custom option, you can select a preferred browser palette, such as Internet Explorer or Navigator, but the Adaptive option seems to be more universally good looking.) Export schmexport; use a screen capture and save some time (see Figure 27-13).*

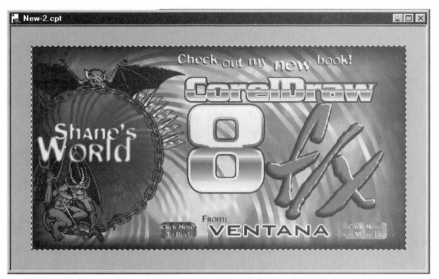

*Figure 27-13: Use the built-in screen capture capabilities of Win95 to paste an image into PhotoPaint. Then use the Crop To Mask command to isolate the desired Web graphic. This graphic can then be subdivided further to facilitate animating sections of the image.*

 **Audience-Specific Design**

The first thing you need to do when you set out to develop a Web site is determine the technical abilities of the target audience. You need to establish the average modem speed, screen size, color depth, and also a user profile to make sure your graphics and interface are appropriate. It is a common trap for designers to fall into, with our big screens, fancy computers, and fast Internet access, to design Web pages that are inappropriate for the market. Until very recently, the largest user base was still limited technically to browsers that did not support frames, JavaScript, or even animation. That is not necessarily the case now, but you still need to consider these issues and design with the target market in mind. Try to view your site via different access providers and a variety of modem speeds, and try using different brands of computers, operating systems, and browsers to get a feel for how your page will really look. For example, I had to abandon my original test pages because they did not build correctly in Netscape Navigator, but they looked fine in Microsoft Internet Explorer. It's a good thing I checked or the pages on the CD would have looked awful for anyone using Navigator. A few years from now, there may be universal standards, but for now, you have to do your homework!

CorelDRAW gives you plenty of Webbing options. Obviously you don't have to break up a Web image as I did, but for the Web site design I had in mind, it was the only way to go. With four separate images instead of just one, I was able to create an animation for the bat and the Shane's World graphic. These images need load only once, and are on all of the subsequent pages. Also, this scheme allowed me to use the same background image for the opening graphics and for the other main sections of my Web site. It's a very atypical way to build a Web site, but if you wanted normal, you would have stuck to the CorelDRAW tutorials!

Going back to the theme of ruthless creativity, remember that you can tweak CorelDRAW-generated Web pages indefinitely. The HTML code is editable with any text editor (e.g., Windows WordPad), so you can go in and add functionality that is not available otherwise. For example, you can assemble the sections of my full-page graphic in CorelDRAW and then have the program generate the HTML code with the complex table formatting of the Publish to Internet feature. Then you can substitute other same-size graphics (like my GIF animations) or add more coding to the HTML text (I added sound files, for example). No one says you have to leave well enough alone!

The Web page demo, seen in Figure 27-10, is in the color section and is also available in several electronic formats. The CorelDRAW file is called newworld.cdr and is in the \Chapt27\ subdirectory on the Companion CD-ROM. Also in that directory are the Web-pages generated using that file for you to load and dissect. Using your favorite Web browser, load the file called index.htm from the \Chapt27\ subdirectory. This will bring up the CorelDRAW 8 test page, with all the graphics and animations in place, but no links. It will give you a much better idea of how a full-screen CorelDRAW graphic migrates to the Web in smaller, Web-friendly chunks. The image needs to be divided up to facilitate the addition of text and the use of multiple-frame animated GIFs, and also to try out specialized Web "tricks." For example, the chain page-break graphic is actually made by repeating one small bitmap four times across, which saves load time and makes your page build faster (see Chapter 28 for an explanation on building repeating tiles). In Chapter 29 we will discover how to animate the gears, which are in fact only two repeating images but look like perpetually spinning objects. When this page is eventually live on the Internet, the gear animation will also have a corresponding image map so that clicking on each gear will launch you to another section of the Web site. Image maps don't work on local systems universally, so the files on the Companion CD-ROM are just for looks. For the real thing, you will have to look up the real Web site on the Web.

## Moving On

In this chapter, we looked at how CorelDRAW can help you create onscreen applications. CorelDRAW is a natural for creating images for Web sites and multimedia applications. With the handy, fat Corel clip-art and font libraries at your disposal, your Web sites should be bursting with creative imagery! The versatile nature of CorelDRAW artwork makes Web site management a snap and also facilitates easy Web-promotion, with the artwork migrating painlessly to print applications. Without question, CorelDRAW is an indispensable weapon in the sticky World Wide Web war.

In the next chapter, we will continue to look at ways to use CorelDRAW for Web enhancement by using the program to create interesting patterns. To add interest to Web pages without adding much download time, you can use CorelDRAW to create seamless tiles for background images and also to create never-ending bitmaps that connect together to create page breaks of any width or length. Keep that browser warm and don't adjust your television sets; we are out to spin us some fine digital tapestries and electronic patterns.

▼ **Beyond f/x**

Onscreen designs, with their high-tech buttons and navigation panels, can also be used for traditional offset printing. You can get a high-tech look by using icons and graphics associated with electronic publishing technology. I have seen many ads use the computer-screen analogy, with pull-down menus and buttons suggesting interaction and motion. The same kind of trick can be used to create a Web browser look for an ad or brochure, which is also a good way to promote a Web site.

Beyond the literal look of onscreen interfaces in print, more esoteric concepts of worldwide connectivity or electronic communication can benefit from tangible artwork like buttons or screens. Of course, buttons and screen designs work the best for Web applications or multimedia events, where CorelDRAW's design flexibility turns into dynamic interaction. Multiple-graphic objects, such as buttons that change or animations, make onscreen experiences much more interesting. Just don't get too crazy and make everything sing and dance or your interactive audience may just sit there, too dazzled to move!

# chapter 28

# Tessellations, Patterns & Tiles

**M**any applications, from the World Wide Web to textiles, need interesting designs and patterns. Repeating patterns are a visually interesting addition to a design and can do a lot to set the tone of the artwork. You can reinforce a concept or product or even set a mood with a repeating image (a "good" page could have an angels background, a "bad" one, little devils, etc.). With textures, you can create the look of wood, marble, or other traditional building materials to set the stage for the rest of the design. CorelDRAW ships with many premade patterns and tiles, but it is also the perfect medium to create your own unique repeating images.

There are many tools within CorelDRAW to create patterns. The Tools | Create | Pattern command lets you create a bitmap pattern by designating an area onscreen, which then is available as a tile for use in the Bitmap Pattern Fill dialog. Or, as we will see in this section the tiling option on the Symbols library also makes great patterns. In addition, with a little creative program tweaking, you can generate all kinds of patterns in CorelDRAW for many applications. Once again, if you can imagine it, you can build it one way or another in CorelDRAW!

In this chapter we will look at creating interesting background artwork using patterns of repeating images. First, we will create images that repeat endlessly in one direction for such uses as Web page dividers. Next, we will create an "Escheresque" tessellation pattern of tight-fitting objects using "clones" and node-editing. Then, using the Tile option on the Symbols roll-up, we'll create a unique background pattern with repeating star shapes. Finally, we'll create seamless tiles to use as repeating images that extend endlessly in all directions for Web page backgrounds or other patterning applications. Man, I'm getting dizzy already!

## Never-Ending Designs

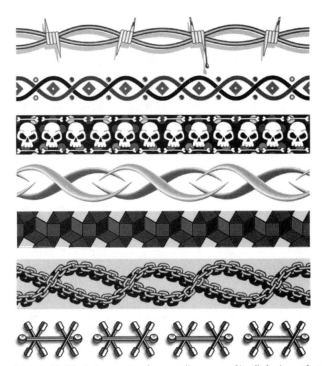

*Figure 28-01: It is easy to plan out "never-ending" designs that repeat forever for horizontal or tubular applications.*

Using graphics as page separators for banners and Web pages is very common. The challenge with the Web is to create as small a tile as possible, fooling the viewer with a bitmap that connects into itself to create a never-ending graphic. This way, one tile can be repeated over and over and connect into a row as long as you wish without increasing download time.

These same techniques can be applied to any application where you need a pattern to merge back into itself. Any tubular design, from embroidered socks to tea cups, uses this same kind of never-ending pattern. With some specialized modifications, these patterns could also be used for bracelet or anklet tattoo designs (see Chapter 12). There are several ways to create repeating patterns, with the results reflecting the amount of work involved (unfortunately, in this case, "more is better").

## Easy

As you may have noticed, you can use a reflection technique to create a seamless row of any image. This is a really easy way to make a bitmap that connects into itself indefinitely. The downside is that it is hard to hide the "repeat" because the images are sometimes very obviously mirrored. The upside is that it is "easy"! For perfection, you will have to buckle up and head into "hard" territory! Here is how to build a never-ending image with the mirroring technique:

1. Start with the image you wish to tile. Like I said, the upside is this technique will work with anything, including abstract patterns. If you want to use a texture fill as I have, you will have to first convert it to a bitmap.

2. Duplicate the object and flip it horizontally by dragging the left-center sizing handle to the right while holding down the Ctrl key. Bang. You are done! The two tiles flipped together create a tile that will endlessly repeat end to end (see Figure 28-2).

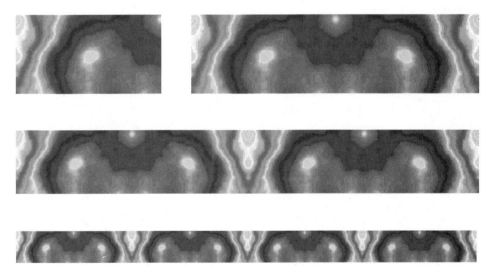

*Figure 28-2: Any object will connect seamlessly into its reflection. The top left tile is duplicated and flip-flopped horizontally to create the never-ending pattern on the top right. This bitmap will butt into itself endlessly, as shown in the bottom two rows.*

3. You can take this one step further and expand the image into a never-ending tile that goes both ways, perfect for a Web page background. Simply take your horizontal tile (made of two copies of the original), duplicate it, and then flip it vertically. Now you have a tile that will

connect endlessly in both directions for a background image like no other! You can change the proportions in either direction, and the tile will still mesh into itself (see Figure 28-3).

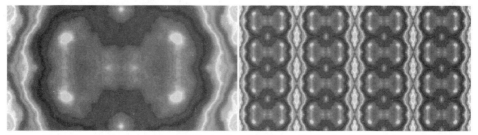

*Figure 28-3: Duplicating and flipping the horizontal tile vertically (on left) creates an image that will repeat endlessly in all directions (as seen on right).*

Okay then. So that was easy! Now on to "medium"...

## Medium

The "easy" tile is quick and dirty, but not always a solution. Some graphics, like a string of words, for example, simply can not be mirrored. With just a little more effort, You can create a never-ending tile. Here is what you do:

1. Start with a graphic that you want to string along, like my chain from the sample Web pages (Chapter 27). The chain as described in Chapter 15 uses perfectly symmetrical curves, so it is a great way to start. (You can open the tubepat.cdr file in the \Chapt28\ subdirectory on the Companion CD-ROM and grab the chains from that file. They are in a PowerClip, but you know what to do!)

2. Draw a box around the area that looks like the "repeat" of the rolling chain segment. With the chain, it is easy to see where this area is—at the bottom of the "swoop." Draw the square at a best-guess so that each side slices through the center of a "flat" link (see Figure 28-4).

*Figure 28-4: A pattern starts with the target image, and a rectangle is drawn around to define the "repeat."*

3. Delete all but the pieces necessary for the repeat. Also delete one of the protruding links. It is much easier to start and stop with the same object. Now draw two vertical lines and align them with the left and right ends of the rectangle (see Figure 28-5).

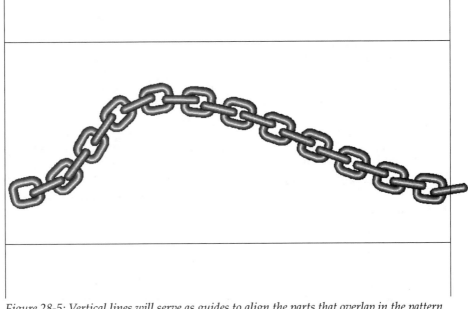

*Figure 28-5: Vertical lines will serve as guides to align the parts that overlap in the pattern "repeat."*

4. Select the right flat link and align it to the vertical center of the right vertical guideline. Duplicate the link and align the duplicate to the left vertical guideline. Basically, that's it! (Okay, maybe this rates as "easy" as well!) Because the links are duplicates of each other, they are already aligned vertically. Use the guidelines to ensure that they are also in alignment for the patterning.

5. Select all of the chain bits, including the two that overhang, and stuff them into the reference rectangle with the PowerClip function. Remove the outline of the rectangle and you have a never-ending tile that will create endless chains to divide your Web pages! Test your tile by duplicating it and aligning the tiles. The links should melt seamlessly into each other (see Figure 28-6).

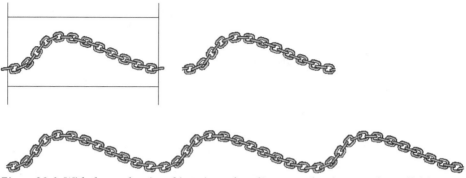

*Figure 28-6: With the overlapping objects in perfect alignment, the pieces can be stuffed into a rectangle with the PowerClip function to create a seamless tile.*

The chain is a "medium" example, as is any artwork that is made up of smaller pieces. The chain, razor wire, rope, and other examples will work well. Making a pattern out of smaller objects that can be aligned to the reference points isn't a big deal. Now on to horizontally tiling objects that are not segmented.

## Hard

Some artwork takes a little more effort to make into a pattern. It isn't really "hard," but does take some guesswork. Here is how to tile other artwork:

1. Start with your art that isn't made of smaller objects; in this case, two tribal-looking bits stolen from Chapter 14. You could just create a bitmap "as is" and bump these images together end to end for a page divider, but that wouldn't result in the inter-meshing optical illusion we want. So group the original pieces, duplicate, and move them horizontally (while holding down the Ctrl key to guarantee no vertical movement) until you get to the point where you want the pieces to overlap. Duplicate the two again and repeat until you get an idea of the pattern (see Figure 28-7).

2. Switch to Wireframe view, zoom in, and draw a rectangle from each point at the overlap for reference. You are looking to define the area of overlap, so find a recognizable shape, such as the diamond area created by the overlapping points. Draw the rectangle so that it just touches each endpoint on this area (see Figure 28-8).

*Figure 28-7: Arrange the pattern pieces by eye into the desired design.*

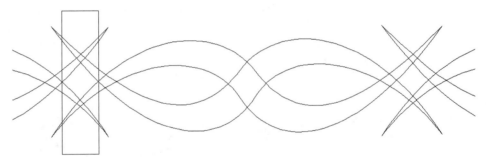

*Figure 28-8: Draw a rectangle to define the area of overlap.*

3. Duplicate the rectangle and move it to the same place over on the right of the target piece. You will find that your "eyeball" pattern was probably way off the mark, with the right set of tribal curves too close or too far away from the group to the left of it. Use the reference rectangle to measure out the position of the right group so it is in the same orientation as the left, using the same reference points as before (see Figure 28-9).

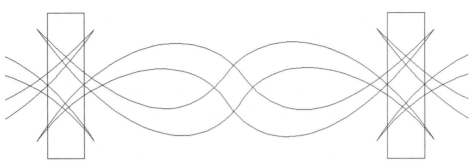

*Figure 28-9: Use the reference rectangles as guides to position both the left and right art pieces the same distance from the center group.*

4. Draw a vertical line and align it to the center of the left reference rectangle and repeat for the right. Delete the reference rectangles. Use the lines as guides to draw another rectangle around the art, starting and stopping at the reference lines. The rectangle should have no fill or outline values (see Figure 28-10).

*Figure 28-10: Draw two more reference lines; then draw a box within the lines.*

5. Delete the reference lines, select all three of the duplicate pieces, and use the PowerClip command to stuff them into the rectangle. The result is a bitmap that will create an endlessly repeating row when butted up end to end (see Figure 28-11).

*Figure 28-11: The art is stuffed inside of the rectangle with the PowerClip command, which creates a tile that will endlessly repeat.*

Creating tiled artwork is just one of those little tricks to make your Web page load faster. The file is called tribalpat.cdr in the \Chapt28\ subdirectory on the Companion CD-ROM if you want to take a peek. This technique has many applications; you can design literally in circles. The same process works in both planes to create seamless tiles that work both ways. That's coming up!

## Tessellate, Schmessellate

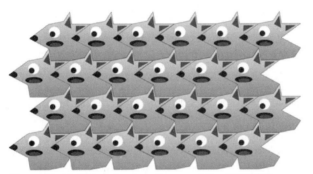

*Figure 28-12: Using the clone feature of CorelDRAW, you can design and manipulate an endlessly repeating pattern of like geometric objects (a tessellation).*

Chalk this example up to children's television. I was baby-sitting my niece and desperately tying to get her interested in the television so I could go do something else. Well this brilliant plan backfired, as I ended up fascinated with a kid's program on tessellations, which are patterns made from like geometric objects (I am easily amused; what can I say?). A brick wall, for example, is a very simple tessellation. You have already built a tessellation, whether you know it or not, back in Chapter 10 when we built the honeycomb. In any case, my niece spent the afternoon playing with the hot wheel set I got her, and I fiddled with tessellations in CorelDRAW!

Tessellations make for cool patterns on Web sites or any other application where you want a unique, eye-catching pattern. Report covers or ads can benefit from a "themed" tessellation, using an object that relates back to the topic at hand (the puppies in Figure 28-12 would work well for a dog or cartooning theme). They are by no means easy to make, and I am not M.C. Escher, so most of this is "theory"! (Hey, they made you learn about atomic theory in school, and you have ever seen an atom either.) The PostScript texture fills in CorelDRAW (accessed from the fill fly-out) contain several tessellations: birds, reptiles, fishscale, patio. These fills only output on PostScript printers, but you can at least see them if you don't have a supported printer by clicking the Preview Fill option in the PostScript Texture dialog. (For more on the subject, do a keyword search on *tessellation* on the World Wide Web. There are many sites dedicated to this topic, some with some very concise, step-by-step lessons!)

The trick behind tessellations and other patterns in CorelDRAW is cloning. Instead of copying an object, you clone it. What this does is create child objects that will reflect any changes you make to the original object, the parent. This has some handy uses beyond patterning. Think of a unique headline graphic you use repeatedly for a catalog or menu project. If you use clones instead of duplicates, when your client asks you change them all from blue to green, you need only change the original parent and all of the clones will automatically follow suit! Please, please, no thanks necessary. Just another handy tip from your crazy Uncle Shane!

Where clones aid in tessellation is during the building stages. By placing clones around the parent, you can see how a change is reflected in all of the objects and how they work to create a pattern. It is a strange way to work, with all of the clones changing "magically" when you change the parent, but it is a great visual aid and the only way I can create a tessellation more complex than a brick wall! Here is how to use clones to create a tessellation:

1. Use the Polygon tool to draw a six-sided shape, holding the Ctrl key as you drag to create a perfect hexagon. With the hexagon selected, choose Clone from the Edit menu. This will create a clone of the original, which will automatically reflect any changes that you make to the parent. Position this clone below and to the right of the original so it fits perfectly like a honeycomb. Now with the clone selected, you can duplicate it with the + key to create another clone. Continue to duplicate and position the clones until they surround the original for a total of four hexagons (see Figure 28-13).

2. Select the original hexagon and convert it to curves. Now use the Shape tool to drag the control nodes into a shape that works as a tessellation. This is a trial-and-error process, but with the three clones butted up against the original, you have immediate feedback and know if the shape you are making will work or not. To make things easier, shift-select opposing node pairs instead of just one node at a time. By selecting a pair, you are ensured that the opposite side will mate up in true tessellation fashion! See Figure 28-14.

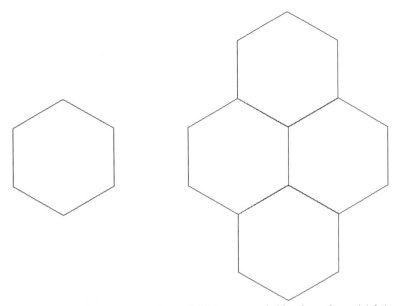

*Figure 28-13: An original hexagon (left) is surrounded by three clones (right).*

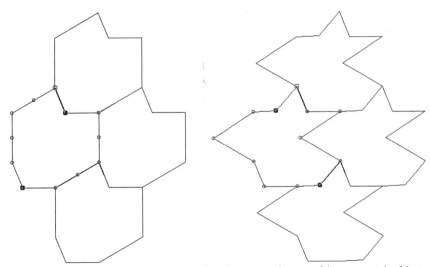

*Figure 28-14: Selecting and moving node pairs creates intermeshing geometric objects.*

3. When you get a shape that starts to look like something, in this case an animated puppy head, you can stop the node-editing phase and start coloring. You can delete the three clone shapes, as they will not reflect the addition of additional objects to the parent curve. The clones were only a visual aide to facilitate the creation of the primary shape. Use the Ellipse tool to draw eyes and a mouth and the Bezier tool to click in some ear details. The nose is a circle trimmed to the shape of the head with the Intersection command.

4. Select all of the objects in your cyber-puppy, and again from the Edit menu, choose Clone. Now move and duplicate the clone groups as before to create a pattern of tessellated pooches (see Figure 28-15).

*Figure 28-15: Simple shapes bring the image to life, which is grouped and again cloned to create a pattern.*

5. You can duplicate and move the clones to create as complicated or as simple a pattern as you wish. You can even use this type of pattern to create the "seamless" tiles as outlined in the last section of this chapter.

The beauty of a pattern made from clones is that all you need to do is change the parent object and all of the obedient clones will follow. You can select a single object in the parent group by holding the Ctrl key when you click on it and then change the fill or outline. Or you can drag and drop new fill attributes on to the objects in the parent group, and all cloned objects will follow suit (see Figure 28-16).

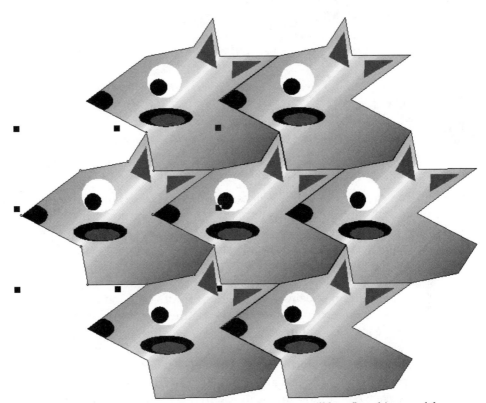

*Figure 28-16: Changes in the attributes in the parent group will be reflected in any of the corresponding clones.*

The tessellation is in the color section as well as in the pooches.cdr file found in the \Chapt28\ subdirectory on the Companion CD-ROM. The clones are still "alive" in the top group and "frozen" in the bottom. If you drag and drop different colors on to the objects in the parent pooch, you can see how this changes things in all of the duplicates. Not sheep, but cloning nonetheless!

## Propeller Heads

*Figure 28-17: Starting with a pattern set up by tiling a symbol, a star object becomes an interesting background for a Web site or advertisement.*

Yes, my "Velcro-brain" strikes again. While innocently browsing through the CD bins at the local music store, I saw an album cover that really appealed to me. It was very similar to the graphic in Figure 28-17, with a photo in the center, a star background pattern, and crisp text elements. I find this style very clean, interesting, and legible. Hmm, imagine that? Text you can read?? Someone should tell the folks over at *WIRED* magazine.

In addition to being a great source for images and icons, the Symbols rollup is also set up for patterning. Using the Tile option, any symbol you choose can be instantly set up as a pattern for any use you can imagine. Unlike the tessellation example, these objects do not interlock, although you can change the density, size, and spacing of the pieces. These patterns by default are spaced in an even grid arrangement of horizontal and vertical rows, which works well for most applications. In this example, however, I decided to break up the grid pattern into a slightly different variant by offsetting every alternative row of symbols. Either way, the Symbols roll-up makes for easy patterning so you can move on and concentrate on the design as a whole. Here is how to use the Symbols roll-up to create a pattern.

1. Start a new design (Ctrl+N) and open the Symbols docker (Ctrl+F11). Locate the Stars1 library and star #40. Now change the size to .25 and click on the Tile Options button. From the Tile Options dialog, change the grid size to .5 inches Horizontal and .5 inches Vertical, and then click OK. Now drag the star onto your page and watch the pattern emerge (see Figure 28-18).

*Figure 28-18: With the Tiling option enabled, many duplicates of a symbol create a design.*

2. Getting the density and spacing right with this feature is a bit of a crapshoot. Experiment with different size numbers and grid sizes until you get what you want. Remember you can always enlarge or decrease the pattern, so worry about only density and spacing at this stage.

3. A pattern set up in this fashion is really the original parent shape; the rest of the duplicates are clones. Select the top-left star and change the fill to cyan and give it a .023-inch ice blue outline (see Figure 28-19).

*Figure 28-19: Selecting and changing attributes of the parent shape will change all of the "clone" objects in the pattern grid.*

4. The grid pattern is nice, but too regimented. To create a more seamless pattern, shift the stars in every other row one star length to the right. To select all of the stars in each alternate row, hold down the Shift key while dragging around them. In this way, you can easily select all of the stars in every second row and move them slightly to the right. Try to align the stars in the rows you are moving so that the top point of each star is midway between the two stars above it (see Figure 28-20).

5. To make the pattern look less uniform and yet retain the structure of the layout, combine all of the shapes into one curve. Now you can create an interesting pattern using a blue-to-white conical fountain fill (see Figure 28-21).

*Figure 28-20: Create a less regimented pattern by moving every other row to the right.*

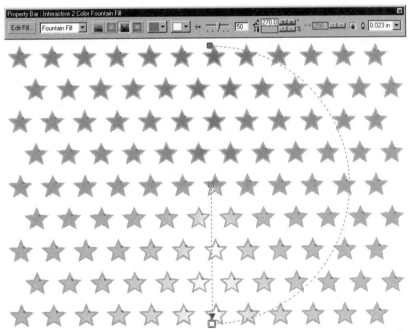

*Figure 28-21: Get away from a flat pattern to a more stylized one by combining all of the elements into a single curve and then coloring it with a conical fountain fill.*

6. For an even more striking effect, use the Contour roll-up to create a second, slightly larger set of stars behind the original. Then use the Arrange | Separate and Arrange | Ungroup All commands to break the two curves into separate curves. Now use a linear fountain fill from baby blue to white, with the angle set at –135 degrees for the front stars and the same fill with the angle set at 45 degrees for the back stars. The fountain fills flow into each other to create a reflected-negative image (see Figure 28-22).

You could go crazy with these two curve shapes, assigning each a different color to create all kinds of patterns. You could even create a very strange graphic by stuffing bitmaps into each of the star shapes with the PowerClip function, much like the octagon example from Chapter 10. Or, draw a box around both sets of stars, combine the three objects into one, then import a bitmap behind this curve, and finally, fill the curve with a Heat Map lens for some very trippy results (see Figure 28-23).

*Figure 28-22: The Contour roll-up creates a second set of stars, which is given the same fill but the exact opposite fill angle to create a "negative" reflection.*

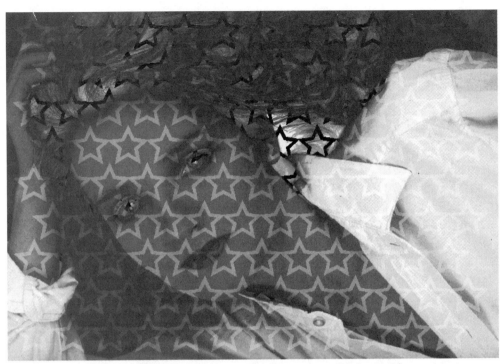

*Figure 28-23: Combining both star curves to a rectangle creates a solid shape with star cutouts. If this shape is placed over a bitmap and given a lens, the result is a patterned and recolored image.*

The star lens pattern is not in the color section, so I insist you load the stargirl.cdr file in the \Chapt28\ subdirectory on the Companion CD-ROM and take a look! Combining a pattern with other effects can make for some very cool imagery. The results belie the ease of creation!

The original stars pattern is in the beanie.cdr file, also in the \Chapt28\ subdirectory and in the color section. This is a good example of a clean use of a geometric pattern as a background image.

The beanie is from the \objects\ directory of the CorelDRAW clip-art CD, which has bitmaps with transparent backgrounds in it. When you import these files for use, they are grouped with a background object. To make them "float," ungroup the objects, then drag the object to where you want it, and then select and delete the remaining background bitmap.

## Tiles: Non-Ceramic

Background patterns are very popular and easy to use to personalize and make a Web page or other art project unique. The challenge with Web pages is to create interesting graphics without using bitmaps that are big and slow to download. This is why background tiles are so popular, as you need download only one small image to fill the screen with a unique pattern. We already saw how using the reflection technique will make anything a tile, and even how to create horizontal "never-ending" tiles, so now we just need to work in both directions simultaneously!

The challenge with creating Web tiles is to create an image that is not immediately recognizable as a background tile. If your pattern tile has an awkward or stark transition, the duplicate tiles will not merge together smoothly and thus will look choppy or, as we saw with the reflection technique, create an abstract pattern. Bad tiles also look literally like bad tiles because bitmaps are unavoidably rectangular by nature and consequently can become a distracting array of boxes in the background if you are not careful.

### ▼ Patterns and Underwear

At this point, I need to take a moment and thank the powers that be for women's underwear. What the heck am I babbling about? Well, all of my pattern and smooth tiling knowledge comes from a stint in the art department of a major underwear manufacturer. Yes, for many months I was busy arranging flowers and paisleys on sexy negligees and sleepwear (I even did a design for Fredricks). The experience taught me, among other things, about how patterns repeat and the need to hide the repeat.

A good pattern dissolves seamlessly into itself to create a never-ending series of images. Most everything that has a pattern, from wallpaper to the aforementioned underwear, is actually just a small pattern repeating over and over. A relatively small silk-screen press is responsible for repeatedly printing on the fabric, creating the endless roll that eventually becomes the garments. The trick is that the right side of the pattern merges into the left, and the top with the bottom. To get a seamless repeat the old-fashioned way, a designer would tape a piece of paper into a tube and then sketch out the image so that the image would go round and round indefinitely. When you untape the paper, you have a left-right seamless tile. The process is repeated for the top and bottom, resulting in a square block that will fit into duplicates of itself to create a smooth, never-ending design.

"Hurrah and hallelujah, underwear boy," you think, "but how does this help me out?" Well, the concept of a seamless tile works great in creating backgrounds for Web pages. If you design a tile that is "seamless" (like our previous chain example, only this time in all directions), it will create a smooth, seemingly endless image that flows together in a way that defies its simple, single-bitmap origin. Create a good seamless tile and your viewers will wonder how you defied the rules of physics and got such a huge background image to download so quickly!

## Webs for the Web

**COLOR STUDIO**  *Figure 28-24: A seamless tile can create an interesting background for a Web page, advertisement, or both.*

Remember, you need to work the background into the whole design scheme of the Web page. Web tiles can very easily make a Web page illegible and defeat the purpose of your efforts. The background tile in Figure 28-24, which assembles into a spider Web, was a good way to build both the Web site and also the printed promotional material. For the Web, you could decrease the contrast to keep the page legible, and for print, keep it as is. Here is how to design a seamless Web tile:

1. For patterning, it is a good idea to start with a perfect square. Draw two lines to criss-cross through the center of the square. Then use the Intersection roll-up to trim the lines to within the square (see Figure 28-25).

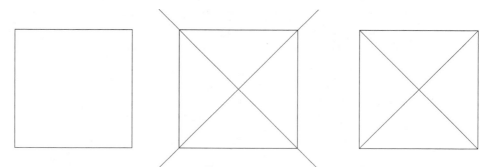

*Figure 28-25: A perfect square perfectly bisected by two lines is our starting point.*

### ▼ Lookit Whut I Kin Do, Ma!

I hate the see-what-I-can-do design mentality that thrives on the Web, with pages full of gimmicks and gizmos that are put there simply for the sake of showing off the programmer's talent. They are disorganized collections of dizzying, random, pointless distractions that fail every traditional design test. If these sites would only come with some sort of virtual aspirin dispenser...

2. Duplicate the x-square and flip it horizontally. Select both of these squares, duplicate, and flip vertically. Now you have a set of squares that already create a seamless tile, with each angled line exiting the square on one side only to reenter on the opposite side. This is the key to this pattern.

3. Now you can use the Shape tool to node-edit the straight lines into the sweeping configuration that is the look of the spider Web. You can combine the smaller lines so that they connect at the center into a larger $x$ as long as you don't change the position of where the lines exit the square. As long as you don't change the exit points, you can change the way the lines curve within the square as much as you wish (see Figure 28-26).

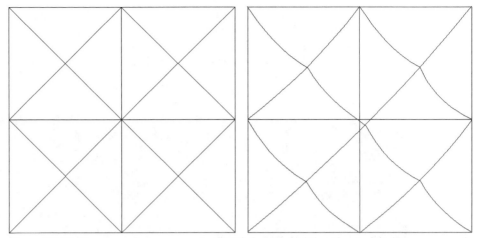

*Figure 28-26: The array of squares creates the tile layout, and then the straight lines are curved to suggest spider Webbing.*

4. Using the small squares as a guide, draw another square the size of the four smaller squares and in the exact same location. Fill it with black or another subtle dark fill and then delete the smaller squares. Give the lines a fat .033-inch dark blue outline. Duplicate the Web lines, give the duplicates a smaller .008-inch white outline, and offset them a hair up and to the right. This creates the dark, spooky Web graphics (see Figure 28-27).

*Figure 28-27: Dark coloring in the square and lighter shades on the lines create the Web.*

5. Select all of the lines and use the PowerClip command to place them inside of the dark boundary square. The PowerClip step trims away the parts of the line that stick over the edge when you give them heavier line weights. This finishes up the tile, which is ready to spin into a Web tile (see Figure 28-28).

*Figure 28-28: With everything constrained within a square, the image is tile-ready.*

6. Select the PowerClip and export it to create a bitmap suitable for the Web.

This and the next example can be seen in the color section and also loaded in a Web browser to see the tile in action. With your Web browser running, open the corelmag.htm file found in the \Chapt28\ subdirectory on the Companion CD-ROM. The Web pages in this chapter are still in development, so the graphics are really too big and unruly to download off of the Web, but they work great right off the CD-ROM! The native file is called Webtiles.cdr and is in the same directory.

**CD-ROM**

## Lava Lamp Not Included

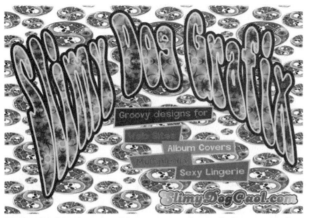

*Figure 28-29: Any graphic group can be made into a seamless tile; then, using the Pattern Fill option in CorelDRAW, it can be used to fill any object.*

Like working with the chain link for the horizontal tile, any graphic made up of smaller units can easily be constructed into a never-ending seamless tile. The freaky background in this psychedelic design is a seamless tile created using a round Deadhead paisley image I had lying around (see Figure 28-29). Yes, you read right, a paisley design using skulls. I found it on a backup tape recently and loved it. Perusing my archives is sort of a digital scavenger hunt!

I created this tile in a flat configuration with the intention of using it as a square tile. When I was using the Pattern Fill feature to create the background for the title graphic, I remembered that you can change the horizontal and vertical tile size. Reducing the vertical dimension of the tile makes the circles look like they are floating at an angle, so I left it like that! For the Web tile, just squish the bitmap in PhotoPaint horizontally or vertically to get this effect. Here is how to make the floating disks seamless tile:

1. Start again with a perfect square; then draw and align guidelines to all four sides of the square. Now import the item that you want to make into a tile, in this case the deadhead paisley. Align the object to the center of the right vertical reference line. Duplicate the object and align the duplicate to the left vertical line. You are ready to start getting seamless (see Figure 28-30).

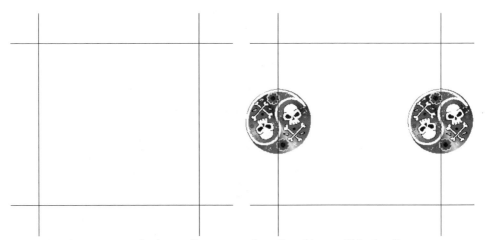

*Figure 28-30: A square and reference lines are used to align objects within the tile area.*

2. With the square defining the area of the tile, and with the art objects aligned horizontally and also exactly at the center of each of the boundary lines, your seamless tile is already at work. Where the paisley exits the rectangle on the left is the exact point that it enters on the right. Cake. It is the distance between the two objects, determined by aligning to the reference lines, that is critical. Now you can select the paisley pair and move them around to create a unique arrangement for this pattern. Any of the objects can stick out beyond the boundary box as long as you first start with a pair of objects. Align the object pair to opposing reference lines; then you can move them as a pair freely and still maintain the seamless tile orientation in the square boundary box (see Figure 28-31).

3. After you have placed all of the object pairs around the square, you can take a deep breath and throw some more objects inside the rectangle. Anything within the image tile needs no special attention. Only the hang-overs need to be properly aligned so that they enter and exit the square in exactly the right orientation. When finished, stuff all of the objects into a perfect square (with no outline) to create your seamless tile (see Figure 28-32).

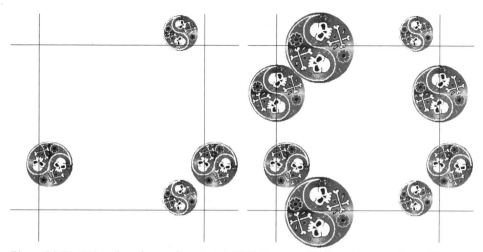

*Figure 28-31: Using the reference lines to establish the correct distance between them, object pairs can be moved around to create the pattern while still maintaining a seamless orientation.*

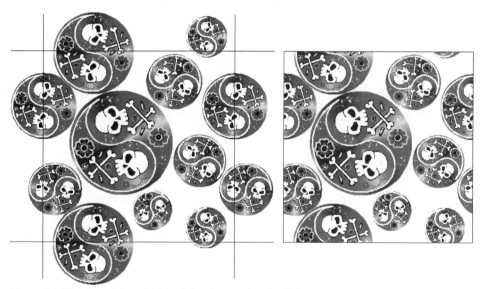

*Figure 28-32: More objects inside of the tile area finish off the pattern, which creates a seamless tile with the PowerClip function.*

4. Select the tile and export it as a bitmap appropriate to your current project. For a Web tile, that is 72 dpi with an RGB color depth. For printed applications, you will want a 300-dpi image with a CMYK color scheme. For a Web tile, you can add the code to your HTML file to get the tile to appear. In CorelDRAW, you can fill any object with the tile using the Bitmap Pattern Fill. Open the Pattern Fill from the Fill tool flyout and click Load to find the freshly made tile. You can use the same height and width values or experiment with different values to make the disks flatter or wider (see Figure 28-33).

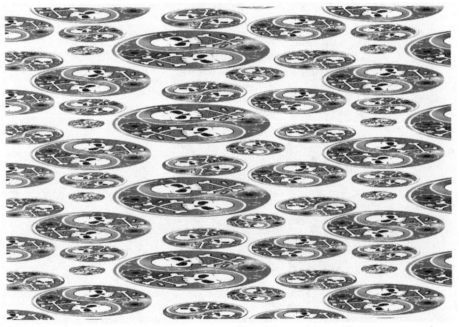

*Figure 28-33: The Bitmap Pattern Fill option lets you fill any object with your new seamless tiles.*

This mind trip can be seen in the color section and also in the Webtiles.cdr file. It is also available as a Web page, called slimy.htm, in the same \Chapt28\ subdirectory on the Companion CD-ROM. You can see how a single seamless tile fills the background with a seemingly solid image. The nice thing is that no matter how big or small you resize your screen or browser, a Web tile will re-calculate to fill the whole screen. A clever background tile and a bitmap on top that takes advantage of the transparency options available in the GIF image format can come together to create a pretty cool Web page. Now it's your turn!

## Moving On

In this chapter, we looked at many ways to create patterns for use in a variety of applications. From freaky tessellations to simplistic backgrounds made with the Symbols roll-up, there are many interesting variants available with CorelDRAW. Once you have artwork finished, you can take it a step further to create seamless tiles for horizontal, vertical, and "all-ways" applications. These patterns are perfect for both Web and print applications as main design elements or secondary background images.

In the next chapter, we will continue to look at ways to use CorelDRAW in nonprint applications. We will take objects and art files and add simple animation techniques to bring them to life on your screen. We will make icons dance, text shimmy, words shake, and images pop. Hey, you don't have to be Walt Disney to get animated, my friend.

### ▼ Beyond f/x

Patterns are everywhere, and with the World Wide Web offering more and more opportunities in design, they are no longer a specialized phenomenon. They can be used to set a mood in a design (a fluffy cloud background sets a much different tone than, say, red hot lava) or to establish the nature of a Web site (a children's Web page with big fun icons in the background; or perhaps a business Web site with a subdued marble background). Patterns can be used in advertising, playing off of the concept with phrases like "We have designs on the future," or "Patterned for success." Holiday theme backgrounds, with little hearts or candy canes, or pumpkins, or whatever icon suggest the time at hand, are an easy way to add a timely feel to a monthly newsletter or other periodical. There are entire industries devoted to the creation of patterns for their products. From high-end silk ties to cheap wrapping paper, you will find patterns everywhere. Textiles alone are huge. Think about it. Beyond clothing, there is upholstery, bedding, drapery, even rugs, all of which need patterning skills to create. It's an interesting and rewarding career in itself, and if you can handle working with underwear all day, I can even give you a few leads!

# chapter 29

# Animation Action

Images that create the illusion of movement are becoming very common-place. With everyone clambering to get on the Web, many designers are being pulled into the electronic design forum by their clients. Multimedia and Web applications are both a blessing and a nightmare, as the new opportunities bring along a host of technical difficulties. Suddenly designers are supposed to be programmers, 3D artists, audio-engineers, and yes, of course, animators!

It does make sense that electronic print designers would take on the tasks of electronic formats. If you have the artwork for other projects in the computer, you are ready to take on the Web or multimedia projects. The art is in place; you just need to get to find some ways to make it more alive. Luckily, with a few tricks, even the most animation-challenged artists can bring artwork to life in CorelDRAW.

Animation goes beyond the traditional sense of creating happy dancing cartoon characters. With contemporary media, things like advertising banners, buttons, pointers, even text, can all be image stacks that refresh in sequence to create live images.

We have already touched on the theory of adding motion and other effects to bring artwork alive in many examples in this book and the Companion CD-ROM. Now we will walk through the complete process of transforming artwork into a set of *cells*, which can be assembled into an interesting, ani-mated entity for your Web site or other onscreen application.

First, we will see how using a transparency effect to change the background coloring can give a static illustration a sense of motion and tension. Then, we will create a word out of jiggling gelatin and alter the background colors to electrify and bring an ad to life. After that, we'll use animated text effects with multiple images and also lens effects to get the headlines on your Web site noticed. Finally, we will create perpetual motion by using frames for the intermeshing gears animation found in the Chapter 27 Web examples. You may think cartoons are for kids, but I guarantee that animations will be a part of your very adult design world if you continue to function as an electronic artist now and into the future!

## Biking Madness

*Figure 29-1: Use a lens to alter the background of an illustration to bring a dynamic sense of motion to animate static image.*

The problem with animation for many commercial applications is that it is way out of the budget of most projects. I already charge an exorbitant amount for a single illustration; imagine the cost of, say, 10 illustrations for a complex animation. Now also consider the insane amount of work to organize and orchestrate such an undertaking. To get our hero in Figure 29-1 to ride and leap would require a lengthy photography session to get the necessary reference material, weeks to ink up the illustrations, and then hours of colorizing and assembling the images in the computer. It's the kind of project that is just not going to happen with your average client.

However, with a few simple tricks you can get a dynamic sense of motion without actually moving anything. Your goal is just to create an interesting animated graphic out of a static image in order to make your Web pages dance and sing like everyone else's. It is little tricks like this that bridge the gap between expensive animation and low-budget images that bring a Web page to life. Here is how to get attention and add interest to an existing graphic by adding a flashing background color effect:

1. This project started as—big surprise—one of my ink illustrations. It was scanned as a 1-bit bitmap, imported into CorelDRAW, and then colorized in the now all-too-familiar process (Chapter 18 for you skip-ahead readers!). I won't bore you with redundant details. The file is called foes.cdr in the \Chapt29\ subdirectory on the Companion CD-ROM if you want to see things firsthand. The ink illustration turned out to be the limiting factor in this project. Because I had no intentions of using this illustration for anything but its original purpose (a bold T-shirt design), the image of the cyclist is connected to the black background. Not the kind of graphic that lends itself easily to animation, but I really wanted it on the Web site. Left with few options, I came up with the flashing color scheme, similar to the angels.avi from Chapter 16, only I didn't have the luxury of foreground/background flexibility.

2. In order to create a different color scheme for the Web animation, draw a yellow rectangle and place it in front of the background coloring elements, but behind the rest of the design. The easiest way to do this is to work in Wireframe view, send the rectangle to the back, then use the Arrange | Order | In Front Of command, and click on the background coloring object. Now it should be in place within the image stack.

3. Select the Interactive Transparency tool, change the Type setting on the Property Bar to Fountain, and then click the Radial button. Done. The transparent yellow mixes with the existing background colors to create new colors, just like on an artist's palette. In this illustration, the yellows mix with the colors underneath to make oranges and yellowish browns.

4. Export the image as a Web-friendly, 72-dpi, RGB bitmap in the TIF format. Don't be too concerned about actual size or color depth at this point; just export at 72 dpi and RGB (16 Million Colors) and we can

CD-ROM

tweak the images specifically for the Web later, as discussed. When we assemble these images in PhotoPaint, we will also tweak the size and color palette to exactly what we need. Remember to number the cell, like foes1.tif, so each file is unique for each unique cell. Be sure to use the same settings for each export, as even a slight variant will be noticeable. (For example, I didn't enable Super-Sampling for one of the cells in the queen.avi animation back in \Chapt4\, and the result was a fuzzy-flash effect.) See Figure 29-2.

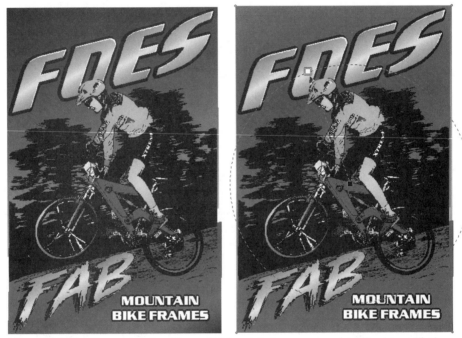

Figure 29-2: A yellow rectangle with a radial fountain transparency (right) mixes with the original background colors (left) to create a cell in the color flash animation (see color section).

**TIP**    *You can use the Windows screen capture feature (Alt+Print Screen) to copy and paste images for Web animations. However, you will have to work with the entire screen intact through most of the process to ensure that each cell is exactly the same size. This is why the Export feature might be a better option, as CorelDRAW is very good about creating exactly the same size image each time and you can selectively pick parts of a design to export with the Selected Only option. I created the animations in Chapter 27 (in the sample Web sites) using screen captures. The examples in this chapter were all created with cells made with the Export function.*

5. With the transparency rectangle selected, change the fill value from yellow to cyan and repeat the export process for cell number two. Then fill it with magenta and export for cell number three. Finally, fill it with black, and export for cell number four. Save your CorelDRAW file and exit the application.

6. Start PhotoPaint and then open all of the cells you just created. PhotoPaint is nice in that it lets you shift-select more than one file at a time to open. Go grab a soda while PhotoPaint opens all of the files, or take a moment to exercise your eyes (see the sidebar, "Repetitive Motion Injuries").

▼ **Repetitive Motion Injuries**

Public service announcement time. As I used to be in charge of office automation for So Cal's number-one grocery chain, I am also an expert on proper workstation habits (I preach to all my friends; bugs the crap out of them!). Make sure you are in a natural work environment in which you are comfortable and that you are using proper posture. Get a good chair with solid lumbar support and a computer desk that has an adjustable keyboard rest so your keyboard will be in a position that is comfortable for you. The new ergonomic mice and keyboards are nice. Position your monitor so you can look either directly at it or slightly down at it (as if you were talking to someone your height or slightly shorter). Make sure no surrounding lights are reflecting back at you in the screen. And on a regular basis, get up and stretch your back and neck, touch your toes, and exercise your eye muscles.

Many problems, like headaches and the inability to focus after working for long periods, are the result of not stretching your eye muscles. When you stare at your computer monitor all day, you end up using a very narrow range of your eye muscles. Take a break now and then and focus on something really far away, like mountains, planes, or the person walking past your window (or cubicle). Then focus on something really close, like your finger near your nose, your elbow, your next deadline, and so forth. This will stretch your eye muscles. Repeat this exercise a few times a day, especially before you get into the car and try to drive. Nothing is more frightening than trying to drive after a day at the computer and everything past the windshield is just a big fuzzy blur! Stretch everything before and after the commute and you will in much better shape. Oh, and don't forget to drink plenty of liquids, defrag your hard drive, and remember to write timely thank-you notes.

7. Select the Foes1.tif image, and from the View menu, choose Zoom | 50%. You need to be able to see all of the image in the window so you can work with it. Notice that there is an unwanted white area on the right of the image. This is because something, perhaps the bitmap or some other object, made the width of the exported bitmap larger than anticipated. This isn't a problem as long as all of the bitmaps are exactly the same. We will remove it in a later step.

8. From the Movie menu, choose Create From Document. This will transform the TIF image into an AVI, which is a multiframe movie format. Notice how there are now additional controls and also the location, Frame1, at the bottom of the selected frame. To add more frames to this one frame movie, click on the right + button. From the Insert Frames dialog, insert as many frames as you wish (you can delete extras later). In this example, we have four total images for a simple loop, so with one image already in the AVI, we only need to add three more. Click OK to add the frames (see Figure 29-3).

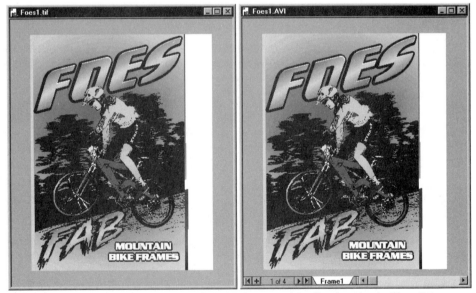

*Figure 29-3: A single-frame bitmap can be made into a multi-cell animation in PhotoPaint.*

9. Use the left of the dual right arrows to advance to the next frame (the other arrow advances to the last frame). Now select foes3.tif and copy the image (Ctrl+C). Select the AVI again (use the Window menu to toggle

between open files) and paste the graphic (Ctrl+V) into place. It should fall exactly into place. If it does not (and randomly it doesn't), delete the pasted graphic (Del key) and stretch the AVI window so it appears larger on the screen. Try the paste again. If it is still not perfectly aligned to the background box, use the arrow keys to nudge it perfectly into place. When it's in place, use the Ctrl+Down Arrow keys to deselect the mask and merge the image with the empty frame. Click the back arrow to see if the image is in line with the first cell (stationary parts of the animation should not hop around from cell to cell). If things are not exact, use the Mask tool to select the image in frame2 and then use the nudge keys until the images are exactly in the same orientation from cell to cell. In this example, I had to nudge each image up and to the left one tap of the arrow key after each paste. When you're finished, use the arrow button at the bottom of the AVI window to advance to the next frame.

**TIP** *To speed up the animation process, use the Insert From File command from the Movie menu to add images into your movie. This helps avoid the out-of-registration problems and also is faster overall. The downside is you can only add a frame before or after the one selected, which means you may have to delete the extra frames later.*

10. Repeat the copy/paste process until each of the bitmap cells created in CorelDRAW is in its own frame in the animation. To view the animation at this stage, use the Movie | Control | Play Movie command. The Esc key or Movie | Control | Stop Movie will halt the player. Take a moment and save the AVI to disk.

11. With the movie working and all the frames in place for smooth animation, we can start to fine-tune the image. For starters, we need to get rid of all that dead space to the right. From the Image menu, choose Paper Size to open the Paper Size dialog where we can trim things down. First disable the Maintain Aspect Ration option or any changes we make to the width will also affect the height. Change the Placement to Centered Left, so our changes will only be to the right-hand side. Now decrease the Width value, using the preview window as a guide. Keep downsizing until all of the white is trimmed away from the right and click OK. Even though you can only view one cell in the Paper Size preview, the changes affect all cells (see Figure 29-4).

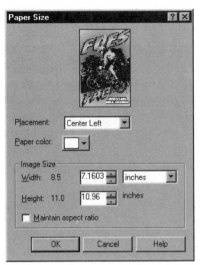

*Figure 29-4: The Paper Size dialog lets you change the size of the image area and trim away unwanted material from all cells in a movie.*

12. You can repeat the trimming process as many times as necessary to reduce and remove the image down to just the desired material. With the movie working and appearing perfectly, it is time to manipulate it further for your application. From the Image menu, select Resample to open the Resample dialog. Here we can control the physical size of the movie and its resolution. First of all, change the Resolution value to 72 dpi, which is what onscreen applications call for. Now change the Image Size setting to the exact size that you need and click OK. All of cells in the movie will resize in unison.

13. If you want to use the animation as an AVI for multimedia applications or what have you, the RGB format is fine. For an image stack to use in a Web page, you need to convert the graphic to a 256 color palette. No sweat, PhotoPaint is here to serve you! From the Image menu again, choose Convert To | Paletted (8-bit). This will open the Convert to Paletted Image dialog, where you have a few options. Choose the Custom Palette type and then the Error Diffusion or Ordered Dither type (the None option will look really awful. The other two choices are personal preference. Experiment to find the dithering algorithm that suits your taste). Click OK to open the Color Table dialog. Here you can choose the standard System palette (the most common choice) or color

tables from specific Web browsers, such as Netscape Navigator or Microsoft Explorer. If you have a specific need (for instance, if you are building a Web site for an intranet where everyone is using a specific browser), pick that specific color table. If not, System is probably your best and most versatile choice. Make your choice and click OK. Save this image in the GIF format, and you can use the animation in a Web page.

**TRAP**

*It is a very common mistake to build a Web site using a color table that is specific to your machine and not your audience's. A buddy of mine built an entire Web site on his PC to show his client, and it looked awesome. When he went to his client's office, his client was using a Mac, which has a different system palette. They loaded up the site and it looked awful. Not a good way to make an impression! In a situation like this, find out the exact color table that the big guy decision maker is using so your presentation will go better. If you have no idea, and you want to make your Web site as universally viewable as possible, select the Adaptive color palette from the Convert to Paletted Image dialog.*

Hanna and Barbera should be shakin' in their shoes, because that's all there is to it! This movie is called foes.avi and is located in the \Chapt29\ subdirectory of the Companion CD-ROM. Also there is foes2.avi, where I took a cell from the first animation and created a new one from there. I used PhotoPaint's tools to copy the rider, change the background, and then paste him back into place. This made for two frames of moving background, which assemble into another movie. You can animate any stack of bitmaps into a movie or GIF file using PhotoPaint; you can also take advantage of the program's built-in bitmap editing features. Not only can you assemble a stack of images, you can also trim down the animation to size and change the color depth to customize the animation for its specific assignment. There is no better or easier way to take an AVI and make it into a GIF for the Web. It is the kind of power that is easy to abuse, as can be seen in the silly dance.avi file, also found in the \Chapt29\ subdirectory of the Companion CD. I created this movie from a brochure that I had made many years ago and just happened to stumble across; the movie is a series of still images of me dancing around like an idiot. (I am my own favorite parody victim, as I almost never sue myself!)

If you want to work through the tutorial step-by-step, you'll also find the original bicycle file, foes.cdr, in the \Chapt29\ subdirectory. It is an easy enough concept to grasp, and I won't bore you with the step-by-step details of assembling the frames in PhotoPaint for the following examples. Once you know how to do it, you can create an animation out of nearly anything!

▼ **Progress, Progress, Progress**

In the passing years, as technology has so rapidly changed, so has the nature of a commercial art studio such as ours (and I am betting yours, too!). At first, our office was essentially a big warehouse filled with tables for pasteup, mechanical-drawing machines, a giant stat-camera, rollers and waxers, and a pukey little computer for bookkeeping. Over the years, those pasteup tools were all tossed, the pricey mechanical-illustration machines were declared worthless, and even the trusty camera was chucked in favor of its digital counterpart. Soon everything was electronic, and even things like ink illustrations began to fade away in favor of high-tech, computer-generated images. Just when we got really good at making pretty pictures for print (we even moved next to our service bureau to work out Mac versus PC output issues and take care of that hassle), our clients started asking about multimedia and World Wide Web projects. The challenges just never stop!

When we first got a copy of CorelMove, an application that let us build an animation, my buddy Eddie and I were thrilled to finally have a way to create our own cartoon. Well, after about 12 hours of learning the program, scanning and coloring the illustrations, adding a few sounds, and assembling the frames, we had a movie of about 15 seconds. It was a caricature of our friend Dave inside a television, sticking his tongue out. I have had undying respect for animation ever since!

## Jay-Eee-Ell-Ell-Oh, You Know?

This animation (jello.avi in the \Chapt29\ directory on the Companion CD-ROM) came from a conversation with the marketing staff at Ventana. For those of you unfamiliar with the world of publishing (and it is a strange world indeed), the marketing people start promoting the title long before it is even finished. They were picking my brain at the beginning of the project for features they could promote, and in the course of the conversation, somehow jiggling Jell-O got thrown into the mix. They loved the idea, and I hung up the phone thinking, "Well, now I have to figure out how the heck to do that!" Nothing like agreeing to the unknown!

The solution to creating cells for jiggling text came from the Brian the BrainBot example (from Chapter 24). If a blend could build and rebuild the robot arms automatically, then why not the jiggling gelatin? The attraction of using a blend like the robot arm example is that you can select and move one of the control curves and the image will rebuild automatically. That's the kind of automation I am after! The same kind of trick works here to rebuild the Jell-O after each move. Here is how to make text jiggle on top with a rigid base:

1. Start with text that is at an angle and use the Perspective function to alter it. Fill it with a dark red and duplicate it. Move the duplicate above the original and fill it with pink. Now shift-select both objects and create a 200-step blend between them. This will create a 3D-like object (see Figure 29-5).

*Figure 29-5: Create a solid gelatin text object by blending two objects together.*

2. Select the top control object and duplicate it. Now from the Fountain Fill dialog, use the Cylinder 22 preset to give the top of the gelatin a nice set of reflections. (You don't want the whole blend to have this fill, just the top, so that is why you duplicate the control object first.)

3. Now you have the live Jell-O word ready to get a jigglin'! Select the top copy with the custom color blend and then press the Tab key. This will toggle and select the control curve right below it. Hold down the Shift key and select the very top piece again. Now you have both top pieces (which you can not group together because of the live blend, so you have to do this little tab-shift-select cha cha each time). With both the top coloring object and the control object beneath it selected, you can move them around anywhere, and the blend will rebuild to create a new jiggle. You can move, resize, twist, slant, whatever, for mild-to-wild gelatin activity! See Figure 29-6.

*Figure 29-6: Moving the top coloring and blend control objects will create cells for a jiggling animation.*

4. Set your gelatin text in any stage setting you choose. My set was a campy '50s-looking ad, with the text centered in a white burst made with the Polygon tool. The text is arched along a circular path at the top, and the font is called Beatsville, which looked sufficiently corny for this application!

5. With the stage set, now you can set out to generate each animation cell. I wanted to use this as a Web animation, so that usually means trying to milk the most animation out of the fewest cells. The minimal number of cells to get the gelatin word to jiggle back and forth is four, with cell two repeated twice to create an endless loop. It goes like this: left-center-right-center. This animation will repeat endlessly as left-center-right-center-left-center-right-center-left-center-right-center, and so on. So basically you need to generate three cells; left, center, and right.

6. Working out the logic for this animation also revealed an interesting possibility for a flashing background effect. If you notice, every other cell is in the center, so if you change the background on that cell to another color, it will cause the graphic to flash. So that is what I did!

Export each cell, moving the top pieces as shown to create a stack of images that will assemble into a jiggling gelatin text object. Change the background color every other image for a flashing effect. The movie is called jello.avi and is found in the \Chapt29\ subdirectory on the Companion CD-ROM. The parent file also there; it's called jello.cdr. If you load the CorelDRAW file, you can see how selecting the top two pieces of the Jell-O and moving them causes the blend to rebuild the rest of the object in the new orientation. Blends make for quick and easy animations, and the color flash technique makes for eye-catching icons on a Web site.

CD-ROM

## Text That Lives!

There are so many ways to animate text to grab attention on a Web site it is nauseating! You can create multiple copies of a headline (like in the world.cdr file from Chapter 16) and create cells where each duplicate is moved slightly (check the animation called jitters.avi in the \Chapt29\ subdirectory, for example). You can create spinning logos with the Extrude feature (as outlined in Chapter 7 and also seen there in the fxspin.avi file) or by creating a stack of 12 images by exporting a text element after spinning it in 30-degree increments. Even complex still images can get a new level of interest by just exporting two cells with slightly different backgrounds and using different anti-aliasing settings for each cell (check out weenie.avi in the \Chapt29\ subdirectory to see what I mean). If you can think of it, you can animate it.

There are some effects, however, that are so cool they defy their easy CorelDRAW origins! The text-thru-a-keyhole effect (fisheye.avi in the \Chapt29\ subdirectory) is a perfect addition to a Web site; it is the result of the simple task of moving a lens over some type. Another great payoff with just a little investment! Here is how to create the fisheye text:

1. Start by using the Artistic text tool to type out the phrase you want to appear in the keyhole. I used a font called AmerType, which looks like it was typed on an old-fashioned typewriter. Color this text white (or any color).

**TIP** *Colors: 256=256. It's interesting to note that a file created with a 256 color palette is often the same size as one created with 256 shades of gray. You may not save any file size by creating black-and-white images for animated Web GIFs. Since you can't save a GIF in the 1-bit black-and-white color depth to take advantage of a smaller file size, you have to use the 256 shades of gray option. That could create a file that is the same size as one that uses 256 colors! So go for the color option, and see if it isn't much bigger than black and white.*

2. Rest your text on a black (or any color) background object. Now draw another box on top of the text and give this object the Fish Eye lens at a rate of 150%. This will bug out the text beneath it (see Figure 29-7).

*Figure 29-7: A text object (in Wireframe view above) is distorted by a rectangle with the Fish Eye lens.*

3. Start with the lens over the left side of the text, and with the lens object selected, open the Export dialog. If you use the Selected Only option, only the rectangle will export, but because it is also a lens, it will export the distorted text. This makes lens effects ideal for creating animation cells; each cell is the exact same size as the lens object, so you don't have to trim down the image with other tricks (like the PowerClip feature, for example) before each export.

4. Repeat the export process many times, each time moving the lens object a little to the right before the export. The bigger the move, the fewer the cells in the animation. You can get away with just a few connecting images for a Web graphic, but if you use too few, it will be hard to read the text. I created 23 cells for a smoother, easier-to-read, fisheye animation.

Lens effects lend themselves to all kinds of animations. If you place a Heat Map lens over an object, for example, and then change the Palette rotation value for a stack of animation cells, you can get a very freaky effect. Or use a Transparency lens over an object, varying the opacity in each cell to fade to or from black. The variety of animations you can generate in CorelDRAW is only limited by your energy and imagination!

## Perpetual Gears

**CD-ROM**

The animated gears that will serve as navigation buttons (see the index.htm file in the \Chapt27\ subdirectory on the Companion CD-ROM) are a great example of something that looks hard to create but isn't. It is also a perfect example of *closure* (see the sidebar, "Closure"). The animation is only two frames, but it repeats endlessly to look like turning gears. Here is how to get the machine moving:

▼ **Closure**

*Closure* is more than ending an experience in your life; it is also your eye's natural tendency to fill in the blanks to make things whole even when they are not. When you watch a movie or cartoon, it is really a series of static images, but you see it as a solid stream of motion. Another example is water flowing out of a faucet or hose. It looks to be a solid stream, but is really round bursts of water one after another. (If you blink your eyes really fast, sometimes you can catch the droplets in the stream. If not, high-speed cameras will convince you!)

Your stupid eyes that don't see what is really there make things like movies, television, laser light shows, and even your computer monitor possible. Your monitor is actually a single row of pixels refreshing from top to bottom. This row refreshes so fast that you think it is a solid image.

To prove to yourself that this is actually happening, stand in front of your monitor, stick your tongue out, and make an obscene raspberry noise. This will vibrate your head and eyes and break up the closure phenomenon enough to see the scan lines in the screen. Vary the pitch and frequency of your tongue vibration and you can see the screen begin to flash, wiggle, and wave (works best on monitors with a slow refresh rate). Now wipe the spit off of the screen, and try to explain to the other people in the office what the heck you are doing. (It may be easier just to say you were critiquing some software!) For more proof (or to avoid spitting on your expensive computer equipment), try taking a picture of your television screen with a high shutter speed, and you will see the scan lines.

1. Start with a set of gears as outlined in Chapter 24. Arrange them inside of a boundary box, which will again guarantee that both bitmap cells have the same physical dimensions.

2. Position the gears as you desire and combine them into one group. Duplicate this gear shape and boundary box and move off to the side. Select and duplicate the gear shape in the first group one more time. Break apart this duplicate back into the individual gears again so you can manipulate each one individually. Select each free gear and rotate until the gear teeth are exactly in between those below it. Repeat this for all of the gears.

3. With the top gears in the rotated orientation, select them all and combine them back into one curve again. Now delete the reference curve for this set, and you should have two gear groups (see Figure 29-8).

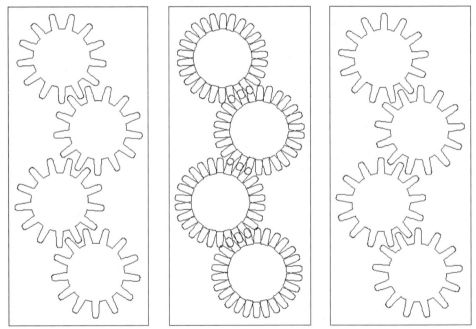

*Figure 29-8: An original set of gears is duplicated and each object is rotated to create the in-between gear orientation.*

4. Shift-select both of the gear curves and fill them with an appropriate color. I used the Gold Plated fountain fill preset to give the objects a metallic look. Now select just one of the gear curves and open the Extrude roll-up. From the Extrude roll-up, create the beveled, dimensional look just like we did before with the gear shapes in Chapter 24. Be sure that the vanishing point for the extrude is set to VP Locked to Object and not To Page before you click Apply. This immediately makes the gears look amazing!

5. Select the non-extruded gears and use the Copy | Extrude command to use the extrude values from the first set of gears in the next set. Sometimes the vanishing point goes perquacky during this process, making the duplicate look wrong. If this is the case, select the original extrude group, open the second page on the Vanishing Point tab of the Extrude roll-up, and write down the Horizontal and Vertical values. Now switch back to the duplicate and change the values to match (see Figure 29-9).

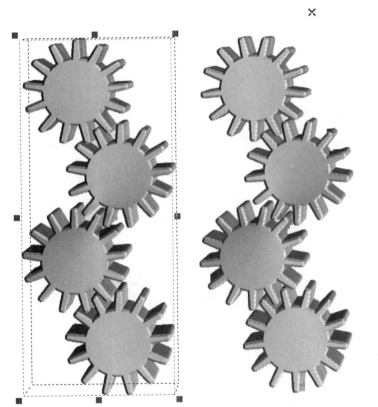

*Figure 29-9: Add depth and shading with the Extrude roll-up on a gear curve; then copy the values to the second gear group.*

There you have it! You have the two frames needed to create the perpetual motion gear animation! You can watch the gears twirl in the Web example in Chapter 27 or in the gears.avi file found in the \Chapt29\ subdirectory on the Companion CD-ROM. Even though there are only two frames, you could swear the gears are counter-rotating like a fancy piece of machinery! Aren't optical illusions fun?

## Moving On

In this chapter, we looked at many examples of how to assemble images created in CorelDRAW into animations. You can use these animations in many applications, including Web pages and multimedia programs. Virtually any stack of images can be made into a playable movie using the animation power of PhotoPaint. It's a simple process, with only your time and patience limiting the complexities of your animations.

In the next and final chapter, we will look at another high-tech trend in the world of design: 3D modeling. Now that CorelDRAW ships with CorelDream as a companion product, your designs can benefit from the magic of virtual reality. Relax, there are no special goggles needed to enter this cyberspace, just your mouse, keyboard, and a little creativity!

▼ **Beyond f/x**

With and more traditional designers being pulled into new media markets, animation is becoming a more common task. You can use animations to add interest and gain attention in many applications, the most obvious being Web pages. Things like information kiosks to automatic teller machines make use of the kind of animation you can produce right this very minute with the hardware and software sitting in front of you! Even print media can benefit from animation; for example, you can use a set of cells as a border element to suggest motion (see Figure 29-10). Animated buttons or those annoying ad banners that show up everywhere on the Web are just a few of the things you could be creating with multiframe images in CorelDRAW, and you would be fattening up your bank account in the process. So get cracking—or perhaps I should say get *stacking*!

*Figure 29-10: Animation techniques can add a sense of motion to a static image, such as this flyer, where animation cells are placed in a movie-like film strip border element.*

# chapter 30

# Beyond Two Dimensions

In desktop publishing, there are many ways to achieve a look that is much more than just flat images lying on the page. Throughout this book, we have added depth with highlights and shadows, created the illusion of dimension with the Perspective and Extrude tools, and even spun objects in a virtual space.

To communicate with others involved in a project (as in the box art example in this chapter), you will want to take flat artwork and arrange it in a 3D-like orientation. By using the skew features within CorelDRAW, you can get a convincing look from your existing working illustrations.

There are times, though, when the 3D capabilities of CorelDRAW will simply not be enough. There are just too many challenges to get the kind of subtle depth, shadow, and reflection in CorelDRAW that some projects will demand (imagine trying to render an image of a poster stuck to a corrugated aluminum wall). These kinds of tasks are achieved with relatively little effort in the new virtual 3D applications such as CorelDream. We have already seen how you can use intricate and complex dimensional objects from CorelDream directly in your CorelDRAW publications with the use of the 3DMF file format, but we have not explored other ways to use these two programs concurrently.

In this chapter, we will start with two-dimensional art files and examine ways to add depth to your designs, both in CorelDRAW and in CorelDream. In the first example, we will use flat packaging artwork to create a 3D mock-up of the finished box directly in CorelDRAW. Then we will walk through a similar project again, only this time we'll create pieces in CorelDRAW to build bitmap stickers to stick on a box in the true 3D environment of CorelDream. Finally, we will examine other ways to mix and match the power of

CorelDRAW and CorelDream to create objects that would be impossible or very difficult to create in either of the programs alone. We will use CorelDRAW to create the specialized shapes that, when manipulated in CorelDream, turn into true 3D objects. We will walk through the process of creating basic CorelDRAW shapes that we will transform into pulleys, gears, bottles, and vases in CorelDream. All of these examples are fairly simple, but my goal here is not to wow you with art, but to reveal some techniques that I use to create cool 3D objects with relatively little effort. We are in for a lot of 3D fun, and you don't even have to wear those goofy glasses!

## Turbo-Charged Box Art

*Figure 30-1: By skewing flat artwork, you can create 3D-like images, which are helpful for visualizing a finished 3D product.*

Prototypes are a huge hassle in design. Starting from scratch to create new packaging ideas or any other project that does not already exist in one way or another can be quite a challenge. More often than not, the biggest difficulty is not creating the necessary artwork, but creating images for the noncreative people involved so that they can share in your visions. Creating artwork to aid in the visualization process is also important to avoid any screw-ups by anyone in the production loop.

The best way to work out problems with a packaging design is to create a physical mock-up of the item (see the sidebar, "Wow 'Em"). Boxes have strange design parameters that depend on the project and the nature of the items to be packaged, so the more reference material for everyone involved, the fewer chances of communication errors and mistakes. In general, boxes are *die-cut* from a single piece of flat cardboard that has been imprinted with the appropriate artwork laid out in the correct orientation (more often with a full-color sticker stuck on to the cardboard) for each panel. CorelDRAW is pretty stable dimensionally, so you can design both the artwork and the *die guide* (the artwork used to create the actual cutting template) right on your desktop. The top half of the graphic in Figure 30-1 (which is also in the color section) shows how a die-cut box looks after it is printed and cut out.

## ▼ Wow 'Em

The best way to blow away your client, and also provide an idiot-proof reference for the production people, is to create an actual mock-up of the box project. Output the box at actual size using a color printer. Most service bureaus offer a large format (tabloid) printer at close to proofing quality. If you can't fit the box on a single sheet, output the panels separately and then glue them onto cardboard. Use a utility knife to cut along your guidelines and then fold and assemble the box. It's easy and will really impress your customer. This is an especially useful tool to use when you have clients who are insecure or dragging their feet on a project. With the box sitting on their desk, they usually lose any fears that you can't make it happen! And it is a handy trick when you need packaging for a photo shoot and the packages don't exist yet!

In this next example, we will take the panels from a box art project and use the skew feature to place them in a 3D orientation. This kind of project is common, where you take existing artwork, like a client's logo, and place it in an angled 3D orientation. You can use the same kind of technique not only to fashion boxes, but also to mock up store displays, billboards, tractor trailers, wherever you want to stick a piece of existing artwork on. This really only works for flat surfaces. If you want to stick artwork on a more complicated surface, say a dimpled metal wall, you will want to create a bitmap in CorelDRAW and then stick it to the 3D surface using techniques outlined in the next section. Here is how to get flat artwork to look three-dimensional in CorelDRAW:

1. Start with the artwork needed to actually print and die-cut the box. This file is called turbobox.cdr in the \Chapt30\ subdirectory on the Companion CD-ROM and is set up in the working mechanicals layout, to give the production people so they can create the box. It has the artwork and also the outlines necessary to create the die for cutting. It isn't very interesting in Normal view (it is mostly black), but the Wireframe view will show you the die-lines, folds, and other details necessary for production.

2. Isolate the artwork for the panels that will show in the 3D configuration. In this case, the front, top, and left sides are needed. Select the art for those sections and delete the rest (see Figure 30-2).

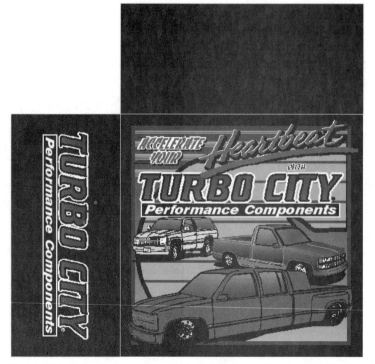

*Figure 30-2: From the box mechanicals, select the top, front, and left side artwork.*

3. Select the artwork for each section and group it. This will just make it easier to select the three main panels. Select the front group and double-click to review the rotation and skew arrows. Select the left-center skew arrows and drag down while holding the Ctrl key to skew the objects 30 degrees. Now select the right group, and using the right center skew arrows, skew the objects 30 degrees (see Figure 30-3).

*Figure 30-3: Use the rotation and skew arrows to give the sides a slanted orientation.*

4. Align the front and side object groups to the bottom. Pull a guideline off of the left vertical ruler so that it runs up the left side of side panel. Now select the graphic for the top and use the top skew arrows to slant 45 degrees to the left (see Figure 30-4). Notice how this meets the guideline.

*Figure 30-4: Drag the arrows to skew the top piece 45 degrees.*

5. Select the top; now use the left-center skew handles and drag down 30 degrees. This just about fits things together, but not quite.

6. In Wireframe view, grab the left panel and use the left-center skew arrows to drop down the left side until it is perfectly aligned with the top angle. Finito! See Figure 30-5.

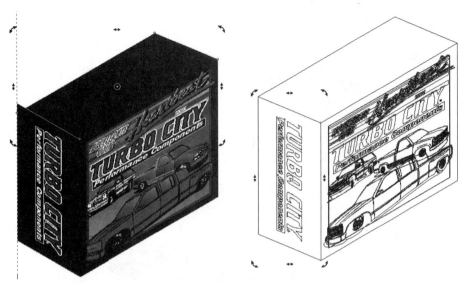

*Figure 30-5: When you skew the top down, it almost fits, but not until the left front panel is skewed a little more.*

This is what I call a quick-and-dirty solution. It looks good and is convincing enough for most applications. If you want to get real technically correct, you could use the Perspective function to place the sides in a perfect 3D orientation. I'm just a big fan of idealized reality, as you know!

## Joe's "Camel" Box

*Figure 30-6: Use CorelDRAW to create both the dimension box sides and the inlaid marble bitmap image for an ornate jewelry box and then assemble it within CorelDream.*

When you use CorelDRAW to create 3D mock-ups, they occasionally fall together easily with acceptable results. You will find, however, that more and more the power and versatility of virtual 3D packages look very attractive. The virtual workspace of CorelDream and other 3D applications allow you to build all kinds of amazing dimensional objects, and you are not limited to the simple box like the one in the previous example. CorelDream lets you construct any object, no matter what the shape or the level of complexity. This power is enhanced even more when you add the simplicity and familiarity of working within CorelDRAW to the creation of pieces for assembly in the virtual world of CorelDream. In this example, the top, sides, and bottom of the box started as CorelDRAW objects, as did the interesting inlaid marble pattern.

Even the amazing power of CorelDream is essentially limited to sculpting objects. To go that extra mile and custom-tailor a unique coloring scheme or pattern, you need to use our old pal, CorelDRAW. Since CorelDRAW has all of the power to create flat artwork, it just makes sense to marry the two technologies.

In this example, we create artwork in CorelDRAW that will be exported as a bitmap and used to paste onto a CorelDream object like a virtual sticker. CorelDream objects can be painted with an almost endless variety of textures and colors, including bitmaps from external sources. Take advantage of that power and design specialized artwork in CorelDRAW to use in CorelDream for patterns, signs, you name it. Here is how to prepare 2D artwork in CorelDRAW for coloring in CorelDream:

1. First, prepare artwork in CorelDRAW to use as a sticker in CorelDream. I created shapes and filled them with the Alabaster texture fill found in the Samples Library. It has a marbled look, and by changing the color scheme, you can get different colors for different shapes. I used symbols for the camel and palm trees and used other basic shapes to create an ornate design that looks like inlaid marble. To save time, you can copy and paste the pieces for use on the other two sides. In Figure 30-7, you see the wireframe of the shapes used to create the flat graphics. Check out the color section to see them filled in.

*Figure 30-7: Build graphics in CorelDRAW using simple shapes and symbols for an inlaid marble look.*

2. Drag-select the objects in each section and group them. Then select the group and use the Export function to create a bitmap for use in CorelDream. Be sure to export each image in the Windows bitmap (BMP) format, which is suitable for CorelDream, and enable the Selected Only option to create a unique graphic for each side. Export the bitmap at 16 million (RGB) colors and at a resolution that is suitable for your application. Repeat the process to produce a separate bitmap for each side and exit CorelDRAW.

3. Start CorelDream and construct the basic box using the cube primitive. This technique will allow for the application of a decal on one side of an object, so you will want to build the box out of thin rectangles, like boards.

4. From the Shaders browser, choose Shader | New, title the shader TOP, and click OK. This will create a new default shader sphere (in red). Double-click on it to open the Shader Editor. Now change the view to Flat Preview, and from the Type menu, choose Texture Map. Locate and click on the bitmap you created for the top of the box and click Open. Now you have the sticker inside of CorelDream (see Figure 30-8).

*Figure 30-8: Use the Shader Editor to load a bitmap for use in CorelDream.*

5. The new image should appear in the Shaders browser. Under the Objects tab in the hierarchy window, locate the object you want to stick this image to. Right-click over the object name and choose Properties. Under the Object Properties dialog, click the Shading tab to reveal the desired options. Under Mapping Mode, click the Box Mapping button; then click on the side of the box you want the sticker to appear on. Click OK when finished (see Figure 30-9).

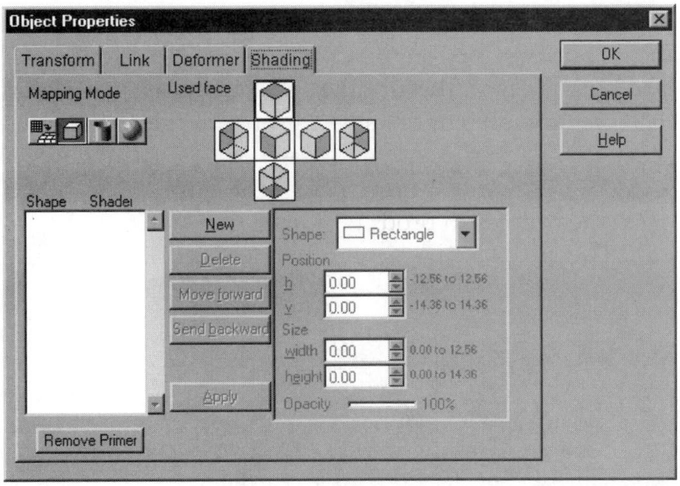

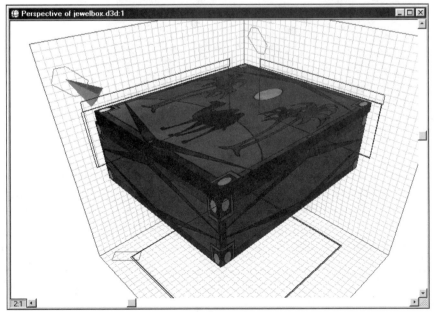

*Figure 30-9: Use the Object Properties dialog to chose where the sticker will appear on the cube.*

6. Now when you drag the sticker image from the Shaders browser onto your cube, it will color the selected side. If nothing seems to happen, change the options under the View menu to Default Quality | Better Preview and Object Quality | Better Preview. Stick 'em up! Repeat this process to add the CorelDRAW image to each side of a CorelDream object (see Figure 30-10).

*Figure 30-10: Any graphic can be stuck to a CorelDream object.*

The box reveals its treasures in the color section and in the camelbox.cdr file in the \Chapt30\ subdirectory on the Companion CD-ROM. The CorelDream file, jewelbox.d3d, is a demo file with the stickers attached to cubes. If you load it, you can see how each of the object properties has been adjusted to make the sticker appear on the correct side.

## 2D to 3D

*Figure 30-11: Objects created in CorelDRAW get depth and dimension in CorelDream to populate a littered digital landscape.*

Like I said before, I am far from a CorelDream expert. It has been a slow, arduous task for me to evolve into the world of virtual space. I just don't have a brain that works well with objects in three dimensions, like some sort of digital depth perception! (Is it a cone or a tunnel? A tunnel or a cone? I can't tell! AAGH!)

The wagon in Figure 30-11 is my coffee table. It has a long and interesting history, but I'll leave that story for those curious enough to browse my Web site. The significance here is that I used a measuring tape to figure out the actual dimensions and then created those pieces in CorelDRAW, where dimensioning is easy. I created a flat rectangle for the base, more rectangles for the sides, and circles at the right size for the tires. Then I exported the pieces as an AutoCAD (DXF) file and imported them into a 3D application (Caligari TrueSpace, actually. This was before CorelDream existed). With all the pieces at the correct size in proportion to one another, it was easy to then extrude the rectangles into boards and build the wagon. When you use each application for its strong points, the process is smoother. There are many instances where CorelDRAW is just easier to work with than these 3D virtual work spaces, especially when creating flat objects. Save yourself a lot of hassle and start creating basic objects in CorelDRAW; then use CorelDream to bring them depth and substance. I could write volumes on the topic of using CorelDRAW with CorelDream, but here I am just going to show you a couple of my favorite, and perhaps not so obvious, tricks. I recommend you get a copy of *Ray Dream 5 f/x* (Ventana 1997), by Shamms Mortier, if you are serious about 3D modeling. I am just a Dream-dabbler!

## Gears

As we have seen, gears can be very easily created in all sizes and shapes within CorelDRAW (see Chapter 24). Instead of using the Extrude roll-up in CorelDRAW, you can give curves depth in CorelDream. It is very simple process, with most of the work happening in CorelDRAW. Here is how to get 3D gears:

1. Just like before, create a gear shape as we have many times based upon the lessons in Chapter 24. This time, add an interesting spoke pattern in the center.

2. Select the gear shape and give it no fill and just a black hairline outline (Figure 30-12). Now select and export the shape as an Adobe Illustrator (.AI) file. This is a vector format that CorelDream can use. Save the CDR file of the gears and exit CorelDRAW.

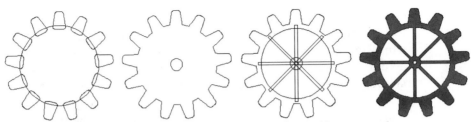

*Figure 30-12: Use the CorelDRAW tools to create a gear shape with cutout spokes.*

3. Start CorelDream and create an empty scene. Grab the Free Form Modeler icon and drag it into the Perspective window. Name the object gear and click OK. Now from the File menu, import the Adobe Illustrator gear file you just created in CorelDRAW. Dream may warn you that the image is complex, but just click Proceed to continue. This will import the wireframe and also "extrude" it, but at very strange proportions (see Figure 30-13).

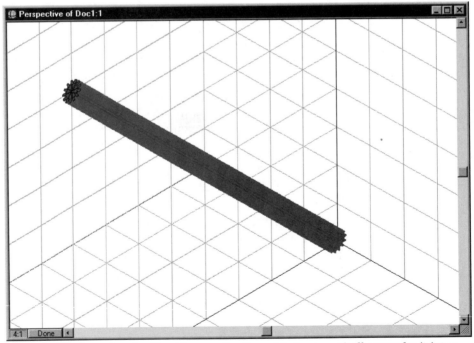

*Figure 30-13: Importing the AI outline as a free form object automatically extrudes it into a 3D object.*

4. To bring the extrusion back into the desired proportions, use the selection tool to click on the pink line (sweep path) on the right wall. Grab the right point of the sweep path and drag it left while holding down the Shift key until the gear has the dimensions you desire (see Figure 30-14). Now you can manipulate the object within CorelDream just like any other object and create your own mechanical illustrations!

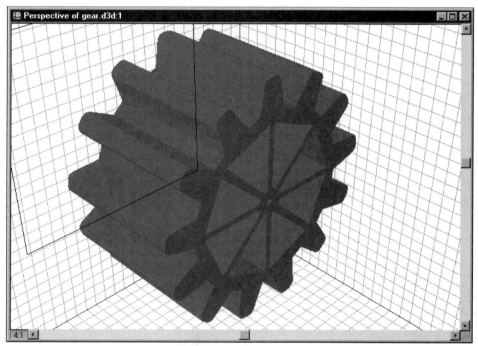

*Figure 30-14. Reducing the sweep path brings the dimensions of the gear back to normal.*

That's all there is to it! This file is called gear.d3d and is found in the \Chapt30\ subdirectory on the Companion CD-ROM (all of these examples are there in the CorelDream format if you want to steal them for your own dreamy designs). You can use this sweep function to add depth to any wireframe generated in CorelDRAW; for example, you can take your company logo and launch it into the world of 3D. The sky is the limit here, and this is probably the most common use of the DRAW/Dream duo.

## Pulleys

An obvious way to get your objects into the 3D world is to add depth with sweeping (the CorelDream equivalent to Extruding in CorelDRAW), as we did in the last example. These next examples use a technique I love to use to get shapes and figures that look far from common. The basic premise is to design a shape in CorelDRAW that is a cross section of the shape you want and then cut it in half. With this one-half cross section prepared in CorelDRAW, you are ready to bring it to life in CorelDream, where you spin it into existence! The trick here is using the Torus preset in CorelDream to create the three-dimensional object from the cross section. Here is how to spin your objects into the third dimension:

1. Again, this is one of those tricks where the work in CorelDRAW is critical. This first example is pretty easy and will unlock the mystery of this
   technique for the more difficult examples to come. Draw an oval and two
   rectangles. Weld the two rectangles together and use the Trim function to
   cut out the round end of one rectangle, as shown in Figure 30-15. This is
   the half of a cross section of a pulley. Select the shape and as before,
   export it as an Adobe Illustrator file.

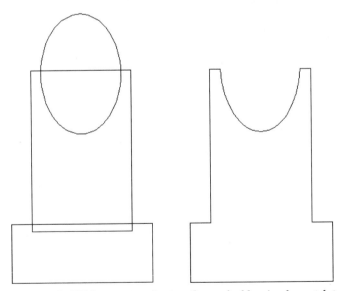

*Figure 30-15: Weld two rectangles together and add a circular notch to create the shape for a pulley object.*

2. Create an empty scene in CorelDream and once again drag the Free Form icon into the Perspective view. Name this object Pulley and click OK. Now from the File menu, import the pulley shape from CorelDRAW. This will automatically sweep it as before, which is not what we want, but don't worry about that at this point.

3. From the Geometry menu, choose Extrusion Preset | Torus. This is the command to spin the wireframe object into a 3D object. In the Torus dialog, change the Distance to Axis value to 1 inch (this is a guessing game at this point, but for the pulley example it isn't critical). Click OK and watch the fun! The Torus preset spins the outline around 360 degrees on the axis you set in the Torus dialog to create a 3D object (see Figure 30-16).

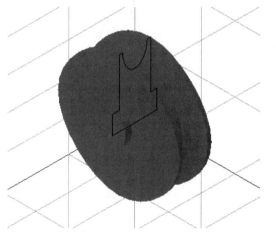

*Figure 30-16: The Torus command spins an outline on an axis 360 degrees to create a solid object.*

4. Once spun into a CorelDream object, you can manipulate the object in any way imaginable using any of the programs fill or texture effects.

Again, this is another simple shape made into something pretty cool in CorelDream. This file, pulley.d3d, is also in the \Chapt30\ subdirectory on the Companion CD-ROM.

## Bottle

In this example, we'll use the same Torus technique we used to create the pulley, but we'll use it on a much more complex shape created in CorelDRAW. Here is how to make a glass bottle:

1. Starting in CorelDRAW, use rectangles and ovals to map out a simple bottle shape. Use the Shape tool to round out the corners of the rect-angles. Now combine all of the shapes into one object using the Weld function. Round out any harsh corners and perform some fine-tuning with the Shape tool. Draw a vertical line and center it to the bottle shape. Using the centered line as a reference, draw a rectangle that covers half of the shape and then use the Trim command to cut away half of the bottle (see Figure 30-17).

*Figure 30-17: Use simple shapes to build a bottle outline and then draw a rectangle to cut the bottle in half with the Trim function.*

2. Now, just as you did with the pulley shape, you can spin this bottle outline into a solid bottle shape in CorelDream. This would probably work in most cases, but with a few more steps you can create the outline that will become a true 3D bottle, with a solid bottom, hollow interior

and open end. Select the bottle outline and use the Contour roll-up to create another shape inside of the curve at the width you want your glass to be. Separate and freeze the contour shape so you can combine it with the original bottle outline. Then draw another shape with the Freehand tool, as shown in Figure 30-18, to use as a template so you can cut away the right side of the bottle curve with the Trim function. This will leave you with your glass shape. Rotate the outline –90 degrees and export as an AI file. Exit CorelDRAW.

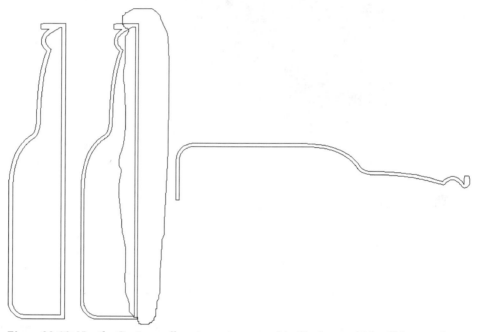

*Figure 30-18: Use the Contour roll-up to create a second inside shape, which will become the "glass" outline when the excess is trimmed away.*

3. Start CorelDream. Follow the same steps you used with the pulley, only enter a smaller value, like .55 inch, in the Torus dialog. This should spin into a nice bottle shape, which will look just like a real bottle, complete with open neck and hollow interior. Use a semi-opaque glass fill for some cool effects in CorelDream (see Figure 30-19).

*Figure 30-19: The outline is made into a perfect 3D bottle using the Torus feature.*

 This image can be swiped out of the bottle.d3d file in the \Chapt30\ subdirectory. Unfortunately, these bottles are all empty!

## Vases

This is a variant of the bottle technique, only the shape is designed to exaggerate the hollow interior of the object; in this case, a flower vase. Here is how to make a vase:

1. Again, the magic happens in CorelDRAW with simple shapes. This time I wanted a definitive lip at the edge of the vase so I used half-circle shapes as primitives to get the angle. It's not a difficult process; it's exactly the same one we used with the bottle, but we'll end up with a shape that will spin into a vase. This time I didn't worry about bisecting the artwork exactly. Concentrate on the left side only, knowing the rest will be trimmed away (see Figure 39-20).

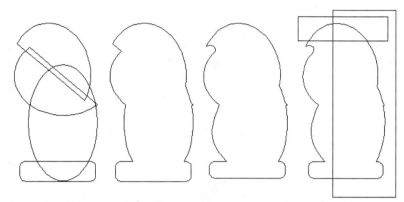

*Figure 39-20: Strange shapes merge together to create a cross section of the vase.*

2. With the basic vase outline in place, again use the Contour roll-up to create the inside line (see Figure 30-21). It can be as thick or thin as you like (but if it's too thick, your vase will look like it is made of concrete). Trim away the excess, rotate –90 degrees, and again export as an AI file. Close CorelDRAW and ready the virtual bouquet....

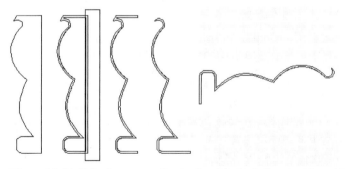

*Figure 30-21: Take the vase outline and create the hollow insides with the Contour and trimming steps.*

3. In CorelDream again, you can spin the object into a lovely addition to any virtual living room! If only decorating my real living room was this easy! The value to use in the Torus dialog is again just a good guess (try 1 inch). Use a marble or other shader to make the vase look good in CorelDream (see Figure 30-22).

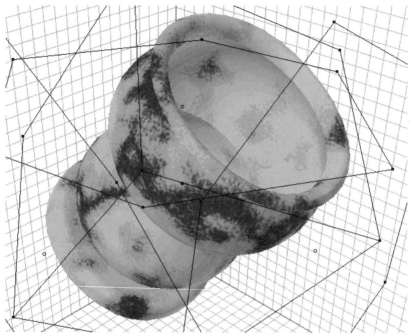

*Figure 30-22: The strange shape from CorelDRAW results in a nice vase in CorelDream.*

**CD-ROM**

This file is called vase.d3d in the \Chapt30\ subdirectory on the Companion CD-ROM. You can release the proverbial bull in that china closet, no fear. Smash all you want, I'll make more! Remember too that you can export all of these pieces in the 3D Metafile (3DMF) format from CorelDream for manipulation back in CorelDRAW (see Chapter 20). There is no penalty for playing ring around the rosey with all the applications in your CorelDRAW design suite!

CorelDream is a great program, but I don't like to work in it without first preparing some artwork in CorelDRAW. Creating artwork like the marbled patters for the box or a product label (see "She Devil Salsa" example in Chapter 12) adds much more visual interest than the 3D objects can generate on their own. It is also a huge time-saver, I find, to generate the parent shapes in CorelDRAW and then bring them to life in CorelDream rather than just work in CorelDream alone. When you plan a project in advance and lay out all the pieces ahead of time using whatever program you need, it makes for a much smoother and more productive workday. The triple threat of CorelDRAW, CorelDream, and Corel PhotoPaint serves to increase your design potential threefold. You paid for the privilege, so don't hesitate to unleash the power in the box!

### ▼ Working Backward, Again.

I have seen several magnificent pieces of artwork created in CorelDRAW and wondered, "Hmm, how did they work out all of the geometry for that virtual landscape?" With a totally fictitious landscape, there is no reference material, yet all the laws of illustration apply.

The answer lies in another working backward technique. A scene is blocked out in CorelDream and then rendered as a bitmap. This bitmap can then be altered even further, say with a fish-eye-type lens, to create a very surreal landscape. The image is then imported into CorelDRAW, where it serves as a reference image to redraw the shapes. It seems like a long way around, but it isn't as crazy as it sounds. Things like mirrored reflections, chrome effects, and so on can all be easily worked out in CorelDream; then the image can be duplicated in CorelDRAW to regain all of the resolution flexibility and other benefits of that program. A CorelDRAW file is crisp at any size, it can be enlarged or reduced without changing the file size, and the file size itself is usually markedly smaller than a bitmap image or even a native CorelDream file. Just log this as miscellaneous information, and someday you may use it to solve a unique illustration problem!

### ▼ Beyond f/x

These days, 3D applications continue to emerge as the avant-garde design field of choice. Everything from movies to magazines are taking advantage of this technology to render incredible images that would simply be impossible or too expensive to create in any other way. This makes the look of 3D very popular, and even traditional artists are being called upon to create these kinds of images.

Corel Corporation understands this evolving market, which is why CorelDream is bundled in the CorelDRAW 8 design suite. Use the technology when it makes sense in your projects and you may find a new source of revenue, but trying to use it where it isn't appropriate may be the digital equivalent of opening Pandora's box!

Here are some ideas to spark your imagination. Create full-color stickers and apply them to CorelDream objects to transform flat artwork into something totally unique. Imagine your client's logo altered to look like a fuel additive and then wrapped around an oilcan for a get up and go campaign. Or extrude a logo and create an animation of it spinning around in space in CorelDream. There are plenty of applications for the technology (all of the buttons on my original Web site started as wireframes in CorelDRAW and were then made into pools of metallic fluid in CorelDream). Remember that 3D media is literally and figuratively without boundaries!

## Conclusion

In this last chapter, we solved some 3D design problems in both CorelDRAW and CorelDream. We took flat box artwork and created a mock-up using the slant feature in CorelDRAW. We also saw how to use CorelDRAW to create objects and images for use within CorelDream. We created full-color stickers to apply to CorelDream objects, which gave us unlimited coloring options within that program. Finally, we saw how to use simple shapes generated inside CorelDRAW as the starting point in CorelDream to make some very unique 3D items. With these tricks, you can build and color anything within the virtual design landscape of CorelDream. Get in there and get crazy.

And as they say in Hollywood, "That's a wrap!" I hope you have found this book to be a worthwhile purchase and an entertaining read. I have tried to squeeze as much as I could get away with into this monster (it was only supposed to be 400 pages long! Psyche!). Anyway, I had a great time putting this beast together and discovered many great techniques along the way. Why are you still reading? Fire up CorelDRAW and get busy!

# Appendix A

# About the Companion CD-ROM

The Companion CD-ROM included with your copy of *CorelDRAW 8 f/x* contains all the art from the book in native CorelDRAW format, demos of commercial plug-in filters, art for the tutorials, and cutting-edge font samples.

## Navigating the CD-ROM

Your choices for navigating the CD-ROM appear on the opening screen. You can install the software or quit the viewer. If the viewer does not run properly on your machine, follow the following instructions for optimum performance:

1. Copy the LAUNCHME.EXE and LAUNCHME.INI files to the same directory on your hard drive.

2. Open the LAUNCHME.INI file in a text editor such as Notepad.

3. Find the section in the .INI file that reads:
   ```
   [Memory]
   ;ExtraMemory=400
   ; Amount of kBytes over and above physical memory for use by a
   projector.
   ```

4. If your computer has enough memory to do so, delete the semicolon from the ExtraMemory line, and change the ExtraMemory setting to a higher number.

5. Save the changes to the LAUNCHME.INI file, and close the text editor.

6. With the CD-ROM still inserted, launch the viewer from the hard drive.

If the viewer still does not run properly on your machine, you can access the material on the CD-ROM directly through File Manager (Windows 3.x) or Windows Explorer (Windows 95).

## Software

The software provided on the Companion CD-ROM is described below in Table A-1.

| | |
|---|---|
| Photo/Graphics Edges 3.0 | Photo/Graphics Edges is a demo version of Auto F/X's Photoshop plug-in compatible graphic design product. Visit http://www.autofx.com for more information. |
| GarageFonts Typefaces | Four unusual typefaces from GarageFonts: Oakmyopia, Pooty, Kindee, Poltergeist and Lobat. These are limited edition fonts. To order full version fonts from their great collection, visit http://www.garagefonts.com. |
| The Ultimate Texture Collection 1.0 | A demo version of Auto F/X's Photoshop plug-in compatible graphic design product, including 3 sample textures and an example of a lighting tile. This is a full working demo and will fuse a texture like the full version, but it will only work with demo version textures. The full version will work with any texture file. Visit http://www.autofx.com for more information. |
| Typo/Graphics Edges 3.0 | A demo version of Auto F/X's Photoshop plug-in compatible graphic design product. Visit http://www.autofx.com for more information. |
| Clikette | Clikette allows you to create pictorial 3D buttons that can be linked to multiple URL destinations. In short, this means that you can now make The Button That Launched A Thousand Links! Well, maybe not a thousand, but 50 at a time is probably enough to keep you and your Web page readers cruising the Internet in finest style. |

| | |
|---|---|
| Flash | Sausage Software's Flash is a user-friendly little tool that allows you to display scrolling text on a browser's status line—sort of like tickertape. In this latest version of Flash, you can pause the scrolling to display status-bar URLs. It's a great way to pass subtle bits of info to your viewers! Check out http://www.sausage.com. |
| Jackhammar | Next time you hit road work on the information super-highway, Sausage Software's Jackhammer will help you dig yourself out of the hole. Whenever you find a site that's too busy to get onto, or an FTP server that's always full, paste the URL into Jackhammer. Set it hammering and it will try the sites until it can get on. Then Jackhammer will launch a new browser window for you or automatically download the file! |
| Mousetrap | Mousetrap brings true user interactivity to your Web pages. Armed with only the barest essentials of HTML, you can create Java enhanced Web pages that play sounds and change pictures or text, depending only on where the surfer moves the mouse. |
| SiteFX | SiteFX is a collection of compact JavaTM-based applications, each of which performs its specialty very well. Thanks to the intuitive interface and superb built-in Help files, SiteFX is very user-friendly. In one handy bundle, SiteFX provides efficient tools that are all you need to bring your Web pages to life. Go to http://www.sausage.com. |
| Eye Candy 3.0 | A demo of the new set of Photoshop plug-ins from Alien Skin Software. Eye Candy 3.0 (formerly known as The Black Box) is the answer to serious Photoshop users' prayers. These filters create special effects in seconds that would normally require hours of hand tweaking. You have probably heard experts explain complex 12-step processes for creating 3D bevels or flames. Now you can stop trying to follow those frustrating recipes and simply use Eye Candy. Version 3.0 makes professional effects even easier by giving you flexible previews and a thumbnail for rapidly navigating your image. Visit http://www.alienskin.com. |

*Table A-1: Contents of the Companion CD-ROM.*

## Limits of Liability & Disclaimer of Warranty

The author and publisher of this book have used their best efforts in preparing the CD-ROM and the programs contained in it. These efforts include the development, research, and testing of the theories and programs to determine their effectiveness. The author and publisher make no warranty of any kind expressed or implied, with regard to these programs or the documentation contained in this book.

The author and publisher shall not be liable in the event of incidental or consequential damages in connection with, or arising out of, the furnishing, performance, or use of the programs, associated instructions, and/or claims of productivity gains.

Some of the software on this CD-ROM is shareware; there may be additional charges (owed to the software authors/makers) incurred for their registration and continued use. See individual program's README or VREADME.TXT files for more information.

# Index